Successful Public Speaking

Nelson.

D0066486

DEVRY INSTITUTE OF TECHNOLOGY
LIBRARY
MISSISSAUGA, ONTARIO

From the Wadsworth Series in Communication Studies

Successful Public Speaking

▼ ▼ ▼ *Nelson*

Cheryl Hamilton

Wadsworth Publishing Company
I(T)P® An International Thomson Publishing Company

Belmont • Albany • Bonn • Boston • Cincinnati • Detroit • London • Madrid • Melbourne
Mexico City • New York • Paris • San Francisco • Singapore • Tokyo • Toronto • Washington

Communication Studies Editor: Todd R. Armstrong
Editorial Assistant: Michael Gillespie
Development Editor: Sherry Symington
Project Development Editor: Lewis DeSimone
Production Editor: Vicki Friedberg
Text and Cover Designer: Ann Butler
Art Editor: Kevin Berry
Photo Editor: Roberta Broyer
Print Buyer: Barbara Britton
Permissions Editor: Robert M. Kauser
Copy Editor: Tom Briggs
Compositor: Joan Olson/Wadsworth Digital Productions
Photo Researcher: Sarah Everston
Illustrator: Precision Graphics
PowerPoint Art: Patrice Wheeler
Cover Illustration: Celia Johnson
Color Separation: GTS Graphics, Inc.
Printer: R.R. Donnelley & Sons, Crawfordsville

Chapter Opening Photos: Chapter 1: IBM; Chapter 2: © Superstock; Chapter 3: © Bob Daemmrich/Stock, Boston; Chapter 4: © Superstock; Chapter 5: © North Wind Pictures; Chapter 6: © Charles Gupton/Tony Stone Images, Inc.; Chapter 7: © Anne Dowie; Chapter 8: © Charles Gupton/The Stock Market; Chapter 9: Richard Hutchings/PhotoEdit; Chapter 10: © David Young-Wolff/PhotoEdit; Chapter 11: © Anne Dowie; Chapter 12: © Anne Dowie; Chapter 13: UPI/(Acme); Chapter 14: © Wally McNamee/Sygma; Chapter 15: © Anne Dowie; Chapter 16: © Jon Jones/Sygma

COPYRIGHT © 1996 by Wadsworth Publishing Company
A Division of International Thomson Publishing Inc.
I(T)P   The ITP logo is a registered trademark under license.

Printed in the United States of America
1 2 3 4 5 6 7 8 9 10

For more information, contact Wadsworth Publishing Company.

Wadsworth Publishing Company
10 Davis Drive
Belmont, California 94002, USA

International Thomson Publishing Europe
Berkshire House 168-173
High Holborn
London, WC1V 7AA, England

Thomas Nelson Australia
102 Dodds Street
South Melbourne 3205
Victoria, Australia

Nelson Canada
1120 Birchmount Road
Scarborough, Ontario
Canada M1K 5G4

International Thomson Editores
Campos Eliseos 385, Piso 7
Col. Polanco
11560 México D.F. México

International Thomson Publishing GmbH
Königswinterer Strasse 418
53227 Bonn, Germany

International Thomson Publishing Asia
221 Henderson Road
#05-10 Henderson Building
Singapore 0315

International Thomson Publishing Japan
Hirakawacho Kyowa Building, 3F
2-2-1 Hirakawacho
Chiyoda-ku, Tokyo 102, Japan

All rights reserved. No part of this work covered by the copyright hereon may be reproduced or used in any form or by any means—graphic, electronic, or mechanical, including photocopying, recording, taping, or information storage and retrieval systems—without the written permission of the publisher.

Library of Congress Cataloging-in-Publication Data
Hamilton, Cheryl.
   Successful public speaking / Cheryl Hamilton.
      p.   cm.
   Includes bibliographical references and index.
   ISBN 0-534-15564-2
   1. Public speaking.   I. Title.
PN4121.H19   1996
808.5'1—dc20   95–36126

To Doris Redd,
who has always encouraged me to write.
As a mother she willingly read and critiqued my
stories when I was a child. As a professional she
willingly read and critiqued each draft of this text.
Thanks, Mom.

Brief Contents

▼ ▼ ▼

Contents

Four ■ Persuasive Speaking

Chapter 13
Persuasive Speaking:
An Overview 325

Chapter 14
Persuasive Appeals 355

Preface

*S*uccessful *Public Speaking* was created for students of all ages who wish to improve their speaking skills. Although the text is based on classical rhetorical theory and contemporary research, it takes a very practical, reader-friendly approach. Concepts and skills aren't just explained; they are illustrated with examples and actual student speeches. The reader is invited to take an active role in the learning process by evaluating various items, taking quizzes, and making decisions about his or her own speeches. There are some very real differences between this text and other public speaking texts—differences that result in specific benefits for both students and teachers.

Teaching/Learning Benefits

Attention to confidence building Speaker anxiety often keeps students from achieving success. Unfortunately no amount of lecture, encouragement, or practice will make someone into a confident, professional speaker as long as deep down inside that person believes himself or herself to be a "poor" speaker. For this reason *Successful Public Speaking* approaches anxiety head-on in Chapter 3 so students can have improvements well under way by the time the first major speech is due. Although a variety of confidence-building techniques is discussed, Chapter 3 concentrates on positive imagery (a technique fairly new to communication journals but well established in athletics). Positive imagery requires only minor instructor guidance and does not need special out-of-class sessions to be successful. In fact, interested students can use positive imagery successfully on their own simply by following the text.

Focus on visual communication Today's society is a visual society. Music videos, television programs, and advertisements use sophisticated computer technology and art composition. Audiences expect it. Yet many public speaking texts address visual aids as an afterthought. Although they may mention various types of visual aids, rarely is the reader told how to create quality visuals. For example, do students know what size type should be used for the titles and body of transparencies, slides, or flip charts to make sure everyone in the audience can easily see them? Shouldn't speakers know that people with red-green color blindness can't distinguish between red and green bars in a bar graph? Or that research has proven that it is easier to read lower- and uppercase type than text written in all-caps? It's time to equip ourselves and our students with needed information on visual aids.

Successful Public Speaking demonstrates why speakers should no longer consider visual aids as optional but should think in terms of verbal/visual/vocal teamwork. Unit Two, "Verbal/Visual/Vocal Teamwork," presents research on why visual aids are so effective and includes detailed information on designing and using visual aids of all types. Student and professional visuals (both effective and ineffective) are used to illustrate basic design concepts.

High-tech visual support for instructors   To assist instructors who are using the text, *Successful Public Speaking* comes with a *PowerPoint* multimedia package that brings high technology into the classroom. Using an LCD panel, *PowerPoint* color images for each chapter can be projected directly from a computer screen to the regular classroom screen. Each item in a particular visual can be called up with a simple click of the mouse, adding movement and interest to lectures and class discussions.

Student speeches early in the semester   Most instructors want students to begin speaking early in the semester but know that to do well students need information not available until later chapters. As a result, many instructors resort to jumping around to adapt most public speaking texts to their course. *Successful Public Speaking*, however, is organized so students can begin giving quality speeches immediately without having to jump ahead for needed information. Chapter 2 discusses the basic characteristics of a successful public speaker and gives an overview of the speaking process by introducing the FLOW sequence (focus, lead-in, organized body, and wrap-up steps). The FLOW sequence, which makes speech organization easy to understand and remember, is applied throughout the text. Beginning speeches (such as the speech of introduction, the humorous incident speech, the artifact speech, the pet peeve speech, or the one-point speech) can be given successfully in the first or second week of class.

Useful chapter order   Chapters on informative and persuasive speaking are usually the last two or three chapters in a public speaking text. Yet few instructors wait until the end of the course to assign informative speeches. To more closely resemble the way public speaking is actually taught, *Successful Public Speaking* divides the chapters into four units: "Foundations," "Verbal/Visual/Vocal Teamwork," "Informative Speaking," and "Persuasive Speaking." This organization allows each unit to build on the skills from previous units while still presenting informative speaking much sooner—making the text more user-friendly. Each unit begins with an overview chapter so students can start choosing topics and researching and organizing their speeches without waiting until they complete the entire unit. Each overview chapter also includes a quiz to pretest student knowledge of unit information and to stimulate interest.

Specific Features

Successful Public Speaking contains a variety of useful features, including the following:

1. Coverage of ethical speaking. The importance of ethical speaking is presented in Chapter 1 and reinforced throughout the text.

2. Unique approach to listening. Instead of concentrating on how to become a better listener, the listening chapter focuses on what successful *speakers* need to know about listeners and the listening process in order to improve their speaking.

3. Sample student speeches with visuals. Real student speeches (transcribed from classroom videotapes) are used throughout the text. Each speech is accompanied by the actual visual aids the students used as well as sample outlines (or storyboards) and speaking notes.

4. Speeches that FLOW. An easy-to-remember sequence (FLOW) is presented for organizing speeches.

5. Introduction of storyboards. Storyboarding is suggested as an alternative to formal outlining and is recommended for students who have a strong aversion to outlines or who prefer a more visual approach to outlining.

6. Sample speech topics. To stimulate student creativity and inspiration in choosing speech topics, sample topics are included throughout the text.

7. Helpful aids for students. Formats for preparing informative and persuasive speeches, as well as evaluation forms, are included for student use.

8. Mind maps. The mind map is presented as a visual, easy-to-remember approach to speaker notes.

9. Tips. Scattered through the text are "Tips" designed to assist students in preparing and delivering quality speeches.

10. Practice suggestions. To encourage students to reflect and expand on what they have read, practice suggestions are included at the end of each chapter.

Instructional Resources

PowerPoint **multimedia presentation** No other public speaking text includes such an innovative computer package for use during lectures and discussions. Instructors who have a computer and an LCD projection panel available for class use may want to use the colorful multimedia computer disk that accompanies each chapter instead of the transparency acetates. This program allows instructors to display the title for a visual aid, such as "Stages of Listening," and then with a click of the mouse add each stage as the lecture or discussion requires it. Both instructors and students soon find this classroom aid indispensable. Even experienced instructors will find the *PowerPoint* multimedia package an exciting visual addition to their usual routine.

Videotape   The videotape designed especially for this text illustrates a broad range of speaking behaviors by reviewing excerpts from several ineffective speeches and by presenting and discussing two effective speeches——one informative and one persuasive. Pointers for effective visual aids, speech organization, speaking delivery, and confidence building also are given.

Transparency acetates   Fifty beautiful color transparencies that model the design features presented in Chapter 7 are available for instructor use. These visuals add excitement and interest to lectures and classroom discussions and model correct visual aids for students.

Instructor's Resource Manual   This handy guide is designed for beginning as well as for seasoned instructors. It includes suggested course syllabi and schedules, teaching ideas, lecture outlines, audiovisual materials, ready-to-use evaluation forms, classroom exercises, ideas for using the practice suggestions in each text chapter, and test questions for each chapter.

Computer test bank   The multiple-choice, true-false, and essay questions from the Instructor's Resource Manual are available on computer disk for DOS, Windows, or Macintosh environments. Instructors may add their own questions to the test bank as well.

Acknowledgments

Anyone who thinks that an author does most of the work in producing a quality book surely hasn't written one yet. I appreciate the valuable assistance of the many people who took an active role in creating *Successful Public Speaking*. First, of course, is the editor, Todd Armstrong—a creative communicator who makes things happen.

Second are the reviewers who did a wonderful job shaping and enhancing each chapter with their pedagogical and academic expertise: Kathy German, Miami University of Ohio; Mark Hickson III, University of Alabama-Birmingham; Ralph Hillman, Middle Tennessee State University; Susan Huxman, Wichita State University; JoAnn Lawlor, West Valley College; Lois Leubitz, Cedar Valley College; Neil Patten, Ferris State University; Deborah Stollery, Xavier University; Mark Stoner, California State University at Sacramento; and Loretta Walker, Salt Lake Community College.

Third are the students who not only tried out the materials in class but allowed their speeches and visual aids to be used as samples. Thanks goes to Karen Gemmer, Tricia Lewis, Robert McDermott, Lorna McElaney, Lynda Ross, Lucy Setliff, Christina Stanton, and Monica Wolfe.

The fourth group of people deserving thanks are the Wadsworth professionals—creative, hard-working, and fun-loving. Special appreciation goes to Sherry Symington, senior development editor by title but friend, hand-holder, and communicator par excellence as well; Vicki Friedberg who did a marvelous job producing this book on time despite a more-than-hectic schedule; and Ann Butler who designed a very appealing, readable text. Additional thanks goes to Gary Carlson, Editorial Director; Lewis DeSimone, for coordinating the appendixes and the supplements package; Kevin Berry and Bobbie Broyer, for managing the art and photos; Bob Kauser, for his help with permissions; Joan Olson, compositor extraordinaire; and Debbie Dennis, David Leach, and Joanne Terhaar in Marketing.

Two freelance professionals also provided invaluable assistance in creating this book: Tom Briggs, who polished the manuscript with his copy editing, and Patrice Wheeler, who produced all the student visuals in the text as well as the state-of-the-art transparencies and the *PowerPoint* multimedia package that dazzles everyone who sees it.

A special thanks goes to Bill Hobson, artist and trainer, for introducing me to the full power of visual aids, and Roy Schwartzman, Director of the Basic Course at the University of South Carolina, for writing both the Instructor's Resource Manual and Appendix A as well as assisting in the writing of Appendix B.

And finally, I wish to express my heartfelt gratitude to my husband, Howard, my daughter, Erin, and my mother, Doris, for their clever ideas and loving support.

Cheryl Hamilton
Fort Worth, Texas

Successful Public Speaking

Before you begin reading **Successful Public Speaking**, I invite you to take a few minutes to look through the *Guide to Learning* on the next several pages. It highlights the special features of this book and how it differs from other public speaking texts.

Research confirms that a speech with strong *verbal, visual,* and *vocal* elements is significantly more memorable than a speech in which any one of these elements is lacking. You'll find that this book emphasizes all three areas, including the visual component, which is given little attention in most texts. Here, you'll find extensive coverage on how to create and use effective visual aids—tools that make the difference between an unforgettable speech and a lackluster one.

Successful Public Speaking offers several other unique features that will help you become a confident public speaker. You'll learn about positive imagery and its role in helping you overcome speech anxiety. You'll look at listening from the speaker's point of view and discover what speakers can do to enhance audience listening. You'll also read about an extremely useful organizational tool called FLOW (Focus, Lead-in, Organize and Support, and Wrap-up) that will help you organize your presentation.

This *Guide to Learning* will assist you in familiarizing yourself with the main elements of this text and help you get the most out of it. As you learn about all three elements of effective speechmaking—verbal, visual, and vocal—plus the importance of positive imagery in building confidence, you'll discover that there's more to being a successful public speaker than meets the ear!

A Strong Emphasis on the Verbal, Visual, and Vocal Aspects of Speechmaking...

Verbal, Visual, and Vocal Codes

Your messages are carried to your audience by codes consisting of symbols (light waves and sound waves). Each time you speak to an audience, three different communication codes carry your messages: (1) the **verbal code** (as defined in this text) includes spoken and written words; (2) the **visual code** includes anything nonverbal such as personal appearance, facial expression, eye contact, and visual aids; and (3) the **vocal code** includes tone of voice, volume, pitch, rate, emphasis, and vocal quality. The difference among the codes can be illustrated in the following example. Suppose you arrive home after a hard day at work or class. As you walk in, you slam the door, plop down on your favorite recliner, and let out a long sigh. When asked, "How was your day?" you reply, "Oh, it was fine." In this instance, to which code would the questioner pay more attention—the slamming of the door (visual), the loud sigh (vocal), or the actual words (verbal)? Or suppose one of your professors told you that you were doing good work in class but at the same time frowned slightly and sounded rather impersonal. Would you believe the verbal message and ignore the visual and vocal ones?

Studies have found that when adults attempt to determine the meaning of a statement, they rely more heavily on vocal and visual cues than they do on the words that are actually spoken.[17] Unfortunately many speakers think that the only really important code is the verbal code and tend to overlook the other two codes. Unit Two focuses on how to use all three codes to make your presentations powerful and memorable.

Feedback

When you observe your own speaking behavior and determine your strengths and weaknesses, when you ask a friend to give an opinion on a practice speech or an actual speech, or when audience members respond to your presentation (positively or negatively), you are experiencing feedback. **Feedback** refers to people's verbal, visual, and vocal responses to messages. Not only is feedback

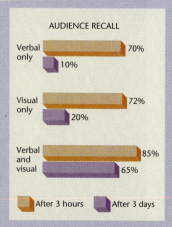

AUDIENCE RECALL

Verbal only — 70% / 10%

Visual only — 72% / 20%

Verbal and visual — 85% / 65%

After 3 hours   After 3 days

Effective Use of the "Three Vs " = Effective Speeches

Verbal skills. Visuals. Vocal delivery . . . This excerpt from *Chapter 1: Public Speaking and You* gives a brief overview of the importance each of these elements plays in delivering effective speeches. As the chart from *Chapter 6: Verbal/Visual/Vocal Teamwork: An Overview* illustrates, audience recall of speeches with both verbal and visual components is more than six times higher three days later than their recall of speeches with no visuals.

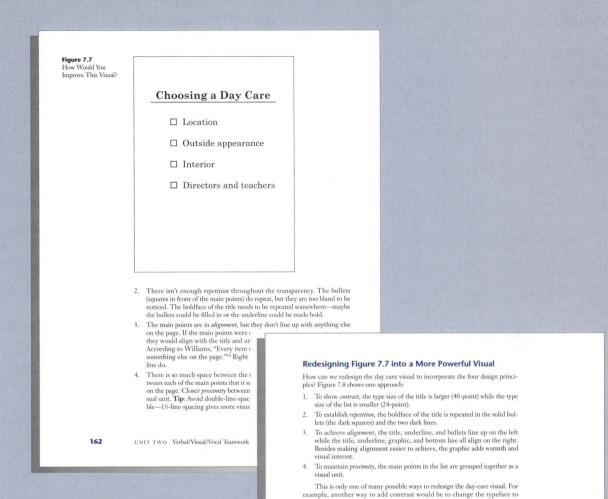

Figure 7.7
How Would You
Improve This Visual?

Choosing a Day Care

- ☐ Location
- ☐ Outside appearance
- ☐ Interior
- ☐ Directors and teachers

2. There isn't enough *repetition* throughout the transparency. The bullets (squares in front of the main points) do repeat, but they are too bland to be noticed. The boldface of the title needs to be repeated somewhere—maybe the bullets could be filled in or the underline could be made bold.

3. The main points are in *alignment*, but they don't line up with anything else on the page. If the main points were [ ] they would align with the title and un[ ] According to Williams, "Every item s[ ] something else on the page."[10] Right [ ] line do.

4. There is so much space between the [ ] tween each of the main points that it se[ ] on the page. Closer *proximity* between [ ] sual unit. **Tip:** Avoid double-line-spac[ ] ble—1½-line-spacing gives more visua[ ]

Redesigning Figure 7.7 into a More Powerful Visual

How can we redesign the day care visual to incorporate the four design principles? Figure 7.8 shows one approach:

1. To show *contrast*, the type size of the title is larger (40-point) while the type size of the list is smaller (24-point).

2. To establish *repetition*, the boldface of the title is repeated in the solid bullets (the dark squares) and the two dark lines.

3. To achieve *alignment*, the title, underline, and bullets line up on the left while the title, underline, graphic, and bottom line all align on the right. Besides making alignment easier to achieve, the graphic adds warmth and visual interest.

4. To maintain *proximity*, the main points in the list are grouped together as a visual unit.

This is only one of many possible ways to redesign the day-care visual. For example, another way to add contrast would be to change the typeface to

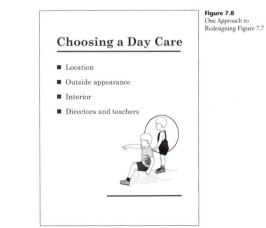

Figure 7.8
One Approach to
Redesigning Figure 7.7

Choosing a Day Care

- ■ Location
- ■ Outside appearance
- ■ Interior
- ■ Directors and teachers

Extensive Coverage of Visual Aids

Discussion of visual aids is featured throughout the text. In addition, entire chapters are devoted to covering the why, what, and how of visual aids. This excerpt from *Chapter 7: Designing Your Visual Message* gives several simple, very specific suggestions on how to improve a visual to increase its effectiveness.

Other Unique Features...

Using Positive Imagery to Overcome Speech Anxiety

In this book, you'll discover the power of positive imagery in enabling you to become an assured, effective speaker and to remain so after your public speaking course is over. This topic is given particularly thorough coverage in *Chapter 3: Building Speaker Confidence,* which includes positive imagery exercises, one of which is excerpted here.

Positive Imagery Exercises

In addition to visualizing your positive statements, tape yourself reading the following positive imagery exercises. For the best results play these tapes (or your own version of them) at least once a week and the night before each scheduled speech. As you listen, *see* and *feel* yourself giving a successful speech. Two recent studies found that speakers who participated in similar exercises only one time had less communication anxiety than speakers who did not use them or who used some other anxiety reduction method.[35] Such visualization exercises also have a long-lasting effect.[36]

Positive Imagery Exercise 1[37]

It's important to get in the mood to visualize. Close your eyes and get as comfortable as you can in your chair. For the next fifteen minutes or so, try to keep an open body posture with your feet flat on the floor and your arms resting comfortably but not touching. Now, take in a deep breath . . . hold it as you count slowly to three . . . and exhale slowly. As you exhale feel the tension in your neck and shoulders draining down your arms and out your fingers; feel the tension in your back and hips draining down your legs and out your toes. Take another deep breath . . . hold it . . . and slowly release it through your mouth (if possible). Feel the tension leaving your body. Now one more time, breathe deeply . . . hold it . . . slowly exhale and begin normal breathing.

Imagine yourself at the sink in your bathroom. You lean toward the mirror to get a better look at your face. See your face? The mirror suddenly clouds over and when it clears again, you are looking through the mirror into the future. You can see yourself getting up on a day in which you are going to give a particularly important speech. You jump out of bed full of energy, full of confidence, and looking forward to the day. You are putting on one of your favorite outfits that makes you feel professional and confident. See how good you look and feel? Imagine yourself arriving relaxed at the speaking site. When you arrive, people comment on your appearance and how relaxed you appear. You feel thoroughly prepared for this presentation. You have researched carefully, have professional visual aids, and have practiced several times. Now see yourself standing or sitting in the room where you will make your speech, talking very comfortably and confidently with others in the room. Everyone seems friendly and supportive. You feel absolutely sure of your material and of your ability to present the information in a forceful, convincing, positive manner. It's time for the speech. See ̲idently to the front and smile at the audience. They smile ̲ our visual aids and begin your presentation.

̲ rself speaking. Your introduction goes the way you had it ̲ dynamic, forceful, and interesting. Your speaking rate is ̲ uses and emphasis couldn't be better; your gestures and ̲ are powerful. As you flow from one main point to the ̲ smiles and nods their heads. They are really paying at-̲ impressed by your visual and verbal supporting material.

---

same listener glances at his watch continually, looks aimlessly around the room, and shifts uncomfortably in his seat (three collaborating behaviors), you can feel much more certain that he is probably tuning you out. And if several audience members are showing similar behaviors, it's time to take a break, switch to a more interesting point, or show a catchy visual. If your speech is almost finished, you can recapture audience attention with such statements as, "I have one last point to make before concluding my speech," or "In conclusion. . . ." The audience will visibly relax and give you a few more minutes of attention.

Telltale Signs of Nonlistening

Now that you know about the potential dangers of assigning meaning to nonverbal behaviors, let's look at some nonverbal behaviors that generally indicate that a typical U.S. audience is not listening.

Signs of Nonlistening	Signs of Listening
Practically no movement, faces void of expression, unwavering eye contact, drooping eyelids, slouched posture.	Normal movement, smiles (or interested looks on faces), occasional direct eye contact, upright or forward-leaning posture.
Restless movement, aimless looks around the room, drumming fingers or tapping pencils, repeated glances at watches.	Occasional movement (maybe even some doodling), occasional glances at watches—usually near the end of the presentation.
Frowns, narrowed eyes or skeptical looks, arms locked across chests, raised eyebrows or rolling eyes.	Open posture, changing facial expressions depending on speech content, occasional nods of head.

Effective speakers constantly monitor nonverbal feedback from their listeners. Based on the feedback they receive, they fine-tune their speeches as they go. The preceding list of nonverbal behaviors (which often occur simultaneously) should give you an idea of when listeners are probably not listening or, at least, not listening effectively. Remember that audiences rarely sit perfectly still unless they are daydreaming. Listening is not passive—it's active and requires conscious effort. On the other hand, too much movement is an indication of boredom and low-level listening.

Listening from the Speaker's Point of View

The text gives in-depth coverage on the important topic of how to read your audience. This excerpt from *Chapter 4: What Speakers Should Know About Listeners* gives you specific guidelines for analyzing audience response while giving your speech.

FLOW and Other Effective Organizational Tools

One of the essential steps in delivering an effective speech is getting your materials organized well at the outset. This excerpt from *Chapter 2: Public Speaking: Getting Started* briefly describes the FLOW sequence, an effective technique for organizing your presentation. FLOW will make speech presentation easier to understand and remember.

For more complex speeches, the book includes "Formats," outlines that guide you in preparing your own speech outlines more easily. In Chapter 12, you'll learn about "Storyboarding," a great visual alternative to traditional outlining and organizing of your speeches.

Organize Carefully to Improve Understanding and Recall

Effective, well-organized presentations seem to flow from idea to idea, from one main point to the next. You will always be well organized if, in preparing and presenting your speech, you remember the acronym *FLOW*.

F   *Focus* audience attention and interest.
L   *Lead in* to your topic.
O   *Organize* and *support* your main ideas with visual and verbal materials.
W   *Wrap-up* or conclude.

The FLOW sequence will be discussed in more detail later in this chapter. Chapters 11 and 15 explain how to use the FLOW sequence to develop effective informative and persuasive speeches.

Each time you put on a new transparency, make sure the top or bottom of the frame is pushed against the pencil—perfect alignment without looking. This is easier than trying to line up the frame with the top edge of the projection glass.

Some speakers make the mistake of leaving a transparency on the screen until they are ready for the next one even though they are no longer referring to it. After you have finished discussing each transparency, you can turn off the projector or block the projector light with a small piece of cardboard. When the cardboard cover is flipped upward, the light shines on the screen as usual; when the cardboard cover is lowered, no light shines. **Tip:** Constantly turning the projector off and on can be irritating and distracting, so don't turn off the projector or lower the cardboard cover if you are planning to remove one transparency and immediately show another one. Simply remove the used transparency with one hand while you position the new transparency with the other hand. Practice will make this a fast and smooth operation.

Using slides   More practice is required to use slides effectively than most other types of visuals. First of all, you must learn how to use the remote control switch that allows you to change slides (in the dark it's easy to push the reverse button instead of the advance button). Or, if someone else is going to forward

Helpful Tips Throughout

These invaluable tidbits offering specific practical advice are scattered throughout the book. This helpful tip is from *Chapter 8: Delivering Your Message.*

End-of-Chapter Learning Aids...

At the end of each chapter are several useful learning tools. The excerpts shown here are from *Chapter 8: Delivering Your Message*.

Summaries

The summary at the end of each chapter offers a succinct yet thorough summation of the chapter's main points.

Practice Suggestions

These useful, involving exercises following the summaries will enable you to reinforce the chapter content through individual and group activities.

Notes

At the very end of the chapter, you'll find extensive listings for the material footnoted in the chapter proper. These references will enable you to access more information on any referenced topic.

Summary
▼ ▼ ▼

Successfully delivering your message depends on three important aspects of delivery—verbal, visual, and vocal codes. Effective verbal delivery results from the use of vivid, specific, simple, and bias-free language. It is also important that your verbal message fit the frames of reference of your listeners. Effective visual delivery entails paying close attention to your appearance, facial expressions, eye contact, posture, movement and gestures, as well as the content and handling of your visual aids. Effective vocal delivery is achieved by varying volume, pitch, emphasis, and rate, as well as making sure pauses, phrasing, articulation, and pronunciation are effective. The best speaking voice is one that sounds conversational, natural and enthusiastic. Rarely will you achieve your best speaking voice without practice.

Your delivery can be enhanced by using immediacy behaviors such as making direct eye contact, smiling, being vocally expressive, using humor, and referring to your audience as "we." These behaviors reduce the psychological distance that often exists between speaker and audience.

In addition to your verbal, visual, and vocal delivery, the method of delivery you choose can affect the success of your speech. In most cases speaking from a manuscript or memorizing your speech should be avoided. Impromptu speaking is a good way to gain confidence in speaking. If you can add a personal or humorous instance, not only will your audience enjoy your speech, but you will feel more relaxed as well. The preferred method of delivery for major classroom speeches is extemporaneous speaking, which involves preparing carefully but speaking from brief notes.

The only way to transfer what you have learned from this chapter into a dynamic, believable delivery is to practice. To prepare yourself, first visualize yourself giving a successful speech. Then practice your speech aloud with your

---

1. To get an idea of how your voice sounds to others, leave a detailed message on your answering machine or voice mail system. Do this regularly until your vocal variety and tone project the warmth, enthusiasm, or authority you desire.[23]

2. For one week, whenever you make a call or someone calls you, record the conversation on a cassette recorder. Listen to your voice quality. After a week listen to your first recording to assess your improvement.

3. Keep a brief log of any really good speeches you see live or on TV. What specific verbal, visual, and vocal techniques made the speeches so good?

4. In Chapter 7 you selected the manuscript of a speech given previously by someone else and prepared at least two visual aids that you thought would clarify and add power to the speech. Read the manuscript (or at least a two-minute portion of it) to the class using the visuals you prepared. Follow the guidelines in this chapter for reading from a manuscript. As you read, make your delivery as effective as possible. Not only will this assignment show you how difficult it is to speak from a manuscript and why your instructor required extemporaneous speeches, but it will give you a chance to polish your verbal, visual, and vocal delivery without having to worry about speech content.

Practice Suggestions
▼ ▼ ▼

Notes

1. Bert Decker, *You've Got to Be Believed to Be Heard* (New York: St. Martin's Press, 1992).
2. Lee Iacocca and William Novak, *Iacocca: An Autobiography* (New York: Bantam Books, 1984).
3. *The New York Times* (July 15, 1980) as reported in the *Current Biography Yearbook*, 1987, p. 259.
4. Oprah Winfrey, *Current Biography Yearbook*, 1987, pp. 610–614.

17. Diana K. Ivy, L. Bullis-Moore, K. Norvell, Phil Backlund, and M. Javidi, *The Lawyer, the Babysitter, and the Student: Non-sexist Language Usage and Instruction.* Paper presented at the annual meeting of the Western States Communication Association, Albuquerque, NM, February 1993.
18. Diana K. Ivy and Phil Backlund, *Exploring Gender Speak: Personal Effectiveness in Gender Communication* (New

Foundations

1

Public Speaking and You

▼ ▼ ▼

Public Speaking: What Roles Can It Play in Your Life?
Enhancing Your Personal Development
Influencing Your World
Boosting Your Career

The Right Speech for the Occasion
Informative vs. Persuasive Speeches
Special Occasion Speeches

The Communication Process and the Public Speaker
Speakers/Listeners
Stimulus and Motivation
Message Encoding and Decoding
Verbal, Visual, and Vocal Codes
Feedback
Environment
Noise

Ethics: The Public Speaker's Obligation
Examples of Unethical Behavior
The Cost of Unethical Behavior
Exaggeration, Distortion, and Plagiarism
Classroom Ethics

Quiz: Avoiding Public Speaking Misconceptions

Summary

Practice Suggestions

Notes

DO YOU ENJOY MAKING SPEECHES? If your answer is no, you are not alone. Not only do many people not enjoy making speeches, they actively dislike and even fear it. You may be thinking, "It doesn't matter that I don't know how to give a speech; my job and personal life won't require it." Are you sure? In this chapter we'll look at the potential roles of public speaking in your life, as well as the elements and ethics of the communication process.

> Before reading this chapter, complete the brief questionnaire in Appendix D and turn in your scores to your instructor. All scores will be kept completely confidential.

Public Speaking: What Roles Can It Play in Your Life?

▼ ▼ ▼

As you become successful in your career, get involved in the community, or pursue various causes or activities, you will be surprised at how many opportunities there are to give speeches. These opportunities can benefit you personally, can influence society, and can boost your career or profession.

Enhancing Your Personal Development

One of the greatest benefits of learning to give quality speeches is the personal satisfaction it brings. It's a wonderful feeling to be able to stand in front of a group of people and present a well-organized, dynamic speech that your listeners obviously appreciate. Also, once you learn to give effective speeches, you can stop dreading the possibility that someone (a boss, a professor, or a friend) will ask you to speak. For example, on the first day of class, a student told me that she had dropped the course five times before and that she would probably drop it again because she simply couldn't give a speech. However, when she looked at the confidence-building techniques in Chapter 3, she was intrigued enough to give it a try. Four weeks later no one could believe this woman. Not only did she get up in class and present an excellent speech—one she seemed to enjoy giving—she also volunteered to give her speech in her psychology class and to an organization in her community. After repeatedly dropping the course because of her dread of giving a speech, the relief and pride she felt was obvious to all.

Being able to speak in public also creates personal satisfaction because it gives you more control over your life. That is, knowing how to research, conceptualize, organize and present your own arguments keeps you from feeling frustrated when trying to get your ideas across to others. Likewise, knowing

At a rally in support of Chinese human rights, this student is using his public speaking skills to have a positive impact on the world.

© Mary Kate Denny/PhotoEdit

how to evaluate the persuasive arguments of others keeps you from feeling manipulated. In addition, most public speakers discover that learning to analyze audiences and to adapt ideas and arguments to specific audiences makes them both more flexible communicators and more critical thinkers. In short, although you may find it difficult to believe right now, learning to speak in public can be very personally satisfying.

Influencing Your World

Learning to give speeches can be both personally satisfying and beneficial to society. Because our form of government depends on citizen participation, noncareer opportunities to speak are almost limitless. Start with your own neighborhood. Many neighborhoods hold regular meetings in which community problems are discussed and solved. Is your neighborhood associated with the city's crime watch program? If so, someone had to speak in favor of it. If not, maybe you should be the one to propose this for your neighborhood. Similarly citizens are permitted to address key issues at city council meetings. If the council decides to run a highway through your neighborhood, you and many neighbors may decide to speak out against it. How about political debates among candidates for office or about controversial issues? If you are a member of a political club or organization, you likely will be asked to make your opinions known. And what about issues on your campus? The student council's stance on a faculty member's dismissal, the English club's position on political correctness, and the independent student association's campaign to keep the library open longer hours—all are situations requiring public speakers. Even college courses often require you to share information in front of the class or give you the option of making an oral presentation in place of a written paper. It's hard to find a situation that doesn't require or wouldn't benefit from public speaking.

Candy Lightner is an example of a person who is influencing her world through her public speaking. In 1980 her 13-year-old daughter was walking to a party when she was killed by a teenage drunk driver. Not only did Lightner found Mothers Against Drunk Driving (MADD), but she also lobbied state legislatures to enact stiffer penalties against drunk drivers and Congress to approve the "21" amendment, which denied federal highway funds to states that refused to raise the drinking age to 21.[1] Her speaking skills, which were minimal at first, are now as polished and professional as the politicians with whom she deals. She is no longer the head of MADD, but she regularly gives lectures on grieving and victimization.[2] Although your reason for speaking out in your college, organization, or community may not be as compelling as Candy Lightner's, society needs responsible, vocal citizens who know how to present themselves and their ideas effectively.

Boosting Your Career

Not only is learning to speak in public personally satisfying and beneficial to society, it can also enhance your career. Suppose you could ask one question of people in any career field that would allow you to adequately predict each person's earning power. What question would you ask? In 1987 AT&T and Stanford University set out to find such a question.[3] They thought it might be something like "How many years have you been working in your career?" or "Do you have an MBA degree?" However, the single best question to predict a person's earning power surprised even the researchers. It was, "Do you enjoy giving speeches?" Those who answered that they did enjoy it were earning the highest salaries; those who said, "You've got to be kidding!" were making much less.

For example, learning to speak was certainly a benefit for one engineer who, at the urging of a friend, reluctantly enrolled in a public speaking seminar through the training department at Bell Helicopter. The class met for two hours once a week for six weeks. By the time the class was finished, this woman had improved so much that less than two months later she was promoted from engineer to senior engineer because, as her boss stated, her presentations were now "so professional."[4]

If you are thinking about a career in business, you should know that the longer you are with an organization and the higher you climb up the organizational ladder, the more likely you are to be asked to speak not only within the organization but also to the general public. According to one manager, "From the chairman of the board to the assistant manager of the most obscure department, nearly everyone in business speaks in public or makes a speech at some time or other."[5]

Although most of us expect that executives in large businesses such as IBM, General Motors, and McDonnell Douglas would have to give speeches, smaller organizations and businesses also need employees who are skilled in speaking. For example, a high school coach may wish to sell the school board on purchasing new equipment or to motivate the team; parents may want to convince other members of the PTA that the dress code is too strict; dentists and dental technicians will have to deal with patients and supply companies; salespeople must present their products and ideas to customers, nurses and doctors, fire and police personnel, and paralegal and parafinancial personnel; and so on. Even assembly line workers at General Motors participate in decision making and formally present group ideas to management. The fact is, no matter what job you choose, you will need the speaking skills discussed throughout this book.

Speakers' bureau   Many companies and industries rely on their own speakers' bureau as a public relations tool. A company speakers' bureau is made up of ordinary employees who have expertise in some aspect of the company and are willing to share it with interested groups looking for a guest speaker. Bell Telephone, Dow Chemical, Xerox, and the United States Army and Navy are but a few of the diverse organizations that communicate with the general public through their speakers' bureaus. Chances are, almost any business, profession, or service organization you might work for will have a speakers' bureau.

Oral communication skills   If you still aren't convinced that speeches are important in your particular career choice, consult one of the periodical guides in your school library and look for articles written by people in your profession. You will be amazed at the number of articles dealing with oral communication skills. For example, an article in *Engineering Education* reported that five hundred engineering leaders ranked communication skills (including speaking) to be more important than technical skills.[6] You will find many other articles in which employees agree that speaking skills are more important to job success than are specific technical skills.[7] For example, Michigan State University conducted a study of over 479 personnel directors from major companies, government agencies, and nonprofit organizations asking them to list the top ten most desired skills in new recruits. Oral and written skills were ranked first and second respectively, while technical job skills ranked seventh.[8] Furthermore, a twenty-year study of MBA graduates from Stanford University has concluded that no skill is more important to a successful career in business than good communication (especially the ability to persuade).[9]

Although you may not feel comfortable yet giving formal speeches, you most likely already give informal talks fairly regularly. Common examples of informal presentations include giving instructions on a class assignment to several classmates who missed the previous class, suggesting an idea to your boss, and discussing a possible money-making project with a group of volunteers. Therefore, even though you may not have realized it, you already have many of the skills necessary for successful public speaking. Learning to give effective speeches is simply a matter of building on what you already know. For example, you already know that there are different types of speeches. The next section will help you identify these types.

The Right Speech for the Occasion
▼ ▼ ▼

The types of speeches you may be asked to give—whether in class, at work, or in the community—can be divided into three basic categories: informative, persuasive, and special occasion speeches.[10]

Informative vs. Persuasive Speeches

If your purpose is to get your listeners to change their beliefs, then your presentation is a persuasive one. However, if your intent is simply to make the listeners aware of a subject or to present some new ideas or information, then the presentation is an informative one. In other words, **informative speeches** promote understanding of an idea or convey a body of related facts. Examples of topics for an informative speech include the following:

> How to perform the Heimlich maneuver
> How stress affects your body
> How to collect information on day-care centers
> How airplanes fly
> How regular exercise affects your body

By contrast, **persuasive speeches** seek to influence choices or opinions. Examples of topics for persuasive speeches include these:

> Why everyone should make out a will
> Why people should use a designated driver when they drink
> Why sexist language is offensive
> Why on-campus parking lots should be expanded
> Why regular exercise is important

As a speaker you need to determine whether your speech is informative or persuasive before you begin preparing because the two types require very different approaches (which will be discussed in detail in Units 3 and 4). Nevertheless, only a thin line actually divides informative and persuasive presentations. For example, persuasive presentations must inform as well as persuade. How can a speaker persuade listeners unless they are informed of the facts? In the same way, many informative presentations are indirectly persuasive. For example, an informative report on a particular subject, such as the effects of exercise, might indirectly persuade listeners to take action. However, unless your intent was to try to influence your listeners to agree with your position on the subject, your speech would be classified as informative.

Special Occasion Speeches

Special occasion speeches lend a sense of distinction to important events in our lives. These speeches typically are given at such events as funerals, job promotions, award ceremonies, and luncheons. For example, Tom Hanks's Academy Award acceptance speech, President Reagan's eulogy for the victims of the *Challenger* explosion, and Barbara Jordan's keynote address at the 1992 Democratic National Convention are all examples of special occasion speeches. Suppose you introduce another student in the class, accept an award, give an entertaining speech, or pay tribute to a retiring professor—these are also special occasion speeches. The special occasion speeches that you are the most likely to give will be discussed in detail in Appendix A.

The Communication Process and the Public Speaker

▼ ▼ ▼

You already know a lot about communication. You even may have studied about it in another class—English, perhaps. However, you probably have not viewed communication from a public speaking perspective. By understanding the communication process, you should be able to anticipate and, therefore, minimize misunderstandings.

The *Oxford English Dictionary* lists the Latin root of *communicate* as *communicare*, which means "to make common to many, share."[11] According to this definition, when people communicate, they express their ideas and feelings in a way that is understandable (common) to other people. Therefore, communication is the process of people sharing thoughts, ideas, and feelings with each other in commonly understandable ways. The model in Figure 1.1 shows the basic elements of the communication process: speaker/listeners, stimulus and motivation, message encoding and decoding, code, feedback, environment, and noise. Let's look at each of these communication elements to see how they relate to your speaking success.

Speakers/Listeners

Although the speaker is generally considered the sender of the message and the listeners the receivers of the message, both are simultaneously sending and receiving throughout the speech. For example, as audience members go

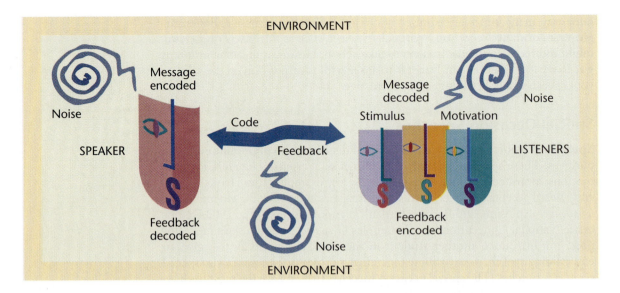

Figure 1.1

Basic Model of
Communication

through the various stages of listening (discussed in Chapter 4), they are sending messages at the same time—through laughter, frowns, bored looks, or sometimes questions. Similarly, while you are speaking, you also are receiving audience responses and making minor adjustments to your speech based on those responses. Minor adjustments might include speaking louder, giving a more detailed explanation, showing another visual aid, or adding another example. Being able to interpret your audience's nonverbal cues is so important to speaking success that an entire section in Chapter 4 is devoted to this topic.

Stimulus and Motivation

Before people take the initiative to communicate, they must be sufficiently stimulated and motivated. First, a **stimulus** triggers a thought, which in turn triggers the desire to communicate. However, a stimulus alone is not enough to prompt communication; sufficient **motivation** (or desire) is also necessary. To illustrate, think about how many times an instructor has asked a question in class and, even though you thought you knew the answer (were stimulated), you did not respond. Perhaps you were not sufficiently motivated—that is, you saw no personal benefit in answering. Or perhaps you saw greater benefit in not answering—you feared being criticized by the professor or looking foolish by risking a wrong answer. Of course, if you knew that the professor graded on class participation, your motivation to answer likely would be greater.

Similarly an audience must also be stimulated and then motivated to listen. Just because audience members are sitting in chairs facing you doesn't mean that they are paying attention. They may be preoccupied with problems at home or work (internal stimulus) or be distracted by a person or object (external stimulus), such as the good-looking person sitting nearby. As a speaker, you must provide the stimulus that grabs your audience's attention and focuses it on your topic. At the same time, you need to motivate audience members to continue listening by showing them how your presentation will be of personal value to them. Will your speech be entertaining? Fascinating? Will it help listeners save money, look and feel healthier, enjoy life more, or what? If you provide both stimulus and motivation for your listeners, their internal problems or concerns are less likely to keep them from paying attention to your speech. See Chapter 4 for more specific information on stimulus and motivation.

Message Encoding and Decoding

The process of deciding how best to convey your message to your specific audience is called **encoding**. Such things as language choice, speech volume and tone of voice, facial expressions, and gestures must be considered. Careful audience analysis (see Chapter 5) makes encoding more effective. When your listeners pick up your message, they try to determine exactly what you mean. Thus, **decoding** is the process the listeners go through in interpreting the sender's meaning.

Although encoding and decoding sound simple enough, they are responsible for some of the main misunderstandings that occur between speakers and listeners. As a speaker, you use your own **frame of reference**—your experience and background—to encode messages. However, listeners use their own frames of reference to decode those messages. There would be no problems if speakers and listeners had the same frames of reference, but of course, they don't. Because people's frames of reference include educational background, race, sex, hometown, parents, attitudes, personality, past experiences, and much more, no two of us will have exactly the same frame of reference. Having different frames of reference increases the probability that speakers and audience members will have difficulty interpreting each other's messages. This is especially true when there are cultural differences, as the following examples illustrate:

- Talking about the importance of completing a project on schedule when some audience members are Muslims could cause interpretation problems. "Muslims believe that human efforts are determined by the will of Allah, not by a schedule."[12]

- Being direct and getting right to the point, which is generally valued as open and honest by speakers in the United States, may be seen as intrusive and brash by listeners from such countries as China, Korea, and Japan, as well as many Arab countries. In these countries an indirect, slowly-work-up-to-the-point approach is preferred.[13]

- When audience members nod their heads in Bulgaria, they mean no, rather than yes.[14]

- The "A-OK" gesture speakers make by forming a circle with thumb and forefinger has different meanings in other countries. In France it means

If this American coach were visiting Australia or Germany, the audience would view his "A-OK" gesture as obscene.

© Bob Daemmrich/Stock, Boston

zero or worthless; in Australia, Brazil, and Germany it is considered to be an obscene gesture.[15]

▸ The "Come Alive with Pepsi" commercial that was so successful in the United States didn't translate well into other languages. In Germany it translates to "Come Out of the Grave with Pepsi," and in many Asian countries it translates to "Bring Your Ancestors Back from the Grave."[16]

To minimize encoding/decoding problems between you and your audience, you should always keep the audience's frame of reference in your mind. Try to anticipate possible misunderstandings and, by carefully choosing your words and examples, correct as many potential problems as possible ahead of time.

Verbal, Visual, and Vocal Codes

Your messages are carried to your audience by codes consisting of symbols (light waves and sound waves). Each time you speak to an audience, three different communication codes carry your messages: (1) the **verbal code** (as defined in this text) includes spoken and written words; (2) the **visual code** includes anything nonverbal such as personal appearance, facial expression, eye contact, and visual aids; and (3) the **vocal code** includes tone of voice, volume, pitch, rate, emphasis, and vocal quality. The difference among the codes can be illustrated in the following example. Suppose you arrive home after a hard day at work or class. As you walk in, you slam the door, plop down on your favorite recliner, and let out a long sigh. When asked, "How was your day?" you reply, "Oh, it was fine." In this instance, to which code would the questioner pay more attention—the slamming of the door (visual), the loud sigh (vocal), or the actual words (verbal)? Or suppose one of your professors told you that you were doing good work in class but at the same time frowned slightly and sounded rather impersonal. Would you believe the verbal message and ignore the visual and vocal ones?

Studies have found that when adults attempt to determine the meaning of a statement, they rely more heavily on vocal and visual cues than they do on the words that are actually spoken.[17] Unfortunately many speakers think that the only really important code is the verbal code and tend to overlook the other two codes. Unit Two focuses on how to use all three codes to make your presentations powerful and memorable.

Feedback

When you observe your own speaking behavior and determine your strengths and weaknesses, when you ask a friend to give an opinion on a practice speech or an actual speech, or when audience members respond to your presentation (positively or negatively), you are experiencing feedback. **Feedback** refers to people's verbal, visual, and vocal responses to messages. Not only is feedback helpful for self-monitoring (which involves evaluating and modifying behavior until it meets personal expectations), but it is the only way a speaker can know whether messages have been interpreted by the listeners as intended. Usually feedback from an audience is visual (such as facial expressions or posture) or vocal (such as a collective sigh, laughter, or groans). Occasionally a listener will make a verbal comment or ask a question. Without feedback a speaker can only assume that the messages have been received correctly. Therefore, as a speaker, you will want to pay close attention to the feedback from your audience.

Environment

The **environment** includes the time, place, and physical and social surroundings in which the speech occurs.[18] A speech scheduled during the evening mealtime (when people wish they were eating) or right after lunch (when they might be feeling groggy) will probably be less successful than a speech given either in the morning or later in the evening. The size of the room, the brightness of the lights, the room temperature, and the comfort and arrangement of chairs can certainly affect the success of a speech. For example, forty people crowded into a small conference room gives the impression that the speaker must be really good to attract such a crowd; however, the same forty people scattered in an auditorium gives the impression that the speaker must not be very compelling or more people would be there. The effective speaker plans and controls the environment as much as possible. Specific environmental suggestions are included in Chapter 8.

Noise

Anything that interferes with communication by distorting or blocking the message is called **noise**. *External noise* includes distractions in the environment, such

What does the feedback from this audience tell you about the speaker?

© Sepp Seitz/Woodfin Camp & Associates, Inc.

as people talking, too bright or too dim lighting, or even the speaker's poor grammar. *Internal noise* refers to conditions inside the listeners, such as headaches, preoccupation with other problems, or lack of knowledge of the topic. Internal noises can also affect you as a speaker. For example, if you are tired from studying too late the night before or are worried about something, you are experiencing internal noise. When possible, select speaking environments that are relatively free of any external noises and try to reduce your internal noise.

As you can see, successful communication involves more than just talking and listening—it's hard work and requires careful preparation. However, the reward of all the work and preparation is an enthusiastic, powerful speech. Successful speakers (1) stimulate and motivate their listeners, (2) do their best to encode their presentations for each specific audience, (3) realize that their visual and vocal communication is as important as their verbal message, and (4) pay careful attention to audience feedback, the speaking environment, and possible noise factors. In addition to preparing a speech that communicates with your audience, you have another very important responsibility, as discussed in the following section: to be an ethical speaker.

Ethics: The Public Speaker's Obligation

▼ ▼ ▼

Because speakers are in a position to influence a large number of people, they need be ethical—to research information carefully and completely, to present only truthful information, and to give credit for all ideas and words that are not original with them. According to Gallup Poll surveys, the American public is fairly skeptical about the honesty and ethics of politicians and many other professional people.[19] For example, since 1976 pollsters have asked this question: "How would you rate the honesty and ethical standards of people in these different fields—very high, high, average, low, or very low?" As you can see in Table 1.1, in 1994 only dentists, college teachers, clergy, and druggists/pharmacists scored 50 percent or better. U.S. senators, state office-holders, and congressmen scored near the bottom, with their ethical standards judged to be higher only than persons selling cars or insurance. Apparently, the American public has little faith in the honesty or ethics of its elected officials.

Examples of Unethical Behavior

Let's take a look at some of the recent cases that may have led to the loss of public confidence. Of course, scandals such as Watergate (which ended with the resignation of President Nixon), the Iran-Contra affair (which raised questions about congressional ethics), and now Whitewatergate (which alleged financial wrongdoing by Bill and Hillary Clinton) have had a lot to do with the erosion of public confidence in our leaders. Other cases, such as those of Senator Joe Biden and Commissioner Lena Guerrero, have contributed to the gradual erosion.

In 1987 Biden, a senator from Delaware, had a good chance of winning the Democratic presidential nomination. In a debate before a crowd at the Iowa State Fair, he delivered an especially powerful closing statement that left the crowd speechless. His remarks were based on a political ad by Neil Kinnock, the British Labour party leader.[20] In fact, Biden had used Kinnock's ideas several times before, but always giving credit: "You know, I saw a speech by the British Labour party leader, Neil Kinnock, and he said something that I think is important."[21] This time, however, he did not give credit: "I started thinking, as I was coming over here . . ."[22] Basically Biden gave Kinnock's speech word for word. He even included the section in which Kinnock referred to his coal-miner heritage (Biden had no coal-miner ancestors). When the press compared tapes of Biden's rousing conclusion and Kinnock's ad, they found that even the gestures and pauses were the same. At first, Biden explained the incident as an accident— after all, he had given credit in previous speeches. However, when the press discovered that he had also used Robert Kennedy's exact words in one of his speeches, had flunked a college course on suspicion of cheating, had not graduated with three degrees as he had claimed in response to a hostile question from the audience, and had been accused of plagiarizing a paper when he was a law student, his presidential bid was over.[23]

Table 1.1

▼▼▼

Profession	Rating									
Percentage of Respondents Rating Each Profession as Having "High" or "Very High" Ethical Standards										
	1977	1981	1983	1985	1988	1990	1991	1992	1993	1994
Druggists, pharmacists	NA	59%	61%	65%	66%	62%	60%	66%	65%	62%
Clergy	61	63	64	67	60	55	57	54	53	54
Dentists	NA	52	51	56	51	52	50	50	50	51
College teachers	46	45	47	53	54	51	45	50	52	50
Engineers	46	48	45	53	48	50	45	48	49	49
Medical doctors	51	50	52	58	53	52	54	52	51	47
Policemen	37	44	41	47	47	49	43	42	50	46
Funeral directors	26	30	29	32	24	35	35	35	34	30
Public opinion pollsters	NA	NA	NA	NA	NA	NA	NA	NA	NA	27
Bankers	39	39	38	38	26	32	30	27	28	27
Business executives	19	19	18	23	16	25	21	18	20	22
TV reporters/ commentators	NA	36	33	33	22	32	29	31	28	22
Journalists	33	32	28	31	23	30	26	27	26	20
Local officeholders	14	14	16	18	14	21	19	15	19	18
Building contractors	18	19	18	21	22	20	20	19	20	17
Newspaper reporters	NA	30	26	29	22	24	24	25	22	17
Lawyers	26	25	24	27	18	22	22	18	16	17
Stockbrokers	NA	21	19	20	13	14	14	13	13	15
Real estate agents	13	14	13	15	13	16	17	14	15	14
Labor union leaders	13	14	12	13	14	15	13	14	14	14
State officeholders	11	12	13	15	11	17	14	11	14	12
Advertising practitioners	10	9	9	12	7	12	12	10	8	12
Senators	19	20	16	23	19	24	19	13	18	12
Insurance salesmen	15	11	13	10	10	13	14	9	10	9
Congressmen	16	15	14	20	16	20	19	11	14	9
Car salesmen	8	6	6	5	6	6	8	5	6	6

SOURCE: Leslie McAneny and David W. Moore, "Congress and Media Sink in Public Esteem," *The Gallup Poll Monthly 349* (October 1994), 4.

Texas railroad commissioner Lena Guerrero lost a promising career in politics because of falsehoods in one of her speeches.

© Ron Edmonds/Wide World Photos, Inc.

In 1991 Lena Guerrero was appointed railroad commissioner by Texas Governor Ann Richards. According to her resume, Guerrero had a degree from the University of Texas and was a member of Phi Beta Kappa, a scholastic honor society. In an address to the graduating class of Texas A&M, she commiserated with the graduates by saying that she knew just how they felt at that moment because she remembered her graduation so well. In actual fact Guerrero had never graduated (she still needed to complete six courses) and was not an honor student.[24] When she was first asked about the inaccuracies, Guerrero denied them. Later she said she was "stunned to learn she had not graduated from UT," and finally, twelve days after the inaccuracies came to light, she admitted that she had lied and resigned from public office.[25]

The media, which are supposed to be objective in reporting the news, also have ethical problems. In their book *Communication Ethics: Methods of Analysis*, James Jaksa and Michael Pritchard report the following:

> On November 17, 1992, NBC's *Dateline* featured a controversy over General Motors' 1973–1987 pickup trucks. The models during those years were designed with fuel tanks mounted on the sides of the vehicle. *Dateline* set out to show that this location renders the tanks highly vulnerable to

leaks and fiery explosions on side impact. Seen by an estimated 17 million viewers, a short segment of the feature showed a side collision with one of the pickups resulting in just such an explosion.

Unfortunately, *Dateline* failed to make clear to its viewers that its consultants had installed remote-control, electrical "igniters" under the two pickups it tested. Initially denying that it had improperly "rigged" the explosion, NBC eventually extended an elaborate apology to General Motors and viewers for its misleading footage.[26]

In 1994, in an even more startling case, breast cancer researcher Roger Poisson of the Saint-Luc Hospital at the University of Montreal was found to have "falsified the results of some of his experiments over the last 15 years and fabricated data for others" and that the Cancer Institute knew of the problem but did not report it.[27] The Cancer Institute claims that the falsified and fabricated data do not change the outcome of the study. The research is particularly important to women because it found that in preventing the spread of cancer, a lumpectomy is as effective as a mastectomy. In a lumpectomy only the cancerous breast tissue is removed; in a mastectomy the entire breast is removed.[28] Unfortunately, according to Representative Pat Schroeder, "Once again women cannot be sure of the science behind their doctors' recommendations on the treatment of breast cancer."[29]

The Cost of Unethical Behavior

Not only has each of these cases added to the erosion of confidence that the American public has in politicians, professionals, and the media, but the people involved in these cases have seen an end to their dreams. Senator Biden lost his chance to be president; Lena Guerrero lost her chance for a promising career in politics and the chance to be a role model for women and Hispanics; and not only is Dr. Poisson's career undoubtedly over, but the director of the research project, Dr. Bernard Fisher of the University of Pittsburgh, was also asked to resign. As for NBC and "Dateline NBC," their reputation for fair and accurate reporting has been incalculably damaged, and only an elaborate on-air apology kept them from being sued.[30] In addition, the president of NBC, Michael Gartner, as well as the show's executive producer, senior producer, and story producer, were pressured into resigning.[31]

Exaggeration, Distortion, and Plagiarism

As these examples illustrate, to be an ethical speaker you must be careful to tell only the truth, without exaggeration or distortion. Although people describing the size of the fish they caught may exaggerate and distort the "facts," listeners expect only the truth from public speakers. Unfortunately, when speakers feel threatened or insecure, they may abandon ethical standards and exaggerate or distort the facts. **Exaggeration** involves overstating or presenting something as greater or more important than it is; **distortion** involves misrepresenting or twisting facts or stating something as true when it is only partially true or not true at all. Both exaggeration and distortion are forms of lying and, as such, are unethical. For example, Senator Biden was angry with the question about his education, which seemed to imply something negative about his intellect, so he distorted his record and claimed he had earned three degrees (he actually had two). Biden also loved the approach that Kinnock had taken in his ad—it expressed exactly how Biden felt. Richard Cramer, author of *What It Takes: The Way to the White House*, reports that Biden "knew that stuff from the Kinnock tape like a song in his head."[32] Under pressure to finish the debate with a stirring conclusion, Biden chose the words that expressed his feelings exactly—even though they were someone else's words. At the time it may have seemed a harmless distortion to Biden, but the American public didn't agree.

As a public speaker you must keep in mind that exaggeration and distortion are only half a step away from overt lying. When Lena Guerrero resigned from office, she told reporters:

> I now realize I have been in a hurry all my life. In my haste, I was reckless. . . . I allowed misperceptions, embellishments and errors of fact about my academic record to go uncorrected. . . . I've done a lot of soul-searching about how that happened. And the only thing I can say to you is perhaps you want something to be so much that you begin to believe it is.[33]

Perhaps Guerrero believed she was only an "embellishment" away from graduating—she had six more courses to complete. However, to the American public the embellishment was a falsehood that remained on her resume for twelve years before it was finally challenged.

In addition to researching carefully and reporting the truth, you must be careful not to plagiarize. If you read an article (or hear an ad or watch a TV program) and then use the information in that article, ad, or program in your speech without citing the source(s), you are plagiarizing even if you paraphrase the content. **Plagiarism** is using the ideas of someone else (whether paraphrased or word for word) without giving them credit. Biden apparently plagiarized a paper in college and parts of at least two of his speeches as a politician. As a result, people lost trust in him. College students who plagiarize all or part of their speeches receive a failing grade for the speech and sometimes for the course and may even be expelled from school. Chapter 10 discusses how to conduct your search for speech information so as to avoid accidental plagiarism.

Classroom Ethics

One of my public speaking classes was given the assignment of coming up with a code of ethics agreeable to everyone in the class. One student said that he didn't see why everyone was so hung up on ethics in using facts and statistics. After all, he said, speaking is entertainment, and if it made the speech more entertaining, why shouldn't he make up information? He added that when he was in debates in high school, he had always made up evidence and statistics and no one had ever said anything. Another student agreed and said that in a previous speech

(text continues on p. 22)

Avoiding Public Speaking Misconceptions

The following questionnaire is designed to call attention to common misconceptions about public speaking. Some of the following statements are sound public speaking principles based on research discussed throughout this book; other statements are misconceptions often thought to be true by beginning speakers.

Directions: If you think a statement is generally accurate, mark it "T"; if you think the statement is a myth, mark it "F." Then compare your answers with the explanations that follow.

_____ 1. In persuasive speeches, your most important persuasive tools are logic and evidence.

_____ 2. Good speakers rarely get nervous.

_____ 3. Visual aids are nice but are not essential to a speech.

_____ 4. Speakers should be experts in the field on which they are speaking.

_____ 5. Red is an excellent color for highlighting graphs and transparencies and emphasizing key data.

_____ 6. Audiences consider male speakers to be more credible than female speakers.

_____ 7. Handouts passed out during the speech help keep the audience's attention.

_____ 8. In a small conference room where the audience is seated around a table, the speaker should stand.

_____ 9. Wearing bright, colorful clothing and accessories adds to your power and credibility as a speaker.

_____ 10. Only accomplished public speakers can deliver effective presentations.

Answers:

1. *False*. Although logic and supporting evidence are important in persuading others, research has indicated that these alone cannot sway most listeners. In fact, one study found that most audience members couldn't distinguish the logical arguments in a presentation from the illogical ones.[34] However, when the speaker used words and phrases that implied a logical progression of thought (such as "It is obvious that," "Therefore," "As a result," and "It is possible to conclude that"), people judged the speech to be logical even if it was not. Furthermore, when listeners favor the speaker's proposal and/or

consider the speaker to be credible, they likely will judge a speech as having convincing evidence even when it does not. However, no matter how strong your logic and evidence may be, your most persuasive tool is to relate your arguments to the personal and organizational needs of your listeners. (Unit Four discusses persuasive speeches in detail.)

2. *False*. Although good speakers may feel more positive about speaking than inexperienced speakers, every new situation causes a certain amount of anxiety or "butterflies" for all speakers. Good speakers have learned to view this feeling as a sign that their body is sending them the additional energy needed for energetic speaking; poor speakers see it as a sign that they are falling apart and are going to do a lousy job. (Chapter 3 offers more information on coping with speech anxiety.) Good speakers also build self-confidence by being well prepared. Disaster can result when you haven't researched your audience, haven't carefully planned and supported your main ideas for this particular audience, don't have professional-looking visual aids, and haven't anticipated possible audience questions and objections. In general, the more you prepare and practice, the more confident you will be.

3. *False*. This may be one of the biggest misconceptions of all. Although you can give a speech without visual aids, research has indicated that we learn and remember more when we can "see" the speaker's ideas at the same time we "hear" them. This is especially true for speeches that are technical or cover complicated information, such as "How a 747 Gets Off the Ground" or "Three Football Plays Everyone Should Know." In fact, visuals are so powerful that when a speech is over, audience members are more likely to remember what they saw than what they heard. Therefore make sure your visual aids are accurate and directly relate to what you want the audience to remember. *Use of visual aids is the rule, not the exception*. (Chapter 6 focuses on how to develop and use visual aids.)

4. *False*. You don't have to be an expert to give an excellent talk on a subject. In fact, sometimes experts are so immersed in the subject matter that they have difficulty communicating to a general audience unfamiliar with the jargon. In some cases, such as when you're giving a talk at your job, you might arrange to have an expert available in the audience to field any technical questions. Or, if no expert is present, you could refer technical questions to the appropriate person for a later response.

5. *False*. Red is an exciting and vibrant color. However, using red on visual aids has one big problem—some members of your audience may be color-blind to reds and greens. The majority of people with red-green color blindness are men, but some women are affected as well. Blue is a safer color to use.

6. *True*. Although changes are definitely occurring, audiences unfortunately still consider male speakers to be more knowledgeable and credible than female speakers. One source points out that "on professional newscasts, males are viewed as more credible anchors than females [and that] 92 percent of commercial voice-overs employ male voices."[35]

7. *False*. Actually, giving out handouts during a speech almost ensures audience *inattention*. The distractions (both visual and verbal) that are created as papers or other materials are passed from person to person makes paying attention to the speaker almost impossible. Furthermore, audience members who begin reading a handout will tend to

(continued)

(continued)

tune out the speaker completely. Unless your listeners need to refer to the handout while you are talking, don't pass it out until the end of the speech.

8. *True.* Normally the only time the speaker should sit down is if he or she is blocking audience view of any visual aids. Standing gives the speaker a better view of audience reactions and adds to the speaker's authority and power. When a speaker is seated and everyone appears to have equal status, audience members are more likely to interact with one another and less likely to listen to the speaker. Or, if they are argumentative, they are more likely to argue with one another, as well as the speaker.

9. *False.* Although bright, colorful clothing and accessories are appropriate in some situations (for example, the fashion industry), many professions and businesses prefer more conservative colors and minimal accessories. In fact, wearing a dark suit or jacket while speaking will automatically give both men and women the appearance of personal power and authority. Dress consultants tell us two important things: (1) jackets and suits broadcast professionalism, and (2) the darker the jacket or suit, the more authority it conveys.[36] If you feel your organization is more casual or you wish to downplay your authority, a lighter color may be appropriate, or you may wish to remove your jacket before or during the presentation. (Chapter 8 contains more information on delivery and appearance.)

10. *False.* Accomplished public speakers, often through trial and error, have learned the "dos and don'ts" of effective speaking presented in this book. There is nothing mysterious about this knowledge. Anyone, even someone who has never made a speech before, can give an effective presentation simply by following the guidelines covered throughout this book.

class she had used a detailed illustration about her grandmother dying from cancer as an attention-getter. The illustration had touched her audience; several people in the class even had tears in their eyes. Actually, she told us, her grandmother never had cancer, but if she had used a hypothetical example, she felt the speech would not have been as moving or effective. As you can imagine, a lively discussion followed. What do you think about these two students' arguments?

Summary
▼ ▼ ▼

You will have many opportunities during your life to give speeches that can benefit your career, your self-esteem, and even society. There are three basic types of speeches: (1) informative speeches, which promote understanding of an idea or convey a body of related facts, (2) persuasive speeches, which influence opinions or choices, and (3) special occasion speeches, which are given at such events as funerals, job promotions, award ceremonies, and luncheons.

To minimize misunderstandings between you and your audiences, you need to pay particular attention to frame of reference (a person's background and experiences). Different frames of reference increase the probability that speakers and audience members will have difficulty interpreting one another's messages.

You also need to consider the three types of communication codes—verbal, visual, vocal—as inseparable. Communication is greatly improved when speakers use all three codes effectively. Studies have found that when adults attempt to determine the meaning of a statement, they rely more heavily on vocal and visual cues than on verbal cues.

Be especially careful about exaggeration and plagiarism—both can cause others to judge you as unethical and untrustworthy.

1. If you haven't yet completed the questionnaire in Appendix D, please do so now and turn in your scores to your instructor. It's important to do this now because you will retake the questionnaire during the last week of class, compare your "before" and "after" scores, and analyze your progress during the course. All scores will be kept completely confidential and will be used only to assist your instructor in designing a course that will benefit you the most.

2. Think over the past year and make a list of the opportunities to give speeches that came your way (regardless of whether you accepted). Consider your community, your campus, any clubs or organizations including religious ones, your job (if you had one), any volunteer work, and any classroom opportunities. If you spoke in any of these settings, what was the outcome? If you didn't give any speeches last year, imagine what benefits could have resulted if you had agreed to speak in one or more of these settings. Share your list with a classmate.

3. Find out whether your business, profession, or favorite volunteer organization has a speakers' bureau. If so, ask what type of speeches members give and to what kinds of audiences. If possible, get one of their information sheets to share with the class.

4. Sit in on a city council meeting. Which of the basic elements of the communication process seemed to cause the council members the most trouble? Describe any differences in frames of reference that you observed.

5. In groups of four or five, decide on a code of ethics for your class, for both listeners and speakers. Once each group has agreed on a list, narrow and combine them into one list that is agreeable to everyone, including your instructor.[37]

6. Select someone in your class whom you don't know personally. For fifteen minutes or less, interview each other to find out all the normal information people usually share (for example, major and minor field of study, home state, marital status, hobbies, and so on). In addition to the usual information, find out something unusual or unique about each other. This could be something that is true today or something that happened years ago (for example, one of you is from a family of ten, is an identical twin, fought in the Persian Gulf War, reads three to five books each week, and so on). If you take notes, keep them brief—words or phrases work best. When your interview time is up, introduce each other to at least one other person in the class or to the entire class.

Notes

1. Margie B. Sellinger, "Candy Lightner Prods Congress," *People Weekly* 22 (9 July 1984), 102, 105.

2. Candy Lightner, *Giving Sorrow Words: How to Cope with Grief and Get on with Your Life* (New York: Warner Books, 1990).

3. Kurt Sandholtz, "Do You Have What It Takes?" *Managing Your Career*, published by *The Wall Street Journal* (Fall 1987), p. 10.

4. This event occurred when I was consulting at Bell Helicopter.

5. "The Science of Speechmaking," *Dun's Review and Modern Industry* (December 1962), p. 32.

6. William R. Kimel and Melford E. Monsees, "Engineering Graduates: How Good Are They?" *Engineering Education* (November 1979), 210–212.

7. A summary of studies showing the importance of communication skills can be found in Samuel L. Becker and Leah R. V. Ekdom, "That Forgotten Basic Skill: Oral Communication," *Iowa Journal of Speech Communication* 12 (Fall 1980), 1–18.

8. Suggested by Neil Patten, Ferris State College, Michigan.

9. T. W. Harrell and M. S. Harrell, *Stanford MBA Careers: A 20-Year Longitudinal Study* (Stanford, CA: Graduate School of Business Research Paper No. 723, 1984).

10. The first known "handbook" of speaking was Aristotle's *Rhetoric*. In it Aristotle listed three similar categories of rhetoric or speaking: forensic (speaking in court), deliberative (political or legislative speaking), and epideictic (ceremonial speaking). For a detailed look at classical or neoclassical rhetorical criticism, see James J. Murphy, ed., *A Synoptic History of Classical Rhetoric* (Davis, CA: Hermagoras Press, 1983); S. K. Foss, *Rhetorical Criticism: Exploration and Practice* (Prospect Heights, IL: Waveland Press, 1989); or Malcolm O. Sillars, *Messages, Meanings, and Culture: Approaches to Communication Criticism* (New York: HarperCollins, 1991).

11. *The Oxford English Dictionary*, 2nd ed., vol. II (Oxford: Clarendon, 1961), p. 699.

12. Mary Munter, "Cross-Cultural Communication for Managers," *Business Horizons* 36 (May–June 1993), 69.

13. Munter, "Cross-Cultural Communications," p. 74.

14. Munter, "Cross-Cultural Communications," p. 76.

15. Roger E. Axtell, *Gestures: The Do's and Taboos of Body Language Around the World* (New York: Wiley, 1991), p. 47.

16. David A. Ricks, *Big Business Blunders* (Homewood, IL: Dow Jones–Irwin, 1983).

17. T. A. Seay and M. K. Altekruse, "Verbal and Nonverbal Behavior in Judgments of Facilitative Conditions," *Journal of Counseling Psychology* 26, 108–119; Judee K. Burgoon, "Nonverbal Signals," in Mark L. Knapp and Gerald R. Miller, eds., *Handbook of Interpersonal Communication* (Beverly Hills, CA: Sage, 1985), pp. 346–347.

18. James N. Holm, *Business and Professional Communication* (Boston: American Press, 1981), p. 22.

19. Leslie McAneny and David W. Moore, "Congress and Media Sink in Public Esteem," *The Gallup Poll Monthly* 349 (October 1994), 2–4. For more information see "A Crisis of Confidence" in James A. Jaksa and Michael S. Pritchard, *Communication Ethics: Methods of Analysis*, 2nd ed. (Belmont, CA: Wadsworth, 1994), pp. 35–62.

20. Richard Ben Cramer, *What It Takes: The Way to the White House* (New York: Random House, 1992), p. 538.

21. Cramer, *What It Takes*, p. 544.

22. Cramer, *What It Takes*, p. 545.

23. Cramer, *What It Takes*, pp. 627, 630, 647, 656, 660, 662.

24. *Facts on File* 52 (26 November 1992), 893; and *Fort Worth Star-Telegram*, (24 September 1992), pp. A1, A10, A17.

25. *Fort Worth Star-Telegram* (25 September 1992), pp. A1, A5, A26.

26. Jaksa and Pritchard, *Communication Ethics*, p. 61.

27. Stephen Burd, "Critics Say Cancer Institute Hid Fraud in Breast-Cancer Project," *The Chronicle of Higher Education* 40 (13 April 1994), A28.

28. Burd, "Critics Say," p. A28.

29. Burd, "Critics Say," p. A28.

30. Jaksa and Pritchard, *Communication Ethics*, p. 62.

31. *Facts on File* 52 (8 April 1993), 250.

32. Cramer, *What It Takes*, p. 544.

33. The Associated Press, "Excerpts from Guerrero's Announcement," *Fort Worth Star-Telegram* (25 September 1992), p. A4.

34. Erwin P. Bettinghouse and Michael J. Cody, *Persuasive Communication*, 4th ed. (New York: Holt, Rinehart & Winston, 1987), pp. 150–152.

35. Hazel J. Rozema and John W. Gray, "How Wide Is Your Communication Gender Gap," *Personnel Journal* 66 (July 1988), pp. 98–105.

36. We suggest that you read Nancy Golden, *Dress Right for Success* (New York: Gregg Division, McGraw-Hill, 1986); and John T. Molloy, *The New Dress for Success* and *The Woman's Dress for Success Book* (New York: Warner Books, 1989 and 1987, respectively). These, and many similar books, are available at most bookstores. The following article is also recommended: Anne Russell, "Fine-Tuning Your Corporate Image," *Black Enterprise* (May 1992), pp. 74–80.

37. Adapted from an application exercise in Michael Osborn and Suzanne Osborn, *Public Speaking*, 3rd ed. (Boston: Houghton Mifflin, 1994), p. 26.

2

Public Speaking: Getting Started

INSTITUTE OF TECHNOLOGY LIBRARY MISSISSAUGA, ONTARIO

TAKE A CAREFUL LOOK AT YOUR classmates. Can you tell just by looking (and by listening to the comments they have made in class) which ones will give the best speeches? Are you thinking that they look more confident than you feel? If so, rest assured that they are thinking the same thing about you. Although one or a few of your classmates may have a special knack for speaking, most people know nothing about speech making when they begin this course. Your feelings at this point may be similar to this student as he looked back on his first speech in the course:

> I put off taking speech for as long as possible. I was scared to death to get up in front of people. Two weeks before we started our speeches, I had trouble sleeping at night. The night before my first speech I didn't sleep at all. Once I did my speech and saw it on videotape, I realized that it wasn't nearly as bad as I had anticipated. I didn't go blank while speaking like I usually do; nobody laughed at me; and I even spoke louder than I normally do . . . I don't want to sound self-centered, but I feel as if I have improved on everything I attempted.

This chapter will introduce you to the characteristics of good speakers and give you an overview of how to plan and prepare an effective speech. Guidelines for building your confidence as a speaker are discussed in the next chapter.

Becoming a Good Public Speaker
▼ ▼ ▼

No doubt you have been to your share of dull, uninteresting lectures. Maybe it was a professor droning on about nonprofit institutions and tax inequities or a long-winded colleague explaining changes in the company's insurance benefits. These dreary presentations reflect the fact that many speakers are unaware of the basic characteristics of good public speaking. To ensure that your speeches are successful, you need to keep the following principles in mind.

Respect the Diversity of Audience Members

Instead of considering their audiences as fair game for manipulation and/or ignoring cultural or gender differences, good speakers respect the opinions and diversity of audience members. Listeners are considered equal participants in the communication process. Before planning a speech, you should first analyze your audience for their knowledge of your topic, their beliefs and values, their cultural makeup, and their age and gender. (Chapter 5 gives detailed information on audience analysis.) You can then use this information as a guide in selecting your topic as well as planning your verbal style, examples, and supporting evidence for the most effective presentation possible.

Speaking to a diverse audience can be enjoyable as long as you expect and prepare for individual and cultural differences. For instance, will all your exam-

Good speakers respect the opinions and diversity of their audience.

© Chip Henderson/Tony Stone Images, Inc.

ples be equally instructive and enjoyable for male as well as female listeners? For Hispanic as well as Native American audiences? Might a certain example cause a negative reaction for retired listeners but not for younger audience members just beginning their careers? The more you know and respect your audience, the better you can prepare your message to fit their frames of reference (their viewpoints and opinions) and the better your communication with them will be.

Know as Much as Possible About Listening

Good speakers realize that successful communication is a two-way street. No matter how polished the speech, it will not succeed unless the listeners do a good job of listening. Unfortunately, without help from a skilled speaker, listeners typically remember only about 10–25 percent of the ideas in a speech.[1] Therefore it's important to know the five stages of listening, the potential pitfalls for listeners in each stage, and ways to reduce listening problems (covered in Chapter 4). For example, in the initial "sensing" stage listeners pay attention only to things that are important or of interest to them and tune out everything else. As a result, it's crucial in this first stage to show how important and/or interesting your ideas are. (One effective way of grabbing—and keeping—audience attention is by using interesting, powerful visual aids, as described in Chapter 7.)

Organize Carefully to Improve Understanding and Recall

Effective, well-organized presentations seem to flow from idea to idea, from one main point to the next. You will always be well organized if, in preparing and presenting your speech, you remember the acronym *FLOW*.

F *Focus* audience attention and interest.
L *Lead in* to your topic.
O *Organize* and *support* your main ideas with visual and verbal materials.
W *Wrap-up* or conclude.

The FLOW sequence will be discussed in more detail later in this chapter. Chapters 11 and 15 explain how to use the FLOW sequence to develop effective informative and persuasive speeches.

Use Language Effectively

Although well-defined acronyms can be useful as a memory aid for your audience, it is generally advisable to limit use of jargon, including unfamiliar acronyms, that might confuse your listeners. For example, an educator who tells new freshmen, "The SPE 1633 course which meets on MWF is required for a BS. Of course, you can't enroll until your SAT and TASP scores are received," likely will quickly lose most listeners. Similarly a manager who refers to a RAM (required action memorandum) may confuse some of his computer-literate listeners, who think he is talking about RAM (random access memory).

Using jargon and acronyms will work if you are addressing a small audience of specialists, because they are likely to interpret this kind of language as a sign that you are "one of the team." However, most audiences are so diverse that you cannot assume that everyone is familiar with the same terminology as you are. Therefore, the first time you use jargon or an acronym, briefly explain its meaning.

In addition to limiting use of jargon and acronyms, you should keep your language simple, specific, and brief. A speech is not like a televised football game—there is no instant replay. If listeners have to work hard at understanding you, they will give up and think about something else. This is especially true if your speech includes instructions of some kind. Even fairly common words like *perpendicular*, *tangent*, and *circumference* could be confusing to a listener who is not feeling well, is preoccupied with personal problems, or is experiencing a high level of stress. The following example highlights the importance of matching your language to your audience's knowledge level:

> A plumber wrote to the U.S. Bureau of Standards about using hydrochloric acid to clean drain pipes. . . .

© Myrleen Ferguson Cate/PhotoEdit

The best speakers are natural and enthusiastic.

Several days later he received this reply, "The efficacy of hydrochloric acid is indisputable but the corrosive residue is incompatible with metallic permanence."

Confused, he wrote again and asked if the acid is "okay to use or not."

A second letter advised him, "We cannot assume responsibility for the production of toxic and noxious residue and suggest that you use an alternative procedure."

Still baffled, he wrote, "Do you mean it's okay to use hydrochloric acid?"

A final letter resolved the question. "Don't use hydrochloric acid. It eats the hell out of pipes!"[2]

Simple language makes your speeches more powerful and memorable. The more words you use (especially if they are not specific), the more likely you are to cause confusion. A short but information-packed speech will be remembered and appreciated by your listeners.

Sound Natural and Enthusiastic

Beginning speakers have a tendency either to memorize their speeches or to use too many notes. As a result, their delivery sounds awkward and unnatural. If you want people to listen to you, try to talk in the same natural and enthusiastic way you do when you are discussing a favorite subject with a

Remember:

Good public speakers . . .

▶ Respect the diversity of audience members.

▶ Know as much as possible about listeners.

▶ Organize speeches carefully to improve understanding and recall.

▶ Use language effectively.

▶ Sound natural and enthusiastic.

▶ Regularly use quality visual aids.

▶ Give only ethical speeches.

friend. Chapter 8 offers specific suggestions for improving both your verbal and nonverbal delivery. For now just remember that you shouldn't put on a "speaking disguise" when you talk; instead, try to sound basically the way you do in ordinary conversations.

Use Quality Visual Aids

A **visual aid** is anything you present for your listeners to *see* that supplements the information they *hear*.[3] As discussed in Chapter 6, visual aids make it possible for an audience to comprehend your ideas faster and remember them better. Visual aids also add to your credibility as a speaker and make you feel more confident while speaking. Of course, sloppy, cluttered, or poorly designed visuals have few, if any, benefits. Chapter 7 focuses on how to make quality visual aids such as overhead transparencies, slides, flipcharts and posters, markerboards, objects, models, and more. Regardless of the type, good speakers consider visuals as important as the verbal part of their speeches and prepare them with equal care.

Give Only Ethical Speeches

Obviously listeners cannot make informed choices if a speaker's information is false or distorted or inadequate. Therefore you need to research each speech topic to make sure your information is accurate and complete. In addition, as discussed in Chapter 1, you must be careful not to plagiarize or to invent, falsify, or exaggerate your information or evidence. Likewise, ethical persuasion does not involve manipulation, trickery, coercion, or force. Using sound logic and solid evidence to show why your alternative is the best choice is ethical persuasion; falsifying or twisting evidence impairs an audience's right to make choices and definitely is unethical, regardless of how "good" your intent may be. Good speakers want listeners to change their beliefs, values, or behaviors in a way that is "voluntary" rather than "forced" by unethical practices.[4]

Sample Student Speech 1

▼ ▼ ▼

The following sample speech is an artifact speech in which a student, Monica Wolfe, discusses how her collection of T-shirts reflects important events in her life. Her assignment specified a two-to-three minute speech on one or more artifacts that, if found by an archaeologist in the future, would reveal the most about her. This speech, which was the first speech Monica gave to her public speaking class, was transcribed from the actual videotape filmed in class. Throughout the remainder of this chapter, Monica's speech will be used to illustrate basic speech organization. A second student speech is located later in this chapter.

Sample Speech 1

Closet Artifacts

by Monica E. Wolfe

IN THIS BOX ARE the archaeological ruins of my closet. As my very southern mother says, "You can tell a lot about a lady by her closet." Although I don't think this is what she had in mind, I'm going to let the T-shirts in my closet tell you about me. My T-shirts will show how my life has changed from my first try at college to world travel as a flight attendant to settled married life and another go at college.

I was born and raised in Austin, Texas. I had never been anywhere but Austin so, of course, I went to the University of Texas. I joined a sorority [T-shirt] and went for two years until they hounded me to say what my major was going to be but I had no idea.

So I left and became a flight attendant for Continental Airlines [T-shirt]. While I was a flight attendant, I had a lot of great experiences. I went to Australia [T-shirt] which I loved—got to hug a koala bear. I went to Mexico [T-shirt] and all around the United States.

One of the best things about being a flight attendant is on a trip I met this T-shirt [T-shirt]. His name is John and he is from Newport Beach, California. This is pretty ragged [T-shirt] because it is his favorite T-shirt. John is a pilot—at the time for Continental Airlines as well, so we had the chance to work together and travel together.

On one of our trips we went to Hawaii [T-shirt] and while we were in Hawaii, we decided to combine our closet space and got married.

A few months after we got married, he decided to get a new job with American Airlines [T-shirt] and this is how we ended up in the Fort Worth/Dallas area [Cowboy T-shirt].

After we were here for about one year, we took another vacation to Ruidoso, New Mexico [T-shirt], and I taught him to ski, which was very interesting. We had a really good time.

When we got back from Ruidoso, I had to wear this shirt [maternity T-shirt]. I know it looks plain but after 9 months, I had this shirt [T-shirt turned around to show baby T-shirt pinned on it]. She is now two years old and the joy of our lives.

As you can see, the T-shirts found in the archaeological ruins of my closet tell a lot about my life. But this last shirt is the shirt that we all wear [imaginary T-shirt held up] because we are unsure of what it says or where we are going but we hope that it will be as well worn as all of these [imaginary T-shirt added to stack of other shirts].

Basic Speech Preparation Steps

1. Analyze your potential listeners.
2. Determine your topic, exact purpose, and main points.
3. Organize and outline your speech.
4. Rehearse your speech using visual aids.

Steps to Success: Planning and Preparing a Speech

▼ ▼ ▼

Although detailed steps in planning and preparing informative, persuasive, and special occasion speeches will be covered later in the text, the basic steps are presented now to help you prepare for your first speeches.

Step 1: Analyze Your Potential Listeners

Your first speeches likely will be given to your classmates. If you can keep the interest and attention of your classmates—who are a captive audience preoccupied with giving their own speeches—you are well on your way to becoming an effective speaker. As discussed earlier, the more you know about your audience (see Chapters 4 and 5 for specifics), the better you will be able to relate your topic to them. For example, how large is the class? How many men and women are in the class? What races and ethnic backgrounds are represented? What is the age range? How many in the class work part-time? Full-time? What major fields of study are represented in the class? Based on your answers to these questions, what beliefs, values, and interests are your audience members likely to hold? How much do they know about the topic you are considering? To obtain answers to questions that are not obvious, briefly chat with various classmates to obtain the needed information. When you feel you have a good grasp of your audience, you are ready for the next step.

Step 2: Determine Your Topic, Exact Purpose, and Main Points

In some cases speakers are assigned a specific topic. Usually, however, you will be assigned a general type of speech (either an informative, persuasive, or special occasion speech) while the specific topic will be up to you. For example, for your first speech you may be asked to give a short special occasion speech (such as a speech of introduction or a humorous incident speech) or a brief informative or persuasive speech (such as an artifact speech, a one-point speech, a pet peeve speech, or a personal opinion speech).

In a *speech of introduction*, you introduce yourself or a classmate. You could highlight several interesting facts about yourself or the other person (such as major field of study, goals in life, travels, or reasons for taking a speech course), or you could focus the speech on what makes you or the other person unique. (A sample student speech of introduction is included at the end of this chapter.)

In a *humorous incident speech* you share a funny incident from your life. For example, one student told about a hilarious camping trip on which several items needed to pitch the tent and cook the food (like tent pegs and cooking and eating utensils) were left at home and what her family did to improvise.

In an *artifact speech* you choose an item or group of items as the focal point for your speech. For example, in the sample artifact speech, Monica discussed how her collection of T-shirts reflects important events in her life. Another way to think about an artifact speech is to begin with the assumption that a nearby volcano suddenly erupted and covered your home with lava.[5] You are to select one or more objects (artifacts) that would reveal the most about you if found by an archaeologist excavating your home site in the future.

In a *one-point speech* you select a single idea (such as "students who eat breakfast get higher grades" or "worry is nonproductive") and spend your time supporting or clarifying the idea.

In a *pet-peeve speech* you select something that really irritates you (such as slow drivers who poke along in the fast lane or professors who read to the class from the textbook) and tell why it bothers you so much.

Finally, in a *personal opinion speech* you state a personal opinion and explain why you feel the way you do. For example, one student gave a speech on why he thought the concept of "political correctness" had no place on a college campus. It stirred up so much discussion that another student, who had already prepared a humorous incident speech, decided to change her topic and speak in favor of political correctness on the campus.

To help you in choosing a topic once you have determined what type of speech you will be giving, consider these guidelines:

▶ *Select a topic you already know about.* You will feel much more relaxed discussing something you know about (as Monica did in her artifact speech on T-shirts) than you will looking through the *Reader's Digest* and finding a topic that you know nothing about (like "How Apes Learn to Talk").

▶ *Select a topic you are interested in talking about.* You may know a fair amount about several topics but not be really interested in them. Avoid such topics. It's difficult to interest an audience in a topic that doesn't interest you.

▶ *Select a topic that you can make interesting and/or valuable to your audience.* Your audience doesn't have to be interested in your topic before you speak, but they should be when you are finished speaking. A topic like "Why Everyone Should Enroll in a Latin Class" would probably be of little value or interest to most audiences. If you analyze your audience, you should have a fairly good idea of their interests.

▶ *Select a topic that fits the requirements of the assignment.* A topic suitable for an artifact speech would hardly be appropriate for a persuasive speech; a one-point speech topic would not be appropriate for a ten-minute informative speech. Make sure you know the type of speech, the time limits, and any other requirements, and select your topic accordingly. (For more information on choosing a topic, see Chapter 9.)

Once you have selected your general topic, you are ready to narrow it down based on your audience's interests and needs. You should be able to state the exact purpose of your speech in one clear and brief sentence. If you can't, your topic is too broad. For example, your exact purpose might be stated as follows:

"After hearing my speech, the audience will understand why my goal in life is to become a doctor."

Next you need to decide on the main points (main ideas) and key supporting arguments you want to include in your speech. On a sheet of paper, brainstorm a list of as many points or reasons as possible (try to list at least six items). While you are brainstorming, don't try to think of only "intelligent" or "impressive" ideas. List anything that comes to mind. You can eliminate weak or ridiculous ideas later. For example, if your topic is "Why My Goal in Life Is to Become a Doctor," your list might include the following:

1. I feel the need to help people
2. My best friend wants to be a doctor
3. Both my mother and grandfather are doctors
4. To get out of the house
5. To make money
6. I hope to help discover a cure for AIDS
7. I felt so helpless when my brother died of cancer
8. I am good at chemistry and physics

Now you are ready to narrow and combine ideas until you decide on which ideas to include in your speech—two or three main ideas are plenty for a short, beginning speech. The final outline of your speech might contain the following:

Purpose: To explain why my dream is to become a doctor
Main points:

  I. Family tradition
 II. Helping others
III. Stable income

The Far Side cartoon by Gary Larson is reprinted by permission of Chronicle Features, San Francisco CA. All rights reserved.

Step 3: Organize and Outline Your Speech

Now that you've identified your exact purpose and selected your main ideas, you're ready to organize your ideas so they **FLOW**.

FOCUS audience attention and interest   The best way to engage listeners is to begin with some type of attention-getter. Common examples include a personal experience ("The first time I jumped out of a plane . . ."), a question ("Did you know you lose 10 billion skin cells every day?"), or a startling statement ("Dinosaurs aren't extinct—every time you see a songbird you're looking at a survivor from the Paleozoic era"). The key is to establish a feeling of rapport with the audience—to make them want to listen to you. Maintain eye contact, smile when appropriate, and speak in an enthusiastic, dynamic manner.

▼ ▼ ▼   **Focus Step:** Closet Artifacts

In this box are the archaeological ruins of my closet. As my very southern mother says, "You can tell a lot about a lady by her closet."

LEAD IN to the topic   Once you have the audience's attention, you can state your purpose and summarize the main ideas you will be including in the speech. In certain circumstances, you might omit the preview of main ideas. Omit a preview if you want to build suspense or if you feel that an audience is hostile and that a summary of your key points might cause them to tune out completely. In most cases, however, previewing your main points helps listeners remember your ideas better.

> ▼ ▼ ▼   **Lead-in Step:** Closet Artifacts
>
> *Although I don't think this is what she had in mind, I'm going to let the T-shirts in my closet tell you about me. My T-shirts will show how my life has changed from my first try at college to world travel as a flight attendant to settled married life and another go at college.*

ORGANIZE and support your main ideas   Now you're ready to organize your main points and provide a variety of visual and verbal supports. The key is to make your main points and supporting materials easy to identify and remember. When people leave your speech remembering the key ideas you covered, you know you have given an excellent talk.

There are several things you can do to make your main ideas memorable. First, *limit yourself to no more than three to five main points*. Research on memory suggests that five bits of information is about all the average person can remember with accuracy at one time.[6] For most speeches three to five main ideas are plenty. In the unlikely event that your speech has to include more than five ideas (for example, in a step-by-step procedure), you're still better off trying to group them into five or fewer categories.

Second, to make them memorable, *keep your main points brief and use parallel structures when possible*. In both the lead-in and the wrap-up stages of your speech, it is a good idea to summarize your main points for the audience. Keep in mind, however, that if your main points are written in detailed, sentence form, a summary of them will be both awkward sounding and difficult for the audience to grasp. For example, read aloud the following speech preview:[7]

> As nurses, let's take another look at the most common human ailment in the world, the common cold. Let's consider:
> I. Over the years people have tried many remedies to combat the common cold.
> II. The traditional modern therapy—get plenty of rest, take aspirin, and drink lots of liquid—is still the best.
> III. Many people believe in curing the cold with vitamin C.

Wouldn't a smoother, easier-to-remember preview read as follows?

Remember:

When you organize . . .

▶ Present no more than three to five main points.

▶ State main points as single words or brief phrases.

▶ Keep main points parallel.

▶ Place the most important main point first or last.

▶ Use rhymes or acronyms to aid memory when appropriate.

▶ Highlight main points with visual aids.

As nurses, let's take another look at the most common human ailment in the world, the common cold. Let's review three aspects of a cold:

I. Ancient remedies

II. Modern therapy

III. Vitamin C cure

To keep your main points *parallel*, use similar phrasing and sentence structure, and use the same voice (either active or passive). For example, "Many remedies have been tried," "Modern therapy is best," and "Curing the cold with Vitamin C" are not parallel. Instead the first two items are complete sentences (one in passive voice and one in active voice) and the third one is a sentence fragment. "Ancient remedies, Modern therapy, and Vitamin C cure" are parallel—three noun phrases.

Third, *arrange your material so that you cover your most important point either first or last*. Research has found that people tend to better remember information presented at the beginning (primacy effect) and at the end (recency effect) of a speech.[8] Although visual aids are helpful throughout a presentation, they are especially important in the middle, when listeners are less likely to recall key points.

Fourth, when possible, *make your main points memorable by creating your own rhyme or acronym*. Your acronym could be a word formed by the first letter of each of your main points. For example, in a speech on "Tips for Communicating with Your Roommate," the following acronym would add interest and make the main points easier to remember:

T Tell each other when you are unhappy.

I Identify potential problem areas needing discussion.

P Participate equally in all discussions.

S Schedule regular discussion sessions.

I. College
   A. UT
   B. Sorority [T-shirt]
II. Career
   A. Flight attendant for Continental Airlines
   B. Travel
      1. Australia [T-shirt]
      2. Mexico [T-shirt]
III. Marriage
   A. Met John
      1. From Newport Beach, CA [T-shirt]
      2. Pilot [T-shirt]
   B. Worked and traveled together
      1. Trip to Hawaii [T-shirt]
      2. Married in Hawaii [T-shirt]
IV. Family
   A. Vacation to Ruidoso [T-shirt]
   B. Pregnant [T-shirt]
   C. Baby [T-shirt]

Not only should your main points be well organized, they should also be supported with a variety of visual and verbal materials. Your main points are the skeleton of the speech; the supporting materials are the meat of the speech. Visual supports for your first speeches could include pictures, objects, or posters; verbal supports could include explanations, comparisons, and personal experiences.

One way to check the organization of your main points and the placement of your supporting materials is to put them into an outline. Outlining will be examined in detail in Chapters 12 and 15. For now use the FLOW sequence as your outline.

WRAP-UP your speech   In the wrap-up stage of your speech, you will briefly summarize your talk and then finish with a closing statement. You can give a general summary of the overall topic of your speech or a more specific summary that details the main points you covered. The purpose of the summary is to clarify again your basic purpose and main points and anchor them in your listeners' memories. The wrap-up ends with a closing statement that can be a general thought or a challenge designed to refocus listeners' interest and keep them thinking about your speech long after it is completed.

As you can see, the T-shirts found in the archaeological ruins of my closet tell a lot about my life. But this last shirt is the shirt that we all wear [imaginary T-shirt held up] because we are unsure of what it says or where we are going but we hope that it will be as well worn as all of these [imaginary T-shirt added to stack of other shirts].

Step 4: Rehearse Your Speech Using Your Visual Aids

You will feel much more confident while speaking if you have rehearsed your speech at least two or three times. Be sure to practice aloud using your notes and visual aids. Reading a speech silently to yourself does not prepare you to use notes and visual aids effectively, nor does it help your words to flow smoothly. If possible, tape record or videotape your speech to get a better idea of how you will sound—and look. Then make any needed changes, such as speaking louder or more distinctly, using smoother gestures, lengthening or shortening your speech, and so on.

This speaker is checking for gestures and facial expressions as he rehearses his wedding toast.

© *Michael Newman/PhotoEdit*

Sample Student Speech 2

▼ ▼ ▼

In the following speech Lynda Ross, a student enrolled in a public speaking class, introduces herself to her classmates by telling of an important event in her life. The assignment specified a three- to five-minute *speech of introduction* to be presented without notes. Lynda's speech was transcribed from the actual videotape filmed in class. As you read this speech, see if you can tell whether Lynda included all of the steps from the FLOW sequence.

Sample Speech 2

I Can

by Lynda Ross

Can you identify where each step of the FLOW sequence begins?

REMEMBER THE SAYING, "Sticks and stones may break my bones, but words will never harm me?" It's really not true, is it? Words can be more powerful than physical strength—whether they are working against us or for us. What I would like to share with you today is how two very small, very simple, little words changed my life dramatically.

Let me begin with a little history. Go back with me to my junior year in high school. I needed to take an elective course because I had already fulfilled all my academic requirements. So you know as a typical junior, all I was looking to do was take an easy course. Little did I know what I was getting ready to put myself through. You see, the name of the course had only two words in it. It was a Zig Ziegler course called "I Can." Now, at the time the theory of "I Can" had no meaning in my life—I didn't even know that it was a concept or philosophy. I had absolutely no idea what was involved. However, even at the tender age of sixteen, I was beginning to understand that I had some unhappiness in my life, some self-doubts, some uneasiness about myself. But I didn't know what this problem was—I had no name for it. I didn't know why it was in my life and I obviously didn't know how to fix it.

It was literally this course that brought my problem to light. What I found out through "I Can" was that I was suffering from what is called a low self-esteem. A good thing about "I Can"—it didn't just tell me I had a problem, those two words began to fix my problem. I realized this through repetition—it's just like it was yesterday—the course was called "I Can," the book was called "I Can," the first page said "I Can," the second page said "I Can," the third . . . you get the point. Throughout the entire course these words were repeated until I began to believe that I could. I could change my low self-esteem; I could be happy; I could have better relationships; I could get along with my parents. So this was the foundation that I began to build everything else on.

I'm sure by now that most of you have heard of Zig Ziegler. But you have to understand that for me (this was several years ago), at first all I could think about Zig Ziegler was that he had a weird name; it's got to be made up; it sounds pretty goofy. If you've ever heard him on tape or live, you know he also sounds sort of weird. So I didn't give him much credit until he started teaching the second lesson. It was in the second lesson that we learned about the concept of "stinking-thinking." I had absolutely no idea that I was such a victim of this. The thing was, I was the criminal. I was victimizing myself. It was me that was putting all the self-doubt into my own head. It was such a revelation that basically it stopped me in my tracks. I mean, it literally stopped my world. It was as if I could pull that garbage from my head, put it in a sack, and put it out on the side of the street for the garbage collectors. From that day forward I realized that I would no longer continue this kind of thinking—that I would start positive thinking, that I would do the self affirmations, that I would do the visualization techniques. That became something that I did from that day forward until today and that I plan to do from today until the day I die.

One of the final lessons I got from this class was—it wasn't even a lesson, it was more of a gift. Through this class, I realized that I had been giving control of my life (I'm talking ambitions, moods, behaviors, attitudes, morals) to other people. These were social people in my life and obviously my parents, too. But I also realized that there were a lot of really negative people out there and they were controlling my every waking moment. Once I realized this, I said, "I need to get this control back. I need to take all these pieces and put them back into a unit—back into my heart, my body, and my mind." I could do this. So that was the gift. The gift was not control, the gift that I got from "I Can" was realizing my own independence. As Zig Ziegler teaches, "If it is to be, it's up to me."

I think I've demonstrated here how two very small, little bitsy words, when believed, can change a life. They changed mine. No longer will I allow a low self-esteem to hold me back. No longer will I allow stinking-thinking in my world. (Really, if I get with anybody else, I don't allow it in theirs either.) And no longer will I let people who don't need control of my life have any influence. I think you'll understand when I say, "Honestly, folks, I truly believe that both you and *I can*."

Summary
▼ ▼ ▼

To become an effective speaker, it helps to know what characteristics good public speakers have in common. Good speakers (1) respect the individual differences of their audience members, (2) understand the communication process and are listener-centered, (3) make sure their main points are easy to identify and recall, (4) use language effectively, (5) speak in a natural and enthusiastic way, (6) regularly use quality visual aids, (7) and are ethical.

Successful speakers also know the basic steps in planning and preparing a speech. First, analyze your potential listeners. Second, determine your topic, exact purpose, and main points. Third, organize and outline your speech. Finally, rehearse your speech using your visual aids.

To develop effective speeches, use the FLOW method of organization: *Focus* audience attention and interest, *Lead in* to your topic, *Organize* and support your main ideas with a variety of visual and verbal supports, and *Wrap up* your speech with a summary and closing statement.

Concentrate on making each speech better than the last. By the end of the course, you will be amazed at how your speaking skills have improved.

1. Attend an organizational meeting where a speaker is scheduled. Note how well the speaker exhibits the characteristics of good speakers discussed in this chapter. Which traits of the speaker were the most effective, and which one(s) were the least effective? Explain why you feel this way. Assign the speaker a grade of excellent, average, or poor. Turn in your evaluation of the speaker to your instructor.

2. Select one of the types of speeches described in this chapter (speech of introduction, humorous incident speech, artifact speech, one-point speech, pet peeve speech, or personal opinion speech) and prepare a two- to three-minute speech using the FLOW sequence. Also prepare a brief outline to hand in to your instructor on the day of your speech. Practice by giving your talk to a family member or friend.

3. Begin to keep a list of possible speech topics you might want to use during the course. Get in the habit of carrying a notepad or a few notecards in your purse or wallet. Anytime you read or hear about a topic that interests you or think of something you know a lot about, write it down—along with the source when relevant. If you get in the habit of doing this, you will be ready the next time you need to select a topic.

4. Select Lynda's speech of introduction included in this chapter or a student speech or a professional speech from Appendix C and make an outline of the speech following the four steps of the FLOW sequence. When you are finished, compare your outline with the outline of a classmate. If the two outlines aren't the same, discuss why they are different. If you need help, speak with your instructor.

Notes

1. E. P. Zayas-Baya, "Instructional Media in the Total Language Picture," *International Journal of Instructional Media* 5 (1977–1978), 145–150; Ralph G. Nichols and Leonard A. Stevens, *Are You Listening?* (New York: Mc-Graw-Hill, 1957); Florence J. Wolff, Nadine C. Marsnik, William S. Tracey, and Ralph G. Nichols, *Perceptive Listening* (New York: Holt, 1983).

2. John Dunworth, "Six Barriers to Basics: Education Depends on You," *Vital Speeches* 46 (1 January 1980), 190.

3. Adapted from Cheryl Hamilton with Cordell Parker, *Communicating for Results: A Guide for Business and the Professions* (Belmont, CA: Wadsworth, 1993), p. 373.

4. James A. Jaksa and Michael S. Pritchard, *Communication Ethics: Methods of Analysis* (Belmont, CA: Wadsworth, 1994), p. 76.

5. The volcano analogy explaining the artifact speech came from Bonnie Creel, Tarrant County Junior College, North East Campus. Used with permission.

6. In 1956 Miller declared that the human memory span was seven, plus or minus two. However, in 1967 Mandler argued that a more realistic number was five.

Finally, in 1975, Broadbent argued that even five was too high; a more accurate number was three. For more specific information see G. A. Miller, "The Magical Number Seven, Plus or Minus Two: Some Limits on Our Capacity for Processing Information," *Psychological Review* 63 (1956), 81–97; G. Mandler, "Organization and Memory," in K. W. Spence and J. T. Spencer, eds., *The Psychology of Learning and Motivation: Advances in Research and Theory*, Vol. 1 (New York: Academic Press, 1967), pp. 327–372; and D. E. Broadbent, "The Magic Number Seven After 15 Years," in A. Kennedy and A. Wilkes, eds., *Studies in Long-Term Memory* (London: Wiley, 1975), pp. 3–18.

7. The main points were taken from a speech entitled "The Common Cold," in Stephen E. Lucas, *The Art of Public Speaking* (New York: Random House, 1989), pp. 195–197.

8. J. C. Jahnke, "Serial Position Effects in Immediate Serial Recall," *Journal of Verbal Learning and Verbal Behavior* 2 (1963), 284–287.

Building Speaker Confidence

I F THE THOUGHT OF GIVING a speech makes you anxious, you aren't alone! A study by R. H. Bruskin Associates found that the fear of public speaking is the number one fear of Americans—even greater than the fear of death.[1] Unfortunately, individuals who experience a high level of anxiety while speaking and in other communication situations are at a great disadvantage when compared to more talkative, confident people. For example, people who feel comfortable expressing themselves are perceived as more competent, make a better impression during job interviews, and are more likely to be promoted to supervisory positions than anxious people.[2]

In Chapter 1 we discussed why speaker confidence creates a positive impression while high anxiety causes a negative one. When we speak, we are communicating three ways—verbally, visually, and vocally. Our verbal message may be clear and well organized, but when we are nervous, listeners are more likely to key in on negative vocal and visual cues (such as lack of eye contact, poor posture, hesitant delivery, and strained vocal quality). However, when we are confident and our verbal, visual, and vocal signals are in harmony, we are more likely to be believed. According to Bert Decker, author of *You've Got to Be Believed to Be Heard*, "Believability is an emotional quality."[3] He warns,

> If you don't believe in someone on an emotional level, little if any of what they have to say will get through. It will be screened out by your distrust, your anxiety, your irritation, or your indifference. Even if the facts and content are great by themselves, they are forever locked out because the person delivering them lacks believability.[4]

Therefore, if we want people to believe us when we speak, if we want to enhance the positive impressions we make on others, we need to build up our speaker confidence. This chapter will give you some suggestions on how to manage communication anxiety in order to develop a more confident, professional delivery.

Understanding Anxiety

▼ ▼ ▼

B efore you can manage your anxiety, you need to know what kind of anxiety you have—situational or trait. **Situational anxiety** refers to factors present in a specific situation that may cause anxiety (for example, speaking before a *new* audience or in front of the *boss* or being *graded or critiqued* while speaking).[5] **Trait anxiety** refers to internal anxieties an individual brings to the speaking situation (for example, feelings of inadequacy when in a group or fear of looking like a fool in front of others).[6] In other words, situational anxiety is caused by a new or different situation while trait anxiety is caused by personal feelings inside the speaker that exist regardless of the situation. Your own anxiety may be situational, trait, or a combination of the two.

Job interviews create situational anxiety for most people.

© *Jeff Greenberg/PhotoEdit*

Situational Anxiety

Feeling nervous prior to a new communication situation is perfectly normal. Telling a troublesome employee that he is fired, interviewing for a position, or presenting a controversial idea before your classmates are all examples of situations that can trigger that butterflies-in-the-stomach feeling. Any time we become anxious, afraid, or excited, our body's nervous system prepares us for action:

> First, the heart begins pumping more blood to the brain, the muscles, and skin. Blood is also diverted away from the stomach and intestines in order to supply those same organs. As a result, the digestive system slows to a crawl, and the central nervous system, heart, and muscles receive extra oxygen and energy necessary for clear thinking, quick reaction, and intense physical exertion. At the same time, the pupils of the eyes dilate to produce sharper vision, the level of blood sugar rises to provide added energy, and the skin perspires in order to flush out excess wastes and to cool the body.[7]

As alarming as all that may sound, we should be glad for this extra boost from our nervous system. Can you imagine an athlete with absolutely no anxiety before a big game, race, or match? His or her performance no doubt would fall far short of winning the "big prize." For instance, speed skater Bonnie Blair, winner of gold medals in two consecutive Olympic games, told reporters that she always gets nervous before a race.

Neither age nor experience seems to cure situational anxiety. For example, Mike Wallace, longtime news journalist for "60 Minutes," still gets butterflies before conducting an interview. Nevertheless, he is a successful speaker. One key to his success may be that he views any symptoms of situational anxiety—such as increased heart rate, dry mouth, and sweaty palms—as normal excitement necessary for dynamic communication. In fact, with this positive attitude anxiety not only becomes manageable but often disappears completely. Poor communicators, who tend to view the physical symptoms of situational anxiety with fear and as further proof that they are poor speakers, often find that their anxiety becomes worse as the speech proceeds. The next time you are in a situation that makes you anxious, don't think of your anxiety in a negative, self-defeating way; instead, view it as normal "excitement" that can aid effective communication.

Trait Anxiety

Whereas basically everyone experiences situational anxiety, fewer people experience trait anxiety. Trait anxiety, or *communication apprehension*, is more of a personal, internal feeling about communication. People with high trait anxiety often (1) feel that they are dissimilar from other speakers ("I'm more nervous than anyone else in my department or class"), (2) have a history of negative speaking experiences (whether real or perceived), and (3) consider themselves to have subordinate status to others.[8] Let's look more closely at each of these characteristics and discuss how they can be overcome.

Dissimilarity   As you look at your classmates in your speech class, you may say to yourself, "Everyone else looks confident. I must be the only one who is really nervous about speaking." One researcher took an informal survey of the students enrolled in all the public speaking classes in his department and found that the apprehensive students felt that "they experienced the highest anxiety levels of all those enrolled in the course. Ironically, about one-third of those interviewed held such a belief."[9]

Dissimilarity obviously is a false belief. We wrongly assume that we are different from everyone else because no one else seems to be nervous. Although some people do show outward signs of nervousness, most nervousness is internal and is barely obvious to an audience. The best way to prove this to yourself is to see yourself on videotape. Most people are amazed that their inner turmoil isn't visible at all or is only slightly visible.

Speaking history   If your prior speaking experiences have been mostly positive, you are less likely to have high trait anxiety. James McCroskey's PRCA (Personal Report of Communication Anxiety) will help you determine your Communication Apprehension (CA) score.[10] Recall that you took the PRCA (located in Appendix D) before reading Chapter 1. Researchers have found the public speaking section of the PRCA to be a good measure of one's speaking history.[11] Feeling that you are going to do poorly as a speaker because you have always been a poor speaker is a vicious cycle. If you have a high PRCA score, especially a high public speaking score, we urge you to pay particular attention to the section in this chapter on managing trait anxiety.

Subordinate status   Not only do highly anxious speakers consider themselves to be subordinate to the person in charge (who sets the rules for appropriate behavior), but, because they generally have low self-concepts, they also feel subordinate to their audience. For example, if you worry that your audience will know more about your topic than you do, you are feeling subordinate. To overcome this feeling, you have several options. First, find two or more expert sources that agree with your viewpoint and cite them during your speech. Second, personalize your speech (with at least one personal story or experience) to show your own unique slant on the topic.

In summary, if you believe you are more nervous than anyone else in your group or have had several negative speaking experiences in the past, or if you are worried that your audience will know more about your topic than you and could probably do a better job of presenting it, there is a good chance that you have trait anxiety.

Once you have identified which type of anxiety is causing your lack of confidence, you can do something to correct or manage it. Although situational anxiety is easier to manage than trait anxiety, both can be controlled.

Managing Situational Anxiety
▼ ▼ ▼

Accept the fact that every speaking situation will cause butterflies. According to the legendary news reporter Edward R. Murrow, "The only difference between the pros and the novices is that the pros have trained their butterflies to fly in formation."[12] The following suggestions will help you control your butterflies:[13]

Prepare and Practice

Nothing will make you more nervous than knowing you are not adequately prepared. After all, isn't your nervousness really fear that you will look foolish in the eyes of your coworkers, classmates, or friends? Lack of preparation makes such a possibility much more likely.

To prepare properly, first analyze your audience and plan your presentation and any visual aids for this particular group. Next, prepare easy-to-follow notes. Using these notes, rehearse your presentation three or more times from beginning to end—*always speaking out loud*. Mentally thinking through your speech is *not* the same as practicing aloud. The environment you practice in should be as close as possible to the actual speaking environment. For example, if you will be standing during your presentation, stand while practicing; if you will be using visual aids, practice using them. As you rehearse, time yourself to see if you need to shorten or lengthen the presentation. Finally, anticipate possible audience questions and prepare answers for them. Knowing that you are well prepared will help ease much of your anxiety. Chapter 2 gave you a brief overview of how to prepare a speech; Chapters 9 and 13 discuss in detail how to prepare for informative and persuasive speeches.

Warm Up First

Speakers are no different from singers who warm up their voices, musicians who warm up their fingers, or athletes who warm up their muscles before a performance. Prior to giving your presentation, you'll want to warm up your voice and loosen your muscles. A variety of techniques will help you do this. For example, try singing up and down the scale, as singers do before a concert. Read aloud a memo or page from a book, varying your volume, pitch, emphasis, and rate. Do several stretching exercises such as touching your toes and rolling your head from side to side. Practice various gestures such as pointing, pounding your fist, or shrugging your shoulders. As with musicians and athletes, these warm-up exercises will help you relax and ensure that you are ready to perform at your best.

Use Deep Breathing

One quick way to calm your nervousness is through deep breathing. This involves taking in a deep breath through your nose, holding it while you count to five, and then slowly exhaling through your mouth. As you exhale, imagine that the stress and tension are slowly draining down your arms and out your fingertips, down your body and legs and out your toes. Repeat the process a second or third time if needed. A more detailed explanation of deep breathing will be given later in this chapter.

Plan an Introduction That Will Relax You and Your Listeners

Most speakers find that once they get a favorable audience reaction, they relax. This is one reason so many speakers start with humor—it relaxes them as well as their listeners. If a humorous introduction is inappropriate or you are not comfortable with humor, relating a personal example or experience is another option. Whatever your preference, make your introduction work to put *you* at ease. See Chapter 11 for a detailed discussion of various types of attention-getters.

Concentrate on Meaning

Instead of worrying about how you look or sound and whether you are impressing your audience, center your energy on getting your *meaning* across to your listeners. In other words, make sure your listeners are following the organization of your speech and understanding your points. Pay close attention to their

Putting your audience at ease right from the start will help you to relax and set the tone for the rest of the speech.

© Bob Daemmrich/The Image Works

nonverbal reactions. If they look confused, explain the idea again or add another example. A speaker who is concentrating on the listeners soon forgets about being nervous. Chapter 4 contains a detailed discussion of listeners and how to read their nonverbal reactions.

Use Visual Aids

Visual aids (discussed in detail in Unit Two) make listening easier for your audience and add to your confidence as a speaker. Visual aids make it almost impossible to forget your main ideas—if you're not sure of the next point, just put up your next visual aid. Also, using visual aids such as posters, flipcharts, or actual objects not only adds eye-catching movement to your presentation but also keeps you too busy to worry about gestures.

Managing Trait Anxiety: Positive Imagery

▼ ▼ ▼

A good way to manage trait anxiety that you can do on your own is called positive imagery, or visualization.[14] This surprisingly simple technique can help make public speaking much more enjoyable.

What Positive Imagery Is

With **positive imagery** you use your mind to create a positive, vivid, and detailed mental image of yourself giving a successful and confident speech. When you imagine yourself speaking confidently, you become more confident. One psychologist defines *imagery* as "a sensory-type experience in the mind without an actual corresponding situation providing the immediate sense stimulus."[15] In other words, in your mind you can create a very real situation that stimulates feelings (of pride, for example) even when no actual situation exists.

Although positive imagery has been applied only recently to speaker confidence,[16] it has been used successfully in sports for years. One of the first studies of positive imagery investigated its effects on basketball players. Students were divided into three groups and shown how to shoot a basket effectively. Group 1 was then told to practice shooting baskets twenty minutes a day for three weeks. Group 2 was told not to touch a basketball for three weeks but to spend twenty minutes a day *imagining* themselves shooting baskets; if they imagined a "miss," they were to correct it and continue practicing. Group 3 had no physical or mental practice of any kind. After three weeks the students in all three groups were tested. Those who had practiced mentally had improved by the same amount as the students who had practiced physically—about 24 percent. However, the students who had practiced neither physically or mentally had not improved at all.[17] Before the 1980 Olympics, Soviet researchers found that skilled athletes whose final training was 25 percent physical and 75 percent mental improved significantly more than athletes trained in any of the following ways: (1) 50 percent physical and 50 percent mental, (2) 75 percent physical and 25 percent mental, and (3) 100 percent physical.[18]

Sports psychologist Jim Loehr says that "studies indicate that 80 to 85 percent of the top athletes consider positive imagery an asset in their training."[19] Tennis great Martina Navratilova, gymnast Mary Lou Retton, and figure skaters Brian Boitano and Kristi Yamaguchi are just a few of the athletes who have made regular use of positive imagery. Speaking of her 1984 Olympic gold-medal-winning performance, Retton recalls: "Before I dropped off to sleep inside the Olympic Village, I did what I always do before a major competition—mind-scripted it completely. I mentally ran through each routine, every move, imagining everything done perfectly."[20]

Of course, visualization alone didn't make these athletes into winners. They practiced long and hard as well. In the same way, using positive imagery is un-

Athletes such as this golfer, David Duval, commonly use visualization to enhance performance. Here, he is checking out the lay of the green for his putt and visualizing the path he wants the ball to take.

© Al Behrman/AP Laserphoto

likely to give you the results you want unless you also prepare and practice your speech carefully.

Positive imagery can be applied in many other areas as well. It can help us control our anxiety in employment interviews, problem-solving discussions, testing situations, or any situation in which our confidence needs a boost. For example, one student used positive imagery to overcome her extreme fear of going to the dentist. Two weeks before a dental appointment, she would begin to get nervous, thinking of all the pain she might experience. Sometimes her leg and arm muscles would get so tense that they ached. However, after several weeks of practicing positive imagery, she not only began to relax but once actually fell asleep while the dentist was drilling.

Why Positive Imagery Works

According to Gail Dusa, president of the National Council for Self-Esteem, "Visualization, in many ways, is nothing more complicated than involving your imagination in goal-setting. It's not hocus-pocus or magic. When you use your imagination to enhance goal-setting you get fired up, excited. This enthusiasm equips you with more mental energy to put into the task."[21]

This mental energy has many of the same effects as physical action. Researchers have known for some time that "vividly experienced imagery, imagery that is both seen and felt, can substantially affect brain waves, blood flow, heart rate, skin temperature, gastric secretions, and immune response."[22] In other words, imagining yourself being attacked in a parking lot creates many of the same physiological responses as actually being attacked. Using brain-imaging technology, British, German, and U.S. neuroscientists recently have demonstrated why visualization works for athletes. In this study athletes who imagined a movement, activated the same areas in the brain as the athletes who performed the actual movement.[23] Another recent study found similar results in the language sphere—both imagined and spoken words activated the same prefrontal and premotor areas of the brain.[24]

Another reason positive imagery works is more difficult to explain. Psychologists tell us that the role of our subconscious mind is to keep us true to our "picture" of ourselves.[25] Every time we react to something we have done or respond to a compliment or criticism, we are sending messages to our subconscious about how we see ourselves. Our present thoughts and words determine our picture of ourselves, which in turn helps determine our future reactions. In other words, we act as the person we "see" ourselves to be. If you say to yourself, "I don't see myself as a confident speaker" or "I couldn't possibly give a talk to a group of people," then you won't.

According to the authors of *The Mental Athlete*, "If you 'visualize' yourself as a mediocre athlete, if you go into a workout or competition 'seeing' yourself performing on an average level or slower or less perfectly than those around you, this is the way you will perform in reality."[26] In an article for *World Tennis*, the same authors talk about an interview with runner Mary Decker Slaney, who fell during the 3,000-meter race in the 1984 Olympics: "She was asked if she had visualized the race. She said she had dreamed about it and visualized it for weeks, even months. She paused, and then said, 'But I never saw myself finishing the race.'"[27]

On the other hand, Alpine skier Jean Claude Killy (winner of gold medals in three events) reports that one of his best performances occurred when an accident prevented him from practicing on the snow, so that the only practice he had was to mentally ski the course.[28]

One of the roles of our subconscious is to make sure that we stay in our "comfort zones" and do only those things we "see" ourselves as doing. *Comfort zone* simply refers to what we feel comfortable doing, thinking, or feeling. In other words, we feel comfortable with whatever fits our idea or picture of ourselves.

Although we can *force* ourselves to speak out in meetings and get up in front of large groups of people, the stress and anxiety can become almost unbearable. Speaking becomes a dreaded chore, not a desired activity.

Why Forcing Yourself Doesn't Work

Forcing yourself to do something outside your comfort zone is like grabbing yourself around the neck and saying, "I *will* go on several interviews" or "I *will* be more outgoing with strangers" or "I *will* give that speech." If you "try hard," you may go on an interview, introduce yourself to a classmate, and even force yourself to give a speech. However, the minute you release this grip on yourself, what happens? Most of us decide that one interview is enough, find that we are too busy to meet new people this semester, and avoid speaking situations.

The problems involved in "trying hard" are illustrated in the following example.[29] Suppose that you and some friends are going to go deep sea fishing. You hire a boat and a guide and head for deep water. The guide picks a spot, sets the boat's automatic pilot on a northeasterly direction, and tells you to begin fishing. After several hours with very few nibbles, you decide that you need to change the boat's direction, so you grab the helm and turn the boat toward the northwest. As soon as the boat is heading in a northwesterly direction, you let go of the wheel and resume fishing. What is going to happen? Will the boat stay heading northwest? No. Because you didn't change the automatic pilot, the boat will slowly return to a northeasterly direction. Without resetting the automatic pilot, the only way to keep the boat heading northwest is to keep your hands on the helm.

We are just like the fishing boat. Our automatic pilot (the subconscious) will direct us as *we see ourselves to be*: "I'm an ineffective interviewee"; "I'm too shy to meet new people"; "I'm certainly not a professional speaker." To answer interview questions effectively, to enjoy meeting new people, and to become a professional speaker we need to first change our internal pictures of ourselves. If I "see" myself as an effective interviewee, as a people-person, and as a confident public speaker, then I no longer need to "try hard." My subconscious (guiding me as I see myself to be) will make the changes automatically and gradually.

Teachers and trainers of aspiring public speakers have long been frustrated by their inability to turn "poor" speakers into "excellent" speakers in a single seminar or semester. The participants usually show some improvement, but they seldom develop into the confident, polished speakers that they and the instructor had hoped. Why not? Because they don't *see* themselves as professional speakers. *No amount of lecture, encouragement, or practice will make you into a confident public speaker as long as, deep down inside, you believe yourself to be a nervous or ineffective speaker.*

Mastering Positive Imagery in Three Steps

So far we have defined positive imagery, discussed why it works, and explained why trying to use force does not work. This section will show you how to use positive imagery to manage your own trait anxiety and begin to see yourself as a confident speaker.

Step 1: develop the habit of positive self-talk   Is your self-talk negative? When you make a mistake, what do you say to yourself? "There I go again. How could I be so stupid? It's just like me to mess up like this! I can't get anything right!" When someone compliments you on a speech, do you reject it by saying, "Oh, it was just dumb luck," or "Well, I did mess up on my visual aids," and so on? Dr. Kay Porter, who teaches mental training techniques to athletes, says that an athlete's self-talk between points and between games can make the difference between winning and losing. She uses herself as an example of what not to do:

> In the years between age 10 and 22, I played tennis. While I never quite mastered my tennis game, I mastered the negative game totally, doing everything that I have spent the last few years teaching people not to do. I choked, blew my concentration, cursed myself, mentally abused myself, and considered myself a total loser when it came to tennis. I was a master of self-defeat.[30]

Your subconscious doesn't know the difference between words you don't mean and words you do mean. It believes what you say and think. Therefore, use only positive self-talk. For example, if you are a basketball player and you miss an easy shot, avoid thinking, "You idiot! You really messed that up!" Think instead, "Calm down. You know you are a good player. It's OK!" If you are in the middle of a speech and suddenly realize that you have forgotten to use your visual aid for the first main point, don't abuse yourself by thinking, "It figures I'd do a stupid thing like that!" Instead use positive self-talk: "That's not like me. The next time I'll practice using my visuals." And when you are complimented for your speech, accept it as credit due without dwelling on whatever faults you think it had. Say, "Thank you, I worked hard on that speech" even though you feel it was not "perfect."

With positive self-talk you also avoid saying to yourself, "I have to/ought to/need to . . ." Such thinking only makes you feel obligated to do certain things, and your subconscious tries hard to get you out of it. Think about what happens when you say to yourself, "I *have to* get up early to prepare tomorrow's report." How many times has the alarm failed to go off, or you felt ill, or you were so sleepy that you couldn't drag yourself out of bed? The trick is to substitute positive trigger words for negatives ones: "I want to/like to/enjoy/choose to . . ." For example, avoid saying, "I've *got to* work on my speech"; instead, say, "I *want to* prepare my speech" or "I'm *looking forward to* working on my speech." Although you may not actually want to do it, you are looking forward to finishing it, aren't you? Then you can enjoy something else without feeling guilty. It's amazing how using positive words instead of negative ones can change your attitude. Instead of resisting the task, you can now spend your time completing it.

Step 2: refocus negative mental pictures into positive ones   The method discussed here is currently used in many athletic programs across the nation[31] and is taught by Louis Tice in his business seminars.[32] To begin the refocusing process, look two or three months into the future (perhaps to the end of the semester) and picture yourself as the speaker you would like to be. What specific speaking characteristics would you like to possess? To help you see the "ideal you," imagine that you are giving a speech to a class, club, or organization three months from now. How do you look, sound, and feel? How is the audience responding? Are you confident, organized, dynamic, and so on? Get a complete picture of the "ideal you" in your mind.

Reprinted by permission of Joe Martin.

© 1994 Tribune Media Services, Inc. All Rights Reserved

Stop reading at this point and make a list of the speaking characteristics you wish to develop.

As a guide consider the following list of speaking characteristics one student hoped to achieve:

I would like to be able to look audience members in the eye.
I want to feel relaxed and confident while speaking.
I would like to sound dynamic when I speak.
I would like to do something constructive with my hands.
I want people to be able to hear me—I'm usually too soft.
I want my speeches to be interesting.
I don't want to worry so much about what my audience thinks of me.
I want to be able to use gestures like my friend Alicia.
I want my speeches to be organized and easy to follow.

When you have completed your list of characteristics, use them as the basis for writing five to ten positive statements that describe you exactly as you want to be. In other words, describe yourself as though the future is now and the changes you want have already occurred. Don't say, "I want/I will/I hope . . ."; say, "I am. . . ." Use the present tense, action verbs, and words that will trigger positive feelings. The following are some sample statements:

1. I feel as relaxed and confident giving a formal speech as I do entertaining good friends in my own living room.

2. People respond well to my speeches.

3. When I'm in front of a group, words flow easily for me. *or* It's easy for me to get my thoughts across to my audience.

4. I enjoy giving speeches regardless of the size of the audience.

5. I handle visual aids confidently and smoothly.

6. I am a dynamic speaker. *or* My delivery is as dynamic and enthusiastic as it is when I talk about an exciting football game.

7. While speaking, I retain my composure and train of thought regardless of interruptions or distractions.

8. While speaking, I do not worry about pleasing everyone; rather, I please myself with what I have to say.

9. I give speeches that are clear, understandable, and well organized.

10. I am a warm, relaxed, and entertaining speaker.

11. I find it easy to look directly at individual audience members and respond to their feedback.

12. I find question-and-answer sessions stimulating and enjoyable.

As you write your positive statements, be sure to phrase them as if they are true right now (even if you know they aren't) and get rid of all negative wording. For example, saying, "I will try to make eye contact with audience members when I speak," implies that you can't make eye contact now. Better to omit the "will try to" and say, "I make direct eye contact with audience members when I speak." How about this statement: "My voice does not shake when I speak." It is written in the present rather than the future tense, but it creates a negative image of a shaky voice. Better to say, "My voice is strong and steady when I speak."

Once you have completed your positive statements, it's time to begin visualizing them. Every morning and evening for about a month, *read* the statements out loud. After reading each one, take a few seconds to close your eyes and mentally *picture* yourself being the person the statement describes. At the same time *feel* relaxed, confident, and competent. For example, if your statement reads, "I find it easy to make eye contact while speaking," see yourself standing confidently in front of the room looking intently at various audience members as you give a clear, well-organized, and entertaining talk. Experience a feeling of confidence and relaxation as you make eye contact with individual members. If your statement reads, "I handle visual aids confidently and smoothly," see yourself standing confidently beside the overhead projector, calmly placing and removing transparencies. Feel a sense of satisfaction in your performance.

It's important to realize that for positive imagery to work—to refocus the negative pictures you have of yourself into more positive ones—you must do more than merely read your statements. For change to occur, you need to *say them* (concrete words), *see them* (vivid mental pictures), and *feel them*.[33] If you have trouble with the "feeling" part of some of your positive statements, build feeling cues into those statements that give you trouble. For example, if you can't "feel" confident while looking listeners in the eye, think of a situation in which you do feel confident making eye contact and add it to your statement. Instead of saying, "I find it easy to make eye contact with my listeners," change the statement to, "It's as easy for me to make direct eye contact with my audience as it is when I speak to a group of children in Sunday school."

> **R e m e m b e r :**
>
> **To create positive mental pictures . . .**
>
> 1. Look two or three months into the future.
> 2. Picture yourself as the "ideal" speaker you would like to be.
> 3. Write five to ten positive statements that describe this "ideal" you.
> 4. Twice a day for four weeks, *read*, *visualize*, and *feel* yourself successfully performing each statement.

Your subconscious can't tell the difference between your giving a successful speech and your mentally picturing yourself giving a successful speech. Therefore, each time you create a vivid mental picture of yourself speaking successfully and feel the confidence and pride that comes with success, you are one step closer to being a confident speaker. A student in one of my classes said that she viewed her past speaking history like a videotape. Although she couldn't erase any of her past failures, she could tape over them with both real and imagined speaking experiences. Once she had taped over all the negative experiences, she started to see herself as a good speaker and actually began to enjoy speaking.

Step 3: don't compare yourself to others   No matter who you are or how long you have been speaking, there will always be people who are better than you. At the same time, you will always be better than some people. It's not a contest between you and the other students in your class. If someone who is really outstanding gives a speech right before you, resist the temptation to say, "There's no way I can follow such a good speech. I can never be that good," or, "I wish I could speak as well as Mario." Your goal isn't to be better than other speakers. Your goal is to be the best speaker you can be—you are only in competition with yourself.

At the same time, however, it's perfectly all right to borrow techniques from other speakers (students as well as professionals). For example, if the colors Jack used on his visuals made them come alive, you might try using the same colors. Or if Monica's gestures seemed especially sincere and expressive, you might try using similar gestures. You may even wish to ask Monica if she uses any special techniques or has any pointers for you. Borrowing public speaking ideas and practices from a person is not the same as wanting to be that person. It simply represents another tool for becoming the best speaker possible.

If you use positive imagery as outlined here, in about four weeks you will begin to feel comfortable with the "new" you.[34] You will have changed your automatic pilot so you no longer need to force yourself to give an effective speech.

Positive Imagery Exercises

In addition to visualizing your positive statements, tape yourself reading the following positive imagery exercises. For the best results play these tapes (or your own version of them) at least once a week and the night before each scheduled speech. As you listen, *see* and *feel* yourself giving a successful speech. Two recent studies found that speakers who participated in similar exercises only one time had less communication anxiety than speakers who did not use them or who used some other anxiety reduction method.[35] Such visualization exercises also have a long-lasting effect.[36]

Positive Imagery Exercise 1[37]

It's important to get in the mood to visualize. Close your eyes and get as comfortable as you can in your chair. For the next fifteen minutes or so, try to keep an open body posture with your feet flat on the floor and your arms resting comfortably but not touching. Now, take in a deep breath . . . hold it as you count slowly to three . . . and exhale slowly. As you exhale feel the tension in your neck and shoulders draining down your arms and out your fingers; feel the tension in your back and hips draining down your legs and out your toes. Take another deep breath . . . hold it . . . and slowly release it through your mouth (if possible). Feel the tension leaving your body. Now one more time, breathe deeply . . . hold it . . . slowly exhale and begin normal breathing.

Imagine yourself at the sink in your bathroom. You lean toward the mirror to get a better look at your face. See your face? The mirror suddenly clouds over and when it clears again, you are looking through the mirror into the future. You can see yourself getting up on a day in which you are going to give a particularly important speech. You jump out of bed full of energy, full of confidence, and looking forward to the day. You are putting on one of your favorite outfits that makes you feel professional and confident. See how good you look and feel? Imagine yourself arriving relaxed at the speaking site. When you arrive, people comment on your appearance and how relaxed you appear. You feel thoroughly prepared for this presentation. You have researched carefully, have professional visual aids, and have practiced several times. Now see yourself standing or sitting in the room where you will make your speech, talking very comfortably and confidently with others in the room. Everyone seems friendly and supportive. You feel absolutely sure of your material and of your ability to present the information in a forceful, convincing, positive manner. It's time for the speech. See yourself walk confidently to the front and smile at the audience. They smile back. You set up your visual aids and begin your presentation.

Now see yourself speaking. Your introduction goes the way you had it planned. You are dynamic, forceful, and interesting. Your speaking rate is just right; your pauses and emphasis couldn't be better; your gestures and body movements are powerful. As you flow from one main point to the next the audience smiles and nods their heads. They are really paying attention and seem impressed by your visual and verbal supporting material.

As you wrap up your main points, you have the feeling that it could not have gone better. The audience applauds with enthusiasm. Hear the applause? Now see yourself answering questions with the same confidence and energy you displayed in the actual speech. The speech is over. People come up and shake your hand and congratulate you. You accept their thanks in a relaxed and pleased manner. You are filled with energy, purpose, and a sense of general well-being. Congratulate yourself on a job well done!

The future fades and the mirror again shows your reflection—but the confident smile on your face remains. Now take a deep breath . . . hold it . . . and slowly let it out. Do this several more times and slowly return to the room.

If you can't actually "see" yourself while doing this exercise, don't be concerned. Positive imagery is easier for some people than for others.[38] If you have difficulty seeing any images at all, "think of what it might be like if you *could* see the pictures you're thinking about"[39] and concentrate on the "feeling" part of the exercise.

If you are used to negative images of your speaking abilities, trying to picture yourself in a positive light may seem not only phony but almost impossible. Some of us may need more practice before we can see ourselves giving a confident speech. When I ask students and seminar participants to say out loud together, "I am an excellent speaker," most of them say they feel like phonies and some of them can't even say the words. How about you? Try saying, "I am an excellent speaker," and make it sound like you mean it. Keep this point in mind: if we can't even say it, how can we expect to do it? Once you begin to *see* yourself as a good speaker, you will notice that it is easier to *be* a good speaker.

The next exercise was written by a student and highlights specific speaking qualities she wanted to develop. You may want to write your own positive imagery exercise and tailor it to fit your specific goals. Begin with the same relaxation and deep breathing described in Exercise 1. When you feel relaxed, play your taped version of the exercise.

Positive Imagery Exercise 2[40]

I am looking at myself sitting in my usual seat in speech class on the day of my first speech. It is my turn to speak. As I rise from my seat, I direct the butterflies of excitement in my stomach into positive energy. I can do this because I have practiced carefully and know I am well prepared. As I turn to face my fellow classmates, I draw in a deep breath, stand up straight, and begin to speak. An aura of confidence radiates from within as I speak. My body shows no tension. My breathing is paced. My motions are fluid, and my gestures are graceful. My shoulders stay relaxed and down. My voice does not quiver or shake. It is pitched low and is well modulated and easy for everyone to hear. My eyes scan from student to student drawing their complete attention. My mind is rested and calm, allowing my words to flow evenly and to be clear and concise. As I speak, I have no trouble remembering each point of my speech. I can see the outline of my speech clearly in my mind and refer to my notes only briefly. I make use of dramatic pauses to stress important points within the speech. It is obvious that the class is understanding what I am saying and that they are enjoying my speech. My words continue to flow smoothly and my transitions are especially good. Each idea is spoken clearly and confidently. There are no mistakes. As the speech winds down, my words are chosen carefully and powerfully. The audience is paying complete attention. I end with a bang! I know from the enthusiastic applause and positive comments that my speech has been a total success! I pause, then ask if there are any questions. As I rephrase each question, I continue to feel relaxed and confident. My answers are brief and to the point. I can tell the audience is impressed with the visual aid I use to answer a question. When the Q & A is over, I pause for effect, then present my final wrap-up. Again the audience applauds with enthusiasm. I feel proud and confident as I walk back to my seat.

Managing Trait Anxiety: Other Methods
▼ ▼ ▼

Positive imagery isn't the only method for reducing trait anxiety (although it is one of the few methods that you can do on your own). Other confidence-building methods (usually offered as a seminar or one-hour course) include systematic desensitization, cognitive restructuring, and rhetoritherapy (a form of skills training).[41] All three of these methods require the help of trained professionals. If your anxiety level is especially high, you may find that one or more of these methods combined with positive imagery may work better for you than any one method alone.[42] Let's take a brief look at each of these methods.

Systematic Desensitization

Systematic desensitization simply means learning to feel relaxed instead of anxious.[43] It involves two basic steps: (1) learning to relax using deep muscle relaxation and breathing,[44] and (2) learning to remain relaxed while visualizing a series of communication situations that begin with low-anxiety situations and progress to high-anxiety situations. Deep muscle relaxation involves tensing and then relaxing various muscle groups until a sense of deep relaxation occurs. James McCroskey lists the following fifteen muscle groups and suggests that each be tensed for approximately 5–10 seconds, followed by 10–15 seconds of relaxation.

1. *Hands*: clench and unclench right hand, then left hand.
2. *Biceps and triceps*: bend right hand upward at wrist, pointing fingers toward ceiling, relax, then left hand; bring both hands up toward shoulders, flex biceps, then relax, repeat.
3. *Shoulders*: shrug shoulders, hold, relax.

4. *Neck*: push head against chair, relax; lean forward, relax.
5. *Mouth*: press lips tightly together, then relax.
6. *Tongue*: extend, hold, retract.
7. *Tongue*: press mouth roof, relax; press mouth floor, relax.
8. *Eyes and forehead*: close eyes tightly, relax; wrinkle forehead, relax.
9. *Breathing*: inhale, hold, exhale.
10. *Back*: arch back, hold, relax.
11. *Midsection*: clench muscles, hold, relax.
12. *Thighs*: clench muscles, hold, relax.
13. *Stomach*: suck in stomach, hold, relax.
14. *Calves and feet*: stretch out both legs, hold, relax.
15. *Toes*: point toes toward ceiling, hold, relax; point toes downward, hold, relax.[45]

Once you are relaxed, begin visualizing various communication situations your instructor or trainer helped you develop. Begin with the least threatening and work up to the more threatening situations. Low-anxiety situations might include hearing that you will be giving a speech later in the semester, being assigned a speech due in two weeks, and researching for speech sources in the library. Higher-anxiety situations might include rehearsing for your speech, arriving at the classroom on the day of your speech, and walking to the front of the classroom to give your speech.[46]

If at any time during the process, you begin to feel tense and anxious, stop visualizing and reestablish a relaxed state. When you can maintain this relaxed state without effort, try visualizing the situation again. Continue this process (which will take many sessions) until you can visualize all problem situations without anxiety.

Cognitive Restructuring[47]

Cognitive restructuring is based on the assumption that speaking anxiety is a result of irrational thoughts that produce negative images and unrealistic expectations about speech-making. "Believing that everyone must like your speech, that everyone should be persuaded by your speech, and that, if you mispronounce one word, everyone will think you are uneducated"[48] are examples of irrational thoughts that contribute to speaker anxiety. To help you overcome any irrational thoughts, cognitive restructuring involves (1) identifying irrational self-talk that produces speaker anxiety, (2) developing alternative coping statements to replace these irrational thoughts, and (3) practicing using the coping statements in stressful situations (such as group discussions or speaking situations).[49]

Rhetoritherapy[50]

Rhetoritherapy focuses on speaking *skills* rather than *feelings* and, as developed by G. M. Phillips,[51] covers communication skills in interpersonal, small-group, and public speaking situations.[52] The skills needed by a public speaker include many of the same skills needed in interpersonal and group settings. In each case the natural way to overcome anxiety is by covering the less threatening one-on-one interpersonal situations first, then building to group situations, and ending with the more threatening public speaking situations. Ideally, as your skills increase, your anxiety decreases.

In focusing on skills, rhetoritherapy deals with goal analysis. In rhetoritherapy you are asked to (1) identify reasonable speaking goals, (2) determine specific behaviors or practices needed to complete the goal, and (3) develop procedures for judging the success of each goal.[53] For example, one goal might be to improve your delivery skills. Specific desired behaviors for this goal might be to speak loud enough to be heard, to use gestures while speaking, and to make direct eye contact with as many audience members as possible.[54] The goal might be judged successful when audience evaluations of your speech indicate that your volume was good, your gestures were effective, and at least half the listeners found your eye contact to be direct and sincere.

Summary
▼ ▼ ▼

"I am relaxed and in control while giving speeches" is a good positive statement to sum up this chapter. There is no reason to let nervousness and anxiety consume us when we speak. Taking control of nervousness and anxiety is much easier once we can identify it.

Situational anxiety is something almost everyone experiences in new situations. We can manage this type of anxiety by preparing and practicing, warming up first, concentrating on our message, planning introductions that relax us as well as our audience, and using visual aids effectively.

Trait anxieties are personal anxieties that we bring to a speaking situation. Although more difficult to control than situational anxiety, trait anxiety can be effectively managed through positive imagery. For example, positive imagery can be used to help you control your anxiety in employment interviews, problem-solving discussions, or any situation where your confidence needs a boost.

Trait anxiety can also be reduced through methods such as systematic desensitization, cognitive restructuring, and rhetoritherapy. Each of these methods requires help from a trained professional. Your college may offer seminars or workshops in one or a combination of these methods. If positive imagery doesn't seem to work for you, ask your professor if instruction in one of these other methods is available. With a little time and effort, your situational and/or trait anxiety can be managed so you can give confident, successful speeches.

Practice Suggestions
▼ ▼ ▼

1. Have you given one of the introductory speeches described in Chapter 2 yet? If so, did you have more or less anxiety than you expected? What type of anxiety did you experience: situational, trait, or both?

2. Have you determined what type(s) of anxiety are likely to give you the most trouble when you speak? What specific actions do you plan to take to manage your anxiety? Write out a brief plan of action and make a copy of it.

Give one copy to your instructor; save the other copy so you can refer to it before each presentation.

3. If you haven't already done so, write out five to ten positive statements that represent the speaking characteristics you wish to develop or polish. Make sure that each statement is written in the present tense (as if it is true right now) and avoids negative words. Ask a classmate to check the wording of your statements. If necessary, make minor changes.

4. One way people indicate confidence is by saying their names using a falling pitch. In other words, if you say your name with a rising pitch (as if you're asking a question) instead of with a falling pitch (as if you're making a statement), you will sound less confident to others. Practice saying your name until you can do so with both a rising pitch and with a falling pitch. Can you hear the difference? Now, one at a time, each of you should walk confidently to the front of the room and say, "Hello, my name is ___ ___" (with a falling pitch), pause, read two positive statements about yourself (making them sound completely true), and walk confidently back and sit down. Be careful not to roll your eyes or do anything else that indicates anxiety. With other class members, discuss how you felt during this activity.

5. If you are feeling some dissimilarity (that you are probably the only one in your class who's really nervous about speaking), ask your classmates to respond to the following two questions:

   a. *How good a speaker do you consider yourself to be?*

Poor	Fair	Average	Good	Excellent

   b. *How much personal anxiety do you usually experience when speaking?*

None	A little	Some	Moderate	Great

   If there are other sections of your course being taught this term, your professor may wish to combine the answers from all sections. How many other students are in the same categories as you? You may wish to share your experiences with one or more of them.

6. In addition to positive imagery (which is a method of overcoming anxiety that you can do on your own), the speech communication department on your campus may offer a seminar or one-hour course using other confidence building methods such as systematic desensitization, cognitive restructuring, rhetoritherapy, or a combination of methods. If your PRCA scores (see Appendix D) indicate that you have moderate to high trait anxiety, you may wish to enroll in one of these programs and benefit from the help of a trained professional. Ask your professor for more information.

Notes

1. "Fears," *Spectra* 9 (December 1973), 4.
2. Virginia P. Richmond and James C. McCroskey, *Communication: Apprehension, Avoidance, and Effectiveness*, 4th ed. (Scottsdale, AZ: Gorsuch Scarisbrick, 1995), pp. 74–75.
3. Bert Decker with James Denney, *You've Got to Be Believed to Be Heard* (New York: St. Martin's Press, 1992), p. 35.
4. Decker, *You've Got to Be Believed*, p. 36.
5. Situational anxiety is often referred to by researchers as "state" anxiety. See M. Motley, "Stage Fright Manipulation by (False) Heart Rate Feedback," *Central States Speech Journal* 27 (1976), 186–191; and S. Booth-Butterfield, "Action Assembly Theory and Communication Apprehension," *Human Communication Research* 13 (1987), 388–398.
6. Trait anxiety is often referred to by researchers as "communication apprehension," or CA. See James A. Daly and Gustav W. Friedrich, "The Development of Communication Apprehension: A Retrospective Analysis of Contributory Correlates," *Communication Quarterly* 29 (1981), 243–255.
7. Robert N. Bostrom, *Communicating in Public: Speaking and Listening* (Santa Rosa, CA: Burges, 1988), p. 55.
8. Michael J. Beatty, "Situational and Predispositional Correlates of Public Speaking Anxiety," *Communication Education* 37 (January 1988), 28–39. See also Michael J. Beatty, Gary L. Balfantz, and Alison Y. Kuwabara, "Trait-Like Qualities of Selected Variables Assumed to Be Transient Causes of Performance State Anxiety," *Communication Education* 38 (July 1989), 277–289.
9. Beatty, "Situational and Predispositional Correlates," p. 37.
10. James C. McCroskey, "Oral Communication Apprehension: A Reconceptualization," in M. Burgoon, ed. *Communication Yearbook* 6 (Beverly Hills, CA: Sage, 1982), p. 140.
11. For a review of the research see Michael J. Beatty, "Physiological Assessment," in J. A. Daly and J. C. McCroskey (eds.), *Avoiding Communication Shyness, Reticence and Communication Apprehension* (Beverly Hills, CA: Sage, 1984), pp. 95–106.
12. Quote reported in Robert N. Bostrom, *Communicating in Public: Speaking and Listening* (Edina, MN: Burgess, 1988), p. 57.
13. From Cheryl Hamilton with Cordell Parker, *Communicating for Results*, 4th ed. (Belmont, CA: Wadsworth, 1993). Used by permission.
14. Research has found positive imagery (visualization) to be especially effective for trait anxiety, to have a long-term effect, and to be easier to administer. See Joe Ayres and Theodore S. Hopf, "The Long-Term Effect of Visualization in the Classroom: A Brief Research Report," *Communication Education* 39 (January 1990), 75–78; Ayres and Hopf, "Visualization: Is It More Than Extra-Attention?" *Communication Education* 38 (January 1989), 1–5; and Ayres and Hopf, "Visualization: A Means of Reducing Speech Anxiety," *Communication Education* 34 (1985), 318–323. See also Joe Ayres, "Coping with Speech Anxiety: The Power of Positive Thinking," *Communication Education* 37 (October 1988), 289–295; and John Bourhis and Mike Allen, "Meta-Analysis of the Relationship Between Communication Apprehension and Cognitive Performance," *Communication Education* 41 (January 1992), 68–76.
15. Peter Russell, *The Brain Book* (New York: Dutton, 1979), p. 110.
16. See Beatty, "Physiological Assessment."
17. Alan Richardson, *Mental Imagery* (New York: Springer, 1952), p. 56.
18. Kay Porter and Judy Foster, "In Your Mind's Eye: Incredible, but True, You Can Visualize Your Tennis Success," *World Tennis* 35 (January 1988), 22.
19. Jim Loehr, "Seeing Is Believing," *World Tennis* 36 (March 1989), 16+; Steve McKee, "Body Talk: Kristi Yamaguchi," *American Health* (January/February 1992), 34.
20. Robert McGarvey, "Rehearsing for Success: Tap the Power of the Mind Through Visualization," *Executive Female* (January/February 1990), 35.
21. McGarvey, "Rehearsing for Success," p. 35.
22. Jean Houston, *The Possible Human* (Los Angeles: Tarcher, 1982), p. 11.
23. K. M. Stephan, G. R. Fink, R. E. Passingham, D. Silbersweig, A. O. Ceballos-Baumann, C. D. Frith, and R. S. J. Frackowiak, "Functional Anatomy of the Mental Representation of Upper Extremity Movements in Healthy Subjects," *Journal of Neurophysiology* 73 (January 1995), 373–385.
24. R. Wise, F. Chollet, U. Hadar, L. Friston, E. Hoffner, and R. Frackowiak, "Distribution of Cortical Neural Networks Involved in Word Comprehension and Word Retrieval," *Brain* 114 (1991), 1803–1817.
25. Maxwell Maltz, *Psycho-Cybernetics* (New York: Prentice-Hall, 1960), p. 2.
26. Kay Porter and Judy Foster, *The Mental Athlete: Inner Training for Peak Performance* (New York: Ballantine Books, 1986), p. 71.
27. Porter and Foster, "In Your Mind's Eye," pp. 22, 24.
28. Anees A. Sheikh, ed., *Imagery: Current Theory, Research, and Application* (New York: Wiley, 1983), p. 514.
29. Louis Tice, *Investment in Excellence* (cassette series, tape no. 1) (Seattle: The Pacific Institute, 1980).
30. Porter and Foster, *The Mental Athlete*, p. 225.
31. For one example, see Porter and Foster, *The Mental Athlete*.
32. For one example, see Tice, *Investment in Excellence*.
33. Kenneth S. Zagacki, Renee Edwards, and James M. Honeycutt, "The Role of Mental Imagery and Emotion in

Imagined Interaction," *Communication Quarterly* 40 (Winter 1992), 56–68.

34. Louis Tice, *Achieving Your Potential: Family Program* (cassette series, tape no. 10) (Seattle: The Pacific Institute, 1979).

35. Ayres and Hopf, "Visualization: Is It More Than Extra Attention?" Ayres and Hopf, "Visualization: A Means of Reducing Speech Anxiety."

36. Ayres and Hopf, "The Long-Term Effect of Visualization in the Classroom," pp. 75–78.

37. The first visualization exercise is based on Ayres and Hopf, "Visualization," 2–3. See also Joe Ayres and Tim Hopf, *Coping with Speech Anxiety* (Norwood, NJ: Ablex, 1993), pp. 31–47.

38. Anne R. Isaac and David F. Marks, "Individual Differences in Mental Imagery Experience: Developmental Changes and Specialization," *British Journal of Psychology* 85 (November 1994), 479–497.

39. Norma Carr-Ruffino, *The Promotable Woman: Becoming a Successful Manager*, 3d ed. (Belmont, CA: Wadsworth, 1985), p. 152.

40. Hamilton with Parker, *Communicating for Results*, pp. 173–174.

41. An excellent description of anxiety reduction methods is included in Richmond and McCroskey, *Communication: Apprehension, Avoidance, and Effectiveness*; and Ayres and Hopf, *Coping with Speech Anxiety*.

42. Joe Ayres and Tim Hopf, *Coping with Public Speaking Anxiety: An Examination of Various Combinations of Systematic Desensitization, Skills Training, and Visualization*. Paper presented at the Speech Communication Association convention, New Orleans, November 1994.

43. The originator of systematic desensitization is J. Wolpe, *Psychotherapy by Reciprocal Inhibition* (Stanford, CA: Stanford University Press, 1958).

44. James C. McCroskey, *Deep Muscular Relaxation: Audio-Tape* (Annandale, VA: Speech Communication Association).

45. McCroskey, *Communication: Apprehension, Avoidance, and Effectiveness*, p. 101.

46. Susan Koester and Joanna Pucel, "Systematic Desensitization," in *Communication Apprehension Intervention*. A short course offered at the Speech Communication Association convention, Miami Beach, November 1993.

47. A. Ellis, *Reason and Emotion in Psychotherapy* (New York: Stuart, 1962); and D. Meichenbaum, *Cognitive Behavior Modification* (New York: Plenum, 1977).

48. Ayres and Hopf, *Coping with Speech Anxiety*, p. 13.

49. William J. Fremouw and Michael D. Scott, "Cognitive Restructuring: An Alternative Method for the Treatment of Communication Apprehension," *Communication Education* (May 1979), 129–133.

50. G. M. Phillips, *Communication Incompetencies: A Theory of Training Oral Performance Behavior* (Carbondale: Southern Illinois University Press, 1991).

51. G. M. Phillips, "Rhetoritherapy Versus the Medical Model: Dealing With Reticence," *Communication Education* 26 (1977), 34–43.

52. L. Kelley, "Implementing a Skills Training Program for Reticent Communicators," *Communication Education* 38 (1989), 85–101.

53. James Keaten, "Rhetoritherapy," in *Communication Apprehension Intervention*. A short course offered at the Speech Communication Association convention, Miami Beach, November 1993.

54. Ayres and Hopf, *Coping with Speech Anxiety*, pp. 72–73.

What Speakers Should Know About Listeners

Stages of Listening
Sensing Stage
Interpreting Stage
Evaluating Stage
Responding Stage
Memory Stage

Attention-Grabbers: Stimulation and Motivation
External vs. Internal Stimulation
Motivation

100 Percent Communication: A Listening Myth
Variations in Frames of Reference
What They See vs. What They Hear

How Listeners Avoid Being Persuaded
Criticizing the Speaker's Credibility
Doubting the Credibility of the Speaker's Sources
Misinterpreting the Speaker's Ideas
Thinking of Something Other Than the Speech

Reading Listeners' Nonverbal Cues
Nonverbal Cues and Context
Misinterpretation of Single Nonverbal Behaviors
Telltale Signs of Nonlistening

Making Listening Easier
Personalize Your Speeches
Increase Your Speaking Rate
Don't State Key Ideas in the First or Second Sentence
Use Visuals to Enhance Listening
Verbally Highlight Important Ideas

WHAT DO THESE TWO SITUATIONS have in common?

Situation 1: You have worked long and hard on a business proposal to present to a Japanese business firm. With the help of an interpreter, you have even prepared your transparencies (visuals) in Japanese. After the introductions you and the interpreter get right to business and outline what you know to be an excellent presentation. The Japanese seem to be nodding in agreement so you feel fairly confident that things are going well. At the end of the presentation, the Japanese promise to look over the proposal and get back in touch with you. But they never do. Whenever you call, they politely give a reason for not meeting with you "at this time."[1]

Situation 2: You are the last speaker of the day. The previous speakers each took more than their allotted time. Even though there are only twenty minutes remaining before the program is scheduled to end, the director assures you that you may have your full time. As you speak you are impressed that the audience seems to be listening so well—most of them are looking directly at you and sitting totally still. By omitting the less important items, you manage to end on time and conclude with a startling bit of information. However, you are surprised that no one acknowledges your unexpected information as they file out of the room.

Can you tell what each of these speakers failed to do? Both apparently prepared their presentations carefully and took their specific audiences into consideration. The first speaker even prepared transparencies in Japanese. The second speaker ended the presentation with a startling statement designed to reestablish audience interest. However, neither speaker really understood audience members as listeners. Read this chapter to see if you can determine what listener characteristic each speaker overlooked. In this chapter we will discuss why listening is not just the responsibility of an audience and what you need to know about listening and listeners to succeed as a speaker.

Stages of Listening
▼ ▼ ▼

To better understand listeners, speakers first need to know what is involved in effective listening. As shown in Figure 4.1, the basic stages of listening are sensing, interpreting, evaluating, responding, and, if the other steps are completed correctly, memory of the speaker's message.[2]

Sensing Stage

In this stage listeners select or ignore one or more stimuli from the multitude of stimuli that bombard all of us continually. It's impossible to notice every sound, sight, and smell or to acknowledge every event or feeling that occurs around us.

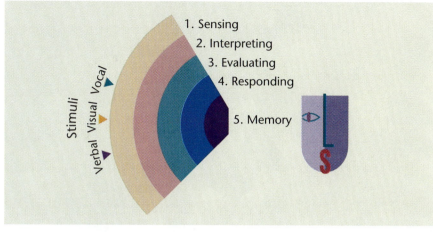

Figure 4.1
Stages of Listening

We learn to become highly selective; we pay attention to things that are important or of interest to us and essentially tune out everything else. For example, how many times have you traveled down a certain street without realizing that it housed a certain specialty shop until you needed something that the shop contained? Listening is the same. In his book *Listen for Success*, Arthur K. Robertson cites another example:

> Eugene Raudsepp of Princeton Creative Research tells the story of a zoologist walking down a busy city street with a friend amid honking horns and screeching tires. He says to his friend, "Listen to that cricket!" The friend looks at him with astonishment. "You hear a cricket in the middle of all this noise?" The zoologist takes out a coin and flips it into the air. As it clinks to the sidewalk a dozen heads turn in response. The zoologist says quietly, "We hear what we listen for."[3]

In addition to needs and interests, listeners' sensing abilities are affected by gender, age, cultural background, bias, emotion, and environmental distractions, to name a few. The goal of the speaker is to get listeners to focus their senses on the message at hand. Suggestions for how to do this are discussed later in the chapter.

Interpreting Stage

At this stage listeners supply meaning to the messages that they have seen, heard, and felt in the sensing stage. In other words, they try to figure out what the speaker really means. The problem is that we often have different meanings for the same word. For example, suppose your boss, in a formal presentation to you and your coworkers, says that raises this year are "likely." What percentage of certainty is implied by the word "likely"? What's the chance that your interpretation and the boss's interpretation will be the same? Or suppose your boss gives

*Multiple stimuli are compet-
ing for the attention of these
listeners.*

© *Thomas Croke/Liaison International*

you a "rush" assignment. How much time would you have to complete the task? One printing company had so many misunderstandings over the use of the word *rush* that it posted the following definitions:

"As soon as possible": Do within two or three days.
"Rush": Do by the end of today.
"Hot": Don't drop what you're doing, but do it next.
"Now": Drop everything.

The same factors that cause faulty sensing also can cause faulty interpretation. Listeners often "assume" that they understand and don't bother to ask questions or to paraphrase (summarize the speaker's ideas in their own words). Sometimes they are so sure they understand that they stop listening. For example, suppose you gave the following drawing instructions to a group of architectural students: "In the center of your paper, draw a one-inch square. Now, we need to label the corners as reference points. Starting with the upper left-hand corner, label that corner 'a.' Label the upper right-hand corner 'b.'" At this point most audience members would stop listening and complete the labeling on their own. But which of the two labeling schemes shown below would they follow? How about you? How would you have labeled the square? In an actual class exercise over half of the students labeled their square following pattern 1 below even though the speaker gave clear instructions for pattern 2.

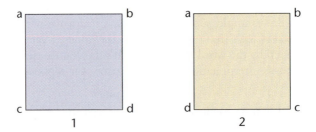

Some of the most serious listening problems occur in the interpreting stage. Sometimes they result from listeners jumping to conclusions (as the labeling example shows) or from fatigue or information overload. However, many times problems with interpretation occur because both speakers and listeners believe that if the speakers are clear and the listeners are paying attention, 100 percent understanding will result—one of the biggest communication myths around. Why this belief is a myth that causes interpretation problems and what speakers should do about it will be discussed later in the chapter.

Evaluating Stage

In this stage listeners "think about the message, make more extensive inferences, evaluate and judge the speaker and the message."[4] In assigning a value judgment to what they have sensed and understood, listeners must decide whether the speaker seems qualified, the information and evidence appear accurate, and the comments are relevant and worth the time. What value judgment do you think the listeners in the picture on the next page are making?

Listeners' evaluations often are affected by their attitude toward the speaker. Imagine yourself speaking before audience members who think you are too young or resent you for your gender or ethnic group or mistrust the organization you represent. Listeners' evaluations also are affected by their previous experiences, their expectations, and even their beliefs and emotional conditions. As a result, listeners sometimes make evaluations based on assumptions without waiting to make sure they have all the facts. A rescue squad member related this incident about a call for help the squad received from a police officer:

> A 38-year-old man had pulled off the road and hit an obstruction. [After calling the rescue squad, the] patrolman had called back: "Cancel the call. The man is not really injured. He's just complaining of chest pains and probably bumped into the steering wheel." The squad went out anyway. When they arrived they could see immediately that the man was having a heart attack. "What happened," he told them between gasps, "was that I had this chest pain and went off the road." And with that he passed out. We got to work on him right away and got him to a hospital, but it was too late. Now he had told the patrolman the same thing he had told us—"I had this chest pain and went off the road." The patrolman heard him, perhaps understood him, but despite his knowledge and experience did not evaluate what he heard and in this case not evaluating correctly was fatal. I never forgot that.[5]

Speakers need to be aware that listener interpretations and evaluations often depend on the verbal, visual, and vocal impressions listeners receive from them. Your words (verbal code), your appearance, gestures, and visual aids (visual code), and your speaking voice (vocal code) are as important to your listeners as your ideas.

What value judgment do you think the listeners in this picture are making?

© Bob Daemmrich/The Image Works

Responding Stage

Once listeners have sensed, interpreted, and evaluated you and your ideas, they respond (give feedback). This stage is very important because, without feedback, speakers can only assume that they have communicated. Listeners won't always agree, but their responses show whether they were listening and whether they understood. Listener response can come in many forms, and it isn't always easy to interpret. Ideally listeners will communicate their agreement, disagreement, or confusion through obvious nonverbal facial expressions (such as frowning or nodding). If the situation allows, they might make comments and ask questions during the speech or during the question-and-answer period following the speech. Many listeners will come up to congratulate you or ask questions after the presentation is over. Some will even drop you a note in the mail. All of these responses will be invaluable to you in judging the success of your presentation.

However, sometimes listeners won't make any obvious responses, in which case you must try to interpret their unintentional responses to see if they understand or are even listening. Although accurately interpreting nonverbal responses is very difficult, later in this chapter we will discuss groups of nonverbal cues that indicate whether your audience members are or are not listening.

Also, keep in mind that listeners often fake attention to speakers. Just because everyone is staring at you doesn't mean that they are listening attentively. Speak-

Remember:

In the five stages of listening, listeners . . .

1. *Sense*—they hear what is important to them.
2. *Interpret*—they assign meaning to what they see, hear, and feel.
3. *Evaluate*—they determine speaker credibility and message importance.
4. *Respond*—they react to the speech, usually through nonverbal cues.
5. *Remember*—they retain parts of the message in memory.

ers make a big mistake when they assume that attentive posture and intent eyes equals listening. People who are actually listening tend to shift around in their seats, doodle on their papers, cough, glance at the clock and the floor, and so on. Normally, *the only people who sit perfectly still are people who are mentally someplace else.* When listeners are silent and their eyes become glazed, listening has ceased.

Memory Stage

Memory storage is the end result of effective listening. Once listeners have completed the sensing, interpreting, evaluating, and responding stages they decide what parts, if any, of the speech to retain and then attempt to store them in memory. Unfortunately, no matter how brilliant your speech or how intently the audience listens, most audience members will remember only about 10–25 percent of your presentation the next day, week, or month.[6] The parts they don't recall may have been impressive and may have contributed to their favorable evaluation of your talk, but the specific facts will have eluded them.

Because so little of the overall presentation is committed to memory, it becomes crucial for you to try to control what is remembered. Being organized, using good delivery, repeating important ideas, and relating the presentation to listeners' backgrounds and interests are all important and will be discussed later in this chapter. However, *the most effective tool for improving poor audience memory is visual communication.* The power of visual aids cannot be overstated. Audience retention and comprehension are definitely increased when visual and verbal communication are properly teamed. (Chapter 6 discusses the benefits and power of using visual aids.)

Knowing the stages that are involved in effective listening can help speakers better understand listeners. Unfortunately you likely will lose some of your listeners at each stage. Fortunately you can use a variety of techniques to help you retain audience attention at each listening stage. Techniques to combat major listener pitfalls will be discussed in the following sections.

Attention-Grabbers: Stimulation and Motivation

▼ ▼ ▼

When customers come to a department store during a sale, there is no guarantee that they will buy anything. Similarly, just because people show up at a meeting or walk into a classroom doesn't mean that they are going to listen to the speaker. In the sensing stage audience members must be stimulated and then motivated if careful listening is to occur.

External vs. Internal Stimulation

A stimulus can be either internal or external. An **external stimulus** is a person or object external to the listener that triggers an idea in the listener; an **internal stimulus** is a thought generated by the listener that triggers additional thought or action. Suppose you are waiting for a speech to begin and you suddenly remember that you did not return an important phone call (internal stimulus). You begin to ponder the problem. If you go back to your office, you will miss the speech; however, if you wait until the speech is over, it will be too late to return the call. You become so engrossed in your problem that you are unaware that the speech has begun.

Prior to the start of a speech, most audience members are dwelling on something other than the speaker's topic. Therefore, the speaker's first task is to focus the attention and interest of the listeners on the chosen topic and away from any distracting interests. Effective speakers often focus on some external stimulus in an attempt to overpower each listener's internal stimuli. Beginning your presentation with a statement of purpose works only for those few listeners who are already excited about the topic. The typical listener is more likely to tune in if you begin your speech with such attention-getters as a startling statement, two or three brief examples, a personal experience (brief or detailed), a short demonstration, a question, or a humorous anecdote or joke that relates directly to the speech topic. These and other methods of stimulating audience attention are discussed in detail in Chapter 11.

Motivation

No matter how effective they are, external stimuli won't guarantee continued audience attention; sufficient motivation also is necessary. To *motivate* an audience to continue to listen, you must convince them that your presentation will benefit them or people they care about in some way. The key issue is, why should listeners with many problems and concerns needing their attention give you their precious time? If they perceive that your topic has no personal value for them, their attention will soon drift to another, more pressing topic. Figure 4.2 contains a list of possible audience motivators; add as many others as you can and refer back to this list each time you plan a speech.

▶ Reduce stress and anxiety	▶ Improve rank/position with new skill
▶ Earn more money	▶ Gain a feeling of pride in the job
▶ Gain personal satisfaction	▶ Reach more customers
▶ Impress others and gain needed esteem	▶ Increase job stability and security
▶ Develop self-confidence	▶ Look more attractive
▶ Try something new and exciting	▶ Become healthier
▶ Solve a pressing problem	▶ Improve parenting skills
▶ Achieve desired goals with less effort	▶ Help others
▶ Improve prestige or power	▶ Make a difference in the world

Figure 4.2
Needs That Motivate Listeners

Can you think of any others?

Although we have all heard speakers begin with nothing more than a statement of their purpose (such as, "Today I'm going to talk about caring for your pets"), these speakers are taking a big risk. Without external stimuli and motivation provided by the speaker, most listeners' worries, problems, and concerns (internal stimulus) keep them from paying full attention to the presenter. Outstanding presenters are aware of the importance of stimulation and motivation and make effective use of them in the first step of their speeches, the "focus" step. (See Chapters 2, 11, and 15 for more on the FLOW sequence of organizing a speech.)

100 Percent Communication: A Listening Myth

▼ ▼ ▼

As noted previously, many speakers believe that if they give a good speech and their listeners are paying attention, 100 percent communication is possible. Basically *100 percent communication is highly unlikely.* Therefore you need to prepare for possible misunderstanding ahead of time. By anticipating and recognizing potential sources of misunderstanding in the interpreting stage of listening, you can prevent many communication breakdowns from happening.

One hundred percent communication rarely happens for two reasons: (1) no two people have the same frame of reference, and (2) your actual words may mean less to your audience than how you speak or what you show them. Let's look at each of these.

Variations in Frames of Reference

After stimulating and motivating an audience, you must clearly communicate a specific message. Communicating a message with 100 percent clarity is extremely difficult, however, because your frame of reference will be different from each audience member's. A person's *frame of reference* includes his or her parents, place of origin, educational background, race, gender, attitudes, personality, past experiences, and much more. Think of your frame of reference as an imaginary window. Everything you see, touch, taste, smell, and hear must be filtered through your own window. With so many different life experiences, it is highly unlikely that any two people will have an identical frame of reference on any topic.

When speakers decide what to say and how to say it (a process described in Chapter 1 as *encoding*), they normally use their own frames of reference because they assume that the listeners' perspectives are similar. However, listeners interpret the speaker's meaning (a process called *decoding*) according to their *own* frames of reference. Because no two people have the same frame of reference, the sent message and the received message will not be identical. Close, perhaps; but not identical. Consider the following event that made two world leaders extremely angry:

> When the two most powerful world leaders, President Reagan and General Secretary Gorbachev, met at the Reykjavik, Iceland, summit on October 10–12, 1986, the two sides disagreed about what specific issues had been discussed [earlier at the summit]. The Soviets stated that both had agreed to "the elimination of all strategic nuclear offensive arms" over a period of ten years. The Americans, however, stated that, although the elimination of all nuclear weapons had been briefly discussed, the two sides had agreed only "to destroy all ballistic missiles [manufactured] in the last five years, leaving intact the other nuclear weapons."[7]

Have you ever disagreed with someone over what you said or meant? When you think of how different Reagan's and Gorbachev's life experiences (and thus their frames of reference) were, such disagreement is not really surprising.

What They See vs. What They Hear

What you say means less to an audience than *how* you say it or *what* they see. Each time you speak to an audience, you are communicating not only verbally but also visually and vocally. As you'll recall from Chapter 1, *verbal* communication includes spoken and written language; *visual* communication includes anything nonverbal such as personal appearance, facial expressions, eye contact, and visual aids; and *vocal* communication includes tone of voice, volume, pitch, rate, emphasis, and vocal quality. Listener interpretation in stage two is made more difficult because many speakers assume that the only important code is the verbal code. Researchers have found, however, that language alone does not carry the entire meaning of a message. In fact, many studies have found that when adults attempt to determine the meaning of a statement, they rely more heavily on vocal and visual cues than they do on verbal cues—that is, what is actually said.[8] This seems to be true regardless of whether the situation involves first impressions, attitudes, job inter-

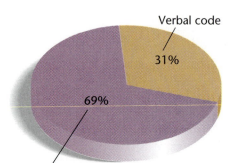

Verbal code

31%

69%

Visual and vocal codes

Figure 4.3

Verbal, Visual, and Vocal Codes

To interpret what speakers mean, listeners rely more heavily on the vocal code (how you speak) and visual code (what they see) than on the verbal code (what you say).

views, or boss-employee conversations.[9] Analyzing results from twenty-three studies, J. S. Philpott found that the language code accounted for 31 percent of the variance in meanings while the vocal and visual codes accounted for the remaining variance.[10] In other words, as Figure 4.3 shows, 69 percent of the meaning in a message is carried by the visual and vocal codes.

The difference among the verbal, visual, and vocal codes can be illustrated in the following example. Suppose that you have purchased a new outfit you plan to wear on a special occasion. As the occasion draws nearer, however, you begin to wonder if the outfit is appropriate and ask a friend for advice. When the friend responds, "It looks great on you!" do you breathe a sigh of relief and take the verbal words at face value, ignoring your friend's tone of voice and facial expression? Or do you look closely at the friend's facial expression and listen carefully to the tone of voice for any indication that the friend is just being nice or may not mean what he or she is saying? For example, a slight raise of the eyebrows and a brief pause after the word "great" could give a completely different meaning.

To communicate effectively, speakers must send the same message in all three codes. However, speakers often send conflicting messages. Take, for example, a company presenter speaking to a hostile group of customers who incorrectly think the company has been overcharging them. Although the presentation is well organized and clearly justifies the company prices, the presenter acts nervous, speaks hesitantly in a fairly high pitch, and fails to make direct eye contact with listeners. If you were a customer, which code would you believe: the verbal, which says that all is well; the vocal, which indicates nervousness; or the visual, which suggests that the presenter is lying? Combining verbal and vocal communication, one researcher found that "with initially equated signals the nonverbal messages outweighed the verbal ones at least 5 to 1, and where they were in conflict the verbal messages were virtually disregarded."[11] Therefore, even if your words are completely clear to the audience, your visual or vocal communication might not be. Furthermore, if your visual or vocal communication is inconsistent with your words, the audience likely will disregard *what* you say and pay more attention to *how* you say it.

Given that your chances of communicating 100 percent with an audience are highly unlikely, what can you do about it? First, do your homework and carefully analyze your audience (Chapter 5 focuses on audience analysis). Do your best to encode your presentation from the listeners' frames of reference, not your own. For example, an army sergeant speaking to a group of former Marines would not refer to his or her audience as "soldiers." *Soldier* is an army term; Marines refer to themselves as "Marines." Second, remember that *the only message that counts is the one actually received*. It doesn't matter what you *really* said, what you *thought* you said, or what you *meant* to say; what's important is what the receivers understood you to say. Third, remember that what you say to an audience and how you say it may mean less to them than what they see. Therefore make sure that what your audience sees adds to rather than detracts from your intended message. Obviously visual aids can be a very powerful tool (Chapter 6 discusses the importance of visuals). And finally recognize that although you may get close, it is highly unlikely you will achieve 100 percent communication. This simple realization can change your whole approach to the way you communicate.

How Listeners Avoid Being Persuaded

▼ ▼ ▼

When you speak on a controversial topic, audience attitudes toward your position will fall somewhere on the continuum from enthusiastic agreement to absolute opposition. Listeners who disagree strongly are obviously the most difficult to persuade. In fact, even those who mildly disagree likely will do their best to avoid being persuaded. Change is not something most people are willing to do without a struggle. As a result, during the evaluating stage listeners use a variety of methods to avoid being persuaded—or even informed. Let's examine the most typically used listener-avoidance methods and some tactics you can use to foil them.

Criticizing the Speaker's Credibility

A credible person is someone whom people find believable—someone who inspires their confidence. Research has found that the greater a speaker's credibility, the more persuasive he or she is.[12] Therefore one of the easiest ways for a listener to avoid being persuaded is to devalue the speaker's credibility. If you don't believe the speaker, there's certainly no reason to believe the message. For example, suppose Julianne is making a good, forceful argument that women are paid less than men for equal work, but John doesn't want to believe it. He feels internal dissonance (discomfort) with her data until he realizes that Julianne is at least ten years younger than anyone in the room. Obviously she is too young to really know how to collect first-hand information. John begins to relax. The dissonance is gone; he has avoided persuasion.

To keep listeners from using this ploy, you need to make sure that you are perceived by audience members as trustworthy and qualified to speak on the topic. You will be considered more credible if you give a presentation that is well organized, include examples from personal experience as well as evidence from known experts, use quality visuals, and deliver your speech in a confident, dynamic manner. If you feel that your credibility might be in question , you can do the following:

▶ Have a highly credible expert on the topic introduce you as a competent and trustworthy speaker.

▶ Identify your views with known experts valued by the audience.

▶ Establish a common feeling with your listeners by identifying beliefs, organizations, or problems you have in common with them.

© Paul Conklin/PhotoEdit

How did you judge Anita Hill's credibility?

Don't forget that if you want people to see you as confident, you must look and sound confident. If needed, review the suggestions for confidence building in Chapter 3.

Doubting the Credibility of the Speaker's Sources

If the listener trying to avoid persuasion can't successfully devalue your credibility, his or her next tactic will be to criticize your sources. Most people seek out information that supports their personal beliefs.[13] In other words, if they are conservative, they read conservative newspapers; if they are liberal, they read liberal newspapers. Therefore, although listeners may know the sources on their side of an issue, what they know about sources on the speaker's side of the issue may be mostly hearsay. Unsupported hearsay (such as, "I read somewhere that the mayor is only marginally qualified to run this city," or "Someone told me that the mayor's honesty is in question") may be enough to keep your listeners from being persuaded. Therefore, to enhance the credibility of your sources, do the following:

▶ Clearly establish the qualifications of your sources.

▶ Refute any expected criticisms.

▶ Show some important quality your sources and your listeners have in common.

R e m e m b e r :

To avoid being persuaded, listeners . . .

▶ Question the speaker's credibility.

▶ Criticize the speaker's sources.

▶ Deliberately misunderstand the speaker's message.

▶ Hear only selected parts of the message.

▶ Decide the message doesn't apply to them.

▶ Try to tune out.

Misinterpreting the Speaker's Ideas

Listeners have a tendency to mentally evade persuasive messages that cause discomfort and, instead, to hear what they want to hear.[14] Listeners evade messages by (1) deliberately misunderstanding the speaker's message, (2) hearing (and remembering) only parts of the message while completely ignoring the more discomforting parts, and (3) changing the focus of the message so that it doesn't apply specifically to them. For example, if an audience were shown cartoons of prejudiced people, the younger listeners could decide that the cartoons were about the prejudice of "older" people, not them. Or female listeners might tell themselves that the cartoons were about the prejudice of men and therefore eliminate themselves from any need for change.[15]

To keep listeners from misinterpreting your persuasive message, first make sure that your ideas are clear and well organized. In addition, you might use one of the following tactics to make a change of opinion less threatening to listeners:

▶ Make it clear that you view the "problem" as fairly universal—it isn't the fault or responsibility of only a few individuals or only your listeners.

▶ Show that your solution won't be a strain on anyone if everyone helps a little.

▶ Show that your view is only a small step from the listeners' current views—a small, hardly noticeable change in opinion that has the potential to benefit all.

Thinking of Something Other Than the Speech

Unfortunately many listeners simply tune out a speaker. Some of them stop listening because they always tune out when they hear complicated information, some because of an emotional reaction to something the speaker said, and some because of internal distractions. However, sometimes listeners will stop listening because they disagree so completely with the speaker. It's easier to think of something else than to listen to arguments that create internal discomfort or anger. In other words, these audience members aren't taking any chances of being persuaded.

If you can't capture the attention of these listeners, you have no chance of persuading them. The following suggestions should make it very difficult for these listeners to avoid paying attention to you:

- Use a dynamic style of delivery—including unexpected volume changes and plenty of movement and gestures (see Chapter 8).
- Include powerful stories and personal instances (see Chapter 10).
- Add humor to the presentation (see Chapter 11).
- Use colorful, entertaining visuals (see Chapter 7).

Of course, there are undoubtedly additional ways that listeners avoid being persuaded. Only the major methods are discussed here to give you an idea of what to expect from listeners. (Unit Four examines persuasive speaking in detail.) Look at the listener ploys summarized in the Remember box on page 84 and decide which speaker tactics you feel will be most useful in counteracting these ploys.

Reading Listeners' Nonverbal Cues
▼ ▼ ▼

Because audience members do not always have obvious reactions, you must learn to "read" listeners' nonverbal responses. Certain nonverbal behaviors can tip you off that your audience is drifting away mentally. Before we discuss these behaviors, however, keep in mind that it is easy to misinterpret nonverbal cues. For example, a student was giving a speech in class on the mysterious stone monoliths of Easter Island. In the middle of comparing the faulty theories of the past with today's more accurate assessment of these objects, he abruptly stopped, said, "Well, if that's how you're going to act, I quit!" and sat down. His classmates looked at one another in stunned silence. The speaker had observed several classmates with foreheads wrinkled in thought and decided that these "frowns" meant they were rejecting his speech. When the class finally convinced him that he had misinterpreted their responses, he agreed to finish his presentation.

Nonverbal Cues and Context

You need to be aware of nonverbal cues without overreacting to them and to remember that context is important in interpreting nonverbal behaviors. That is, before you assume you know what a nonverbal behavior means, consider the specific situation, environment, time of day, and cultural background and personal frames of reference of the listener(s) involved. For example, several listeners with their arms locked across their chests (often a sign of disapproval) takes

Which people are showing nonverbal signs of not listening?

© Sepp Seitz/Woodfin Camp & Associates, Inc.

on a different meaning in a room where the air conditioner is set so low that everyone is freezing. A puzzling lack of audience participation during a question-and-answer period can be more easily interpreted once the speaker realizes that the company president has entered the room. A roomful of nodding heads may mean different things depending on the culture of the listeners. For instance, American listeners tend to nod their heads when they are in agreement. However, when Japanese listeners nod their heads during a presentation, it generally means only that they have received the message, not that they agree. In England listeners at formal presentations avoid head nodding and instead blink their eyes—an indication of polite attention but not necessarily agreement.[16]

Misinterpretation of Single Nonverbal Behaviors

Basing audience evaluation on a single nonverbal behavior rather than on several simultaneous responses can result in misinterpretation. For example, someone who glances at his watch during your speech might be bored with your talk, but he might have other reasons for this gesture. He might be checking the time in the hope that plenty of time remains; he might be consulting his watch for the date in reference to something you said; or he might habitually look at his watch at this time of day because that is when school gets out. Of course, if this same listener glances at his watch continually, looks aimlessly around the room, and shifts uncomfortably in his seat (three collaborating behaviors), you can feel much more certain that he is probably tuning you out. And if several audience members are showing similar behaviors, it's time to take a break, switch to a more interesting point, or show a catchy visual. If your speech is almost finished, you can recapture audience attention with such statements as, "I have one last point to make before concluding my speech," or "In conclusion. . . ." The audience will visibly relax and give you a few more minutes of attention.

Telltale Signs of Nonlistening

Now that you know about the potential dangers of assigning meaning to nonverbal behaviors, let's look at some nonverbal behaviors that generally indicate that a typical U.S. audience is not listening.

Signs of Nonlistening	Signs of Listening
Practically no movement, faces void of expression, unwavering eye contact, drooping eyelids, slouched posture.	Normal movement, smiles (or interested looks on faces), occasional direct eye contact, upright or forward-leaning posture.
Restless movement, aimless looks around the room, drumming fingers or tapping pencils, repeated glances at watches.	Occasional movement (maybe even some doodling), occasional glances at watches—usually near the end of the presentation.
Frowns, narrowed eyes or skeptical looks, arms locked across chests, raised eyebrows or rolling eyes.	Open posture, changing facial expressions depending on speech content, occasional nods of head.

Effective speakers constantly monitor nonverbal feedback from their listeners. Based on the feedback they receive, they fine-tune their speeches as they go. The preceding list of nonverbal behaviors (which often occur simultaneously) should give you an idea of when listeners are probably not listening or, at least, not listening effectively. Remember that audiences rarely sit perfectly still unless they are daydreaming. Listening is not passive—it's active and requires conscious effort. On the other hand, too much movement is an indication of boredom and low-level listening.

Making Listening Easier

▼ ▼ ▼

You must take responsibility for making your presentations interesting and valuable enough for listeners to sense, interpret, evaluate, respond to, and remember your messages. The following suggestions are designed to promote better audience listening and retention.

Personalize Your Speeches

One of the surest ways to guarantee that an audience will listen to you is to share something about yourself. We all enjoy hearing a speaker talk about real-life experiences—it makes us feel as if we know the speaker personally and it adds to the speaker's credibility. For example, in a speech on "How to Earn an MBWA Degree," James H. Lavenson told this personal experience (MBWA stands for Management by Walking Around):

> A couple of years ago, I was asked to consult with the management of the Tour Hassan Hotel in Rabat, Morocco. They had service problems and profit problems and they wanted me to help fix them. . . . I flew to Morocco not having the remotest idea how to start and just checked into the hotel like any other guest. The first morning I wanted my breakfast in the room and walked around trying to figure out how to order it. There were two buttons over the bed with a single sign over both saying "Service" in English. I pushed one button, waited five minutes and then pushed the other one. Nothing happened, so I got dressed and went downstairs for breakfast. The hotel's manager was there and again, like any guest, I was quick to tell him his buttons didn't work. He wasn't the least bit upset. "They've never worked since I've been here and that's five years. You have to call for room service on the phone," he said casually.
>
> "Can't you get them fixed?" I asked.
>
> "Cost too much," was his answer, which I've learned to expect from management in almost any business.
>
> "How much?" I wanted to know.
>
> "A lot" was his enlightening answer.
>
> Not satisfied, I went to the controller and asked if he'd seen a bid on repairing the buzzer system from the rooms. He hadn't, but he knew it would cost too much. I went to the chief engineer and asked him how much it would cost. Do you know what he said? He told me it wouldn't cost anything because there was nothing wrong with the system. It was just turned off. All that was required to make it work was to throw a switch. So why was it turned off? Because, since the two buttons were never identified as to which was which—food or maid—guests batting an even .500 would push the wrong button every other time. The maids got exasperated, the room service waiters were sick of people crying "Wolf, Wolf," or rather, "food, food," when what they really wanted was a clean towel. So the housekeeper persuaded the chief engineer to throw the switch. Nobody had told the manager, and he never asked to find out. Believe it or not, I got a citation from the king of Morocco for a stroke of sheer genius . . . putting labels over each of the two buttons, marking one "food" and one "maid" and asking the engineer to throw the switch.[17]

If you don't have a personal example that relates to the point you wish to make, tell about an experience that happened to someone you know (a family member or friend) or even to someone you have read about. The key is to give enough details to paint a clear and interesting picture to promote listener attention.

Increase Your Speaking Rate

Another way to stimulate audience listening is by speaking a little faster than you normally do. Most speakers talk at a rate of about 100–175 words per minute. However, your listeners can think at a rate of 400–800 words per minute.[18] This means that listeners can easily follow every word you speak and still have some spare time. Although attentive listeners use most of that spare time to think about your ideas, check your evidence, and even memorize important facts, less dedicated listeners tend to while away the time daydreaming, which often leads to total disconnection. These listeners become so engrossed in their own thoughts (an important meeting, a weekend activity, a problem) that they forget to check back with you and miss the majority of your speech. By delivering more than 100–175 words per minute, you give your listeners less time to daydream. According to researchers, "The optimal speaking rate for comprehension appears to be between 275 and 300 words per minute."[19]

Of course, while speaking faster you can't speak in a "mushmouth" fashion (as if you have a mouthful of potato chips). Clear articulation is absolutely necessary. Also, don't speak continuously at a fast pace. Instead, occasionally slow your rate and use pauses to emphasize key points, to create suspense, and to add variety. By the way, if you have been told in the past that you speak too rapidly, consider this a bonus. Except in rare cases, you won't need to slow down—you simply need to articulate clearly and pause more often (especially after main ideas) to let the listeners absorb your ideas.

Don't State Key Ideas in the First or Second Sentence

When a speech begins, most audience members are getting settled in their seats, talking with one another, or thinking of something they need to be doing. Yet speakers expect everyone to suddenly listen attentively. Unfortunately, because listeners aren't ready to listen, most of them completely miss the first sentence (or two) of the speaker's introduction. Therefore stating your central idea or some key fact in your first two sentences is sure to catch many listeners off guard. And if listeners can't figure out the main idea fairly rapidly, they usually blame the speaker and feel justified in thinking of something more "important." Therefore, at the very beginning of your talk, do something to capture and focus audience attention. This helps entice audience members who were expecting to be bored and gives the typical listener time to tune in.

Use Visuals to Enhance Listening

Have you ever seen a speaker set up a visual aid such as a poster before it was time to mention it? Was the audience listening to the speaker or reading the poster? Reading the poster, of course. For some reason, when audience members see something in print, they immediately begin reading it. In the same way, a poorly prepared visual, such as the one shown in Figure 4.4, can actually throw an audience into a "reading" mode rather than a "listening" mode. Because

FACTS ABOUT U.S. TRANSPLANTATION

ON AUGUST 18, 1994 THERE WERE:

- 18,952 patients waiting for a *kidney* transplant.
- 1,495 patients waiting for a *liver* transplant.
- 610 patients waiting for a *pancreas* transplant.
- 2,170 patients waiting for a *heart* transplant.
- 152 patients waiting for a *heart-lung* transplant.
- 570 patients waiting for a *lung* transplant.

23,949 TOTAL

TRANSPLANTS PERFORMED IN 1993:

- 9,433 *kidney* transplants performed.
- 2,534 *liver* transplants performed.
- 529 *pancreas* transplants performed.
- 1,998 *heart* transplants performed.
- 52 *heart-lung* transplants performed.
- 187 *lung* transplants performed.

14,733 TOTAL

Figure 4.5
Well-Designed Visual

Although it includes the same information as in Figure 4.4, this visual is designed to encourage listening.

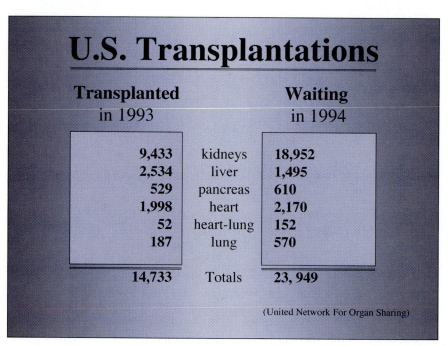

U.S. Transplantations

Transplanted in 1993		Waiting in 1994
9,433	kidneys	18,952
2,534	liver	1,495
529	pancreas	610
1,998	heart	2,170
52	heart-lung	152
187	lung	570
14,733	Totals	23, 949

(United Network For Organ Sharing)

audience members can't concentrate on both reading and listening at the same time, the speaker is basically ignored for as long as it takes to read the visual. Properly prepared text and graphic visuals, such as the one shown in Figure 4.5, should allow listeners to absorb the content in one glance (around three to six seconds) and then refocus their attention on the speaker. You can have considerably more impact and help rivet the attention of your audience if you rely on properly designed visuals, display them only when ready to speak about them, and remove them from audience view when not referring directly to them. (Chapter 7 offers guidelines for preparing successful visual aids.)

Verbally Highlight Important Ideas

When you highlight the important ideas in your speeches, it's much easier for listeners both to follow and to remember your messages. Also, if listeners drift off for a moment, they have a better chance of reorienting themselves when your speeches include various highlighting techniques. There are four effective ways to highlight your points.

Signposts   Think of *signposts* as road signs for listeners—they clearly indicate where the speaker is going and make the speech easy to follow. For example, instead of saying, "And the next step is . . . ," say, "The *third* step is . . ." Instead of saying, "Another benefit that occurs when you stop smoking is . . . ," say, "The *second* benefit that occurs when you stop smoking is . . ."

Internal summaries   Don't wait until the conclusion of the speech to summarize. Give occasional internal summaries, as in these examples:

> "So far I've covered two important points to consider in choosing a day care—the location, and the outside appearance of the facility. Both are fairly easy to research. The next item is just as important, but much more difficult to research. . . ."

> "I hope I've made clear the benefits of walking as a form of exercise. Unlike running, which often causes as many injuries as it prevents, walking is a gentle but no less effective way to keep in shape. Regular walking at a brisk pace strengthens the heart, increases lung capacity, improves blood circulation, and burns calories—all without strain on the knees and ankles caused by running. Now let's look at a third type of exercise—swimming."[20]

Transitions   *Transitions* generally show relationships between ideas. They are similar to signposts and internal summaries in that they make it easier for listeners to follow the development of a speaker's ideas. *Words* such as "also," "although," "but," "because," and "however" and *phrases* such as "in addition," "on the other hand," "for example," and "in other words" are very helpful transitions that speakers don't use often enough. To show listeners which ideas are

Remember:

Speakers can make listening easier by . . .

▶ Illustrating points with personal experiences.

▶ Speaking more rapidly than normal.

▶ Focusing audience attention before stating key ideas.

▶ Using properly designed visuals.

▶ Highlighting important ideas with signposts, internal summaries, transitions, repetition, and restatement.

particularly important or difficult to understand, brief *sentences* such as the following can also be used:

"If you don't remember anything else from this speech, be sure to remember this."

"This next point will be of special interest to all parents."

"Pay special attention to my next idea."

"No mistake can be more costly than this last one."

"Although my third point sounds complicated, in reality it's the easiest process of all."

Repetition and restatement   Listeners seem to realize the importance of ideas or facts that are repeated or points that are restated, so don't be afraid to use both techniques. *Repetition* is used when you want the exact words or figures to be remembered. The following examples use repetition:

"The business community spends more than $100 billion per year to fill out federal government forms. Imagine! $100 billion a year just to fill out forms! Based on my salary, I can't even fathom how much $100 billion really is."

"But I've always been fond of quoting Eleanor Roosevelt on the subject of self-confidence and it was she who said, 'No one can make you feel inferior without your consent.' Think about that for a moment. 'No one can make you feel inferior without your consent.' Isn't that a remarkable statement?"[21]

Instead of using the exact words or figures, *restatement* uses different words to make an idea stand out in the listeners' minds. For example:

"Each year in the United States, 350,000 people die premature deaths caused by smoking—that's equivalent to 920 fully loaded 747 jumbo jets crashing."

To help listeners follow and remember your ideas, try using several or all of these techniques to highlight your messages. Listeners have many important concerns demanding their attention besides your speech. It's up to speakers to make speeches so interesting and easy to follow that listeners can't help but listen. If they are interested and can follow the points, there is a good chance that they will remember them.

Summary
▼ ▼ ▼

Think back to the two communication situations presented at the beginning of the chapter. Have you determined what listener characteristic each speaker had overlooked? The first situation involved a business proposal to a Japanese firm. The speaker felt sure that the Japanese were going to accept the proposal because they were nodding their heads in agreement. However, the speaker had misinterpreted the nonverbal cues—in Japan, nodding one's head does not mean agreement, but merely that the message was received. In the second situation the speaker was impressed that the audience was listening so well because members were sitting totally still and making eye contact. However, the speaker was unaware that listeners with almost no movement and unwavering eye contact are probably not listening but are someplace else mentally.

Attentive listeners progress through the stages of sensing, interpreting, evaluating, responding, and remembering. However, at each stage listeners may tune out or misunderstand. Effective speakers are aware of these problems and use various methods to help listeners stay on track. For example, using stimulation and motivation to grab audience attention definitely will help your listeners get started, and careful analysis of your audience's frame of reference can decrease the possibility of decoding problems. Knowing the ways that listeners may attempt to avoid being persuaded (such as criticizing your credibility) can help you develop tactics to counteract them. Knowing the telltale signs of nonlistening will help you monitor nonverbal feedback from your listeners. In addition, you can make listening easier for your audience by adding personal references, increasing your speaking speed, using visual aids, and verbally highlighting important ideas you want your listeners to remember.

Practice Suggestions
▼ ▼ ▼

1. Do you consider yourself a good listener? Check your general listening skills with this questionnaire.[22]

   Directions: For each of the following statements, circle the appropriate response. Tally the results in the space provided.

a. I feel comfortable when listening to others on the phone.	Yes	Sometimes	No
b. It is often difficult for me to concentrate on what others are saying.	Yes	Sometimes	No
c. I feet tense when listening to new ideas.	Yes	Sometimes	No
d. I have difficulty concentrating on instructions others give me.	Yes	Sometimes	No

e. I dislike being a listener when I'm a member of an audience.	Yes	Sometimes	No
f. I seldom seek out the opportunity to listen to new ideas.	Yes	Sometimes	No
g. I find myself daydreaming when others seem to ramble on.	Yes	Sometimes	No
h. I often argue mentally or aloud with what someone is saying even before he or she finishes.	Yes	Sometimes	No
i. I find that others are always repeating things to me.	Yes	Sometimes	No
j. I seem to find out about important events too late.	Yes	Sometimes	No

Number of times I answered "Yes" _____
Number of times I answered "Sometimes" _____
Number of times I answered "No" _____

If you answered "Yes" or "Sometimes" on less than three questions, you perceive yourself to be a good listener. If you answered "Yes" or "Sometimes" on three to six questions, you are an average listener. If you answered "Yes" or "Sometimes" on seven or more questions, you need immediate improvement of your listening skills.

2. Select a person on campus or in your community who is recognized as a good speaker. Attend one of their presentations and look for the answers to these questions:

   a. How did the speaker focus the attention and interest of the audience on his or her topic and away from distracting interests? Did the speaker win your attention immediately?

   b. Was there any place where the speaker's meaning was not clear? What did you do about it?

   c. Were you convinced that the speaker was qualified to speak on the subject? Did you believe what the speaker told you? What words or nonverbal behavior or visuals helped convince you?

   d. What feedback did audience members give the speaker? Did the speaker seem to respond to their reactions? How?

   e. What techniques did the speaker use to help the listeners remember his or her main points? Can you list three important ideas that were presented?

3. Do you think it is ethically OK to deliberately pretend to be listening to a speaker when you are thinking of something else? Discuss your opinion with a classmate or friend.

4. Think of a speaker you recently found difficult to listen to. At what stage of the listening process did the difficulty occur? What caused the problem? Was it an internal stimulus or an external stimulus? Describe what the speaker was doing at the time.

5. Ask one of your friends to get permission from his or her instructor for you to visit class one day. Observe the nonverbal reactions of the students. Record evidences of listening and identify evidences of poor listening.

6. During the next week watch for times when you are "tuning out" a speaker (such as at a meeting, lecture class, church, and so on). Record what you were thinking about when you realized you had tuned out. Why did you stop listening? What could the speaker have done to keep you motivated to listen?

Notes

1. Cheryl Hamilton with Cordell Parker, *Communicating for Results* (Belmont, CA: Wadsworth, 1993), pp. 155–156.

2. Based on the SIER Listening Model in Lyman K. Steil, Larry L. Barker, and Kittie W. Watson, *Effective Listening: Key to Your Success* (Reading, Mass.: Addison-Wesley, 1983), p. 21.

3. Arthur K. Robertson, *Listen for Success: A Guide to Effective Listening* (Burr Ridge, IL: Irwin Professional Publishing, 1994), p. 45.

4. Blaine Goss, "Listening as Information Processing," *Communication Quarterly* 30 (1982), 306.

5. Lyman K. Steil, Joanne Summerfield, and George deMare, *Listening—It Can Change Your Life: A Handbook for Scientists and Engineers* (New York: Wiley, 1983), pp. 27–28.

6. Ralph G. Nichols and Leonard A. Stevens, *Are You Listening?* (New York: McGraw-Hill, 1957).

7. Sheldon Metcalfe, *Building a Speech* (Fort Worth, TX: Holt, Rinehart & Winston, 1991), p. 61.

8. T. A. Seay and M. K. Altekruse, "Verbal and Nonverbal Behavior in Judgments of Facilitative Conditions," *Journal of Counseling Psychology* 26 (1979), 108–119; D. T. Tepper and R. F. Haase, "Verbal and Nonverbal Communication of Facilitative Conditions," *Journal of Counseling Psychology* 25 (1978), 35–44; D. Archer and R. M. Akert, "Words and Everything Else: Verbal and Nonverbal Cues in Social Interpretation," *Journal of Personality and Social Psychology* 35 (1977), 443–449; A. G. Gitter, H. Black, and J. E. Fishman, "Effect of Race, Sex, Nonverbal Communication and Verbal Communication on Perception of Leadership," *Sociology and Social Research* 60 (1975), 46–57; G. L. Zahn, "Cognitive Integration of Verbal and Vocal Information in Spoken Sentences," *Journal of Experimental Social Psychology* 9 (1973), 320–334.

9. Judee K. Burgoon, "Nonverbal Signals," in Mark L. Knapp and Gerald R. Miller, eds., *Handbook of Interpersonal Communication* (Beverly Hills, CA: Sage, 1985), pp. 346–347.

10. J. S. Philpott, "The Relative Contribution to Meaning of Verbal and Nonverbal Channels of Communication: A Meta-Analysis" (unpublished Master's thesis, University of Nebraska, 1983). In Burgoon, "Nonverbal Signals," p. 346.

11. M. Argyle, "The Syntaxes of Bodily Communication," *International Journal of Psycholinguistics* 2 (1973), 78; see also Timothy Hegstron, "Message Impact: What Percentage Is Nonverbal?" *Western Journal of Speech Communication* 43 (1979), 134–142.

12. Carl I. Hovland and Walter Weiss, "The Influence of Source Credibility on Communication Effectiveness," *Public Opinion Quarterly* 15 (1951), 635–650; Mary John Smith, *Persuasion and Human Action* (Belmont, CA: Wadsworth, 1982), pp. 213–240.

13. Charles U. Larson, *Persuasion: Reception and Responsibility*, 6th ed. (Belmont, CA: Wadsworth, 1992), p. 75.

14. Larson, *Persuasion*, pp. 73–76.

15. Eunice Cooper and Marie Jahoda, "The Evasion of Propaganda: How Prejudiced People Respond to Anti-prejudiced Propaganda," *Journal of Psychology* 23 (1966), 36–43.

16. E. T. Hall, *The Hidden Dimension* (Garden City, NY: Doubleday/Anchor Books, 1969), p. 143.

17. James H. Lavenson, "How to Earn an MBWA Degree," *Vital Speeches* (April 15, 1976), 411.

18. Florence I. Wolff, Nadine C. Marsnik, William S. Tacey, and Ralph G. Nichols, *Perceptive Listening* (New York: Holt, Rinehart & Winston, 1983), pp. 158–159.

19. Andrew D. Wolvin and Carolyn G. Coakley, *Listening*, 2nd ed. (Dubuque, IA: Wm. C. Brown, 1985), p. 178.

20. Stephen E. Lucas, *The Art of Public Speaking*, 4th ed. (New York: McGraw-Hill, 1992), p. 164.

21. Max D. Isaacson, "Public Speaking and Other Coronary Threats," *Vital Speeches* 46 (March 15, 1980), 352.

22. Adapted from L. Wheeless, "An Investigation of Receiver Apprehension and Social Context Dimensions of Communication Apprehension," *The Speech Teacher* 24 (1975), 261–263.

5

Analyzing Your Audience

AUDIENCE ANALYSIS IS NOT A difficult process. It simply involves knowing your listeners well enough that you can organize your verbal, visual, and vocal messages to fit into their frames of reference. As Patricia Ward Brash explains, Christopher Columbus certainly knew the importance of audience analysis:

> Before Columbus met the King and Queen of Spain, navigational experts in both Portugal and Spain had already recommended against backing his rather unusual proposal to reach the Far East by sailing in the opposite direction—westward.
>
> But Columbus understood the art of persuasion, of tailoring the message to the audience, and he knew how to put together an effective presentation. He knew, for example, that the Queen had a fervent desire to win more converts to her religion. So he made frequent references to the teeming masses of the Orient, just waiting to be converted.
>
> Columbus learned that the Queen loved falcons and exotic birds, so he searched carefully through the accounts of Marco Polo's travels to the Orient and marked in the margin all references to those kingdoms where there were falcons and exotic birds.
>
> He knew the King wanted to expand Spain's commercial power, so he made frequent references to gold, spices, and other fabulous riches of the East.
>
> All these points were worked into his presentation, which won the backing that [he desired].[1]

Although your attempts may not have been as dramatic as Columbus's, you have been using audience analysis since you were a child. Think back to when you first began driving the family car. When you wanted to borrow the car, did you use the same arguments for needing the car regardless of which parent you were asking? For example, suppose you had heard your dad say he was disgusted with members of his carpool who didn't do their fair share of driving; you probably mentioned that you needed the car to drive to basketball practice because your friend had driven the last three times. However, suppose you had heard your mother complain about careless teenage drivers; you probably mentioned that you needed the car to drive to basketball practice because your friend who usually drove tended to speed and made you nervous. Regardless of what you actually said (as long as it was true), if you altered your approach depending on whom you were asking, you were using audience analysis.

Even Peggy Noonan, speechwriter for former Presidents Reagan and Bush, learned the importance of audience analysis when she was a child. According to Noonan:

> All speechwriters have things they think of when they write. I think of being a child in my family at the dinner table, with seven kids and hubbub and parents distracted by worries and responsibilities. Before I would say anything at the table, before I would approach my parents, I would plan what I would say. I would map out the narrative, sharpen the details, add color, plan momentum. This way I could hold their attention. This way I became a writer.[2]

We learn the importance of audience analysis when we are children.

© Michael Newman/PhotoEdit

When you analyze an audience, you aren't trying to trick, manipulate, or coerce them; you are simply making sure that your message fits their frames of reference so they will give you a fair hearing. In the previous chapter you learned about the listening weaknesses of the typical audience and ways to adapt your message and delivery to improve listener attention and understanding. When analyzing an audience, effective speakers consider much more than just listening ability. This chapter will cover additional aspects of audience analysis you will need to know to accurately match your message to your listeners.

Analyzing Your Audience: Situational Information

▼ ▼ ▼

Before preparing your speech, you will want to learn as much as you can about the speaking situation. Situational information includes audience size, members' general expectations about the topic, and the inclusion of other speakers at the event. In gathering situational information for your speech, keep the following questions in mind.

First, *are audience members attending voluntarily because they have a particular interest in hearing you or your topic?* Or are they attending because someone is requiring them to do so? Voluntary audiences tend to be relatively more homogeneous—that is, members have a fair amount in common with one another. Because your classroom audience is an involuntary or "captive" audience, it is probably fairly heterogeneous—that is, members differ in a variety of ways including interests, major and minor fields of study, work experience, and even ages. If your classroom is heterogeneous, you will need to pay particular attention to demographic characteristics and values/belief systems, which are discussed later in this chapter.

Second, *how many people will be attending*? As you will see in Chapter 7, the size of your audience is a crucial factor in deciding which visual aids will work best. For example, a flipchart works well for small audiences but is ineffective for audiences of thirty or more members. Similarly gestures and vocal variety, discussed in Chapter 8, also change with audience size.

Third, *how much does your audience know (or think they know) about your topic*? If the topic is discussed frequently in the mass media, your audience likely will be at least familiar with it. If so, you won't have to give much background information. However, if your topic is a fairly new one or is not covered much in the mass media, audience members may be unfamiliar with it or may think they know more than they actually do. In this case you will need to present specific background information and dispel any misconceptions about the topic. In addition, the less the audience knows about your topic, the more important it is for your introduction to stimulate interest in the subject or issue. Chapter 11 gives detailed information on attention-getters.

Fourth, *what does your audience know about you, and what general opinions does it have of you*? If members have heard you give speeches in the past or know of you through other activities or events, they probably have already formed an opinion of you. If their opinions of you are positive, they are more likely to also feel positive about your speech topic. However, if they don't know you or have a negative opinion of your expertise, it will be important for you to establish your credibility. Methods for doing so include citing statistics and sources your audience considers highly credible, preparing professional visuals, and using a controlled, forceful delivery. Chapter 14 gives additional information on developing credibility in the eyes of an audience.

Fifth, *what type of presentation is your audience expecting*? If your audience is expecting a multimedia presentation with color and sound but you give an intimate speech with only black-and-white transparencies, members will be disappointed no matter how excellent your speech. Likewise, if the audience is expecting a serious, scholarly speech but you present a humorous, after-dinner-type talk, members will not feel satisfied either. Knowing your audience expectations helps you choose appropriate topics, visual aids, delivery style, and appearance.

Finally, *will anyone be speaking before you*? If so, about what? In political rallies, conventions, and college classrooms, often several speakers in a row address the audience. Here the atmosphere created by each speech (whether positive or negative) lingers into the next speech. For example, the previous speakers may have droned on to the point that audience members have quit listening. Or your speech topic may be serious, but as you step up to the lectern you can see that the audience is still amused by the previous humorous speech.

When you follow another speaker, the introduction to your speech is even more important than usual. If the topic of one of the previous speeches relates to yours in some way, it's a good idea to mention it in your introduction. Also, if the atmosphere created by the previous speech is not appropriate for your

Remember:

Situational information includes . . .

▶ Whether attendance is voluntary or required.

▶ The number of people expected to attend.

▶ Audience knowledge of the topic.

▶ Audience knowledge and opinions of the speaker.

▶ The type of presentation the audience is expecting.

▶ Other speakers and their topics.

speech, mention how your speech will differ or make a startling statement to shock the audience into another mood. For example, read the following introduction that one student used in her speech entitled "Plutonium 238: NASA's Fuel of Choice" and see if you agree that her audience would not have continued to chuckle over the previous humorous speech for very long:

> On January 28, 1986, the American Space Program suffered the worst disaster in its more than 30-year history. The entire world was shocked when the space shuttle *Challenger* exploded seconds after lift-off, claiming the lives of seven brave astronauts and crippling our entire space agenda. I suppose the oldest cliche in our culture, spoken on battlegrounds and indeed virtually anywhere Americans die, is "We must press forward, so we can say they did not die in vain." Rest assured. They didn't. The deaths of our seven astronauts probably saved the lives of untold thousands of Americans.
>
> For, you see, if the O-rings had not failed on January 28, 1986, but rather on May 20, 1987, the next scheduled shuttle launch, in the words of Dr. John Gofman, Professor Emeritus at the University of California at Berkeley, you could have "kissed Florida goodbye."
>
> Because the next shuttle, the one that was to have explored the atmosphere of Jupiter was to carry 47 pounds of Plutonium 238, which is, again according to Dr. Gofman, the most toxic substance on the face of the earth. Dr. Helen Caldicott corroborates Dr. Gofman's claim in her book *Nuclear Madness* when she cites studies estimating that one ounce of widely dispersed Plutonium 238 particles as having the toxicity to induce lung cancer in every person on earth.[3]

This introduction was compelling enough to cause audience members to forget about the humor contained in any previous speech and to focus on the seriousness of her presentation.

How might the interests of this audience differ from those of an audience of college sophomores?

© *David Young-Wolff/PhotoEdit*

Analyzing Your Audience: Demographic Information

▼ ▼ ▼

In addition to evaluating situational information, you will need to consider basic demographic information as you plan your speech. This includes general audience characteristics such as age, gender, marital status, education, economic status, occupations (or current jobs), major or minor field of study, political beliefs, religion, cultural background, and group identification. If you are familiar with the audience (your classmates, for example), you can observe many of these characteristics yourself. If you are unfamiliar with the audience, ask for input from the person who invited you to speak, as well as two or three members of the prospective audience.

Identifying Specific Demographic Characteristics

It's a good idea to find out as much about each audience as possible. Although audiences are made up of individuals, members often share similar attributes or demographic characteristics. To give you an idea of what demographic information could be helpful in planning your speech, let's look at each characteristic in more detail.

Age Because age is related to interests, knowledge of group members' age can guide you in selecting a topic and picking appropriate supporting materials to interest and persuade your audience. For example, what age group would prefer listening to Johnny Mathis, Tony Bennett, and Peter, Paul and Mary? Would they be older or younger than the age group that prefers listening to the Smashing Pumpkins, the Cranberries, and the Jazz Masters? Although knowing the general age of audience members can be very helpful, it may also be misleading unless you explore other demographic factors as well. For example, high school and college students often enjoy listening to "golden oldies" from the fifties and sixties (such as the Beatles, Beach Boys, and Lovin' Spoonful) as much as their parents do.

In any case, in selecting topics and examples for your speeches, be sensitive to the ages of your listeners. Keep in mind, too, that in your speech class there is probably a fairly wide range of ages. For example, the mean age of students enrolled at four-year colleges and universities is around twenty-four,[4] while the mean age at two-year colleges is approximately twenty-five.[5] Make sure your speech relates to *all* ages, not just your own age group.

Ethnic and cultural background   Another demographic characteristic you need to be especially sensitive to is the ethnic and cultural background of your audience. Members of culturally diverse groups can have different interests and expectations of what makes a good speech. Also your classroom audience may be more diverse than the population of your hometown. For example, although blacks tend to be spread fairly evenly across the country, Hispanics and Asians tend to be grouped in regions. As Peter Morrison, researcher and senior demographer for the RAND Corporation in California, notes, "Three-fourths of Hispanics live in California, Texas, New York, and Florida; one-half of Asian-Americans live in California and Hawaii."[6] Morrison continues:

> The country we once called a great melting pot is now a racial and ethnic mosaic in which different peoples tend to keep their identities. It is made up not just of whites, blacks, and Hispanics, but a multitude of nationalities and ethnic subgroups as well.
>
> The mosaic varies from city to city. In St. Paul and Missoula, it contains Hmongs from Southeast Asia; in Atlanta and Providence, Cambodians; in Des Moines and Sioux City, Tai Dam and Vietnamese; in Arlington, Virginia, Salvadorans and other Central Americans; in Hartford, Jamaicans, Puerto Ricans, and assorted Asian populations. California's cities contain a dazzling array of nationalities and ethnic groups, including Filipinos, Koreans, Vietnamese, Hmong, Armenians, and Japanese [as well as blacks, Hispanics, and whites].[7]

When you are speaking to a culturally diverse audience, research the different cultural groups carefully to make sure that both your speech topic and speech content are appropriate for your particular audience. In addition, you will need to be especially sensitive to the effect of your visual and verbal delivery. For example, Chinese, Asian, Thai, and Indian audiences generally prefer speakers to avoid making direct eye contact or even focusing on individual faces in the audience.[8] On the other hand, if you are from a culture that typically avoids looking directly at audience members, keep in mind that your college audience (as well as your professor) may view lack of direct eye contact as a sign of nervousness or inexperience.

If your audience is culturally diverse, you should also pay special attention to your visual aids. People from certain cultures might be offended at the informal way Americans have of writing on flip charts during a presentation. To them a speaker who doesn't prepare visuals ahead of time doesn't value the audience.[9] Also, when speaking to Japanese audiences, remember that animated facial expressions and spontaneous gestures, which are valued in the United States, may appear brash and egotistical to some listeners. The Japanese tend to admire people who "are, for the most part, distinguished by their modest demeanor, lack of eloquence, their public modesty."[10] At the same time, if you have a Japanese cultural background, you may need to add more animation to your delivery when you address your classmates.

In addition to selecting your visual messages with care, you need to ensure that your verbal messages show cultural sensitivity. In the United States many audiences value straight talk and respond negatively to speakers who take forever to get to the point. As a result, speakers tend to present their main ideas up front. However, "many people (notably those in Japanese, Latin American, and Arabic cultures) consider such directness to be brash and inappropriate."[11] Thus, for audiences dominated by members of these cultures, you should present ideas more slowly—perhaps concluding with the main point rather than beginning with it. Also, always choose your words with care. For example, avoid referring to your audience as "you people" or beginning an example with, "I'm not prejudiced or anything, but . . ." Obviously the more you know about your audience, the more you will be able to relate to their cultural expectations.

Gender   Another demographic characteristic that can give you clues to possible audience interests is gender. However, be careful to avoid gender stereotyping. To assume that all men enjoy sports (while women do not) and that all women are interested in cooking (while men are not) would likely lead to some negative audience reactions. If you have both men and women in your audience, you need to relate your topic to both genders; if you can't, select a different topic.

When speaking to a mixed audience, be sure that your word choices show gender sensitivity. It's best to avoid masculine or feminine terms and expressions and to substitute more gender-sensitive words. For example, instead of "policeman" or "policewoman," say "police officer"; instead of "stewardess" or "steward," say "flight attendant." A more detailed discussion of gender-sensitive words and phrases is included in Chapter 8.

Group affiliation   Another demographic characteristic that can help you relate your speech to your listeners' frames of reference is group affiliation. Most people are very proud of the groups to which they belong—whether it be the National Rifle Association, Toastmasters, Woman's Auxiliary, Meals on Wheels, Young Republicans, Campus Crusade for Christ, the drama club, a sorority, and so on. Knowing that your audience members belong to a particular social, religious, or political group (even though your topic isn't about their group) can help you identify what is important to them and what questions they are likely to ask. Referring to this group during your speech lets members know that you are aware of them and are speaking to them personally.

If your topic is a religious one, you need to be especially sensitive to listeners' faiths. As the United States becomes more culturally diverse, religions are becoming more diverse as well. In addition to the familiar Catholic and Protestant churches and Jewish synagogues, it is not uncommon to see Buddhist temples, Muslim mosques, and Hindu temples.[12] People of all faiths tend to get emotional if they feel their beliefs are being attacked. Make sure you are sensitive to your audience's religious as well as other group orientations.

Marital status and children   Knowing whether your listeners are predominantly single, married, divorced, or cohabiting and whether they have children can help you select examples that will relate rather than offend. Again, be careful of stereotypical statements such as, "Good mothers don't work." Today 60 percent of mothers with young children under the age of six are working as compared to only 12 percent in 1950.[13] Other facts of interest related to marital status and parenthood include the following:[14]

▶ One half of all marriages end in divorce.

▶ Divorce affects over one million children each year.

▶ Five percent of U.S. households are comprised of unmarried couples living together.

▶ One-fourth of all babies are born to unmarried women.

If you wish to give a speech on a subject related to marriage, divorce, or children, don't forget your classmates who are not married or don't plan on ever marrying and who have no children or don't plan on ever having any children. If you can't relate your speech to them personally, you may be able to relate it indirectly. For instance, they likely have relatives, close friends, and even neighbors who have children, so that your topic still can have relevance to them.

Occupation, education, major or minor, and economic status   Focusing on one or more of these demographic characteristics could provide you with valuable information on audience members and their interests. Do you think an audience of well-paid professionals would have different interests than an audience of less well-paid nonprofessionals? If you knew your audience members had college degrees, would your choice of topic, vocabulary, and examples be different than if your audience members had only high school diplomas, or were high school dropouts? For your college speech class, your classmates' majors and minors could be helpful. For example, if the majority of your classmates are majoring in the same subject as you, you can go into your subject in much more depth.

All of the demographic characteristics discussed here can help you understand the frames of reference of your audience members and thus identify ways to communicate better with them. The question is, do you use all of the demographic characteristics for each speech?

Remember:

Demographic information includes . . .

▶ Age.
▶ Ethnic and cultural background.
▶ Gender.
▶ Group affiliations.
▶ Marital status and children.
▶ Occupations, education, major or minor, and economic status.

Determining Which Demographic Characteristics to Use

The nature of your topic determines which demographic characteristics to use for a particular speech. Suppose you wanted to give a speech on the importance of regular exercise. Political beliefs, major field of study, religion, occupation, and cultural background would probably not be important considerations, but the age and gender of your audience members could be. For example, if your audience consisted of traditional college-age students, you might want to stress the value of regular exercise for maintaining a healthy, attractive body; to identify the local club or the campus gym as a place to socialize and meet new people; and to suggest that exercise breaks make the long hours of study less tedious. However, if your audience was comprised mainly of thirty- to forty-year-olds, a change of focus might be needed. This group is likely involved in raising children and/or establishing careers and have probably slacked off on exercising. You might want to mention how valuable exercise is in reducing the stress associated with children and career; how athletic clubs cater to parents by offering child-care facilities; how inexpensive, foldaway treadmills and exercise bikes make exercise at home convenient; and how exercising with a colleague during lunch or after work makes exercise more fun. Obviously, if you were speaking to an audience of senior citizens, your focus would shift again. You might stress that walking and using weight machines add years of mobility and enjoyment to people's lives even if they rarely exercised when younger.

For all three of these audiences, the basic topic is the same but the speech focus changes to relate to the interests and needs of each audience. Of course, as with all your speeches, no matter what approach you take, you will need to cite sources and give examples to convince listeners that you know what you are talking about. Chapter 10 discusses researching and supporting ideas in detail.

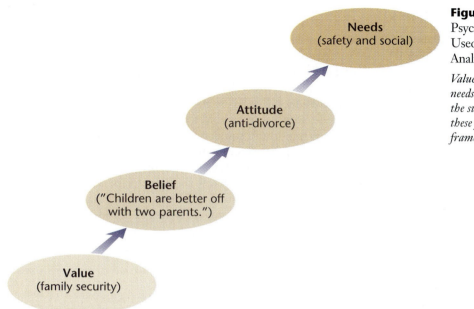

Figure 5.1
Psychological Factors
Used in Audience
Analysis

*Values, beliefs, attitudes, and
needs build on one another;
the successful speaker relates
these factors to listeners'
frames of reference.*

Analyzing Your Audience: Psychological Information

▼ ▼ ▼

Determining your audience's psychological characteristics—their attitudes, beliefs, values, and needs—also is important in preparing a speech that relates specifically to listeners' frames of reference. See Figure 5.1 for a pictorial view of how these characteristics relate to each other.

Attitudes

An **attitude** is a *feeling* of liking or disliking, of approval or disapproval, toward a person, group, idea, or event. For example, you might support gay rights but oppose women in the military; you might be pro–term limits and pro–animal rights but anti–government and anti–Greek organizations on campus; you might approve of "Take Your Daughters to Work Day" but disapprove of "The Great American Smoke-out." In any event, your search for psychological information about your audience should begin with your audience's attitudes. Will they approve or disapprove of your topic? Will they favor or oppose your proposal?

Beliefs

A **belief** is the mental acceptance that something is true even if we can't prove that it is true. For example, even though they may not be able to cite any definite sources, individuals may believe that college is important, that women are discriminated against, that lateness shows disrespect, and that nothing can be done about the national debt. Beliefs are the reasons people hold the attitudes they do.[15] For example, someone may hold a pro-college attitude based on the belief that education is important; someone may have a favorable attitude toward equal rights legislation based on the belief that women are discriminated against. Therefore, in your psychological analysis, discovering your audience's attitudes isn't enough. You must also know the reasons for those attitudes. If you discover that a belief is based on false information or that the audience thinks they know more than they do, you will have a better idea of what information and arguments to present in your speech.

Values

Values are deep-seated principles that serve as personal guidelines for behavior.[16] They usually are learned from social institutions such as the family, church, school, and so on. Values provide the underlying support for our many beliefs and attitudes. Researcher Milton Rokeach identified two types of values—instrumental and terminal. Although we possess only a few *terminal values* (ideal states of being), we possess a great many *instrumental values* (guides for conduct in fulfilling terminal values).[17] For example, "We get an education (instrumental value) so we can find a rewarding career (terminal value). We work hard (instrumental value) so that we can have a comfortable life (terminal value)."[18] For three decades Rokeach researched how Americans ranked eighteen key terminal values:[19]

1. world peace
2. family security
3. freedom
4. a comfortable life
5. happiness
6. self-respect
7. a sense of accomplishment
8. wisdom
9. equality
10. national security
11. true friendship
12. salvation
13. inner harmony
14. mature love
15. a world of beauty
16. social recognition
17. pleasure
18. an exciting life

Rokeach found the rankings to be highly stable across time, with only minor changes occurring over three decades. In addition, only minor differences existed between the rankings of men and women and between blacks and whites. However, as you might expect, there were sizable differences between Americans and people from other cultures (for example, Australians, Canadians, and Israelis).[20] Thus, when you are speaking to multicultural audiences, don't automatically assume that your high-ranked values are necessarily the same as listeners' high-ranked values. Although the list of values may be the same, the importance placed on each value may differ.

Because values are so stable, they are more difficult to change than beliefs or attitudes. In fact, in a single speech you are unlikely to change high-ranked audience values. However, you may be able to show your audience that a particular value is more important (or less important) now than it used to be.[21] Normally you will highlight (or reinforce) one or more audience values and show how your ideas or proposal fits into those values. Also, knowing your audiences' values will help you determine what evidence and emotional appeals will be needed to convince listeners that a particular belief or attitude conflicts with their basic values.

Needs

A **need** is a state in which some sort of unsatisfied condition exists. Needs are a result of our attitudes, beliefs, and values. We all have needs or wants in our lives that serve to motivate us. If you can show how a listener's need will be completely or partially satisfied by information to be presented in your speech, the listener will pay close attention. Likewise, if you can show how taking a particular action will partially or completely satisfy a need, the listener likely will be persuaded to take the action. In some cases you may have to show an audience that a need exists before you can use it to motivate behavior. For example, you won't be very successful selling a new type of lock to audience members who feel safe at home. However, when you show them the police statistics on how many homes have been broken into in their community during the past six months and demonstrate how easy it is to pick the typical lock that most of them have on their front doors, they realize that their feelings of security were misplaced. And if you can anchor an unsatisfied need to audience beliefs or values (such as, "It is the responsibility of parents to provide a safe home environment for children"), your audience is even more likely to listen and be persuaded.

Maslow's hierarchy of needs   According to sociologist, Abraham Maslow, human needs can be categorized into five basic levels: physiological, safety, social, esteem, and self-actualization (see Figure 5.2).[22] Think of these needs as the rungs of a ladder. Although people may be motivated by several levels at a time, usually a lower rung must be satisfied before the next level becomes important. Maslow's five categories of needs are useful guidelines for adapting your speech to your audience's needs and wants. Let's look at each of these basic needs:

1. *Physiological needs*—include food, shelter, clothing, air, water, and sleep.
2. *Safety needs*—include a job and financial security; law and order; protection from injury, poor health, harm, or death; and freedom from fear.
3. *Social needs*—include love, companionship, friendship, and a feeling of belonging to one or more groups.
4. *Esteem needs*—include pride, recognition from others, status and prestige, and self-recognition.

Figure 5.2

Maslow's Basic Hierarchy
of Human Needs

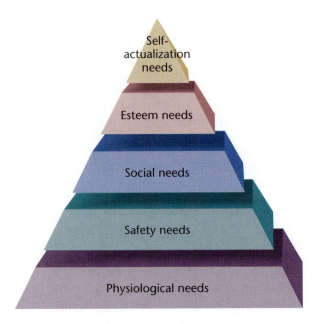

5. *Self-actualization needs*—involve becoming the best person one can—developing to one's fullest capabilities and achieving worthwhile goals.[23]

Applying needs analysis Because audience members have different frames of reference, it's unlikely that they will all be concerned and motivated by the same needs. Therefore you need to select two or three of the lowest levels that represent your audience needs and use them as motivators in your speech. As illustrated in Figure 5.1, needs grow out of attitudes, beliefs, and values. If you have determined some of your audience's attitudes, beliefs and values, their basic needs should be fairly obvious. For example, an audience member who *values* freedom, *believes* that a woman has the right to control her own body, and has a pro-choice *attitude*, likely will be concerned with safety needs (freedom from restraint) on the topic of abortion. On the other hand, an audience member who *values* life, *believes* that life begins at conception, and has a pro-life *attitude* will also be concerned with safety needs but for a different reason (fear of death).

Remember that before your listeners can focus on the higher needs cited in Maslow's model, their needs at the lower level must be mostly satisfied. For example, if your audience is concerned about safety issues (perhaps a series of drive-by shootings has everyone very nervous), appealing to the high-level ideals of self-actualization and esteem aren't likely to interest or persuade. On the other hand, a need that has already been met (the gang members were caught and the community again feels safe) is no longer a motivator. Suppose you were giving a motivational speech to students enrolled in a work-study program. If your listeners were primarily concerned with having enough money to pay their rent and school expenses (safety needs), appealing to their desire for self-actualization or their sense of pride would most likely be an ineffective way to encourage them to work harder. A better solution would be to explain how increased

Remember:

Psychological information includes . . .

▶ Audience attitudes.
▶ Audience beliefs.
▶ Audience values.
▶ Audience needs.

productivity would not only secure their jobs as work-study participants for another semester but also likely get them raises at the next evaluation period. Chapter 14 discusses using audience needs to persuade in detail.

The Hazards of Incomplete Psychological Analysis

To illustrate what can happen when the analysis of an audience's attitudes, beliefs, values, and needs is incomplete, consider the following scenario. In 1984–85 Coca-Cola decided to change the 100-year-old formula used to make America's most popular soft drink. A blind taste-test had shown that consumers preferred the new sweeter taste by a 6 percent margin, but "no one had examined the psychological ramifications of withdrawing the old formula."[24] When the change in Coke was announced, American consumers reacted unexpectedly. Within a week the company was receiving more than 1,000 irate calls per day, and the number eventually climbed to more than 8,000 calls per day. "They talk as if Coca-Cola had just killed God," reported an employee monitoring the consumer hot line.[25] Protest letters (which numbered up to 40,000 per day) included comments like, "Changing Coke is just like breaking the American dream, like not selling hot dogs at a game."[26] Generations of Americans had grown up sipping Coca-Colas at Little League games, at birthday parties, on first dates, and on many other occasions. It was an important part of their culture that they couldn't imagine changing. One woman even used her umbrella to attack a Coca-Cola delivery man who was stocking the new Coke on a supermarket shelf. Reaction was so intense, and sales dropped so drastically, that within three months the company reinstated the old Coke as "Coca-Cola Classic." Eventually the new Coke was removed from the market and the old Coca-Cola formula again became the only Coke formula.

Coca-Cola's incomplete audience analysis (overlooking the psychological factor) led to unexpected customer reactions. As mentioned at the beginning of the chapter, if Christopher Columbus had ignored the psychological factor in his analysis of the king and queen of Spain, it's unlikely that they would have agreed to finance his expedition. Audience analysis includes more than just situational and demographic characteristics; it also involves psychological characteristics in the form of attitudes, beliefs, values, and needs of your listeners. The end result of incomplete audience analysis could be nothing more than bored listeners, but it also could result in angry, disbelieving listeners willing to work against your position. Although inadequate audience analysis is unlikely to cause a completely negative reaction from a classroom audience, treat your classroom as a laboratory setting and try to find out as much about your classmates as possible. Use them to sharpen your audience analysis skills.

Analyzing for Audience Type

▼ ▼ ▼

Once you have analyzed your audience according to situational, demographic, and psychological characteristics, you need to factor in how generally receptive they will be to you. To do this, you place them into one of four basic types of audiences: (1) friendly; (2) neutral or impartial; (3) uninterested or indifferent; and (4) hostile.[27] Although you need to be careful not to overstereotype an audience, it is easier to organize your speech, select supporting materials, and plan your delivery when you can place your audience into a general category. Table 5.1 summarizes strategies for dealing with each audience type.

The Friendly Audience

This is the audience that has already heard you speak before or has heard positive things about you or is simply sold on your topic. These listeners are looking forward to your speech and are expecting to enjoy themselves. Organizing your speech for this type of audience is easy—just about any organizational pattern will work. Feel free to try something new, to be creative. If you can find a way for audience members to participate, they will probably be even more enthusiastic. Selecting appropriate supporting materials for the friendly audience is also quite easy. Supporting materials include quotations, statistics, personal instances (brief or detailed), and comparisons to clarify and prove your main points. Because audience frames of reference differ so widely, all speeches should use a variety of supporting materials. Humor and personal instances work especially well to build an intimate relationship with an audience that's already sold on you. In addition, you can use pictures or computer clip art on your visuals (in addition to text) to give the visuals a personal touch. Although your delivery will vary depending on your topic, generally a warm, relaxed, but enthusiastic style with lots of eye contact, smiles, and gestures will work best. The positive reaction you will get from this audience (and the more they respond, the more you are likely to give) makes speaking a joy.

Table 5.1

Strategies for Dealing with Four Types of Audiences

	Strategies		
Audience Type	**Organization**	**Delivery**	**Supporting Material**
Friendly (predisposed to like you and your topic)	Any pattern. Try something new; ask for audience participation.	Warm, friendly, open. Make lots of eye contact, smile, gesture, and use vocal variety.	Humor, examples, personal experiences.
Neutral (consider themselves calm and rational; have minds already made up but think they are objective)	Pro-con or problem-solution patterns. Present both side of the issue. Save time for audience questions.	Controlled, even; nothing "showy." Use confident, small gestures.	Facts, statistics, expert opinion, comparision and contrast. Avoid humor, personal stories, and flashy visuals.
Uninterested (short attention span, present against their wills)	Brief—no more than three points. Avoid topical and pro-con patterns that seem long to the audience.	Dynamic and entertaining. Move around; use large gestures.	Humor, cartoons, colorful visuals, powerful quotations, startling statistics.
	Do not: Darken the room, stand motionless behind the podium, pass out handouts, use boring view-graphs, or expect audience to participate.		
Hostile (looking for chances to take charge or ridicule speaker; emotional)	Noncontroversial pattern such as topical, chronological, or geographical.	Calm and controlled. Speak slowly and evenly.	Objective data and expert opinion. Avoid anecdotes and jokes.
	Avoid: Question-answer period if possible. Otherwise, use a moderator or accept only written questions.		

The Neutral Audience

The neutral audience can be just as satisfying to talk to if you are prepared. These audience members consider themselves objective, rational, and open to new information. However, many of them already have made up their minds. Usually they are sure that emotion will play no role in their response to your ideas. "Just give us the facts," they say. As a result, you must organize your speech logically. If you're discussing a controversial topic, you will need to present both sides of the issue and use a pro-con or problem-solution method of organization. Select sources that this group will consider objective and credible and include graphs and statistics on your visual aids. Make sure your delivery is controlled, even, and confident. Your appearance will be especially important when dealing with a skeptical audience. Adopt a look that signals credibility and authority to them, and avoid anything "showy," including dramatic gestures—unless you are addressing an audience (such as one comprised of actors or artists) that values a flamboyant style.

The Uninterested Audience

The uninterested audience can be a challenge unless you plan carefully. These listeners have a short attention span and are often attending your presentation even though they would rather be someplace (probably anyplace) else. Like many classroom audiences they feel trapped in a situation that they expect to be either a waste of time or a bore. They probably will be polite but also will plan to take a "mental holiday" during your presentation. To jolt them into attentiveness, inform them that your presentation will be brief. Offer no more than three main points and avoid using topical or pro-con patterns of organization, which can seem unbearably long to such listeners. To maintain interest, use supporting materials such as humorous anecdotes, powerful quotations, or startling statistics. In addition, use colorful and interesting visuals (maybe even a cartoon or two), and change them often to keep a fast pace. A dynamic and entertaining delivery with good pitch, varied emphasis, and volume changes will help keep listeners focused. Without pacing methodically like a caged tiger, move often and use large, expressive gestures. Do *not* darken the room to use slides, stand motionless behind the lectern, pass out handouts, or expect the audience to participate—they will mentally drift away. If you plan for this audience carefully, you will enjoy seeing them listen in spite of themselves.

The Hostile Audience

The hostile audience can be the greatest challenge of all because these listeners are predisposed to dislike you, your topic, or both. Their attitudes may be due to prejudice or jealousy or bad experiences with other speakers. In any case a key to overcoming the hostile audience is to be neither intimidated nor defensive. Organize your speech in a noncontroversial pattern—by topic, by time, or by geographical location. Supporting material should include objective data and expert opinion. Your visual aids should generally be conservative and emphasize facts and statistics. If any of your audience members have written papers or articles on the subject that support your views, be sure to cite them. Otherwise, use authorities that your audience members consider to be experts and show how your speech agrees with or was inspired by them. If you can get even one of these hostile listeners to side openly with you, others will be more receptive to your message. Avoid anecdotes and jokes since that might imply to them that you are not taking the speech seriously. You also may want to avoid the question and answer period altogether if you sense it will be hostile. Or you can use a moderator to ask for and rephrase questions for you or accept only written questions that someone gathers up at the end of your speech. Any obvious traps or obnoxious questions can be ignored. Above all, *stay in charge*.

Using Audience Analysis in Your Verbal/Visual/Vocal Messages

▼ ▼ ▼

What you discover in your audience analysis should affect your verbal, visual, and vocal messages. Let's look first at your verbal messages. Your vocabulary, choice of words, supporting materials, and humor will depend on the situational, demographic, and psychological information you discover about your potential audience, as well as on your analysis of audience receptiveness. For example, jargon and examples that a typical college-age audience would relate to (such as GRE and STDs and finals-week stress) would likely differ from the jargon and examples that an older, career-oriented audience would relate to (such as TQM and EEOC and boss-employee stress). In addition, a friendly audience will enjoy humor and personal examples. An uninterested audience also benefits from humor, but it's best to avoid being personal. For neutral and hostile audiences, lend your message authority by citing expert opinions and using statistics and facts.

Audience analysis can also affect your visual messages—such as choice of gestures, eye contact, and visual aids. For example, the spontaneity and informality provided by flipcharts, animated facial expressions, and lively gestures would not be effective with cultures that prefer modest speaker demeanor but would work well with most friendly or uninterested American audiences. If you expect your audience to be neutral or hostile, your credibility will be enhanced with visual aids that are conservative in use of color and design and with small, controlled gestures. At the same time, if you can get these audiences involved with your visual aids, they are likely to become less hostile. For example, in the O. J. Simpson trial, the DNA expert for the prosecution, Dr. Robin Cotton, gave visuals to the jury and got them involved in matching DNA strands.

Your vocal messages may also change depending on the results of your audience analysis. If you expect a friendly audience, a warm, conversational tone of voice is recommended. When the audience is uninterested, a more dynamic, theatrical voice is needed. However, when the audience is neutral or hostile, an authoritative yet calm and controlled voice works best.

Collecting Audience Information

▼ ▼ ▼

You should collect situational, demographic, and psychological information, as well as information on potential audience receptivity (type), before your speeches to enable you to adapt to audience frames of references. After your speeches you need to collect information on audience reactions in order to evaluate the success of your presentation and plan for needed changes in future speeches.

Before the Speech

To gather all four types of information (situational, demographic, psychological, and receptivity) about your classroom audience, begin by observing and listening. Many demographic and situational traits become obvious through simple observation. Listening to your classmates' comments and opinions should give you a good idea of many of their beliefs and values. You also might interview a few classmates for additional information or give everyone a short questionnaire to complete at least one week before your speech. Keep in mind, however, that distributing large numbers of questionnaires generally is both impractical and intrusive. Therefore you would be better off preparing a simple questionnaire as a guide for interviewing by phone the person who originally asked you to speak. The questionnaire should include *situational questions* (for example, the name of the organization, audience size, the seating arrangement, the reason you were asked to speak, audience familiarity with your topic), *demographic questions* (for example, general audience ages, gender breakdown, occupations, marital status, children, cultural backgrounds, and any important group affiliations), *psychological questions* (for example, attitudes toward your topic, beliefs relating to your topic, basic needs of the group), and *receptivity questions* (for example, "How would you classify the response to my topic: friendly, neutral, uninterested, or hostile?"). As the person answers your questions, jot down his or her responses. If you feel you still need more information, ask for the names of two people to interview who are familiar with the expected audience and call them.

There is one final way to obtain audience information prior to presenting the speech. Arrive at the speech site early. After checking to make sure that the lectern and any equipment needed for visual aids is in place, greet the first few audience members as they arrive. Introduce yourself and politely ask about their interest in your speech and motivation for attending. Not only will you feel that you have some friends in the audience when you get up to speak, but your conversation may help you verify areas you have in common with your listeners. If you discover any new information, you may wish to make a last-minute adjust-

© Lee Celano/Reuters/Bettmann

© Sygma

After a test audience found her "aggressive" and "pushy," the prosecutor for the O. J. Simpson trial, Marcia Clark, softened her look (right).

ment to your introduction. The more things you and your audience have in common, the more believable you will be to them.

During the pretrial hearing for the O. J. Simpson trial, prosecutor Marcia Clark used focus groups (as similar as possible to the actual jurors) to determine how her verbal, visual, and vocal communication might affect their opinions of her.[28] What she found was that her hairstyle and power suits, as well as her hard-hitting words and vocal tone, made her come across as an "aggressive," "pushy," and "aloof" courtroom attorney instead of the friendly, caring, yet sharp attorney the mock jurors said they preferred. As a result, she adopted a "softer" hairstyle, changed her wardrobe to feature soft colors and designs, altered her tone of voice and words to come across as friendlier and less aggressive, and smiled and even laughed in the courtroom. All of Marcia Clark's changes were an attempt to relate to the jurors' frames of reference so they would listen and believe what she said in court. As this book goes to print, the trial is still proceeding. Time will tell whether her attempts were successful.

After the Speech

Although the need for audience analysis prior to the speech should be fairly obvious, many speakers fail to recognize the importance of soliciting feedback after the speech. Assessing listener reactions is the only way you can tell if the analysis you conducted before the speech was adequate; if it wasn't, you'll want to make changes before your next speech. Of course, the most immediate feedback you will receive after a speech is the applause. If your speech ended with emotion or was particularly profound or startling, there may be a moment of

Taking time to talk to audience members after your speech is a good way to get valuable feedback.

©Sepp Seitz/Woodfin Camp & Associates, Inc.

silence before the applause while the audience absorbs your conclusion. You can tell the difference between an enthusiastic response and a lukewarm one.

Make yourself available after the speech so audience members can offer their comments. Except in the classroom (where another speech begins almost immediately), audience members will tend to come up and thank the speaker, ask questions, and offer valuable feedback. If you are off in the corner talking with officials or are busy putting away equipment, however, most people will leave without speaking to you—a missed opportunity.

A brief questionnaire, similar to the one shown in Figure 5.3, is another way to get feedback after your speech. You can place the questionnaire on a table by the door for audience members to complete as they leave, or you can send a thank-you letter and copies of your questionnaire to your contact person with a request to have three or four people from the audience fill it out. Or you may simply ask specific questions of one or two people you know who attended the speech.

A final way to get significant feedback is to have someone videotape your talk. If your contact person doesn't have a video camera, bring your own or rent one. Ask a friend to come along with you to tape both your speech and some audience reactions if possible. Once your speech is over, it's very difficult to remember exactly what you said, what gestures you used, and so on. Viewing a videotape of yourself is the only way you can really determine what your verbal, visual, and vocal presentation sounded and looked like. You will find things you like and things you don't like. The things you don't like you can correct with practice.

	1	2	3	4	5	6	7	
Dull	—	—	—	—	—	—	—	Exciting
Disorganized	—	—	—	—	—	—	—	Organized
Weakly supported	—	—	—	—	—	—	—	Well supported
Sources questionable	—	—	—	—	—	—	—	Sources believable
Poor delivery	—	—	—	—	—	—	—	Dynamic delivery
Unpleasant voice	—	—	—	—	—	—	—	Pleasant voice
Limited eye contact	—	—	—	—	—	—	—	Direct eye contact
Confusing visuals	—	—	—	—	—	—	—	Helpful visuals
Too soft	—	—	—	—	—	—	—	Easily heard
Poor overall	—	—	—	—	—	—	—	Excellent overall

Figure 5.3
Sample Speech Evaluation Questionnaire

Summary
▼ ▼ ▼

You can collect four types of information to successfully analyze your audience: situational, demographic, psychological, and audience type. *Situational information* (such as audience size and expectations and the possible inclusion of other speakers) helps you plan your speech to fit the specific situation. *Demographic information* (such as age, ethnic and cultural background, gender, group affiliation, marital status and children, occupation, and education) helps you know as much as possible about your audience and aids in selecting your topic and supporting materials. *Psychological information* also is very important in planning your speech. To interest audience members in your topic or to persuade them to take some action, you must identify their attitudes, beliefs, values, and needs in order to decide what information or appeals will be most effective. Once you have gathered situational, demographic, and psychological information on your audience, you are ready to determine *audience receptivity*—how receptive the audience will likely be to you and your topic. Audiences can be friendly, neutral, uninterested, or hostile. Each audience type requires different verbal, visual, and vocal approaches.

All four types of audience information are gathered before your speech to allow you to adapt your presentation to listeners' frames of reference. Without this information your chances of communicating successfully with your audience are diminished; with it you can feel confident that your presentation will succeed. Similar information is collected after the speech to enable you to evaluate your speech and to plan for needed changes in future speeches.

Practice Suggestions

▼ ▼ ▼

1. Try to find out which organizations in your community have a speakers' bureau. Maybe an organization to which you belong has one. By phone obtain the name of a speaker and ask this person how he or she analyzes the audience before each presentation. Compare the answer with the suggestions made in this chapter.

2. Select one of the speeches from Appendix C. Look for things the speaker says that seem to be a result of specific audience analysis. Try to find examples of at least one situational, one demographic, and one psychological adaptation. What do these adaptations indicate about the audience?

3. Clip an advertisement out of a newspaper or magazine. What specific customer group is this ad targeting? How does the ad adapt to the needs or desires of the target group? Select a different target group and explain how you would change this ad to appeal to the new group. Be specific. Share your ideas with an individual classmate or a group of classmates.

4. Find an ad for walking shoes that targets eighteen- to twenty-five-year-olds. What in the ad made you decide it was targeting this age group? How would you change the ad to reach people who like to travel? Senior citizens? People involved in organized sports? Share your ad and interpretation with a small group of classmates. As a group select the best ad and prepare to present it to the entire class.

5. List ten topics you feel would interest your classmates and ask your classmates to select the five topics they would be most interested in hearing. Tabulate your results and compare them with the findings of five other students. Save this information for use in selecting speech topics to be assigned later.

6. In small groups prepare a questionnaire that could be used to analyze the demographic characteristics of your speech class. Representatives from each group should then meet to compare questionnaires and select the best questions from each. Distribute the final questionnaire to all class members. Results should be tabulated for future use.

7. Are you still visualizing your positive statements once or twice a day? If not, spend the next ten minutes going over them. Remember to read, visualize, and feel confident performing each of your statements. If you can't seem to find time to work on all your statements, select the one that you most hope to achieve and concentrate on it for the next week. Every chance you get (whether while showering, driving or walking to class, getting ready for bed, or performing some other activity alone), visualize yourself successfully completing your statement for the week. Don't forget to feel confident and pleased while you are visualizing. When the week is over, select another positive statement and spend the next week working on it.

Notes

1. Patricia Ward Brash, "Beyond Giving a Speech," *Vital Speeches* 59 (15 November 1992), 83–84.

2. Peggy Noonan, *What I Saw at the Revolution* (New York: Ivy Books, 1990), p. 71.

3. Jenny Clanton, "Plutonium 238: NASA's Fuel of Choice," *Vital Speeches* (1 April 1989), 375–376.

4. Cathy Cummins, " 'Old-Timers' at USF Now Have a Place to Go," *Tampa Tribune* (27 March 1995), p. 1.

5. Illinois Community College Board, *Student Enrollment Data and Trends in the Public Community Colleges of Illinois, Fall 1989* (ERIC Document Reproduction Service No. ED-314-112, 1990).

6. Peter A. Morrison, "Congress and the Year 2000: Peering into the Demographic Future," *Business Horizons* 36 (November/December 1993), 59.

7. Morrison, "Congress and the Year 2000," p. 59.

8. Edward Hall, *The Hidden Dimension* (Garden City, NY: Anchor Books, 1969), and in personal conversations with natives of these countries.

9. Ronald E. Dulek, John S. Fielden, and John S. Hill, "International Communication: An Executive Primer," *Business Horizons* (January/February 1991), 22.

10. Dean C. Barnlund, *Communicative Styles of Japanese and Americans: Images and Realities* (Belmont, CA: Wadsworth, 1989), p. 115.

11. Mary Ellen Guffey, *Business Communication: Process and Product* (Belmont, CA: Wadsworth, 1994), pp. 436–437.

12. Richard N. Ostling, "One Nation Under Gods," *Time* (Fall 1993), p. 62.

13. Bruce A. Chadwick and Tim B. Heaton, *Statistical Handbook on the American Family* (Phoenix: Prux Press, 1992), p. 198.

14. Chadwick and Heaton, *Statistical Handbook*, pp. 83, 169; Morrison, "Congress and the Year 2000," 55.

15. William J. McGuire, "Attitudes and Attitude Change," in Gardner Lindzey and Elliot Aronson, eds., *The Handbook of Social Psychology*, vol. 2, 2nd ed. (New York: Random House, 1985), pp. 287–288.

16. Garth S. Jowett and Victoria O'Donnell, *Propaganda and Persuasion*, 2nd ed. (Newbury Park, CA: Sage, 1992), p. 23.

17. Milton Rokeach, *The Nature of Human Values* (New York: Free Press, 1973), pp. 7–8.

18. Barbara Warnick and Edward S. Inch, *Critical Thinking and Communication: The Use of Reason in Argument*, 2nd ed. (New York: Macmillan, 1994), p. 213.

19. Warnick and Inch, *Critical Thinking*, pp. 213–215, comment on research by Milton Rokeach and Sandra J. Ball-Rokeach, "Stability and Change in American Value Priorities," *American Psychologist* 44 (1989).

20. Warnick and Inch, *Critical Thinking and Communication*, p. 215.

21. Nicholas Rescher, *Introduction to Value Theory* (Englewood Cliffs, NJ: Prentice-Hall, 1969), pp. 111–118.

22. A. H. Maslow, "A Theory of Human Motivation," in Richard J. Lowry, ed., *Dominance, Self-Esteem, Self-Actualization: Germinal Papers of A. H. Maslow* (Monterey, CA: Brooks/Cole, 1973), pp. 153–173.

23. M. A. Wahba and L. T. Bridwell, "Maslow Reconsidered: A Review of Research on the Need Hierarchy Theory," *Organizational Behavior and Human Performance* 15 (1976), 212–240.

24. Mark Pendergrast, *For God, Country, and Coca-Cola: The Unauthorized History of the Great American Soft Drink and the Company That Makes It* (New York: Scribner's, 1993), p. 360.

25. Pendergrast, *For God, Country, and Coca-Cola*, p. 364.

26. Pendergrast, *For God, Country, and Coca-Cola*, p. 363.

27. Janet E. Elsea, "Strategies for Effective Presentations," *Personnel Journal* 64 (September 1985), 31–33.

28. Betsy Streisand, "Can He Get a Fair Trial?" *U.S. News & World Report* 117 (3 October 1994), pp. 62–63; and Lynda Gorov, "Simpson Prosecutor Gets Makeover on Expert's Advice," *Boston Globe*, syndicated (16 October 1994).

Verbal/Visual/Vocal Teamwork

6

Verbal/Visual/Vocal Teamwork: An Overview

OF ALL THE INSTRUCTORS YOU have observed since you have been in college, how many of them regularly used visual aids while speaking or lecturing? Probably not very many. Of those who did use visual aids, how many used overhead transparencies? Was the content of their transparencies interesting and even exciting? Did these transparencies make it easier to understand and remember the content of their lectures? Or did they look as if the instructor had simply copied a page out of your textbook—no color, no illustrations, just lines and lines of tiny print. If your instructors used visual aids that were interesting and exciting, you were very lucky. Unfortunately many instructors and speakers either don't use visual aids at all or use overcrowded, difficult-to-read visuals that make it impossible for listeners to comprehend the visual's content, take notes, and listen to the lecture all at the same time.

Don't let any negative experiences lead you to conclude that visuals aren't important or that they should be little more than an afterthought in your speech preparations. Visual communication (including a speaker's visual aids, appearance, and delivery) is as important to speaker success as either verbal or vocal communication. In fact, successful speakers view verbal, visual, and vocal communication as a team. You've already learned that what listeners *see* during a speech means as much or more to them than what the speaker *says* or *how* the speaker says it. This chapter will demonstrate exactly why visual communication is so important and why it deserves equal team status with verbal and vocal communication. How to design successful visual aids will be covered in Chapter 7; how to deliver your verbal, visual, and vocal messages will be addressed in Chapter 8.

Seeing Is Believing

▼ ▼ ▼

Chances are you have attended only a few speeches and/or lectures in which visual aids were used. The majority of speakers make very little use of them.[1] Why is it that visual aids have been given only scant attention by most speakers? In some cases it may be because some time is required to prepare them or because most visual aids are cumbersome to carry around and the equipment needed to use them is not always available. However, in most cases speakers simply are not aware of the power of visual aids.

Well-constructed visuals are generally acknowledged to have more "power" (overall impact and influence) than spoken words.[2] Unfortunately, many speakers have discovered the power of visual aids the hard way. Consider the speaker who put up his visual aid at the beginning of his speech even though he planned to refer to it later. He found that his audience was paying more attention to the visual than to what he was saying. Or consider another speaker who, while taking one last look at her visuals, found an error in an important statistic but decided to use the visual anyway and just make a *verbal* correction during her speech. She spent the following week answering calls from audi-

© D. Walker/Gamma Liaison

Effective speakers no longer consider visual aids optional.

ence members telling her about the "error" in her statistics. Even though they *heard* her correction, what they actually *saw* (the incorrect statistic) was what they remembered.

Because quality visual aids *anchor* your audience to the fact, concept, or idea you are presenting, visuals have a greater initial impact and longer-lasting influence (in other words, more "power" to affect your audience) than spoken words only.[3] For example, when trying to recall a fact or name, how many times have you remembered that the information appeared on a page accompanied by a picture, cartoon, or graph of some sort? The visual item was serving as an anchor for the written information. Probably, as soon as you recalled the details of the visual, you remembered the information as well. Because of this anchoring effect, audience members are more likely to remember your main points if, while you are discussing or summarizing them *verbally* and *vocally*, you are also showing them the list *visually*.[4] If the list of main points also is anchored by a picture or line drawing that portrays or conceptualizes the basic idea, audience recall will be even better.[5]

Of course, overuse of visual or verbal content in a speech can have negative consequences also. For example, when a speech includes too much verbal information, audience members are more likely to get bored, drift off into their own worlds, and naturally remember less of the presentation. When a speech includes too many visuals (even visuals that are effectively designed and include pictures and graphs), the audience is likely to get information overload, lose interest, and stop paying attention. How many is too many depends on your topic and the type of visuals used. Chapter 7 discusses various types of visual aids and suggests guidelines for determining the appropriate number of visuals.

As you read this chapter, keep in mind that poorly designed visuals have very little power and are just as ineffective as too many or too few visuals. Poorly constructed visual aids simply take too much time for an audience to comprehend. As a result, audience members must choose between listening to the speaker or reading the visual aid—and you know which they will choose. Therefore, in preparing visuals, keep in mind that if listeners must spend longer than three to six seconds to grasp the content, they likely will slip into a reading mode.[6] As mentioned in Chapter 4, when audiences are thrown into a reading mode, they hear almost nothing the speaker says. The remainder of this chapter will elaborate on the benefits of visual aids and explain why they have so much power.

The Power of Visual Aids

▼ ▼ ▼

The benefits of using visual aids are so great that speakers who know about them are hesitant to give presentations without the "power" visuals can supply. Let's examine the many ways properly designed visual aids can enhance a presentation.

Figure 6.1
Audience Recall Rates Are Greater When Speakers Use Visual Aids

Visual Aids Improve Audience Memory

Ralph Nichols, the father of research on listening, has long maintained that a few days after a verbal presentation, listeners have forgotten most of what they heard. He theorized that good listeners might remember no more than 25 percent—and probably much less. The percent remembered is the same whether it is a business audience, a college audience, a PTA audience, or whatever.[7] In fact, as shown in Figure 6.1, "less" is a more accurate assessment of listener recall— 10 percent recall is all you can expect from listeners in the typical speech that uses no visual aids.[8]

Imagine giving an important speech to fellow students in the campus auditorium or to a group of potential clients and realizing that only 10 percent of what you say will likely be remembered. Discouraging, isn't it? However, speakers who use quality visual aids don't need to settle for such depressing statistics. Recent research by the University of Minnesota and 3M Corporation found that speeches using visual aids (especially color visuals) significantly improved audience retention.[9] Likewise research by the Industrial Audio Association indicates that average listeners remember 50 percent of what they *see and hear*.[10] Summarizing research in instructional media, E. P. Zayas-Baya presents statistics showing that when verbal and visual information are presented together, audiences may retain as much as 65 percent (see Figure 6.1).[11] After all the

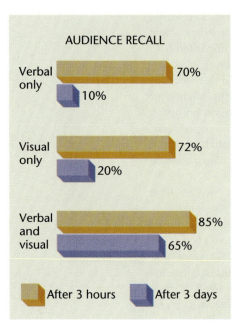

AUDIENCE RECALL

Verbal only — 70% / 10%

Visual only — 72% / 20%

Verbal and visual — 85% / 65%

After 3 hours / After 3 days

work involved in preparing a speech, which amount would you rather have your audience remember—10 or 65 percent?

Picture memory   To understand why visual aids cause such an improvement in listener recall, let's look at the research on memory. As indicated by statistics, *visual images are easier to remember than either spoken or printed words.*[12] In fact, our memory of pictures is almost perfect.[13] (This shouldn't come as a surprise in light of the discussion of the power of positive imagery in Chapter 3—imagery is just a "mental" visual aid.) In one of the first studies to determine the power of picture memory, subjects were shown 2,560 photographic slides—one slide every ten seconds over several days, for a total of seven hours of viewing. One hour after the last picture was shown, the subjects were shown 280 pairs of slides, with each pair containing one picture they had already seen and one they had not seen (although it was similar to a previous picture). Subjects were able to pick out the previously viewed picture 85–95 percent of the time. Even when they were allowed to view the pictures for only one second and some of the pictures were reversed so the left-hand side became the right-hand side, recognition rates were the same. The researcher concluded that "these experiments with pictorial stimuli suggest that recognition of pictures is essentially perfect. The results would probably have been the same if we had used 25,000 pictures instead of 2,500."[14]

Other researchers have reached the same conclusion. A Canadian researcher showed subjects 10,000 pictures, some of which were "vivid" while others were "normal." This study found that subjects were able to correctly identify 99.6 percent of the vivid pictures as ones they had already seen.[15] A vivid picture contained especially interesting subject matter. For example, a photo of a dog would be considered a normal picture, but a picture of a dog with a pipe in its mouth would be considered a vivid picture; a normal picture might show an airplane while a vivid picture might show a plane crash. Another researcher also showed subjects 10,000 pictures. This time subjects were required to select the previously viewed pictures out of groups of thirty-two pictures. Even so, subjects were able to identify 92 percent of the pictures they had already seen, again suggesting that "the capacity of recognition memory for pictures is almost limitless."[16]

Not only is our recognition of pictures almost perfect, it is long-lasting. In one study subjects were shown yearbook pictures of their former high school classmates (class sizes ranged from 90 to 800). Each picture was grouped with three other pictures of nonclassmates. Even up to thirty-five years after high school graduation, recognition rates were over 90 percent accurate.[17]

Text visuals   Research on memory has given speakers a definite reason for using **graphic visuals**—visual aids such as maps, charts, graphs, diagrams, and pictures with very few words. Listener memory for visual images is simply greater than memory for spoken or printed words. Research on memory also indicates that speakers should use pictures of some sort on **text visuals**—visual aids that normally include only text or printed words. However, improved listener memory does not apply to poorly designed or cluttered visuals. In one study in which pictures shown to subjects were intentionally designed to be misleading and confusingly complex, picture memory was found to be poor.[18]

What about text visuals that include only printed words? For example, would a transparency that included the title of a speech and a list of the main points (but no pictures) still aid audience memory? The answer is yes—if it was designed following the suggestions in Chapter 7, if the speaker reads or refers directly to each item on the visual, and if vivid words are used as often as possible. In one study, subject recall of verses of English poetry was tested. One group saw the written verses on a slide projector, one group heard the verses read to them, and one group saw and heard them at the same time. Not surprisingly, the group that saw the verses on the screen at the same time they heard them read had recall superior to the other two groups. Not only did they remember more information correctly, they also were the least distracted from listening by background noises. There was, however, no difference in recall between the other two groups, which relied exclusively on either the visual or verbal.[19] These results indicate that seeing the list of main points while hearing the speaker refer to them will result in more recall than if you simply show the visual without referring to each item on it.

Research has also found that when subjects are shown lists of words and then tested on their recall of the words, they remember more when the words are concrete (vivid) and easily stimulate mental images in their minds (high-imagery words). They are less likely to remember words that are abstract and do not stimulate mental images (low-imagery words).[20] For example, words like *friend*, *snake*, and *corpse* are concrete, high-imagery words while *devotion*, *greed*, and *cost* are more abstract, low-imagery words. Adding some vivid adjectives to the concrete words will enhance the imagery even further (for example, *the long, slimy snake*). Although speech and language have long been associated with the left hemisphere of the brain,[21] it now appears that high-imagery words and even emotional words are encoded both verbally and pictorially[22] and activate both the left and right hemispheres.[23] Thus recall is greater. (Brain hemispheres are explained in the next section.)

Realizing that concrete words are remembered better than abstract words, the FTC recommended in 1979 that warning messages for such items as cigarettes and alcohol should contain more concrete and vivid warnings. For example, "This product could be hazardous to your health," they suggested, would be better changed to "Consuming this product will increase the user's chance of death by 5%."[24]

Therefore, it is a good idea not only to use text visuals to reinforce your words but, whenever possible, to use vivid, expressive words on your text visuals. And because printed words, even vivid ones, are not as easy to remember as pictures, include a picture or drawing on as many of your text visuals as possible. To be effective, the pictures should illustrate (conceptualize) the ideas you are presenting.[25]

Visual Aids Speed Up Listener Comprehension

Not only are visual aids easier to remember, but when complex, technical information is presented visually, audiences understand it more quickly than if they just listen to a lecture. A look at right-brain/left-brain thinking explains why visuals speed listener comprehension. While the left hemisphere seems to specialize in step-by-step, analytic processing of information and pays close attention to details, the right hemisphere seems to specialize in simultaneous processing of information as a whole and pays little attention to details. In other words,

> The human mind is divided into two halves that "think" differently. The left side of the brain controls logical thought. When you hear words, it is your left brain that understands what you hear. The right brain, the creative side, controls conceptual thought. It enables you to comprehend complex information with blinding speed . . . in fact, in as little time as it takes you to just glance at a picture.[26]

Speakers who use no visual aids or only data charts loaded with statistics are asking the left side of their listeners' brains to do all the work. After a while, even a good left-brain thinker suffers from information overload, begins to make mistakes in reasoning, and loses interest. In computer terminology "the system shuts down." On the other hand, in only one glance the right brain can understand complex ideas presented in graphic form.

To illustrate this point, let's look at two different versions of the same data. First, look at the statistical data on cost-benefit analysis in Figure 6.2. In three

COST-BENEFIT ANALYSIS		Alternatives	
	Current system	Terminal	Personal computer
Initial development costs			
Hardware	$ 0	$ 1,500	$ 7,000
Software	0	0	500
Total	$ 0	$ 1,500	$ 7,500
Yearly operating costs			
Phone lines	$ 0	$ 3,500	$ 500
Supplies	250	1,000	500
Labor (overtime)	2,000	0	0
Maintenance	0	50	250
Lost sales	4,000	0	0
Total	$ 6,250	$ 4,550	$ 1,250
Annual cost savings	$ 0	$ 1,700	$ 5,000

Figure 6.2
Statistical Data in Table Form Often Can Be Difficult to Grasp

(From Living with Computers, *Second Edition, by Patrick G. McKeown, copyright © 1988 by Harcourt Brace Jovanovich, Inc. Reprinted by permission of the publishers.)*

to six seconds, can you tell which computer system would be the cheapest in the long run? Probably not. In fact, some people simply give up when they see a statistical table. Now look at the same data presented in graph form in Figure 6.3. At a glance you can tell that although the initial cost of switching from the current system to personal computers would be greater, by the end of the second year the personal computer would cost the least money. Therefore, when complicated data needs to be included in a speech, comprehension will be more complete and occur more quickly if you present the data in graphic form.

Using visual aids is a fast way to trigger the right brain. It is also possible to use language to trigger mental pictures and visual associations in the minds of your listeners—imagery is also a right-brain activity. To show you what we

Figure 6.3
Statistical Data in Graph Form Is Much Easier to Grasp

(From Living with Computers, *Second Edition, by Patrick G. McKeown, copyright © 1988 by Harcourt Brace Jovanovich, Inc. Reprinted by permission of the publishers.)*

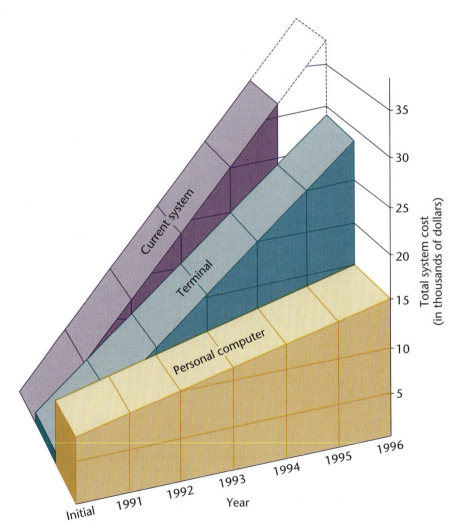

COST-BENEFIT ANALYSIS

mean, try this experiment. Take any personal experience (walking in the park; playing cards; meeting a special friend; or just sitting in a room). Now sit down with pen and paper and describe that experience in words. Include as much detail as possible and be as accurate as possible. As you write, are you picturing the incident in your mind? If so, you are drawing on stored visual impressions of that experience—a right-brain activity.

Using the right side of the brain isn't something that only artists and musicians do. Many of the most successful people combine creativity and analytical thinking. To show you why they are successful, let's take a look at Albert Einstein:

> As soon as you see his name, you probably think of a great scientist, the supreme rational thinker, the great mathematician surrounded by figures and equations, a logical left-hemisphere thinker. Yet Einstein's ideas initially came to him as pictures and images, and only subsequently did he put them into words and mathematical symbols. When Einstein hit upon the theory of relativity, it was not through rational analysis. He did not sit down with pen and paper and step by step work out the theory, eventually arriving at the logical conclusion. The theory was born when Einstein was lying on a grassy hillside one summer's afternoon. He was gazing up at the sun through half-closed eyelids, playing with the light that came through his eyelashes, when he began to wonder what it would be like to travel down a light beam. He lay there in a dream state letting his mind wander freely, imagining himself traveling down a light beam, when suddenly he realized (one almost has to say in a flash) just what it would be like. This realization was the essence of the theory of relativity, and it came to him not as a logical deduction, but as a creative, intuitive insight, the result of synthetic rather than analytic thinking.[27]

Even logical, scientific types (including the late Einstein) make use of right-brain, creative thinking.
© *Photo Collection CIT Archives*

Although neither we nor our audiences may be in quite the same league with Albert Einstein, we can all benefit by using both sides of our brain.

Visual Aids Decrease Presentation Time

One of the biggest complaints heard in most organizations is, "I can't get anything done because I spend so much of my time in meetings." One researcher estimates that the average supervisor spends as much as 40 percent of the workweek in meetings and conferences.[28] Because people can comprehend information faster and more completely when visual aids accompany the verbal explanation, less meeting time is required. Even if nothing more than a list of the options to be considered were written on a chalkboard, seeing the list while discussing it could shorten the time required for group members to reach a consensus. A study by the U.S. Department of Education found that instructors using overhead projectors could cut fifteen minutes off each one-hour lecture.[29] Similarly, the study by the University of Minnesota and the 3M Corporation, mentioned previously, found that the use of visuals could reduce the length of the average business meeting by 28 percent![30] If you are a member of an organization that has long, drawn-out discussions, try using visual aids and see what happens.

Visual Aids Add to Speaker Credibility

If you are in a situation in which you have fairly low credibility (such as when you are new to a company, younger than most others in the same position, or unknown to audience members), use of visuals could be very important. One researcher found that low-credibility speakers who use visual aids (1) can overcome an audience's view of them as untrustworthy and nonauthoritative by using quality visual aids, and (2) can elicit the same level of audience retention as high-credibility speakers.[31] The study conducted by the University of Minnesota and the 3M Corporation also found that an "average" presenter who uses visuals can be as effective as an "expert" presenter who uses no visuals.[32]

By the time you give your second speech in class, you will already have some type of credibility in the eyes of your classmates. For example, isn't there someone in your class that when he or she walks to the front of class to give a speech, everyone thinks, "Great, I'm really going to enjoy this"? This person has high credibility with the class. On the other hand, is there someone in your class whom you expect to do something crazy or to be unprepared for his or her speeches? This person's credibility is low or at best questionable, but this same person could increase his or her credibility with the audience simply by using quality visual aids. The minute the class sees the first visual aid they will be surprised; by the second visual aid they likely will decide that the speaker is obviously prepared and settle back to enjoy the speech.

Visual Aids Decrease Speaker Nervousness

Researchers have found that anxious speakers feel more confident when they use visual aids.[33] There are several reasons visual aids are so helpful.

NANCY® by Jerry Scott, reprinted by permission of UFS, Inc.

Dry, technical, or complex information can be more enjoyable when explained with visuals.

© Mike Yamashita/Woodfin Camp & Associates, Inc.

Visual aids give you something to do with your hands   When you are turning the pages of a flipchart, changing transparencies on the overhead projector, holding an object in your hands, or pointing to information on a screen or chart, your accompanying gestures look natural. Of course, you will need to practice using your visuals to appear really confident. Practice at least once (more if time allows) giving the speech using your actual visuals. Remember, the trick is to continue talking while manipulating the visuals and maintaining eye contact with the audience. Practice shifting from visual to visual as smoothly as possible so you won't distract audience attention from what you are saying.

Visual aids draw audience attention away from you   If you feel nervous because everyone is looking directly at you, you will love using visual aids. Each time you put up a visual, audience attention is immediately drawn to the visual and away from you, the speaker. To illustrate this point, have a classmate or your instructor put up a really interesting transparency (one with some color if possible) but continue talking about something unrelated to the visual. Everyone in the class should try to look only at the speaker, not the visual. The urge to look at the visual is overwhelming, isn't it? Although the audience shift in attention from you to the visual aid will only last a few seconds, this gives you enough time to mentally relax and regain your confidence.

Remember:

Visual aids have the power to . . .

▶ Improve audience memory.

▶ Speed up listener comprehension.

▶ Decrease presentation time.

▶ Add to speaker credibility.

▶ Decrease speaker nervousness

▶ Add listener interest and enjoyment.

Visual aids make it almost impossible to forget what you want to say

Suppose that you are ready to move to your last point when your mind suddenly goes blank. If you have prepared a visual aid for each point, all you have to do is put up the next visual and you will instantly remember what you want to say. There is also no need to worry about remembering specific facts or statistics when that information is included on a text or graphic visual. Many speakers who use flip charts write notes to themselves lightly in pencil on the chart. No one but the speaker can even see the notes. The frames around transparencies are also excellent places for notes. Keep your notes brief—key words or phrases are usually enough. When you use visual aids, you can feel confident that you will not forget any major ideas or information.

Visual Aids Add to Listener Interest and Enjoyment

How many speeches or lectures have you attended in which you stayed interested and enjoyed the speaker? Probably not many. The content of many lectures and presentations by guest speakers seems to deal with dry, technical, complex information. However, if the information is important enough that you must interrupt your work or study time to attend the lecture or presentation, then it must be important enough to remember. There are many ways to liven up a speech, including dynamic delivery, effective use of language, good verbal supporting materials, and, of course, effective visual aids. All of these techniques are discussed in detail later in this book.

Given a choice, would you prefer to listen to a speech from a tape recorder or attend the speech in person? It's much more interesting if you can see the speaker, isn't it? If the speaker uses powerful visual aids during the speech, it will be even more interesting and enjoyable.

Checking Your Verbal/Visual/ Vocal Awareness

The following questionnaire is designed to call attention to some common misunderstandings about the verbal, visual, and vocal aspects of speaking that will be discussed in this unit. Some of the following statements are true; some are commonly held ideas that have been proven false by research.

Directions: If you think a statement is generally accurate, mark it "T"; if you think the statement is inaccurate, mark it "F." Then compare your answers to the explanations at the end of the quiz.

_____ 1. The main reason for using visual aids is to entertain your audience.

_____ 2. If you can use words to create mental pictures in the minds of your listeners, it isn't necessary to use visual aids.

_____ 3. An audience typically waits until after you have completed the introduction to decide whether your speech is interesting enough to listen to.

_____ 4. When you are speaking, you should either look just over your audience's heads or find one or two people who seem to be listening and talk to them.

_____ 5. Using a markerboard or chalkboard as a visual aid is good because you already know how to use them—practice is seldom necessary.

_____ 6. To make your visual aids more interesting, use several colors and several different typefaces.

_____ 7. You should avoid using sexist language because some of your audience members may be turned off by it and not listen to your message.

_____ 8. If practicing your speech out loud is embarrassing or inconvenient, going over it mentally will be just as good.

_____ 9. In order to make the text easy to read, you should use all-capital letters on your visuals.

_____ 10. If you have a good memory, it is better to memorize your speech than to take a chance on forgetting part of it.

Answers

1.   _False._ Although using visual aids does add to the interest and enjoyment of the audience, that is only one of many reasons effective speakers use them. A more important reason is to help the listeners remember the main points of the message. You may have been surprised to learn in this chapter that average listeners remember only 10 percent of what they hear but as much as 65 percent of what they hear _and_ see. _(continued)_

(continued)

2. *False.* Certainly an audience will listen more attentively and, therefore, remember your ideas better when scenes and events are described so vividly as to paint mental pictures for listeners. However, some well-designed visuals will make your presentation still more powerful.

3. *False.* Would you believe that audience members have largely made up their minds as to whether they want to listen to a speaker after only a few words? Listeners assess visual messages (whether intended or not) before they even hear any vocal and verbal messages. This means that preparation is critical. Chapter 8 will give you the information you need to have your audience eagerly waiting to hear what you have to say.

4. *False.* Besides being a valuable source of feedback from your audience, making eye contact with listeners throughout the audience makes them feel that you are one of them and that you care about them. When an audience feels friendly toward you, they listen more attentively and are more likely to believe what you are saying.

5. *False.* Regardless of the type of visuals you use, practice is essential if you want to feel confident and give an effective speech. Markerboards and chalkboards have their uses, but for most speaking occasions a more polished visual aid is recommended.

6. *False.* With the capability of computer software, it is tempting to fill your visuals (especially transparencies) with different typefaces, to add clip art, and to splash color generously. Although you may have created a lovely piece of art, it will not be as effective as a visual with limited typefaces and color used mainly for emphasis and for grouping of related data. Chapter 7 will give you the information needed to produce visual aids that are the envy of your classmates and colleagues.

7. *True.* You don't want to alienate your listeners by using sexist language. Figure 8.3 lists some masculine and feminine terms and expressions that often upset audience members and suggests alternative, gender-neutral words.

8. *False.* Mentally thinking through your speech does not help make the connection between the brain and the mouth. There is no substitute for practicing your speech aloud while using your notes and visuals. Oral practice will make you feel confident and allow you to give a speech both you and your audience will enjoy.

9. *False.* Although some textbooks favor using only capital letters on your visuals and media departments in many organizations use them, research shows that words written in all-capital letters are more difficult to read than those written in capital and lowercase letters.

10. *False.* Although memorizing your opening and closing statements is all right if it makes you feel more comfortable, memorizing the entire speech has several drawbacks, as covered in Chapter 8. Speaking from key-word notes is preferable because it allows you to speak in a relaxed, warm, conversational way that isn't possible when speaking from memory.

We have all heard of great speakers who were riveting without the help of visuals. Winston Churchill and Martin Luther King, Jr. come quickly to mind. These speakers created mental pictures (visuals) in the minds of their audiences through use of vivid words, illustrations, stories, analogies, and other supporting materials. Such techniques are very important but they don't replace the power of visual aids, especially in speeches containing complex, technical information. Remember, too, that this is the media age—the types of computer-generated graphics we see on television are incredible, and we "listen" to music by watching videos of the artists as they play or sing. You may be one of those rare people who can hold an audience spellbound without visual aids, but why take the chance?

The need for verbal/visual/vocal teamwork and the benefits of using visual aids in speeches cannot be overemphasized. Visual aids have so much power because they (1) improve audience memory, (2) speed up listener comprehension, (3) decrease the time needed to present a message, (4) add to speaker credibility, and (5) decrease speaker nervousness. In short, *speakers should no longer consider visual aids as optional*. Speakers who fail to think in terms of verbal/visual/vocal teamwork are shortchanging their audiences and themselves.

1. Interview from five to ten students asking the following questions. Share your information with your classmates.

    a. How many of your instructors (now or in the past) regularly use(d) visual aids while lecturing?

    b. List the types of visuals used: Transparencies, chalkboard, slides, flip charts, computer visuals, objects or models, other.

    c. If they used transparencies, how would you rank them?

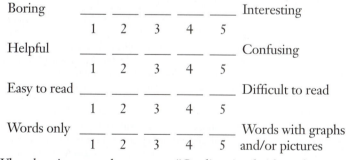

Boring   ___ ___ ___ ___ ___   Interesting
           1   2   3   4   5

Helpful   ___ ___ ___ ___ ___   Confusing
           1   2   3   4   5

Easy to read   ___ ___ ___ ___ ___   Difficult to read
           1   2   3   4   5

Words only   ___ ___ ___ ___ ___   Words with graphs
           1   2   3   4   5   and/or pictures

2. What does it mean when we say, "Quality visual aids anchor your audience to the fact, concept, or idea you are presenting?" Share your interpretation with a classmate.

3. Which of the advantages of using visual aids (improved memory, faster comprehension, shorter presentation time, added credibility, decreased nervousness, or listener enjoyment) do you feel will be the most beneficial for you and/or your listeners when you speak? If you have used visual aids

while speaking, did you notice any of these benefits? Share your experiences with the class.

4. If you haven't already done so, take the quiz at the end of the chapter. What percent did you get correct? Are there any answers that seem incorrect to you? Discuss your reasons with a classmate. At the end of this unit (after reading Chapters 6–8), return to the questions and see if you still feel the way you do now. If so, ask your instructor for his or her opinion. Feel free to write the author for additional information as well.

5. If your instructor has a stack of visual aids (transparencies) from student speeches of past semesters, try the following impromptu speaking exercises: Place student names in a hat and stir. The instructor draws a name from the hat, reads it out loud, and hands the student two unrelated visual aids. The student walks to the front and presents an impromptu speech of approximately one minute using the two visuals. The speech may be humorous or serious. This assignment gives students practice in using visual aids and is fun as well.

Notes

1. For example, "A Profile of Meetings in Corporate America: Results of the 3M Meeting Effectiveness Study" (Austin, Texas: 3M Corporation Meeting Management Institute and the Annenberg School of Communications at the University of Southern California in Los Angeles, 1989) reports that the majority of business speeches include no visuals at all; of those that do use visuals, 47 percent of them rely on handouts, 13 percent use chalkboards, 13 percent use overhead transparencies, and the remaining 27 percent use a combination of flip charts, slides, videos, and computer presentations.

2. K. L. Alesandrini, "Imagery-Eliciting Strategies and Meaningful Learning," *Journal of Mental Imagery* 6 (1982), 125–140; Allan Paivio, *Imagery and Verbal Processes* (New York: Holt, Rinehart & Winston, 1971).

3. Alesandrini, "Imagery-Eliciting Strategies," pp. 125–140.

4. Valerie A. Thompson and Allan Paivio, "Memory for Pictures and Sounds: Independence of Auditory and Visual Codes," *Canadian Journal of Experimental Psychology* 48(3) (September 1994), 380–395; see also F. M. Dwyer and H. De Melo, "Effects of Mode of Instruction, Testing, Order of Testing, and Cued Recall on Student Achievement," *The Journal of Experimental Education* 52(2) (1984), pp. 86–94.

5. Paivio, *Imagery and Verbal Processes*.

6. Richard Scoville, "Ten Graphs (and How to Use Them)," *PC World* 6 (September 1988), 217.

7. Ralph G. Nichols, "Listening Is a 10-Part Skill," *Nation's Business* 45 (July 1957), 56; see also Ralph B. Nichols and Leonard A. Stevens, *Are You Listening?* (New York: McGraw-Hill, 1957); and Florence I. Wolff, Nadine C. Marsnik, William S. Tracey, and Ralph G. Nichols, *Perceptive Listening* (New York: Holt, Rinehart & Winston, 1983).

8. E. P. Zayas-Baya, "Instructional Media in the Total Language Picture," *International Journal of Instructional Media* 5 (1977–78), 145–150.

9. Douglas R. Vogel, Gary W. Dickson, and John A. Lehman, "Persuasion and the Role of Visual Presentation Support: The UM/3M Study," *3M Corporation In-House Publication* (St. Paul, MN, 1986), pp. 1–20.

10. Research results available from Audio Visual Management Association, P.O. Box 821, Royal Oak, MI 48068.

11. Zayas-Baya, "Instructional Media," 145–150.

12. Ellen Perecman, editor of *Cognitive Processing in the Right Hemisphere* (New York: Academic Press, 1983), says on page 222 that "pictures and highly imageable words are most likely to be dually coded and consequently stored in and retrieved from memory more readily than other stimuli." See also A. N. Katz and A. Paivio, "Imagery Variables in Concept Identification," *Journal of Verbal Learning and Verbal Behavior* 14 (1975), 284–297.

13. Peter Russell, *The Brain Book* (New York: Dutton, 1979), p. 114.

14. Ralph N. Haber, "How We Remember What We See," *Scientific American* (May 1970), 105.

15. R. S. Nickerson, "Short-Term Memory for Complex Meaningful Visual Configurations: Demonstration of

Capacity," *Canadian Journal of Psychology* 19 (1980), 155–160.

16. Lionel Standing, "Learning 10,000 Pictures," *Quarterly Journal of Experimental Psychology* 25 (1973), 207–222.

17. H. P. Babrick, P. O. Babrick, and R. P. Wittlinger, "Fifty Years of Memory for Names and Faces: A Cross-Sectional Approach," *Journal of Experimental Psychology* 104 (1975), 54–75.

18. A. G. Goldstein and J. E. Chance, "Visual Recognition Memory for Complex Configurations," *Perceptions and Psychophysics* 9 (1970), 237–241.

19. Hower J. Hsia, "Output, Error, Equivocation, and Recalled Information in Auditory, Visual, and Audiovisual Information Processing with Constraint and Noise," *The Journal of Communication* 18 (December 1968), 325–345.

20. M. P. Bryden and Robert G. Ley, "Right Hemispheric Involvement in Imagery and Affect," in Ellen Perecman, ed., *Cognitive Processing in the Right Hemisphere* (New York: Academic Press, 1983), pp. 116–117; see also S. Hishitani, "Vividness of Image and Retrieval Time," *Perception and Motor Skills* 73 (1991), 115–123.

21. Russell, *Brain Book*, p. 53.

22. Katz and Paivio, "Imagery Variables," 284–297.

23. Bryden and Ley, "Right Hemispheric Involvement," p. 119; see also Joseph B. Hellige, "Hemispheric Asymmetry," *Annual Review of Psychology* 41 (1990), 55–80.

24. Federal Trade Commission, *Consumer Information Remedies* (Washington, DC: U.S. Government Printing Office, 1979).

25. Alesandrini, "Image Eliciting Strategies," 125–140.

26. In a brochure advertising *Picture Perfect* and *Diagraph*®, both business graphics software by Computer Support. *Diagraph*® is a registered trademark licensed to Computer Support Corporation.

27. Russell, *Brain Book*, p. 56.

28. Thomas R. Tortoriello, Stephen J. Blatt, and Sue DeWine, *Communication in the Organization: An Applied Approach* (New York: McGraw-Hill, 1978), p. 81.

29. C. W. Chance, "Experiments in the Adaptation of the Overhead Projector in Teaching Engineering Descriptive Geometry Curriculum," U.S. Office of Education, Project 243 (microfilm No. 61–3680), Austin, University of Texas, 1960.

30. Vogel, Dickson, and Lehman, "The UM/3M Study," as reported in Michael Antonoff, "Presentations That Persuade," *Personal Computing* 14 (27 July 1990), 62.

31. William J. Seiler, "The Conjunctive Influence of Source Credibility and the Use of Visual Materials on Communication Effectiveness," *Southern Speech Communication Journal* 37 (Winter 1971), 174–185.

32. Vogel, Dickson, and Lehman, "Persuasion and the Role of Visual Presentation Support."

33. Ayres, Joe, "Using Visual Aids to Reduce Speech Anxiety," *Communication Research Reports* 8 (June/December, 1991), 73–79.

Designing Your Visual Message

▼ ▼ ▼

O NE OF THE EASIEST AND most enjoyable ways you can help ensure the success of a speech is to prepare interesting and powerful visual aids. You have, no doubt, attended lectures in which the visual aids were anything but interesting and powerful. So you already know some of the pitfalls to avoid when using visuals. Hopefully you also have had the pleasure of observing a master presenter hold an audience spellbound with a well-orchestrated combination of content, delivery, and visual aids. If so, you already have an idea of some of the types of visual aids that you might like to try in your own speeches.

There is no great mystery to preparing eye-catching visual aids. Even if you haven't yet used visuals in a speech, your experience as an audience member has taught you many dos and don'ts. Figure 7.1 shows a transparency used by a student in an informative speech. Based on your past observations of visual aids, what changes would you suggest to transform this visual into a more powerful one? (Hint: there are at least six changes that would add to its effectiveness.) Jot down your ideas, and then read the chapter to discover the basic design rules for effective visual aids that you will want to use in your own speeches. As you read, occasionally refer back to Figure 7.1 to see if you can identify any additional problems.

Types of Visual Aids
▼ ▼ ▼

B efore discussing how to design an effective visual aid, let's take a brief look at the types of visual aids you might want to use in your speeches. Although the options for visual aids are limited only by your imagination and the specific speaking situation, the following types are used most often: overhead transparencies; slides; flip charts and posters; objects, models, and handouts; markerboards and chalkboards; and projected computer visuals. Each has advantages and disadvantages as discussed in the following section.

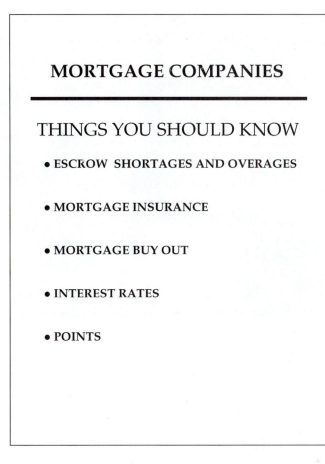

Figure 7.1
What Changes Would
Make This a More
Powerful Visual?

Overhead Transparencies

A **transparency** is a piece of transparent acetate with text and/or pictures that can be projected onto a screen from an overhead projector. Transparencies lend a polish and excitement that can greatly enhance the impact of your speech. When you get more involved in your career, you will probably discover that transparencies are used more than any other visual aid. Even though you may feel more comfortable using posters and charts (because you are familiar with them), it will be well worth your time to learn to prepare and use quality transparencies. Start by using transparencies in a class report and see the reaction you get from your classmates and your instructor.

One reason that transparencies (often called *viewgraphs* or *overheads*) are used so often is because you can project them in normal room light while facing your audience. This allows you to maintain eye contact with the audience (necessary in establishing rapport and interpreting nonverbal reactions) and still glance down at the transparency on the overhead projector as needed. Also, the frame around each transparency is an excellent place to put notes and personal

Overhead transparencies lend a polish and excitement that can greatly enhance the impact of your speech.

© David Young-Wolff/PhotoEdit

reminders. Chapter 8 discusses techniques for effectively handling your transparencies and the overhead projector.

Another advantage of transparencies is that you can make them yourself with minimal effort. All you need is a computer, a copy machine, and the appropriate acetate sheets. Most college computer labs have software (such as *WordPerfect*, *PowerPoint*, *PageMaker*, or *Harvard Graphics*) and a variety of typefaces and *clip art* (ready-to-use drawings and pictures) you can use to create text and graphics for your transparencies. Many labs have laser printers that allow you to print your copy directly onto the transparency acetate (film). You also can produce transparencies on a copy machine using special transparency acetate or you can go to a local copy shop, which can produce color transparencies and even print color photographs on your transparency film for a reasonable price. You can even add color to transparencies by using tinted acetate instead of the standard colorless acetate or by using a special marker that can write on acetate (such as a Sharpee brand marker).

The usable area of an overhead transparency is approximately 7½ by 9½ inches. Transparencies can be used with the long side placed either vertically or horizontally. Keep in mind, however, that it is easier to stack, carry, and use transparencies if they are all designed to face in the same direction.

Another advantage of transparencies is the ease with which you can use **overlays**—pieces of clear or colored acetate that are taped to the frame and folded back until needed. The overlays can be nothing more than strips of colored acetate used to highlight ideas (see visual 1 in Figure 7.2). Overlays can also contain main points, bar graphs, or clip art to allow you to reveal your speech content gradually. Overlays lend themselves to surprise conclusions as well. For example, one student finished his speech on budgeting guidelines by first projecting a clear transparency showing the words "Family Budget 1996." He then said, "Unless you follow the guidelines I have presented, your family budget in 1996 [here he lowered a red overlay with the word "Bankrupt" in white letters] may be bankrupt in 1997." This was a powerful conclusion that visualized the importance of his topic.

Of course, there are some disadvantages to using overhead transparencies. For example, they are bulky to carry around and tend to scratch easily. To reduce scratching, transport and store them with sheets of paper between them. **Tip**: Transparencies produced on a thermofax machine (used by many businesses and schools) rarely, if ever, scratch. They don't scratch because the thermofax burns the image into the film instead of laying the image on top of the film as copy machines and laser printers do.

35-Millimeter Slides

Unless you happen to have slides already on hand, you probably won't use them in your classroom speeches. A major disadvantage is the time required to produce them. Once you have created your visual aid masters, you still must photograph them with slide film and then send the film out for processing. As a result, last-minute changes are close to impossible. Another disadvantage is that the room must be darkened for projection, which makes interaction with your audience difficult and reference to your notes impossible. However, slides have certain advantages over transparencies. For one thing, because slides can have dark and even black backgrounds and use intense colors, they can look very professional. For another, they are easy to transport.

If you design the copy for each slide to fit inside a 6- by 9-inch space, it will reduce at the correct slide ratio. As with transparencies you can use slides in either the vertical or horizontal position, but it is better to use the same position for all the slides in any one speech. **Tip**: If you plan to use your slides more than once or to project certain slides for longer than a few minutes, request that your photo processor use glass mounts. Cardboard mounts tend to warp when exposed to extended projector heat, and warping causes focus problems.

Flip Charts and Posters

No doubt you have seen posters and flip charts used during class reports or lectures. Because they can be hard to read for large audiences, flip charts and posters work best with groups of no more than thirty people. The advantages of using posters and flip charts are that they tend to set an informal mood (*if* you make sure the print is large enough to be seen easily), they are simple to prepare, and they can add a feeling of spontaneity to your speech if you write on them as you speak.

Posters and flip charts do have disadvantages, however. Both poster boards and the newsprint pads used as flip charts are awkward to transport and even more awkward to store. Because markers tend to bleed through newsprint, it's a good idea to leave a blank page between each page you plan to write on during the speech. **Tip**: Water based markers will not bleed through newsprint.

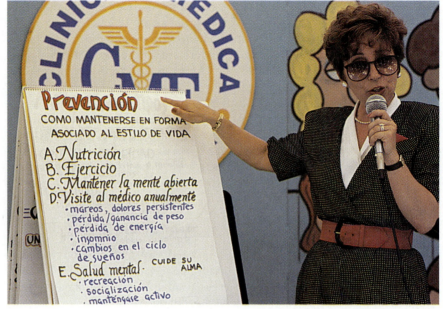

To ensure neatness and readability, this speaker has prepared her flip charts ahead of time. She is also standing next to the easel so she won't block the audience's view.

© David Young-Wolff/PhotoEdit

To use posters and flip charts effectively, learn to write on them without blocking the audience's view and to talk and write at the same time—both of these take practice. While you are experimenting with posters and flip charts, try either writing on them ahead of time or penciling in guidelines to trace over during your talk. These lightly penciled markings will be invisible to the audience but will free you from worry over misspelled words or forgotten points. **Tip**: To keep posters from sagging when placed on an easel, mount them on foam-core board or gatorboard, available in most campus bookstores.[1]

Objects, Models, and Handouts

Objects can be very effective visual aids as long as they are large enough to be seen yet small enough so you can transport and display them easily. For example, in a speech about computer graphics, you might bring in a small computer terminal and printer and let the audience actually watch the entire process from input to final printed graphic. Or, in a speech on CPR, you might use a manikin to show the proper head position. **Tip**: Although some objects might be small enough to be passed around the audience for a closer view, you're better off waiting until your speech is completed to do this. Otherwise audience members will be distracted from what you are saying.

If an object is either too small, too large, or too dangerous to be used as a visual aid, you might want to use a model instead. For example, a model car, a model office layout, or a model of an atom would all serve as effective visual aids.

Handouts can be both a blessing and a curse. Although handouts reduce the necessity for listeners to take notes, the typical audience member will read the handout instead of listening to you. So, unless you need listeners to actually *do* something with the material while you are speaking (such as fill out a checklist to determine their risk of a heart attack), it's better to pass out handouts at the end of your speech. However, don't forget to tell your audience in your speech introduction that a handout will be provided.

Markerboards and Chalkboards

Markerboards usually are preferable to chalkboards because the glossy white of the markerboard is more attractive and there's no messy chalk residue. Also, small markerboards can be placed on easels and moved closer to the audience for a more personal feel. However, both markerboards and chalkboards have several drawbacks.[2] First, *practice is vital for success*. Without practice you might write either too small to see or so large that you run out of space; or you might have to erase your sketch or repeat it several times to get the proportions correct; or you might forget the spelling of a key word. Actually it will probably take you more practice to effectively use a markerboard or chalkboard than to use transparencies, slides, objects, or posters. Second, because drawing on the board takes valuable speaking time, *you must be able to speak and draw at the same time*, which also takes a great deal of practice. Third, *while writing on the board, your back is toward the audience*. This not only affects audience interest and denies you valuable audience feedback but also makes it difficult for you to project your voice to the back of the room. A markerboard is somewhat better because you can stand beside it and still look at the audience occasionally. Finally, *using the chalkboard makes you look less prepared and less professional* than using other types of visuals.

Because of these disadvantages, markerboards and chalkboards should be used only as a last resort. If you must use a chalkboard, have your information on note cards ready to transfer to the board.

Projected Computer Visuals

Computer technology is advancing so rapidly that it's difficult to keep up with all the developments. Affordable computer hardware and software now make it possible to produce sophisticated shows with color, animation, and sound. Although such screen shows are good for sales and special occasions, most speakers depend on static computer visuals similar to those used for transparencies and slides. In a small group (probably not more than eight) your computer visuals can be viewed directly on the computer screen. In larger groups you will need to project the images onto a larger screen, using a portable LCD flat-panel that sits on top of a regular overhead projector. Or you may have access to one of the new self-contained LCD projection systems that attach directly to your computer and need no overhead projector. **Tip**: If you use a laptop or notebook computer with the portable LCD panel or projection system, your visuals will be almost as easy to transport as a stack of transparencies or a slide carousel.

There are several advantages to using projected computer visuals. For one thing, once the visuals are designed, they are ready for instant use. For another,

This speaker is using the LitePro® 580 self-contained LCD projection system. It connects directly to her laptop computer and requires no overhead projector.

© InFocus Systems. Used by permission.

the colors that appear on the computer screen are the colors the audience will see (when screen colors are translated onto a transparency by a color printer or turned into a slide, the colors are often not what the speaker expected[3]). Also, last-minute updates or changes are easy to do. The only disadvantages are the cost and the availability of equipment. However, if you have the equipment, it's hard to beat a computer presentation.

Selecting the Right Type of Visual Aid

▼ ▼ ▼

Once you have decided on your topic and analyzed your audience (following the suggestions in Chapter 5), you have all the basic information you need to select the appropriate type of visuals for your speech. Simply apply the information already gathered to answer the following questions:

▶ *How big will the audience be?* For a small audience of 5–10 people, you can select from all the visuals discussed. For audiences of 30 or so people, all visuals except the computer screen will work. However, if your audience numbers more than 50, only transparencies, slides, or an LCD panel will project an image large enough for easy viewing. For most classroom audiences any type of visual (except the average-sized computer screen) works well.

▶ *What equipment is available?* Most educational, professional, and business environments have easels for holding flip charts and posters, as well as projection screens, overhead projectors, and chalkboards or markerboards. Fewer have slide projectors, LCD panels, or laptop computers available for speaker use.

▶ *Which visual aid best fits the purpose of the speech?* Although most types of visual aids can be effective regardless of the speech purpose (informative, persuasive, or entertaining), transparencies, flip charts, markerboards, and objects are especially good in working or learning situations. Slides work well in more formal situations or in persuasive and motivational situations. Computer screen shows are especially good for entertaining situations.

▶ *Would a low-light situation work for this audience?* Slides and LCD projected computer images require low-light conditions for ease of viewing; all of the other types of visual aids can be used in normal room light. For example, in choosing between slides (which require low light or no lighting) and transparencies (which use normal room lighting), consider what happens when the lights are turned low. First of all, in a low-light environment an audience tends to be more relaxed and passive—an entertainment or "movie theater" atmosphere is created. Obviously this is not the kind of atmosphere you would want in either a working/learning presentation requiring listener participation or in a speech to an "uninterested" audience (discussed in Chapter 5) that may not be motivated to pay attention. However, a low-light atmosphere might be perfect for an entertaining speech. In addition, when the lights are turned low, eye contact between speaker and audience is no longer possible. Lack of eye contact diminishes your control as a speaker and puts added importance on your voice and your visual aids. Therefore, to attract and hold audience attention, you'll want to make your voice more animated and interesting, your examples more personal, and your visual aids clearer and more interesting. This type of speaking can be a lot of fun, but it requires practice and experience. Try it only after giving several speeches in normal light conditions. The visual design skills needed to succeed in low-light situations are covered later in this chapter; the vocal delivery skills needed are discussed in Chapter 8.

Designing Text and Graphic Visuals

▼ ▼ ▼

Now that you know what types of visuals are available and how to decide which one(s) to use in each of your speeches, you are ready to discover how much fun it is to create visuals. It's so much fun that some speakers use too many visuals in their speeches. **Tip**: To keep your audience from experiencing visual overload, try this formula when deciding how many visuals to use:

$$\frac{\text{Length of speech}}{2} + 1 = \text{maximum number of visuals}$$

For example, for a six-minute speech, you would want a maximum of four visuals (6 divided by 2 plus 1); for a ten-minute speech you would want a maximum of six visuals (10 divided by 2 plus 1). Of course, this formula is only a guide. Fewer visuals could certainly be used; more visuals should be used with caution.

Distinguishing Between Text and Graphic Visuals

As we discussed in Chapter 6, visual aids can be divided into two basic groups: text visuals and graphic visuals. **Text visuals** include mainly text or printed words with one or two clip art drawings or pictures. The majority of visual aids used in speeches are text visuals. Text visuals are especially helpful during the introduction of your speech as you list your main points, during the conclusion of your speech as you summarize the main points, and at any other times when lists of information are needed. **Graphic visuals** include organizational charts and flowcharts, diagrams and schematic drawings, maps, pictures, and graphs with just enough words to clarify the visual.

You can choose from many types of graphs, including line graphs; vertical, horizontal, and stacked bar graphs; pictographs; and pie charts. *Line graphs* show relationship changes over time; *bar graphs* compare countable data at a specific moment in time; *pie charts* and *stacked bar graphs* show parts of the whole or percentages; and *pictographs* replace bars with graphic symbols or icons. **Tip**: When you take a pie chart and tilt it into a 3-D pie chart, be aware that wedges in the foreground are distorted into looking more important while wedges in the back are distorted into looking smaller and less important than they really are.[4]

Because graphic visuals trigger the right brain and allow for faster comprehension of complicated data, they are especially useful in informative speeches. Sample student-produced text and graphic visuals are shown in Figure 7.2; professionally prepared visuals are shown in Figure 7.3.

Using the Correct Type Size

One of the most common mistakes that speakers (even experienced speakers) make in preparing visuals is to use text that is too small for easy audience viewing. Think back over your experiences as an audience member. Remember how frustrating it was to have a speaker hold up a poster or put up an overhead transparency with letters too small to read and say, "As you can see . . ."? To avoid this pitfall as you make the text for your posters, flip charts, chalkboards, and markerboards, keep the following guidelines in mind:

▶ *Titles* should be approximately 3 inches high.
▶ *Subtitles*, if used, should be 2 to 2½ inches high.
▶ *Text* should be 1½ inches high.

Figure 7.2
Student-Produced Text and Graphic Visuals

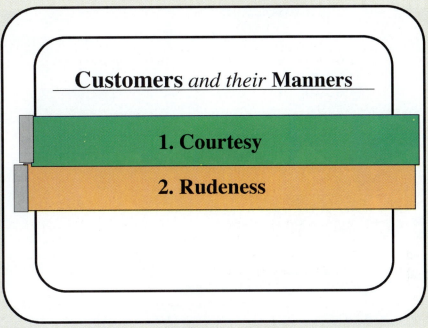

Visual 1   Transparency with color acetate overlays to highlight main points.

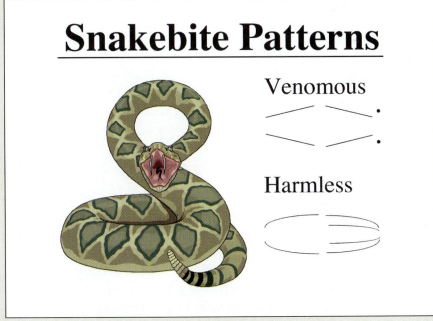

Visual 2   Text visual with clip art and hand-drawn snakebite patterns.

Figure 7.2 (continued)
Student-Produced Text and Graphic Visuals

Visual 3   Text visual with clip art.

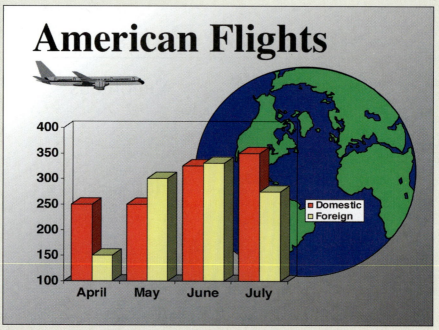

Visual 4   Clustered vertical bar graphs with background image.

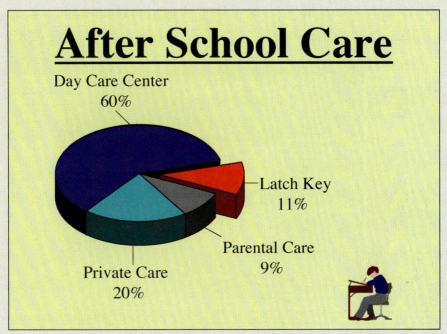

Visual 5   3-D pie chart with emphasized slice.

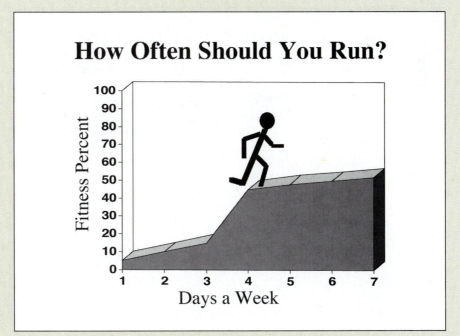

Visual 6   3-D filled line graph and pictograph.

Figure 7.3
Professionally Prepared Visuals

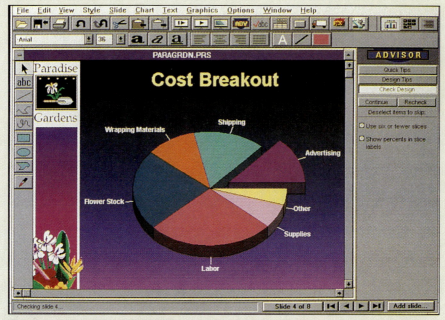

Visual 1   3-D pie chart shown being prepared on Harvard Graphics™ *(Software Publishing Corporation).*

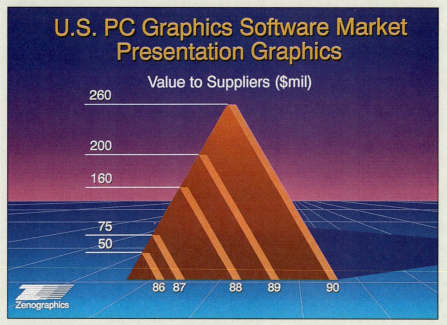

Visual 2   Stacked pyramids (a creative version of 3-D bar graphs) created by Pixie© *(Zenographics, Inc.).*

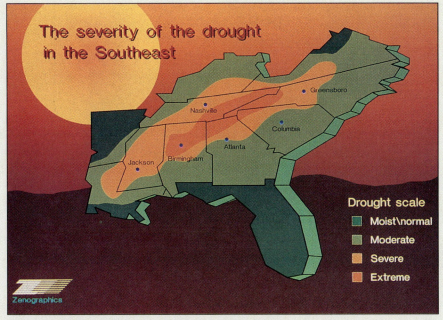

Visual 3   3-D map created by Pixie© *(Zenographics, Inc.).*

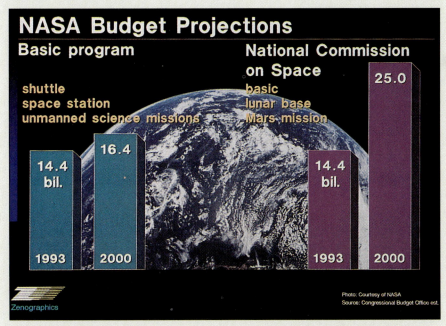

Visual 4   Bar graphs in front of scanned background photo by Mirage© *(Zenographics, Inc.).*

Figure 7.4
Determining Type Sizes in Points or Inches (measure only capital letters)

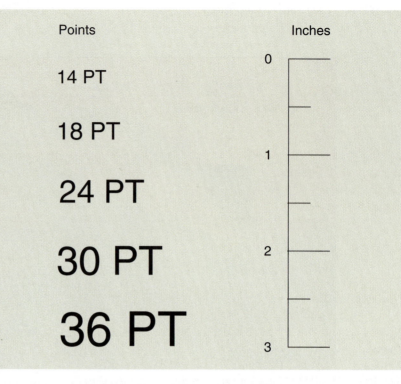

Although these size recommendations may seem too large at first, they will ensure that even the people in the back row can see your message clearly.

When you use slides, transparencies, and projected computer visuals, type size is measured in points. Your listeners will have no problems if you use the following suggested point sizes (see Figure 7.4):

	Title	Subtitle	Text
Transparencies	30–36 pt.	24 pt.	18 pt. (24 pt. if no subtitle)
Computer visuals	30–36 pt.	24 pt.	18 pt. (24 pt. if no subtitle)
Slides	24 pt.	18 pt.	14 pt. (18 pt. if no subtitle)

Remember, you can always use larger type sizes if needed, but you should never use type sizes smaller than those recommended here. Obviously regular typewriter and computer print sizes will *not* work! Compare the size of the type used in this paragraph (10 point) to the suggested type sizes for titles, subtitles, and text as shown in Figure 7.4.

Selecting the Correct Typeface

There are over 10,000 different typefaces in existence and over 1,000 readily available typefaces for personal computer users.[5] With so many choices it is important to know how to select the correct typefaces for your visuals. Typefaces can affect the readability of your visuals and will either harmonize with or distract from the overall tone or style of your speech.

Typeface explained   A typeface is a collection of upper and lowercase letters, punctuation marks, symbols, and figures that are stylistically consistent.[6] Suggested typefaces for visuals include Helvetica, Times Roman, Century, Garamond, Palatino, Optima, Bodoni, Futura, and Poster Bodoni. In the terminology of desktop publishing programs, the word *font* is now used interchangeably with *typeface*.

In preparing text for visuals, it's important to distinguish between serif and sans serif typefaces. A **serif** typeface has small lines or finishing strokes (feet) that extend from the main letter stems to varying degrees (for example, Century). A **sans serif** typeface, on the other hand, has no serifs or varying strokes and is more geometric looking (for example, Helvetica). Serif typefaces, such as Times Roman, Palatino, and Garamond, work well for the text of a visual and are excellent to use when you need a readable yet small type for bar graphs or pie charts. Sans serif typefaces, such as Helvetica and Futura, are boring in long passages of text but are excellent for visuals (especially titles and subtitles) because they project so well.

Typeface connotations   A typeface can affect both the readability and power of a visual. Therefore selecting the right typeface is similar in importance to selecting the proper clothes for a specific occasion—whether casual, corporate, or formal. Different typefaces have a different image or tone, and the best visual aids include typefaces that harmonize with the content and style of your speech. Figure 7.5 shows some sample typefaces and the tone or image they

Figure 7.5
Nine Different Typefaces, Each Displaying the Image or Connotation It Generally Suggests to Audiences

Title	Text	Image
Helvetica with Times Roman		Classical business look
Helvetica with Century		Traditional, nostalgic look
Helvetica with Garamond		Bold, direct look
Helvetica with Helvetica		Modern, urban look
Times Roman with Times Roman		Official, confidence-inspiring look
Century with Century		Reassuring, friendly, lively look
Futura with Bodoni		Collegiate or athletic look
Futura with Garamond		Corporate look
Futura with Times Roman		High fashion, "tabloid" look
Poster Bodoni with Times Roman		Sophisticated, trendy look
Poster Bodoni with Futura		Light, artistic look
Optima with *Garamond Italic*		Glamorous, elegant look
Optima with Palatino		Soft, gentle look
Optima with Optima		Restrained, formal look
Palatino Italic with Palatino		Fresh, modern, upbeat look
Helvetica Extended with **Bodoni Bold**		**Fitness club look**
Helvetica Extended with Futura		Modern, clean look

Figure 7.6

Successful Typeface Combinations and Projected Connotations

tend to portray. Imagine the confusion an audience would feel if you were giving a speech on a serious topic but your visuals used Poster Bodoni, a playful typeface. Sometimes the typeface you choose depends as much on your audience as on the topic. For example, if you were speaking to a group of skeptical parents about the educational values of a day-care facility, a Times Roman typeface would give your visuals an official, confidence-inspiring look. However, if you were speaking on the personal, loving attention that the day-care facility gives to each child, Century would be a good choice because it portrays a friendly, caring tone.

Sometimes the only way to be sure that your visuals are sending the message you desire is to see them projected on a screen—once they are enlarged, the tone is more obvious. Combining typefaces is not always easy. Figure 7.6 gives you some successful typeface combinations and their projected images.[7] **Tip**: Generally use no more than two different typefaces per visual, and be consistent in your use of typefaces for all visuals used in a particular speech.

General Design Principles

▼ ▼ ▼

Before we discuss specific design rules for text and graphic visuals, let's look at four general design principles that apply to all visuals, whether text or graphic. A summary of these design principles discussed by Robin Williams in *The Non-Designer's Design Book*[8] follows:

Contrast
The idea behind contrast is to avoid elements on the page that are merely *similar*. If the elements (type, color, size, line thickness, shape, etc.) are not the *same*, then make them **very different**. Contrast is often the most important visual attraction on a page.

Repetition
Repeat visual elements of the design through the piece. You can repeat color, shape, texture, spatial relationships, line thicknesses, sizes, etc. This helps develop the organization and strengthens the unity.

Alignment
Nothing should be placed on the page arbitrarily. Every element should have some visual connection with another element on the page. This creates a clean, sophisticated, fresh look.

Proximity
Items relating to each other should be grouped close together. When several items are in close proximity to each other, they become one visual unit rather than several separate units. This helps organize information and reduces clutter.[9]

Analyzing Figure 7.7 Using Design Principles

Let's illustrate how these four design principles can really make a difference in the quality of a visual aid by applying them to an actual visual from a speech on choosing a day care. Look at the transparency shown in Figure 7.7. What's right about this transparency? The speaker has chosen Century as the typeface (a typeface that gives a caring, friendly impression), which seems appropriate for the topic. The type is large enough for easy audience viewing (the title is 36-point and the main ideas are 30-point), and only necessary words have been used on the visual. Also, a two-line underline separates the title from the main points, which helps the audience grasp the organization of the visual. This visual, then, is basically good.

So, what's wrong? It's fairly bland, isn't it? Nothing attracts the eye. This transparency does not follow the four general design principles presented by Williams:

1. Even with the title in boldface, there isn't enough *contrast*. The type sizes of the main points and the title are too similar for contrast.

Figure 7.7
How Would You
Improve This Visual?

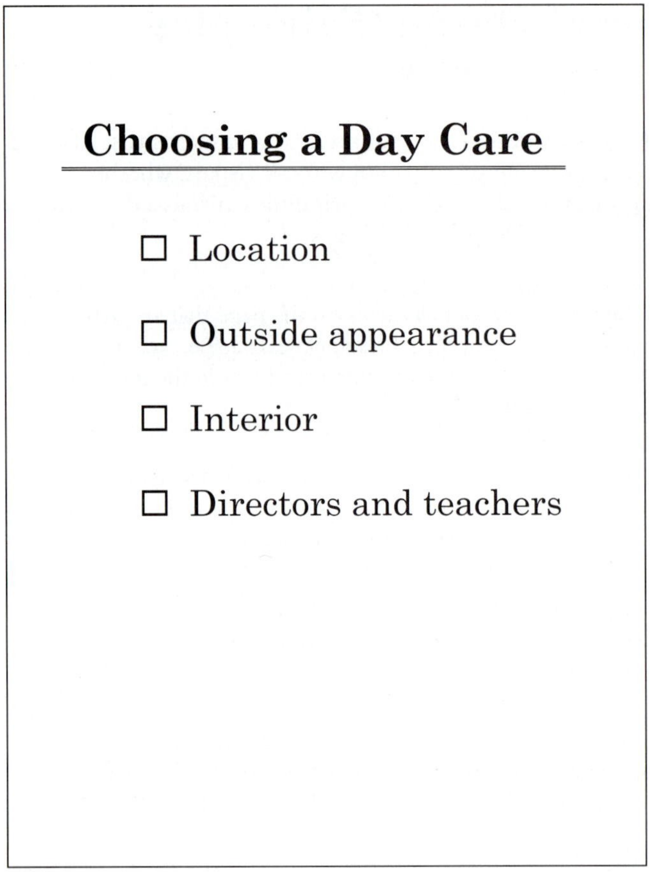

Choosing a Day Care

☐ Location

☐ Outside appearance

☐ Interior

☐ Directors and teachers

2.   There isn't enough *repetition* throughout the transparency. The bullets (squares in front of the main points) do repeat, but they are too bland to be noticed. The boldface of the title needs to be repeated somewhere—maybe the bullets could be filled in or the underline could be made bold.

3.   The main points are in *alignment*, but they don't line up with anything else on the page. If the main points were centered (normally not a good idea), they would align with the title and underline, which are already centered. According to Williams, "Every item should have a visual connection with something else on the page."[10] Right now, neither the title nor the underline do.

4.   There is so much space between the title and the first main point and between each of the main points that it seems as if there are five separate items on the page. Closer *proximity* between items is needed so they become a visual unit. **Tip**: Avoid double-line-spacing between main points when possible—1½-line-spacing gives more visual proximity.

Redesigning Figure 7.7 into a More Powerful Visual

How can we redesign the day care visual to incorporate the four design principles? Figure 7.8 shows one approach:

1. To show *contrast*, the type size of the title is larger (40-point) while the type size of the list is smaller (24-point).

2. To establish *repetition*, the boldface of the title is repeated in the solid bullets (the dark squares) and the two dark lines.

3. To achieve *alignment*, the title, underline, and bullets line up on the left while the title, underline, graphic, and bottom line all align on the right. Besides making alignment easier to achieve, the graphic adds warmth and visual interest.

4. To maintain *proximity*, the main points in the list are grouped together as a visual unit.

This is only one of many possible ways to redesign the day-care visual. For example, another way to add contrast would be to change the typeface to

Figure 7.8
One Approach to
Redesigning Figure 7.7

Optima bold (36-point) for the title and Garamond italic (24-point) for the main points. This change in typeface would suggest a more classy day-care environment. Color would also add power to the visual. **Tip:** When time allows, prepare two or more versions of each transparency to experiment with design possibilities.

Text Visuals: Specific Rules[11]

▼ ▼ ▼

The rules for text visuals are summarized in Figure 7.9. Before reading further, look at Figure 7.9 to see how many of the rules listed in the visual are violated in this figure. Then, continue reading and see if you were correct. Remember, if visual aids require effort to read, the audience is forced into a reading mode rather than a listening mode. Listeners can't pay attention to what you are saying while they are reading your visual; therefore a good visual should make sense in six seconds or less.

Use No More Than Four to Six Lines of Text

Not counting the title and subtitle(s), a visual containing more than six lines of text takes too long for your audience to grasp. Of course, if the text is a list containing single words, seven or eight lines might be fine. In general, if you need

Figure 7.9
Effective Visuals Can Be Read in Six Seconds or Less. How Much of This Visual Can You Read in Six Seconds?

DESIGN RULES FOR TEXT VISUALS

- YOU SHOULD USE ONLY FOUR TO SIX LINES OF TYPE PER VISUAL.

- BE SURE TO LIMIT EACH LINE TO NOT MORE THAN FORTY CHARACTERS.

- IT IS BEST TO USE PHRASES RATHER THAN SENTENCES.

- IF YOU USE UPPER- AND LOWERCASE TYPE, IT IS EASIER TO READ.

- USING A SIMPLE TYPEFACE IS EASIER TO READ AND DOES NOT DETRACT FROM YOUR PRESENTATION.

- IF YOU ALLOW THE SAME AMOUNT OF SPACE AT THE TOP OF EACH VISUAL, YOU MAKE IT EASIER FOR YOUR LISTENER TO FOLLOW YOU.

- YOU CAN EMPHASIZE YOUR MAIN POINTS WITH COLOR AND LARGE TYPE.

more than six lines of text, you probably should either split the information into two visuals or narrow and simplify your text. **Tip**: If you feel the audience needs more information than you can place on your visuals, put it in a handout. (Figure 8.2 in the next chapter shows a sample handout that includes reduced copies of speaker transparencies along with additional text.)

Limit Each Line to Forty Characters

If your text contains more than forty characters per line (including letters *and* spaces), you aren't leaving enough *white space* (space that contains no text or graphics). White space is essential for fast comprehension and keeps your visual from looking cluttered and unorganized. Use white space between items and on all four sides of your visual. Keep in mind, however, that although some white space between lines makes the text easier to read, too much white space (such as in Figure 7.1) makes the lines of text look unrelated.

Use Phrases Rather Than Sentences

Eliminate unnecessary words so listeners can grasp the content of your visual in six seconds or less. In Figure 7.9, note how full sentences slow down comprehension. Figure 7.10 presents the same key information using easy-to-comprehend phrases. Which visual would you rather have an instructor use in a lecture?

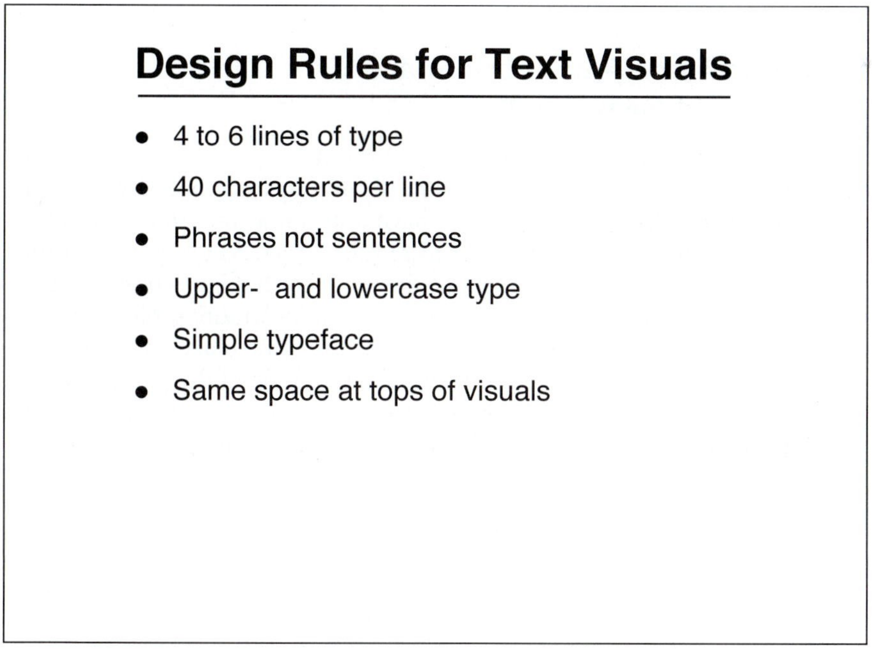

Design Rules for Text Visuals

- 4 to 6 lines of type
- 40 characters per line
- Phrases not sentences
- Upper- and lowercase type
- Simple typeface
- Same space at tops of visuals

Figure 7.10
Which Transparency Would You Rather Have an Instructor Use in Class—This One or the One in Figure 7.9?

Use Upper- and Lowercase Type

ONE OF THE EASIEST WAYS TO IMPROVE AUDIENCE COMPREHENSION OF YOUR VISUALS IS TO USE UPPER AND LOWERCASE LETTERS RATHER THAN ALL-CAPITALS ON YOUR TITLES, SUBTITLES, AND TEXT. If you need a larger title, use a larger type size—don't use all-capitals. Research has shown that text in all-capitals is more difficult to read and comprehend. To illustrate why this is true, try a brief experiment using Figure 7.11. The word *official* has been divided into two parts. Hold your hand over the top part and ask at least four people to read the bottom part. Now hold your hand over the bottom part and ask four other people to read the top part. Which part were more people able to read correctly? The reason the top part was easier to read is that word recognition comes mainly from the upper half of lowercase letters. However, when the word *official* is put in all-capitals (OFFICIAL), it becomes a shapeless box that cannot be instantly recognized.[12] Therefore use all caps only for special emphasis.

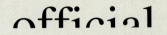

Figure 7.11
Word Recognition Experiment

Word recognition comes mainly from the upper half of lowercase letters, which is why all-caps are difficult to read.

Source: *J. Michael Adams, David D. Faux, and Lloyd J. Rieber, Printing Technology, 3rd ed. (Albany, NY: Delmar, 1988), p. 48.*

Use Simple Typefaces

Many of the typefaces available for use on personal **computers are completely inappropriate** and basically illegible **except for special emphasis.** You will want to select a typeface that harmonizes with your topic and that is visually interesting yet easy to read. The typefaces suggested earlier in this chapter have stood the test of time and are known to work for visual aids. Feel free to experiment, but don't get carried away.

Leave the Same Amount of Space at the Top of Each Visual

Many speakers incorrectly center the content on each of their visuals vertically—that is, they leave an equal amount of white space above and below the text. This means that some visual aids have only a few lines in the middle of the page while others have an entire page full of text. As a result, each time you project a transparency or slide onto the screen or hold up a poster, the audience has to search for the title. Your visuals will look more professional and be easier to comprehend if the text begins at the same place on each visual. For transparencies place the title 2 inches from the top of the page; for slides locate the title 1½ inches from the top; for posters and flip charts place the title approximately 3 inches from the top (some exceptions may be necessary, of course).

Use Clip Art, Larger Type, and Color for Emphasis

In the section on design principles, we discussed the importance of contrast. Three ways to add contrast and emphasis are by using clip art, larger type, and color. For example, clip art (as well as pictures, photos, and freehand drawings) serves to anchor the content of your visual in the minds of the audience. Look back at the visual in Figure 7.1. Did you discover at least six ways to make the visual more powerful? If you didn't, here's one hint: What about a picture of a house or a for-sale sign? Even if you made no other changes, the visual would be improved by adding some clip art.

Large-sized type and color are both excellent ways to direct the eye to areas you wish to emphasize. The largest and boldest type will always be read first unless you have also used color to emphasize. When you first started reading this section, did your eye latch onto the phrase *Figure 7.1* because of its bright color? If you want to direct your audience's attention to a portion of a complicated diagram, color is the way to do it. Even on a color visual, a bright, contrasting color will focus your audience's attention. We will discuss the use of color further in the last section of this chapter.

Graphic Visuals: Specific Rules[13]

▼ ▼ ▼

In order for graphic visuals (which emphasize illustrations over words) to trigger the right brain and allow for comprehension of complicated data in only six seconds, the visuals must be carefully designed. In addition to the general design principles of contrast, repetition, alignment, and proximity discussed earlier in this chapter, some specific rules apply just to graphic visuals. Let's look at these rules.

Limit Data to What Is Absolutely Necessary

Figure 7.12 illustrates the importance of using only the data needed to support your verbal points. Because the speech deals with sales, the line graphs for earnings and dividends (as well as the distracting grid lines) are not necessary and actually obscure the seriousness of the sales decline. It is always a good idea, however, to have additional materials ready in case of audience questions. For example, the earnings and dividends line graphs would make excellent overlays that you could use to answer a question. Figure 7.13 illustrates how much more effective it is to eliminate the distracting data point markers and to label individual line graphs when more than one line graph is included.

Figure 7.12
Limiting Data

Limit data to what is needed to support your verbal point and eliminate distracting grid lines.

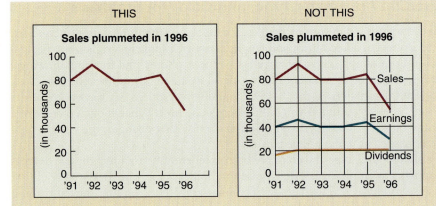

Figure 7.13
Eliminating Data Points

Use more than one line graph when necessary, but for viewing ease, eliminate data points.

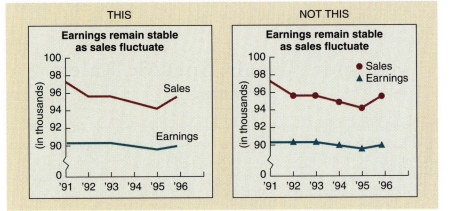

Group Data When Possible

Even after you have limited the data to only what is absolutely necessary, try grouping smaller categories of data into one larger category. Figure 7.14 illustrates the principle of grouping data. When seven small categories of costs were grouped under the general heading of "Other expenses," the amount of time needed to grasp the pie chart was greatly reduced. You could follow this visual with a second one that lists the content of "Other expenses." **Tip**: Although you may be tempted to put more than one graph on a visual, remember that multiple graphs are more difficult to comprehend and take longer to read.

Keep Background Lines and Data Points to a Minimum

In most cases grid lines (like those used in Figure 7.12) and data points (like those in Figure 7.13) should be eliminated from your visuals. Grid lines and data points are distracting, take too much time to interpret, and are not necessary for understanding. If you know your audience (say, a group of engineering students) expects grid lines and data points, then use them, but include only essential data points and make the grid lines lighter than the data lines.

Make Bars Wider Than the Spaces Between Them

When the white space between the bars is wider than the bars themselves, as in Figure 7.15, the "trapped" white space visually pushes the bars apart, making them seem unrelated.[14] Therefore, for faster audience viewing, make sure that the bars are wider than the spaces between them, regardless of whether the bars are placed horizontally or vertically.

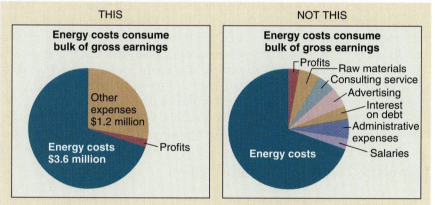

Figure 7.14
Grouping Data

Group distracting data under a general heading.

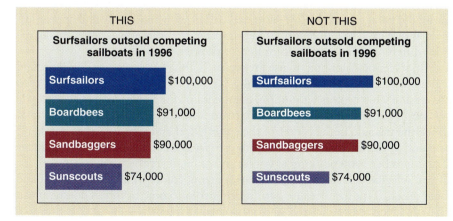

Figure 7.15
Limiting White Space

For viewing ease, make the space between bars narrower than the bars.

Always Use Headings

Whether your graphic visual is a chart, graph, map, or picture, always use a title or heading to reinforce your point. For example, a hand-drawing of a skier in the correct position to begin water skiing might seem obvious to you as a speaker, but without a title or heading, the exact purpose of the visual wouldn't be immediately clear to your audience.

Visual Aids and Color
▼ ▼ ▼

Designing color into your visuals is so much fun that it's easy to go overboard. Don't forget that when color is poorly used, it can be as great a distraction as too many words or a cluttered graph. However, if used to highlight, organize, or add interest, color has real benefits. A study conducted by the University of Minnesota and the 3M Corporation found that color transparencies were more persuasive and produced better recall than black-and-white transparencies.[15] In a related study the Bureau of Advertising found that readers are 80 percent more likely to read a color ad than a black-and-white ad and that sales from color ads were 50–80 percent greater than sales from noncolor ads. They also found that recall of ad content was 55–78 percent greater for color ads than black-and-white ads.[16] Also, colors are known to produce an emotional response. For example, cool colors such as blue and green generally have a calming effect on viewers; warm colors such as red and orange generally have a stimulating, invigorating, and sometimes anger-producing effect.[17]

Using the Twelve-Hue Color Wheel

One of the safest ways to pick color combinations is by using a color wheel such as the twelve-hue wheel shown in Figure 7.16.[18] **Hue** is the actual color selected from available colors—each color on the color wheel is a different hue. **Saturation**, on the other hand, is the amount of color used in the selected shade (fully saturated colors are vivid; low-saturated colors show more gray and appear less colorful). **Tip**: Use different hues for unrelated items; however, use a single hue with different saturation levels for items that are related.[19]

In selecting color hues to use for accent, highlights, graphs, and background colors, usually pick colors that visually *harmonize* (are pleasing to the eye). To determine which colors harmonize, use the following method:[20] Make a triangle the same size as the one in Figure 7.16 and number the corners from 1 to 3. Place the triangle in the center of the color wheel and turn it so that number 1 is pointing to a color you would like to use (say, green). The colors that number 2 and number 3 are pointing to (violet and orange) are the harmonizing colors. If you selected yellow-orange, the harmonizing colors would be red-violet and blue-green. **Tip**: Just because harmonizing colors come in threes doesn't mean that you need to use all three; one or two may be plenty.

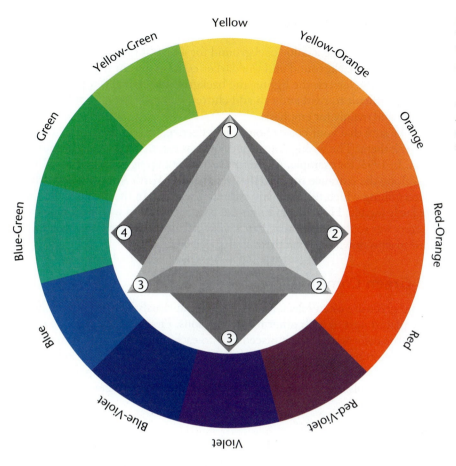

Figure 7.16
Twelve-Hue Color
Wheel Used in Picking
Colors for Visual Aids

*The triangle is used to find
colors that harmonize; the
square is used to find pairs of
opposite colors that complement each other.*

Another way to use the color wheel is to find pairs of complementary colors that work well together. *Complementary* colors are opposites on the color
wheel (like red and green or blue and orange) and are less relaxing than harmonizing colors. Although opposites tend to vibrate (seem to move on the page)
when placed side by side, when used with two other opposite colors, they can
make eye-catching visual aids. To find two pairs of opposite colors, use the following method:[21] Make a square like the one in Figure 7.16 and number the
corners from 1 to 4. Put the square in the center of the twelve-hue color wheel
and point the number 1 toward a color you like. The other corners of the square
will identify three other colors that complement the selected color. For example, if you selected the color yellow, the other three colors would be red-orange,
violet, and blue-green (colors 1 and 3 and colors 2 and 4 are opposites). Just remember not to place opposite colors side by side because the vibration makes it
difficult to focus on them. Complementary colors are especially good to use
when emphasis is needed.

A third way to use the color wheel is to select spectral hues (colors that
are next to each other on the color wheel). Spectral hues have low contrast

but are perfect for the subtle effect needed for shadowing or suggesting three dimensions.[22]

If you wish to use a color background for a text or graphic visual, use the lighter color as background and the darker color as accent or for the letters. The smaller the letters, the lighter the background.[23] However, because they are more difficult to read and can add clutter, colored letters should be used sparingly and mainly for emphasis.

To be sure that your color choices are effective, project them onto a screen and check them. The wrong color combinations can make your visuals difficult to read. In 1993, for example, American Airlines put up signs (each listing 15–20 cities) along the entrance roads to the Dallas–Fort Worth Airport to aid drivers in determining which terminal and gate they wanted. In the daylight the signs were fairly legible. However, at night the blue background with dark blue capital letters was so difficult to read that several accidents occurred as drivers were forced to slow down to locate their destination city.[24]

Red-Green Combination

Red and green are often selected for bar graphs in visuals. However, they should not be placed next to each other for two reasons. First, because they are opposites on the color wheel, when placed next to each other, they appear to vibrate, creating eyestrain. Second, many people have red-green color blindness, often without even knowing it. Why take the chance that one or more people in your audience may misinterpret your data because they can't distinguish between red and green?

Final Thoughts on Color

As you add colors to your visuals, keep these additional suggestions in mind:

▶ It's not a good idea to select colors at random. Use the color wheel to select harmonizing and complementary colors that won't be jarring on the eye.

▶ Whatever colors you select, be consistent throughout the visuals for any one speech. For example, you wouldn't want to use a different-color background for each visual.

▶ Although dark backgrounds are often used on slides, the study conducted by the University of Minnesota and the 3M Corporation, mentioned earlier, found that color slides were judged to be more difficult to read and less effective than color transparencies unless the slides had light-color backgrounds and were shown in a completely dark room.[25] The same study found color transparencies to be more effective than any of the other types of visual aids, including slides.[26]

▶ Color photographs can be as effective on transparencies as on slides. Even posters or flip charts can use color markers to highlight areas of importance. **Tip**: Use the brightest colors to highlight the most important information.

Don't be afraid to use color, but do limit the number of colors you use—more than four colors usually makes visuals look cluttered and slows down audience comprehension time.

After reading the chapter, did you find at least six changes that would make the mortgage visual in Figure 7.1 more powerful? Figure 7.17 illustrates one possible way to redesign this visual. Compare your recommendations with the following suggested changes:

1. Change the type from all-capitals to upper and lowercase letters.
2. Revise the title—the main points are about mortgages, not mortgage companies.
3. Add more contrast between the title, subtitle, and main points. In the original visual all three were in boldface. Both the title and subtitle were 30-point Palatino; the main points were 20-point. Now the title is 40-point,

Summary
▼ ▼ ▼

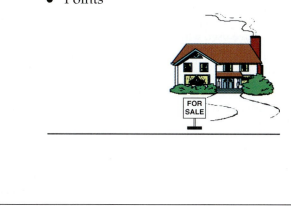

Figure 7.17
A Redesigned and More Powerful Version of the Visual in Figure 7.1

the subtitle is 30-point, and the main points are 24-point. For additional contrast the title is now in boldface and the subtitle in Garamond italic.

4. Add clip art to provide contrast and interest and to visually conceptualize the topic for the audience.

5. Improve the alignment. Before the only things in alignment were the main points, but they didn't align with either the title, subtitle, or underline. Now the title, subtitle, and underline all align on the left; both lines, the clip art, and the first main point align on the right; and the bullets align with the line at the bottom.

6. Improve proximity by grouping main points closer together. Originally each line on the visual looked like an unrelated item. Now the eye sees a visual unit.

7. Use repetition by adding a line at the bottom of the visual that is parallel to the title underline. The two dark lines, the dark bullets, and the dark underline also add repetition to the visual.

By selecting and designing effective visuals, you will help your listeners maintain their interest and remember the important points in your speech. As you read the section on types of visuals, was there one in which you were especially interested? An overhead projector with transparencies is probably the most commonly used type of visual aid. You will certainly want to practice designing and using transparencies until you are comfortable with them.

When designing your text and graphic visuals, remember to select your typefaces with care and to use a type size that is large enough for the audience to read with ease. Also design your visuals keeping the four design principles—contrast, repetition, alignment, and proximity—in mind. And, of course, have fun with color, but use it with caution.

Practice Suggestions
▼ ▼ ▼

1. Select the manuscript of a speech that you would like to deliver to the class at a later date. For speech ideas look in *Vital Speeches* (a magazine in your campus library) or Appendix C in this text. Be sure to select a subject you can speak on with enthusiasm. Decide what kinds of visuals would be best to use with this presentation. Prepare two visuals that the original speaker could have used with the speech.

2. Based on this chapter prepare a list of the ten most important dos and don'ts for designing visual aids. Compare your list with one or two classmate's lists, and justify your choices.

3. Prepare a *chart* or *graph* using the information in the following paragraph:

> From the beginning of creation to 1850 A.D. world population grew to one billion. It grew to two billion by 1930, three billion by 1960, four billion by 1979, and five billion by 1987, with six billion en route. Every 33 months, the current population of America, 257,000,000 people, is added to the planet.[27]

Ask two or three friends to help you think of ways that your chart or graph might be improved.

4. Be creative and prepare a *text visual* that conveys the main idea in this paragraph:

> In a *Time Magazine* cover story entitled, "Drowsy America," the director of Stanford University's sleep center concluded that, "Most Americans no longer know what it feels like to be fully alert." Lacking a balance between work and play, responsibility and respite, "getting things done" can become an end-all. We function like human doings instead of human beings. We begin to link executing the items on our growing "to do" lists with feelings of self-worth. As the list keeps growing longer, the lingering sense of more to do infiltrates our sense of self-acceptance. What's worse, our entire society seems to be irrevocably headed toward a new epoch of human existence. Is frantic, however, any way to exist as a nation? Is it any way to run your life?[28]

Compare your visual with that of a classmate. Decide what is best about each visual and what could be improved. Make the changes. Do you agree that the changes improved the effectiveness of your visual?

5. Practice the design rules covered in this chapter by redesigning one or more of the visual aids in the chapter. The visuals in Figure 7.2 (prepared by students) and Figure 7.3 (prepared by professionals) would be especially interesting to redesign. If your instructor is willing, why not have everyone in the class redesign the same two or three visuals. Ask three people from the community or from the department to serve as judges and select the three best visual aids.

Notes

1. Margaret Y. Rabb, *The Presentation Design Book: Tips, Techniques and Advice for Creating Effective, Attractive Slides, Overheads, Multimedia Presentations, Screen Shows and More*, 2nd ed. (Chapel Hill, NC: Ventana Press, 1993), p. 49.
2. Cheryl Hamilton with Cordell Parker, *Communicating for Results: A Guide for Business and the Professions*, 4th ed. (Belmont, CA: Wadsworth, 1993), pp. 393–394.
3. R. Kaufmann and M. O. O'Neill, "Color Names and Focal Colours on Electronic Displays," *Ergonomics* 30 (August 1993), 881–890.
4. Michael Talman, *Understanding Presentation Graphics* (Alameda, CA: SYBEX, Inc., 1992), p. 247.
5. Steve Byers, *The Electronic Type Catalog* (New York: Bantam Books, 1992), p. xii.
6. Byers, *Electronic Type Catalog*, p. 4.
7. These typeface combinations and their likely connotations were compiled from the following sources: Carol Buchanan, *Quick Solutions for Great Type Combinations* (Cincinnati, OH: North Light Books, 1993), and Don Dewsnap, *Desktop Publisher's Easy Type Guide: The 150 Most Important Typefaces* (Rockport, MA: Rockport Publishers, 1992).
8. Robin Williams, *The Non-Designer's Design Book: Design and Typographic Principles for the Visual Novice* (Berkeley, CA: Peachpit Press, 1994), p. 14.
9. Williams, *Non-Designer's Design Book*, p. 14.
10. Williams, *Non-Designer's Design Book*, p. 27.
11. Revised from Marya W. Holcombe and Judith K. Stein, *Presentations for Decision Makers: Strategies for Structuring and Delivering Your Ideas* (Belmont, CA: Lifetime Learning Publications, 1983), pp. 76–79.

12. Revised from Floyd K. Baskette, Jack Z. Sissors, and Brian S. Brooks, *The Art of Editing*, 5th ed. (New York: Macmillan, 1992), p. 267.

13. Based on Holcombe and Stein, *Presentations*, pp. 79–97; Figures 7.12–7.15 from Holcombe and Stein, pp. 76–79.

14. Williams, *Non-Designer's Design Book*, p. 22.

15. D. R. Vogel, G. W. Dickson, and J. A. Lehman, *Persuasion and the Role of Visual Presentation Support: The UM/3M Study* (St. Paul, MN: 3M General Offices, 1986).

16. Cited in Virginia Johnson, "Picture Perfect Presentations," *The Toastmaster* (February 1990), 7.

17. Ana C. Gardano, "Cultural Influence on Emotional Response to Color: A Research Study Comparing Hispanics and Non-Hispanics," *American Journal of Art Therapy* 24 (May 1986), 119–124.

18. Johannes Itten, *The Art of Color*, translated by Ernst van Haagen (New York: Van Nostrand Reinhold, 1973), pp. 34–35.

19. J. A. Conway, "The Interaction of Color Code Type and Information Type on the Perception and Interpretation of Visual Displays," *Dissertation Abstracts International* 48 (1988), 2123–2124.

20. Itten, *Art of Color*, pp. 118–119.

21. Itten, *Art of Color*, pp. 118–119.

22. Rabb, *Presentation Design Book*, p. 123.

23. Russell N. Baird, Arthur T. Turnbull, and Duncan McDonald, *The Graphics of Communication*, 5th ed. (New York: Holt, Rinehart & Winston, 1987), p. 241.

24. J. Lynn Lunsford, "D/FW Signs Blamed for More Crashes: 3 Incidents in Two Weeks Attributed to Billboards," *Dallas Morning News* (September 4, 1994), pp. 31A and 36 A.

25. Vogel, Dickson, and Lehman, *Persuasion*, pp. 9–10.

26. Vogel, Dickson, and Lehman, *Persuasion*, pp. 11–12.

27. Jefferson Davidson, "Overworked Americans or Overwhelmed Americans," *Vital Speeches* 15 (May 15, 1993), 471.

28. Davidson, "Overworked Americans," p. 471.

PROJECTED EARNINGS
10
8
6
4
2
0
NOV
JAN
Projections
se Market
ish Satellite
ove Productivity
D Funding

Delivering Your Message

W HAT DO LEE IACOCCA, Oprah Winfrey, and Norman Schwarzkopf have in common?[1] They are public speakers who really know how to connect with an audience. They are enthusiastic, interesting, powerful, persuasive, caring, and—most important of all—believable.

Lee Iacocca took over Chrysler Corporation when it was several billion dollars in the red. He was able to convince Congress to approve a $1.5-billion loan guarantee. He was also able to convince Chrysler workers who had received huge wage cuts and Chrysler dealers who were being wooed by Japanese franchises to pull together to get the company back on its feet. And finally, he was able to persuade the American public to buy Chrysler cars through his personal appearances in advertisements. Chrysler was able to pay back the federal loan seven years before it was due.[2] What made Iacocca so effective? "Iacocca was able to get people to cooperate because they believed in him," Maryann N. Keller, Wall Street auto analyst, told *The New York Times*.[3]

Oprah Winfrey became a popular talk-show host when it seemed that no one could compete with Phil Donahue. One month after she arrived in Chicago, her show "A. M. Chicago" drew even with "Donahue," and after three months it nosed ahead.[4] Oprah's show (now on national TV) continues to lead the talk-show ratings after nine years. How does she do it? She makes it seem as if she is speaking directly to each of her listeners, she is real, and she is believable.

General "Stormin'" Norman Schwarzkopf inspired the American people and his troops to feel loyalty and confidence in him during Operation Desert Storm. His press briefing at the conclusion of the Persian Gulf War became a best-selling videocassette. During that briefing he explained his "Hail Mary" surprise plan with clarity. His dynamic, warm voice cracked with emotion for the lost soldiers, and he was believable. He was equally effective when speaking before a joint session of Congress a month later. The speech, which lasted only 16½ minutes, was interrupted by standing ovations dozens of times.[5] (You can read the speech General Schwarzkopf gave to the departing troops at Dhahran on March 8, 1991, in Appendix C.)

These three speakers do more than just prepare convincing and well-organized ideas; they present their ideas in a believable manner. They communicate verbally, visually, and vocally with their audiences. And so can you. These speakers weren't always so good. They learned through their mistakes, just like George Bush, the forty-first President of the United States. When Bush first ran in the Republican primaries, critics referred to him as "The Wimp" because of his "high-pitched, reedy, and whiny" voice.[6] Yet when he ran for president, his voice sounded much stronger, more sincere, and authoritative. How did he do it? With the coaching of political media advisor Roger Ailes, he was able to "bring his voice down into a deeper, more authoritative range."[7] Bush didn't suddenly become more knowledgeable or more sincere; he simply learned better how to communicate his knowledge and sincerity to others. When his vocal code began to send the same message as his visual and verbal codes, he became more believable.

As Lee Iacocca said in his autobiography, "You can have brilliant ideas, but if you can't get them across, your brains won't get you anywhere."[8] Your delivery

Effective speakers communicate verbally, visually, and vocally with their audiences.

© *Mike Theiler/Reuters/Bettmann*

isn't more important than what you have to say, but without good delivery your audience may never hear what you have to say. To make your presentation believable to your audience, your verbal, visual, and vocal delivery must all be effective. This chapter will give you suggestions for effectively using all three codes.

Visual Delivery

▼ ▼ ▼

Since the first impression listeners form comes more from what they see than from what they hear, visual delivery will be discussed first—specifically, how you appear to your listeners and how you handle your visual aids.

Visual Delivery and You

As a speaker, your overall appearance, facial expressions, eye contact, posture, and gestures all affect how you are perceived by the audience.

Appearance   Right or wrong, audience members use your appearance as their first clue to your status, credibility, knowledge, and believability. Unless you are certain about what is appropriate for the audience and the occasion, the safest thing is to dress on the conservative side. For women this means suits or dresses in classic styles with nondistracting hairstyles and minimal jewelry. For men this means dress slacks and a sports coat or suit and tie with dark shoes. John T. Molloy, image consultant and author of *New Dress for Success* and *The Woman's Dress for Success Book*, has found that in general dark clothes communicate authority.[9] **Tip**: Even informally dressed audiences generally expect a guest speaker to have a professional, polished look.

Facial expressions and eye contact   We all enjoy listening to speakers who smile appropriately, look at us while speaking, and seem to enjoy giving speeches. With speakers who appear tense, don't smile, and only rarely make eye contract, listeners will probably react in one of two ways:

1. *Observation*: The speaker is nervous.

    Reason: The speaker's not prepared, is inexperienced, or is uncertain.

    Conclusion: Listening is not worth my time.

2. *Observation*: The speaker is lying.

    Reason: The speaker isn't an ethical, trustworthy person; is trying to manipulate us; or doesn't respect us.

    Conclusion: Listening is not worth my time.

In either case, your audience will tune out. On the other hand, listeners are much more likely to listen when you smile appropriately and make direct eye contact with them. In making eye contact, hold your gaze for three to five seconds before moving on to someone else; if your eyes dart too quickly, you will appear nervous. Also be sure to look at people in all parts of the room—some speakers inadvertently favor one side or the other.

Posture, movement, and gestures   A relaxed yet upright *posture* makes you look confident, friendly, and energetic. Avoid slumping your shoulders and putting your weight on one hip, both of which make you look less confident and less believable. Speakers have a tendency to concentrate on their posture from the waist up and to forget that their lower bodies may be sending conflicting messages. For example, the confidence indicated by upright, upper-body posture is sabotaged by nervous foot tapping or the "I-wish-I-were-someplace-else" look projected when you stand with your weight on one hip. For the best posture take a comfortable open stance with one foot slightly ahead of the other, and lean slightly forward without locking your knees. This posture gets you ready to move in any direction yet makes it almost impossible to sway or rock as some speakers do. Also, leaning slightly forward indicates that you have a positive feeling toward the audience.

Don't be afraid to move around occasionally. *Movement* can add interest, energy, and confidence to your presentation. To add emphasis, try moving at the beginning of an idea or as a transition between ideas. If you are using transparencies, be sure you are back at the overhead projector when it's time to put on the next transparency.

The best *gestures* are natural ones. If you don't worry about them, gestures will usually occur naturally. When speaking to a group of friends about an exciting event, you don't worry about when or how to gesture, do you? In the same way, if you concentrate on getting your meaning across while speaking, your gestures (such as a shrug of the shoulders) will come naturally. For example, imagine that it's the seventh-inning stretch at a baseball game and you're talking to a group of friends seated several rows away about the unbelievable catch made by the third baseman. Not only will you automatically speak louder, you will also exaggerate your gestures. The same should be true when speaking before an audience. The larger the audience, the bigger your gestures must be. Therefore, when speaking before a large audience, gesture as though you were in a large, noisy place.

If possible, videotape yourself while practicing your speech or have a friend observe you and make suggestions. Make sure that your gestures are clearly noticeable and look out for any distracting ones. If you notice a nervous gesture (such as playing with your hair or rubbing your nose), make a concerted effort to stop it or to replace it with a more appropriate gesture. When not gesturing, rest a hand on the lectern or let your hands fall naturally at your sides. By the way, using visual aids will keep your hands so busy that you won't have time to worry about them. Check your awareness of which gestures stimulate or hinder listening by answering the questions in Figure 8.1. Keep in mind that the context of the message may often influence the appropriateness of your gestures.

Visual Delivery and Your Visual Aids

Besides gestures another important part of your visual delivery is handling your visual aids. When you practice your speech, also practice using your visual aids. Let's look at ways for handling each type of visual aid.

Using transparencies   After placing a transparency on an overhead projector, most speakers turn around (with their backs to their audiences) to see if the overhead looks straight on the screen and is in focus. The first time you practice using transparencies, you will discover how strong this urge is to turn and look. However, turning your back on your audience not only looks unprofessional but keeps you from observing audience reactions to the visual. You won't need to look at the screen if you make sure that the projector is focused and the image is centered on the screen *before* your speech begins—and preferably before the audience arrives. **Tip**: Right above or below the projection glass, most overhead projectors have an indentation designed to hold a pointer. If you put a pencil in that indentation, you have a perfect alignment edge for your transparencies.

Directions: Put an "S" by those behaviors you think would *stimulate* listening. Put an "H" by those behaviors you think would *hinder* listening.

____ 1. Constantly moving eyes	____ 16. Looking delighted
____ 2. Smiling	____ 17. Puffing cheeks
____ 3. Nodding	____ 18. Looking straight at listeners
____ 4. Leaning forward	____ 19. Drumming fingers
____ 5. Pausing	____ 20. Shuffling papers
____ 6. Frowning	____ 21. Showing enthusiasm
____ 7. Looking at upper corner of room	____ 22. Hanging head down
____ 8. Rolling eyes	____ 23. Tilting head down
____ 9. Having relaxed body posture	____ 24. Narrowing eyes
____ 10. Folding arms across chest	____ 25. Scowling
____ 11. Pacing	____ 26. Playing with pointer
____ 12. Making eye contact	____ 27. Clearing throat often
____ 13. Jingling coins	____ 28. Moving about calmly
____ 14. Gesturing	____ 29. Sighing
____ 15. Looking out window	____ 30. Walking to side of podium

Answers

Behaviors 2–5, 9, 12, 14, 16, 18, 21, 23, 28, and 30 would stimulate listening. The remaining behaviors would most likely hinder listening.

Figure 8.1

Nonverbal Awareness
Check

*Check your awareness of a
speaker's nonverbal behaviors by completing the following scale.*

Each time you put on a new transparency, make sure the top or bottom of the frame is pushed against the pencil—perfect alignment without looking. This is easier than trying to line up the frame with the top edge of the projection glass.

Some speakers make the mistake of leaving a transparency on the screen until they are ready for the next one even though they are no longer referring to it. After you have finished discussing each transparency, you can turn off the projector or block the projector light with a small piece of cardboard. When the cardboard cover is flipped upward, the light shines on the screen as usual; when the cardboard cover is lowered, no light shines. **Tip**: Constantly turning the projector off and on can be irritating and distracting, so don't turn off the projector or lower the cardboard cover if you are planning to remove one transparency and immediately show another one. Simply remove the used transparency with one hand while you position the new transparency with the other hand. Practice will make this a fast and smooth operation.

Using slides   More practice is required to use slides effectively than most other types of visuals. First of all, you must learn how to use the remote control switch that allows you to change slides (in the dark it's easy to push the reverse button instead of the advance button). Or, if someone else is going to forward slides for you, you must practice so the helper knows when to advance the next slide without your having constantly to say, "Next slide, please." Second, since slides don't project well unless the room is dark, you will need to check on lighting options. In most speaking environments only two choices exist. Either the

Remember:

When using transparencies . . .

▶ *Don't turn and look at the screen behind you.* Instead, look at your audience or at the transparency on the projection glass.

▶ When placing and removing transparencies, *don't turn on the projector until your transparency is in place.* As soon as you are finished discussing each transparency, immediately replace it with another or turn off the projector (or block the projection light).

▶ *Bring an extra projector bulb and an extension cord* with you in case the bulb burns out or you need to rearrange the placement of the projector.

▶ *Arrive early* to do the following: Check to see that the projector is working and that the projection glass is clean. Place the projector in the correct position for the largest, clearest picture. Focus the projector using your first transparency. Determine where you should stand.

▶ When pointing to the screen, *take a couple of steps back so you are beside the screen* rather than in front of the screen, which is sure to block someone's view.

▶ When using a transparency containing a list of items, *read the list* so the audience will know what is coming and then *cover all but the first item with a heavy piece of cardboard* (the projector's fan will blow a regular sheet of paper onto the floor). Uncover each point as you are ready to discuss it.

room is put in total darkness (which is best for slide clarity) or the dimmers can be set so some light is on the speaker, which means that the screen is also bathed in light. If the background of your slides is a light color, some light won't hurt the readability of the slides; they just won't look as nice. However, if you are using dark-colored or black backgrounds on your slides, a dark environment is necessary for legibility. Also, unless there's a spotlight on you, the audience will have to depend on your verbal and vocal delivery in the darkened room since they can't see your facial expressions and gestures. This means you will need to practice more. **Tip**: Bring a pencil flashlight with you to place on the lectern so you can see your notes if the lectern doesn't have a light.

Using posters and flip charts   Although most speaking environments will have some type of easel to hold posters, they might not have an easel with a T-bar, necessary to hold up most flip chart pads. The safest thing might be for you to purchase your own inexpensive, light-weight easel with detachable T-bar. Most easels also have collapsible legs so they can be used as table easels. Or you might wish to purchase the type of flip chart pad that comes with a rigid backing board that folds into a self-standing easel you can set on a table. In any case make sure that you have a way to display your posters and flip charts in clear

Remember:

When using slides . . .

▶ *Practice several times* using the remote control and coping with a dark room.

▶ *Bring an extra projector bulb and an extension cord* with you in case they are needed.

▶ *Arrive early* to do the following: Make sure all necessary equipment is there and arranged as you want it. Check to see if dimmer switches will light the lectern yet leave the screen in darkness. If necessary, move the lectern to a lighted area.

▶ *Make sure that your slide carousel fits the projector* (not all carousels fit all projectors) and project two or three slides to *make sure that the slides are positioned in the tray correctly*. After your speech has begun, it's embarrassing to discover that your slides are in upside down or sideways.

view of your audience. Avoid setting posters in the tray of a wall-mounted chalkboard or markerboard if at all possible—both you and your posters will likely be too far from the audience.

Although posters are usually prepared ahead of time, flip charts are normally written in front of the audience for a spontaneous effect. As suggested in Chapter 7, prepare lightly penciled guidelines ahead of time that you can trace during the speech. This way you won't need notes and you avoid misspelling a word, making your letters too small, or writing at an angle.

Using objects, models, and handouts   The value of using objects to clarify points and add interest can easily be seen by watching a painting, cooking, or sewing program on television. Inspired by the way people on these programs use objects, one student, speaking on how to select the correct jogging shoe, used four shoes as well as a cutaway model of the inside of a jogging shoe to illustrate his points. Make sure your object is large enough for the audience to see clearly. If it's not, use a drawing or an enlarged model of the object, but have the "real" object on hand for the audience to view after your speech is finished.

Remember that objects (as well as any visual aid) can distract from your speech and your credibility as a speaker if not handled well. One student, speaking on bowling, brought in his bowling ball and dropped it on the floor as an attention-getter, but the audience wasn't impressed. Another speaker brought in a kitchen knife designed to cut through anything, but when he tried to slice through an aluminum can, he failed.

Handouts can also cause problems if not used correctly. Unless you plan for the audience to refer to your handouts in some way during the speech, wait until

Remember:

When using posters and flip charts . . .

▸ *Try using light green or pale blue poster boards* instead of white—they are less glaring for your audience to look at.

▸ When writing on posters, *use dark or black marker pens for your text with contrasting colors for emphasis.* Never write on posters in pastel colors (like yellow, pink, or light blue)—the audience will be unable to read them.

▸ *Try a flip chart pad with self-stick adhesive on the back of each sheet.* This way, when speaking to small groups, the completed sheets can be placed on the wall (in clear view of the audience) and referred to later in the speech or during the question-and-answer period.

▸ *Use watercolor markers on flip chart pads* because they won't bleed through the paper onto the next sheet the way permanent markers will.

▸ When referring to a poster or flip chart, be sure to *stand to the side of the easel and near to it so you won't block the visual from anyone's view.* If you will be using a lectern, position the easel near enough to the lectern so that only a step or two is required to reach your posters or to draw on the flip chart.

the speech is over to distribute them. Otherwise, audience members will likely read them instead of listening to you. If the handouts are needed during the speech, be prepared for a loss of attention as they are distributed.

In some professions speakers are expected to give paper copies of their transparencies to audience members as a handout. If you decide to do this, reduce them to 80 percent to keep them "from looking too bold and overwhelming."[10] If you want your handout to include both a reproduction of a transparency or slide and some explanatory text, make the copies of each visual even smaller, as illustrated in Figure 8.2, so there is room for the text.

Using markerboards and chalkboards   Markerboards and chalkboards should be used only as a last resort. As you'll recall from Chapter 7, you need to practice to use them effectively, you must be able to speak and draw at the same time, and you will look less prepared and less professional. Of the two, markerboards that are not attached to a wall are preferred because you can position them just as you would an easel—at an angle and close to the lectern. Also, since your markerboard is at an angle, you can still make occasional eye contact with your audience as you write. By contrast, when you are writing on a chalkboard, your back is toward the audience. Because of the time required to write on markerboards (or chalkboards), they are best used only when drawing brief diagrams and charts or showing the spelling of an unusual term. More complicated

*Models clarify and add
interest to your presentation.*

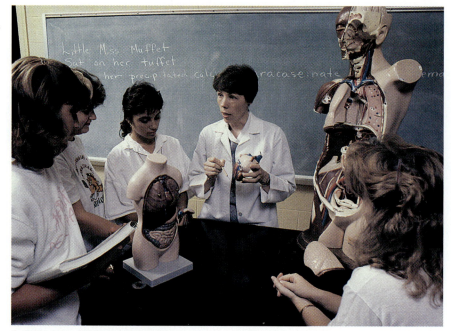

© Charles Gupton/TSW-Click/Chicago Ltd.

information should be presented on a poster or transparency. **Tip**: Don't forget to make your text approximately 1½ inches high for easy audience viewing—titles should be approximately 3 inches (see Chapter 7).

Using projected computer visuals and audiovisual aids

If your audience numbers less than ten, you can show your computer-generated visuals directly on the computer screen. For larger groups, use an LCD panel or self-contained LCD projector discussed in Chapter 7. If you have the equipment, you can even present a sophisticated screen show with color, animation, and sound. However, keep in mind that for classroom speeches your visuals should add to your speech, not become the speech. Therefore, most speakers who use computer visuals project static visuals like those used on transparencies and slides.

Audiovisual aids, when used with extreme care, can also add an interesting dimension to your speech. For example, if a VCR is available, you could use a videotape to show a brief segment of a rafting trip down the Colorado River or a demonstration of how to break out of an attacker's hold. You could even put the tape on slow motion, pause the tape to point out something of special interest, or replay a segment if needed for emphasis or clarity. Make sure the videotape is set to begin at the correct spot, that the television is placed where everyone can see it, and that the sound is loud enough to be heard at the back of the room. Unless the sound is essential, you may want to turn it off and talk during the tape as you would with other visuals. Be sure to practice using the videotape.

"Our State of Health" by Lucy Tisdale Setliff

#3

Cancer's Warning Signs

1. Bowel/bladder changes
2. Non-healing sore
3. Unusual bleeding/discharge
4. Thickening or lump
5. Indigestion/difficulty swallowing
6. Change in wart/mole
7. Cough/hoarseness

Nat. Cancer Institute

#4

Heart Attack Warnings

- Pressure, fullness, squeezing, pain
- Spreading to shoulders/neck/arms
- Lightheadedness, fainting, sweating, nausea or shortness of breath

American Heart Assoc.

#5

Blood Pressure Warnings

- Systolic pressure above 140
- Diastolic pressure above 90
- Frequent headaches, feelings of tension and irritability, dizziness, and fatigue

Life & Health,
Levy, Dignon, & Shirreffs

Can you list cancer's 7 warning signals without looking? According to the National Cancer Institute, "None of these symptoms is a sure sign of cancer, but if any of them last longer than two weeks, see a doctor."

Don't wait for your symptoms to become painful. The National Cancer Institute warns that "pain is *not* an early cancer sign." By the time you feel serious pain, it may be too late.

According to the American Heart Association, "Sharp, stabbing twinges usually are *not* signals of heart attack." However, if you feel uncomfortable pressure, fullness, squeezing, or pain in the center of the chest that lasts more than a few minutes, take immediate action. Call 911 and tell them you suspect a heart attack or, if you are near a hospital with a cardiac unit, have someone drive you. Every minute counts. Some experts also recommend that you immediately chew and swallow an aspirin tablet as well.

Blood pressure is measured in two numbers. Systolic pressure (the top number) measures the force of the blood as it travels from the heart into the arteries. Diastolic pressure (the lower number) indicates your blood pressure in between beats.

If you suspect high blood pressure, have your pressure checked regularly and see a physician.

Figure 8.2
Sample Handout with Reduced Copies of Speaker Transparencies Along with Additional Text (see actual speech in Chapter 9)

Audiotapes and CDs (compact discs) are other examples of audiovisual aids that can enhance your speech. For example, a speech on humpback whales would be much more interesting if you played a brief taped segment of the singing noises of the whales; a speech on types of jazz would be much more informative if the audience could hear brief cuts from well-known jazz selections.

Guidelines for Using All Types of Visuals

▶ *Make sure your visuals add to your presentation*, not upstage you or distract from the content of your presentation.

▶ *Don't show your visuals until you are ready to use them.* When you are finished referring to them, remove them from audience view. Objects and models should be covered or, if there is space, place them inside the lectern until you are ready for them. Posters should be covered from view by a blank poster. When it's time to show the first poster, simply remove the cover and slide it behind the first poster. Unless your flip charts are already filled out, no cover is needed. If a cover is needed, leave a blank sheet at the beginning and between each filled sheet.

▶ *Make sure your back does not face a window* because the glare from the window will make it very difficult for the audience to see your facial expressions.

▶ If possible, *arrange the chairs so that the doors are at the back of the room.* This way latecomers can enter without causing a disturbance.

▶ *Practice using your pointer.* If you lay your pointer or pencil directly onto the transparency itself, be careful not to dislodge the transparency. Lay the pointer down between visuals so it won't be distracting. Some speakers will tap it on the desk or, if it is a telescoping pointer, nervously move the pointer in and out. Even laser pointers require practice for effective use.

▶ *Practice giving your speech without visuals.* There's always a slight possibility that you will forget to bring some or all of them, that the equipment won't be there or will quit working, or that the power will go off (here's where having a handout comes in handy). If you have practiced without your visuals at least once, you'll feel more confident should a problem occur.

If you use an audiotape or CD, select a brief portion, cue it to the exact spot, set the volume, and practice smoothly integrating it into your speech.

Vocal Delivery
▼ ▼ ▼

The best speaking voice is one that sounds conversational, natural, and enthusiastic. An audience is more likely to listen closely to your speech and to understand your ideas if you speak much as you do in normal conversation. Most people speaking with a friend automatically use excellent vocal variety. *Vocal variety*, the key to a conversational voice, is achieved by varying volume, pitch, emphasis, rate, and pauses in a natural manner, as well as articulating and pronouncing words clearly.

Volume and Pitch

Volume and pitch are easily noticed and make a big impression on an audience. If your vocal variety needs some polishing, begin with volume and pitch.

Volume, the loudness and softness of your voice, is important to your success in several ways. First, you must speak loudly enough to be heard easily from all parts of the room. Second, you need to vary the volume of your voice to make the speech interesting. Third, use increases and decreases in your volume to emphasize words or phrases. To increase your volume, increase the amount and force of the air you expel while speaking. However, increasing your volume should not involve straining your neck muscles or raising your shoulders while breathing.

To check your volume, ask a friend to sit at the back of a large room while you stand at the front. Practice saying the word *stop* emphasizing the *ah* vowel sound while rapidly expelling as much air as possible. Imagine that a child is starting to walk into the street and you are calling through an open window. Say the word *stop* loud enough for the child to hear. Don't yell; just speak loudly and project your voice. When your friend says that you are loud enough to be heard easily, it will probably sound much too loud to you. Practice speaking at this new, louder volume until it feels comfortable.

Pitch, the highness and lowness of vocal tones, is also important to vocal variety. Too little variety in pitch can make your voice a dull and uninteresting monotone (like a piano repeating one note). However, extreme changes in pitch can make you sound unnatural and insincere. Effective speakers use two types of moderate pitch changes: (1) steps in pitch (high, medium, and low pitch) and (2) pitch inflection (rising or falling pitch). Together, these pitch changes add interest and enthusiasm to speaker voices and communicate subtle or implied meanings.

First, let's look at *steps in pitch*. Read these sentences aloud following the indicated step changes in pitch and decide which one sounds the best:

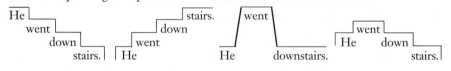

Now, let's look at *pitch inflection*. A rising pitch at the end of a sentence usually signals a question (*She stole the money* ⤴?) while a falling pitch indicates a statement or understanding (*She stole the money* ⤵). On the other hand, a drawn-out rising pitch implies doubt (*really* ♩?), a drawn-out high falling pitch implies a light-bulb type understanding (*Oh* ⤸, *now I understand*), and a low falling pitch indicates boredom (*Sure* ↓). Read aloud the following words using the pitch inflection indicated by the arrow to imply the meaning suggested in parentheses:[11]

well ⌒ (I'm waiting)	*go* ⌒ (On a red light?)
my ⌢ (I'm surprised)	*say* ⌢ (That's excellent)
oh ⌒ (Is that so?)	*You* ⌒ (He meant you?)
stop ⌢ (Right there)	*now* ⌢ (Don't wait)

Some speakers (especially during a question-and-answer session) use an upward pitch inflection (called "upspeak") at the end of declarative sentences and phrases. The audience will likely perceive this as a sign of the speaker's insecurity or desire to gain approval. Say the following sentences ending each with a downward inflection:

Hello, my name is _____ _____ ⌢ . I am a confident speaker ⌢ .

Now say the same two sentences each ending with upward inflections:

Hello, my name is _____ _____ ⌒ . I am a confident speaker ⌒ .

Could you hear the difference? With downward inflections the sentences sound confident; with upward inflections the sentences sound as if you are asking for verification or for approval. Both pitch step and pitch inflection can add to your effectiveness by making you sound more interesting and authoritative and by allowing you to add appropriate subtle meaning to your speeches.

Emphasis, Rate, and Pauses

Good vocal variety requires more than just effective use of volume and pitch. To make your voice as expressive as possible, you also need to develop your use of emphasis, rate, and pauses.

Emphasis, stressing a word with your voice to give the word significance, is another important ingredient of vocal variety. In emphasizing a word, two things happen: (1) your pitch goes up (usually followed immediately by a downward inflection) and (2) your volume increases. Courtroom lawyers certainly know the value of emphasis. They can repeat the exact words of a witness yet make the sentence sound entirely different. For a demonstration of this point, say the following sentence five times, each time emphasizing a different word as shown. Listen to your pitch and volume as you speak. You should be able to give five different meanings to the sentence.

Why did you fire him?
Why *did* you fire him?
Why did *you* fire him?
Why did you *fire* him?
Why did you fire *him*?

Rate, how fast or how slowly you speak, is especially important in maintaining listener attention. Constantly speaking at the same rate can lull your listeners to sleep. Work on varying your speaking rate. Try speaking faster to show excitement or enthusiasm and to emphasize key points; speak slower to indicate importance or emphasis, to build suspense, and to indicate boredom.

Pauses, referred to as "live silence," and *phrases*, groups of words preceded and followed by pauses, also add to listener interest and understanding. If your phrases are too long or too choppy because you use too few or too many pauses, listeners will have difficulty understanding you. Pauses and phrases can be short, medium, or long. If you have ever been told that you speak too fast, it probably means that you don't pause long enough or often enough for the audience to absorb your ideas. Pauses not only make phrases easier to understand but also add suspense and dramatic effect. Read the following sentence, each time pausing when indicated with a slash:

That / outfit / looks great / on / you.	(Too many pauses for effective phrasing.)
That outfit looks great on you.	(No pauses needed; the speaker sounds sincere.)
That outfit looks great / on you.	(Pause after "great" makes it sound as if you may like it, but no one else would consider wearing it.)

Don't forget that a pause is a *live silence*. Try not to fill the silence with distracting vocalizations like "ah," "uh," "um," "OK," "and uh," "well uh," or "you know." Silence may seem awkward at first, but pauses give your listeners time to absorb and consider your ideas.

Articulation and Pronunciation

Both articulation and pronunciation are important for maximum audience understanding. Although often mistaken for each other, they are really very different processes.

Articulation, the clear and distinct production of speech sounds, is vital for clear audience understanding. Many speakers are lazy articulators and tend to run words together or leave off some word endings. For example, you might say, "Whadayamean" instead of "What do you mean," "Seeya" instead of "See you," or "Goin' " instead of "Going." Practice making your articulation crisp and clear by exaggerating all sounds as you read aloud the following nonsense rhyme:

> *To sit in solemn silence in a dull, dark dock.*
> *In a pestilential prison with a life long lock.*
> *Awaiting the sensation of a short, sharp shock.*
> *From a chippy chippy chopper on a big black block.*[12]

Pronunciation, speaking words with all the sounds and accents that are in general usage in a population, is not always easy. Words that a speaker pronounces "incorrectly" are difficult for audience members to ignore—they attack the ears. If your speech includes several mispronounced words, especially if the mispronunciation is major, the audience may begin to doubt your credibility. For example, the chancellor of a large college continually mispronounced the word *registration* when speaking to the faculty. Instead of *rej-i-stra'-shun* the chancellor always said *red-ster-a'-shun*, which made him sound uneducated. Take a look at the following list of commonly mispronounced words to see if you need to work on any of them.

Word	Correct	Incorrect
arctic	arc'-tic	ar'-tic
ask	ask	aks
athlete	ath'-lete	ath'-a-lete
February	Feb'-ru-ary	Feb'-yu-ary
get	get	git
library	ly'-brery	ly'-berry
picture	pic'-ture	pitch'-er
secretary	sek'-ra-terry	sek'-a-terry
with	with	wit or wid

Now that you have read the section on vocal delivery, which two or three areas do you think you need to improve or polish the most? Each time you speak, try to work on an additional vocal skill. Remember, however, that you can't expect to perfect everything at once. For your first speeches concentrate on speaking loud enough and using effective pitch changes so you will sound conversational and interesting.

Verbal Delivery

▼ ▼ ▼

In addition to your visual delivery (you and your visual aids) and vocal delivery (your style of speaking), listeners will pay attention to your verbal delivery (the words you choose and the way you construct sentences). Listeners expect speakers to use a more informal language style than is typical for written reports. For example, in oral communication it is best to use short, simple sentences, and it isn't always necessary to use complete sentences. Also, it is perfectly all right to use personal pronouns such as *I*, *we*, *you*, and *us* and contractions such as *I've* and *won't*—forms often avoided in formal written English.

One of the most serious mistakes a speaker can make is to use long or extremely technical words or jargon in an attempt to impress listeners. Even if you are speaking in a professional setting, don't assume that your audience uses or understands the same technical terms and jargon that you do. The best language is *vivid* (paints a picture for the listener), *specific* (give details), and *simple* (is easy to understand).

To drive home this point, one writing professor who was training a class of individuals responsible for writing government forms and regulations created a sample of the worst of government writing:

We respectfully petition, request, and entreat that due and adequate provision be made, this day and date herein under subscribed, for the satisfying of these petitioners' nutritional requirements and for the organizing of such methods of allocation and distribution as may be deemed necessary and proper to assure the reception by and for said petitioners of such quantities of cereal products as shall, in the judgment of the aforementioned petitioners, constitute a sufficient supply thereof.[13]

Were you able to interpret what this paragraph really says? According to the professor this paragraph illustrated how most bureaucrats would write, "Give us this day our daily bread."[14]

Alexander Haig, who served as chairman of the Joint Chiefs of Staff and later as secretary of state, gave us many other examples of confusing language. Haig, who combined the language of diplomacy with the language of his previous job as general, confused people with such phrases as " 'careful caution,' 'caveat my response,' 'epistemologicallywise,' 'nuanced departures,' 'definitizing an answer,' and 'saddle myself with a statistical fence.' "[15]

Another mistake many speakers make is using sexist language that risks alienating their audience. For example, you should avoid using the pronoun *he* as a generic term to refer to both males and females. Research indicates that *he* conjures up masculine images in the minds of an audience.[16] A study of college students conducted in 1993 found that both male and female students tended to use masculine pronouns when referring to judges, engineers, and lawyers, and feminine pronouns when referring to nurses, librarians, and teachers.[17] According to Diana K. Ivy and Phil Backlund in *Exploring Gender Speak*, when speakers use generic masculine terms (like *he*, *mankind*, *sportsman*, and *workmanship*) and feminine terms (like *stewardess*, *waitress*, and *actress*), they are helping to maintain sex-biased perceptions.[18] Figure 8.3 lists some masculine and feminine terms and expressions with suggested alternative words.

Putting your ideas into simple, easy-to-understand language that fits the frames of reference of your listeners and is vivid, specific, and bias-free can be hard at first. As you work on the basics of delivery, however, keep the principles discussed here in mind and your language and speaking style will improve. You will have a chance to hone these skills further in Chapter 16.

"Immediacy" Behaviors and Your Delivery

▼ ▼ ▼

Verbal, visual, and vocal behaviors that instructors use to promote a sense of closeness and personal interaction with students during lectures have been labeled **immediacy behaviors**. Research has found that students learn significantly more and have an improved attitude toward the classroom experience when instructors use immediacy behaviors.[19] Also, in general, as the

Figure 8.3

Selected Masculine and Feminine Terms and Expressions with Suggested Alternatives

Source: Diana K. Ivy and Phil Backlund, Exploring Gender Speak: Personal Effectiveness in Gender Communication *(New York: McGraw-Hill, 1994), pp. 78, 80, 93–94.*

▼ **Masculine Terms**
anchorman
chairman
mailman/postman
man-eating
mankind
man-made
policeman

▼ **Alternative Terms**
anchor; newscaster
chair; chairperson
mail carrier; postal worker
flesh-eating; carnivorous
humankind; humanity
artificial; handmade
police officer

▼ **Feminine Terms**
actress
comedienne
heiress
hostess
lady, girl, gal, or doll
stewardess

▼ **Alternative Terms**
actor*
comedian*
heir*
host*
woman
flight attendant

▼ **Expressions**
a dumb blonde
a gentleman's agreement
father time
fellow classmates
I'm not my brother's keeper
like father, like son
modern man

mother earth
mother hen
nervous nellie
signing your John Hancock

▼ **Alternative Expressions**
an unintelligent person
an informal agreement or promise
time
classmates
It's none of my business
following in one's footsteps
modern people; modern
    civilization
earth
being protective
worrywart
signing your name

*Omit the suffix and use the original term.

class size increases, the importance of immediacy behaviors increases.[20] Although research on immediacy behavior has focused on teachers and students, the similarity between a classroom and a public speaking environment is close enough for us to benefit as well.

The three speakers mentioned at the beginning of this chapter (Lee Iacocca, Oprah Winfrey, and Norman Schwarzkopf) certainly use immediacy behaviors—these behaviors are what make them so believable. What are these behaviors? *Verbal behaviors* include using humor sensitively; citing personal instances and experiences during the speech; referring to the group as "we" and "our"; praising individuals for their work, actions, or comments; referring to individuals by name (especially when giving praise); occasionally asking for opinions and questions; and conversing with the audience before and after the presentation. *Visual behaviors* include making eye contact, smiling at appropriate times at individuals as well as the group as a whole, keeping a relaxed body posture, gesturing naturally, and moving around rather than staying behind the lectern. *Vocal behavior* involves being vocally expressive—that is, using good volume, pitch, emphasis, rate, and so on. Therefore, to break down the feeling of psychological distance between you and your listeners and replace it with a feeling of closeness and personal contact, make your verbal, visual, and vocal behaviors work for you.

Methods of Delivery

▼ ▼ ▼

Often the success of your presentation depends on the method of delivery you select: speaking from written manuscript, from memory, impromptu (off the top of your head), or extemporaneously (from brief notes).

Speaking from a Manuscript

Although it might seem that reading your speech would be easy, speaking from a manuscript is much harder than speaking from notes. It's difficult to use good vocal variety while maintaining direct eye contact when you are reading a speech word for word. Also, unless you deviate from the manuscript occasionally, you cannot respond to verbal or nonverbal listener feedback, so your talk will likely seem somewhat stiff and remote.

Manuscript speeches are usually given by politicians and top-level business and professional people who must give out copies of their speeches ahead of time to the media (like a president of the United States prior to the state of the union address), who need to make sure that what they say is exact enough to avoid misinterpretation, especially in an emergency situation (like the CEO of Exxon after the *Valdez* oil spill in Alaska), and who want to guard against saying something unintentionally.

If you must use a manuscript sometime in the future, be sure to practice reading it until your pitch, rate, volume, and emphasis make you sound authoritative yet conversational and until you are able to glance up and make eye contact with your listeners often enough to look natural. To show you how difficult it is to speak effectively from a manuscript and why speech teachers don't want you to give your class speeches from a manuscript, try activity 4 at the end of this chapter.

Speaking from Memory

Speaking from memory has even more drawbacks than reading your speech. First, it takes a great deal of time and effort to memorize a manuscript. Second, speaking from memory makes it difficult or impossible to react to listener feedback. A question from a listener can throw you off so much that you forget the next sentence or maybe even the rest of your speech. Even if listeners make no verbal comments, they make plenty of nonverbal ones. If you spot facial expressions that indicate audience confusion, you can hardly risk deviating from your practiced speech to add another example—you might lose your concentration or forget the speech entirely. Also, it will be much more difficult to make your delivery relaxed, warm, spontaneous, and believable if you are focusing on recalling memorized text. There's another drawback to depending on memorized speeches: What will you do in the future when someone (probably your boss) asks you to give a speech to an unexpected group of visitors? You won't have time to memorize the speech, only time to decide on your main points and find the necessary supporting materials (statistics, examples, and so on). Always memorizing your speeches is a crutch that could easily work against you in the future.

If you select a speech topic that you already know a lot about and that interests you, you won't need to memorize it—you already know the material. However, some speakers do feel more comfortable memorizing their opening and closing remarks and sometimes the transitions between main points. Memorizing small segments such as these shouldn't cause a problem; just avoid memorizing the entire speech.

Impromptu Speaking

Impromptu speaking, speaking without prior preparation and without notes or manuscript, is obviously a hazardous way to give your major classroom speeches. However, anytime you are unexpectedly asked a question (in class by an instructor, at a PTA meeting, by your boss), your response is an impromptu speech. Likewise, if you are called on sometime to explain some process to a group, that's an impromptu speech. Ideally, even though you have no time to prepare, you will sound intelligent, authoritative, and confident! A hesitant, apologetic, or stumbling answer does not project the image you want. When asked to do impromptu speaking, try the following:[21]

▶ *Appear confident* (even if you must pretend).

▶ *Decide on your conclusion first*, so that everything you say can lead up to the conclusion in an organized manner.

▶ *Begin with a general statement or background information* to give yourself time to think of one, two, or three supporting reasons for your conclusion.

▶ *Introduce your supporting reasons with the word "because"* until you can stay organized without it. For example:

Q: Do you think speech training should be a requirement for all college students?

A: *Because* most college students have to give presentations in upper-level courses, and *because* many college students will be getting jobs that demand speaking skills, I see speech training as an important requirement for all college students.

▶ *Answer the question directly and honestly*. However, in those rare instances when you are asked a question you don't wish to answer or one for which you don't have an answer (and you feel it would be unacceptable to say, "I don't know"), it may be justifiable to change the topic to one you do want to answer. Politicians are very good at changing subjects with such comments as:

"That's an important question—almost as important as . . ."

"I was hoping someone would ask me that question because it gives me an opportunity to talk about . . ."

"Could I come back to that question? I've been wanting to reply to the remark this gentleman made earlier. He said . . ."

"I think we need to look at the problem from a different angle . . ."

If this advice seems too complicated, you might prefer to answer impromptu questions by following a simple three-step process:[22]

1. Make a single point.
2. Support that point.
3. Restate that point.

In an impromptu situation you may not have figures and sources at your fingertips. If not, give a personal, family, or humorous instance to clarify and support your point. For example, in an impromptu speech on "What type animals make the best pets?" a student supported her point that the best pets are dogs by telling the audience about her three dogs. She told what kind of dogs she had, gave their names, and described an instance that showed what good companions they were. The instance was both humorous and heart-warming. The audience loved her speech. Chapter 10 gives more examples of instances.

Question-and-answer sessions after your presentation are another type of impromptu speaking. Even though you should plan for possible questions ahead of time, many will be unexpected and require an impromptu response. The three-step approach would be a good one to use in this situation.

"Well, I see my time is up . . ."

Reprinted from the Saturday Evening Post. © *The Curtis Publishing Company. Used by permission of Mrs. Joe Zeis and Rev. Gabriel Zeis, T.O.R.*

There's no telling when your next impromptu speaking opportunity may occur, but it could be one of the most important and even the most successful short speeches you give. You will probably have several opportunities to give impromptu speeches in class. Try a variety of the techniques suggested here until you find the one that works best for you.

Speaking Extemporaneously

For most speeches you will be most effective and connect best with your audience if you speak extemporaneously. An extemporaneous speech is not memorized or written out word for word; instead, the speech is developed and presented from brief notes (discussed in Chapter 12). In planning an extemporaneous speech, you first list the main points you wish to include in the speech. Next you decide what verbal and visual supporting materials to use to prove and clarify each of your main ideas, listing these in outline fashion. Once an introduction and conclusion are added, you practice aloud using your visuals and note cards for guidance until you feel comfortable using them. Each time the presentation is given, it will be a little different unless it has been memorized. Speaking from brief key-word notes allows you to sound conversational, to maintain good eye contact with your listeners, and to alter your speech if listener feedback indicates confusion.

Practicing Your Speech
▼ ▼ ▼

There is a big difference between reading about how to deliver a speech effectively and actually doing it. The only way to transfer what you have read into what you can do is to *practice*. Remember that your goal is to sound confident and natural—just the way you do when talking to friends. If you have been visualizing yourself giving an effective speech since reading Chapter 3, you have taken an important first step to confident delivery. If you haven't been visualizing, go back and find the positive statements you wrote about yourself as a speaker and read them several times. As you read each one (for example, "It's easy for me to make direct eye contact with my audience while speaking"), picture yourself in front of the class looking directly at the audience and feeling good about it. Also play a tape of the positive imagery exercise on page 62 several times or have someone read it to you.

Feeling confident while speaking is one of the benefits of rehearsing. The best results are obtained when you prepare two ways: (1) by visualizing yourself giving a successful speech and (2) by actually practicing your speech aloud. The following suggestions will help you as you practice your speech:

▶ If you haven't already done so, *turn your formal preparation outline into key-word notes* and copy them onto one or two note cards. If you have any quotes, put each one on a separate note card—typed and double-spaced for ease of read-

© Loren Santow/Tony Stone Images, Inc.

This speaker is videotaping his speech while a friend takes notes on how he's coming across. This practice session would have been even more realistic if he could have been standing at a lectern.

ing. If you are using transparencies, decide what notes, if any, to put on each transparency frame.

▶ Remember that thinking through your speech silently does not count as practice. It may help you to check for organization problems and to familiarize yourself with the content, but it won't help at all with your vocal or visual delivery and only a little with your verbal delivery. *There is no substitute for practicing out loud*—standing on your feet, using your notes and visual aids, practicing your gestures and eye contact, and speaking aloud.

▶ *Practice alone at first.* Tape-record yourself to get feedback on your vocal delivery or practice in front of a mirror. If possible, practice in a room similar to the one in which you will be speaking. If your practice room does not have the equipment necessary to use your visuals, simulate handling them. If you are reading a manuscript, be sure that it is double- or triple-spaced in 14- or 16-point type. Use a hole punch and place manuscript pages into a stiff binder. Practice holding the binder up high enough that your eyes can glance down at the manuscript without having to bob your head.

▶ After you begin to feel comfortable with your speech, *practice it in front of a friend or family member.* Ask them for specific comments on your verbal, visual, and vocal delivery. Practice making direct eye contact and using gestures. If you have a video camera, let a friend film you so you can observe yourself. If you discover any awkward spots in your talk, decide how to alter the speech to smooth them out.

▶   At least once before the actual speech (two or three times would be better), *practice using your visual aids with all the needed equipment.* Videotape yourself if possible or ask a friend to observe one of your final practices.

▶   Try to *get plenty of sleep the night before your speech* (hopefully you won't wait until the last minute to finish the speech). *On the day of the speech, get to class early* so you can compose yourself, check to see that your notes and visuals are in the proper order, and read through your outline one last time.

Remember, no one expects perfection. If you make a mistake, correct it if necessary and go on. Then forget it. If you have practiced until you feel comfortable with your speech and have visualized yourself giving a successful speech, you should feel excited but confident.

Summary
▼ ▼ ▼

Successfully delivering your message depends on three important aspects of delivery—verbal, visual, and vocal codes. Effective verbal delivery results from the use of vivid, specific, simple, and bias-free language. It is also important that your verbal message fit the frames of reference of your listeners. Effective visual delivery entails paying close attention to your appearance, facial expressions, eye contact, posture, movement and gestures, as well as the content and handling of your visual aids. Effective vocal delivery is achieved by varying volume, pitch, emphasis, and rate, as well as making sure pauses, phrasing, articulation, and pronunciation are effective. The best speaking voice is one that sounds conversational, natural and enthusiastic. Rarely will you achieve your best speaking voice without practice.

Your delivery can be enhanced by using immediacy behaviors such as making direct eye contact, smiling, being vocally expressive, using humor, and referring to your audience as "we." These behaviors reduce the psychological distance that often exists between speaker and audience.

In addition to your verbal, visual, and vocal delivery, the method of delivery you choose can affect the success of your speech. In most cases speaking from a manuscript or memorizing your speech should be avoided. Impromptu speaking is a good way to gain confidence in speaking. If you can add a personal or humorous instance, not only will your audience enjoy your speech, but you will feel more relaxed as well. The preferred method of delivery for major classroom speeches is extemporaneous speaking, which involves preparing carefully but speaking from brief notes.

The only way to transfer what you have learned from this chapter into a dynamic, believable delivery is to practice. To prepare yourself, first visualize yourself giving a successful speech. Then practice your speech aloud with your visual aids. You will soon find yourself getting compliments on the way you deliver your speeches.

1. To get an idea of how your voice sounds to others, leave a detailed message on your answering machine or voice mail system. Do this regularly until your vocal variety and tone project the warmth, enthusiasm, or authority you desire.[23]

2. For one week, whenever you make a call or someone calls you, record the conversation on a cassette recorder. Listen to your voice quality. After a week listen to your first recording to assess your improvement.

3. Keep a brief log of any really good speeches you see live or on TV. What specific verbal, visual, and vocal techniques made the speeches so good?

4. In Chapter 7 you selected the manuscript of a speech given previously by someone else and prepared at least two visual aids that you thought would clarify and add power to the speech. Read the manuscript (or at least a two-minute portion of it) to the class using the visuals you prepared. Follow the guidelines in this chapter for reading from a manuscript. As you read, make your delivery as effective as possible. Not only will this assignment show you how difficult it is to speak from a manuscript and why your instructor required extemporaneous speeches, but it will give you a chance to polish your verbal, visual, and vocal delivery without having to worry about speech content.

5. With a group of classmates, select a cutting from a play, a short story, or a children's storybook such as a Dr. Seuss book. Assign characters or parts to each and practice presenting it as a readers' theater. Make your vocal and visual cues fit the story.

6. Practice reading to a small group of your classmates the following excerpt from Michael Warder's speech "The Politics of Cultural War." Try to present the speech as you think he would have delivered it at the 1993 Chicago Conservative Conference. Then discuss with classmates how you could read this excerpt so that an audience would realize that you do not believe what you are saying. Take turns reading it aloud before the class.

> Foolish? I'll tell you what's foolish. Foolish is setting up another federal program to fix the family, fix education, fix race relations, fix out-of-wedlock births, fix urban housing, or any other federal program that's supposed to fix a personal or social problem. I can't think of any institution more ill-suited to solve these kinds of problems. Seeking to involve the federal government in our social lives is a little like an ant inviting an elephant over to its home for dinner. The federal government tends to crush whatever small things with which it comes in contact.[24]

7. Using a humorous incident speech (discussed in Chapter 2), have a "talk-down" between you and one other student. See which of you (using the delivery suggestions covered in this chapter) is the most successful at capturing and holding audience attention. At the end of one or two minutes, have the audience vote on which speaker held their attention more of the time. This activity could include all members of the class or only four to six volunteers. Remember, the more chances you get to practice speaking, the better you will become.

Notes

1. Bert Decker, *You've Got to Be Believed to Be Heard* (New York: St. Martin's Press, 1992).
2. Lee Iacocca and William Novak, *Iacocca: An Autobiography* (New York: Bantam Books, 1984).
3. *The New York Times* (July 15, 1980) as reported in the *Current Biography Yearbook*, 1987, p. 259.
4. Oprah Winfrey, *Current Biography Yearbook*, 1987, pp. 610–614.
5. Richard Pyle, *Schwarzkopf: The Man, The Mission, and The Triumph* (New York: Signet/Penguin Books USA, 1991), pp. 3–9.
6. Decker, *You've Got to Be Believed*, p. 123.
7. Decker, *You've Got to Be Believed*, p. 124.
8. Iacocca, *Iacocca*, p. 16.
9. John T. Molloy, *New Dress for Success* (New York: Warner Books, 1988); John T. Molloy, *The Woman's Dress for Success Book* (New York: Warner Books, 1978).
10. Margaret Y. Rabb, *The Presentation Design Book: Tips, Techniques and Advice for Creating Effective, Attractive Slides, Overheads, Multimedia Presentations, Screen Shows and More*, 2nd ed. (Chapel Hill, NC: Ventana Press, 1993), p. 245.
11. Grant Fairbanks, *Voice and Articulation Drillbook*, 2nd ed. (New York: Harper & Row, 1960), p. 132.
12. Source unknown.
13. Carl Wayne Hensley, "What You Share Is What You Get: Tips for Effective Communication," *Vital Speeches* 59 (December 1, 1992), 117.
14. Hensley, "What You Share," p. 117.
15. Robert B. Rackleff, "The Art of Speech Writing," *Vital Speeches* 54 (March 1, 1988), 312.
16. L. C. Hamilton, "Using Masculine Generics: Does Generic 'He' Increase Male Bias in the User's Imagery?" *Sex Roles* 19 (1988), 785–799.
17. Diana K. Ivy, L. Bullis-Moore, K. Norvell, Phil Backlund, and M. Javidi, *The Lawyer, the Babysitter, and the Student: Non-sexist Language Usage and Instruction*. Paper presented at the annual meeting of the Western States Communication Association, Albuquerque, NM, February 1993.
18. Diana K. Ivy and Phil Backlund, *Exploring Gender Speak: Personal Effectiveness in Gender Communication* (New York: McGraw-Hill, 1994), p. 75.
19. Joan Gorham, "The Relationship Between Verbal Teacher Immediacy Behaviors and Student Learning," *Communication Education* 37 (January 1988), 40–53; Derek G. Kelley and Joan Gorham, "Effects of Immediacy on Recall of Information," *Communication Education* 37 (July 1988), 198–207; Joan Gorham and Diane M. Christophel, "The Relationship of Teachers' Use of Humor in the Classroom to Immediacy and Student Learning," *Communication Education* 39 (January 1990), 46–62; Judith A. Sanders and Richard L. Wiseman, "The Effects of Verbal and Nonverbal Teacher Immediacy on Perceived Cognitive, Affective, and Behavioral Learning in the Multicultural Classroom," *Communication Education* 39 (October 1990), 341–353.
20. Gorham, "The Relationship," p. 51.
21. Adapted from Janet Stone and Jane Bachner, "Speaking Impromptu," in *Speaking Up: A Book for Every Woman Who Wants to Speak Effectively* (New York: McGraw-Hill, 1977), pp. 153–161.
22. Suggested by Dr. Susan Huxman, Wichita State University.
23. Suggested by Decker, *You've Got to Be Believed*, p. 226.
24. Michael Warder, "The Politics of Cultural War," *Vital Speeches* 21 (August 15, 1993), 654.

Informative Speaking

9

Informative Speaking: An Overview

S INCE THE COURSE STARTED, YOU have been gaining steadily in speaking ability. You've learned how to prepare and deliver a short speech. In addition, you've learned how to use verbal/visual/vocal teamwork, how to design and prepare visual aids, how to use words and vocal expression effectively, how to manage both trait and situational anxiety, how to be an ethical speaker, and how to analyze listeners before and after your speech. It's now time to apply those skills to longer, more involved speeches.

The chapters in this unit on informative speaking will expand and fine-tune those skills that you learned in Chapters 1–8. Specifically this chapter will give you an overview of informative speaking, with special emphasis on picking a topic and deciding what main points to include in preparing an informative speech. Chapter 10 will cover researching and supporting your informative speech. Chapter 11 will focus on how to organize your main points and how to begin and end your speech. Finally Chapter 12 will discuss why and how to outline a speech (when done correctly, outlining is not only easy but a handy tool you won't want to be without).

Types of Informative Speeches

▼ ▼ ▼

A s discussed in Chapter 1, you are giving an informative speech when you make your listeners aware of a subject, present ideas or information designed to promote understanding, or convey a body of related facts. Informative speeches are not meant to influence choices or opinions—persuasive speeches do this. Of course, an informative speech may be indirectly persuasive. For example, a listener might decide to become a volunteer just from hearing an informative speech on various community organizations. There are many different ways to categorize informative speeches, but for our purposes informative speeches will be divided into two basic categories: (1) demonstration speeches and (2) informational speeches.

Demonstration Speeches

Both demonstration and informational speeches promote understanding and convey a body of related facts. A **demonstration speech** "promotes understanding" by showing how to do or make something—right in front of the listeners so they can see the steps necessary to achieve the same results. Hopefully your audience will have learned so well that they can carry out the operation themselves. For instance, suppose you work in a flower shop and want to give a demonstration speech on flower arranging. You might cover the dos and don'ts of making beautiful flower arrangements (transparencies listing the dos and don'ts would be nice), but the main focus of your presentation would be the demonstration of each step, resulting in one or more completed arrangements. You would bring flowers, vases, art objects, water, preservatives—all the sup-

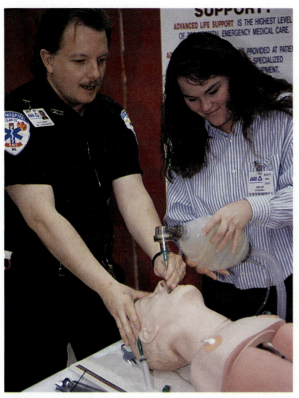

A demonstration speech promotes understanding by showing how to do or make something.

© D. & I. MacDonald/The Picture Cube, Inc.

plies and visuals you need to explain and show each step in the process of creating a lovely arrangement. Or suppose you wanted to give a demonstration speech on how to prepare delicious nonalcoholic drinks to serve on special occasions. You would bring in all the ingredients and actually prepare the drinks in front of the audience, explaining each step as you go. You might have volunteers try their hand at squeezing lemons or blending the ingredients to just the right consistency. Passing out samples of the recipes you have demonstrated also might be a good idea. **Tip**: Be aware that a demonstration speech usually takes more time than an informational speech—especially when audience participation is involved. To make sure you won't run out of time while giving your demonstration speech, add one minute to your practice time.

Informational Speeches

An **informational speech** uses verbal, visual, and vocal messages to create awareness of a subject, to present ideas or information promoting understanding, or to convey a body of related facts. The focus of the informational presentation is on content and ideas, not on how to do or make something. Even though a minidemonstration might be used as an attention-getter or as a way to

> ### Remember the differences between types of informative speeches:
>
> **A demonstration speech . . .**
>
> ▶ Promotes a skill—making or doing.
> ▶ Shows how to accomplish a task by doing it step by step.
>
> **An informational speech . . .**
>
> ▶ Promotes understanding—knowing.
> ▶ Focuses on content and ideas; may discuss how something is made but will not actually make it.

clarify a point in an informational speech, the focus of the speech is on the speech content, not on the demonstration. (See Chapter 11 for suggested attention-getters.)

Suppose you wanted to do an informational speech on flower arrangements instead of a demonstration speech. You could talk about the aesthetic value of flowers, flower selection, and flower placement while using transparencies (one listing main points, one showing an effective arrangement, and one showing a poor arrangement) and conclude the speech by showing an actual flower arrangement. Be aware that most informational speeches (such as the sample student speech on unhealthiness that follows) cover topics that would not be appropriate for demonstration speeches (for example, youth fads, stress prevention, or vacation suggestions).

Listener Retention: Tips from Previous Chapters
▼ ▼ ▼

Regardless of whether your speech is a demonstration or an informational one, you will want to do everything possible to increase listener retention. As we learned in Chapter 4, without specific help from the speaker, the typical listener retains only approximately 10–25 percent of the information in a speech. To help you help your listeners, Figure 9.1 includes a review of the major verbal, visual, and vocal tips from previous chapters. These tips should help you make your ideas easier to understand and more likely to be remembered.

▼ Verbal Tips

Use verbal immediacy behaviors (for example, personal examples, references to "we" and "our," reference to individuals by name, and praise).

Use external stimulus to overcome internal listener noise.

Avoid jargon and limit acronyms.

Make language brief, vivid, and specific.

Organize ideas so they flow.

Highlight ideas by using signposting, internal summaries, transitions, repetition, and restatement.

Place the most important points either first or last in your outline

▼ Visual Tips

Use nonverbal immediacy behaviors (for example, relaxed body posture, gestures, and eye contact).

Use powerful visual aids that can be grasped in 3–6 seconds.

Make sure text visuals include:
fonts that harmonize with content
type sizes from 18 to 36 point
upper- and lowercase type
no more than 6 lines
phrases not sentences
clip art, color, and large type for emphasis

Make sure graphic visuals:
limit and group data
always include headings
minimize background lines
have bars wider than space between them
avoid too much color or red/green bar graphs

▼ Vocal Tips

Use vocal immediacy behaviors (for example, vocal expressiveness and interest).

Use a natural, enthusiastic delivery.

Increase your speaking rate.

Use good vocal variety by varying:
pitch
volume
rate
emphasis

Figure 9.1
Verbal, Visual, and Vocal Tips

Sample Student Speech 3

▼ ▼ ▼

The following informative speech, "Our State of Health," was given by Lucy Tisdale Setliff to her speech class and was transcribed from the actual videotape. Minor changes were made by Lucy to the transcribed speech to make it less indirectly persuasive. The assignment specified a 5- to 7-minute informational speech followed by a 1½- to 3-minute question-and-answer period and a 1-minute (or less) final wrap-up. Lucy's speech will be referred to throughout the chapters in this unit to illustrate how she went through the process of preparing her speech. Specific steps include selecting the topic and organizing the main points, making a rough draft and a preparation outline, researching for information, developing verbal and visual supporting materials, finalizing the introduction and conclusion, and practicing—all leading up to her actual class speech. As you read this speech, think about changes you would make if speaking on the same topic. Another sample informative speech by a student is located at the end of Chapter 12. See Appendix C for additional informative speeches.

Sample Speech 3

Our State of Health

by Lucy Tisdale Setliff

Focus Step HIPPOCRATES ONCE SAID THAT health is the greatest of human blessings. Health—what exactly does that mean to each of us? Well, as defined in Webster's Dictionary, "Health is the absence of disease." Health became very important to me when I lost my father to heart disease. The day before he died, he said, "Lucy, I'm going to fight this thing." But, you know, he couldn't because the disease had completely taken over his heart. After he died, I became better informed about our state of health and I learned that the nation's two leading causes of death are heart disease and cancer, according to former Surgeon General C. Everett Koop. I also discovered that these and other diseases that kill us are caused partially by our own habits. Through improper diet and lack of exercise, we pay the price in the way of medical bills, plus we decrease our chances of spending our "golden years" in relatively good health

Lead-in Step So, this morning, I would like to look at our State of Health. I'll focus on three aspects of health: First, we'll identify major risk factors to health. [Transparency #1] Second, we'll review cancer and heart attack warning signs. Third, we'll explore diet and exercise guidelines.

Organize Body Step: So let's go back to the
1st Main Point first item and identify risk factors. [Transparency #2]. Levy, Dignan & Shirreffs in a text called *Life & Health* point out a number of risk

Transparency # 1

factors involved in the development of disease. How many of us know them? The risk factors include heredity, genetics, improper diet, and lack of exercise. True, the risk factors of heredity and genetics remain beyond our control, but we can control the factors of improper diet and lack of exercise. So, how great a risk is

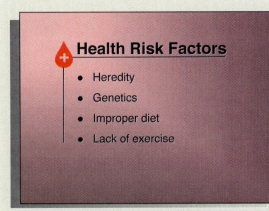

Transparency # 2

improper diet and lack of exercise? A study by the American Heart Association shows that more than 66 million Americans or one in four people have some form of heart disease related to a high fat diet and lack of exercise. Over one million Americans die each year from heart disease. Additionally, the American Heart Association states that cancer kills one out of every five people and cancer experts conclude that 75 percent of these deaths could be avoided through a healthier lifestyle including lower intake of fat and more exercise. Yet the National Sporting Goods Association states that 45 percent of Americans do not participate in any type of physical activity. And there's high risk involved for this type of behavior because the American Heart Associ-

ation states that sedentary individuals run five times the risk of developing disease compared to active individuals. So we see that cancer and heart disease are directly related to the risk factors of poor diet and lack of exercise.

2nd Main Point We've identified risk factors; now let's review warning signs that may indicate we have a disease. [Transparency #3] Can you list cancer's 7 warning signals? They are: 1) Change in bowel or bladder habits, 2) a sore that does not heal, 3) unusual bleeding or discharge, 4) thickening or lump in breast or

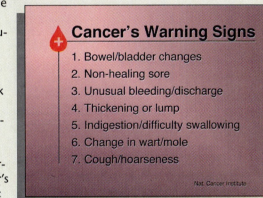

Transparency # 3

elsewhere, 5) indigestion or difficulty in swallowing, 6) obvious change in wart or mole, and 7) nagging cough or hoarseness. According to the National Cancer Institute, "None of these symptoms is a sure sign of cancer, but if any of them last longer than two weeks, see a doctor."

There are also warning signs that indicate a heart attack. Most people are less aware of these signs than they are the cancer warning signs. According to the American Heart Association, "Sharp, stabbing twinges usually are *not* signals of heart attack." However, the following symptoms are definite indicators of possible heart attack: [Transparency #4] 1) Uncomfortable pressure, fullness, squeezing or pain in the center of the chest that lasts more than a few minutes, 2) pain that spreads to the shoulders, neck or arms, and 3) chest

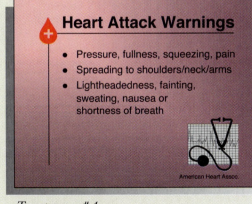

Transparency # 4

discomfort with lightheadedness, fainting, sweating, nausea or shortness of breath.

If these symptoms occur, every minute counts. My family did not know these symptoms and waited an extra day after my father had suffered a heart attack before taking him to the hospital. He died a week later. So you see, what we do not know can hurt us.

3rd Main Point   So far we've identified major risk factors to health and reviewed cancer and heart attack warning signals. Diet and fitness guidelines are the final focus of our state of health. First, let's look at diet guidelines. If it seems like nothing's safe to eat anymore, you'll be happy to know that in 1992, the U.S. Department of Agriculture released guidelines for an improved diet called the Food Pyramid. [Transparency #5] As we look at the diagram, we see the base of the pyramid forms the foundation of your diet consisting of breads, cereals, rice and pasta. As we move up the pyramid, the next emphasis is on fruits and vegetables followed by lesser amounts of meats and dairy products. The tip of the pyramid shows those foods to use sparingly—those consisting of fats, oils, and sugar.

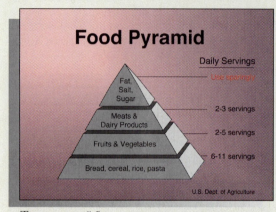

Transparency # 5

The tip of the pyramid needs to be our real concern, especially if you eat a lot of fast foods. The American Heart Association recommends that fats should be less than 30 percent of total calorie intake. This means for the average woman approximately 65 grams and for the average man only 80 grams of fat per day. Yet look at the fat in some of our favorite fast foods.

According to a recent issue of *Good Housekeeping*, Burger King's Double Whopper with Cheese has 63 grams of fat; Jack-in-the-Box's Colossus Burger contains 60 grams of fat; McDonald's Quarter Pounder with Cheese has 29 grams of fat; while Wendy's Big Bacon Classic contains 36 grams of fat. If you are thinking, that's why I eat chicken and fish instead, listen to this: Jack-in-the-Box's Fish Supreme Sandwich has 32 grams of fat; Burger King's BK Big Fish Sandwich contains 43 grams of fat and their BK Broiler has 29 grams of fat. McDonald's McChicken Sandwich also has 29 grams of fat—the same as their Quarter Pounder with Cheese.

Along with the diet guidelines are the exercise guidelines. Fortunately, exercise guidelines, as established by the American Heart Association, are fairly simple. They recommend that a minimum of 15 minutes of exercise three times a week will help control our blood pressure and help us control our weight. To lose weight, more exercise is required—as much as one hour three times a week. However, jogging isn't necessary; a brisk walk can be just as effective.

Initial Wrap-up   We should take a long look at the way we continue living life. Part of the great challenge of living is grasping opportunities and making the best choices we can. If we know the risk factors involved with disease, learn the warning signals that indicate disease, and discover diet and exercise guidelines, we improve our chances of preventing disease. Only then can we obtain health, the greatest of human blessings.

Questions and Answers   Are there any questions?

QUESTION: Of all the types of exercises that are currently out there—I mean, I've heard all kinds of different things you can do. Probably most of us know all the things you can do but really don't like doing them. Is there one that's favored over others for cardiovascular health?

ANSWER: That's a good question, Les. As the American Medical Association states, the more exercise you do the better it is for your heart. When you do strenuous exercise such as cycling or use machines such as Nordic Track, stationary bicycles, or treadmills, you will strengthen your heart even more. However, less strenuous exercise such as brisk walking is recommended as well. Walking will help a lot in the long run.

QUESTION: Lucy, is it important to know your family history as far as health is concerned?

ANSWER: Very important. Glad you asked, Leona. We need to be aware of our family health history because diseases and illnesses are passed down generation after generation. If we know that disease runs in the family, then we can be alert to that disease and start taking precautions now to prevent the problem from escalating. For example, high blood pressure runs in my family. My grandmother had it, my mother now has it. I now need to be alert to the possibility that I, too, may inherit it. So, right now I'm taking measures such as watching my salt intake and exercising to keep it down.

QUESTION: Now I don't know if this is a myth or what, but I always thought that on the food pyramid that if you have too many carbohydrates . . . I mean, I could eat pasta all day long but I would gain weight.

ANSWER: Right, Kelly. The number of servings [refers to Transparency #4] depend on how active you are. So, shoot really for the minimum because that provides the minimum nutrients. But if you are really active, if you do a lot of sports, you probably need to increase the amounts.

Final Wrap-up   Thank you for your questions and your attention this morning. I think that we'll all agree that our health is what we choose to make it. How we take care of our bodies today will determine if we suffer problems later on. Health begins with awareness. Don't wait until later to get interested in your health. As it was with my father—later may be too late.

Informative Speech
Preparation Steps

▼ ▼ ▼

Your beginning speeches probably seemed fairly simple to prepare. The longer speeches you will be making now will require more preparation time and more attention to detail—much like the difference between studying for a quiz and studying for a midterm or final exam. The following steps for preparing an informative speech are obviously similar to but more extensive than the basic steps presented in Chapter 2.

Step 1: Carefully Analyze Your Potential Audience

The importance of analyzing your audience was introduced briefly in Chapter 2 and discussed more fully in Chapter 5, so you already know why speech preparation begins with this step. Before you finalize your topic selection and begin researching, review the situational, demographic, and psychological characteristics of your classroom audience. Specifically, you might ask yourself the following questions (Lucy's answers to these questions regarding her speech, "Our State of Health," are in italics):

▶ At this point in the course, will my classmates' current opinions of me add to my credibility or take away from it? What can I do to make my credibility higher?

Lucy knew that she was well liked by most students in her class, but she knew that she hadn't made a very good impression with her introductory speech because she had been so nervous. She decided to add to her credibility by making her delivery more conversational and by citing several impressive sources—so research was definitely needed.

▶ How much do my classmates know about the general topics I am considering? (If you don't have any specific topics in mind yet, come back to this question when you do.)

Lucy had tentatively decided to give her informational speech on the general topic of health—specifically what, she wasn't sure.

▶ What type of visual aids will be more likely to impress my audience? What type of attention-getters will interest these listeners the most (for example, personal instance, startling statement, or quote)?

When Lucy checked with the other speakers scheduled to speak on the same day and found that most of them were using transparencies, she decided to use overhead transparencies as well. As Chapter 7 explains, transparencies create a more professional, polished presentation, which adds to the overall credibility of a speaker—something Lucy felt she needed.

▶ Based on the demographic characteristics of my class (for example, ages, marital status, children, majors, group memberships, hobbies), how can I

Informative Speech Preparation Steps

1. Analyze your potential audience.
2. Determine topic, exact purpose, and main points.
3. Rough out an outline of main points and possible supporting information.
4. Research topic to find needed supporting information.
5. Determine how best to organize main points.
6. Expand rough-draft outline into preparation outline or storyboards.
7. Develop the focus, lead-in, and wrap-up steps.
8. Prepare visual aids and speaking notes.
9. Rehearse speech.

make my possible topics interesting and beneficial to them? (If you can't think of a way, you probably need to select a different topic.)

Although the demographics of her class varied widely, the only ones that seemed important were age (ages ranged from eighteen to thirty) and group membership (several students were members of a health club). Lucy felt that audience members would be interested in maintaining their health. However, because of a lack of information on health, many of them placed studying and work ahead of exercise and proper diet.

▶ What attitudes, beliefs, or values relevant to my topic already exist in the minds of my classmates? How can I use these psychological factors to better communicate my ideas?

Before-class conversations with several of her classmates convinced Lucy that the students in her class already believed that exercise was beneficial and that health was important. She could use those beliefs to communicate her ideas on health—as soon as she decided how to narrow down the topic.

▶ What basic needs (physiological, safety, social, self-esteem, or self-actualization) do most of my classmates have that will make the need for my topic obvious?

Lucy decided that safety, social, and self-esteem needs were basic audience needs that best related to the topic of health. Her classmates all wanted to avoid poor health (safety need), would enjoy the companionship and sense of belonging that exercising at a club or with a friend brings (social needs), and would feel a sense of pride at knowing that they had taken steps to ensure their health (self-esteem needs).

Most likely your classroom audience will be the "friendly" type of audience, like Lucy's. These listeners will know what you are going through and be rooting for your success. Personal examples and humor will be especially effective. Also, any extra effort you put into your visual aids (such as clip art or color as discussed in Chapter 7) will be recognized and appreciated. You can also add to class enjoyment if you refer to a speech given by an earlier speaker or cite the behavior or statements of a student from the class as an example to support your own ideas. If, by chance, your class does not fall into the "friendly" audience category, review Chapter 5 to categorize the degree of negativity ("neutral," "uninterested," or "hostile") and adjust your speech accordingly. Remember that your purpose for analyzing your audience is to make your communication as effective as possible.

Step 2: Determine Your Topic, Exact Purpose, and Main Points

If, as suggested at the end of Chapter 2, you began carrying a note card in your purse or wallet and used it to record possible speech topics as they occurred to you, you likely have more speech topics than you know what to do with. All you have to do is decide which one(s) to use. However, if you haven't been keeping a list of possible speech topics, don't despair. Finding a good topic isn't that difficult. Start with the guidelines for topic selection.

Selecting your topic   The following four guidelines (introduced in Chapter 2) apply regardless of which types of speeches you are asked to give in this unit—demonstration, informational, or both:

▶   *Select a topic that fits the requirements of the assignment.* Once you know whether you are to give a demonstration speech or an informational speech, go back to the beginning of the chapter and make sure you are clear about the distinction between the two types of speeches. Many topics that would make ideal informational speeches would not work as demonstration speeches at all. The reverse is also true. For example, "Preparing an Effective Resume" or "Lowering Your Cholesterol" would make good informational speeches but would be almost impossible to actually demonstrate. In the same way, "How to Fold a Flag" or "How to Play the Drums" would make excellent demonstration speeches but wouldn't be nearly as effective as informational speeches.

Also, make sure your speech fits the time requirement. The only way you can be sure is to practice the actual speech and time it. Thinking it through in your mind is not a reliable way to check the length of a speech, as one student found out the hard way. Layla was presenting a demonstration speech on "How to Wrap Attractive Gifts." She started off by showing a hilarious example of how her parents wrapped her Christmas gifts when she was a child. The box looked like it had fallen down the stairs and been rescued by a pet. Then she showed the audience a beautifully wrapped gift and suggested that listeners could do it themselves in three easy steps. The problem was, by this point in her speech she had used up over half of the allotted time and was forced to end without covering all the steps. Had she practiced her speech out loud, she would have realized that the introduction was too long and that it takes longer to actually wrap a gift than it does to talk about it.

▶ *Select a topic you already know a lot about*. You will feel more relaxed and confident giving your speech if you select a topic that is familiar—either because of personal experience or previous research. If you have been keeping a list of speech topics, you likely have discovered there are many subjects that you know a lot about. If you haven't been keeping a list, brainstorm possible speech topics for each of the following topic areas: job (current or past), college-related topics, family, hobbies, things that you spend most of your time on, skills or accomplishments you are especially proud of, and research papers you've written. As you brainstorm each topic area, list anything that comes to mind no matter how crazy it seems. These crazy ideas often lead to a really good topic that you never would have thought of without the "crazy" topic to stimulate your thinking. Continue until you have at least three items for each category.

> Stop reading at this point and brainstorm your list of topics.

When you have completed your list, look at the sample topics in Figures 9.2 and 9.3. Hopefully these sample topics will cause you to think of additional topics. Add them to your list. Now select from this list those topics you feel might be appropriate for your assigned speech.

After Lucy had brainstormed for possible topics and crossed out the inappropriate ones, she was left with five possible speech topics that fit her assignment:

1. *"Vacationing in Germany" (she had lived in Germany for seven years).*
2. *"Basic health maintenance" (she had done a report on health the previous semester; also, several years earlier she had seen her father die of heart disease and her uncle struggle with diabetes).*
3. *"The logistics of taking televised courses" (she had taken several ITV courses).*
4. *"The adult with braces" (she had new braces placed on her teeth only days before the course began).*
5. *"Cross-stitching as a hobby" (she had found cross-stitching to be a relaxing hobby).*

▶ *Select a topic you are interested in talking about*. Use this criterion to narrow down your list of possible speech topics. Mark off those topics you may know a lot about but that do not interest you. It's very difficult to interest your audience in a topic that you don't care about. Select a topic that you are enthusiastic about, and this enthusiasm will carry over to your audience. **Tip**: Don't waste time trying to find the "perfect" topic. Just find a topic that you enjoy that fits the other criteria and go with it.

By eliminating those topics that interested her the least, Lucy narrowed her possible speech topics to two: basic health maintenance and the logistics of taking televised courses. Either topic would be fine—she had personal experience with both topics as well as some outside research on each. She was

Family/Miscellaneous
Make a puppet from a sock
Make a shadow puppet
Pack a lunch a child will eat
Press a shirt/blouse with sleeves
Program your VCR
Shine shoes
Sew on a button/repair a hem
Change a cloth diaper
Properly introduce younger and older persons

Hobbies
Load/unload a camera
Take a really good picture
Keep score in bridge
Play bridge
Juggle
Make artificial flowers using tissue paper
Make fishing flies
Mat and frame pictures
Do macrame
Apply clown makeup
Draw a cartoon figure
Whittle a wooden figure
Use a miter box
Use a metal detector correctly
Erect a tent

Food/Beverages
Decorate holiday foods
Make a noncook dessert (fudge)
Make a piña colada
Make a great cup of coffee
Make a pitcher of Koolaid

Pets/Animals
Build a birdhouse or bird feeder
Groom a pet
Teach your dog a trick

Holiday/Gift/Home
Refinish furniture
Decorate holiday cakes
Fold a flag
Make gift bows
Make Christmas tree ornaments
Make a flower arrangement
Fold napkins for a party
Clean and store silver items

Magic/Games/Music
Do origami (Japanese paper-folding)
Play a guitar or harmonica
Do magic tricks
Do rope tricks
Play the drums

Health
Tape ankles (knees, wrists) to prevent injury
Save a choking person using the Heimlich maneuver
Take your blood pressure
Apply a splint
Give CPR to an adult/child

Sports/Exercise
Dribble a basketball
Hit a baseball
Keep score in tennis
Keep score in bowling
Interpret football signals
Swing a golf club
Select the proper jogging shoe
Do warm-up exercises

Personal
Balance a checkbook
Defend yourself
Tie a necktie (or bow tie)
Read a person's palm
Use the *Readers' Guide to Periodical Literature*
Use an overhead projector
Pack an overnight bag

Figure 9.2
Sample Demonstration Speech Topics (How to . . .)

able to decide between the two topics on the basis of audience interest—the next criterion to be discussed.

▶ *Select a topic that you can make interesting and/or valuable to your audience.* As was mentioned in Chapter 2, audience members don't have to be interested in your topic *before* you begin speaking, but they should be interested by the time you finish. The audience analysis you did in step 1 will help you select a topic that will interest your listeners and benefit them in some way as well. Ask yourself: What will my topic do for my listeners? Will it make them healthier,

Family
- Dealing with Alzheimer's
- The blended family
- Wills and living trusts
- Latchkey children

Business
- Changes in the workplace
- Using the Internet
- Sales techniques that work
- How to dress professionally
- Dressing on a budget
- Whole-life or term insurance?
- New computer software

Miscellaneous
- A famous person
- A vacation spot
- Topic related to your job
- Topic related to your major
- Review of a favorite book
- Who benefits from college?

Personal
- Building lasting relationships
- Dealing with stress
- Study techniques
- Preparing an effective resume
- How to improve your memory
- Protecting your car from theft
- Car repairs you can do yourself
- Living in a small town

Food/Beverages
- Illnesses from uncooked foods
- The fat content of fast foods
- Ethnic food
- Shopping on a budget
- Low-calorie cooking

Pets/Animals
- Animals that make good pets
- Selecting a pet for your child
- Teaching your dog tricks
- Disciplining your pet

Holiday/Gift/Home
- Gifts everyone will love
- Holiday safety tips
- Holiday depression
- Home protection services

Social Issues
- Neighborhood gangs
- Immigration
- Americans with Disabilities Act
- AIDS
- Charity scams
- What is political correctness?

Sports/Hobbies
- Tennis tips
- Reflective clothing for joggers
- How to watch football— for the non-football fan
- Collecting baseball cards

Health
- Lowering your cholesterol
- Music as a way to relax
- Streptococcus B
- The Heimlich maneuver
- Sleep disorders
- Effects of second-hand smoke
- Eating disorders
- CPR: basic steps
- Exercise and health
- Safe dieting
- Antidotes for household poisons
- Attention Deficit Disorder
- Vitamins
- Killer bees: not a joke anymore

National
- Social Security benefits
- Television and children
- Space station
- Airline safety features
- Environmental programs
- The new military
- NAFTA/GATT
- The role of congressional lobbyists

Multicultural*
- Mexican vaqueros, the original cowboys
- Diversity training at work
- Nonverbal cultural differences
- Japanese educational system
- African American politicians

*Marlene C. Cohen, Susan L. Richardson, and Tony D. Hawkins, *Multicultural Activities for the Speech Communication Classroom* (Geneva, IL: Houghton Mifflin, 1994), p. 133.

Figure 9.3
Sample Informational Speech Topics

happier, or more aware? Will it show them how to save money? Save lives? Communicate better with dates or parents? Study more productively for exams? Learn something new? Will it dispel a myth? Or add more excitement to their lives? In other words, a good speech topic should not only interest both you and your audience but also benefit your listeners in some way.

> Although both health and ITV courses interested Lucy, she decided that not all students were self-motivated enough to benefit from televised instruction. However, everyone in her class was interested in maintaining their health. By questioning a few of the students in her class, she also decided that a talk on health would benefit her audience more than one on televised instruction. She was now ready to determine her exact purpose and possible main points.

Tip: If you simply cannot decide between two possible topics, go to the college library and do some initial research. Check the *Readers' Guide to Periodical Literature* for current articles and the online catalog (or card catalog) for current books. (If you're not sure how to use the library to research topics, ask for help at the main desk—most college libraries have research librarians who are there *to help you*.) Why not select the topic with the most information available?

Deciding on your exact purpose   Now that you have analyzed your audience and decided on a general topic, you are ready to narrow your topic so that it will fit the time limit and the specific needs and interests of your audience. Although narrowing your topic may sound like a fairly simple process, it is one of the most difficult tasks a speaker faces, no matter how experienced the speaker is. **Tip**: It is better to cover fewer points and to thoroughly illustrate and support each point than it is to skim over a larger number of points in an attempt to "say it all." Audiences appreciate and remember well-supported points but tend to daydream when the speaker skims over too much material.

To illustrate the importance of narrowing your topic, let's assume that you are an avid professional football fan who has selected football as your general speech topic. You have five minutes to present an informative speech—how will you narrow the topic? Start by making a list of possible speeches on football, writing each in the form of an exact purpose (see the list below). An **exact purpose** should be written in one clear and simple sentence beginning with, "After hearing my speech, the audience will . . ." Can you tell which of the following purposes are still too broad for a five-minute speech?

Exact purpose: After hearing my speech, the audience will be able to . . .

1. Explain the divisions and conferences that make up the NFL.
2. Understand the steps required for a team to make it to the Super Bowl.
3. Understand the role of the Competition Committee in making game rules.
4. Realize why the instant replay rule was removed.
5. Contrast and compare the role of referee, umpire, and linesman.
6. Explain the job of coaching.

7. Realize how much power the commissioner of the NFL really has.

8. Identify the qualities needed in a winning quarterback.

9. Understand the size, speed, and psychological requirements of each football position.

10. Perceive football as a money-maker.

11. Associate football players with their commercial endorsements.

12. Explain the argument over artificial versus natural turf.

13. Describe the personality of football fans in several different cities.

14. Understand three facts viewers need to know to watch football intelligently.

15. Perceive football cheerleaders as goodwill ambassadors.

16. Know the history of Emmitt Smith (or player of the speaker's choice).

17. Demonstrate how the football is held when thrown versus when caught.

18. Understand the history of the National Football Conference (or the AFC).

Although several of these purposes could be narrowed down if the speaker so desired, purposes 6, 9, and 18 are definitely too broad. For example, there are several different types of coaches in football—head coach, assistant coach, offensive and defensive coordinators, special teams coach, line coach, quarterback coach, linebacker coach, and so on. Since it would be impossible to include them all, purpose 6 should specify which coach is being discussed (maybe the head coach or the offensive coordinator). Purpose 9 also needs narrowing—it would be difficult to include all football positions in a short speech. However, it would be possible in a short speech to compare and contrast the positions of tight end and wide receiver. In the case of purpose 18, the history of the NFL covers more than seventy-five years and encompasses a variety of teams and personalities. It would be better to narrow the purpose to something like "How the NFL got started" or "The early years of the NFL." Of course, exactly how you narrow your topic will depend on your own interests and the interests of your audience.

> Few general topics require as much narrowing as the football example discussed above. Even so, once Lucy decided to speak on the basics of health maintenance, she knew she would need to narrow the topic somewhat. After listing several exact purposes, she decided on the following—Exact purpose: After hearing my speech, the audience will be more aware of major health risk factors, cancer and heart attack warning signs, and diet and fitness guidelines.

Determining your main points   Since you have selected a topic that you already know quite a bit about, it's a good idea at this time to decide on the main points you plan to include. This helps you to complete the research step much faster because you're more focused. Of course, in your research you may uncover additional information that you wish to include in the speech or discover that one of your points should be discarded. **Tip:** In the future, if you are

Figure 9.4

Lucy's Rough-Draft Outline

Notice how it indicates where research is needed.

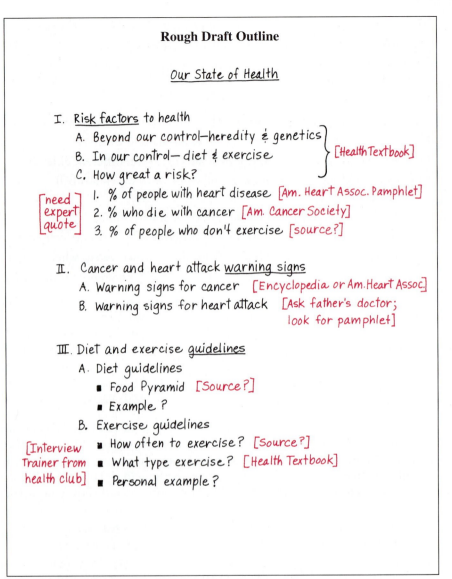

Rough Draft Outline

<u>Our State of Health</u>

I. <u>Risk factors</u> to health
   A. Beyond our control—heredity & genetics ⎤
   B. In our control— diet & exercise   ⎬ [Health Textbook]
   C. How great a risk?   ⎦
      [need expert quote]
      1. % of people with heart disease [Am. Heart Assoc. Pamphlet]
      2. % who die with cancer [Am. Cancer Society]
      3. % of people who don't exercise [source?]

II. Cancer and heart attack <u>warning signs</u>
   A. Warning signs for cancer [Encyclopedia or Am. Heart Assoc.]
   B. Warning signs for heart attack [Ask father's doctor;
                                         look for pamphlet]

III. Diet and exercise <u>guidelines</u>
   A. Diet guidelines
      ▪ Food Pyramid [Source?]
      ▪ Example ?
   B. Exercise guidelines
      [Interview Trainer from health club]
      ▪ How often to exercise? [Source?]
      ▪ What type exercise? [Health Textbook]
      ▪ Personal example?

assigned a topic that you know very little about, you'll need to do some initial research just to discover what main points will work best.

It's possible that you will know exactly what main points you wish to include since you are so familiar with your topic. However, if you are not sure, try the brainstorming method suggested earlier. In five minutes or less make a list of every possible content idea that comes to mind. Then consider each one, combining and eliminating until you settle on the three to five main points that will be the most beneficial to your audience. (Refer back to Chapter 2 for more on main point selection.)

Preparing a rough-draft outline before you begin your research (as this student is doing) will save you valuable research time.

© Hangarter/The Picture Cube, Inc.

Since Lucy had previously researched her topic of health maintenance for a paper in another class, she already knew that she wanted to include (1) health risk factors, (2) cancer and heart attack warning signs, and (3) diet and fitness guidelines. Although her instructor pointed out that any one of these main points could be developed into a complete speech, Lucy felt that for her listeners to get a clear picture of health maintenance, they needed information from all three areas. She was now ready to rough out an outline of her main points and possible supporting materials to help her determine what research needed updating and what supporting materials were lacking.

Step 3: Rough Out an Outline of Your Main Points and Possible Supporting Information

Unless you are familiar with your topic, you will need to do research before making a detailed outline. However, even before beginning your research, make a rough outline of the main points and supporting information you think you might use. With a rough outline as a guide, you will avoid researching areas that won't be included in your speech. Figure 9.4 shows Lucy's rough-draft outline.

Tip: Keep in mind that a rough-draft outline is exactly as it sounds—rough. Don't worry about following the rules for outlining. Later, when you are ready to expand your rough draft into either a preparation outline or storyboards, you will need to be more aware of procedure. If formal outlines make you break out in a cold sweat, you may want to use *storyboards* instead of a preparation *outline*. Storyboards don't require the structure or symbols used in formal outlines, plus they allow for a rough sketch of visual aids and provide space for transitions between main points. Preparation outlines and storyboards are discussed more completely in Chapter 12.

Step 4: Research Your Topic to Find Needed Supporting Materials

Analyzing your audience, selecting an interesting and beneficial topic, and making sure that your main points are clear by roughing out an outline are important steps in speech preparation. However, without adequate verbal and visual supporting materials, your speech will still be weak. You already know about the different types of visual supports from Chapters 6 and 7. Verbal supporting materials (such as explanations, illustrations, statistics, quotations, and examples) are used to clarify and prove the main ideas in your speech. Ideally some of your supporting materials should come from your own personal experiences. As you learned in Chapter 4, when you share something about yourself (a real-life experience), your audience can relate to you better. However, it's also important to gather supporting materials from books, magazines, encyclopedias, and journal articles. Using information from respected sources adds to your credibility as a speaker. Chapter 10 will cover various types of supporting materials and where and how to research for them.

Step 5: Determine How Best to Organize Your Main Points

Once you have completed your research and made any necessary changes to your main points, you will need to decide how best to organize those points. Chapter 11 will present four popular patterns for organizing the body of informative speeches: *topical*, *chronological*, *geographical*, and *causal*. Basically points organized causally follow a cause-effect or effect-cause pattern; points organized geographically follow a north/east/south/west or bottom/middle/top spatial pattern; points organized chronologically follow a time pattern such as first/second/third or in 1990/in 1992/in 1994; and finally points organized topically are related by subject. Speakers tend to use the topical pattern more often than any other. For example, Lucy uses the topical pattern when she discusses risk factors, warning signs, and diet and fitness guidelines. **Tip**: Since the unusual tends to attract interest, one of the less used organizational patterns (chronological, geographical, or causal) might create more immediate listener interest. Don't just assume that topical is the way to go.

Before deciding on any one organizational pattern, try forming your topic into all four patterns. Then select the pattern that will generate the most listener interest. Below is Lucy's topic on health maintenance organized into all four patterns. Do you think she chose the most interesting pattern?

Topical Pattern	Chronological Pattern
▶ Risk factors	▶ Risk factors for youth
▶ Warning signs	▶ Risk factors for adults
▶ Guidelines	▶ Risk factors for elderly

Geographical Pattern	Causal Pattern
▶ Health of eastern U.S.	▶ Cause: Many Americans have poor health habits.
▶ Health of middle U.S.	
▶ Health of western U.S.	▶ Effect: Poor health habits can lead to cancer and heart disease.

Step 6: Expand Your Rough-Draft Outline into a Preparation Outline (or Storyboards)

You are now ready to expand your rough-draft outline into either a preparation outline or several storyboards—either one will help you fine tune your speech. Preparation outlines are more formal; storyboards are less formal and include sketches of your visuals. (See Chapter 12 for details.)

At this point in the speech preparation process, many inexperienced speakers make a key mistake—they begin writing their speech as though it were a paper. Does this sound like you? Unfortunately writing out your speech word for word is more of a handicap than a help.

Instead, try the following method: Formalize your rough outline into either a phrase or complete-sentence outline or several storyboards. (See Figures 12.3 and 12.6 for samples.) Make sure all quotes and statistics are complete. Now, realizing that the beginning and ending of the speech are missing, read or talk through the speech. If you find that something is awkward, adjust as needed and proceed through the speech again. You may decide to add another example or remove one. You may even decide to do some more research. Whatever you do, don't memorize the speech—an extemporaneous speech will be a little different each time it's given.

Using this expanded outline/storyboard approach instead of writing out your speech word for word has many advantages:

▶ You can prepare an outline/storyboard much faster than you can write a paper.

▶ You can spot and correct needed changes (such as confusing organization or not enough supporting materials) much more easily.

▶ You can make notes to speak from in a snap.

▶ You are less likely to feel the need to memorize the speech (memorized speeches almost always are less effective and receive lower grades).

When you decide that the body of your speech is in good shape, you are ready for the next step.

Step 7: Develop the Focus, Lead-in, and Wrap-up Sections of Your Speech

Once you have completed the body of your speech (main points, supporting materials, and transitions), you are ready to add the beginning (focus and lead-in steps) and the ending (wrap-up step). Although there is nothing wrong with preparing the focus and lead-in steps before you complete the body of your

Figure 9.5

Part of Lucy's Speaking Notes on a 4- by 6-inch Note Card

speech, you will save yourself time and frustration by waiting until the body of your talk is completed. It's almost impossible to know how to introduce a speech that may change several times before it is completed. Specific guidelines on preparing the focus, lead-in and wrap-up steps (including Q & A sessions) are covered in Chapter 11. Examples from real speeches are used to illustrate each guideline.

Step 8: Prepare Visual Aids and Speaking Notes

If you organized your speech by using storyboards, you already have a good idea of the visual aids you want to use. If not, look at your expanded outline and rough out some possible visuals. One of your visuals could be a text visual listing the main points in your speech. Another visual might include a graph of some statistics or a picture that illustrates a point. Before finalizing your visuals, review Chapter 7 for design suggestions.

Your speaking notes are the last thing you need to prepare. Although there are several types of speaking notes (some speakers prefer a single, 8½- by 11-inch page, others prefer to use several smaller note cards; some speakers put

Careful speech rehearsal (including speaking aloud while using your speaking notes and visual aids) leads to a confident, professional-looking speech.

© *Sepp Seitz/Woodfin Camp & Associates, Inc.*

their notes in outline form, others do not), they all have one thing in common—they are brief. Beginning speakers often want to have a detailed sentence outline or a word-for-word manuscript with them when they speak. However, experienced speakers will tell you that this is a mistake—the words all blend in together and become more of a hindrance than a help.

Basically *speaking notes* are brief key-words or phrases that guide the speaker through the speech. Important words are usually underlined in a bright color, and personal notes may be written in the margins. Quotes are the only things written out word for word. (See Chapter 12 for more information and Figure 12.7 for a look at Lucy's one-page speaking notes.) If Lucy had chosen to use note cards, the first card might have looked like the one in Figure 9.5. After practicing, she might have decided to use even fewer words on her speaking notes.

Step 9: Rehearse Your Speech

As you learned in Chapter 8, mentally thinking through your speech will not have the same result as practicing aloud. A successful speech rehearsal involves your standing up and using your speaking notes and visual aids (including equipment if possible), in an environment similar to the one in which you will speak.

> Lucy rehearsed her speech several times in her living room using the high back of the sofa as a lectern. Her practice included use of her transparencies—she even pretended that she had an overhead projector and pushed the off/on button on the machine to ensure that her movements would be

smooth during her speech. The first time she practiced, she taped her speech to see how she sounded—she wanted her tone to indicate the seriousness of the topic without sounding glum. Later, her husband and daughter served as her audience and made some valuable comments. For example, her husband said that her hand movements were so expressive that they were distracting; her daughter assured her that her eye contact was excellent. She tried to give her speech in front of a mirror so she could see her facial expressions, but she gave it up when she couldn't keep from laughing. On the day of her speech, she managed to get to class early so she could run through her speech one time using a real overhead projector. Practice made Lucy feel confident that she would do a good job.

This chapter has presented a capsule look at what's involved in preparing and presenting an informative speech so that you can begin preparing your speech right away—even while looking forward to getting more detailed information in the remaining chapters of this unit. You can check your level of readiness by taking the following quiz.

Quiz
▼

Testing Your Knowledge of Informative Speaking

The following questionnaire is designed to call attention to some misconceptions you may have about informative speaking.

Directions: If you think a statement is generally accurate, mark it "T"; if you think the statement is a myth, mark it "F." Then compare your answers to the brief explanations that follow.

____ 1. Although explanations are necessary to clarify and define, when this type of supporting material is overused (as it is by many speakers), the result is a dull and boring speech.

____ 2. Because first impressions are the most important, you should normally develop the focus and lead-in steps before developing the body of your speech.

____ 3. After a question-and-answer session, it is very important to reestablish control and leave the audience with a feeling of closure. Therefore, end the Q & A in time to give a final, memorable wrap-up.

_____ 4. Because outlines are planning tools, it's a good idea to rough out your thoughts in outline form even before beginning to research your topic.

_____ 5. Statistics should be used as often as possible in informative speeches because listeners are impressed when you can back up your arguments with statistics.

_____ 6. A storyboard is a type of poster you can use to illustrate your speech.

_____ 7. If you're nervous, it's a good idea to tell the audience so they will make allowances for you and because you will feel more relaxed.

_____ 8. It is a good idea to avoid using humor in informative speeches unless you are a professional entertainer.

_____ 9. Although plagiarism should be a concern when speaking in public, it's only a minor concern to you as a classroom speaker because no one will know.

_____ 10. The basic procedure for beginning an informative speech is as follows: You walk to the front, pause for a second, state your topic and purpose, and then present your attention-getter.

Answers

1. *True*. As you will discover when you read Chapter 10, the one thing that is the most responsible for creating deadly dull speeches (and uninteresting English papers, for that matter) is the overuse of explanation. Instead of presenting statistics to illustrate the seriousness of a problem, speakers will "explain" how serious it is; instead of giving a real-life, personal instance to show how rude drivers are today, speakers again will "explain" that drivers are rude. Which of the following speeches do you think would be the most interesting?

Speech 1	Speech 2
I. First main point	I. First main point
A. Explanation	A. Personal instance
B. Explanation	B. Figurative comparison
C. Explanation	C. Statistics
II. Second main point	II. Second main point
A. Statistics	A. Explanation
B. Explanation	B. Quotation
C. Explanation	C. Humorous instance
III. etc.	III. etc.

2. *False*. An introduction (focus and lead-in steps) that grabs the attention of your audience is very important—otherwise, your audience may take a mental holiday during the body of your speech. However, preparing the introduction before developing your main points is usually a waste of time. Speakers normally change the direction of their speech and even add and remove main points several times before they are satisfied. Each time you make a change in the body of your speech, you will probably have to change the introduction as well.

3. *True*. Speakers often make the mistake of letting the Q & A period get out of control (audience members may begin arguing with each other or with the speaker) and/or run on *(continued)*

(continued)

too long. When this happens, audience members may forget how positive they felt about your speech and go home feeling disappointed or empty. To avoid this, thank the audience for their participation, finish up any final responses to questions, and direct your audience back to your speech topic. Using a visual aid during this final wrap-up section can be very effective. See Chapter 11 for more suggestions on how to handle the Q & A period.

4. *True.* If you know nothing about your topic, you will need to do some research before making an outline. However, if you followed the advice in this chapter for topic selection, you will know enough about your topic to rough out an outline. This will save time because it will limit and direct the amount of research needed. Remember, it is better to develop your speech through an outline than it is to write it out word for word.

5. *False.* Although statistics may lend clarity and support to your ideas, they can confuse, bore, and overload listeners when used incorrectly. Basically you need to relate statistics to your listeners' frames of reference. For example, telling a classroom audience that smoke-related diseases kill half a million people a year may leave them yawning unless you also tell them that this would be 50 people an hour, 1,200 a day, and 8,400 a week—every week for a year—until half a million people die.[1] That would be like eliminating a city the size of Fort Worth, Texas, every year! Using statistics too often is another way to bore and overload listeners. Any supporting material used too often loses its effectiveness. Chapter 10 discusses other guidelines for using statistics effectively.

6. *False.* If you read this chapter before taking the quiz, you no doubt got this one right. A storyboard is not a poster. It is an alternative way of organizing your speech that is less formal and more visual than outlining. Storyboards do not require careful use of numerals and letters, and they allow space for possible visual aids and transition statements.

7. *False.* It's never a good idea to tell your audience that you are nervous or unprepared. Even though you may momentarily feel better by confessing, your listeners will likely feel anxious, embarrassed, and uncomfortable. Your credibility in the eyes of your audience sinks as well. Also, don't forget that your feelings of anxiety rarely show—unless you confess.

8. *False.* There is a big difference between using humor and telling jokes. Few speakers are able to tell jokes effectively. If you are one of those speakers who forgets the punch line or leaves out a pertinent fact so that the punch line is meaningless, you had better leave the jokes to the pros. However, most speakers can add humor to their speeches with well-placed examples or unexpected facial or vocal expressions. As long as it doesn't work against the seriousness of your topic, humor is very appropriate in informative speeches. Information on using humorous instances is included in Chapter 10.

9. *False.* The ethical speaker is always careful not to plagiarize—it doesn't matter how unlikely it is that anyone would ever know. Using other people's material without giving them credit is always unethical. If you are concerned about plagiarism, read the section in Chapter 10 that gives pointers on how to use supporting materials and avoid unintentional plagiarism.

10. *False.* If you answered true to this question, don't feel alone. Many students follow this procedure. They walk to the front, pause, then make a statement like, "This morning, I want to cover the importance of exercise in maintaining the quality of our lives," and finally give their attention-getter. The correct procedure is to walk to the front, pause, and immediately begin with an attention-getter ("Last week, my favorite uncle was playing basketball with his two teenage sons when . . .") and then state your purpose.

There are two basic types of informative speeches—demonstration and informational. In a demonstration speech visuals become the focus of the speech; in an informational speech visuals are used only to augment and clarify.

When preparing an informative speech, the following nine steps are recommended: (1) analyze your audience; (2) determine your topic, exact purpose, and main points; (3) rough out an outline of main points and supporting information; (4) research the topic to find supporting materials; (5) determine how to organize your main points; (6) expand the rough outline into a preparation outline or storyboards; (7) develop the focus, lead-in, and wrap-up sections; (8) prepare your visual aids and speaking notes; and (9) rehearse your speech. Although the exact order of steps can be varied, until you are an experienced speaker, try to use the steps in the order suggested.

The remaining chapters in Unit Three will add details and examples to several of the steps listed above. The quiz you took in this chapter should give you a good idea of which of the remaining chapters you will need to concentrate on the most. Good luck on your own informative speech.

1. Prepare a three- to four-minute demonstration speech. Follow the guidelines in this chapter in selecting, preparing, and rehearsing your speech. Refer back to Chapter 7 for suggestions on what visuals to use and how to prepare them.

2. Begin preparation for a four- to five-minute informational speech to be followed by up to two minutes of questions from the audience and a one-minute (or less) final wrap-up. This speech will be given later in the semester after all the chapters in Unit Three have been read and discussed. Unless your instructor indicates otherwise, prepare a minimum of two transparencies—other types of visuals may be used in addition. Follow the guidelines in this chapter in selecting, preparing, and rehearsing your speech.

3. Once you have decided on a specific topic for your informative speech, decide on your exact purpose and possible main points, and prepare a rough outline. Get feedback from one or more classmates, revise your rough outline, and then discuss it with your instructor. Once you clear your exact purpose and rough outline with your instructor, you are ready to read Chapter 10 and begin your research.

4. Are you still working on the positive statements that you wrote in Chapter 3? Twice a day as you read each one aloud, are you picturing yourself successfully accomplishing the skill and feeling confident about it at the same time? Remember, changing negative thoughts and habits into positive ones requires that we "say," "see," and "feel" ourselves succeeding. If you have slacked off on your positive statements, it's not too late to begin working on them again.

Note

1. Lonnie R. Bristow, "Protecting Youth from the Tobacco Industry," *Vital Speeches* 60 (15 March 1994), 333.

10

Researching and Supporting Your Ideas

S O YOU DON'T WANT TO spend weeks in the library researching your topic? You won't need to if you followed the suggestions in Chapter 9: (1) select a topic you already know a lot about and (2) rough out an outline or storyboard. Being familiar with your topic and knowing what main points you plan to include in your speech will help you avoid researching areas you don't need and save you time. However, as you research, stay open to the possibility of revising your main points. In addition, if you were able to sketch out information needed to support your main points (as Lucy did in her rough outline in Figure 9.4), you will simplify your research even more. For example, Lucy knew that she needed to find statistics on how many people have heart disease and how many people contract and/or die from cancer—and she was able to find this information quickly and easily. And, of course, selecting a topic with which you are familiar will help cut your research time even more because you will be able to use your own knowledge and experience as supporting material. To speed you in your research, this chapter discusses where to look for needed information and what type of supporting materials you will want to look for as you research.

Where to Look for Information

▼ ▼ ▼

In researching their topics, beginning speakers tend to make one of two mistakes: (1) either they do too little research (planning to rely primarily or completely on their personal knowledge and experience) or (2) they spend too much time researching (trying to read every possible source on the topic). Either way is a mistake. Even if you have a great deal of personal experience with your topic (for example, you plan to talk on yard and garden care and you have your own landscaping service, or your topic is the advantages of ITV courses and you have taken several televised courses), it's a good idea to have *at least two additional sources*. Using information from other respected sources shows that you are an objective and informed speaker and adds to your credibility.

Although you will need to research enough information to support your main points effectively and to be able to answer any questions from the audience, it is possible to spend so much time researching that there isn't enough time left for planning and practicing your speech. Keep in mind, however, that effective speakers know much more about a topic than just what they include in their speeches. There will always be researched information that you have to leave out due to time limitations—one of the most frustrating things about speaking is that there is never enough time to tell your audience everything you know about a topic.

As you research, look for information in printed materials, computer databases, and personal interviews. If you are relatively unfamiliar with your topic, it's a good idea to begin your search for information by obtaining one or two current books on the topic. Reading them should give you a good overview. However, if you are already fairly knowledgeable on your topic, begin your search for information by conducting one or more computer searches.

Printed Materials

Before you start looking in the library for printed materials, you may want to check out two other excellent sources: (1) look in your college bookstore for textbooks on your topic—not only is the information found in textbooks current, but additional valuable sources will be listed in the footnotes and/or references—and (2) look in the phone book for local agencies (like Mothers Against Drunk Driving, the American Cancer Society, or the National Rifle Association) and call them for printed information on your topic.

Pamphlets Brochures and pamphlets can give you a useful thumbnail sketch of your topic. Contact local or national organizations for pamphlets on your topic that you can pick up or they can mail to you. Libraries usually have a vertical file of pamphlets as well as a *Vertical File Index* that lists available pamphlets.

Books Most college and university libraries now have a computerized or online catalog, which is much faster than the old-fashioned card catalogs. Unless you are looking for a specific title or author, run a subject search for books by typing in your general topic. Don't give up if no books appear under the term you choose—you may need to try several different terms before you find the one used by the library. To save time, check the *Library of Congress Subject Headings* volumes for what term your topic is likely indexed under. **Tip**: If you have a computer with a modem, you may be able to access the online catalog from your own room—ask a librarian for information.

Magazines Magazines are another good place to look for research materials, especially if your topic is current. Most of the magazines you will want to use are indexed in the *Readers' Guide to Periodical Literature*, usually found in the reference section of the library. Select the year in which you are interested, look for a term that likely indexes your topic (general terms are listed alphabetically), and then read through the articles listed under that term. Remember, it may take several tries before you find the term in the index that includes the information you want. For example, suppose you want to give a speech on blood donations, but "blood donations" is not listed. Look under other possible terms (such as "blood," "donations," "American Heart Assoc.," "blood bank," or "American Red Cross"). The librarians will be glad to assist you if you need help.

Don't overlook the more specialized indexes to magazines and journals (such as *Business Periodicals Index, Cumulative Index to Nursing and Allied Health, Education Index, Index to Journals in Communication Studies, PAIS—Public Affairs Information Services,* or the *Social Science Index*) if your topic calls for more advanced information. Depending on your library, the more recent issues of magazines may be on the shelves (either loose or bound) while the magazines dated more than one or two years ago may be located on microfilm or microfiche. **Tip**: Many libraries now have periodical indexes available on CD-ROM for fast computer searching. In addition to the indexes just mentioned, *Academic Abstracts* is an excellent computer index of both general-interest and specialized magazines and journals.

Newspapers   Although newspaper accounts are not always completely accurate, they are more current than magazines and books and contain personal details and quotes that can make good supporting materials for your speeches. Your college library will have national newspapers like *The Wall Street Journal* and *The New York Times*, several large city papers like the *Los Angeles Times* and *The Washington Post*, and some local newspapers. Many libraries also have computer indexes to major newspapers and usually to at least one local newspaper—check with your librarian. One of the most useful computer indexes is the *National Newspaper Index*, which indexes all the newspapers mentioned above. **Tip**: Many computer newspaper indexes allow you to print off complete articles, not just the references, so you can avoid having to hunt for the actual newspaper.

Specialized dictionaries and encyclopedias   If you aren't very familiar with your topic and/or haven't completed the rough outline of possible main points, you might find it helpful to begin your research with a specialized dictionary such as the *Dictionary of American History* or an encyclopedia such as *Encyclopedia of Sociology*, *Encyclopedia of Science and Technology*, or the *Physician's Desk Reference*. These reference books relate to broad subject areas and would give a general overview of your topic. For example, the *Physician's Desk Reference* contains pictures and explanations of the Heimlich maneuver.

Quotation books   You will want to familiarize yourself with the reference shelves that contain books of quotations like *Bartlett's Familiar Quotations*, the *Oxford Dictionary of Quotations*, or the *Speaker's and Toastmaster's Handbook* by Prochnow. Although the content of each book varies, most quotation books include not only quotations but also humorous stories, sayings, and proverbs—excellent supporting materials for your ideas. **Tip**: There is even a *Quotations on CD*, which indexes over 100,000 quotations. Check to see if your library has one.

Yearbooks   If you need to track down a fact or find a little-known statistic, look in the reference section for yearbooks. Besides such well-known annual references as *The Book of Lists*, *The Guinness Book of World Records*, or the *World Almanac*, there are two additional yearbooks you will find indispensable. The first is the *Facts on File Yearbook*, which includes national and international events from the previous year easily accessed by name or by date; the second is the *Statistical Abstract of the United States*, which contains statistical data on a wide variety of topics ranging from weather to the number of women over age forty expecting to give birth.

Other library resources   Although this section has covered the sources of information most likely to be used by speech students, libraries contain much more. If you need more than the sources mentioned above, check with your librarian. For example, your library may have government documents, special collections, and films or videotapes relevant to your topic. Also, you may be able

If you have a computer with a modem, you may be able to access your library's online catalog (as well as other online services) from your own room—ask a librarian for information.

© David Gonzales

to locate additional materials through interlibrary loan services. As discussed in the next section, your librarian can also help you run a computer search on more specialized databases if necessary.

Computer Databases

In addition to computer indexes for the periodicals, newspapers, and quotations, many other more specialized computer databases are available. New and expanded databases that cover books and magazines, journal articles, government documents, and more are constantly being purchased by libraries—so if you don't find what you need today, it may well be available soon. Keep asking. Many larger colleges and universities already offer more than seventy different databases for student use. A few that might be especially helpful for researching your speech are *InfoTrac*, *Periodical Abstracts on Disc*, *Education Index*, *Comm Index*, *ERIC*, *Medline*, and *Psylit*. If a variety of databases are not yet available for student use at your college, the librarian will usually run the search for you for a small fee or may access an information retrieval service to run it (again, for a reasonable fee).

It is amazing how little time it takes to locate materials now that library card catalogs are online and so many computer indexes and databases are available. Of course, reading and analyzing the information will take time, but since you will have picked a topic you enjoy, this part of your speech preparation should be pleasurable.

There are many ways to obtain information for a speech. This student is conducting a personal interview.

© *Michael Newman/PhotoEdit*

Interviews

It is possible that not even your personal knowledge, agency pamphlets, or library research will provide exactly the type of information you want. When this occurs, you can find new information by conducting one or more information-seeking interviews. In many ways conducting an interview is similar to presenting a speech. After you decide on likely candidates for your interviews, you should organize your questioning according to the FLOW model.

Decide who to interview and contact them   The prior research you have done on your topic should have given you one or more ideas on whom to interview. For example, if you were doing a speech on drunk driving, you might decide to interview one of the directors of MADD (Mothers Against Drunk Driving), a police officer assigned to DWI (driving while intoxicated) cases, a mother whose son was killed by a drunk driver, a local politician with the power to help change the state's DWI laws, an ambulance driver who arrived shortly after a recent DWI accident, or a local doctor who might be able to tell you why drunks often seem to escape serious injury. Once selected, contact the appropriate person(s) and arrange a meeting in a convenient, quiet place. When you call, be sure to tell the interviewees who you are, what course you are taking, why you want to interview them, and how much of their time you will need.

Plan the interview carefully   Even though the interview should take only fifteen or twenty minutes, its success will depend on how carefully you plan and conduct each of the following steps:

1. *Focus step*: Thank the interviewee for his or her time and establish a feeling of rapport by talking about your assignment, the weather (if it's unusual), or the reason you especially wanted to speak with this person. Be relaxed and friendly, and make good eye contact.

2. *Lead-in step*: State why you are there (unless already mentioned), how long you expect the interview to take, exactly what information you are looking for (if there are several areas, list them), and how the responses will be used.

3. *Organized step*: Here is where you will ask your questions, which you have already planned carefully. Be sure to write your questions out and bring them with you so you won't forget anything important. In general, most people will be more open and relaxed if you do not record the interview. Just listen carefully and take an occasional note to record an important fact, figure, or main idea. Try to use mainly open-ended questions—you will get more information from them. An *open-ended question* (such as "Tell me about the accident") is a general question that allows for any possible response. Specific questions (like "Was he speeding?" or "How fast was he driving?") should be kept to a minimum. Concentrate more on probing questions like "Tell me more" or "What happened next?" to keep the interviewee talking. To make sure you haven't missed valuable information, end your questioning with, "Is there anything else you think I should know?"

4. *Wrap-up step*: Use this step to verify information and give closure to the interview. Begin with a brief summary of the main areas you covered in the interview (this allows both you and the interviewee to see if anything important was omitted). If you are planning on quoting the interviewee directly, now is the time to review the quote for accuracy and ask for permission to use it in your speech. End by thanking the interviewee, shaking hands, and making a timely exit. On your way home, drop a thank-you note (expressing the value of the interviewer's information to you and your speech) in the mail.

Use the results with care   When you get back from the interview, expand your notes immediately so you won't forget or misrepresent the interviewee's information. In deciding what, if anything, to use in your speech, be sure to keep all confidences.

How to Record Your Research Information

▼ ▼ ▼

Although some instructors may prefer that you write your research notes on 4- by 6-inch note cards, any organized method will work. Instead of taking notes, some students prefer to photocopy the information and articles they find and keep everything together in a special binder. If you use this method, circle or highlight important information and use Post-it notes for summaries, messages, and ideas. What's important is that you find a procedure *that works for you*. Of course, there are some definite advantages to using note cards. For one thing, they are all the same size so they are easy to handle and store. Another advantage is that, because each card contains only one idea, it is easy to move a card from one main point to another until you have decided where it belongs (if at all) in your speech. On the other hand, a disadvantage to using note cards is the length of time it takes to hand-write quotes and summaries of the ideas you might want to use. Another disadvantage is that you may later decide that you want to use more information from the source and have to locate it again. Or the summary that seemed so clear when you wrote it may no longer be so clear when you get ready to prepare your speech.

No matter how you decide to record your research information, *to avoid unintentional plagiarism*, make sure you use a method that does the following:

▶ Provides ready access to materials.

▶ Makes clear those passages that have been paraphrased and those that are quotes. If you use cards or Post-its, always put quotation marks around any materials that are taken directly from the source.

▶ Includes complete source citations (such as complete name of author, source, date, publisher, and page numbers). For books from your college library, you may want to add a call number.

▶ Includes a bibliography. Many experienced speakers prefer to have a separate note card for each source because the cards are so easy to manage. However, a sheet of paper can be used as well. **Tip**: When your bibliography cards or bibliography page includes the complete source information for each reference, each individual note card need include only the last name of the author, title, and page number (see the sample note card in Figure 10.1).

Figure 10.1
Sample Note Card

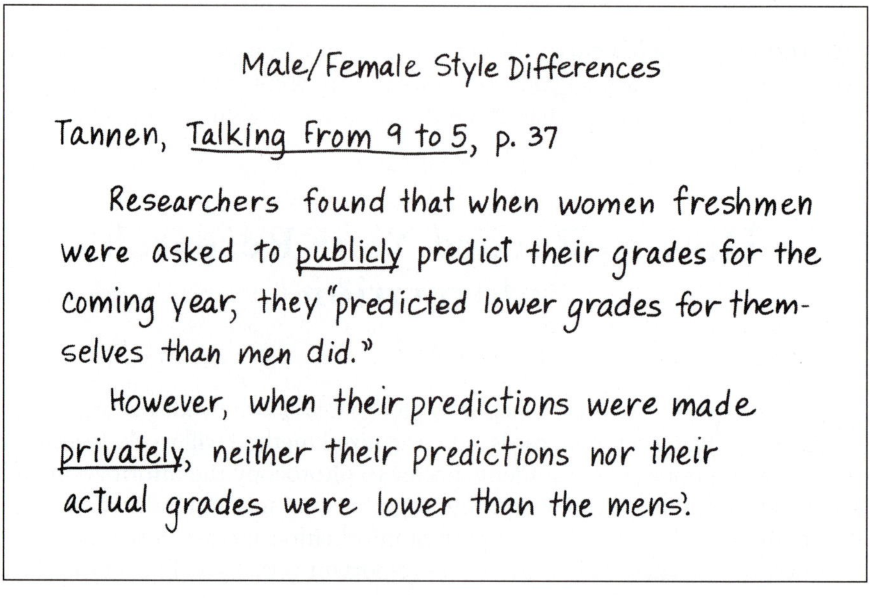

Male/Female Style Differences

Tannen, Talking From 9 to 5, p. 37

Researchers found that when women freshmen were asked to publicly predict their grades for the coming year, they "predicted lower grades for themselves than men did."

However, when their predictions were made privately, neither their predictions nor their actual grades were lower than the mens'.

Supporting Materials to Look for as You Research

▼ ▼ ▼

Now that you know *where* to find research materials for your speech, let's discuss *what* type of information you should be looking for as you research.

Supporting Materials: What They Can Do

Obviously you will want to find the information that best supports your main ideas. This information is referred to as supporting materials. *Supporting materials* are any type of verbal or visual information used to clarify, prove, or add interest to the ideas presented in your speech.

▶ *Supporting materials clarify.* Just because an idea is clear to you doesn't mean that it will be as clear to your audience. As we discussed in Chapter 1, no two people have identical frames of reference. Our experiences, family lifestyle, educational background, personality, and so on cause us to interpret things differently. Therefore it is important for speakers to clarify concepts and terms with both visual supports (such as graphs, charts, and pictures) and verbal supports (such as explanations, specific instances, and comparisons).

▶ *Supporting materials prove.* Rarely will listeners accept your statements without some kind of proof. Verbal supporting materials (such as quotes from experts, statistics, or personal instances) serve as evidence for the ideas and statements presented in a speech. Although supporting materials that prove your points are essential in persuasive speeches, they are also important in informative speeches. **Tip**: *How much proof is needed depends on your topic.* If you are speaking on the advantages and disadvantages of living in a small town, personal and family instances may be enough. However, a speech on campus crime would require not only specific instances you know about but also expert police opinion and statistics to convince the audience that your information is accurate.

▶ *Supporting materials add interest.* Using a variety of different supports is one of the best ways to keep an audience listening to your speech. For example, some listeners may find statistics and expert opinion interesting. Others may tune out statistics but listen carefully to personal or humorous instances. It's very unlikely that all your listeners will respond to the same type of support. **Tip**: For each main point use a minimum of two different types of support—more than two is even better. For example, a point supported only with statistics or only with instances is weak. A point that is supported with statistics (presented in graph form), a humorous instance, and a comparison has a greater chance of appealing to everyone.

Types of Verbal Supporting Materials

As you look for material to support the main points of your speech, try to use a variety of these types of supports: (1) explanations, (2) statistics, (3) instances (including personal, family, famous, business, and humorous instances), (4) comparisons (including literal and figurative comparisons), (5) expert opinion, (6) fables, sayings, poems, and rhymes, and (7) simple demonstrations. Explanations and statistics are the supports that are used too often while the remaining types are not used often enough. Each of these types of support will be described and illustrated in the sections that follow. While you read, note the types of support you feel would be most appropriate for your topic and look for these as you do your research.

Supports That Are Overused— Be Careful!

▼ ▼ ▼

Speakers, especially beginning speakers, tend to overuse explanations and statistics and ignore the other types of supporting materials. When overused, these supports can make a speech terribly dull; when used sparingly, they can add to listener understanding and enjoyment.

Explanations

When used correctly, an **explanation** makes clear the relationship between two or more items, defines or gives more information on a term or topic, or gives instructions on how to do something or information on how something works.

> In the introduction of her speech, Lucy defined "health" as the "absence of disease." This explanation clarified her meaning of health and prepared the way for her three main points: major risk factors to health, cancer and heart attack warning signs, and diet and fitness guidelines.

Newton N. Minnow, director of the Annenberg Washington Program in Communications Policy Studies of Northwestern University, used the following explanation to show the importance of television as an educator in his speech entitled "Television: How Far Has It Come in 30 Years."

> Suppose you were asked this multiple-choice question: Which of the following is the most important educational institution in America? (a) Harvard, (b) Yale, (c) Columbia, (d) the University of California, (e) none of the above. The correct answer is e. The most important educational institution in America is television. More people learn more each day, each year, each lifetime from television than from any other source. All of television is education: the question is, what are we teaching and what are we learning?[1]

Remember:

Explanations . . .

▶ Should be used sparingly because they tend to be dull.

▶ When used, should be brief but specific.

▶ Are more effective when followed by one or two "for instances."

▶ Are used for clarification, not proof.

▶ Tend to be overused by beginning speakers. Whenever possible, replace explanations with other types of support. For example, find a quote or comparison that clarifies the same idea as the explanation you were planning to use.

In a speech on fishing, the speaker explained how worms are gathered by the technique called "grunting":

> A popular method employed by fishermen and others to collect earthworms is the "grunting" technique, in which a stake is violently pounded into the soil and then vibrated. For reasons not fully understood, the vibrations produced drive worms to the surface where they can be collected.[2]

The best explanations are followed with an example or a "for instance" to make sure the concept is clear. Speaking before the Cincinnati chapter of the Public Relations Society of America, Fraser P. Seitel successfully used an explanation followed by four business instances to make his point on the importance of communication in a crisis:

> . . . we must convince those for whom we work that if they are truly to be "trusted" by those with whom they deal . . . then they must *explain* to people not only *what* they're doing—but more important, *why*; that is, the *reasons* for their actions.
>
>   For example, Johnson & Johnson explained why it was removing Tylenol from the shelves. Pepsi-Cola explained why it wasn't removing Diet Pepsi. Both triumphed in the face of adversity. By contrast, NASA with the *Challenger* [explosion] and Exxon in the Gulf of Valdez said little and lost terribly.[3]

When used incorrectly, explanation can produce a dull speech. Nothing is more deadly than a speech with too much explanation. Think of a really boring lecture you've heard lately. Chances are, this lecture included no comparisons, quotations, short or detailed instances, and probably no visual aids or statistics—just explanations. Read the following explanation used in a speech on the economic outlook of the United States and imagine how you would feel if the entire speech were similar to this paragraph.

I am sure that you are all familiar with the weaknesses in the economy. The construction industry suffers from lingering excess supplies due to past overbuilding as well as appropriate hesitancy among many lenders to finance new projects. Demographics are also contributing to the sluggish housing market. The aging of the population means that there are not as many first-time home buyers as there were when we came out of the last recession in 1982. Besides the adverse demographics, we had eight years of expansion in which housing demand was very well met. That means very little pent-up demand developed during the recession. . . . All in all, there is no reason to expect that a housing rebound will contribute much to the recovery, as typically has occurred in the past. . . .[4]

Statistics

Statistics are numbers used to show relationships between items. When used correctly, statistics can clarify as well as help prove your ideas. Unfortunately many speakers overuse statistics, which can create a confusing and boring speech. To make sure your statistics are a positive addition to your speeches, follow five simple rules.[5]

Rule 1: *Make your statistics meaningful by relating them to your listeners' frames of reference.* A student was giving a speech on the meteorite crater in Arizona and couldn't understand why the audience seemed unimpressed when she said, "This meteorite crater is two miles wide." After her speech she discovered that very few audience members could picture a two-mile-wide hole. In exasperation she said, "Well, this meteorite crater is large enough to hold our entire college campus with room left over for at least one football field!" Finally the audience was impressed. Another way she could have related the crater size to her listeners' frames of reference was to compare the width of the crater to approximately seventeen football fields placed end-to-end.

Speaking to a group of retired federal employees, George Marotta, research fellow at Stanford's Hoover Institution, did a good job of relating the national debt to his listeners:

> The size of our national debt of $3.7 trillion dollars is utterly incomprehensible. That sounds like a lot of money, but if you divide it by all the citizens of our country, 250 million, it amounts to only $16,000 per person. That means that when our three new granddaughters (Sara, Rebekah, and Megan) were born last year, we as a society gave them a birth present of $16,000 in our country's debt. They will have to pay interest on that debt during their lifetime. . . .[6]

Instead of just telling his Indiana University audience that tobacco kills nearly half a million Americans each year, Lonnie Bristow, M.D. and chair of the Board of Trustees of the American Medical Association, made the statistic more meaningful in the following way:

> I ask you to check your watches. Because in this hour, by the time I'm done speaking, 50 Americans will die from smoke-related diseases. By the time

you sit down to breakfast in the morning, 600 more will have joined them; 8,400 by the end of the week—every week, every month, every year—until it kills nearly half a million Americans, year in, year out.

That's more than all the other preventable causes of death combined. Alcohol, illegal drugs, AIDS, suicide, car accidents, fires, guns—all are killers. But tobacco kills more than all of them put together.[7]

Rule 2: *Eliminate any statistics that are not absolutely necessary*. Even those who generally relate well to statistics can experience overload when too many statistics are presented. In 1992 David Boaz, executive vice president for the Cato Institute, gave a speech on "The Public School Monopoly." If you had been in the audience, how would you have reacted to the following interesting but statistic-laden words?

The public schools are one of the most bureaucratic systems in our society. Between 1960 and 1984 the number of students in the public schools was stable. The number of teachers rose 57 percent, which doesn't say much for productivity, but could mean better education. The number of principals and supervisors grew by 79 percent—and the number of other staffers grew by *500 percent*.

Chicago has 3300 bureaucrats in the central school bureaucracy. The Catholic schools in Chicago serve 40 percent as many students in a larger geographical area with 36 bureaucrats. You find the same pattern in small schools. In 1980 the Berkeley newspaper reported that the Catholic schools in Oakland, California, serve 22,000 students with 2 central administrators. The schools in Richmond, California, have 30,000 students and 24 administrators. New York, of course, is always the best example. The public schools there have 6,000 central administrators. The Catholic schools serve about 20 percent as many students with 25 administrators.[8]

When you have to use a large number of statistics, apply rule 5 for effective use of statistics, as discussed below.

Rule 3: *Round off the numbers to make them easy for your listeners to recall*. The audience is less likely to remember 8,211 than they are 8,200 or, better yet, 8,000. Unless the audience expects it (for example, a group of scientists) or your topic demands it (negotiation figures), exact numbers normally are used only in handout materials and occasionally on graphic visuals. However, when discussing the data on a graphic visual (even exact-number data), round off the numbers.

Rule 4: *Demonstrate the credibility of your statistics* by citing the source, the reason the source is considered expert (if the audience doesn't already know), and the population size from which the statistics were compiled. Since today's sophisticated audiences know how easy it is to distort or even falsify statistics, you want your listeners to feel confident that the statistics you are presenting are accurate. For example, "Four out of five dentists recommend Gleam-on toothpaste" sounds good until you realize that only five dentists had to be interviewed to make that claim. However, if we knew that 300,000 dentists were surveyed and 4 out of 5 of them (240,000) recommend Gleam-on, we could feel more confidence in the results. In a speech about computer online information

Figure 10.2
Graph of Statistics

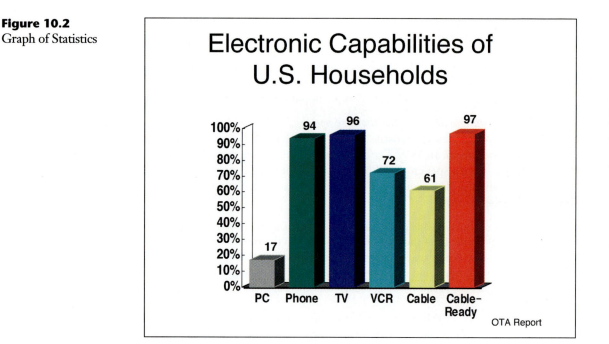

technology, Brent Baker, dean of the College of Communication at Boston University, demonstrated the credibility of his statistics as follows:

> Let's look at the citizen information capabilities: Late last year the Congressional Office of Technology Assessment (OTA) issued a report on "Electronic Delivery of Federal Services." In that report were some interesting facts:
>
> ▶ Only 17 percent of U.S. households own personal computers and only a fraction have modems for on-line services. . . .
> ▶ 94 percent of U.S. households have telephone service.
> ▶ 96 percent of U.S. households have television sets and 72 percent have VCRs.
> ▶ 61 percent of U.S. households subscribe to cable television and 97 percent have the technical capability to be connected.[9]

Rule 5: *Whenever possible present your statistics in graphic form*—your audience will comprehend them faster and remember them longer (as covered in Chapter 6). For example, Figure 10.2 contains a graphic visual of the statistics on citizen information capabilities that Brent Baker could have used in his speech on information technology.

Remember:

Statistics . . .

▶ Are numbers used to show relationships between items.
▶ Are more effective when related to listeners' frames of reference.
▶ Should be used sparingly.
▶ Should be rounded off.
▶ Are more credible when the source and source's qualifications are given.
▶ Are easier to understand and remember when shown in graphic form.

Supports That Are Underused— Maximize Them

▼ ▼ ▼

Just as explanation and statistics are overused by speakers, several effective types of support are underused: factual and hypothetical instances, literal and figurative comparisons, expert opinions, and even fables, sayings, poems, and rhymes. All of these clarify and add interest; in addition, some of them (factual instances, literal comparisons, and expert opinions) also add proof to your arguments.

Instances

One of the surest ways to grab the attention of your audience and keep them listening is to use a variety of instances. An **instance** is an example or specific case used to clarify, add interest, and (in some cases) prove a point.

Types of instances   Although there is no limit to the types of instances you can use in your speeches, the following types are very effective:

▶ Personal instances (something that happened to you or that you observed firsthand)

▶ Family instances (something involving children, parents or grandparents— not necessarily your own)

▶ Famous instances (cases involving famous people)

▶ Business instances (cases involving businesses or business topics)

▶ Humorous instances (any type of experience involving humor)

Instances can be *brief* (contain basic facts only) or *detailed* (paint a vivid picture or narrative); they can be *factual* (actually happened) or *hypothetical* (made up but could happen). Of these four categories, most instances are both factual and detailed. That means that most of your instances should be about things, people, or events that actually happened and that you will tell about in enough detail that your listeners can picture exactly what happened. For example, if you were telling about an accident, you would set the stage by telling what the weather was like that day ("It was a dull, overcast day. It wasn't actually raining, but the mist was so heavy that the roads were shiny and slick") and what emotions the participant(s) were feeling. ("It had taken Karen longer to complete her economics exam than she had planned and now she was going to be late for work. As she approached her office building, she realized that *if* she made it through this last intersection before the light changed, she might be on time").

When you use instances that are brief, it is always better to use two or more. One brief instance by itself is easy to overlook and has less impact than two or more instances. In the previous section on explanation, speaker Fraser Seitel followed his explanation with brief business instances:

> For example, Johnson & Johnson explained why it was removing Tylenol from the shelves. Pepsi-Cola explained why it wasn't removing Diet Pepsi. Both triumphed in the face of adversity. By contrast, NASA with the *Challenger* [explosion] and Exxon in the Gulf of Valdez said little and lost terribly.[10]

He used two brief instances (Johnson & Johnson and Pepsi-Cola) to illustrate what happens when businesses successfully communicate with the public, and two brief instances (NASA and Exxon) to show what happens when businesses fail to communicate with the public. Details weren't needed in these cases because the instances were already well known to his audience. Using only a single instance would not have had nearly the same impact, would it?

Don't overlook the value of hypothetical instances. Whether detailed or brief, hypothetical instances (instances that haven't actually happened but that could happen) are very useful in getting audiences interested and involved. Since a hypothetical instance is created by the speaker, it's very important that it begin in a way that cues the audience that the instance is not "real." Begin hypothetical instances with such words as "Suppose . . . ," "Imagine . . . ," or "What would you do if . . . ?" For example, in a speech on class attendance, you might use the following detailed hypothetical instance:

> Imagine that it's a school day and your alarm has just gone off. You reach over and after several tries finally get that awful noise to quit. You pull the cover from your head, force your eyes open, yawn, and roll over. You're thinking, "Should I get up and go to class, or should I skip the class and sleep in a bit longer. After all the weather is bad today and I do have a cold. . . ."

You'll probably see some sheepish looks on your listeners' faces because they've done a similar thing more than once—maybe even this morning. **Tip:** One of the advantages of using hypothetical instances is that audience members can relate the instance to their own experiences and become more involved in your speech.

Using instances to prove   Although you cannot prove an idea by using only instances, factual instances (whether brief or detailed) are effective ways to add proof to your arguments. Suppose you were trying to prove that the lakes in your state are polluted. You describe in detail the pollution that you and other people who live near a local lake have experienced. You tell about the broken glass on the beach and bottles and cans on the bottom of the lake, the soap scum and trash floating on the surface, the awful smell in the summertime, the sign the city posted on the beach last summer that warned parents not to let their children come into contact with the water, and the disbelief of the community when two teenaged boys died after diving one afternoon in the polluted water. Would describing this one lake be enough to convince your audience that the state's other lakes were polluted? No, of course not. One detailed and vivid instance might raise some doubts, but it wouldn't prove that most lakes were polluted. How about two detailed instances? Better, but still not proof. In fact, there's not enough time in most speeches to give enough detailed instances to prove a point.

Now, imagine that you have presented two detailed factual instances of polluted lakes—one in your community and another one elsewhere in the state. Then you put up a transparency listing ten other lakes and their pollution indexes and say to your audience, "Each lake on this list is as polluted or more polluted than the two I have described to you." Now, would your audience be convinced? Presenting one or two detailed instances followed by several brief instances is a very powerful proof package. Add some statistics and a quote from a water pollution expert, and your proof would be complete. **Tip**: Proof is always more likely when two or more types of supporting material are used. Even statistics, when used alone, are unlikely to completely prove a point.

Personal instances   Instances that happened to you or that you observed firsthand are of special interest to your listeners because they get to know you better through these instances. As Chapter 4 explains, personalizing your speeches is an effective way to promote better audience listening and memory. Everyone listens to personal instances—even the daydreamer. And because they listen, personal instances serve to anchor your ideas in their minds. When they recall the instance, they will most likely recall the point the instance was supporting.

Lucy used a personal instance in the focus step of her speech when she told about the conversation she had with her father the day before he died of heart disease.

In an informative speech on drunk drivers, Ken gave the following detailed personal instance of DWI to his speech classmates:

On July 4th, 1985, I was 18 years old. I got out of work early. A friend of mine bought a case of beer. We went to his house and drank three six-packs in an hour. Then we got this stupid idea to go to the beach. I had to go to my house, about three miles away, to change clothes. There are only three things I remember about that time. I remember turning the key; I remember putting in a Metallica tape; and I remember hitting a tree, head-on. Apparently the police were following me. I was told that I was driving through parking lots screaming with my beer out the window. I don't remember anything about it.

The accident was pretty bad. I was in the hospital for a few weeks. The medical bills alone were $15,000. I didn't break any bones; I wasn't wearing a seat belt. When I hit the tree, I went into the windshield with the top of my head and my arms went through the steering wheel—this elbow [points to his right arm] bent my car key. Both of my knees—one went into the heater duct and one went into the emergency brake—so my knees are real bad off nowadays. But it could have been a lot worse.

This happened in the early evening on the 4th of July, yet there weren't children playing on the corner where I hit the tree. There are always kids playing there—but this time there was nobody there. So, I thank God to this day that I didn't kill anybody. . . .

In a commencement address at Penn State University, Harvey B. Mackay used the following detailed, factual instance:

A few months ago I was in New York and hailed a taxi. It turned out to be one of the most memorable rides of my life.

In my personal opinion, the majority of New York cab drivers are unfriendly, if not downright rude. Most of the cabs are filthy, and almost all of them sport an impenetrable bullet proof partition. This time, I jumped into a cab at LaGuardia Airport and guess what? It was a *clean* cab. There was beautiful music coming out of the sound system and believe it or not, no bullet proof partition.

I said to the driver, "Park Lane Hotel please." He turned around with a big broad smile and said, "Hi, my name is Wally," and he handed me a mission statement. That's right, a *mission statement*! It said he was going to get me there safely, courteously, and on time.

As he pulled away from the curb he held up copies of *The New York Times* and *USA Today* and said, "Be my guest." A few minutes into the ride he motioned to me not to be bashful and to help myself to some of the fruit in the basket on the back seat. He then promptly asked if I preferred to listen to rock and roll or classical music from his audio tape collection. About ten minutes into the ride he held up a cellular telephone and said, "It's a dollar a minute if you would like to make a call."

Somewhat shocked, I blurted out, "Where did you learn this?" He answered, "On a talk show." I then asked, "How long have you been practicing this?" And he answered, "Three or four years." I then said, "I know this is prying, but would you mind sharing with me how much extra money you earn in tips?" He responded proudly, "Twelve to fourteen thousand dollars a year!"

He doesn't know it but he's my hero. He's living proof that you can always shift the odds in your favor if you believe in yourself.[11]

Take a few minutes and think of any personal experiences you have had that relate to your speech topic. Ask your family members and close friends if they can remember an instance involving you and your speech topic (or related topics) that you may have overlooked. Make notes on any personal instances. Remember, you are looking for instances that will clarify, add interest, or provide proof for any of your main points.

Family instances   Instances involving children, parents, spouses, combined families, or in-laws are especially effective because everyone has a family and can relate to both the problems and joys of family life. Family instances may be personal and come from your own family experiences, or they could be about other families that you have heard about. For example, in his speech entitled "Our Kids Deserve Better!" Michigan governor John Engler used several brief family instances to support his point that our schools aren't working:

> We've all heard the stories. About the mom in Detroit who broke the law and was sentenced to probation. Her crime? Sending her daughter to a higher-quality school in the suburbs where she didn't live.
>
> Or how about the Eaton Rapids kindergartner who has to ride a bus two hours a day because his school district won't release him to attend a school 10 minutes down the road.
>
> Or the story about a mother who went to court and gave up custody of her son so he could live with relatives in order to attend a higher-quality school.
>
> Or the stories about school districts hiring "family police" at taxpayer expense to investigate where children live![12]

To come up with family instances, think of the stories that family members tend to tell over and over. Ask your friends for their favorite family stories. If you find one or two family instances that relate to your speech topic, practice telling them with plenty of detail so that your listeners will feel as if they were actually there when the instance occurred. For example, David Powers told this family instance:

> One day I was trying to teach my son the value of sacrificing for the things you really want. At the moment the thing he wanted most was a BB gun. We agreed that whatever he saved out of his allowance I would double for the purchase of that BB gun.
>
> Things went along fine for a while and the fund grew rapidly. Then there was no mention of it. A month or so later I happened to think of it.
>
> "Say, Guy," I began. "Whatever happened to that money you were saving for the BB gun?"
>
> "Oh!" He hesitated. "I spent it for something else."
>
> There was my wonderful lesson gone up in smoke. What trivial thing had he bought now? I was terribly disappointed in him.
>
> "Well, Guy," I began gravely, "it was your money and if you didn't really want the gun . . ."
>
> "But, Daddy, I do want the gun—I even dream about it."
>
> "But what did you buy?"

"I bought a Chinese boy."

"A Chinese boy? How in the name of heaven did you do that?"

"Well, you see, Sister Delphine told us the missions could buy a little Chinese boy and save his life for only five dollars—so I bought one."

A great big man felt very small and hugged his boy. When the world learns to "buy" boys instead of guns there will be peace on earth.[13]

Famous instances   Instances involving famous (or at least well-known) people also capture audience interest and attention and add support for your ideas. To illustrate that public policy on the information superhighway is lagging behind reality, Robert E. Allen, chairman and CEO of AT&T, included an instance with President Clinton in his speech:

It's a bit like going jogging with the President of the United States. I understand that being photographed jogging with the President is one of the hottest photo ops in politics today.

But I've also read that some of the people who want to go jogging with Bill Clinton underestimate how fast he moves along. They run with him for a hundred yards or so and then drop back. So the Secret Service packs them into what's known as the "straggler van."

The winded politicians end up following the President in the straggler van. Then they emerge at the end of the run to have their pictures taken.[14]

In his speech on the importance of keeping a positive attitude, Richard L. Weaver used Abraham Lincoln's win-loss record to make his point:

Probably the most dramatic example in history of what attitude can accomplish occurred in the track record of Abraham Lincoln. Look at his professional accomplishments. He lost his job in 1832. He was defeated for the legislature, also in 1832. He failed in business in 1833. He was elected to the legislature in 1834. His sweetheart died in 1835. He suffered a nervous breakdown in 1836. He was defeated for speaker of the House in 1838. He was defeated for nomination for Congress in 1843. He was elected to Congress in 1846. He lost his renomination for Congress in 1848. He was rejected for land officer in 1849. Lincoln was defeated for Senate in 1854. He was defeated for the nomination for vice-president of the United States in 1856. He was again defeated for Senate in 1858. And Abraham Lincoln was elected president of the United States in 1860.[15]

Business instances   Business instances involve businesses, business topics, or business experiences (your own personal experiences or those of others). Although business instances may not fit all speech topics, when they do fit, they have the same advantages as other types of instances—they clarify, add interest to, and help prove your main points. In a speech on "Succeeding in Business," Jean L. Farinelli, CEO for Creamer Dickson Basford, used the following business instance:

In 1972, I joined Carl Byoir and Associates. At that time, Byoir was the second-largest public relations firm in the world. Most of the role models above me were men. Only one vice president was a woman. Moreover, I noticed that the men did not line up at my office door, taking bakery numbers, for the chance to become my mentor.

So I used guerrilla tactics. Every time I went to lunch, I sat next to a different vice president. I asked each VP how he succeeded, or, in Byoir terms, how they all got to the eighth floor. After a few weeks of lunches, a pattern emerged. I had broken the code. To get to the eighth floor, you managed a large account. Then you had enough work to spread around the firm, helping many of your colleagues fill up their time sheets. . . .

If you have a mentor, that's wonderful and lucky. But even if you don't, you can still get people to help you break the code.[16]

Business instances often include other types of support as well. In a speech entitled "Successful Strategies for Achieving Your Career Goals," the vice-president of Plant Operations for Miller Brewing Company, Virgis Colbert, used a business instance with statistics to support the importance of goal-writing:

Let me illustrate the power of the force that can be released when you write down your goals. A study of Yale University graduates in 1953 found that *only 3 percent* of them wrote down their goals in life. This includes actually:

▶ Listing their objectives
▶ Setting a time limit for accomplishing each goal
▶ Listing the people or organizations who could help them achieve these goals
▶ Listing the obstacles that would have to be overcome
▶ Spelling out what they need to know in order to achieve this goal
▶ Developing a plan of action, and
▶ Spelling out why they wanted to achieve each goal.

The rest of the graduating students didn't bother to write down their goals.

Twenty years later, a follow-up study revealed that the *3 percent who had written down their goals were worth more financially than all the other 97 percent combined.*

That clearly illustrates the power of written goals.[17]

Humorous instances   Humorous instances include any type of instance (personal, family, famous, or business) involving humor. The following humorous instance (also a famous and family instance) could be used in a speech on "Making Mountains out of Molehills":

Toward the end of May 1919, the Roosevelts were returning home from a dinner party when a bomb exploded outside the home of Attorney General A. Mitchell Palmer with an impact that damaged the Roosevelt house across the street. The Roosevelts rushed home to see if their son James was all right. They found him standing half asleep by the window, confused by the uproar. Roosevelt hugged him so tightly that he remembered it for years; but Mrs. Roosevelt said calmly, "Whatever are you doing out of bed at this hour, James? Get yourself to bed." When the boy asked what

A humorous instance is an excellent way to add interest and enjoyment to your speech.

© David Young-Wolff/PhotoEdit

had happened, she said, "Turn right over and go to sleep. It's just a little bomb!" For years after that, in moments of excitement in the Roosevelt household, someone was likely to quote her: "It's just a little bomb."[18]

In addition to the sources cited in the research part of this chapter, a good place to look for humorous instances is in the *Reader's Digest*. For example, Frank Scott sent the following humorous instance into the "Life in These United States" section of *Reader's Digest*:

> When we got married, my wife kept her maiden name. Although it is pronounced exactly as it's spelled—Verderosa—it frequently presents a stumbling block to telephone salesmen and others who don't know her.
>
> On one such call I was addressed as "Mr. Verdonga." Sensing my displeasure, the salesman asked, "Did I pronounce your last name correctly?"
>
> "No," I replied.
>
> "How do you pronounce it?" he asked.
>
> "Scott," I told him.
>
> After a moment of silence, he said, "Boy! It's sure not pronounced like it's spelled, is it?"[19]

This humorous instance would work well in a speech about local words that visitors typically mispronounce or in the introduction of any speech if your own name is often mispronounced. Can you think of other uses for this instance?

When you are reading newspapers, magazines, or books, try to get in the habit of keeping a record of any instances that really catch your interest. You never know when they will come in handy. Of course, before selecting any instance, analyze your audience carefully. Be especially careful to avoid inappropriate or offensive humor.

R e m e m b e r :

Instances . . .

▶ Are brief, detailed, factual, or hypothetical examples used to clarify, add interest to, and (in some cases) prove main points.

▶ When brief, are more effective when two or more are used at a time.

▶ When detailed, should paint a vivid picture for listeners.

▶ Can be of personal, family, famous, business, or humorous events.

▶ Will add spice to a speech and help ensure continued audience attention.

Comparisons: Literal and Figurative

Comparisons are another type of supporting material that is often overlooked by beginning speakers—yet they are easy to use and add greatly to a speech's overall effect. Use a *comparison* when you want to clarify something for your listeners. You do this by comparing (and/or contrasting) something your listeners know a lot about with something they know little or nothing about in order to make the unfamiliar thing clear. Suppose your listeners are very familiar with item A but they know very little about item X. By showing how item X is similar to or different from item A, you have helped your listeners to become familiar with item X as well.

There are two types of comparisons: literal and figurative. A **literal comparison** shows similarities or differences between two or more items of the same class or category. Examples of literal comparisons would be comparing two species of saltwater fish, three study techniques, two well-known diets, or the way the people of two countries view the importance of product packaging. For example, M. George Allen, senior vice president of research and development for the 3M Corporation, used the following literal comparison in a speech on "Succeeding in Japan":

> In Japan, perfection is the baseline expectation from which you begin— not where you end. For example, many Americans wouldn't care if a package is printed poorly—as long as the product inside is a good one. To the Japanese, a less than perfect package is a matter of concern. They ask: "How can you make a good product if you can't get the packaging right?"[20]

Richard D. Lamm, former governor of Colorado, also used a literal comparison when he compared affordable housing in his generation with affordable housing for today's generation:

> Let's look at housing. My wife and I bought our first house in 1963 for $11,900. Our first house payments were $49 a month. Virtually everyone

> **Remember:**
>
> **Comparisons . . .**
>
> ▶ Are especially good for clarifying the unfamiliar—compare or contrast the unknown item or idea with something that the audience knows or understands.
>
> ▶ Are an excellent way to add interest and variety to your speech.
>
> ▶ Can be either literal (comparing things that are of the same type or category) or figurative (comparing things of different types or categories).

in our generation could afford to buy a house. Yet a recent congressional study estimated that significantly fewer of those under 30 would ever be able to buy their own homes. My generation only had to spend 14 percent of our income to buy a median-priced house, where today's average 30-year-old must spend 44 percent of his income to buy a median-priced house. We passed laws that gave ourselves big tax breaks for owning our own homes and government subsidized mortgages on top of that. Yet many of our children will never in their lives be able to own their own homes.[21]

While the literal comparison compares two or more items that are basically alike, the **figurative comparison** shows similarities or differences between two or more items that are basically different—from different classes or categories. Examples of figurative comparisons would be comparing an individual to a snowflake, or the mayor of a city to the helmsperson of a boat, or an in-law to a bulldog. Figurative comparisons are never used for proof, but they do add interest and clarify ideas. For example, the Japanese ambassador to the United States, Takakazu Kuriyama, in a speech delivered at George Washington University, clarified the state of Japanese-American relations by using a figurative comparison:

> Conceptually, the Japanese-U.S. relationship has been compared to the three legs of a stool. The three legs are security, global cooperation and economic relations. The first two legs are strong. Our security ties remain close. We cooperate on a number of global issues. . . . It is the third leg of economic relations that makes the whole stool seem a little wobbly right now. . . .[22]

If you have a concept or main point that you aren't sure will be clear enough to your audience, consider using one or more literal or figurative comparisons. Even if no literal comparison comes to mind, arriving at a figurative comparison is as simple as saying, "This concept is just like . . ." For example, in a speech about overcoming speaker nervousness, you might use this figurative comparison:

The fear involved in giving a speech is similar to the fear you had as a child when you first learned to ride a bike. Remember how nervous you were waiting for your Dad to put you on the bike? But, as soon as you began to ride, your fear was replaced by excitement and by the time the lesson was over, the excitement had turned to a feeling of accomplishment and of being in control. And you wondered why you had been so nervous at all. Well, speaking is much the same. Once you start speaking, nervousness turns to excitement and then to a feeling of accomplishment. You will wonder why you bothered being nervous at all.

Expert Opinions

When you refer to the ideas of another person who is an expert on your topic, you are using a type of support referred to as **expert opinion**. Expert opinion refers to someone other than yourself. Your expertise on the topic will be presented in the form of explanations, personal (or other types of) instances, and comparisons. You wouldn't say, "And then I said, quote . . ."

Expert opinion is an excellent way to add both clarification and proof to your speech, whether you paraphrase the expert or quote him or her directly. When using expert opinion as proof, be sure to (1) state the name of the expert, (2) give a brief description of the expert's qualifications unless you are sure your audience is already familiar with the person, and (3) briefly cite when and where the expert reported this information (in the last issue of *U.S. News and World Report*, in a personal interview you conducted last week, and so on).

When *paraphrasing*—putting the expert's ideas into your own words—make sure that you don't misrepresent the expert's ideas. Here is a sample way to introduce a paraphrase:

In her new book, *Talking from 9 To 5*,[23] Deborah Tannen, university professor and well-known authority on male/female communication, makes the point that . . . [put the information in your own words].

Here is a sample way to introduce a *direct quote*:

In response to a question asking whether men or women tend to be the most indirect in their communication at work, Dr. Tannen, a well-known authority on male/female communication and author of the popular book *Talking from 9 to 5*, answered, [insert quote].

As you read direct quotes, make sure that your delivery is lively and convincing—avoid a dull or monotone presentation.

When your audience is unfamiliar with your experts, you will need to introduce them thoroughly, as Jenny Clanton did in her speech entitled "Plutonium 238: NASA's Fuel of Choice." In her attempt to inform the audience of the danger of Plutonium 238, she used the following paraphrase:

Last July, *Common Cause* magazine contacted Dr. Gofman at Berkeley and asked him to place Plutonium 238 in perspective. Before I share Dr. Gofman's assessment, please understand he's no poster-carrying "anti-nuke." Dr. Gofman was co-discoverer of Uranium 233, and he isolated the

R e m e m b e r :

Expert opinions[24] . . .

▶ May be paraphrased or quoted directly.

▶ Should be kept brief to keep listener interest.

▶ Can be use for both clarification and proof.

▶ Should be quoted as though the expert were actually speaking—not read in a dull or monotone voice.

▶ Should usually include the name and qualifications of the expert and the source and date of the information.

▶ In many cases should be followed by a brief summary or explanation.

isotope first used in nuclear bombs. Dr. Gofman told Karl Grossman, author of the article "Redtape and Radio-activity" that Plutonium 238 is 300 times more radioactive than Plutonium 239, which is the isotope used in atomic bombs.[25]

If your expert is well known to your audience, it is not necessary to cite the expert's qualifications. For example, Max D. Isaacson, vice president of administration for Macmillan Oil Company, used the following quote that needed no detailed introduction:

> But I've always been fond of quoting Eleanor Roosevelt on the subject of self-confidence and it was she who said, "No one can make you feel inferior without your consent." Think about that for a moment. "No one can make you feel inferior without your consent." Isn't that a remarkable statement?[26]

Whether you are paraphrasing or using a direct quote, try to make sure your audience understands what the expert is saying. If you feel there is any chance of confusion, follow the paraphrase or quote with such comments as, "In this quote, _____ is making the same argument I made earlier," or "What is _____ saying? He or she is telling us . . .", or "I cited _____ because . . ."

Fables, Sayings, Poems, and Rhymes

Another category of supporting material that deserves to be used more often includes such items as **fables** (fictitious stories, usually with animal characters, meant to teach moral lessons), **sayings** (pithy expressions of truth or wisdom—usually from unknown sources), **poems** (words written in meter or free verse that express ideas, experiences, and emotions in an imaginative style), and **rhymes** (poems or verses that regularly repeat sounds).[27] Although these supporting materials are used more often in focus and wrap-up steps, they also can be quite effective any place in your speech where clarification and variety are needed. They do not, however, provide proof. For example, Carole M. Howard, a Reader's Digest Association vice president, used a version of the well-known *fable* of the pig and the chicken in her speech on "Advertising and Public Relations":

> It's like the story of the chicken and the pig, who were walking down the road together when they saw a sign in a restaurant advertising ham and eggs. The chicken said, "Look, isn't that nice? Together you and I are the most popular items for people's breakfast."
>
> And the pig replied, "Yes, but for you it's only a part-time job. For me it's a total commitment."
>
> For PR and advertising people, working together needs to be a total commitment.[28]

Farah M. Walters, president and CEO for University Hospitals of Cleveland, clarified Washington's attitude toward health care reform with these words: "It's like that old saying: 'Success has many parents, but failure is an orphan.'"[29] Another *saying* was also used by Theodore J. Forstmann, senior partner of Forstmann Little, in his speech on "The Spirit of Enterprise":

> An old Middle Eastern saying runs as follows: "Lease a man a garden and in time he will leave you a patch of sand. Make a man a full owner of a patch of sand, and in time he will grow there a garden on the land."[30]

As a powerful ending to her speech on DWI, Lorna, a student in a public speaking class, used a *poem* that a listener anonymously sent in to a local radio station (see Chapter 13 for the complete poem):

> I went to a party, Mom;
> I remembered what you said.
> You told me not to drink, Mom,
> So I drank soda instead.
>
> . . . .
>
> As I lay here on the pavement, Mom,
> I hear the policeman say,
> "The other guy is drunk," Mom,
> And now I'm the one who'll pay.
>
> This is the end, Mom.
> I wish I could look you in the eye
> To say these final words, Mom,
> "I love you and good-by."

The following childrens' *rhyme* was used in the focus step of a speech on sexist fairy tales to introduce and clarify the speaker's position that children are introduced to male and female stereotypes while they are still very young:

> What are little boys made of, made of?
> What are little boys made of?

Remember:

Fables, sayings, poems, and rhymes . . .

▶ Add listener interest and clarify meanings.

▶ Should be read with enthusiasm and good vocal variety.

▶ Are especially effective when they are already known to your audience.

Frogs and snails and puppy-dogs' tails,
That's what little boys are made of.

What are little girls made of, made of?
What are little girls made of?
Sugar and spice and all things nice,
That's what little girls are made of.[31]

Demonstrations

"A picture is worth a thousand words" is a saying that expresses the importance of visual *demonstrations*. Telling about the efficiency of a vacuum cleaner may impress a client, but the client's seeing the vacuum suck up a pile of dust makes the sale. One of the reasons that TV infomercials are so successful is that we get to see demonstrations of the products. We see a lady with ordinary hair use the amazing hand-dryer with curling attachment and are impressed with the stunning hairstyle she creates; we see leftover ham chopped into a delicious ham spread in less than two minutes; and we see a knife whack through a frozen block of ice and two soft drink cans and still shave thin slices off a tomato.

Regardless of whether your demonstration involves objects, people or both, there are some basic guidelines you should follow:

▶ If your objects are not large enough to be seen by the entire audience, show pictures of the objects on transparencies or posters.

▶ Practice the demonstration until you can perform it smoothly (thus avoiding unpleasant surprises). For example, one student meant to demonstrate how common drain cleaners are highly caustic, but she didn't practice. She had a clear bowl filled with water sitting in a large, shallow pan of water. She placed a styrofoam cup of water into the clear bowl and planned to show how drain cleaner would eat a hole through the cup. However, instead of carefully measuring the drain crystals, she dumped a whole bunch in. When the drain cleaner hit the water in the styrofoam cup, it began to bubble and fizz, devouring the entire cup and forming a mushroom-type cloud that reached the ceiling. At the same time, foam bubbled up and over the edge of the clear bowl of water, out of the pan of water and over the side of the desk onto the carpet. The fumes were

To keep your listeners from displaying the skepticism you see here, make sure you use supporting materials that prove as well as clarify.

© Bob Daemmrich

so potent that the room had to be cleared. When the room aired out and the class returned, they found that the drain cleaner had blackened the ceiling tile and eaten a hole in the carpet.

▶ Unless you are giving a demonstration speech, keep the demonstration extremely brief—thirty seconds or less. Showing the correct way to hold a racquet or swing a golf club adds clarity and interest to a speech while taking only a few seconds. **Tip**: Clear all demonstrations with your instructor ahead of time.

▶ While doing the demonstration, maintain direct eye contact with your audience and continue speaking as you demonstrate.

Supporting Materials: Clarification or Proof

▼ ▼ ▼

You'll remember that our definition of supporting materials stated that they are used to clarify, prove, or add interest to the ideas presented in your speech. Using supporting materials to keep listeners interested is easy—select supports that relate to your audience and use a *variety* of supporting materials. Selecting supports to clarify and prove is more complicated because some supports are used only for clarification while others are used both for clarification and proof. As a speaker it's important to know the supporting materials that fit into each category. For example, if you were presenting a new procedure to a skeptical audience, you would need to prove the accuracy of your information. Yet your chances of doing this would be minimal if you used only supports that clarified. Here is a handy chart categorizing the supporting materials included in this chapter:

Supports Used Only for Clarification	Supports Used for Both Clarification and Proof
Explanations	Statistics
Hypothetical instances	Factual instances (detailed or brief)
Figurative comparisons	Literal comparisons (a very weak type of proof)
Fables, sayings, poems, and rhymes	Expert opinions
Demonstrations	

Summary
▼ ▼ ▼

As you do your research for your speech topic, you should look for information in at least three types of source materials: (1) printed materials (such as books, magazines, newspapers, specialized dictionaries and encyclopedias, quotations books, and yearbooks), (2) computer databases, and (3) interviews.

Not only is research important for a successful speech, but it's also important to know what type of supporting materials to look for as you research. Supports clarify, add interest to, and provide proof for your ideas. Although explanations and statistics can be successful, they are often overused. The following types of support need to be used more often: instances (personal, family, famous, business, and humorous); figurative and literal comparisons; expert opinions; and fables, sayings, poems, and rhymes. Demonstrations can also be used to clarify information.

Practice Suggestions
▼ ▼ ▼

1. To see how difficult it is to listen to a speech containing nothing but explanations, select a member of your class to read aloud the explanation of the economic outlook of the United States on page 246. The person reading should try to make the explanation sound as interesting as possible. Audience members should not follow along in the text; instead, close your text and listen carefully. When the reading is completed, discuss whether the selection held your attention or whether you kept drifting off. How could the original speaker have made this information more interesting?

2. Talk to family members and come up with at least two favorite family instances. If possible, conclude each instance with a moral. Write down the instances and exchange them with several classmates. Save them for possible use in future speeches.

3. Based on the last activity, each of you should select one detailed family instance and prepare to present it to the class. Use the personal instance by Harvey Mackay on page 252 or the family instance by David Powers on page 253 as a guide. In other words, begin with a simple sentence of explanation, present the instance, and end with a moral or brief comment on the instance. Each presentation should take no longer than one minute.

If you and your instructor prefer, have a "family instance talk-down" in which two students at the same time present their family instance, each trying to capture and hold the audience's attention. This activity could include all members of the class or only four to six volunteers. Not only is this activity a lot of fun, it will demonstrate to the class what type of instances tend to be the most effective. Let the student on the left be speaker A and the student on the right be speaker B. At the end of one minute, ask each audience member to hold up either the letter A or B to indicate which speaker held their attention more of the time. Have an assistant quickly count and record the votes.

4. Read the informative speeches located in Appendix C. Find as many examples as you can for each of the types of supporting material covered in this chapter. Compare your answers with a classmate.

Notes

1. Newton N. Minnow, "Television: How Far Has It Come in 30 Years," *Vital Speeches* 57 (1 July 1991), 554. Used by permission.
2. "Stomping Turtles," *Tropical Fish Hobbyist* 35 (March 1987), 77.
3. Fraser P. Seitel, "The 10 Commandments for Corporate Communications," *Vital Speeches* 60 (15 January 1994), 203.
4. Robert P. Forrestal, "The Outlook for the United States and the Southwest in 1992," *Vital Speeches* 58 (1 February 1992), 227.
5. Cheryl Hamilton with Cordell Parker, *Communicating for Results: A Guide for Business and the Professions*, 4th ed. (Belmont, CA: Wadsworth, 1993), p. 369.
6. George Marotta, "Bureaucracy: The National Debt," *Vital Speeches* 58 (1 June 1992), 499.
7. Lonnie R. Bristow, "Protecting Youth from the Tobacco Industry," *Vital Speeches* 60 (15 March 1994), 333.
8. David Boaz, "The Public School Monopoly: America's Berlin Wall," *Vital Speeches* 58 (1 June 1992), 508.
9. Brent Baker, "Damn the Consumers—Full Speed Ahead: The Electronic Highway," *Vital Speeches* 60 (1 May 1994), 445.
10. Seitel, "The 10 Commandments," p. 203.
11. Harvey B. Mackay, "How to Get a Job: How to Be Successful," *Vital Speeches* 57 (15 August 1991), 658.
12. John Engler, "Our Kids Deserve Better!" *Vital Speeches* 60 (15 November 1993), 73–74.
13. David Guy Powers, *How to Say a Few Words* (Garden City, NY: Dolphin Books, Doubleday, 1953), p. 120.
14. Robert E. Allen, "The Information Superhighway: Moving into the Fast Lane," *Vital Speeches* 60 (15 January 1994), 216.
15. Richard L. Weaver, II, "Attitude, Not Aptitude, Determines Altitude," *Vital Speeches* 59 (15 May 1993), 479.
16. Jean L. Farinelli, "Succeeding in Business: You Can Do It with the Right Strategy," *Vital Speeches* 60 (15 June 1994), 533.
17. Virgis Colbert, "Successful Strategies for Achieving Your Career Goals," *Vital Speeches* 60 (15 December 1993), 142.
18. Paul F. Boller, Jr., *Presidential Anecdotes* (New York: Penguin Books, 1982), p. 265.
19. Frank Scott, "Life in These United States," *Reader's Digest* 145 (December 1994), pp. 83–84.
20. M. George Allen, "Succeeding in Japan," *Vital Speeches* 60 (1 May 1994), 432.
21. Richard D. Lamm, "The Ten Commandments of an Aging Society," *Vital Speeches* 54 (15 December 1987), 135.
22. Takakazu Kuriyama, "U.S. and Japan Trade Relations," *Vital Speeches* 60 (1 May 1994), 422.
23. Deborah Tannen, *Talking from 9 to 5: How Women's and Men's Conversational Styles Affect Who Gets Heard, Who Gets Credit, and What Gets Done at Work* (New York: Morrow, 1994).
24. Adapted from Hamilton with Parker, *Communicating for Results*, 373.
25. Jenny Clanton, "Plutonium 238: NASA's Fuel of Choice," *Vital Speeches* 55 (1 April 1989), 375.
26. Max D. Isaacson, "Public Speaking and Other Coronary Threats," *Vital Speeches* 46 (15 March 1980), 352.
27. The definitions for *fable, saying, poem,* and *rhyme* adapted from *Webster's New World Dictionary of the American Language*, 2nd college ed. (New York: Simon & Schuster, 1984).
28. Carole M. Howard, "Advertising and Public Relations," *Vital Speeches* 60 (15 February 1994), 272.
29. Farah M. Walters, "If It's Broke, Fix It," *Vital Speeches* 59 (1 September 1993), 687.
30. Theodore J. Forstmann, "The Spirit of Enterprise," *Vital Speeches* 58 (1 December 1991), 122.
31. Tome dePaola, "What Are Little Boys Made of?" *Mother Goose* (New York: Putnam, 1985), p. 36.

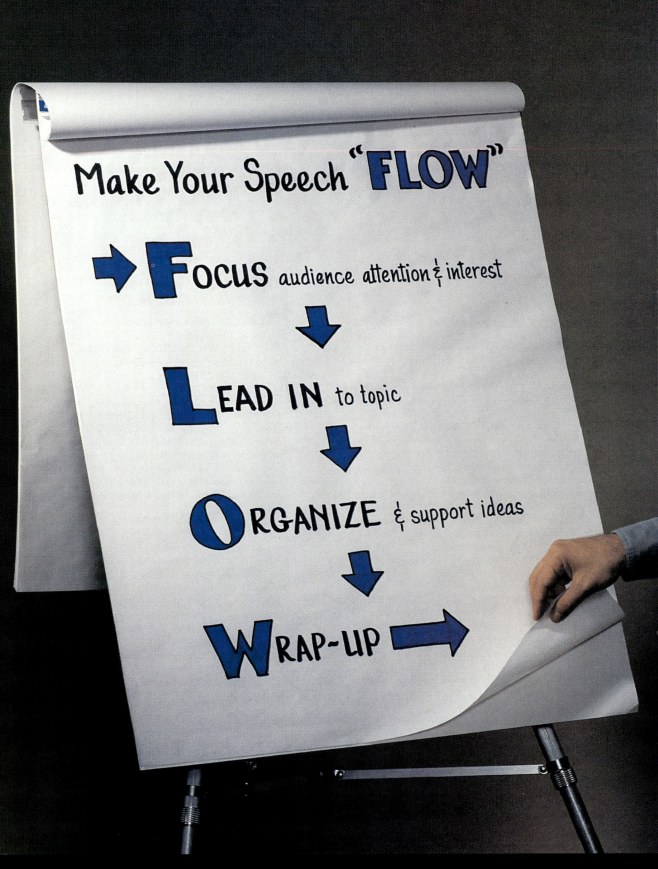

Organizing Your Ideas
So They FLOW

▼ ▼ ▼

Step 1: FOCUS Audience Attention and Interest

Begin with an Attention-Getter

Motivate Your Audience to Listen

Establish Your Credibility

Step 2: LEAD IN to the Topic

State Your Purpose

Preview Your Main Points

Include Necessary Background Information (optional)

Tell Your Audience About Handouts (if any)

Step 3: ORGANIZE and SUPPORT Your Main Ideas

Select a Pattern of Organization

More Than One Pattern at a Time

Make Your Main Points Memorable

Quiz: Test Your Knowledge of Organizational Patterns

Step 4: WRAP-UP

Summarize Main Ideas

Refocus Audience Interest

Use Q & A Effectively

Summary

Practice Suggestions

Notes

Y OU ARE ALREADY FAMILIAR WITH the FLOW sequence for organizing a speech, which was introduced in Chapter 2. Now that you are giving more involved speeches, the FLOW sequence becomes more specific as well. The basic steps of the FLOW sequence as used in informative speeches are outlined in Figure 11.1. When you plan a speech, it is usually better to plan the body of the speech (step 3: organize and support) first and then add steps 1 (focus), 2 (lead-in), and 4 (wrap-up). Otherwise you may find it necessary to change the introduction and conclusion steps each time you make a change in your main points. However, so you can see the FLOW sequence from start to finish, this chapter will describe each step in the order you present them in a speech rather than in the order you would normally prepare them.

Step 1: FOCUS Audience Attention and Interest

▼ ▼ ▼

I magine that it's your turn to speak. You walk confidently to the front of the room. After positioning your visual aids and notes, you look out at the audience and pause. Then you begin to speak: "I'm here to talk to you about NAFTA today. NAFTA stands for North American Free Trade Agreement, and this agreement is eliminating tariffs between the United States, Mexico, and Canada. . . ." What's wrong with beginning a speech this way? Many speakers do it—start their speeches with a statement of their purpose. Even President Clinton began a televised speech to the nation with these words: "Today I want to talk with you about our nation's military involvement in Somalia."[1]

To answer the question of what's wrong with beginning a speech with a statement of your purpose, let's look again at the goal of step 1—*focus* audience attention and interest. Remember in Chapter 4 we learned that in the first stage of listening, the sensing stage, listeners are highly selective. They tend to select (pay attention to) only things that are important to them or of interest to them. They tune out what seems unimportant or uninteresting. Chapter 4 also mentioned another key trait of listeners—few of them ever hear what speakers say in the first sentence or two. They are still getting settled mentally. Therefore we have two reasons for not beginning a speech with a statement of purpose: (1) since it takes a couple of sentences before most listeners are focused enough to listen, chances are they will miss your statement of purpose completely, and (2) listeners will stay alert to your speech only as long as it interests them. If they are not interested (or don't think they are interested), they will stop listening until they hear something that draws them back in.

So the question is, would most listeners immediately perk up when they heard the acronym NAFTA? How many people who caught that the president was speaking on Somalia would immediately click to another channel? Even your classmates will click to another mental channel if they don't think your topic sounds interesting or relevant to them. You can't "assume" that they will

FLOW Sequence for Organizing Informative Speeches

FOCUS audience attention and interest:
  I. Begin with attention-getter
  II Motivate audience to listen
  III. Establish credibility and rapport

LEAD IN to topic:
  I. State purpose
  II. Preview main ideas
  III. Include necessary background information (optional)
  IV. Tell audience about handouts (optional)

ORGANIZE AND SUPPORT main ideas:
  I. Use a clear pattern of organization
    A. Topical pattern
    B. Chronological pattern
    C. Spatial pattern
    D. Causal pattern
  II. Use a variety of verbal supporting materials
    A. Supports that are overused—be careful!
      1. Explanation
      2. Statistics
    B. Supports that are underused—maximize them
      1. Instances
      2. Comparison
      3. Expert opinion
      4. Fables, sayings, poems, and rhymes
      5. Demonstrations
  III. Use visual aids

WRAP-UP:
  I. Summarize main ideas
  II. Refocus audience interest

Figure 11.1
The FLOW Sequence as Used with Informative Speeches

wait until your introduction is finished to make a decision on whether to listen. It's up to you, the speaker, to provide the stimulus that sparks the interest of audience members and focuses their attention on your topic. And the sooner you do it, the better.

Which of the following speech introductions do you think would be likely to grab the interest of listeners?

Today, I want to talk to you about a hobby of mine—using a metal detector to search for metal objects in yards, parks, and around deserted buildings.

It's three days until the end of the month. How many of you could use a little extra money about right now? I certainly could, and I've got some. In my hand is a check for $92 made out in my name. Last month about this time, I received a check for $34. Where did I get this money? No, it wasn't from the lottery. I found it! I found the money represented by these checks by using an inexpensive metal detector. Today, I'm going to tell you about this hobby of mine that pays *me* money instead of costing money.

The first introduction would appeal to listeners already interested in metal detectors, but what about the rest of the audience? On the other hand, it would be difficult not to find the second introduction interesting. For the exact content of a successful focus step, look at Figure 11.1. You will see three specific things you should include: (1) begin with an attention getter, (2) motivate the audience to listen, and (3) establish credibility and rapport. Let's look at each one in more detail.

Begin with an Attention-Getter

So far, we've discussed why it's important to grab attention and spark interest in the beginning of your speech and why launching your speech with a statement of your purpose is a mistake. Of course, if your listeners have come to hear you speak on a certain topic and are eagerly awaiting your talk, then an attention-getter would not be as crucial. The following are a variety of effective ways to win audience attention. Most of them are types of supporting material that were discussed in Chapter 10. Which one to use depends on your own preference and on audience interest. However, to be successful, any attention-getter you choose will need to be practiced until you feel confident and it flows smoothly.

Detailed instance   A detailed factual or hypothetical instance (personal, family, famous, business, or humorous) is an effective way to stimulate listener interest. Remember, the key is to give enough vivid, narrative-type detail that your listeners can picture the event.

Here's a sample factual instance:

Last week something happened to me that shakes my belief in the goodness of Americans. I had decided to shop at the mall for a birthday gift for my sister . . . [in vivid detail, tell the story of what happened].

If you do not have a factual case to draw on, a hypothetical instance (in vivid detail) works well—listeners picture themselves as part of your narrative and get more personally involved. Here's a sample hypothetical instance:

Have you ever considered winning the lottery? Imagine waking up one morning and turning on the radio just in time to hear the last four winning lotto numbers. Those are your numbers! You race to the kitchen where you left the stubs just in time to hear them announce the winning numbers again . . . [in vivid detail, describe the various emotions the winner might feel].

Brief instances   Two or more brief instances (personal, family, famous, business, or humorous; detailed or brief) are very effective at grabbing the attention of an audience. For example, imagine a speech starting with these three factual instances:

In a desert east of Los Angeles, Jude Kendrick found four gold nuggets worth around $1500; in Washington, D.C., Jack Nelson found a quarter-ounce gold nugget shaped like a butterfly; George Massie found 800 ounces of gold nuggets worth over $600,000 in Temecula, California. All three of these finds (and many others) occurred in the last five years to amateur prospectors.[2]

Peter M. Gerhart, a law school dean, used only one brief instance in his speech on "The Future of the Legal Profession," but the instance and his explanation of it were powerful enough to stand alone:

If the legal profession needed a wake-up call, it got it last summer when a prominent brewing company presented a television advertisement showing a rather portly attorney coming out of a rodeo chute and being lassoed by a cowboy as the crowd cheered. Lawyer jokes are one thing, and lawyer bashing has become a part of the political process, but this was different . . . being portrayed as animals of lower intelligence who need to be corralled, lassoed, and hog-tied, rather than as agents of control, deeply affected our sensibilities.[3]

Humor   A joke or humorous instance is such a popular way to introduce a speech that we'll discuss it separately from other types of instances. Keep in mind, however, that in order to use a joke or humorous instance, it must relate to your speech topic. Imagine a speaker telling one or two jokes that are totally unrelated to the speech to come. The audience is relaxed and in a humorous mood when the speaker suddenly pauses and says, "I now want to talk to you about the high cost of funerals." How do you think the audience will react? They will laugh, of course, because the speaker has prepared them for humor, not for a serious speech on funerals. They think this statement is another joke. If the speaker had replaced the original jokes with a humorous incident related to the high cost of funerals, the audience would have been much more focused on and prepared for the speech topic. However, since most would likely consider funeral humor in poor taste, humor is not the best choice to introduce this topic.

When used correctly, however, humor can be very effective. While speaking in London, Robert L. Clarke (an American) used humor in his introduction to get attention and establish a common ground with his listeners:

. . . I will in my remarks tonight remain ever mindful of the linguistic ocean that separates the United Kingdom and the United States. Though I hope you will forgive me if you discover I have lost my bearings between the two shores. The waters are treacherous even for those with greater experience with them than I have. Even Winston Churchill—whose mother, as you know, was American—found himself adrift at times.

During a visit to the United States, Churchill was invited to a buffet luncheon at which cold chicken was served. Returning for more, he asked politely: "May I have some breast?"

His hostess replied: "Mr. Churchill, in this country we ask for white meat or dark meat."

Churchill apologized profusely.

The following morning, the hostess received a magnificent orchid from her guest of honor. The accompanying card read: "I would be most obliged if you would pin this on your white meat."[4]

In deciding whether to use jokes or humorous instances, make sure that humor is appropriate for your topic and that you are good at using it. Although anyone can tell a humorous instance, not everyone *can* tell a joke. Nothing is worse in the beginning of a speech than a joke that falls flat.

Quotation   A quote or paraphrase from a well-known publication or expert can grab the interest of your audience if you read it with good vocal variety and eye contact and if the expert has something of real interest to say. Quotes are more effective when the audience is already familiar with the expert. James V. Schall, a Georgetown University professor, successfully introduced his speech by using expert opinion:

In Woody Allen's book *Without Feathers*, a title I believe that refers to the human condition in its pristine form, he provides a brief list of what he calls "Laws and Proverbs." Allen is definitely an Old Testament type. Three of these laws and proverbs, ones that seem particularly insightful to me, are as follows:

1. "The wicked at heart probably know something."
2. "The lion and the calf shall lie down together but the calf won't get much sleep."
3. "My Lord, my Lord! What hast Thou done, lately?"

Such "laws and proverbs" remain everywhere valid and not a little amusing. The wicked do know something. Evil is not possible without knowledge, without knowledge of what is good, in fact. The calf does not doze comfortably even with a sleeping lion about. We live in a dangerous universe—such is our glory.[5]

Startling fact   Revealing one or more startling facts is another good way to grab listener attention. When your facts involve *statistics*, be sure that you make them meaningful by relating them to your listeners' frames of reference. If you were speaking on smoking, you might begin your speech with the following startling statistics:[6]

Approximately 3,000 children (average age 12½ years old) start smoking *every day*. That's over one million children a year!

To show you how successful the tobacco industry is in targeting these children, look at the success of their Joe Camel Campaign. Before the campaign, sales were approximately $6 million. After the campaign, sales reached $500 million! Before the campaign, ads reached approximately one-half of one percent of children under 18 years of age; after the campaign the ads were reaching 33 percent!

The governor of California, Pete Wilson, began a speech at the Los Angeles town hall with a startling announcement that he was launching a lawsuit against the U.S. government. His statement was an effective attention-getter:

> I've come here this afternoon to announce that I will file suit this week against the federal government for its failure to control our nation's borders. It's not a decision I come to lightly. I would rather resolve this crisis in the Congress than in the courts. But the repeated failure of Congress to confront its responsibility to control illegal immigration and to prevent the terrible unfairness to state taxpayers and to needy legal residents—has driven us to seek redress for our injuries in the courts. The federal government's immigration policy is broken and the time to fix it is now.[7]

Question   Asking a rhetorical or actual question is a good way to get listener involvement and, therefore, their attention. A *rhetorical question* is one designed to make the audience think—no real answer is expected. Asking your audience, "If I could prove that every penny would be spent purchasing items of clothing for the needy, would you be willing to donate from $1 to $5?" is a rhetorical question. However, asking your audience, "How many of you had breakfast

© Bob Daemmrich

This speaker is effectively engaging his listeners and asking them to respond to a question with a show of hands.

before coming to class this morning?" is an example of an *actual question* for which a response is expected. To make sure your audience realizes that you want a show of hands, raise your own hand as you ask the question or say, "I would like a show of hands on this question: How many of you had breakfast before coming to class this morning?"

Reference to occasion   Referring to the specific occasion or event is essential if you have been invited to speak on a special occasion (such as a company's twentieth anniversary). However, for regular classroom speeches there is no need to mention how thrilled you are to be here for the first day of informative presentations.

Fable, saying, poem, and rhyme   Opening with a fable, saying, poem, or rhyme can also be a good way to stimulate listener attention. Speaking on medical ethics, Richard D. Lamm used a fable (he called it a parable) to grab the attention of his audience:

> I would like to start with a parable. In the Christian tradition, there is the story about Saint Martin of Tours who in the Medieval Ages was riding his horse, alone and cold, through the deepening night toward the walled city which was his destination. Right outside the gate to the city, Saint Martin of Tours met a cold and starving beggar. In an act of charity that lives in Christian tradition, Saint Martin of Tours divided his cloak in half and gave it with half of his dinner to the cold and starving beggar. It was clearly the ethical and moral course to take. It has served as an example of Christian charity for centuries.
>
> Yet Brecht, in his play "Mother Courage," raises the issue of what if, instead of one cold and starving beggar, there were 40. Or, if you like, 100. What then is the duty of an ethical and moral person? It obviously does not make any sense to divide one's cloak into 40 or a 100 painfully inadequate pieces. There is no reason to choose one among the many cold and starving beggars, and it is hard to solve this dilemma other than perhaps saying a prayer for them all as you ride past them into the city.
>
> It is my passionate belief that this parable applies to the dilemma we are faced with in health care. There is a new set of realities with which we are confronted; and we must develop a new set of values and a new way of looking at health care if we are to resolve the implications of this brave new world of health care.[8]

Demonstration   A brief demonstration of a procedure or skill is the final suggested method for getting the attention of your audience. Any demonstration used would need to be brief yet impressive. For example, a demonstration speech on how to tie gift bows might begin with the following brief demonstration:

> [On the table in front of the speaker are two beautifully wrapped packages. The speaker points to the one on the left.] The bow on this package can be purchased at most specialty stores for $5. However, the bow on this package [speaker points to the package on the right] cost only 50 cents because I made it myself. Not only is this bow inexpensive, it is easy to make. [The

Remember:

Attention-getters include . . .

▸ A detailed factual or hypothetical instance.

▸ Two or more brief instances.

▸ A joke or humorous instance.

▸ A quote or paraphrase.

▸ One or more startling facts.

▸ A rhetorical or actual question.

▸ Reference to the specific occasion or event.

▸ A fable, saying, poem, or rhyme.

▸ A brief demonstration of a procedure or skill.

speaker then picks up ribbon and a wire and in only a few seconds produces a beautiful, professional-looking bow. She looks at the audience.] Look at the money you could save on birthday and Christmas gifts by making your own bows.

An informational speech on types of dead-bolt locks might use the following brief demonstration as an attention-getter:

[Two miniature door frames are placed on a table by the speaker. One frame is labeled "A"; the other is labeled "B."] The lock on door A is the same lock that 85 percent of you have on your doors. Anyone can pick this type of lock. [The speaker then reaches into his pocket and pulls out a common bobby pin, straightens it, places it in the lock, and in less than two seconds has door A swinging open.] However, the lock on door B has a special dead-bolt lock that no one can pick. In fact, the only way a person could get in this door without a key would be to kick in the door frame. [He then takes out another bobby pin and tries to open door B with no success. He looks directly at his audience.] Which door would you feel safer sleeping behind at night?

Motivate Your Audience to Listen

Unfortunately, just because your listeners laugh at your opening joke or pay attention to your personal instance doesn't mean that they will continue to listen. They must feel that there is some advantage in it for them. In other words, what will your speech do for your listeners? Will it show them how to reduce stress, develop self-confidence, lose weight, solve a pressing problem, have more interesting dates, gain a feeling of pride, improve their health, make better grades, or what? (Refer to Figure 4.2 for a list of additional motivators.) Audience members who find no particular interest or value in your topic are less likely to make the effort to listen. However, when you answer the "So what? Why should I care?" question that goes through listener minds, you are providing them with motivation to listen.

To determine how best to relate your topic to your audience, refer to the demographic and psychological information you discovered earlier when you analyzed your audience. In an informative speech, audience interests (indicated by demographic characteristics), values, and needs (psychological characteristics) are especially useful in determining how best to motivate your audience. If, for some reason, you skipped the audience analysis step, read Chapter 5 and complete it now.

Depending on your topic, it is possible to combine the attention-getting and motivation steps. For example, the gift-wrapping and door-lock demonstrations mentioned earlier as possible attention-getters not only grabbed attention but also included a reason for listening (saving money and increasing personal safety). Here's another example that combines the attention-getter and motivation to listen in just one sentence:

> If I could tell you about a hobby that is inexpensive, is something the whole family can do together, or, if you are single, is a great way to meet members of the opposite sex, would you be interested?

Establish Your Credibility

The third thing that helps focus your audience's attention and interest is establishing your credibility as a speaker. A credible person is someone whom others view as believable—someone in whom they can place their confidence. In other words, do you know what you are talking about? If you have personal experience with your topic, this is the time to mention it ("I have taught CPR for the last five years" or "I have played racquetball since I was old enough to hold a racquet"). There's no need to wear all your medals or bring in your trophies, but it is important to let your audience know of your expertise.

If you don't have personal experience with your topic, your audience will want to know why you selected this subject. Is it something you have studied about in another class? Did you write a paper on it in another class and find that the subject really mattered to you? Are you interested in it because of something that happened to a family member or a friend? Or did you watch a television program or read a newspaper article and decide to research it on your own? Unless it's too personal, sharing this kind of information with your audience will add to your credibility and help establish rapport (feeling of respect and liking) with your audience.

Another way of establishing credibility is to mention the expert sources you have consulted. If your listeners are unfamiliar with your experts, you will need to establish their qualifications. The number of sources you will need to establish your credibility often depends on your topic. If you are discussing the advantages of joining a social Greek fraternity or sorority and you have been a member for two years, you can depend largely on your own personal credibility.

However, if you have never been a member of a Greek social organization, your personal opinion on this topic will not carry weight. You will need to strengthen your credibility by using outside experts.

In Chapter 9 we saw a good example of a student informative speech, "Our State of Health" by Lucy Tisdale Setliff. Let's look at Lucy's focus step in more detail.

▼ ▼ ▼ Focus Step

Analysis

Lucy uses a paraphrase of a well-known quote by Hippocrates and a definition of "health" as her attention-getter.

The brief family instance not only serves as an attention-getter but shows why Lucy is so interested in health and helps establish her credibility. She furthers her credibility by telling us that she has researched the topic of health.

Lucy hopes to motivate the audience by telling them that the price for improper diet and poor exercise is costly bills and poor health.

Speech

Hippocrates once said that health is the greatest of human blessings. Health—what exactly does that mean to each of us? Well, as defined in Webster's Dictionary, "Health is the absence of disease." Health became very important to me when I lost my father to heart disease. The day before he died, he said, "Lucy, I'm going to fight this thing." But, you know, he couldn't because the disease had completely taken over his heart. After he died, I became better informed about our state of health and I learned that the nation's two leading causes of death are heart disease and cancer, according to former Surgeon General C. Everett Koop. I also discovered that these and other diseases that kill us are caused partially by our own habits. Through improper diet and lack of exercise, we pay the price in the way of medical bills, plus we decrease our chances of spending our "golden years" in relatively good health.

Step 2: LEAD IN to the Topic

▼ ▼ ▼

With minor changes this step is similar to the thesis statement required in an English theme. Basically it includes two essential items (statement of purpose and summary of main points) and two optional items (background information and information on handouts, if any). There is no particular order to these steps.

State Your Purpose

It is amazing how many speakers fail to make their purpose clear. Their introduction may make the general topic they are discussing clear, but their exact purpose for this particular speech may not be clear until the speech is completed, if then. You've probably had instructors like this—the general topic under discussion is clear, but the content to be covered that particular day (their specific purpose) is not clear. It makes taking notes much more difficult, doesn't it?

Remember, audience members are not always skilled listeners. If they have to do too much work to figure out your purpose, they will probably take a mental holiday. Unless you need to build suspense, you will want to quickly make your purpose as clear as possible. For example:

> Today we are going to look at three aspects of the Electoral College. [Used by student Robert McDermott in his speech "The Electoral College." The complete speech appears in Chapter 12.]

> Let me give you three tips for effective communication. If you practice these, you have a good chance to establish shared meaning and improve your communication. [Used by communications professor Carl Hensley in his speech "What You Share Is What You Get."[9]]

Preview Your Main Points

Listing your main points after you state your specific purpose will improve the chances that your audience will recall your main ideas. If you plan to use visual aids during your speech, this is an excellent time to present one. A quality visual aid (following the guidelines in Chapter 7) that lists your main points could be used during your introduction and again in your conclusion. Remember, listeners are more likely to remember information that they can see and hear at the same time.

Include Necessary Background Information (optional)

If you need to include some clarifying information but don't wish to spend enough time on it to make it into a main point, cover it as background information in the lead-in step of your speech. For example, in a speech about the causes, results, and cures of anorexia, you probably would want to define "anorexia" and briefly compare it to other types of eating disorders. You might also include some statistics on how many young women in America are afflicted with anorexia (unless you used these statistics as your attention-getter). Such background information would clarify your topic and prepare the audience to get the most from your three main points.

Tell Your Audience About Handouts (if any)

As discussed in Chapter 8, rarely should handouts be distributed during your speech—it's usually better to wait until the end. However, suppose that you were giving a speech on various organizations to which your audience could write for free information and you had a transparency of the organizations and their phone numbers. Many listeners would want to take notes. The shuffle to find paper and pencil would, in itself, become distracting. However, if in your introduction you mentioned that a handout listing the organizations and their phone numbers

© Matthew Borkoski

If you plan on distributing handouts, let your audience know during your lead-in step. This will help them decide whether to take notes.

would be available at the conclusion of your speech, audience members could relax and spend their time listening. If you had no handout, however, it would be a good idea to mention this since listeners might want to take notes.

Tip: In deciding whether to include optional information in your speech, keep this guideline in mind: the *focus and lead-in steps combined* should take no more than 10–15 percent of your total speaking time. Therefore, a speech introduction should last approximately this long: in a 5-minute speech, 30–45 seconds; in a 7-minute speech, 45–60 seconds; and in a 10-minute speech, 1–1½ minutes.

Lucy's lead-in step took about 10 seconds. When combined with her focus step (lasting 40 seconds), the introduction to her 7-minute speech lasted a total of 50 seconds. Let's take a closer look at Lucy's lead-in step.

▼▼▼ Lead-in Step

Analysis

Lucy identifies "looking at our state of health" as her specific purpose and lists three main points. Her transparency adds interest and should make it easier for the listeners to identify and recall her points.

Speech

So, this morning, I would like to look at our State of Health. I'll focus on three aspects of health: First, we'll identify major risk factors to health. [Transparency #1] Second, we'll review cancer and heart attack warning signs. Third, we'll explore diet and exercise guidelines.

Step 3: ORGANIZE and SUPPORT Your Main Ideas

▼ ▼ ▼

The body of your speech includes your main ideas and the material to support your main ideas. Since verbal supporting materials were covered in Chapter 10 and visual supporting materials were covered in Chapter 7, this section will concentrate on patterns of organization typically used in informative speeches.

Tip: Regardless of which pattern you choose, the body of your speech should take approximately 70–80 percent of your total speech time. Therefore, in a 5-minute speech, the body should last approximately 3½–4 minutes; in a 7-minute speech, 5–5½ minutes; and in a 10-minute speech, 7–8 minutes.

Select a Pattern of Organization

Basically there are four organizational patterns used by most informative speakers: (1) topical, (2) chronological, (3) spatial or geographical, and (4) causal. As you read, consider which patterns would best fit the informative speech you are currently working on.

Topical pattern   As was briefly mentioned in Chapter 9, topical arrangement is the most commonly used method of organizing main points. No chronological, geographical, or causal relationship exists between the main points in a *topical* pattern; each is merely one of several ideas related to the same subject. If you are speaking to a business or professional audience, you could organize your main points from the most to the least important since some members of the audience may have to leave before the speech is finished. However, the *best arrangement* for most talks is:

▶ Your most important or interesting point first.

▶ Your second most important or interesting point last.

▶ Your least compelling points in the middle of your speech.

It's important to begin and end with impact. Also, don't forget that listeners tend to remember better the information covered either at the beginning (primacy effect) or the ending (recency effect) of a speech.[10]

In a speech honoring Charles Lindbergh, author and columnist T. Willard Hunter organized the following main points using the topical arrangement (the visual is one he could have used):

   I. What did he do?
  II. Why did he do it?
 III. What does he have to say to us today?[11]

Charles Lindbergh

❑ What did he do?

❑ Why did he do it?

❑ His message for today?

President Clinton used a topical pattern when he organized his October 1993 speech around four questions people were asking about American effort in Somalia (the visual is one he could have used):

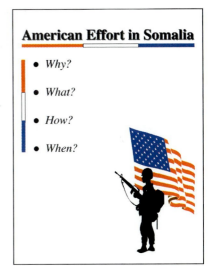

American Effort in Somalia

- *Why?*
- *What?*
- *How?*
- *When?*

I. Why are we still there?
II. What are we trying to accomplish?
III. How did a humanitarian mission turn violent?
IV. When will our people come home?[12]

Although the topical organizational pattern is very effective, don't overlook the possibility that one of the other patterns (chronological, spatial, or causal) might make your speech even more interesting. Briefly consider how your topic might play out when organized according to these four different options (see Chapter 9, pp. 226–227, for Lucy's speech topic organized all four ways). Then, based on what you know of your audience and your own preferences, select one of the patterns.

Chronological pattern   When you arrange your main points by time—either in a step-by-step order or by dates—you are using a *chronological* pattern of organization. For example, a talk on what to do in case of a fire could

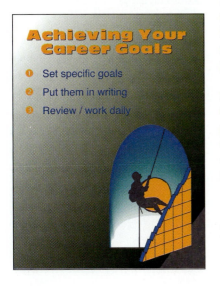

Achieving Your Career Goals

1. Set specific goals
2. Put them in writing
3. Review / work daily

be presented from first step to last. Or the history of your favorite sport could be presented in chronological order from the time it first became popular to the present.

In a speech entitled "Successful Strategies for Achieving Your Career Goals," Virgis Colbert (vice president of plant operations for Miller Brewing Company) organized his goal-setting advice in a chronological pattern (the visual is one he could have used):

I. First, set very specific goals.
II. Second, write down those goals.
III. Third, review them and work toward their accomplishment on a daily basis.[13]

Spatial or geographical pattern   When you arrange your main points according to location in space, such as front to back, left to right, first floor to third floor, or north to east to south to west, you are using a *spatial* pattern.

For example, a speech about a new Super Playground built entirely by community donations of time and money would lend itself to a geographical pattern (the visual is one that could be used):

I. The giant jungle gym at the east entrance.
II. The fort and stockade at the south entrance.
III. The swinging bridge, tunnels, and sandpit at the west entrance.
IV. The super swings at the north entrance.

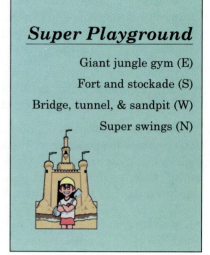

Super Playground

Giant jungle gym (E)

Fort and stockade (S)

Bridge, tunnel, & sandpit (W)

Super swings (N)

Causal pattern When your main points have a cause-effect or effect-cause relationship, you are using the *causal* pattern of arrangement. In this type of organization you would have only two main points—one would be the cause and the other would be the effect. In cause-effect you discuss a problem or condition and then follow with the result or effects of the condition.

For example, a cause-effect speech on the negative effects of spanking might be organized as follows (the visual is one that could be used):

I. Many parents use spanking to discipline their children.
   A. Over 44 percent of all parents discipline by spanking.
   B. Spanking takes many forms.
II. Spanking can result in negative consequences for the child.
   A. Spanking lowers a child's self-esteem.
   B. Spanking teaches that violence is acceptable.[14]

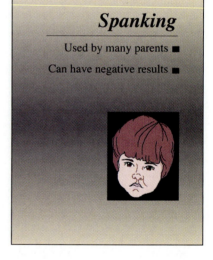

Spanking

Used by many parents ■

Can have negative results ■

This same speech arranged in effect-cause pattern would appear as follows:

I. Spanking can result in negative consequences for the child.
   A. Spanking lowers a child's self-esteem.
   B. Spanking teaches that violence is acceptable.
II. Even so, many parents use physical spanking to discipline their children.
   A. Over 44 percent of all parents discipline by spanking.
   B. Spanking takes many forms.

Remember, if you decide to use a causal pattern, you can't just assert that a causal relationship exists—you will need to cite evidence and use a variety of supporting materials. Notice that the speaker is not trying to persuade the audience to stop spanking. The speaker is merely informing the audience on the causal relationship between spanking and low self-esteem/violence in children.

More Than One Pattern at a Time

Speakers often ask if it is possible for a speech to include more than one pattern of organization. It is possible that the supporting materials for each of your main points may be organized in different patterns, but the main points themselves can use only one pattern at a time. For example, in a speech on racquetball, John organized his three main points (equipment, court, and history) in a topical pattern. However, the supporting points for each main point were organized in a variety of patterns—topical, spatial, and chronological:

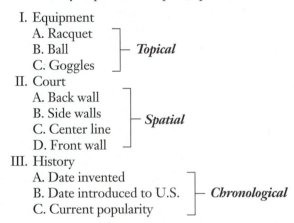

I. Equipment
   A. Racquet
   B. Ball   — *Topical*
   C. Goggles
II. Court
   A. Back wall
   B. Side walls
   C. Center line   — *Spatial*
   D. Front wall
III. History
   A. Date invented
   B. Date introduced to U.S.   — *Chronological*
   C. Current popularity

Make Your Main Points Memorable

Before you take the quiz in the next section of this chapter, take a moment to refer back to Chapter 2 (pp. 39–40) and read about how to make your main points easy to identify and remember. Chapter 2 covered the following points (which will be included in the quiz): (1) limit your main points to five—if your speech must include more than five ideas, group them into three to five categories; (2) compose your main points so they are brief and parallel (examples included in Chapter 2); (3) put your most important point either first or last; (4) occasionally use a clever rhyme or acronym like the "TIPS" example discussed in Chapter 2. Remember, your goal is to phrase your main points in such a way that your audience can't help but remember them—even weeks after you have given the speech.

Testing Your Knowledge of Organizational Patterns[15]

I. Directions: Below are six mini-outlines, each with a title and main points. Identify how the main points of each outline are organized by selecting either (a) topical, (b) chronological, (c) spatial (geographical), or (d) causal. Write the letter of your choice in the appropriate blank.

____ 1. "Ways to Cut Your Taxes"
- ▶ Invest in bank certificates of deposit.
- ▶ Get a social security number for children over five.
- ▶ Keep all receipts for nonreimbursed business expenses.
- ▶ Keep all home-improvement receipts.

____ 2. "Grounding of ATR Aircraft"
- ▶ ATR aircraft were recently grounded where icing may occur.
- ▶ Many airline commuters are experiencing serious delays.

____ 3. "Preparing an Elegant Mincemeat-Pear Tart"
- ▶ Prepare the pastry.
- ▶ Prepare the streusel topping.
- ▶ Bake crust 20 minutes at 350 degrees.
- ▶ Arrange mincemeat and pears into partially baked crust.
- ▶ Add streusel topping and bake 15 to 20 minutes at 425 degrees.

____ 4. "The Best of XYZ Software"
- ▶ XYZ allows typing in columns.
- ▶ XYZ creates perfect footnotes.
- ▶ XYZ automatically outlines and indexes.

____ 5. "The U.S. Space Station—2000 or Bust"
- ▶ The Goddard Space Flight Center in Greenbelt, Maryland
- ▶ The Lewis Research Center in Cleveland, Ohio
- ▶ The Marshall Space Flight Center in Huntsville, Alabama
- ▶ The Johnson Space Flight Center in Houston, Texas

____ 6. "Registration Advice"
- ▶ Always preregister.
- ▶ Select teachers for ability, not personality.

II. Directions: Decide which of the following answers best describes each of the following mini-outlines: (a) the main points are wordy, (b) the main points are not phrased in parallel form, (c) the main points are both wordy and not parallel, or (d) the main points represent an effective outline (for use on a visual aid, or to verbally summarize in the speech intro or conclusion).

_____ 7. "Aspirin: One Tablet a Day"

▶ Prevents heart attacks.

▶ Makes major heart attacks minor.

▶ Minimizes strokes.

_____ 8. "Aspirin: One Tablet a Day"

▶ Aspirin (one tablet a day) helps prevent heart attacks from occurring.

▶ Aspirin helps reduce the seriousness of a heart attack once it has begun.

▶ Aspirin helps prevent death and disability from cerebral thrombosis (stroke).

_____ 9. "Aspirin: One Tablet a Day"

▶ Prevents heart attacks.

▶ Major heart attacks will be turned into minor ones.

▶ Less likelihood of death and disability from strokes.

_____10. "Aspirin: One Tablet a Day"

▶ For people who have never had a heart attack, one tablet a day prevents heart attacks from ever occurring.

▶ If you have an attack, its seriousness will be diminished if you will chew one or two tablets immediately.

▶ Death and disability from strokes were greatly decreased for stroke victims who had taken an aspirin a day.

Answers, Part I

1. (a) _topical._ If you said chronological, look again. There is no time relationship between points—they could be placed in any order.
2. (d) _causal._ This is a cause-effect organizational pattern with the first statement being the problem or cause and the second statement being the result.
3. (b) _chronological._ Each main point must be done in order (time sequence) if the tart is to be completed successfully.
4. (a) _topical._ Since there are no chronological, spatial, or causal relationships among these main points, they must be organized topically.

(continued)

(continued)

5.   (c) *spatial*. Starting with Maryland in the east, the main points work westward as they locate space flight centers responsible for the possible U.S. space station—therefore a spatial pattern is used.

6.   (a) *topical*. Even though this outline has only two main points, it is not causal. There is no causal relationship between preregistering and the ability/personality of teachers. Although most speeches generally have three or more main points, there is no reason that a speech could not have only two (or even one) main points.

Answers, Part II

7.   (d) Of the four speech outlines on aspirin, this one is by far the best. The points are brief and parallel—easy for an audience to comprehend and remember.

8.   (a) Although these main points are definitely parallel (each begins with "Aspirin helps . . ."), they include too many words. The wordiness would make them more difficult to grasp and certainly more difficult for listeners to remember.

9.   (b) In this mini-outline, the main points are relatively brief, but they are not parallel. The first and third points are phrases but are not parallel; the second point is in sentence form. Also the first point speaks in the present while the second point speaks in the future.

10.   (c) The main points in this outline are neither brief nor parallel. The tense changes from present to future to past; the voice changes from "people" to "you." This outline would be the most difficult of all the outlines for your audience to remember.

Before we move to the final step in the FLOW sequence, the wrap-up, let's take a brief look at Lucy's basic speech outline as summarized in her lead-in step. Does it follow the rules discussed above?

"Our State of Health"
   I. Major risk factors
  II. Cancer and heart attack warning signs
 III. Diet and exercise guidelines

Step 4: WRAP-UP

▼ ▼ ▼

A wrap-up includes at least two things—a summary and a final refocusing thought. No speech is complete without a concluding wrap-up, because it helps make sure all points were understood and remembered and provides needed closure. It's very possible that some of your listeners missed a point (maybe they were distracted or were daydreaming for a few moments), misunderstood a point, or simply forgot one of your points. Without a wrap-up there is no way to correct these problems. A wrap-up is also important because audiences like and need closure. Without it they may feel as if they are vacationers left adrift after a pleasure cruise—much of the enjoyment created by the cruise is lost. Closure is especially important if you have a Q & A (question-and-answer) session at the end of your speech. Have a brief wrap-up before the Q & A and another one at the end of the Q & A to tie up any loose ends and to redirect audience attention back to the central ideas presented in your speech.

As you can see, the wrap-up step is too important to take lightly. If you see that time is running out, don't plan on eliminating your wrap-up. It is better to abbreviate your final point (or even skip it entirely) than to short-cut your wrap-up. If you time your speech while practicing, you won't have to worry about a time problem.

Summarize Main Ideas

A **summary**, which is a recap of the highlights of your speech, can be general (referring to the overall topic of the speech) or specific (listing the main points covered). Your choice depends on how important it is for listeners to remember specific points. If you want them to recall specific points, use a visual aid listing the points as you summarize them (the visual used to summarize your main points in the lead-in step could be used again here). Remember that the intent of the summary is to reclarify the purpose of your talk or your main points. In her classroom speech on "Outdoor Oklahoma," Christina used the following summary:

> So the next time you're looking to escape into a corner of wilderness for a moment of solitude—go to Oklahoma and check out four of nature lover's dream spots: Quartz Mountain State Park, Lake Tenkiller, Talimena Drive, and Arbuckle Wilderness. [Christina followed this summary with a refocus statement.] You too will agree that the lines from the state song truly echo Oklahomans' pride: "We know we belong to the land, and the land we belong to is grand!"

Refocus Audience Interest

You don't want your listeners to leave the room after your speech and never think of your ideas again. Try to make your refocusing step so memorable that they continue to think about and talk about your speech long after it's over. Sometimes you can refocus interest with a final thought or challenge, as Linda Reivity did when she was secretary of the Department of Health and Social Services for the state of Wisconsin. In her speech "Women's Achievements Toward Equality," she refocused interest in her topic with the following humorous and thought-provoking conclusion that played on the fact that Grover Cleveland didn't make much of a mark in history:

> I would like to close today with a salute to former President Grover Cleveland who in 1905 said, "Sensible and responsible women do not want to vote."
>
> May all those who display equal enlightenment as [his] attain an equal place in history.[16]

Speaking to a group of businesswomen on "Succeeding in Business," Jean L. Farinelli, CEO of Creamer Dickson Basford, refocused her audience's attention with the following thought and prayer:

> Almost all of us start out in life with about 700,000 hours to live—smokers end up with somewhat fewer hours. This is the greatest form of equality. Almost everyone can expect to be given those same 700,000 hours. The big question is what will we do with that time. It's completely up to us, how we will decide to spend it.
>
> So, when we wake up each morning, we might want to say this prayer: "This is the beginning of a new day. God has given me this day to use as I will. I can waste it or use it for good. What I do today is important, because I am exchanging a day of my life for it. When tomorrow comes, this day will be gone forever, leaving in its place something that I have traded for it. I want it to be gain, not loss; good, not evil; success, not failure; in order that I shall not regret the price I paid for it."[17]

Another effective way to refocus audience attention is to relate back to your focus step. The delightful and compelling speech "Light the Fire: Communicate with Your Child" is an excellent example of tying the introduction and conclusion of a speech together. Joan E. Aitken, assistant professor from the University of Missouri–Kansas City, was speaking at a parents workshop sponsored by the Heart of America Suzuki Teachers Association when she used the following focus and refocus steps:

Focus Step

As I light these four candles, I want to share some things I've heard my five year old child say . . .

CANDLE 1: "Whoops."
CANDLE 2: "Why do elephants put dirt on their backs?"
CANDLE 3: "Knock, knock" ("Who's there?") "Bananas." ("Bananas who?") "Bananas are something monkeys like to eat. Ha, ha, ha, tee-he, ho."
CANDLE 4: "Your lap is my favorite place, Mom."

As I blow out these four candles, I want to share some things I've said to my son . . .

CANDLE 1: "What's the matter with you?"
CANDLE 2: "I don't know why elephants do things."
CANDLE 3: "I don't get it. Is that joke supposed to be funny?"
CANDLE 4: "Ow. You're getting so big. Get off me."

Wrap-up (Refocus) Step

[After a 30-minute speech on how to communicate with your child:]

In closing, I want to light these four candles again, saying other words I try to use.

CANDLE 1: My child said: "Whoops."
And I said: "That's okay. What do you need to do to fix it, Wade?"
CANDLE 2: "Why do elephants put dirt on their backs?"

© David Young-Wolff/PhotoEdit

When you organize your ideas so they flow, you are likely to get this type of audience feedback at the close of your speech.

"You ask the most interesting questions. I've noticed the elephants in the zoo do that. Do you suppose it makes them cool? Maybe it's their sunscreen. What do you think?"

CANDLE 3: "Knock, knock" ("Who's there?") "Bananas." ("Bananas who?") "Bananas are something monkeys like to eat. Ha, ha, ha, tee-he, ho."

"Darlin', I love to hear you laugh."

CANDLE 4: "Your lap is my favorite place, Mom."

"Then, come sit. You are the light of my life!"[18]

Any of the supporting materials used to gain attention in the focus step of your speech (detailed factual or hypothetical instances; two or more brief instances; a joke or humorous instance; a pithy quote or paraphrase; a startling fact; a rhetorical question; a fable, saying, poem, or rhyme; or a brief demonstration), can also be used effectively to end your speech.

Tip: An effective wrap-up step should take no more than 10–15 percent of your total speaking time. Therefore the wrap-up (including the summary and refocus) in a 5-minute speech is approximately 30–45 seconds; in a 7-minute speech, 45–60 seconds; and in a 10-minute speech, 1–1½ minutes.

John J. Ring, chair, president, and CEO of Unocal Corporation, ended his speech with a detailed factual instance and a challenge. However, if you add a summary before this refocus, the wrap-up would be too long for most speeches. On the other hand, the example is really excellent. So, as you read the following section from Ring's speech, think about how it could be shortened and still retain the same effect.

Let me end my comments today with a true story. It was told to me by a senior Soviet official who visited the United States last year.

This was the first time he'd ever been outside his country. He was amazed by almost everything he saw in the United States—especially our personal freedom and our material abundance. They went beyond the wildest rumors he'd heard about America in his home country.

But what really caught his eye was a visit to a local supermarket. To him, the shelves were chock full of an incredible variety of food, beverages, and other products. He assumed that this market was reserved for high government officials and wealthy businessmen.

No, his hosts told him, anybody could just walk right in and buy whatever they liked. He did not believe them.

That night, after dinner, he decided to check it out for himself. He found a supermarket, went up to the front entrance, and just walked right in. No one stopped him, no one questioned him, no one asked to see his credentials. There were no long lines and no one was hoarding food.

He returned to his hotel room, lay down on the bed and cried. He realized that his whole life had been based on a lie.

"Your system of free enterprise works," this official said to me. "My system must change. I will never see such a high quality of life, but perhaps my children or grandchildren will live to enjoy it," he concluded.

Ladies and gentlemen, we live in a great country. Somehow, in recent years, we've begun to lose our way. To get back on track, we must ask ourselves some hard questions and squarely face our responsibilities. We must learn to value our economic rights as well as our political rights. Together, they made America the envy of the world.

Thank you for inviting me to join you today.[19]

Use Q & A Effectively

Let's end this chapter by taking a look at Lucy's wrap-up step and discussing some guidelines you can use if you are asked to include a Q & A session after your speech.

The key to successful Q & A sessions is to really know your topic and to anticipate audience questions. We mentioned earlier in this unit that one of the most frustrating things about speaking is having to eliminate so much important information (both personal and research-based) from your speech due to time limits. However, if you are planning a Q & A session to accompany your speech, it's impossible to know too much about your topic. The more you know, the better your answers will be. **Tip**: Just in case you need to refer to them, bring a note card or two listing several important sources, experts, and organizations.

In addition to knowing your topic, anticipate several questions you think your audience may ask and prepare one or two visual aids to use when answering these questions. Before preparing completely new visuals, see if one or more overlays (for example, one with a bar graph containing new information) could be added to a visual you plan to use in your speech. The overlays would be used only during the Q & A session. Of course, it's always possible that none of these questions will be asked, but if they are, your audience can't help but be impressed. Lucy included a Q & A in her wrap-up step.

Analysis

In the first two sentences Lucy is challenging the listeners to make the best choices possible.

She summarizes her main points and concludes the initial wrap-up by referring back to her opening paraphrase of Hippocrates.

Since Lucy planned a question-and-answer period immediately after her speech, an involved refocus step was not necessary.

After the Q & A, Lucy brings closure to her listeners by including a final wrap-up. Her sincerity, direct eye contact, and reference to her father's death (which ties the introduction and the conclusion together) leaves the audience thinking.

Speech

We should take a long look at the way we continue living life. Part of the great challenge of living is grasping opportunities and making the best choices we can. If we know the risk factors involved with disease, learn the warning signals that indicate disease, and discover diet and exercise guidelines, we improve our chances of preventing disease. Only then can we obtain health, the greatest of human blessings.

[Q & A session]

Thank you for your questions and your attention this morning. I think that we'll all agree that our health is what we choose to make it. How we take care of our bodies today will determine if we suffer problems later on. Health begins with awareness. Don't wait until later to get interested in your health. As it was with my father—later may be too late.

The following list contains additional suggestions to help you with your Q & A session:

▶ Repeat each question before answering it to make sure everyone heard the question.

▶ Rephrase any confusing or negative questions in a clear and positive manner.

▶ Think a moment before answering each question. If you don't know the answer, say so and refer the questioner to someone in the audience who does know or tell the person that it's a good question and that you will find the answer and let him or her know at the next meeting.

▶ If you think a question is irrelevant or will take too long to answer, thank the person for the question and mention that you will talk with him or her personally about the question after the session is over.

▶ Don't argue or get angry or defensive while answering questions. What you say during the Q & A session will affect the audience's overall judgment of your credibility and your speech.

▶ If you anticipate a hostile audience, avoid a Q & A session if at all possible. If not, mention in your lead-in that there will be a short question-and-answer period at the end of your speech and ask audience members to write out questions during your speech. After your initial wrap-up, gather up the questions, select three or four good ones, and answer them—ignoring the less desirable ones.

▶ Watch your time, and end the session with a final wrap-up that refocuses audience attention and brings a pleasing closure to your speech.

Summary
▼ ▼ ▼

Great ideas and outstanding supporting materials will be lost on the audience if your speech is not well organized. Clear, interesting, and memorable presentations that flow smoothly occur when your speech is organized around four important steps.

In the first step, you *focus* audience attention and interest on your topic by beginning with an attention-getter, motivating the audience to want to listen, and establishing credibility and rapport.

In the second step, you *lead in* to the topic by clearly stating your purpose and previewing the main points of the speech. If the main points that you preview are brief and parallel (as well as presented on a transparency or other visual aid), they will be easier for your audience to remember. In this step it may also be necessary to include background information on why you selected this topic and to mention briefly the status of any handouts.

In the third step you *organize and support* the main points that make up the body of the speech. Your main points can be organized into either the topical, chronological, spatial/geographical, or causal patterns. Main points should be clearly stated and backed up with a variety of supporting materials designed to hold the audience's attention as well as clarify and prove your ideas.

In the fourth and final step, you *wrap up* your speech by summarizing the main points and refocusing audience attention so that your listeners will remember your speech long after it is finished. Any supporting materials you can use to get attention in the beginning of the speech can be used to refocus attention at the end of your speech. Be sure to leave the audience with a satisfied feeling of closure, especially after a Q & A session.

The next chapter will include a more detailed look at outlining and storyboarding. Remember, if you don't care for outlining, storyboards may be just what you need. The final chapter in this unit on informative speaking concludes with the complete text of another student speech.

Practice Suggestions
▼ ▼ ▼

1. If you haven't already taken the "Knowledge of Organizational Patterns" quiz on page 284, do so now. Before you look at the suggested answers, compare your responses with those of a classmate.

2. Select at least two of the following speech topics and write four mini-outlines for each topic (one topical, one chronological, one spatial/geographical, and one causal):

   a. Car repairs you can do yourself
   b. Children and discipline

c. Recreational activities [in your state]

d. Exercise tips for good health

e. Pet care

As you phrase the main points, make sure they are brief and parallel. Compare answers with a classmate. Clarify any questions with your instructor.

3. In groups of four or five classmates, select one of the mini-outlines produced from the previous exercise and develop an attention-getter for the focus step and a way to refocus audience attention in the wrap-up step. Also discuss what background information, if any, you would need to include in the lead-in step of your sample speech. Share your ideas with the class.

4. Consider the informative speech you are currently working on. Take a careful look at the organizational pattern you have selected. Is it possible that another pattern could create more audience interest? If you aren't sure, prepare outlines using other patterns and ask a classmate or friend which they like best.

5. Take another look at the refocus example from John J. Ring's speech on page 289. How would you shorten this example so it could be used in a 7- or 10-minute speech? Compare your possible revision with a classmate. Were the two of you in basic agreement?

6. Select an informative speech from Appendix C (student or professional) and see if you can identify the exact line on which each of the four FLOW steps begins and ends. Are any steps missing? Use the evaluation form in Figure 11.2 to critique the speech. Compare the grade you gave with the grades given by your classmates.

7. Your instructor may wish to play a sample videotaped speech for the class. If so, evaluate the speaker using the evaluation form in Figure 11.2. Compare the grade you gave with the grades given by your classmates.

Notes

1. Bill Clinton, "Somalia: Our Troops Will Leave By March 31, 1994," *Vital Speeches* 60 (1 November 1993), 34.

2. Michael Bowker, "Is There Gold in Your Back Yard?" *Reader's Digest* 145 (September 1994), pp. 55–56.

3. Peter M. Gerhart, "The Future of the Legal Profession: The Challenge Is Not Public Relations, It Is Human Relations," *Vital Speeches* 60 (15 March 1994), 347.

4. Robert L. Clarke, "Hard Times and Great Expectations: The Condition of the National Banking System," *Vital Speeches* 54 (1 July 1988), 548.

5. James V. Schall, "On Living Three Years in New Zealand," *Vital Speeches* 57 (1 July 1991), 571.

6. Lonnie R. Bristow, "Protecting Youth from the Tobacco Industry," *Vital Speeches* 60 (15 March 1994), 334.

7. Pete Wilson, "Securing Our Nation's Borders," *Vital Speeches* 60 (15 June 1994), 534.

8. Richard D. Lamm, "New World of Medical Ethics," *Vital Speeches* 59 (1 July 1993), 549–550.

9. Carl Wayne Hensley, "What You Share Is What You Get: Tips for Effective Communication," *Vital Speeches* 59 (1 December 1992), 115.

10. J. C. Jahnke, "Serial Position Effects in Immediate Serial Recall," *Journal of Verbal Learning and Verbal Behavior* 2 (1963), 284–287.

11. T. Willard Hunter, "The Spirit of Charles Lindbergh," *Vital Speeches* 59 (15 September 1993), 722–725.

12. Clinton, "Somalia," 34–36.

13. Virgis Colbert, "Successful Strategies for Achieving Your Career Goals," *Vital Speeches* 60 (15 December 1993), 141–143.

Informative Speech Evaluation Form

Speaker: _____ Topic: _____ Evaluator:_____

Directions: For each step circle the number that best describes the overall performance (1 = poor; 5 = excellent).

FOCUS & LEAD-IN: 1   2   3   4   5
- _____ 1. Begins with attention-getter
- _____ 2. Motivates audience to listen
- _____ 3. Establishes credibility
- _____ 4. States purpose and summarizes main ideas
- _____ 5. Optional: Discusses background information/handouts

ORGANIZATION: 1   2   3   4   5
- _____ 1. Uses clear pattern of organization
- _____ 2. Makes main points easy to follow
- _____ 3. Uses smooth transitions

SUPPORTING MATERIALS: 1   2   3   4   5
- _____ 1. Supports ideas well with data; cites sources
- _____ 2. Uses variety of verbal supports
  (check those used)
  - _____ *Explanation*   _____ *Comparisons*
  - _____ *Statistics*   _____ *Expert opinions*
  - _____ *Brief instances*   _____ *Fables/sayings/poems/rhymes*
  - _____ *Detailed instances*   _____ *Explanations*
- _____ 3. Uses a variety of visual supports
  (check those used)
  - _____ *At least two transparencies used*   _____ *Professional looking*
  - _____ *Legible and easy to read*   _____ *Handled in professional manner*
  - _____ *Simple (one idea per visual)*

WRAP-UP: 1   2   3   4   5
- _____ 1. Summarizes main ideas
- _____ 2. Refocuses attention in memorable way
- _____ 3. Handles Q & A well

DELIVERY: 1   2   3   4   5
- _____ 1. Has relaxed, confident posture
- _____ 2. Maintains eye contact
- _____ 3. Sounds natural and conversational
- _____ 4. Is free of distracting mannerisms (check those used)
  - _____ *Says "uh"/"um"/"and uh"/"You know"/"well"/"OK"*
  - _____ *Plays with pencil, clothes, hair, or pointer*
  - _____ *Laughs or coughs nervously*
  - _____ *Slouches, taps feet, paces, or sways*
- _____ 5. Refers to notes only briefly
- _____ 6. Uses good volume, pitch, rate, and emphasis

OVERALL EFFECTIVENESS: 1   2   3   4   5

Grade:
30
29 A
28
27
26
25 B
24
23
22
21
20 C
19
18

Figure 11.2

14. Bruce A. Chadwick and Tim B. Heaton, eds., *Statistical Handbook on the American Family* (Phoenix: Oryx Press, 1992), p. 251; William Sears and Martha Sears, "8 Reasons Spanking Doesn't Work...And 5 Hands-Off Techniques That Do," *Redbook* 184 (March 1995), pp. 156, 158–159.

15. The mini-outlines in Part I were taken in part from Cheryl Hamilton with Cordell Parker, "Instructor's Manual," *Communicating for Results*, 4th ed. (Belmont, CA: Wadsworth, 1993), pp. 195–196. The information for the mini-outlines on aspirin came from Michael Castleman, "Aspirin: Not Just for Your Heart," *Reader's Digest* 144 (April 1994), pp. 85–89.

16. Linda Reivity, "Women's Achievements Toward Equality," *Vital Speeches* 52 (15 December 1985), 153.

17. Jean L. Farinelli, "Succeeding in Business," *Vital Speeches* 60 (15 June 1994), 533.

18. Joan E. Aitken, "Light the Fire: Communicate with Your Child," *Vital Speeches* 59 (15 May 1993), 473–477.

19. John J. Ring, "Global Competitiveness: Five Steps to Failure," *Vital Speeches* 58 (1 April 1992), 367.

Outlining and Storyboarding

How do you react when you hear the word *outline*? If your immediate reaction is a negative one, maybe you never really learned to outline correctly, or perhaps past experiences with theme-writing bring back less-than-fond memories. Whatever the reason, you aren't alone—many people dislike outlining. This dislike is really unfortunate because, when used correctly, outlines can save you a great deal of time and help you produce a much better speech.

Hopefully your recent experience using the rough-draft outline suggested in Chapter 9 has shown you that an outline can be a valuable tool. If this experience and the additional information on outlining presented in this chapter still don't ease your anxiety about outlines, try using storyboards. Storyboards, discussed in the second half of this chapter, don't require the structure or use of symbols found in regular outlines. Also they provide space for transitions and space to sketch visual aids (thus stimulating right-brain thinking and creativity).

Outlining and Storyboarding: An Overview

▼ ▼ ▼

Although we began this unit by listing the steps involved in preparing an informative speech, as far as outlining and storyboarding are concerned, speech-making can be divided into three basic stages: stage 1 (topic selection and research), stage 2 (planning and organization), and stage 3 (rehearsal and presentation of speech). The only type of outline needed in stage 1 is the rough-draft outline already described in Chapter 9. Stage 2 requires you to polish and expand the rough-draft outline into either a preparation outline or several storyboards (both will be discussed later in this chapter). However, preparation outlines and storyboards are planning tools, not speaking tools. Neither is recommended for use while speaking. Therefore in stage 3 you make brief speaking notes from your polished outline or storyboards. These notes can be in outline form if you prefer, but an outline isn't necessary. Speaking notes will be discussed later in this chapter. See the Remember box for a summary.

Outlining

▼ ▼ ▼

Two different types of outlines are suggested as valuable tools for speakers: the rough-draft outline and the preparation outline. In addition, you may decide to use an optional key-word outline for your speaking notes. You may be wondering, however, why use an outline at all.

Remember:

To aid research, use . . .	To aid planning/ organizing, use . . .	To aid speaking, use . . .
▸ *Rough-draft outline*	▸ *Preparation outline or storyboards*	▸ *Speaking notes*

What's the Real Value of Outlining?

As Chapter 9 indicated, many inexperienced speakers fail to make use of outlines. In fact, if they prepare an outline at all, it's done after the speech is completed and only because the instructor insists. Does this sound like you? If you don't organize your initial thoughts by using a brief, rough-draft outline and revise this rough draft into a more detailed preparation outline (written in phrase or sentence form), you must be writing your speech out word for word. Let's look at the real value of outlining and its advantages over writing out your speech in manuscript form:

Problems with speech easier to detect   When you look at your speech written in manuscript form, can you tell at a glance how your main points are organized? Can you tell which of your main points have too much supporting material and which ones don't have enough? Can you be sure that you have used a variety of supporting material? You will have a hard time identifying areas needing change when your speech is in manuscript form. To understand how difficult written-out speeches can be to analyze, imagine trying to do research in a book that lacks a table of contents (which is basically an outline of what's in the book) and lacks section headings in the chapters. You could not just glance at a book's table of contents or skim the section headings to find the categories of information you need; instead, you would have to read the entire book to tell if it held any valuable information on your topic. Writing your speech in manuscript form causes similar problems. When you can't see your speech in outline form, it's difficult to see the big picture and to know what needs work.

Worthwhile critiques less difficult to solicit   Have you ever handed a speech manuscript to a friend or classmate and asked them to look it over and make some suggestions? If so, they probably said something like, "Looks good to me." It would be an unusual friend who carefully read the entire speech. However, if you handed them an outline, they could read it without too much effort and would likely make more valuable suggestions.

Temptation to memorize diminished   When a speech is written word for word, the tendency to memorize it is great. Inexperienced speakers will often say, "I'll make an outline to speak from later; right now, I'm just practicing with the manuscript until I get familiar with it." The problem is that after you get used to reading your speech (a comfortable crutch), it's difficult to change to a speaking outline. When you speak from an outline, your speech will be slightly different each time you give it—this is positive, not negative. Remember, a spontaneous delivery will be much more interesting for an audience than a memorized speech. (Refer back to Chapter 8 for some of the problems involved in memorized speaking.)

Speaker flexibility increased   One purpose of an education is to increase your flexibility, yet writing a speech in manuscript form limits your speaking flexibility. For example, what if in the future your boss says, "We have an unscheduled team coming from our plant in Akron. They'll be here in thirty minutes and I would like you to present . . ." There is no time to write out the speech word for word. All you have time to do is jot down the main points you want to cover, decide on some supporting facts (you may have to make a couple of phone calls to get the most recent data or statistics), and think of an attention-getter to focus the team on your topic. Learning to use an outline adds to your flexibility as a speaker.

The only way you can see the true value of outlining is to use outlining as it's described in this chapter (and in Chapter 9). It won't be easy if you are used to writing your speech in manuscript form, but the rewards can be great.

General Outlining Tips

There are five simple suggestions for creating outlines that can ensure their readability and usefulness without bogging you down in mechanics. *These principles must be applied to your preparation outline.* However, because your rough-draft outline is expected to be "rough" and your speaking notes don't have to be in outline form at all, it's up to you whether to apply these outlining tips to your rough-draft outline and your speaking notes.

▶ *Use standard numbering.* Since the main steps of the FLOW sequence—focus, lead in, organize and support, and wrap-up—don't need to be preceded by any number or letter, it is recommended that you reserve roman numerals for your main points, use capital letters for the first-level subpoints or supporting material, and standard numbers for second-level supporting materials. Basically the different levels most typically used in speech outlines are:

I. First main point
  A. Subpoint or supporting material
    1. Supporting material

▶ *Indent for faster comprehension.* When each main point and level is indented (instead of left-aligned or centered), you can grasp your general ideas and find needed information more quickly. Beverley's second main point from her speech on ADHD (Attention Deficit Hyperactive Disorder) illustrates the importance of indenting.

Centered:

II. The real trouble begins when the child starts kindergarten.
                        A. First conference
                            B. Testing
                    1. Stanford Binet (IQ test)
                2. Attention Deficit Rating Scale
                    3. Oppositional Defiant Scale
                        4. Physical exam
                C. Recommended treatment
                        1. Ritalin
                        2. Clondine

Left-aligned:

II. The real trouble begins when the child starts kindergarten.
A. First conference
B. Testing
1. Stanford Binet (IQ test)
2. Attention Deficit Rating Scale
3. Oppositional Defiant Scale
4. Physical exam
C. Recommended treatment
1. Ritalin
2. Clondine

Indented:

II. The real trouble begins when the child starts kindergarten.
    A. First conference
    B. Testing
        1. Stanford Binet (IQ test)
        2. Attention Deficit Rating Scale
        3. Oppositional Defiant Scale
        4. Physical exam
    C. Recommended treatment
        1. Ritalin
        2. Clondine

▶ *Include at least two items per level when possible*. In other words, if you have an "A," you need a "B"; if you have a "1," you need at least a "2" (see Figure 12.1). However, don't force an unnatural division just to have two items per level. On rare occasions you might use a single item.

▶ *Use parallel elements in each level*. Therefore, if the item in "A" is a sentence, then "B" should also be a sentence (see Figure 12.1, A, B, and C). However,

Figure 12.1

A Sample from Lucy's
Preparation Outline
Before She Revised It

I. There are several health risk factors.
  A. Two factors are linked to heart disease
     and cancer.
     1. Improper diet
     2. Lack of exercise
  B. Foods high in saturated fats place us
     at risk.
  C. Lack of physical exertion places us
     at risk.
     1. Less than 45 percent of Americans
        participate in any kind of regular
        physical activity.
     2. Sedentary people run five times the
        risk of developing heart disease.
II. Cancer and heart attack warning signs are
    important to know.

both "A" and "B" could be phrases (see Figure 12.1, A1 and A2). Normally it is best to state your main points in sentence form (even if the rest of your outline is in phrases) because sentences contain more information. Notice that Lucy's preparation outline in Figure 12.3 uses complete sentences for all except the third-level supporting information. Robert's preparation outline in Figure 12.4 uses phrases for everything except main points. John's outline in Chapter 11 (page 283) uses key words for everything.

▶ *Capitalize the first word in each level* (see Figure 12.1). It only takes a glance to know where a new level begins when the first word in each level is capitalized.

Although you may choose not to follow these guidelines in your rough-draft outline, when you polish and expand your rough draft into a presentation outline, you will need to adhere to them carefully. Check with your instructor for any additional guidelines. With these general outline tips in mind, let's discuss rough-draft outlines and preparation outlines in more detail.

Rough-Draft Outlines

After you (1) analyze your audience and (2) determine your topic, exact purpose, and possible main points, you are ready to (3) rough out an outline of your main points and possible supporting information, as discussed in Chapter 9. You should prepare this rough-draft outline *before* beginning your research to help you narrow down the items you will be discussing and clarify the supporting materials you'll need to research. Although you will need to research until you have a complete understanding of your topic, your rough outline can focus your research and save valuable time. Of course, if you are speaking on an unfamiliar topic (which is not recommended), you will need to do enough preliminary research to be able to make an intelligent rough-draft outline.

Go back to Chapter 9 and take a second look at Lucy's rough-draft outline in Figure 9.4. Notice that it does not include an introduction or conclusion but contains only the information and supporting materials she thinks she will want to use in the body of her speech. Not all of it was included in her actual speech, and some information that ended up in her speech was not included in her rough-draft outline.

Once your research is completed, the rough-draft outline has served its purpose, and you are ready to turn it into a more detailed and polished preparation outline (or storyboards, to be discussed later).

Preparation Outlines

Instead of succumbing to the temptation to write out your speech word for word, expand your rough-draft outline into a preparation outline. Whereas your rough draft contained only main points and supporting information, your *preparation outline* should include all four steps of the FLOW sequence. Figure 12.2 shows a suggested preparation outline format to use in finalizing your informative speech. These guidelines will help you develop your preparation outline:

▶ Write the focus, lead-in, and wrap-up steps in complete sentences, partial sentences, or phrases. Normally these steps are not outlined, but you may if you wish.

▶ Outline the body of your speech. Your main points are normally written in complete sentences; the subpoints and supporting material may be complete sentences, phrases, key words, or a combination. Whichever you choose, make sure each level of the outline is parallel.

▶ Write out transitions between main points in sentence form.

▶ Include a list of references at the end of the outline.

▶ List the exact page numbers from your references in a column down the right side of the outline along with other types of sources you used. Types of sources include references (books, magazines, newspapers, and so on), personal observations, interviews, and media (radio or television programs).

▶ Identify types of supporting materials in brackets: for example, [statistics]. This allows you to tell at a glance whether you are using a variety of supporting materials for each of your main points. (Review Chapter 10 for the various types of supporting materials.)

▶ Also identify the locations of visual aids in your speech with brackets: for example, [Transparency #1].

The preparation outline format (including all the above categories) is demonstrated in Figures 12.3 and 12.4. Take a look now at Lucy's preparation outline for her speech "Our State of Health" in Figure 12.3, pp. 306–307. (Her complete speech was included in Chapter 9.) Next, look at the preparation

Figure 12.2

Preparation Outline Format

Topic or Title:
Exact Purpose:

	Type of Source
FOCUS: • **Attention-getter:** • **Audience motivation:** • **Credibility:**	(personal observation, interview, media, or reference)

LEAD-IN
• **Purpose statement:**
• **Preview:**
• **Background** (optional)
• **Handout information** (if any)

ORGANIZED BODY with SUPPORTS
 I. **Main Point 1:**
   A. Subpoint or supporting material
     1. Supporting material
     2. Supporting material
   B. Subpoint or supporting material

  [Transition]

 II. **Main point 2:**
   A. Supporting material
   B. Supporting material

  [Transition]

 III. **Main point 3:**
   A. Subpoint or supporting material
   B. Subpoint or supporting material
     1. Supporting material
     2. Supporting material

WRAP-UP
• **Summary:**
• **Refocus:**

References:
(Books, magazines, newspapers, etc.)

outline in Figure 12.4, pp. 308–309, from another student speech entitled "The Electoral College." This speech, given by Robert McDermott, a junior majoring in history and political science, is included at the end of this chapter. You will be surprised (as both these students were) at how easy it is to expand your rough draft simply by following the preparation outline format above.

Storyboarding

▼ ▼ ▼

If you tend to get bogged down in traditional outlining, then storyboarding may be just what you need. Basically a *storyboard* is an informal visual as well as verbal representation of your ideas. In other words, when you use a storyboard to plan your speech, you jot down your main points and supporting information and include visual sketches.

Advantages of Storyboards

Storyboarding is an effective way to prepare a speech and offers some advantages over the traditional method of outlining. Basically storyboards have these benefits:

▶ *Storyboards can be prepared quickly.* Storyboards generally can be prepared more quickly than traditional outlines because you don't have to worry as much about structure. There is no standard numbering system—you can use anything you want (bullets, dashes, numbers, or whatever).

▶ *Storyboards encourage verbal/visual teamwork.* When you are developing a storyboard, you are writing down ideas and also sketching possible graphic and/or text visuals at the same time. In traditional outlining, visuals are an afterthought. As you learned in Chapter 6, visual communication is too powerful a speaker tool to take a back seat to verbal ideas. Both the verbal and visual elements of a speech need to be considered together from the moment topic development begins. Storyboards are an excellent tool for this dual planning.

▶ *Storyboards stimulate right-brain thinking and creativity.* Whereas traditional outlining is basically a left-brain activity, storyboarding takes advantage of right-brain intuitive insight and often inspires creativity. Seeing your ideas in visual form (whether a graphic or text visual) often clarifies your thinking and stimulates new ideas.

▶ *Storyboards are easy for others to read and evaluate.* Just as an outline is easier to read than a manuscript, storyboards are often easier to read than an outline, partly due to the visual sketches that accompany them. Exchanging storyboards with a classmate is a good way to get helpful comments on your speech. If you are involved in a team presentation (see Appendix B for information on team speaking), storyboards are especially effective. It's a good idea to pin or tape all the storyboards to a wall in the order they will be presented. Seeing a verbal list of ideas as well as the accompanying visual aids helps the team quickly grasp the basic elements of each member's part of the speech and identify weaknesses in the overall presentation.

▶ *Storyboards encourage the use of transitions.* Although the preparation outline format in Figure 12.2 does provide space for transitions, most traditional outlines

(text continues on p. 308)

Figure 12.3
Lucy's Preparation Outline

Lucy's Preparation Outline

Title: "Our State of Health" by Lucy Tisdale Setliff
Exact Purpose: After listening to my speech, the audience will be more aware of health risk factors, cancer and heart attack warning signs, and diet and exercise guidelines.

	Type of Source
FOCUS:	
• **Attention-getter:** Hippocrates—"Health is the greatest of human blessings." Webster's definition: "Health is the absence of disease." [Explanation]	Ref. #6, p. 9
• **Audience motivation:** Surgeon General C. Everett Koop—two main causes of death (cancer and heart disease) are caused by our own habits.	Ref. #5, p. 112
• **Credibility:** Health important after my father's death from heart disease; personal research. [Family instance]	Personal
LEAD-IN	
• **Purpose:** To become more aware of our state of health	
• **Preview:** Focus on three aspects of health: **[Transparency #1]** —major risk factors —cancer and heart attack warning signs —diet and exercise guidelines	
ORGANIZED BODY with SUPPORTS	
I. **There are several major risk factors to health.**	
A. There are four basic risk factors to health. **[Transparency #2]**	Ref. #5, p. 321
1. Two of these risk factors (heredity and genetics) remain beyond our control.	
2. Two of these risk factors (diet and exercise) we can control.	
B. Statistics indicate that the health risk from poor diet and lack of exercise is great.	

	Type of Source
1. One in four (or 66 million Americans have some form of heart disease related to a high fat diet and lack of exercise. [Statistics]	Ref. #3, p. 3 and Ref. #5, p. 287
2. Cancer kills one out of every five persons, yet experts conclude that 75% of cancer deaths could be avoided through a healthier lifestyle. [Statistics]	Ref. #1, p. 3 and Ref. #5, p. 318
3. Physical activity is avoided by 45 percent of Americans even though sedentary people run five times the risk of developing heart disease. [Expert opinion and statistics]	Ref. #7, p. 37 and Ref. #5, p. 85
[Transition]: We've identified risk factors; now let's review warning signs that may indicate we have a disease.	
II. **There are specific warning signs for cancer and heart attacks.**	
A. Most people are aware of some of the warning signs for cancer.	Ref. #1, p. 13
1. Cancer's seven warning signs are: **[Transparency #3]**	
a. Change in bowel or bladder habits	
b. A sore that does not heal	
c. Unusual bleeding or discharge	
d. Thickening or lump in breast or elsewhere	
e. Indigestion or difficulty in swallowing	
f. Obvious change in wart or mole	
g. Nagging cough or hoarseness	
2. According to the National Cancer Institute, "None of these symptoms is a sure sign of cancer, but if any of them lasts longer than two weeks, see a doctor." [Expert opinion]	Ref. #1, p. 14
B. Fewer people are aware of the warning signs for heart attack.	

Page 3

	Type of Source
1. According to the American Heart Association, "Sharp, stabbing twinges usually are not signals of heart attack." [Expert opinion]	Ref. #2, p. 1
2. There are three indicators of possible heart attack: [Transparency #4]	Ref. #3, p. 3
a. Uncomfortable pressure, fullness, squeezing, or pain in the center of the chest that last more than a few minutes	
b. Pain that spreads to the shoulders, neck, or arms	
c. Chest discomfort with lightheadedness, fainting, sweating, nausea, or shortness of breath	
3. My family did not know these symptoms and waited an extra day before taking my father to the hospital.	

[Transition]: So far we have identified major risk factors to health and reviewed cancer and heart attack warning signs. Diet and exercise guidelines are the final focus of our state of health.

III. **Fortunately, diet and exercise guidelines are fairly simple.**

	Type of Source
A. The 1992 Food Pyramid provides healthy diet guidelines. [Transparency #5]	Ref. #4, p. 62
1. Each level of the pyramid includes suggested daily servings. [Explanation]	
2. The tip of the pyramid (fat) should be our real concern. [Explanation]	
a. Fats should be less than 30 percent of our total calorie intake—65 grams for an average woman, 80 grams for an average man. [Statistics]	Ref. #5, p. 117
b. Many fast food items contain too much fat. [Instances/statistics]	Ref. #8

Page 4

	Type of Source
B. The American Heart Association suggests simple exercise guidelines.	Ref. #5, pp. 86 and 103.
1. To control blood pressure, exercise 15 minutes a day, 3 times a week. [Expert opinion]	
2. To lose weight, exercise for 1 hour, 3 times a week is required. [Expert opinion]	
3. A brisk walk can be as effective as jogging.	

WRAP-UP

• **Summary:** The challenge of living is grasping our opportunities. If we know the risk factors, learn the warning signs, and discover diet and exercise guidelines, we can improve our chances of preventing disease.

• **Refocus:** Our health is what we choose to make it. How we take care of our bodies today will determine if we suffer problems later on. Health begins with awareness. Don't wait until later to get interested in your health. As it was with my father—later may be too late.

References:
1. American Cancer Society. *Cancer Facts and Figures—1990.* Atlanta: American Cancer Society, 1990.
2. American Heart Association. *Fact Sheet on Heart Attack, Stroke and Risk Factors.* Dallas: American Heart Assoc., 1994.
3. American Heart Association. *1990 Heart and Stroke Facts.* Dallas: American Heart Assoc., 1989.
4. Brownlee, Shannon, and Barnett, Robert. "A Loaf of Bread, a Glass of Wine." *U.S. News & World Report* 117 (July 1994), pp. 62–63.
5. Levy, Marvin R., Dignan, Mark, and Shirreffs, Janet H. *Life and Health: Targeting Wellness.* New York: McGraw-Hill, 1993.
6. Richards, Donna Beck. *Here's to Your Health,* 2nd ed. Dubuque, Iowa: Kendall/Hunt, 1992.
7. Smith, Charles, and Jones, Don. *Exercise Just for the Health of It.* Dubuque, Iowa: Kendall/Hunt, 1981.
8. "The Fast Food Survival Guide." *Good Housekeeping* 220 (May 1995), pp. 118 and 120.

Figure 12.4

Robert's Preparation Outline

Title: "The Electoral College" by Robert McDermott
Exact Purpose: After listening to my speech, the audience will understand how the Electoral College works.

	Type of Source
FOCUS:	
• **Attention-getter:** Hypothetical presidential election [Transparency #1]	
• **Audience motivation:** Few know what it is. Less than 10% can actually tell you how it works.	Interviews, Ref. #3
• **Credibility:** Personal research and study	
LEAD-IN	
• **Background: [Transparency #2]** When you ask people about the Electoral College, they give answers like, "Isn't it that college in New Hampshire?" or "How's its football team?" or "Where is it?" Actually, it's not an institution of higher learning. It's the way our government votes and elects the president of the United States.	Personal observation
• **Purpose:** To look at three aspects of the Electoral College	
• **Preview:** Where did it come from? What is it? How does it work?	

ORGANIZED BODY with SUPPORTS

I. **Where did the Electoral College come from?**	
A. Constitutional Convention in 1787 [Explanation]	
B. Debate: Congress or citizens to elect President?	
C. Concern: Citizen knowledge and ballot-box tampering	
D. Result: Indirect election method—the Electoral College	Figure #2

[Transition] Now that you know where the Electoral College came from, what is it exactly?

II. **What is the Electoral College? [Transparency #3]**	Fig. #2
A. Definition: System using a set number of electoral votes [Explanation]	
B. Example: California vs. Montana [Comparison]	

[Transition] Our last topic to discuss is really the most interesting to me—how does the Electoral College work?

do not. Storyboards have a special section at the bottom for transition sentences. If the transitions allow your arguments to flow smoothly from one to another, you know they are effective.

▶ *Storyboards make organizational problems easy to identify and correct.* Since a storyboard includes a simplified verbal account of the speech as well as a visual representation, identifying organizational problems is easy. When you sketch out a visual using your main ideas, organizational problems that weren't noticed before suddenly become obvious.

	Type of Source
III. How does the Electoral College work?	
A. Vote for elector, not president [Hypothetical instance]	Fig. #1
B. Winner-take-all system [Explanation]	
C. Larger states determine outcome [Explanation and instances]	
WRAP-UP	
• **Summary:** Let's look at the results of the hypothetical presidential election discussed in the beginning of this speech. Candidate B had the most popular votes but Candidate A won the electoral votes. [**Transparency #4**] [Statistics]	
• **Refocus:** Has this ever happened? Yes in 1876 and 1888 election; almost in 1960.	Ref. #2
	Ref. #2,
—candidates view U.S. from distorted view. [**Transparency #5**]	Fig. 3.1, p. 65
—That's why during a presidential election, you will never see a candidate appearing in Wyoming or any place like that because he doesn't need any of those states to win the presidency.	

References:
1. Edwards III, George C., and Wayne, Stephen J. *Presidential Leadership,* 3rd ed. New York: St. Martin's Press, 1994.
2. Watson, Richard A. *The Presidential Contest,* 3rd ed. Washington, DC: Congressional Quarterly Press, 1988.
3. Interview with Dr. Irving Dawson, professor of Political Science, UTA.

Guidelines for Storyboards

Storyboards, like preparation outlines, are planning tools that grow out of your rough-draft outline. If you view outlines as more of a burden than a help, or if you like the idea of combining visuals and outlines, try using storyboards instead of the preparation outline. Figure 12.5 shows a suggested storyboard format to use in finalizing your informative speech.[1] Basically effective storyboards include the following information:

Figure 12.5

Storyboard Format

Topic or Title:
Exact Purpose:

Step or Main Point:

Supporting Statements:	Type of Source	Data, Charts, Tables, etc.

Transition Sentence:

References:

▶ A separate storyboard for each step of the FLOW sequence (although you may want to combine the focus and lead-in steps) and usually a separate storyboard for each main point in the organized body step. Remember to keep everything as brief as possible. You can use key words, phrases, sentences, or a combination of all three.

▶ A transition sentence at the bottom of each storyboard that leads to the next step or topic.

▶ A sketch of planned text and graphic visuals on the right of each storyboard. Once you are satisfied with your visuals, sketch them on regular-sized paper to plan specific details. After you have completed your sketches, you can turn them into polished slides, transparencies, or flip charts.

▶ A list of supporting points and/or supporting statements for each main point. Again, you may use key words, phrases, sentences, or a combination of all three. The goal is to communicate clearly yet briefly.

Figure 12.6 shows some sample storyboards for Christina's speech on "Outdoor Oklahoma." Think about which format you like best—Lucy's preparation outline or Christina's storyboards. For your first informative speech, you may wish to prepare both a preparation outline and several storyboards to determine which you prefer using.

Speaking Notes

▼ ▼ ▼

Once you have read through your preparation outline or your storyboards several times and feel comfortable with the main points and supporting materials contained in the speech, you are ready to prepare your speaking notes. Don't be tempted to speak from your preparation outline or storyboards. Beginning speakers often want to have detailed sentences with them while speaking because they think it will make them feel more secure. However, experienced speakers will tell you that complete sentences usually are no help while speaking. You can't glance down at a main point written in a complete sentence and expect to recognize it immediately—your eyes can't grasp more than three or four words at one time. As a result, speakers who have notes written in complete sentences (or even long sentence fragments) usually find that they must decide between two fairly undesirable choices. Either (1) they end up reading the notes word for word to keep from losing their place, which means they can't make eye contact with the audience and they have a stilted, unnatural speaking voice, or (2) they forget the notes and try to "wing it," which means they usually leave out much of the interesting detail they intended to include. The only thing that should be written out word for word are quotes. Practice until you can read all quotes so they sound interesting and natural.

Basically effective speaking notes are brief, include key words or phrases, use color and underlining so important words will stand out, and include personal notes (like *pause* or *louder*) written in the margins. Your speaking notes may be in outline form if you wish, but it's not necessary. Many speakers prefer to use note cards (one 4- by 6-inch card is usually enough) because they are easy to hold and easy to see, especially when reading a quote. Although some speakers prefer a single 8½- by 11-inch sheet of paper so they can see the entire speech at one time, there are some disadvantages to this approach. If you place your pages of notes on a lectern, chances are the lectern will not be tall enough for easy reading. However, if you decide to hold your notes, the page is large enough to be distracting and it may shake, making you look nervous. Of course, if you use transparencies, you can jot your notes on the cardboard frames and won't need to use

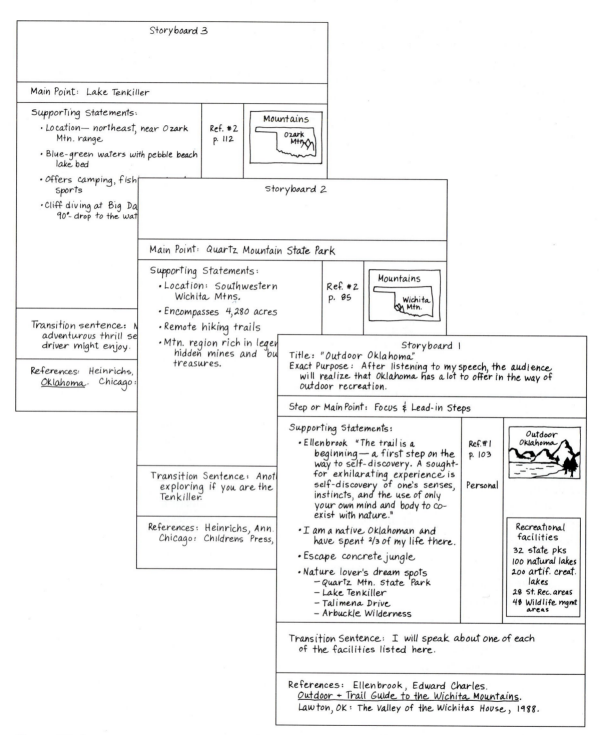

Storyboard 3

Main Point: Lake Tenkiller

Supporting Statements:
- Location— northeast, near Ozark Mtn. range
- Blue-green waters with pebble beach lake bed
- Offers camping, fish[ing]
  sports
- Cliff diving at Big Da[...]
  90'- drop to the wat[er]

Ref. #2
p. 112

Mountains
Ozark Mtn.

Transition sentence: N[...]
adventurous thrill se[...]
driver might enjoy.

References: Heinrichs,
Oklahoma. Chicago:

Storyboard 2

Main Point: Quartz Mountain State Park

Supporting Statements:
- Location: Southwestern Wichita Mtns.
- Encompasses 4,280 acres
- Remote hiking trails
- Mtn. region rich in legen[d...] hidden mines and bu[ried] treasures.

Ref. #2
p. 85

Mountains
Wichita Mtn.

Transition Sentence: Anot[her]
exploring if you are the [...]
Tenkiller.

References: Heinrichs, Ann[...]
Chicago: Childrens Press,

Storyboard 1

Title: "Outdoor Oklahoma"
Exact Purpose: After listening to my speech, the audience will realize that Oklahoma has a lot to offer in the way of outdoor recreation.

Step or Main Point: Focus & Lead-in Steps

Supporting Statements:
- Ellenbrook "The trail is a beginning— a first step on the way to self-discovery. A sought-for exhilarating experience is self-discovery of one's senses, instincts, and the use of only your own mind and body to co-exist with nature."
- I am a native Oklahoman and have spent 2/3 of my life there.
- Escape concrete jungle
- Nature lover's dream spots
  – Quartz Mtn. state Park
  – Lake Tenkiller
  – Talimena Drive
  – Arbuckle Wilderness

Ref.#1
p. 103

Personal

Outdoor Oklahoma

Recreational facilities
32 state pks
100 natural lakes
200 artif. creat. lakes
28 St. Rec. areas
48 Wildlife. mgmt areas

Transition Sentence: I will speak about one of each of the facilities listed here.

References: Ellenbrook, Edward Charles.
Outdoor + Trail Guide to the Wichita Mountains.
Lawton, OK: The Valley of the Wichitas House, 1988.

Figure 12.6
Sample Storyboards from Christina's Speech

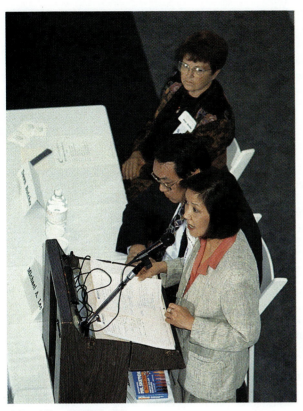

The most useful speaking notes are brief and include key words or phrases rather than sentences.

© David Young-Wolff/PhotoEdit

either cards or other types of notes. Whatever you use, make sure your notes are very brief and that you practice until you can use them comfortably. Chapter 9 includes the first note card of Lucy's speaking notes. Recall that she used various colors to grab her eye, underlined key words so they would stand out, and wrote notes to herself in the margins. However, after practicing with note cards, Lucy decided that she would feel more comfortable using a single sheet of paper so that she could see the entire speech at once. Part of her discomfort may have been due to overly long phrases and too many words per card. Figure 12.7 shows Lucy's one-page speaking notes.

One thing Lucy didn't try might actually have suited her better than either the note cards or the single sheet of paper. She could have used a simple *mind map*—a visual aid for the mind.[2] We've talked about how audience recall is greatly improved with effective visual aids; speaker memory can be improved with visual aids as well. As psychologist Peter Russell describes it, "To make a mind map, one starts in the center of the paper, with the major idea, and works outward in all directions, producing a growing and organized structure composed of key words and key images."[3] He also recommends using color, printed lowercase letters (all-caps should be used sparingly), three-dimensional shapes,

Figure 12.7

Lucy's One-Page Speaking Notes

"Our State of Health"

Focus: Hippocrates—*"Greatest of human blessings"*
Def—*"absence of disease"*
Example of father/Surgeon General C. Everett Koop

Lead-in: Look at 3 aspects: **Risk factors**
Warning signs (trans. #1)
Guidelines

Body:
I.   **Risk factors**
A. 4 risk factors (trans. #2)
B. Statistics indicate high risk
• 1 in 4 (heart disease) = 99 million
• 1 in 5 (cancer); 75% deaths avoidable
• 45% Americans = no exercise; 5 times risk
[Transition]

II.   **Warning signs**
(trans. #3)   A. *Cancer's* 7 warning signs [2 weeks = see Dr.]
B. *Heart attack* warning signs [sharp twinge *not* sign]
(trans. #4)   • Family did not know signs
[Transition]

III.   **Guidelines**
A. Diet — Food Pyramid [fat = 30% total / w = 60g; m = 80g]
(trans. #5)   — Fast food: Dbl Whopper w C = 63g /
C Burger = 60g / 1/4 lb w C = 29g
Fish supreme = 32g / BK fish = 43g
BK Broiler = 29g / McChicken = 29g
B. Exercise — 15 min, 3 times a week = healthy
1 hour, 3 times a week = weight loss

Wrap-up: **The challenge of living . . .** (Q & A) *"questions?"*
**Don't wait to get interested in health. As with my father,
later may be too late!**

---

and arrows to make the maps more visual. In other words, instead of having written notes, you could turn your speaker notes into a visual map designed to stimulate recall of the main points and supporting information you want to include in your speech. Of course, just like all other types of speaker notes, effective mind maps must be brief. Figure 12.8 shows a mind map that Lucy could have used as her speaking notes. Unless your instructor has specific requirements for your speaking notes, you may wish to try several methods to determine which one works best for you.

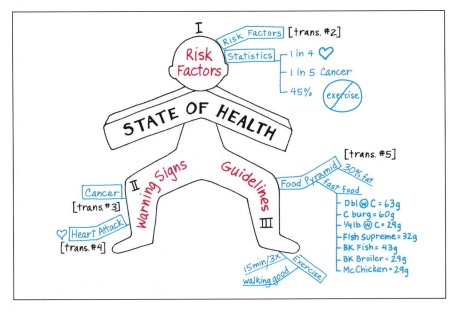

Figure 12.8
Lucy's Speaking Notes in Mind-Map Form

Sample Student Speech 4

▼ ▼ ▼

The following informative speech, "The Electoral College," by Robert McDermott, concludes this chapter and this unit on informative speaking. Robert's speech was transcribed from the videotape of his actual speech. Robert's preparation outline (Figure 12.4) was referred to earlier in the chapter. His assignment specified a four- to six-minute informational speech. As you read this speech, think about changes you might make if you were speaking on the same topic. Pay particular attention to Robert's visual aids. He created and designed all of his visuals from scratch except for the final one, a map of the United States showing a candidate's view of the importance of each state. This visual was scanned from one of his listed references directly into his computer. He removed all unnecessary data from the scanned image before adding a title. He then had it copied onto acetate to create a transparency. Although two of Robert's visuals violate the "no more than six lines of type" guideline from Chapter 7, he felt the need justified his use. What do you think?

The Electoral College

by Robert McDermott

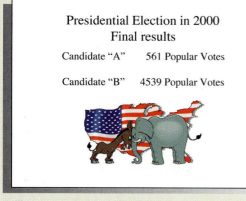

Presidential Election in 2000
Final results

Candidate "A"   561 Popular Votes

Candidate "B"   4539 Popular Votes

Transparency #1

I MAGINE, IF YOU WILL, that the year is 2000 and we are coming up on a presidential election. To make things simpler let's pretend that each state has 100 voters, plus Washington D.C. That's another 100 voters so a total across the United States would be 5100 votes. When you go to the polls on Tuesday morning, you vote for the candidate of your choice. Well, you are real interested in the election, so Wednesday morning you pick up the paper because you'd like to see who won this election. When you open it up, [Transparency #1] the headline reads, "Candidate A received 561 popular votes and Candidate B received 4539 popular votes." Well, you would think to yourself that Candidate B won this election by a large margin, but actually in this scenario Candidate A won the presidential election. And he won it because of an entity in the Constitution called the Electoral College.

Since I began studying the Constitution, I have found out that not many people know about the Electoral College. Less than 10 percent can actually tell you how it works. [Transparency #2] When you ask people about the Electoral College, they give answers like, "Isn't it that college in New Hampshire?" or "How's its football team?" or "Where is it?" Actually, it's not an institution of higher learning. It's the way that our government votes and elects the president of the United States.

Today we are going to look at three aspects of the Electoral College: First, we are going to look at where the Electoral College came from; second, what is it; and third, how in the heck does this thing work.

First of all, where did it come from? In 1787 during our Constitutional Convention our forefathers weren't really sure how to elect a president of the United States. A lot of them really didn't trust the public; they felt that they weren't educated enough to elect the president of the United States. So they wanted Congress to vote for him. But the other half thought that, no the people really need to vote for our president. But they didn't have the transportation or the technology available to gather all the votes across the country and take them to the nation's capital without people tampering with the ballot boxes. So they came up with an indirect way of electing the president that's called the Electoral College.

How's their football team?
Isn't it that college in New Hampshire?

The Electoral College

What kind of degrees do they offer?
Where is it?
?

Transparency #2

Now that you know where the Electoral College came from, what is it exactly? The Electoral College by definition is a system of electing the president by a set number of electoral votes. Each state has electors equal to the number of members it has in Congress [Transparency #3]. There are 535 total people in Congress—100 senators and 435 members in the House of Representatives. Each state automatically has two senators and at least one member in the House of Representatives. The rest of the members in the House of Representatives is based on the state's population. And these same numbers in Congress equal the number of electoral votes they each have. As you can see, a state like California has 54 electoral votes because they have 52 members in the House of Representatives and two senators, where a state like Montana only has 3 electoral votes. Washington, D.C., which has no Senators or voting Representatives, is still represented in the Electoral College; it has 3 electoral votes.

Electoral Votes Per State

State	# Of Votes	State	# Of Votes
California	54	Colorado	8
New York	33	Arizona	8
Texas	32	Connecticut	8
Florida	25	Iowa	7
Pennsylvania	23	Mississippi	7
Illinois	22	Oregon	7
Ohio	21	Arkansas	6
Michigan	18	Kansas	6
New Jersey	15	Nebraska	5
North Carolina	14	West Virginia	5
Virginia	13	New Mexico	5
Georgia	13	Utah	5
Indiana	12	Maine	4
Massachusetts	12	New Hampshire	4
Wisconsin	11	Idaho	4
Missouri	11	Hawaii	4
Tennessee	11	Nevada	4
Washington	11	Rhode Island	4
Minnesota	10	Vermont	3
Maryland	10	North Dakota	3
Alabama	9	South Dakota	3
Louisiana	9	Delaware	3
Oklahoma	8	Montana	3
Kentucky	8	Wyoming	3
South Carolina	8	Alaska	3
		Washington D.C.	3

Total Votes............................538
Total Votes Needed To Win...270

Transparency #3

Our last topic to discuss is really the most interesting to me—how does it work? Well, when you go to the polls to vote for a president, you are not exactly voting for that candidate. You are voting for an elector that you hope votes for that candidate. That sounds—you know it's kind of confusing, so let's take a quick example. New York, for instance, has 33 electoral votes because they have, again, 31 members in the House of Representatives and 2 members in the Senate. Well, let's say I'm running against Ross Perot. OK. And once again there are 100 voters in the state of New York. I receive 51 of the votes and Ross Perot receives 49 of the votes. Well, even though I won this election by two votes only, I still receive all 33 electoral votes that New York has. You see, the Electoral College is a winner-take-all system. Whoever wins by whatever margin, they receive all that state's electoral votes. Why is this important? Well, all a candidate has to do is concentrate on the largest states, because those are the ones that contain most of the electoral votes. So, all a candidate has to do is win a majority of the Electoral College. There are 538 electoral votes, so that means all a candidate has to do is win 270 of the votes to win the election.

Let's go back and look at the results we looked at at the beginning of the speech and see how this actually came about [Transparency #4]. As you can see, Candidate A concentrated on the top eleven most populated states. Even though he only won each one of those states by two votes, he still received all the electoral votes from those states. And the bottom states, they just hated him because all he did was concentrate on the large states—and they didn't even give him one vote. He lost every one of those states 100 to zero. So he came up with 561 popular votes compared to 4539 for Candidate B but the electoral vote is what counts and he received 270 compared to Candidate B's 268. Thus the winner of the presidential election in the year 2000 is Candidate A.

You might ask yourself, well has this ever happened? Not to this extreme it's never happened, but it has happened twice in the history of the United States. It happened in 1876 when Rutherford Hayes lost the popular vote but he won the electoral vote. He lost the popular vote by about 250,000 votes. Now that may not seem like a lot today when you have over 100 million voters but that would be like 2 or 3 million votes nowadays. And it also happened in 1888 with Benjamin Harrison. He lost (the popular vote) by about a thousand or two thousand votes but he still won the Electoral College. And something a little bit more modern—John F. Kennedy, who won the presi-

Hypothetical Election in 2000

State	A	B	State	A	B
California	51	49	Colorado	0	100
New York	51	49	Arizona	0	100
Texas	51	49	Connecticut	0	100
Florida	51	49	Iowa	0	100
Pennsylvania	51	49	Mississippi	0	100
Illinois	51	49	Oregon	0	100
Ohio	51	49	Arkansas	0	100
Michigan	51	49	Kansas	0	100
New Jersey	51	49	Nebraska	0	100
North Carolina	51	49	West Virginia	0	100
Virginia	51	49	New Mexico	0	100
Georgia	0	100	Utah	0	100
Indiana	0	100	Maine	0	100
Massachusetts	0	100	New Hampshire	0	100
Wisconsin	0	100	Idaho	0	100
Missouri	0	100	Hawaii	0	100
Tennessee	0	100	Nevada	0	100
Washington	0	100	Rhode Island	0	100
Minnesota	0	100	Vermont	0	100
Maryland	0	100	North Dakota	0	100
Alabama	0	100	South Dakota	0	100
Louisiana	0	100	Delaware	0	100
Oklahoma	0	100	Montana	0	100
Kentucky	0	100	Wyoming	0	100
South Carolina	0	100	Alaska	0	100
			Washington D.C.	0	100

Total:

Popular Votes		Electoral Votes	
"A"	561	"A"	270
"B"	4539	"B"	268

Winner Is Candidate "A"

Transparency #4

dential election, would have lost the election if he'd had nine thousand less votes in Illinois.

Well, you can see when a candidate embarks on a presidential election, [Transparency #5] he doesn't view the United States the same way as you and I do. He views the United States with a distorted view because he has to concentrate on the states that have more electoral votes if he wants to win the presidency of the United States. He sees states such as New York and California and Texas and Ohio as bigger than all these smaller states like Montana and Wyoming, North Dakota and South Dakota. That's why during a presidential election, on the newscasts you will never see a candidate appearing in Wyoming or any place like that because he doesn't need any of those states to win the presidency.

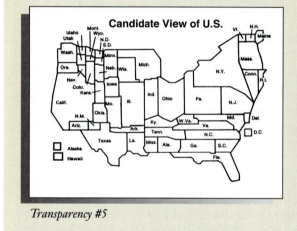

Transparency #5

Summary
▼ ▼ ▼

In stage 1 of the speech-making process (topic selection and research), the rough-draft outline is recommended; in stage 2 (planning and organization), either the preparation outline or storyboards may be used; and in stage 3 (rehearsal and presentation of speech), speaker notes (which may or may not be in outline form) are recommended.

There are two basic types of outlines: the rough-draft outline and the preparation outline. The rough-draft outline helps you narrow your main points and determine areas needing research. Since it is "rough," no special format is required. The preparation outline is a polished and expanded version of the rough-draft outline and follows specific guidelines: (1) use standard numbering, (2) indent for faster comprehension, (3) include at least two points per level, (4) make points parallel, and (5) capitalize the first word of each point.

Storyboards are especially good if you tend to get bogged down in traditional outlining because they don't require strict adherence to mechanics. Storyboards have certain advantages over preparation outlines. They can be prepared quickly, encourage verbal/visual teamwork, stimulate right-brain thinking and creativity, are easy for others to read and evaluate, encourage use of transitions, and readily identify organizational problems.

As long as they are brief, speaking notes can take several forms, including free-style and outline. Some speakers use one or two note cards while others prefer a single sheet of paper. Mind-mapping is an alternative, visual way to prepare your speaker notes. You can experiment with different types of speaker notes until you find the method that suits you best. However, don't be tempted to write your speech out word for word.

Practice Suggestions
▼ ▼ ▼

1. Go back and reread the speech on the Electoral College by Robert McDermott. What organizational pattern (topical, chronological, spatial, or causal) does Robert use to structure his main points? What type of supporting material does he use to gain attention in the beginning and to refocus attention in the end? If you had been giving this speech, what would you have done differently? Why? Share your opinions with a classmate.

2. Use the evaluation form in Chapter 11 (Figure 11.2) to evaluate Robert's speech. (Although you can't analyze his delivery, his instructor gave him a "5" on his overall delivery.) Adding a "5" for delivery, what grade did you assign Robert? How does it compare with the grade given by other people in your speech class?

3. Check your understanding of outlining by taking the scrambled outline shown in Figure 12.9 and organizing it into the preparation outline format using the form in Figure 12.10. By each point from the scrambled outline, mark the outline location. If you prefer, photocopy the scrambled outline and cut each point into strips to be organized into the correct speech. When you have completed the outline, share it with a classmate and then look at the actual outline located in Appendix C.

Notes

1. Adapted from Marya W. Holcombe and Judith K. Stein, *Presentations for Decision Makers: Strategies for Structuring and Delivering Your Ideas* (Belmont, CA: Lifetime Learning Publications, 1983), pp. 63–72.
2. Tony Buzan, *Use Both Sides of Your Brain*, revised and updated ed. (New York: Dutton, 1983), pp. 106–115.

Mind-mapping was developed by Buzan for a British Broadcasting Corporation television series in the early 1970s.
3. Peter Russell, *The Brain Book* (New York: Dutton, 1979), p. 176.

Directions: Using the Preparation Outline Format on p. 322, organize the following outline pieces into a completed outline.

Outline Location	
	—So now that you know what this disease is, how is this disease spread?
	—Approximately 50 percent or one out of every two dogs in our state that are unprotected against this disease will develop it. Now, that's the bad news. The good news is—for you dog owners and future dog owners—that this disease is entirely preventable.
	—A parasite in the heart and adjacent blood vessels
	—After bite, six months from microfilaria to adult worms
	—Now that you know how easily heartworm disease is spread, exactly how can we prevent it?
	—How is heartworm disease prevented?
	—Prescription from veterinarian
	—"Canine Heartworm Disease" by Karen Gemmer
	—Facts about adult heartworms
	1. 14 inches long
	2. 7-year life span
	3. Up to 250 in heart at one time
	4. Microscopic offspring called micropolaria
	—What I am holding in my hand—in this jar—is a dog's heart. And this heart is completely infested with worms. This dog died from a very debilitating and deadly disease called Canine Heartworm Disease.
	—What is heartworm disease?
	—Spreading rapidly
	1. Disease found in all 50 states and Canada

Figure 12.9
Scrambled Outline

Outline Location

2. Heavy infestation in eastern and southern states

—Damage to heart, arteries, and other organs

—After listening to my speech, the audience will be aware of the existence of Canine Heartworm Disease and know how to prevent it.

—They are: (1) What exactly is this disease? (2) How is it spread? (3) How can it be prevented?

—Let's just review real fast what we have covered. All right, we know that this is a disease that affects the heart, as well as other body organs, and it's caused by a parasite. It is spread by the mosquito and it's very easily prevented by a monthly medication.

—There are three main points that I'd like to cover today about heartworm disease:

—Spread from dog to dog by mosquito

—Results: Congestive heart failure and death

—I have two dogs [personal instance of healthy dogs]. Because heartworm disease will strike one of every two dogs here in our state if they are unprotected, right now either Robin or Willie would have heartworm disease. So what I would like you to remember from today is that this disease is out there, and it is deadly. But if the medication is given conscientiously every month, it is entirely preventable.

—At one time, when I thought I was going to be a veterinarian, I worked as a technician for a veterinarian. According to the journals I've read and the doctors I've talked to . . .

—Monthly medication

—How is heartworm disease spread?

Figure 12.10

Preparation Outline Form for Use with the Scrambled Outline

Topic:
Exact Purpose:

FOCUS
- **Attention-getter:**
- **Audience motivation:**
- **Credibility:**

LEAD-IN
- **Purpose:**
- **Preview:**

ORGANIZED BODY with SUPPORTS
   I.
      A.
      B.
      C.
      D.

      [Transition]

   II.
      A.
      B.
      C.

      [Transition]

   III.
      A.
      B.

WRAP-UP
- **Summary:**
- **Refocus:**

Persuasive Speaking

▼ ▼ ▼

13

Persuasive Speaking: An Overview

T HINK OF HOW OFTEN IN your daily conversations at school, at work, with friends, and even with your family that you use persuasion. For example, have you ever:

▶ Convinced a professor that your reasons for turning your paper in late were justified?

▶ Persuaded your boss that a change in procedure (such as ordering paper supplies from a different company) would save the department money?

▶ Convinced your friends, who had planned on a night's entertainment (such as attending a hockey game), that a particular movie would be more fun?

▶ Gotten your family members so interested in a project of yours (such as recycling) that they pitched in to help?

Of course, your persuasive experiences may differ from these examples, and you may not always be successful. The point is, you are already familiar with persuasion. Your knowledge of persuasion and your past speaking experiences have prepared you for one of the most interesting yet involved types of speeches—persuasive speaking. The four chapters in this unit will develop your persuasive speaking skills. Specifically this chapter will outline the types of persuasive speeches and discuss the steps for preparing a successful persuasive speech. Chapter 14 will focus on which persuasive appeals to use and which ones to avoid. Chapter 15 will show you how to organize a persuasive speech using the FLOW sequence. Finally Chapter 16 will cover ways to develop language style appropriate for persuasive speaking.

Persuasion Defined

▼ ▼ ▼

A s indicated in Chapter 1, **persuasion** is communication intended to influence choice.[1] This definition includes two important aspects of persuasion: (1) persuasion is intentional and (2) persuasion involves influence, not control. Let's look at each of these in more detail. First, successful persuasive speakers *intend* to persuade their listeners. They take a definite stand and, through various persuasive appeals, urge their listeners to adopt a certain position, belief, or action. This is different from the ineffective persuasive speaker who presents information and options, hoping that the audience will be persuaded, but who fails to specify which options are best and avoids taking a definite stand. Examples of the two different approaches follow. Which one do you think would be more persuasive?

Approach 1

We've looked at some of the possible solutions to the crisis in our educational system. I hope you will consider them carefully in deciding how best to solve our educational dilemma.

Approach 2

We've looked at a variety of plans for solving our educational crisis. However, there's only one that has a record of success in every district where it has been tried. There's only one that appears to please students, parents, teachers, and taxpayers alike. There's only one that deserves our support—and that plan is. . . .

The first approach presents options with no specific guides as to which option is best and leaves listeners in the dark about which solution the speaker advocates. Considering the many different frames of reference in your audience, it's dangerous to assume that listeners will automatically reach the conclusion you are convinced is best. On the other hand, the second approach leaves no doubt which plan the speaker advocates. This direct approach decreases the chances of misunderstanding and increases the probability of persuasion.[2]

The second important aspect of persuasion is that it involves *influence, not control*. Taking a stand does not mean that you want to control your listeners or force them to do what you want—there is no coercion in persuasion. To *coerce* is to eliminate or exclude options. To *inform* is to increase the number of a person's options or choices (the more listeners know, the more choices they have). To *persuade* is to limit the options that are perceived as acceptable.[3] **Tip**: To limit the options your audience perceives as acceptable, you must really know your audiences' attitudes, beliefs, values, and needs. Successful persuasive speakers begin with audience analysis. Successful persuasive speakers also know the differences between persuasive and informative speeches.

Persuasive vs. Informative Speeches: Main Differences

▼ ▼ ▼

Many speakers seem to think that the only real difference between informative and persuasive speaking is in the conclusion of the two speeches. However, if you have to wait until the conclusion to tell if a speech is persuasive or not, it's not. It takes more than a concluding sentence or two to persuade most people. Persuasion begins with your introductory comments and continues through your concluding remarks. Basically, persuasive speeches differ from informative speeches in four ways.

Need for Supporting Materials

All speeches need to use a variety of supporting materials to keep audience interest and attention and prove the accuracy of information provided. Persuasive speeches, however, must do more—they also must prove that their recommended position, belief, or action is accurate and desirable. Therefore it is critical that persuasive speeches present supporting materials that *prove* (including expert opinion, statistics, brief and detailed factual instances, and literal comparisons).

Language and Style

Although language style (including transitions, word choices, and stylistic devices) are important to all speakers, persuasive speakers are more likely to use emotional appeals as well as emotional words in an effort to get their audiences to relate personally to their positions (see Chapters 14 and 16). Successful persuasive speakers also use more logical-sounding transitions (such as "therefore" and "as a result") than informative speakers.

Delivery

Successful delivery (including verbal, visual, and vocal variety) is important in all types of speeches. However, delivery is even more important in persuasive speeches because delivery can affect how an audience judges a speaker's credibility, which, in turn, can affect the speaker's persuasiveness (see Chapter 14). For example, trustworthiness, a factor in credibility, is affected by a speaker's eye contact, speaking rate, vocal quality, and vocal variety. In general, persuasive delivery must be more forceful and direct than informative delivery.

Organizational Patterns

Informative organizational patterns (such as topical, chronological, and geographical) are intended to present information *without biasing* audience opinions. However, persuasive organizational patterns discussed in Chapter 15 (such as the claim pattern, problem-solution pattern, and criteria satisfaction pattern) are *intended to influence* audience opinions. Effective speakers use organization to help make their speeches more persuasive.

Although we've defined persuasion and discussed the main differences between informative and persuasive speaking, we have yet to acquaint you with the basic types of persuasive speeches.

Types of Persuasive Speeches
▼ ▼ ▼

There are two basic types of persuasive speeches: (1) the speech to convince and (2) the speech to actuate. The two speeches differ in the degree of audience reaction sought—the speech to convince seeks intellectual agreement from listeners while the speech to actuate asks listeners for both intellectual agreement and action of some type.

Speech to Convince

In a speech to convince, you want your audience to agree with your way of thinking. You aren't asking listeners to "do" anything—just believe you or agree with you. For example, in a speech on latchkey children, Karen tried to convince her audience that latchkey children are causing many problems for society and that four relatively simple solutions together could solve these problems, benefiting both the children and society. Karen didn't ask her audience to write to Congress, to vote for a particular bill, or to donate money. She just wanted to convince her audience that 10 million latchkey children represent a serious—but solvable—problem for society. **Tip**: This approach is especially good when your listeners initially disagree with your position and you realize that moving them to action is unlikely. In that case, a less ambitious goal of getting agreement would be more realistic.

Speech to Actuate

In a speech to actuate, you want your audience to go one step past agreement to take a particular action. First you must *convince* listeners of the merits of your ideas; then you want to *actuate* them—move them to action. Most speakers try

This Native American speaker at a protest rally is giving a speech to actuate.

© Bob Daemmrich/Stock, Boston

to persuade the audience to "do" something they haven't been doing (such as write a letter to their local representative, volunteer their time, sign a petition, buy a particular product, or begin exercising three times a week). However, there are three other approaches you can use.[4] You can urge the audience (1) to *continue* doing something (continue eating balanced meals), (2) to *stop* doing something (stop waiting until the last minute to study for exams), or (3) to *never start* doing something (never start smoking cigarettes). Depending on your topic and your audience, you may want to include more than one action request. For example, in a speech on alcohol you might urge audience members who drink to use a designated driver, those drinkers who have used designated drivers to continue to do so, and those who don't drink to never start.

Which type of persuasive speech you pick will depend on your instructor's assignment, your personal preferences, and the topic itself (some topics lend themselves to a particular approach). For example, the cultural bias of standardized tests, the breakdown of the family, and the necessity of teen curfews are topics that might make better speeches to convince than to actuate. These topics seem to lend themselves to *believing* rather than *doing*. On the other hand, the need for volunteers in the community or the health problems resulting from recycled cabin air in commercial airliners are topics that lend themselves to audience action. In the first case you might urge your listeners to spend at least one hour a week as a volunteer. For the second topic you might recommend that your listeners write to commercial airlines, state and national government officials, and the Federal Aviation Administration urging that cabin air be continually replaced with fresh air, not recycled.

Sample Student Speech 5

▼ ▼ ▼

The following persuasive speech, "Drinking and Driving," was given by Lorna McElaney to her public speaking class, who voted her as best speaker. The speech was transcribed from the actual videotape. The assignment specified a four- to seven-minute persuasive speech using visual aids. She chose a speech "to actuate," in which she tries to persuade the audience to sign a petition and join in "Lights on for Life." Lorna's speech will be referred to throughout the chapter to illustrate how she went about preparing the speech. As you read her speech, think about the changes you would make if you were speaking on the same subject. (See Chapter 14 for a sample student speech "to convince.")

Drinking and Driving

by Lorna McElaney

Introduction to Lorna's Speech by Jeanette

In the holiday season we will be hearing a lot about drinking and driving and alcohol-related accidents. Today I would like to introduce you to a mother of two preteen children who worries about her children's safety each holiday. She has already suffered the loss of a high school friend killed in an alcohol-related accident and the daughter of a friend who was involved in an alcohol-related accident is confined to a wheelchair for life. Lorna would like tougher penalties for first-time and repeat offenders. So, today I would like to introduce you to Ms. Lorna McElaney.

Focus Step

THE CHRISTMAS SEASON IS the time for sharing and giving and sweet memories of years gone past. There is a lot of celebrating going on, not only now, but all through the year. Everyone seems to be celebrating one thing or another. How many of you when you are out there celebrating have had a drink, or maybe two or more, and then gotten in your car and driven away? Well last year in December Larry Dotson did the same thing and he hit and killed Natalie Gale, a twenty-year-old girl, and her companion. Perhaps with greater awareness and tougher laws Natalie would be here today and her mother wouldn't be suffering the pain and anguish that she is this Christmas Season. Last Christmas it was Natalie Gale; this Christmas it could be one of us.

Lead-in Step

Today I will share with you some startling facts that show how serious a problem drunk driving has become, recommend several workable solutions, and urge you to join me in writing our senators to demand tougher laws to protect ourselves and those we love.

Organized Body Step:
I. Problem

According to the National Highway Safety Department [Transparency #1] two out of five people in their lifetime will be in an auto/alcohol-related accident. That means three or four of you in this classroom will be in an auto accident involving alcohol. Mothers Against Drunk Driving in their *1994 Summary of Statistics* reports that over seventeen thousand people in the United States were killed in auto/alcohol-related accidents in 1993. Now that's a lot. Although some of you might not think it's a lot compared to our total population. But if it's your brother or your sister or a friend or an acquaintance, that's one too many.

According to an article in the *Dallas Morning News*, last year we had eighteen

Alcohol-Related Facts

- 2 of 5 people in accident
- 17,400 killed in U.S. last year
- 1,800 killed in Texas last year
- Only 20-30% conviction rate

Transparency #1

hundred alcohol-related deaths in Texas—1,800 senseless deaths. You know we Texans boast about our number one Cowboys, and our great state, and we *are* number one in a lot of things. Well, now we are number one in alcohol-related deaths. I don't want to be known for that—do you?

Only twenty to thirty percent of arrests lead to conviction. This sends a clear message to people—you are not going to get caught, or if you do get caught drinking and driving, you are going to get a slap on your hand, maybe a fine, a night in jail and that's it!

Last year at this time Officer Alan Chick was killed by a repeat offender. He was doing his job; he was helping a motorist on the side of the road. And this drunk came along and hit him and killed him. A repeat offender with eight prior convictions! The Chick family won't have new Christmas memories this year. His wife Lisa and two young children will have to rely on past memories. As this example and these statistics show, drunk driving is a serious problem in Texas.

II. Solution

What should be done? There's a lot of things that can be done. According to MADD, Mothers Against Drunk Driving, we need to have more sobriety check-points. You hear about them at holiday time—at Christmas, July Fourth, Memorial Day—but that's not enough. We need them the year round so people will know that they can be stopped any time, not just during the holiday time. Maybe they will think twice before they get behind the wheel.

We also need legislation to lower the legal alcohol level. Right now in Texas before you are considered legally drunk your blood alcohol level must be .10 or higher. MADD is appealing to the legislature to lower that level to .08. The Insurance Institute of Highway Safety says that when a person's alcohol level is at .05, the probability of a crash begins to increase significantly. People are driving around in a lethal weapon—their cars. They can't handle .10. It's obvious with all the deaths that we have.

We also need stronger penalties for drunk driving. As reported by the *Dallas Morning News*, Texas has the most lenient DWI penalties in the nation. Our laws must change. In 1994, Ohio implemented stricter laws for DWI offenders. First-time offenders can now have their license revoked at the scene or a new license plate is put on their vehicle identifying them as a person who has been pulled over for drinking and driving. Second-time offenders can have their cars impounded. So we see there are things that can be done to lessen the DWI problem.

III. Desired Audience
Actions

Action must be taken now. And we must all take part in that action. December is National Drinking and Driving Awareness Month. On December 16th the National Highway Safety and Traffic Administration is calling for "Lights on for Life" day. Please join in this promotion in remembrance of those killed in alcohol- and drug-related traffic accidents and to show our government representatives that we want change.

You can also make a difference by writing your senators. I have a letter here today that I have written to Senator Kay Bailey Hutchison urging her to take the legal actions I have discussed in this speech. If you agree with me, at the end of my presentation, come up and sign this letter.

Wrap-up Step   We must demand more sobriety check points, a lower legal alcohol level, and tougher penalties for drunk driving. If we don't, we can look forward to more senseless deaths this Christmas. And next Christmas, like Natalie's mother and Officer Chick's family, it could be us with nothing but memories of someone dear. The time for action is now. Let's stop these senseless deaths. [Transparency #2] Let's get these drunks off the road before they kill someone we love. I'm going to leave you with a sobering excerpt from a poem called "Prom Night" that was anonymously sent in to a local radio station.

I went to a party, Mom;
I remembered what you said.
You told me not to drink, Mom,
So I drank soda instead.

I felt really proud inside, Mom,
The way you said I would.
I didn't drink and drive, Mom,
Even though others said I
    should.

I know I did the right thing,
    Mom;
I know you are always right.
The party is finally ending, Mom,
And everyone drives out of sight.

As I got into my car, Mom,
I knew I'd get home in one piece
Because of the way you raised me,
    Mom,
So responsible and sweet.

I started to drive away, Mom;
But as I pulled out onto the road,
The other car didn't see me, Mom,
And hit me like a load.

As I lay here on the pavement, Mom,
I hear the policeman say,
"The other guy is drunk," Mom,
And now I'm the one who'll pay.

This is the end, Mom.
I wish I could look you in the eye
To say these final words, Mom,
"I love you and good-bye."

Transparency #2

Persuasive Speech
Preparation Steps

▼ ▼ ▼

You'll be happy to know that the basic FLOW sequence and the general preparation steps are similar for both informative and persuasive speeches. That's one of the values of the FLOW sequence—once you learn it, only simple adjustments are needed to give any type of speech. Of course, as we discussed earlier in this chapter, although the speeches may be similar to prepare, they are different from each other in many important ways. You will make very different choices for the materials in the focus, lead-in, and wrap-up steps, as well as for the body of your speech (Chapter 15 details these choices).

Step 1: Determine Your Topic, Position Statement, and Type of Speech

In persuasive speaking it's hard to decide whether to analyze the audience first or to select your topic and then analyze the audience. Although successful persuasive speakers carefully analyze their audiences, they seldom select their topics with a particular audience in mind as is done in informative speaking. Persuasive speakers usually select their topics because they feel strongly about the value and importance of those topics. They don't reject a topic just because some audience members may disagree with their position. Getting these audience members to reevaluate their beliefs is what persuasion is all about. Persuasive speakers often speak on the same topic to more than one audience—of course, the arguments, supporting materials, and persuasive appeals for each audience will change depending on audience beliefs, attitudes, and values.

For your persuasive speech select a topic that you feel is important. Then, using the information in this unit, try to persuade as many of your classmates as possible to agree with you or even to do something that you recommend. Consider the following guidelines.

Selecting your topic   If you have been keeping a list of possible speech topics on 3- by 5-inch note cards as was recommended in Chapter 2, you probably know exactly which topic you want. However, if you haven't decided on a topic, the following guidelines should help:

▶ *Select a topic that fits the requirements of the assignment*. Your assignment may allow you to give either type of persuasive speech you wish, or you may be instructed which type to give—speech to convince or speech to actuate. Your assignment may allow you to select any organizational pattern you wish, or you may be assigned a specific organizational pattern such as problem-solution or comparative advantages (see Chapter 15). A specific time limit (such as five to seven minutes) will also be assigned. Once you know the specifics of your as-

Persuasive Speech Preparation Steps

1. Determine topic, position statement, and type of speech.
2. Analyze audience attitudes toward topic:
   - Review situational, demographic, and psychological characteristics.
   - Take an attitude poll when appropriate.
   - Determine areas of agreement.
   - Identify possible audience objections.
3. Rough out an outline of main points and possible supporting materials.
4. Research topic:
   - Find supporting materials.
   - List main arguments for and against position.
   - Give answers to audience objections.
   - Identify benefits to position.
5. Decide how best to organize main points.
6. Expand rough-draft outline into preparation outline or storyboards.
7. Develop the focus, lead-in, and wrap-up sections.
8. Make sure speech is ethical.
9. Prepare visual aids and speaking notes.
10. Rehearse speech.

signment, go back to the beginning of this chapter and make sure you understand which type of persuasive speech you will be giving.

- *Select a controversial topic.* A controversial topic is one that has at least two conflicting views. The controversy may be over whether a problem exists or what to do about a problem. For example, everyone may agree that teenage pregnancy is a serious problem but disagree on how to solve the problem.

For *speeches to convince,* controversial topics must be selected. If there's no controversy, there's no need for persuasion. "Everyone should exercise for their health" is a topic that lacks controversy. Is there another side to this topic? Would anyone argue that you're healthier if you don't exercise? On the other hand, the following topics would be controversial for most audiences: "Parents should encourage their children to participate in peewee football," "Irradiated vegetables are unhealthy," and "Sex education should be taught at home, not at school." Even experts disagree on these topics.

For *speeches to actuate,* controversial topics are encouraged but not required. For example, although the need for exercise is not a controversial topic and cannot be used in a speech to convince, you could use it for a speech to actuate. Just because your listeners know that exercise is healthy doesn't mean they do it. As Lucy noted in her informative speech on health, 45 percent of Americans don't exercise at all.[5] Therefore you might wish to persuade your audience to put aside their many excuses and make a commitment to regular exercise. Your position statement might read: "Beginning today, everyone in this class should commit to six months of rigorous exercise involving fifteen to twenty minutes a day at least three times a week."

▶ *Select a topic you feel strongly about.* Persuasion includes more than just logic; it also involves feelings. You will be more confident giving a speech on a topic that arouses strong feelings in you. Are there controversial issues in society or politics, in the workplace, in education or college life, in sports or the media, or in health or personal topics on which you have definite opinions? What changes (if any) in thinking or action would you recommend to your classmates in relation to these issues?

> Stop reading at this point and brainstorm for persuasive speech topics that arouse strong feelings in you. List as many for each of the above categories as possible.

When you have completed your list, look at the sample persuasive topics in Figure 13.1. If you feel strongly about any of these topics or if they cause you to think of additional topics, add them to your list. Now select from this list those topics that would be the most appropriate for your assigned speech.

> *For example, Lorna, who gave the sample speech on drinking and driving presented earlier in this chapter, felt so strongly about the problems involved with drunk driving that no other topic seemed appropriate for her persuasive speech. Because of her friends' experiences with drunk drivers and the fact that her two children will be driving soon, Lorna has a real concern about the high number of accidents involving drunk drivers.*

▶ *If possible, select a topic that you already know a lot about.* Use this criterion to narrow down your list of possible speech topics. The topics that you have the strongest feelings about are probably the topics you know the most about (either from reading or personal experience). If you aren't sure which of two issues to select for your speech, you may want to hold off on deciding until you have written the position statements for each topic, as discussed next. You also might want to poll your audience (see step 2) before you make the final decision.

Deciding on your position statement   A *position statement* is similar to the exact purpose of an informative speech—it is a simple sentence that states exactly how you feel about the issue you have chosen. A single word, like "abortion," is not enough because it does not specify the speaker's exact position. A statement like, "Abortion should be illegal in all cases except where the woman's

Social Issues
Cyberspace piracy
Control of gangs
Care for the homeless
Latchkey children
Teen curfews
Breakdown of the family
Race relations
Nuclear power
Women in the military
Recycling
Closed land fills
Capital punishment
Child abuse/child custody
Racial discrimination
Medical research using aborted fetuses
Driving and drinking
AIDS
Overcrowded prisons
Need for volunteers

Political Issues
Teen curfew
National deficit
National health care
Term limits for Congress
Legalizing marijuana
Space program funding
Airline safety regulations
Environmental issues
DWI laws
War on drugs
Seatbelt legislation
Mandatory AIDS testing
Mandatory drug testing
Acid rain—who should pay?
Government-funded abortion clinics
Abortion laws
Participation in voting
English as the national language
Illegal aliens and constitutional rights

Farm subsidies to tobacco growers
State and federal funding mandates
Minimum wage
Aid to third-world countries
Aid to Russia
Child support laws
Legalized gambling
Prisoners required to work
Gun registration
Limits on liability legislation

Educational Issues
Sleep-deprived schoolchildren
Classes taught in languages other than English
Year-round schooling
Corporal punishment (spanking)
School violence
Busing
Sex education in schools
School distribution of condoms
Cultural bias of SAT and other standardized tests

College Issues
Grade inflation
Fraternity-sorority hazing
Food service on campus
Required community service
Violence at sports events
Equal money for women's sports
Student involvement in politics
Value vs. cost of football programs

Health Issues
Dieting dangers
Blood donations
Recycled vs. fresh cabin air on commercial airliners
Curing sleep disorders
Local smoking legislation
Health problems from electromagnetic fields (i.e., power lines)
Irradiated vegetables

Workplace Issues
Retirement age
Sexual harassment
Sexist language
Hiring the disabled

Personal Issues
Alcohol consumption
Smoking
Sun vs. tanning beds
Premarital sex
Birth control
Eating balanced diets
Making a will
Regular exercise
Steroid use
STDs (sexually transmitted diseases)

Miscellaneous Issues
Television and violence
Salary cap in professional sports
Existence of angels
Life on other planets
Alcohol and cigarette advertising at sports events
Children and bicycle helmets
Medical experiments with animals

Figure 13.1
Sample Persuasive Speech Topics

life is in danger," makes the speaker's exact position clear. Position statements are written as statements of either fact, value, or policy.

▶ *Statement of fact.* A statement of fact indicates that you will present facts and evidence to persuade your listeners that something *is or is not true.* This is different from an informative speech for which facts and evidence are known to be true. A statement of fact deals with issues for which lack of information make an absolute answer impossible—room for debate exists. Sample statements of fact include, "Irradiated vegetables are unhealthy," "Nuclear power plants are a safe energy source," and "Lee Harvey Oswald was part of a conspiracy."

▶ *Statement of value.* A statement of value indicates that you will present arguments, facts, and evidence to persuade listeners that something *is or is not good* (ethical, wise, beautiful, and so on). In other words, in your speech you will present facts while also making value judgments on the worth of an idea, object, or person. Sample statements of value include, "The U.S. space program is a wise use of taxpayer's money," "The death penalty is a civilized and moral form of punishment," and "It is immoral to use animals for medical research."

▶ *Statement of policy.* A statement of policy indicates that you will persuade listeners that something *should or should not be done.* You will use both facts and value judgments in recommending a certain policy or solution to the audience. Sample statements of policy include, "Cigarette advertising should be banned from all sports events," "Drugs should be legalized," and "Home owners should no longer bag their grass clippings."

Unless your assignment specifies the type of position statement to use, take your general speech topic(s) and brainstorm two or three possible statements of fact, value, and policy. This will help you look at a variety of ways you could approach your topic—in other words, help you narrow your topic.

> Although Lorna knew she wanted to speak against drunk drivers, her final position statement could have been any of the following:
> 1. **Statements of fact**: "Stiff DWI penalties deter drunk driving," or "Drivers with blood alcohol levels higher than .08 are incapable of making safe driving decisions."
> 2. **Statements of value**: "Setting the blood alcohol level at .10 is irresponsible," or "The DWI laws of other states are more responsible than DWI laws in Texas."
> 3. **Statements of policy**: "The state of Texas must implement tougher penalties for drunk driving," or "Texas citizens should demand that local and state representatives take stronger measures against drunk drivers."

It is important to know whether you are using a position statement of fact, value, or policy because each type of position statement requires different supporting materials (see step 3) and different persuasive appeals (see Chapter 14), which means that your research will be somewhat different for each. **Tip**: If you have selected an issue that you feel strongly about but don't know much about, you may need to do some initial research before you can feel confident making a position statement.

Deciding on the type of speech   If you haven't already decided whether your speech should be a speech to convince or a speech to actuate, now is the time to make that decision. What exact reaction do you want from your audience? In other words, do you want your audience simply to agree with your position or to actually do something—to take a particular action? It's important to decide which type of speech (convince or actuate) you will use because they are organized somewhat differently (see step 5 and Chapter 15).

> *Lorna decided that she wanted her audience to take some responsibility for getting tougher DWI laws—so she chose a speech to actuate. In her research she looked for specific things her listeners could do to lobby state and national representatives to vote for tougher DWI laws.*

Once you have determined your topic, position statement, and type of persuasive speech, you are ready to analyze your specific audience's attitudes toward your position.

Step 2: Analyze Audience Attitudes Toward Your Position

Since this persuasive speech will be given to the same audience as your earlier informative speech (your classmates), you already know a great deal about them. If you didn't already know your audience, you would need to conduct a detailed analysis like the one you conducted prior to your informative speech (see Chapter 9). Go back and review the situational, demographic, and psychological information you gathered previously on your classmates and update it where necessary. Take a look at the following questions that relate to the ethical and emotional appeals you will wish to use in your speech (see Chapter 14 for a discussion of persuasive appeals):

▶ Will my classmates' current opinions of me add to my credibility (ethical appeal) or take away from it? What can I do to make my credibility higher?

> *Lorna felt that her overall credibility with her classmates was good. She was a few years older than most of the students in the class, and they often came*

B.C. reprinted by permission of Johnny Hart and Creators Syndicate, Inc.

to her for advice. They seemed to view her as open-minded and trustworthy. To make sure she appeared competent on her topic, she knew she would need to cite several respected sources on drinking and driving. She also planned to interview the director of the local MADD (Mothers Against Drunk Drivers) organization. Her one problem was dynamism, an important element of credibility. She was naturally a soft-spoken person and felt embarrassed to show emotion in front of an audience. However, she was determined to be more forceful and personal in her delivery and began practicing in front of a mirror and even videotaped herself several times.

▶ What beliefs and values relevant to my topic already exist in the minds of my classmates? How can I use these beliefs and values to better communicate by arguments?

Although Lorna knew that several of the students in her class drank heavily at parties on weekends, she had heard them mention the importance of having a designated driver and felt that they believed that driving after drinking was irresponsible. Based on previous speeches her classmates had given in class, she also knew that they valued family security and self-respect—two values that are threatened by drunk driving.

▶ What basic needs (physiological, safety, social, self-esteem, or self-actualization) do most of my classmates have that will make the need for my topic obvious?

Lorna decided that safety, social, and self-esteem needs (emotional appeals) were basic audience needs that best related to the topic of drinking and driving. Her classmates wanted their friends and family members to avoid accidents (safety need), yet enjoyed the companionship and sense of belonging that social gatherings bring (social need) and would feel a sense of pride knowing that they had personally taken steps to ensure their own safety as well as the safety of their friends and loved ones (social need).

Once you have reviewed and updated your previous audience analysis notes, you are ready to determine specific audience reactions to the position you have taken on your persuasive topic. To help you in planning your persuasive arguments, you will want to do the following: conduct an audience attitude poll to (1) find areas where you and your audience agree (common ground) and (2) determine specific audience objections to your position. Let's look at each of these in more detail.

Attitude poll   Although an attitude poll is not always appropriate or possible outside the classroom, in the classroom it makes an excellent learning tool. The information you collect from the attitude poll will help you select the type of arguments and evidence to use in your speech. For example, should you look at *both sides* of the issue by discussing some objections people may have to your topic (of course, you will refute these objections by showing how your position is the better choice). Or should you ignore possible audience objections and present only *one side*—those arguments that support your position? Chapter 14 will answer these questions and many more. For now, just be aware that audi-

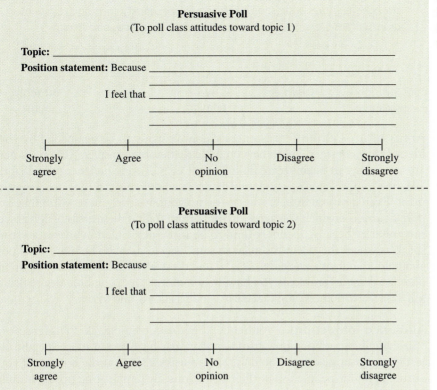

Figure 13.2
Sample Attitude Poll (enlarge on copier for use in class)

ence responses on the attitude poll will help determine the arguments and evidence you will use in your speech.

An *attitude poll* should include your topic, position statement, and the response categories "Strongly disagree," "Disagree," "No opinion," "Agree," and "Strongly agree" (see Figure 13.2). Each potential audience member will read your position statement and check the response category that most closely represents their attitude toward your topic. The more specific your position statement, the more certain you can be of the exactness of the audience responses. Therefore it's a good idea to include some background information (in the form of a "because" statement) before you state your position statement. Also, make sure that your solution is completely clear. For example, your audience may agree that stricter laws are needed to deter drug use but disagree with your interpretation of "stricter."

Lorna avoided vagueness in her position statement by including a background "because" statement and by specifying some of the solutions she had in mind:

Topic: *Drinking and driving*
Position statement: Because *so many needless deaths occur from drunk driving and because Texas has the most lenient DWI penalties in the nation,*

I feel *that we should demand that our government representatives take stronger measures against drunk drivers (more sobriety checkpoints, loss of driver's license for a specified time, a longer jail sentence, and so on).*

	√	√√√	√√√√√ √ √√√√√ √	√√
Strongly disagree	Disagree	No opinion	Agree	Strongly agree

Areas of agreement Listeners are more likely to be persuaded by your ideas if they consider you to be a credible (believable) speaker. Although there are many ways to establish credibility in the eyes of your audience (see Chapter 14), one important way is to focus on areas where you and they are in agreement. Even if several listeners disagree with your position, there will still be important areas on which you agree. It's important to find these areas of agreement or similarity because listeners tend to be more persuaded by messages from speakers whom they view as similar in some way to them.[6] The more you know about your audience, the easier it is to find these areas of agreement—opinions on related issues, problems you have in common, values you hold dear (such as self-respect, happiness, family security, and freedom), and so on.

Audience objections Audience members who check "Disagree" or "Strongly disagree" on your attitude poll clearly have one or more specific objections to your position. You may wish to leave a space at the bottom of your attitude poll for people to put their objections. By anticipating probable audience objections, you can plan ways to refute them during the speech. In situations where polls are not appropriate, you could interview the person in charge as well as one or two other members of the audience. Or you could merely anticipate possible objections based on the belief, attitudes, or values you know are held by the audience.

Step 3: Rough Out an Outline of Main Points and Possible Supporting Materials

Before you conduct any serious research on your topic, make a rough outline of the main points and supporting materials you think you may use. As with your informative speech, a rough outline can narrow your search for information and save you valuable time. Also, seeing your speech in visual form stimulates creative thinking and makes it easier to check for problems.

Lorna's roughed-out persuasive outline is shown in Figure 13.3. For a review of the mechanics of outlining and storyboarding, see Chapter 12. Persuasive preparation outlines and storyboards are covered in Chapter 15.

Step 4: Research Your Topic

Careful research is the key to a successful persuasive speech. Once you have prepared a rough-draft outline, you are ready to begin researching. Although

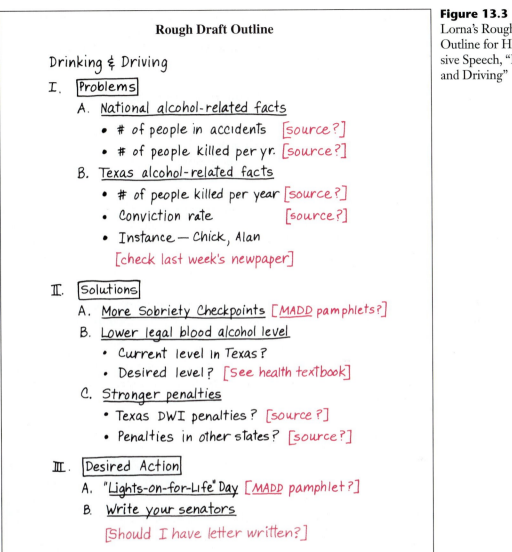

Figure 13.3

Lorna's Rough-Draft Outline for Her Persuasive Speech, "Drinking and Driving"

Rough Draft Outline

Drinking & Driving

I. Problems
   A. National alcohol-related facts
      • # of people in accidents   [source?]
      • # of people killed per yr. [source?]
   B. Texas alcohol-related facts
      • # of people killed per year [source?]
      • Conviction rate   [source?]
      • Instance — Chick, Alan
        [check last week's newpaper]

II. Solutions
   A. More Sobriety Checkpoints [MADD pamphlets?]
   B. Lower legal blood alcohol level
      • Current level In Texas?
      • Desired level? [See health textbook]
   C. Stronger penalties
      • Texas DWI penalties? [source?]
      • Penalties in other states? [source?]

III. Desired Action
   A. "Lights-on-for-Life" Day [MADD pamphlet?]
   B. Write your senators
      [Should I have letter written?]

you will want to include personal experience to help support your arguments, persuasive speeches are supported largely by outside sources. As you locate these sources, you will want to search them for supporting materials, arguments for and against your position, answers to possible audience objections, and benefits to your position.

Research supporting materials   As with your informative speech, you will be looking for both verbal and visual supporting materials to clarify, prove, and add interest to the arguments in your speech. Although it is good to use a variety of supporting materials to clarify and maintain audience interest, persuasive speeches should focus on materials that prove (expert opinion, statistics, brief and detailed factual instances, and literal comparisons). Review Chapter 7 for various types of *visual* supporting materials and Chapter 10 for *verbal* supporting materials and a discussion of *where* to research for information.

Research arguments for and against your position   You should research both sides of your position for several reasons. First, researching both sides is the ethical thing to do—you can assure your audience that you have carefully researched available sources (such as printed materials, computer databases, and interviews with experts). In addition to researching the sources suggested in Chapter 10, try *Editorials on File*—a good source for both sides of most issues. Second, researching both sides ensures that you are using the "best" arguments in your speech. And finally, researching both sides gives you a good idea of probable objections your audience may have to your position. This is especially valuable for situations in which you can't poll your audience. Even though you can't answer all of these objections in your speech, you will be ready for any questions during a Q & A session following your speech.

Research answers to major audience objections   Once you know the basic objections to your position, you can research ways to refute those objections. Some objections may be based on faulty reasoning (see Chapter 14 for a discussion of the types of faulty reasoning), which you can bring to your audience's attention. Some objections may be based on false or misleading information, so you will need to research for the correct information. And some objections may be valid ones that you can't disprove with reasoning or facts. If

Careful research is the key to a successful persuasive speech.

© Elizabeth Crews/Stock, Boston

you find that a particular objection is a valid one, you will need to admit this to your audience. Most audiences are impressed with this type of admission—it shows that you are an ethical speaker who has carefully researched the topic. Of course, you will want to show that this single objection, although true, is a relatively minor one and that the benefits of your position (or plan) far outweigh it. In your research try to find a noted expert you can quote who explains why the objection does not weaken your position.

Research additional benefits   If you can show that your position not only solves the problem under discussion but also provides additional, unexpected benefits, you will be even more persuasive. Weighing the benefits of your position against any disadvantages is one way to refute objections. For example, you might say, "Although my proposal has one disadvantage, it is an insignificant one when compared to its many advantages." Another way to refute objections is to compare the benefits of your proposal with the benefits of a rival proposal. Assuming that both proposals could solve the problem, the more persuasive one would be the one with the greater number of advantages or the more important advantages (see the comparative advantages pattern in Chapter 15).

To increase your chances of persuasion, additional benefits can also be presented during the wrap-up section. Consider, for example, Karen's speech on latchkey children (mentioned earlier in the chapter). To conclude, she summarized the problem and reviewed how her solutions would greatly diminish the problem. She then added to her persuasiveness by presenting a transparency listing six additional benefits to her solutions (such as increased self-esteem and improved social skills of the children).

Step 5: Determine How Best to Organize Your Main Points

Once you have completed your research and made any necessary changes to your main points, you will need to decide how best to organize those main points. Chapter 15 will cover a variety of popular patterns used in organizing the body of a persuasive speech: claim, causal, problem-solution, comparative advantages, and criteria satisfaction. Which type you choose will depend on whether you are giving a speech to convince or to actuate and whether your position is a statement of fact, value, or policy.

Step 6: Expand Your Rough-Draft Outline into a Preparation Outline (or Storyboards)

Once you have completed your research and decided which organizational pattern will best present your ideas, you are ready to revise and expand your rough-draft outline into either a preparation outline or several storyboards. See Figure 13.4 for the preparation outline format and Figure 13.5 for the storyboard format. Which you decide to use will depend on your personal preferences. As you know from your informative speech, the preparation outline is more formal and

Figure 13.4

Persuasive Preparation Outline Format

Topic or Title:
Position Statement:
(Circle answers): Speech to Convince or Actuate? Position statement of fact, value, or policy?

	Type of Source
FOCUS • **Attention-getter:** • **Audience motivation:** • **Credibility:**	(personal observation, interview, media or reference)

LEAD-IN
• **Position statement:**
• **Preview:**
• **Background of problem** (optional)
• **Clarification of terms** (optional)

ORGANIZED BODY with SUPPORTS
*(Use with any of the organizational patterns covered in Chapter 15; below
are two of the most common—claim and problem/solution/action)*

  I. Claim 1 or Problem:
      A. Subpoint or supporting material
         1. Supporting material
         2. Supporting material
      B. Subpoint or supporting material

    [Transition]

  II. Claim 2 or Solution:
      A. Subpoint or supporting material
      B. Subpoint or supporting material
         1. Supporting material
         2. Supporting material

    [Transition]

  III. Claim 3 or Action:

WRAP-UP
• **Summary of arguments, position, or recommendations:**
• **Visualization of future** (optional):
• **Challenge or appeal for action:**
• **Refocus attention:**

References:
  (Books, magazines, newspapers, etc.)

must adhere to the general outlining tips presented in Chapter 12. Storyboards are less formal and are accompanied by sketches of your visual aids. Regardless of which you decide to use, both preparation outlines and storyboards include transitions to link your arguments together, a list of your references, page numbers indicating where information was found, and brackets to indicate where you want to use transparencies and to identify types of supporting materials. Also don't forget that preparation outlines and storyboards contain all four steps of the FLOW sequence (your rough draft contained only the main points). Therefore, before handing them in to your instructor, add preparation step 7.

Figure 13.5

Persuasive Storyboard Format

Topic or Title:

Position Statement:

(Circle answers): Speech to Convince or Actuate? Position statement of fact, value, or policy?

Step or Main Point:

Supporting Arguments:	**Type of Source**	**Data, charts, tables, etc.**

Transition Sentence:

References:

Remember that expanding the body (main arguments) of your speech into a more polished outline or storyboards will improve your flexibility as a speaker far more than writing out your speech word for word. When the outline or storyboards of your speech are completed, you will be able to evaluate your organization and supporting materials at a glance—you can't do this with a manuscript. See how easy it is to read and understand Lorna's preparation outline (located in Chapter 15).

Step 7: Develop the Focus, Lead-in, and Wrap-up Sections of Your Speech

Once you have completed the body of your persuasive speech (main points, supporting materials, evidence, and transitions), you are ready to add the focus, lead-in, and wrap-up sections to your preparation outline. These sections are prepared much the same as they were for your informative speech. The main difference occurs in the wrap-up, where you have the option of visualizing the future for your audience and where you challenge or appeal to the audience to take action. Guidelines for preparing the focus, lead-in, and wrap-up sections are included in Chapter 15.

Step 8: Make Sure Your Speech Is an Ethical One

Ethics are even more important in persuasive speaking than other types of speaking because you are asking your listeners to trust you and change their opinions. Since persuasive speakers have so much influence *on* their audiences, they must be ethical and responsible *to* their audiences. Persuasive speakers use logic, evidence, emotional appeals, and their own credibility to connect with audience members and persuade them. However, as mentioned earlier in this chapter, they should not resort to trickery or coercion. This means that falsifying or misrepresenting information, plagiarizing, or using false reasoning (see Chapter 14 for a discussion of false reasoning) would all be unethical—no matter how "good" or important your cause might be. Before completing your speech, take a minute to check your outline and review your arguments, evidence, and reasoning to make sure your speech is an ethical one. As a persuasive speaker you have the responsibility and obligation to be ethical regardless of how positive you are that your view is the correct one or how strongly you want the audience to agree with you.

Step 9: Prepare Your Visual Aids and Speaking Notes

If you used storyboards in place of a preparation outline, you probably know exactly what visual aids you want to use. If not, sketch out some possible visuals while reading through your outline. For example, you might want to make a text visual showing an important definition or a list of your main arguments or a graphic visual of some important statistics. Before finalizing your visuals, review Chapter 7 for design suggestions.

Your speaking notes are the last thing to prepare. For most people, "the fewer words the better" is a good guide. If you have too many words in your speaking notes, you may be tempted to read them—a sure way to decrease your dynamic delivery. *Speaking notes*, as defined in Chapter 9, are brief, include keywords or phrases, use color and underlining so important words will stand out, and include personal notes (like *pause* or *louder*) written in the margins. Refer to Figure 9.5 for sample speaking notes on note cards, Figure 12.7 for a single-page outline, or Figure 12.8 for speaking notes in mind-map form. If you had any problems with the speaking notes you used for your informative speech, try to correct those problems for this speech.

Step 10: Rehearse Your Speech

Since direct eye contact and a dynamic delivery help determine an audience's overall positive evaluation of your credibility, practice is very important. Remember that mentally thinking through your speech is not as effective as practicing aloud. Basically, successful speech rehearsal involves standing, speaking aloud, using your notes only occasionally (if at all), and using your transparencies in an environment similar to the actual speaking environment.

> Lorna kept her speaking outline and transparencies on the kitchen counter, and every time family members wandered into the kitchen, she handed them a stopwatch and presented her speech. Each time she tried to be more dynamic and to speak louder. Her thirteen-year-old daughter was also taking speech in school so her comments were especially helpful. For example, she suggested that Lorna relax and slow down a bit. Referring to her mother's tendency to get teary when she read the final poem, her daughter said, "This isn't going to work, Mom—it's too sappy." Lorna's husband told her that she was "doing good." On the day of her actual speech, Lorna was confident that her delivery would be dynamic (and it was) and that she could read the final poem in a personal yet non-teary manner (and she did).

In order that you may begin working on your speech right away, this chapter is designed to give you an overview of how to prepare a persuasive speech. You will be learning more details in the remaining chapters in this unit. Check your awareness of persuasive speaking by taking the following quiz.

Quiz
▼

Testing Your Knowledge of Persuasive Speaking

The following questionnaire is designed to call attention to some misconceptions you may have about persuasive speaking.

Directions: If you think a statement is generally accurate, mark it "T"; if you think the statement is a myth, mark it "F." Then, compare your answers to the brief explanations that follow.
(continued)

(continued)

____ 1. When trying to persuade an audience, ethical speakers keep emotional appeal to a minimum.

____ 2. A speaker who seldom makes eye contact with the audience is likely to be judged an untrustworthy person.

____ 3. An audience is generally more persuaded when your transparencies and slides are in color.

____ 4. When evidence is used, simply mentioning the source of the evidence makes the speech more persuasive.

____ 5. It's unethical to use special knowledge of your listeners' needs and wants in order to change their way of thinking.

____ 6. Good logic will persuade almost anyone.

____ 7. If you have low credibility, you can greatly increase your credibility by using professional-looking transparencies.

____ 8. If you give the source of your evidence, it is normally more persuasive to mention the source before presenting the evidence.

____ 9. The most persuasive type of supporting material is your personal experience.

____ 10. If you fail to take a specific stand in the conclusion of your speech, you will be less persuasive than the speaker who urges listeners to adopt a specific belief or action.

Answers

1.　*False*. Although ethical speakers should avoid extreme fear-threat appeals (where listeners are scared into agreeing with them), there is nothing wrong with using emotional appeal. Using emotional appeal is nothing more than relating your arguments to your listeners' frames of reference—showing how your proposal will benefit them personally by allowing them to fulfill a dream or helping them to overcome an obstacle that has kept them from something they value highly. Emotional appeal doesn't mean that the audience is in tears; it simply means that you have shown listeners that your proposal relates to them "personally" because of a need, value, or belief they have. See Chapter 14 for a detailed discussion of audience needs and emotional appeals.

2.　*True*. One important element of your credibility (and persuasive power) is your trustworthiness. Eye contact is one of several factors that seems to determine whether a speaker is viewed as trustworthy. If you avoid eye contact, look over the heads of your listeners instead of directly at them, or shift your eyes rapidly back and forth, listeners may think you have something to hide and trust you less as a result. See Chapter 14 for more detail on credibility and Chapter 16 for a discussion of successful persuasive delivery.

3. *True*. Although much more research needs to be done, it does appear that color (when used correctly) is more persuasive. The University of Minnesota and the 3M Corporation found that color transparencies were more persuasive than black-and-white transparencies; the Bureau of Advertising found that readers are 80 percent more likely to read a color ad and 55–78 percent more likely to purchase an item shown in a color ad.[7]

4. *False*. Although you may have been taught to always cite a source when giving evidence, research indicates that mentioning only the source of the evidence—and not the qualifications of the source—does not make the presentation more persuasive. Actually, citing the source of the evidence without explaining qualifications makes the presentation less persuasive than citing no source at all. See Chapter 14 for additional discussion.

5. *False*. Although coercion, manipulation, and trickery are unethical, analyzing your audience members so you know their needs and wants is simply good research. How else are you going to make sure that your message fits their frames of reference so they will give you a fair hearing?

6. *False*. Many people think that it is logic and only logic that persuades audiences. However, research has found that very few people are persuaded by logic alone. In fact, one study indicated that most people can't even distinguish illogical arguments from logical ones.[8] Have you ever had an argument with someone who refused to believe you even after you showed them proof? Remember that *logic is only logical if your audience views it as such*. And what makes people view an argument as logical is when they can relate to it personally. For example, a listener might be completely uninterested in the S & L scandal until realizing that the bailout is costing every man, woman, and child (including the listener) over $1,000 in taxes.

7. *True*. Professional, colorful, interesting visual aids can't help but impress an audience. Since you obviously worked hard on your visual aids, they enhance your credibility in the eyes of your audience—even if your listeners previously saw you as low in credibility. Research indicates that speakers with low credibility can dramatically increase their credibility by using visual aids (especially overhead transparencies). Credibility is discussed in Chapter 14.

8. *False*. Unless the source is a famous, well-liked person, it is more persuasive to cite the source *after* presenting the evidence. Apparently it is better to let the audience absorb the evidence without the influence of an unknown source. See Chapter 14 for a more detailed discussion.

9. *True*. Most people respect and admire first-hand experience. We are more likely to be persuaded by someone who tells us about his or her personal experience than by someone who presents a summary of statistical data.[9] As you will see in Chapter 14, one of the most persuasive things a speaker can do is to personalize the speech with actual first-hand experiences.

10. *True*. The more explicit you can be in the conclusion of your persuasive speech, the more persuasive you will be. Because individual frames of reference are so different, it is dangerous to assume that listeners will interpret the evidence and automatically reach the same conclusion as you. See Chapter 15 for further discussion.

Summary
▼ ▼ ▼

Persuasion is communication intended to influence choice. This means that although persuasion is intentional, it should influence, not coerce. Persuasive speeches are different from informative speeches in four basic ways: supporting materials, language style, delivery, and organizational patterns. There are two basic types of persuasive speeches: (1) the speech to convince, in which you want audience agreement, and (2) the speech to actuate, in which you want both audience agreement and audience action.

When preparing a persuasive speech, the following ten steps are recommended: (1) determine your topic, position statement, and desired audience reaction; (2) analyze audience attitudes toward your topic; (3) rough out an outline; (4) research your topic; (5) decide how best to organize your arguments; (6) expand your rough outline into a preparation outline or storyboards to clarify organization, evidence, and supporting materials; (7) add the focus, lead-in, and wrap-up steps; (8) make sure your speech is an ethical one; (9) prepare visual aids and a speaking outline; and (10) rehearse your speech. Although the exact order of the steps can be varied, it is recommended that you follow them as closely as possible until you are experienced in persuasive speaking.

The remaining chapters in Unit Four will develop these steps in more detail. The quiz you took in this chapter should give you a good idea of which chapters you will need to concentrate on the most. Good luck on your own persuasive speech.

Practice Suggestions
▼ ▼ ▼

1. If you are having difficulty selecting a persuasive topic, refer back to preparation step 1. Follow the instructions in that section on selecting topics. Make sure that the topics you list are ones that you feel strongly about. Narrow your list by selecting the one or two that you know the most about and will personally enjoy preparing the most.

2. Write three different position statements (fact, value, and policy) for each of the following persuasive issues. Ask one or two classmates to look over each statement to see if they can identify which type each is. If there are some they can't identify or you don't agree with, rewrite them and try again.

   a. Airline safety

   b. Grade inflation

   c. Legalized gambling

   d. Care for the homeless

3. Select one of the persuasive speeches in Appendix C. Decide whether it is a speech to convince or to actuate and what type of position statement the speaker appears to use—fact, value, or policy. Compare answers with a classmate. Discuss your answers with your instructor.

4. Begin preparing for a five- to seven-minute speech to actuate using a position statement of policy that you will give later in the semester. Follow the preparation steps covered in this chapter. Prepare a poll to determine how your audience feels about your topic. Use a copier to enlarge Figure 13.2 (or prepare your own poll). If your instructor doesn't reserve a special day

for you and your classmates to poll each other, pass your poll around immediately before class begins. If you find that several students disagree with your position, ask around to see if you can find out why. As you read the next two chapters, continue working on your speech.

Notes

1. Martha D. Cooper and William L. Nothstine, *Power Persuasion: Moving an Ancient Art into the Media Age* (Greenwood, IN: The Educational Video Group, 1992), pp. 2–5.
2. Daniel J. O'Keefe, *Persuasive Theory and Research* (Newbury Park, CA: Sage, 1990), pp. 159–161. After reviewing the research on explicit vs. implicit conclusions, O'Keefe concludes: "The overwhelmingly predominant finding is that messages that include explicit conclusions or recommendations are more persuasive than messages without such elements" (p. 160).
3. Used by Winston L. Brembeck and William S. Howell in their short course, "Teaching the College Level Course in Persuasion," presented at the Speech Communication Association's 61st annual convention in Houston, December 30, 1975.
4. Wallace C. Fotheringham, *Perspectives on Persuasion* (Boston: Allyn & Bacon, 1966), p. 32.
5. Charles Smith and Don Jones, *Exercise Just for the Health of It* (Dubuque, IA: Kendall/Hunt, 1981), p. 37.
6. For a discussion of similarity, see Richard M. Perloff, *The Dynamics of Persuasion* (Hillsdale, NJ: Lawrence Erlbaum, 1993), pp. 145–149; see also William J. McGuire, "Attitudes and Attitude Change," in G. Lindzey and E. Aronson (eds.), *Handbook of Social Psychology*, 3rd ed., Vol. 2 (New York: Random House, 1985), pp. 233–346.
7. D. R. Vogel, G. W. Dickson, and J. A. Lehman, *Persuasion and the Role of Visual Presentation Support: The UM/3M Study* (St. Paul, MN: 3M General Offices, 1986); the ad studies were cited in Virginia Johnson, "Picture Perfect Presentations," *The Toastmaster* (February 1990), 7.
8. For a discussion of evidence and persuasion, see Kathleen K. Reardon, *Persuasion in Practice* (Newbury Park, CA: Sage, 1991), pp. 107–108; see also James C. McCroskey, "A Summary of Experimental Research on the Effect of Evidence in Persuasive Communication," *Quarterly Journal of Speech* 55 (April 1969), 169–176.
9. Dean C. Kazoleas, "A Comparison of the Persuasive Effectiveness of Qualitative Versus Quantitative Evidence: A Test of Explanatory Hypotheses," *Communication Quarterly* 41 (1993), 40–45; see also T. R. Koballa, Jr., "Persuading Teachers to Reexamine the Innovative Elementary Science Programs of Yesterday: The Effect of Anecdotal Versus Data-Summary Communications," *Journal of Research in Science Teaching* 23 (1986), 437–449.

14

Persuasive Appeals

O NE OF THE MOST ENJOYABLE yet challenging speeches is the persuasive speech. Persuasive speaking is enjoyable because you get to speak on issues that you feel strongly about and, if you do a good job persuading, you can really influence your audience. At the same time that it's enjoyable, persuasive speaking is also challenging—people aren't easily persuaded. For example, politicians can testify to how difficult people are to persuade—many of them have experienced the "boomerang effect" that can result from misjudging an audience. A boomerang effect means that fewer people agree with the speaker at the end of the speech than before he or she began. In his book *Standing Firm*, in the chapter on "How to Lose an Election," Dan Quayle discusses how President Bush and he failed to communicate effectively with the American public. Quayle calls the 1992 Bush/Quayle campaign the "most poorly planned and executed incumbent presidential campaign in this century."[1] Although other factors played a role in their loss, clearly Bush and Quayle failed in their persuasive speaking efforts.

To keep your persuasive speech from being "poorly planned and executed," this chapter covers three main factors or appeals that, depending on your specific audience, will help convince listeners of the importance and relevance of your ideas: (1) the *evidence and logic* of your message, (2) your *credibility* (which includes expertise) as a speaker, and (3) the *psychological needs* of your listeners. Usually all three types of appeals play a role in persuasion, although not necessarily at the same level of importance. This chapter will also identify unethical types of persuasive appeals that should be avoided when you are the speaker as well as recognized and resisted when you are the listener.

Using Evidence and Logic Skillfully[2]

▼ ▼ ▼

O f the three factors or appeals leading to persuasion, the use of evidence and logic is the most ambiguous. Although Americans like to think of themselves as logical people who make logical decisions, and they expect speakers to use logic and evidence in their speeches, they often are swayed more by other factors as discussed below. Nevertheless, when listeners are persuaded, they tend to attribute the persuasion to the superior logic and evidence used by the speaker.

Evidence and Logic Defined

Evidence consists of factual statements and opinions originating, not from the speaker, but from a source other than the speaker.[3] Evidence supports the logical arguments of the speech and may consist of factual instances, expert opinion, statistics, and other types of supporting materials. (See Chapter 10 for additional supporting materials that can serve as evidence.) **Logic** has been defined as "the study of orderly thinking, the sequence and connection of thoughts and ideas as they relate to one another."[4] In other words, it is logic that connects the various pieces of evidence together into a meaningful and persuasive argument.

Evidence and Logic as Persuasive Tools

Researchers have begun to realize that evidence and logic may not be nearly as effective at persuasion as previously thought and that certain ways of using evidence may even be harmful to persuasion. Note the following research findings:

▶ Listeners have difficulty identifying evidence, distinguishing between logical and illogical messages, and telling the difference between high-quality evidence and low-quality evidence.[5] Apparently, even though listeners think logic and evidence are important, often they can't identify them in speeches.

▶ When a large amount of evidence is used, even if it is poor-quality evidence, low-ability listeners who are not personally involved with the topic will tend to be persuaded.[6]

▶ Logical-sounding phrases (such as "therefore," "as a result," "it is only logical that," and "it is possible to conclude") have surprising power to convince listeners that a presentation is logical. In general, speeches without these words are judged to be less logical, no matter what the actual merits of the speech.[7] This finding indicates how unethical speakers who use logical-sounding words are sometimes able to fool their listeners.

▶ Listeners who are already in favor of the speaker's proposal or who see the speaker as credible tend to rate the speech high in evidence even if no actual evidence is presented.[8] However, speakers with shaky credibility can use evidence effectively to increase their perceived credibility and thereby increase their persuasiveness.[9] In most cases listeners' view of the speaker's credibility and their attitude toward the topic are more important persuasive factors than the evidence presented.

▶ When evidence is used, only mentioning the source of the evidence ("according to Kenneth Johnson") without explaining who this "expert" is does not make the presentation more persuasive. In fact, unless the source's qualifications are also mentioned ("according to Kenneth Johnson, research director for Business Color, Inc."), citing an unfamiliar source of evidence actually makes the presentation *less* persuasive.[10]

▶ When giving a source, normally it is more effective to cite the source and his or her qualifications *after* the evidence is presented.[11] For example, " 'There is no scientific evidence that extra-terrestrial beings have ever visited earth,' concludes Dr. Emmy Mendoza, scientist and spokesperson for Aerospace, Inc., in the latest issue of *Science Today* magazine." Speakers should cite the source *before* the evidence only if they know that their listeners consider the source a highly credible one. For example, if you knew that your audience had great respect for Dr. Carl Sagan, professor of astronomy and space sciences at Cornell University, you could introduce him in this manner: "Dr. Carl Sagan, in his book *The Cosmic Connection*, answers the question of whether extraterrestrials have ever visited Earth: 'To a person with an even mildly skeptical mind,' he says, 'the evidence is unconvincing.'"[12]

▶ Speakers who support their assertions by citing first-hand experiences are rated higher in trustworthiness and are more persuasive than speakers who refer only to high-prestige sources.[13] Personal examples and experiences also tend to be more persuasive than statistical or numerical data[14] and to have a longer-lasting persuasive effect.[15]

Four Methods of Presenting Evidence

There are four principal ways of presenting evidence, and you may be surprised to discover that one of the most commonly used methods is the least persuasive. Figure 14.1 shows a comparison of the effectiveness of the four methods.

▶ Method 1—*assertion plus evidence plus source (A + E + S)*: "We need to paint our workroom walls orange [assertion]. Productivity normally increases by 20 percent when walls are painted orange [evidence] according to Kenneth Johnson [source]."

▶ Method 2—*assertion plus evidence (A + E)*: "We need to paint our workroom walls orange [assertion]. Productivity normally increases by 20 percent when walls are painted orange [evidence]." Note that here the evidence is not linked to a source or documented in any way.

▶ Method 3—*assertion plus evidence plus source plus qualifications of source (A + E + S + Q)*: "We need to paint our workroom walls orange [assertion]. Productivity normally increases by 20 percent when walls are painted orange [evidence], according to Kenneth Johnson [source], the research director for Business Color, Inc. [qualifications of source]."

▶ Method 4—*assertion plus first-hand experience (A + F)*: "We need to paint our workroom walls orange [assertion]. Twice I have been in departments that painted their work areas orange and both times productivity increased approximately 20 percent [first-hand experience]."

Figure 14.1

Persuasiveness of Evidence Presented in Four Different Methods

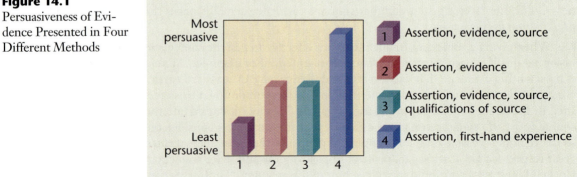

358

© Dennis Brack/Black Star

Ross Perot added to his credibility as a presidential candidate by presenting detailed evidence enhanced by professional-looking visual aids.

Notice that method 1, the method that many of us use, is the least persuasive of all four methods. As discussed earlier, citing a source without giving the qualifications of the source is even less persuasive than presenting evidence with no source at all. Of course, as Figure 14.1 shows, the most persuasive type of evidence is often first-hand experience. So which method should you use?

Best methods to use when you are unknown to your audience
When speaking to audiences that do not know you well, the best methods of presenting evidence are method 3 (assertion plus evidence plus source plus qualifications of source) and method 4 (assertion plus first-hand experience). This would probably include your classroom audience.

There are several reasons for using method 3 for audiences who are unfamiliar with you. Since these listeners do not know you personally, it is a good idea to enhance your credibility by citing sources they consider prestigious. Also, these listeners will expect you to include documented evidence in your speech. To appear credible (and to improve your persuasiveness), you must meet their expectations.

In addition, when speaking to the general public, which is likely to hear other speakers on the same topic, your documented evidence can serve to counteract opposing arguments of these other speakers. Communications researcher James McCroskey found that audiences were less affected by the opposing view of a second speaker if the first speaker's message contained documented evidence.[16] Although undocumented evidence can be persuasive, once your listeners leave the speech environment, they may begin to think about your arguments, realize that no sources were cited, and begin to doubt you. Later, when they hear a second speaker take a different stance, they may abandon your views. However, if you support your arguments with carefully documented, prestigious sources, your listeners may feel more confidence in your arguments and consequently be less likely to succumb to the views of later speakers. For example, consider two speeches on year-round schooling—one in favor (in which the speaker uses logic and examples but fails to cite authoritative sources) and one against (in which the speaker uses logic and examples and cites authoritative sources). If we hear the "pro" speech first and are persuaded, the chances are that when we later hear the "con" speech and realize that the "pro" speaker's sources are weak, we will side with the second speaker. However, if we hear the "con" speech first and are persuaded, when we later hear the "pro" speech we will likely realize that this speaker's sources are inadequate and retain our previous "con" opinion.

If you are already known as an authority, or if the person introducing you presents you to the audience as an authority, then method 4 (assertion supported by first-hand experience) will be especially effective. Who would you find more persuasive—a childless person trying to convince you of the joys of adoption or a parent who has both biological and adopted children? Would you be more persuaded hearing about the effects of drugs on an addict's life from a speaker who quoted from a book on the subject or from an ex-drug addict or relative of a drug addict who had first-hand knowledge of the devastating effects of addiction?

Remember that method 4 should be used only if you have considerable first-hand experience and know more about the topic than most of your listeners. Even so, you should come prepared with more than just personal experience. You should have made an objective and complete search for relevant evidence (both for and against your idea) as part of your speech preparation. If someone asks for additional evidence, be prepared to present it.

Best methods to use when you are known to your audience   When speaking to an audience that knows you well (such as a club, organization, or work group you have belonged to for a period of time), method 2 (assertion plus evidence without sources) and method 4 (assertion plus first-hand experience) are good methods for presenting evidence. Method 2 is especially appropriate when your speaking time is limited. Since your audience already knows you (assuming your credibility and expertise are good), they will tend to view extensive documentation as a waste of time.

Also, extensive citing of sources is often unnecessary for audiences in organizations and work environments because these listeners are usually already somewhat familiar with the topic being discussed. Even if the speech is about a new concept or product, your audience will normally have enough general knowledge in the field to determine whether your figures or evidence are reasonable.

If you are uncertain about whether you should cite your sources, a compromise solution might be to include an abbreviated version of your sources (prestigious sources only) on the transparencies you show the audience. For example, at the bottom of a transparency showing the results of a national survey of business trends, you could print simply, "Dun and Bradstreet."

Whether to Present Only One or
Both Sides of Your Position

Another important decision to make about the evidence you use in your speech is, should you present only the arguments that support your position or should you introduce and then refute opposing arguments (counterarguments) as well? Research indicates the following guidelines:[17]

▶ Present only your side of the argument when the listeners already agree with your proposal. Presenting negative arguments that they had not thought of (even if you refute them well) may create some doubt in the listeners' minds and sabotage your attempt at persuasion (the boomerang effect).

▶ Present only your side of the argument when your listeners know nothing about your topic (too many arguments would cause confusion), when you want them to take an immediate action (such as donating money at the door as they leave), or when there is very little chance that they will hear the other side from another speaker or the news media.

▶ Present both sides of the argument when the listeners are fairly knowledgeable on your topic, when they already disagree with your proposal, when you do not want them to take immediate action, or when there is a good chance that they will hear the other side from another speaker or the news media. Knowledgeable listeners, especially when they disagree with the speaker, are suspicious of speakers who present only one side of the topic. Just as presenting documented evidence in your speech can help listeners resist later speakers' arguments, presenting both sides also serves to "inoculate" the listeners against later opposing arguments.

Inoculation theory   According to William McGuire's "inoculation theory," inoculating a listener against opposing ideas is similar to inoculating a person against a disease.[18] The person who has never heard any negative arguments on a certain topic will be very susceptible to opposing arguments, just as the person who has lived in a germ-free environment is susceptible to catching a disease. Immunity can be produced by giving a shot containing a weakened form of the disease or, in the case of a speech, by presenting a "brief look" at opposing arguments along with their refutation (facts and logic disproving the arguments). This "inoculation" builds a type of immunity in listeners that helps them stay resistant to counterarguments. Then, when the listener hears opposing arguments, he or she can say, "Oh, yes I knew that. However, it's not important (or true) because research shows that . . ." Presenting both sides also seems to make listeners more resistant to additional new arguments that the speaker did not even cover.[19] Apparently, inoculating listeners gives them the immunity needed to continue building their own counterarguments. For example, when hearing a new argument, the listener says, "I haven't heard this specific argument before, but based on the information I know, this argument couldn't be true because . . ."

Deciding on one side or two sides   Once you poll your classmates, you will have a better idea of whether you should include both sides or only one side of your issue. However, based on the above information (and since polling normally is not possible), the safest course is to *present both sides*.[20] Regardless of whether your listeners agree or disagree with you, they will normally be well informed and in a position to hear opposing arguments. Also, presenting both sides shows that you have thoroughly researched the problem—a sure boost to your credibility.[21]

Remember that presenting both sides does not mean that you give your opposition equal time. Presenting the "other side" means that you mention one or two objections to your plan (such as high cost) and then (1) show how each objection is based on inaccurate information or faulty reasoning, or (2) if an objection is accurate, show how this disadvantage is minor compared to the many advantages of your proposal. After all, every view has some disadvantages. The key is to show that any disadvantage to your plan or position is minor. For example, in a speech on the importance of drinking bottled water, you might admit that cost is a disadvantage but that the small increase in the family budget would be minimal compared to the increase in the family's health.

> Stop reading at this point and decide the following:
> ▶ Should I present one side or both sides of my topic?
> ▶ Which of the four methods of presenting evidence will work best for my audience?

Logical Reasoning

Four patterns of reasoning (deductive, inductive, analogical, and causal) are used most often by successful persuasive speakers to organize evidence into logical, persuasive arguments.

Deductive and inductive reasoning   In order for your arguments to be considered logical, the assumptions (premises) you present to your audience must support each argument's conclusion. Deductive and inductive reasoning patterns are two basic ways to make sure your premises support your conclusions.[22] **Deductive reasoning** is reasoning from a general conclusion to specific supporting cases; **inductive reasoning** is reasoning from specific cases to a general conclusion. For example, suppose you believe that your company should provide affordable child care for employees. If you use deductive reasoning, you will state your general conclusion first ("To improve employee satisfaction, Bag It, Inc. should provide child care for the children of its employees") and then support it by discussing specific cases ("Companies A, B, and C have recently begun providing child care, and each has experienced improved employee satisfaction"). However, if you use inductive reasoning, you will present the specific evidence first ("Companies A, B, and C have recently begun providing child care, and each has experienced improved employee satisfaction") and build up to your conclusion ("By providing day care, Bag It, Inc. could increase employee satisfaction also").

Which method to use depends on your audience. For example, if you use the deductive pattern of reasoning on an audience that might be hostile to the general principle or belief you state first, audience members might simply stop listening (a technique listeners use to avoid being persuaded that was discussed in Chapter 4). So, even though your specific evidence might have stimulated them to rethink their positions, you have already lost them. In this instance, the inductive approach would be a better approach, especially if you can catch listeners' interest with powerful stories and vivid personal instances. On the other hand, listeners who already accept the belief or principle that forms the basis of your argument will be drawn in by deductive reasoning since they will feel a rapport with your position immediately and will be more open to hearing how you want to apply it to your specific issue.

Analogical and causal reasoning   It's important to realize that **analogical reasoning** (or reasoning by analogy) is used *to explain and clarify* while **causal reasoning** (especially cause-effect reasoning) is used *to prove*. More specifically, analogical reasoning occurs when you compare an example that is well known to the audience with a less well-known example to show how a particular characteristic of the unknown also applies to the known. For example, suppose you wanted to urge adoption of a state income tax. Using reasoning by analogy, you would show several important similarities between your state and state A. You would then suggest that because state A has a state income tax and has benefited from it, your state would also benefit from a state income tax. Reasoning from analogy cannot serve as absolute proof (because the two items being compared are not identical), but it can be a powerful way to persuade your audience of the merits of your argument. Since no proof is involved in analogical reasoning, you can use either literal or figurative comparisons (see Chapter 10). Comparing joggers wearing cheap jogging shoes to a jogger wearing shoe boxes tied on his or her feet is an example of a *figurative* analogy. Showing similarities between the occasional jogger and a professional jogger and then telling listeners that, like the professional jogger, they should wear only a special type of shoe is an example of a *literal* analogy.

Causal reasoning occurs when you imply a causal link between two items (for example, fatty foods cause high cholesterol levels in humans). According to persuasion expert Charles Larson, cause-effect reasoning (which is the most common type of causal reasoning) is used "to identify events, trends, or facts that have caused certain effects."[23] Since causal reasoning is used to prove, you must make sure that what you are claiming as a cause-effect relationship isn't just a chance association. Ask yourself these questions:[24]

▶ Do the events occur together consistently? (For example, Melissa always sneezes violently when a dog comes near.)

▶ Does the cause consistently precede the effect? (Every time Melissa sneezes violently, a dog is nearby.)

- Is the cause sufficient to produce the effect by itself? (Dogs cause excessive sneezing in many people allergic to dogs.)
- Is it possible that a third factor is the "cause" of the events? (Melissa has taken all the allergy tests, and she's only allergic to dogs.)

If you can answer yes to the first three questions and no to the final one, you can be fairly confident that your cause-effect relationship is real.

Fallacious Reasoning

Unfortunately not all reasoning is logical reasoning; some speakers, knowingly or unknowingly, use various types of **fallacious** (false or faulty) **reasoning**. Seven of the most typically used types of fallacious reasoning are discussed in this section for two reasons: (1) so that you can be sure to avoid using fallacious reasoning and (2) so that, if in your research you find objections to your position (or plan) that involve fallacies, you can recognize them and give an effective rebuttal in your speech.

Ad hominem   Speakers using the *ad hominem* fallacy attempt to divert attention from the real issue or from a question they aren't prepared to answer by attacking the person who presents the argument or asks them the question ("Who are you to question the high cost of my plan—you can't even balance your own checkbook"). Literally, *ad hominem* is a Latin phrase meaning "to or against the person." The idea is that if you can discredit the person in the eyes of the audience, the chances are that the person's idea will be discredited also. There is nothing wrong with questioning a person's credibility if it is relevant to the issue at hand. However, the *ad hominem* fallacy is much more than a credibility check—it is an unwarranted attack (often involving name-calling) designed to distract the audience from a discussion of the issues.

Ad populum   The *ad populum* fallacy is another way to distract attention from an investigation of the issues. However, instead of attacking someone's credibility, the speaker using *ad populum* (a Latin phrase meaning "to the people") argues, "How could this idea possibly be wrong when public opinion says it's right?" In other words, why waste time with unnecessary evidence when it's obvious that a group this size can't be wrong ("You've asked if some German shepherds are vicious, but everyone knows that they are the best and most loyal dogs in the world"). As with most fallacious reasoning, the intent of *ad populum* is to distract the listeners from a careful consideration of the evidence.

Appeal to ignorance (ad ignoratiam)   Speakers who appeal to ignorance (*ad ignoratiam*) are basically saying that since no one can prove that a particular belief is false, it must be true. The purpose of this appeal is to put the opposition on the defensive and to convince the audience that the burden of proof is now on the opposition ("You can't prove that UFOs don't exist, can you? Of course not. No one has ever been able to disprove the existence of UFOs. It's obvious that they do exist"). When the opposition is unable (or unwilling) to disprove the claim, the claim is obviously true, says the speaker. However, arguing from ignorance (arguing that "because something has not been disproved, it has been proved"[25]) is fallacious reasoning.

Begging the question   The speaker who uses begging-the-question reasoning (a type of circular reasoning) "asserts that something is because it is."[26] A 1988 Sony Corporation ad illustrates this type of reasoning. In speaking about the Trinitron XBR television, the ad stated: "The best statement we can make about this television is that it's the best television we've ever made."[27] This was a "catchy" ad—but one that contained no evidence. In begging-the-question arguments, the audience is supposed to "assume" that the question (considered debatable by most people) has already been answered and no longer requires supporting evidence.

Hasty generalization   The hasty generalization fallacy (which is more common with speakers using inductive reasoning) occurs when a general conclusion is based on too few examples and/or on isolated examples. In other words, speakers or audience members who draw conclusions based on samples that are too small or that are not representative of the population they come from are likely to reach faulty and biased conclusions. The following is an example of a hasty generalization:

> A survey of students in one inner-city school found that 20 percent carried weapons.
>
> Last month in our own city, there were two incidents involving handguns.
>
> We need to install gun detection equipment in every school in the state.

Post hoc   The Latin phrase *post hoc* means "after the fact."[28] The *post hoc* fallacy (which is fairly common with speakers using deductive reasoning) occurs when the speaker claims a causal relationship simply because one event followed another event. In other words, just because event B followed event A doesn't prove that A caused B. The following is an example of *post hoc* reasoning:

> People are drinking more carbonated drinks than ever before.
>
> Since carbonated drinks became so popular, incidents of cancer have increased.
>
> Therefore, carbonated drinks cause cancer.

Slippery slope   When a speaker asserts that taking a particular step will lead to a second undesirable step (for example, listening to rock music will lead to drug use among teenagers) and does not provide evidence to support the assertion, slippery slope reasoning has occurred. The phrase "slippery slope" implies that if you take one step, you will inevitably slip down the slope to another, even worse, situation. If no evidence or only inadequate evidence is cited to support the argument, then faulty reasoning results.

Remember:

Fallacious reasoning includes . . .

▶ *Ad hominem*—attacking the person rather than the argument.

▶ *Ad populum*—arguing that since everyone knows an idea is right, it can't be wrong.

▶ *Ad ignoratiam*—arguing that since no one can prove that a particular belief is false, it must be true.

▶ *Begging the question*—asserting that something is because it is.

▶ *Hasty generalization*—basing a general conclusion on too few examples or on isolated examples.

▶ *Post hoc*—claiming a causal relationship simply because one event followed another event.

▶ *Slippery slope*—asserting that taking a particular step automatically will lead to a second undesirable step.

Final Thought: Use Novel Evidence

Research has indicated that audiences are more easily persuaded when the arguments presented by the speaker are novel or new.[29] It makes sense that listeners who disagree with your topic won't be persuaded by the same arguments and evidence that failed to persuade them in the first place. However, new arguments and evidence, or even old arguments presented in a novel or unusual way, could be successful. **Tip**: If your topic is one that has been debated in the media for several years, research for new information and novel ways to present the old information. If you can't find any, seriously consider changing your topic unless you are confident that your audience is unfamiliar with the information you plan to include.

Establishing Speaker Credibility

▼ ▼ ▼

Another important factor or appeal in persuasion is the **credibility** of the speaker. A credible speaker is someone with ethical proof, someone whom listeners perceive as believable—someone in whom they can place their confidence. In general, research has found that the greater your credibility, the more persuasive you are.[30] For example, one study of executives and purchasing directors from seventy metal-working companies found that when they made decisions to award contracts, they were more than twice as likely to base their decisions on the credibility of the suppliers than on any other factor. They felt that finding someone with whom they could work well, someone who was honest and dependable, was even more important than finding a good price.[31]

The business environment isn't the only place where a speaker's credibility impacts his or her ability to persuade. Consider, for example, political candidates running for office in your town or state or on the national level. How about the student who wants your vote for student body president, or the two friends you know who have agreed to run for chairperson of your favorite club or organization? How about an instructor who recommends that you sign up for an additional course that's not on your degree plan? In all these cases, the credibility of the persuader would likely play a role in your decision.

Credibility as a Persuasive Tool

Researchers are beginning to discover that a speaker's credibility depends on such factors as the situation, listeners' involvement with the topic, and their similarity to the speaker. Note the following research findings:

▶ Listeners who have very low involvement with the topic tend to be more persuaded by the expertise of the speaker than by the quality of arguments or evidence. However, listeners who are very involved with the topic are more persuaded by quality arguments than by the credibility of the speaker.[32] One explanation for this finding is that involved listeners are more likely to pay attention to and evaluate the arguments presented by the speaker but that uninvolved listeners are less interested in evaluating arguments and more likely to be influenced by impressions they have formed of the speaker.[33]

© Mathieson/Sygma

Audiences who identify with the speaker are more likely to be persuaded. Colin Powell, former chairman of the Joint Chiefs of Staff, likely won over many Americans who identified with his humble background as the son of a Jamaican immigrant.

▶ When a persuasive message appears in audio or video form, the level of listener persuasion is likely to be determined by the credibility of the speaker; however, when the message is in the print mode, the level of listener persuasion is more likely to be determined by the data and quality of evidence.[34] This may be because print allows time for careful analysis of data while audio and video do not—listeners must base their evaluation of a speaker's evidence on speaker credibility factors such as sincerity and trustworthiness.[35]

▶ Perceived similarity between audience members and the speaker may enhance persuasion.[36] For example, when audience members perceive attitudinal similarities between themselves and the speaker (even when these similarities don't relate specifically to the topic of the speech), the result is increased audience liking for the speaker and a higher rating of *trustworthiness*.[37] Suppose you have a positive attitude toward pet ownership and discover from the speaker's attention-getter that he or she has two pets at home. Would this similarity of attitude cause you to increase your "liking" of the speaker? Even if the speaker's topic happened to be recycling? Research would indicate that this is likely. However, speakers are likely to be judged as more *competent* only when perceived similarities are *relevant* to the topic.[38]

Basic Elements of Credibility

A speaker's credibility results from four basic elements: trustworthiness, competency, dynamism, and objectivity.[39] As you read this section, remember that in order for credibility to aid your persuasiveness, actually *being* a credible person isn't good enough—you must also *appear* to be a credible person in the eyes of your audience.

Trustworthiness Most listeners determine the credibility of various speakers by observing all four elements and "averaging" them together. However, when speakers appear untrustworthy, their credibility is questioned regardless of their other qualities.[40] Therefore trustworthiness (honesty, fairness, integrity) is the most important of the four elements. Several factors seem to affect whether listeners perceive speakers as untrustworthy. For example, speakers who avoid eye contact, shift their eyes rapidly from place to place, or always look over the listeners' heads appear to be ashamed or to have something to hide and, as a result, may be judged untrustworthy. Speakers who don't articulate, who have breathy or nasal voices, or who speak either in a monotone or too rapidly are also perceived as less trustworthy.[41] In addition to having an effective delivery style, you can improve your perceived trustworthiness by presenting both sides of an argument and by appearing friendly and likeable.[42]

Competency Another major factor of credibility is competency. Listeners are more likely to judge a speaker as credible if they perceive that person as competent (knowledgeable, experienced, expert) on the topic. However, speakers who use nonfluencies while speaking are often judged as low on competence. **Nonfluencies** include such things as inaccurate articulation, vocalized

As a news anchor, Walter Cronkite's direct language and style, relaxed delivery, and good eye contact all enhanced audiences' perception of him as trustworthy.

© Bob Daemmrich/Tony Stone Images, Inc.

pauses (like "ah" or "and uh"), and unnecessary repetition of words.[43] In addition to avoiding nonfluencies, you can appear competent by citing personal instances that relate to the topic, by citing sources the listeners feel are prestigious, by speaking in a confident manner, and by using quality visual aids.

Dynamism   Dynamism is another element of credibility. A *dynamic* speaker is one who is forceful and enthusiastic and who uses good vocal variety (discussed in Chapter 8). Have you noticed that you can often tell which person is in charge simply by the forcefulness of his or her delivery? If you avoid direct eye contact, are soft-spoken, use very little vocal emphasis, and appear hesitant, you will give the impression that you are uncertain about what you are saying (incompetent) or that you are trying to deceive your listeners (untrustworthy). As a result, your listeners are less likely to be persuaded.

At the same time, to be fully effective, the dynamic speaker must also sustain a conversational tone. Researchers have found that as speakers move from low to moderate levels of dynamism, they are perceived as more credible (moderately dynamic speakers are still considered conversational). However, as speakers move from moderate to extreme levels of dynamism, in which they overdramatize, they are perceived as less conversational, less trustworthy, and less credible.[44] Speakers who deliver their speech with too much drama and oratorical flair are perceived as unnatural and phony.

Objectivity   The fourth element of speaker credibility is objectivity. An objective speaker is one who is open-minded and fair and who appears to view evidence and arguments in an unbiased manner. You can appear objective by avoiding false reasoning and by discussing both sides of your proposal (of course, you must show why your arguments are best).

Suggestions for Improving Your Credibility

If the listeners don't know you and therefore are unaware of your credibility, or if they see you as having low credibility, you have several options to enhance your standing with them:

▶   Have a highly credible expert on the topic (or someone of higher rank) introduce you and establish you as a competent and trustworthy speaker. However, if you cannot arrange this kind of introduction and your qualifications are not particularly impressive, you are more likely to keep your listeners tuned in if you don't reveal much about yourself until after your talk. By then, audience members will have drawn their own conclusions about you based on the excellence of your speech.

▶   Support your assertions with up-to-date, carefully documented evidence and sources that the listeners consider to be prestigious.[45] Identifying your views with those of a person or institution with an established reputation will increase your credibility considerably.

▶   Present both sides of an issue (the disadvantages as well as the advantages) to show your willingness to be fair and honest.

▶   Present your ideas in a smooth, forceful, and self-assured manner while maintaining good eye contact with the listeners.[46] Careful preparation and practice make self-assured delivery easier.

▶   Use professional-looking visual aids while you speak (see Chapter 6). You can overcome an audience's view of you as untrustworthy or nonauthoritative by using quality visual aids.[47]

▶   Enhance your perceived trustworthiness by identifying attitudes you have in common with your audience; enhance your perceived competence by identifying topic-related similarities between you and your audience. It is also possible to demonstrate similar group membership by your dress and use of jargon. For example, you wouldn't expect to see your doctor walk into the examining room wearing cutoffs and a T-shirt.

One sure way to lose credibility is to fail to acknowledge (in content or delivery) the official status of your listeners and the degree of their knowledge.[48] For example, suppose a student scheduled to present a proposal to a group of administrators shows up late, has to take time to set up the overhead projector, presents roughly drawn charts, and discusses the proposal at a very elementary

R e m e m b e r :

Improve your credibility by . . .

▶ Having a highly credible person introduce you.
▶ Using carefully documented evidence and citing prestigious sources.
▶ Presenting both sides of your issue.
▶ Speaking in a smooth, dynamic, and self-assured manner.
▶ Using quality visual aids.
▶ Identifying similarities you have with your listeners.
▶ Acknowledging the status and knowledge of your listeners.

level. How much credibility would this speaker have by the end of the presentation? Few people like to be treated as though they are less important than their positions in the organization indicate. The administrators would undoubtedly be disgusted and not be persuaded. Similarly male speakers often lose their credibility with female listeners by referring to women as "girls," "gals," "honey," or other terms that disregard the formal status of women.

Unethical Use of Credibility

Unfortunately some speakers give the appearance of credibility to hide the fact that their evidence is incomplete or even misleading. The stereotype of the used car salesperson who gives every outward appearance of being honest to get the customer to buy a car that the seller knows will barely make it out of the lot illustrates this point. Unethical speakers who are forceful and dynamic, who make direct eye contact, and who give every appearance of sincerity and honesty may be able to temporarily persuade an audience to agree with their ideas or buy their products. However, when the listeners eventually realize that these speakers based their arguments on inadequate evidence and/or faulty evidence, they cease to be fooled.

Appealing to Listeners'
Psychological Needs
▼ ▼ ▼

Even though you may be a credible speaker and include logic and evidence in your presentations, you will not be successful at persuasion unless you also adapt your arguments to the psychological needs of your listeners.

If this speaker can show how his idea meets his audience's needs, he will be more persuasive.

© *Charles Gupton/Tony Stone Images, Inc.*

In Chapter 5 a *need* was defined as "a condition in which there is some sort of deficiency." Striving to get these needs (deficiencies or wants) fulfilled is a great motivator for all people. And because they are based on values, beliefs, and attitudes, needs arouse emotions. A certain amount of *emotional appeal* or pathos is needed in a persuasive speech. This doesn't mean that you want audience members to be choked up or teary-eyed. It means that you want them to feel that your topic relates to them personally—that they have a stake in the outcome of your speech.

Personalizing Your Persuasive Argument

Why don't more people participate in blood drives or volunteer an hour each month to charities or vote in important elections? How about you? When was the last time you donated blood? Do you regularly volunteer your time to worthy causes? Do you vote in every election? Many of us fail to participate in these kinds of activities because they don't relate to us personally—we don't feel any emotional stake in them. We expect other people to take care of these good works: "They have more time—everyone knows that students are too busy studying to volunteer" or "I'm too busy working and raising a family—let the students do it" or "My single vote won't make any difference anyway." The challenge of the persuasive speaker is to make us realize that these issues do relate to us. It could easily be an elderly person in our neighborhood who is bedridden and needs volunteers to fix meals; an election we fail to vote in could easily contain an issue that could have a great impact on our lives.

Don't expect logic and evidence to be enough to convince listeners. In fact, your audience may choose not to believe your evidence no matter how good you feel it is. For example, have you ever had an argument with someone and knew you were right, yet when you presented all the facts to that person, the response was, "I don't care. I don't believe it." Frustrating, isn't it? As persuasive speakers we need to remember that *it isn't evidence unless audience members think it's evidence*. However, if you can get your listeners to relate personally to your evidence—to decide that your topic is important to them and their specific needs—they are more likely to consider your evidence as logical and reasonable.

The importance of relating to personal needs is illustrated by the following example:

> A high-performing vice president decided to retire early, much to the dismay of his co-workers. All kinds of inducements (such as a substantial salary increase, more office help, and a new car) were offered to convince him that it was logical and reasonable to stay with the company. When inducements didn't work, his colleagues pointed out how much he was needed. Nothing was successful. On his last day with the company, he was having lunch in the executive dining room with the president and two other executives. The president began to discuss a completely new and risky project the company was contemplating. Almost in jest, the president suggested that the vice president stay and head the new project. He accepted. None of the other appeals were persuasive since they didn't relate to his personal needs. The challenge presented by the new project was something he could not resist.[49]

Maslow's Hierarchy of Needs

Discovering your listeners' basic needs and motives is an essential part of any audience analysis. In Chapter 5 we discussed Maslow's hierarchy of needs as one way to identify basic audience needs: physiological, safety, social, esteem, and self-actualization[50] (for a detailed discussion, refer to Chapter 5). These basic needs can be thought of as resembling a pyramid, as shown in Figure 14.2. Although people may be motivated by several levels at one time, generally the bottom level of the pyramid must be satisfied before the next level becomes important. Rarely will you persuade an audience that is mainly concerned with safety needs by appealing to the higher levels such as esteem or self-actualization. At the same time, needs that have already been satisfied are no longer persuasive either.

To use the hierarchy of needs to help figure out how you can be most persuasive, first decide which audience needs your topic addresses. Next, using Figure 14.3, select specific "motivational appeals" (subcategories of needs) from each need category you plan to use in your speech. Last, develop your persuasive argument around the selected motivational appeals. The following persuasive statements illustrate use of different basic needs and motivational appeals:

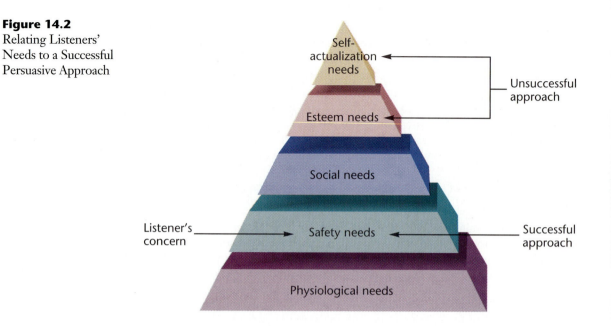

Figure 14.2
Relating Listeners'
Needs to a Successful
Persuasive Approach

- Self-actualization needs
- Esteem needs
- Social needs
- Safety needs
- Physiological needs

Unsuccessful approach

Successful approach

Listener's concern

- ▶ Exercise regularly for a sexier, slimmer you. [physiological need of sexual attraction]

- ▶ It may seem like graduation is a long way off. But anything worth having is worth waiting and working for. [esteem need of sense of achievement]

- ▶ Unless we take a leadership role in this international crisis, America will be viewed as ineffective and weak. We will lose our standing among other nations. [esteem need of status and prestige]

- ▶ Aren't you tired of being a prisoner in your own home each holiday because of the drunks out on the roads? Wouldn't it be nice to be able to take a trip in your car without worrying about possible consequences to your family? [safety need of protection from injury]

- ▶ Let your children know how you feel about them. Send them off to school each day with a nourishing, hot breakfast. [social need to give and receive love]

Fear Appeals

Appeals designed to arouse negative emotions are called *fear appeals*. In other words, fear appeals cause listeners to feel threatened or afraid while positive emotional appeals cause listeners to feel emotions such as pride or sympathy. You'll notice that the motive appeals listed in Figure 14.3 contain both positive and fear appeals.

Although creating a fearlike anxiety in your listeners is not an easy thing to do,[51] recent studies indicate that when it is done successfully, a high level of fear

▼ **Physiological Needs**
Bodily comfort (food, shelter, clothing, air, and water)
Physical enjoyment and activity
Sufficient rest and sleep
Sexual attraction

▼ **Safety Needs**
Freedom from fear and the unknown
Fear of punishment and conflict
Fear of death
Need for conformity
Desire for law and order
Protection from injury or poor health
Financial and job security
Freedom from censorship and restraint
Freedom from boredom

▼ **Social Needs**
Need to give and receive love
Companionship and friendship
Dating, marriage, and family ties
Feeling of belonging
Loyalty
Respect for Deity
Need to give and receive sympathy
Helping the needy

▼ **Esteem Needs**
Feeling of pride
Recognition from self and others
Status, prestige, and reputation
Sense of achievement

Sense of value and worth
Happiness with appearance
Freedom from guilt
Need for power and control

▼ **Self-Actualization Needs**
Developing one's potential
Responsible for own decisions
Need for creative outlets
Curiosity
Reaching worthwhile goals
Being the best person possible
Need to be challenged

Figure 14.3
Motivational Appeals for Each of Maslow's Need Categories

is more likely to result in persuasion than a medium or low level of fear.[52] To make your fear appeals successful, research suggests you do three things in your argument:[53]

1. Show significant and relevant consequences if change does not occur.

2. Show how likely it is that the consequences will occur.

3. Show successful action(s) the audience can take to halt or minimize the consequences.

In other words, in a speech on the importance of exercising regularly, you would (1) show your listeners significant and personally relevant consequences of not exercising regularly (weight gain, heart disease, cancer, loss of energy and so on); (2) show them how likely it is that they will gain weight, lose energy, or get heart disease or cancer if they don't exercise regularly; and (3) explain simple, inexpensive actions they can take to keep these consequences from happening. Without step 3, listeners are likely to feel that nothing they can do will prevent the problem (because of lack of money, time, or knowledge) and, therefore, mentally evade persuasion (see Chapter 4 for ways listeners evade persuasion). In fact, when listeners perceive the threat to be high but the effectiveness (efficacy) of the solution to be low, they may do the opposite of what you are recommending (a boomerang response).[54]

Unethical Use of Emotional Appeals

Emotional appeals are a necessary part of a persuasive speech. However, when emotional appeals are used in place of evidence or are deliberately misused, they are unethical. Here are two unethical psychological appeals you should avoid using in your persuasive speeches.

Fabrication of similarities   Establishing similarities with your audience is a valuable psychological appeal. By showing that you are similar to your audience in some important way, your credibility and, therefore, your persuasiveness are increased. However, in order to gain this advantage, some persuasive speakers fabricate or greatly exaggerate similarities with their audiences. For example, a speaker who played golf only a few times in his life may try to win over his golfing audience by referring himself as a "golf fanatic."

Exaggeration   Speakers who use exaggeration typically overestimate "the costs, problems, or negative consequences of a new proposal."[55] Without giving specifics they phrase their exaggerations in emotional terms designed to get an audience response. For example, the emotion in the statement, "We've received hundreds of phone calls in violent opposition to Senator Johnson's proposal," could get an audience upset enough to forget to look for specific evidence. Exactly how many phone calls? Is this more or less than the usual number of phone calls received? What exactly is "violent" opposition?

Sample Student Speech 6

▼ ▼ ▼

The following persuasive speech "to convince" deals with drug legalization and was given by Tricia Seeley Lewis as a class assignment. The assignment specified a four- to seven-minute speech to convince using visual aids. This speech was transcribed from the videotape of Tricia's actual speech. As you read this speech, notice how Tricia uses logical, emotional, and ethical appeals while at the same time refuting arguments against her position by pointing out the opposition's use of fallacious reasoning. Do you see any fallacious reasoning Tricia may have used in her own arguments?

Drug Legalization

by Tricia Seeley Lewis

Focus Step

MY BROTHER'S FIRST EXPERIENCE with drugs began in the seventh grade locker room where he used steroids and speed to enhance his performance on the football field and in the weight room. Because of this, what some might call innocent experiment with drugs, he's spent the last nine years waging a war against drug addiction. He's been in and out of prison, in drug rehabs, in and out of our home, on the streets. We've experienced financial and emotional devastation, not just in his life but in our family.

Lead-in Step

I urge you that as a society we cannot let our government make the mistake of legalizing drugs. [Transparency #1] We see the flaws in the argument to legalize drugs when we see the fallacies in their reasoning, the hypocrisy of governmental legislation, and the devastation that drugs can cause.

Organized Body Step:

Claim IA

Unless you listen carefully to the arguments of those who want to legalize drugs, you may miss the fallacies in their reasoning. The first fallacy in reasoning is when they say, "Well, we're losing the war on drugs anyway." We *are* losing the war on drugs. It's estimated that this year alone our government will spend $12 billion fighting the drug war. But even though they spend all this money and time in education, cocaine and marijuana and speed are as available on our streets as they were in 1980. In an article from *Christianity Today*, Charles Colson says, "We are losing the war on drugs . . . but does this mean we should surrender? We were losing World War II until the battle of Midway; but no one suggested handing the keys to the Pentagon over to the Japanese." We are losing the war, but it is not time to surrender!

Claim IB

The second fallacy occurs when the pro-legalization advocates say that legalization will work because it has worked in foreign countries—they cite Great Britain and Italy as model programs. According to the 1981 *British Medical Journal*, Britain's experiment with controlled distribution of heroin was a disaster. Between 1959 and 1968 heroin addicts doubled every sixteen months. And in Italy where drugs are now legal, the total number of heroin addicts—over 350,000 of them—is greater than any other Western European country, says Lee

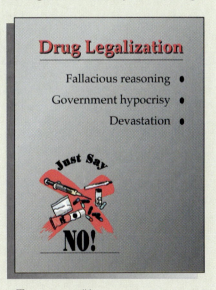

Transparency #1

P. Brown, the director of the National Drug Control Policy. It doesn't sound like legalization is working to me.

Claim IC   And the third fallacy is that since alcohol and nicotine cause death yet they are both legal, all drugs should be legal. Yes, they do cause death; but just because two things that cause death are legal, should we legalize a third thing that is more deadly? These drugs are not even comparable. Tobacco shortens one's life; cocaine debases it. And as James Q. Wilson, who was a former member of the National Council for Drug Abuse Prevention, says, "Nicotine alters one's habits and cocaine alters one's soul. The heavy use of crack, unlike the heavy use of tobacco, corrodes the natural sentiments of sympathy and duty that constitutes our personality." Crack and cocaine can't even be considered in the same class as alcohol and cigarettes.

Claim II   [Transparency #2] But say the government does accept these fallacies and legalizes these drugs, wouldn't they be putting themselves in a state of hypocrisy? I mean, how can they teach our children to "just say no" when they themselves have just said yes?

Claim III   We've talked about issues relating to drugs, but the most important issue is what do drugs do to the victim of drug addiction? I've seen this first-hand. As a result of drugs you lose your self-respect. Nothing matters to you except for that drug. And as a result you lose your sense of responsibility. You can't hold a job. Government handouts help you to live because you are unemployed. You are on the street. And when your mind doesn't function the same way that it used to, you lose your family because you can't express emotions and you can't give to a relationship. And only then, when drugs have taken your self-respect, when they've taken your family, they then take your life.

ARCHAEOLOGICAL DISCOVERY OF THE FUTURE: LATE 20TH CENTURY MAN

Cartoon courtesy of John Branch/San Antonio Express-News.
Transparency #2

Wrap-up Step   We've talked about the fallacies of legalizing drugs. We've discussed the hypocrisy that government would be putting themselves in if they accepted legalization. And we've talked about the destruction drugs cause. My family, for the past nine years, has been on the brink of emotional devastation. Drugs do not just influence the life of one person. They influence the life of the whole family and everyone who is involved.

As a society we cannot let government legalize something that is so deadly, not just to the individual, but to the family and ultimately to society. As James Q. Wilson says, "We all have a stake in ensuring that each of us displays a minimal level of dignity, responsibility and empathy." We cannot, of course, coerce people into goodness, but we can, and should, insist that some standards be met if society itself is to persist.

This chapter covered three of the main factors or appeals that lead to persuasion: (1) evidence and logic of the message, (2) the credibility of the persuader, and (3) the psychological needs of the listeners. Although some people may think that logic and evidence are far more important than other factors, research does not support this notion. In fact, psychological appeals are often needed to convince an audience of the truth and importance of your evidence. Successful persuasive speakers consider all three factors when preparing their speeches.

When you present the source of your evidence, also give the qualifications of the source. Presenting the source by itself is less persuasive. Also, pay particular attention to the types of fallacious reasoning discussed in this chapter: *ad hominem*, *ad populum*, *ad ignoratiam*, begging the question, hasty generalization, *post hoc*, and slippery slope. You may be able to refute objections to your position by pointing out the false reasoning that was used.

When planning how to improve your credibility as a speaker, keep in mind the four elements that make up credibility: trustworthiness, competency, dynamism and objectivity.

When planning how to appeal to the psychological needs of your audience, select specific motive appeals based on the analysis of your audience's attitudes, beliefs, values, and needs. Remember that persuasion requires more than evidence and credibility—emotional appeal that relates directly to your audience's needs is equally important.

1. With two or three of your classmates, compose a specific instance that illustrates each of the seven types of fallacious reasoning. When you are done, exchange lists with another group, read their list, and put a check mark by each instance that you think adequately illustrates the type of reasoning, and an X by each one you don't understand or think needs more work. If time allows, exchange papers with one more group and repeat the process. Then return the papers to the original group. If there are any X's by your instances, revise them with the help of your group. If you aren't sure, check with your instructor.

2. Read Tricia's speech on "Drug Legalization" and evaluate how she used evidence and logic, credibility, psychological appeals, and audience opinions to advance her position. Also look for the different types of faulty reasoning she refuted in her speech. In your opinion, was she effective? What do you think she might have done differently?

3. Select four motive appeals from Figure 14.3. For each motive appeal find a current radio or television commercial that tries to persuade listeners to buy a product by appealing to that specific listener need. Share your examples with your instructor, a classmate, or the entire class.

4. Using the persuasive speech you began preparing in Chapter 13 (Practice Suggestion 4), plan specific logical, ethical, and psychological appeals that will enhance your persuasiveness. Which of the methods for presenting

evidence do you think will work best with your audience? Do you think deductive, inductive, analogical, or causal patterns of reasoning will be most effective? Prepare a brief summary for your instructor.

5. To enhance your persuasiveness by improving your delivery, practice visualizing your positive statements about how effective a speaker you are. Remember that three steps are important for maximum effect of positive imagery: say, see, and feel. In other words, "say" each positive statement, "see" yourself standing in front of the class performing your speech with ease and success, and "feel" confident while visualizing your success.

Notes

1. Dan Quayle, *Standing Firm: A Vice-Presidential Memoir* (New York: HarperCollins, 1994), p. 355.

2. Adapted from Cheryl Hamilton with Cordell Parker, *Communicating for Results: A Guide for Business and the Professions*, 4th ed. (Belmont, CA: Wadsworth, 1993), Chapter 13.

3. James C. McCroskey, "A Summary of Experimental Research on the Effect of Evidence in Persuasive Communication," *Quarterly Journal of Speech* 55 (April 1969), 169–176.

4. Kathleen Bell, *Developing Arguments: Strategies for Reaching Audiences* (Belmont, CA: Wadsworth, 1990), p. 262.

5. Erwin P. Bettinghaus and Michael J. Cody, *Persuasive Communication*, 4th ed. (New York: Holt, Rinehart & Winston, 1987), pp. 150–151; R. C. Ruechelle, "An Experimental Study of Audience Recognition of Emotional and Intellectual Appeals in Persuasion," *Speech Monographs* 25 (1958), 58; W. R. Dresser, "Effects of 'Satisfactory' and 'Unsatisfactory' Evidence in a Speech of Advocacy," *Speech Monographs* 30 (August 1963), 302–306; James C. McCroskey, "The Effects of Evidence in Persuasive Communication," *Western Speech* 3 (1967), 189–199.

6. R. E. Petty and J. T. Cacioppo, "The Effects of Involvement on Response to Argument Quantity and Quality: Central and Peripheral Routes to Persuasion," *Journal of Personality and Social Psychology* 46 (1984), 69–81.

7. Bettinghaus and Cody, *Persuasive Communication*, p. 151.

8. Robert S. Cathcart, "An Experimental Study of the Relative Effectiveness of Four Methods of Presenting Evidence," *Speech Monographs* 22 (August 1955), 227–233; Dresser, "Effects," 302–306.

9. James C. McCroskey, "The Effects of Evidence as an Inhibitor of Counter-Persuasion," *Speech Monographs* 37 (August 1970), 188–194.

10. H. Gilkinson, S. F. Paulson, and D. E. Sikkink, "Effects of Order and Authority in an Argumentative Speech," *Quarterly Journal of Speech* 40 (1954), 183–192; Cathcart, "Experimental Study," 227–233; Robert N. Bostrom and Raymond K. Tucker, "Evidence, Personality, and Attitude Change," *Speech Monographs* 36 (March 1969), 22–27; T. H. Ostermeier, "Effects of Type and Frequency of Reference upon Perceived Source Credibility and Attitude Change," *Speech Monographs* 34 (June 1967), 137–144.

11. A. R. Cohen, *Attitude Change and Social Interaction* (New York: Basic Books, 1964), pp. 6–7.

12. Carl Sagan, *The Cosmic Connection: An Extraterrestrial Perspective*. (Garden City, NY: Doubleday, 1973), p. 207.

13. For the original studies, see Ostermeier, "Effects of Type," 137–144; and D. Papageorgis, "Bartlett Effect and the Persistence of Induced Opinion," *Journal of Abnormal and Social Psychology* 67 (1963), 61–67.

14. Z. Ginossar and Y. Trope, "The Effects of Base Rates and Individuating Information on Judgements About Another Person," *Journal of Experimental Social Psychology* 16 (1980), 228–242; J. Reinard, "The Empirical Study of the Persuasive Effects of Evidence," *Human Communication Research* 15 (1988), 3–59; T. R. Koballa, Jr., "Persuading Teachers to Reexamine the Innovative Elementary Science Programs of Yesterday: The Effect of Anecdotal Versus Data-Summary Communications," *Journal of Research in Science Teaching* 23 (1989), 437–449.

15. Dean C. Kazoleas, "A Comparison of the Persuasive Effectiveness of Qualitative Versus Quantitative Evidence: A Test of Explanatory Hypotheses," *Communication Quarterly* 41 (Winter 1993), 40–50.

16. McCroskey, "The Effects of Evidence as an Inhibitor," 188–194.

17. M. A. Kamins and L. J. Marks, "Advertising Puffery: The Impact of Using Two-sided Claims on Product Attitude and Purchase Intention," *Journal of Advertising* 16 (1987), 6–15; A. Lumsdaine and I. Janis, "Resistance to 'Counter-Propaganda' Produced by a One-Sided Versus a Two-Sided 'Propaganda' Presentation," *Public Opinion Quarterly* 17 (1943), 311–318; C. I. Hovland, A.

A. Lumsdaine, and F. D. Sheffield, *Experiments on Mass Communication* (Princeton, NJ: Princeton University Press, 1949); Hovland, Lumsdaine, and Sheffield, "The Effects of Presenting 'One-Side' vs. 'Both Sides' in Changing Opinions on a Controversial Subject," in Ralph L. Rosnow and Edward J. Robinson, eds., *Experiments in Persuasion* (New York: Academic Press, 1967), pp. 201–225; E. McGinnies, "Studies in Persuasion: III. Reactions of Japanese Students to One-Sided and Two-Sided Communications," *Journal of Social Psychology* 70 (1966), 91–93; J. R. Weston, "Argumentative Message Structure and Message Sidedness and Prior Familiarity as Predictors or Source Credibility," Ph.D. dissertation, Michigan State University, 1967.

18. For a detailed discussion of inoculation theory, see Daniel J. O'Keefe, *Persuasion: Theory and Research* (Newbury Park, CA: Sage, 1990), pp. 179–182. For a review of his work on inoculation theory, see William J. McGuire, "Attitudes and Attitude Change," in G. Lindzey and E. Aronson, eds., *The Handbook of Social Psychology*, 3rd ed., vol. 2 (New York: Random House, 1985), pp. 233–346.

19. B. Pryor and T. M. Steinfatt, "The Effects of Initial Belief Level on Inoculation Theory and Its Proposed Mechanisms," *Human Communication Research* 4 (1978), 217–230. See also D. Papageorgis and William McGuire, "The Generality of Immunity to Persuasion Produced by Pre-exposure to Weakened Counterarguments," *Journal of Abnormal and Social Psychology* 62 (1961), 475–481.

20. Mike Allen, "Meta-Analysis Comparing the Persuasiveness of One-sided and Two-sided Messages," *Western Journal of Speech Communication* 55 (Fall 1991), 390–404.

21. R. G. Hass and D. E. Linder, "Counterargument Availability and the Effects of Message Structure on Persuasion," *Journal of Personality and Social Psychology* 23 (1972), 227.

22. Howard Kahane, *Logic and Contemporary Rhetoric: The Use of Reason in Everyday Life*, 7th ed. (Belmont, CA: Wadsworth, 1995), pp. 10–14.

23. Charles U. Larson, *Persuasion: Reception and Responsibility*, 7th ed. (Belmont, CA: Wadsworth, 1995), p. 206.

24. Adapted from James A. Herrick, *Argumentation: Understanding and Shaping Arguments* (Scottsdale, AZ: Gorsuch Scarisbrick, 1995), pp. 190–193; and Michael Pfau, David A. Thomas, and Walter Ulrich, *Debate and Argument: A Systems Approach to Advocacy* (Glenview, IL: Scott, Foresman, 1987), p. 132–134.

25. Herrick, *Argumentation*, p. 227.

26. Bell, *Developing Arguments*, pp. 278–279.

27. See Bell, *Developing Arguments*, p. 279.

28. The complete Latin phrase is *Post hoc ergo propter hoc*, which means "After this, therefore because of this."

29. Donald D. Morley and K. B. Walker, "The Role of Importance, Novelty, and Plausibility in Producing Belief Change," *Communication Monographs* 54 (1987), 436–442; Donald D. Morley, "Subjective Message Constructs: A Theory of Persuasion," *Communication Monographs* 54 (June 1987), 183–203.

30. For an excellent review of source credibility research, see O'Keefe, *Persuasion*, pp. 130–140; S. Zagona and M. Harter, "Credibility of Source and Recipient's Attitude: Factors in the Perception and Retention of Information on Smoking Behavior," *Perceptual and Motor Skills* 23 (1966), 155–168; C. Hovland and W. Weiss, "The Influence of Source Credibility on Communication Effectiveness," *Public Opinion Quarterly* 15 (1951), 635–650.

31. Roger P. Wilcox, *Communication at Work: Writing and Speaking*, 3rd ed. (Boston: Houghton Mifflin, 1987), pp. 301–302.

32. R. E. Petty and J. T. Cacioppo, "The Elaboration Likelihood Model of Persuasion," in L. Berkowitz, ed., *Advances in Experimental Social Psychology*, Vol. 19 (San Diego: Academic Press, 1986), pp. 123–205. For more recent research see A. Tesser and D. R. Shaffer, "Attitudes and Attitude Change," *Annual Review of Psychology* 41 (1990), 479–523; and S. Ratneshwar and S. Chaiken, "Comprehension's Role in Persuasion: The Case of Its Moderating Effect on the Persuasive Impact of Source Cues," *Journal of Consumer Research* 18 (1991), 52–62.

33. This explanation is suggested by research following the Elaboration Likelihood Model (ELM) developed by R. E. Petty and T. J. Cacioppo, *Attitudes and Persuasion: Classic and Contemporary Approaches* (Dubuque, IA: Brown, 1981). For an explanation see Alice H. Eagly and Shelly Chaiken, *The Psychology of Attitudes* (Ft. Worth, TX: Harcourt Brace Jovanovich, 1993), pp. 305–325; or Kathleen K. Reardon, *Persuasion in Practice* (Newbury Park, CA: Sage, 1991), pp. 68–70.

34. Steve Booth-Butterfield and Christine Gutowski, "Message Modality and Source Credibility Can Interact to Affect Argument Processing," *Communication Quarterly* 41 (Winter 1993), 77–89.

35. S. Chaiken and A. Eagly, "Communication Modality as a Determinant of Persuasion: The Role of Communicator Salience," *Journal of Personality and Social Psychology* 45 (1983), 241–256.

36. For a detailed analysis of research on similarity, see O'Keefe, *Persuasion*, pp. 148–151.

37. E. Berscheid, "Interpersonal Attraction," in Lindzey and Aronson, *Handbook of Social Psychology*, pp. 413–484; R. L. Applbaum and K. W. Anatol, "The Factor Structure of Source Credibility as a Function of the Speaking Situation," *Speech Monographs* 39 (1972), 216–222.

38. O'Keefe, *Persuasion*, p. 150.

39. Raymond G. Smith, "Source Credibility Context Effects," *Speech Monographs* 40 (1973), 303–309; Jack R. Whitehead, "Factors of Source Credibility," *Quarterly Journal of Speech* 54 (1968), 61–63.

40. Smith, "Source Credibility," p. 309.

41. David W. Addington, "The Effects of Vocal Variations on Ratings of Source Credibility," *Speech Monographs* 38 (1971), 242–247.

42. S. Chaiken, "Physical Appearance and Social Influence," in C. P. Herman, M. P. Zanna, and E. T. Higgins, eds., *Physical Appearance, Stigma, and Social Behavior: The Ontario Symposium*, Vol. 3 (Hillsdale, NJ: Lawrence Erlbaum, 1986), pp. 143–177.

43. James C. McCroskey and R. S. Mehrley, "The Effects of Disorganization and Nonfluency on Attitude Change and Source Credibility," *Speech Monographs* 36 (1969), 13–21; James C. McCroskey and T. J. Young, "Ethos and Credibility: The Construct and Its Measurement After Three Decades," *Central States Speech Journal* 32 (1981), 24–34.

44. W. Barnett Pearce and Forrest Conklin, "Nonverbal Vocalic Communication and Perceptions of a Speaker," *Speech Monographs* 38 (1971), 241.

45. R. Norman, "When What Is Said Is Important: A Comparison of Expert and Attractive Sources," *Journal of Experimental Social Psychology* 12 (1976), 83–91.

46. McCroskey, "Summary of Experimental Research," 169–176; R. Rosnow and E. Robinson, eds., *Experiments in Persuasion* (New York: Academic Press, 1967), pp. 2–5; Albert Mehrabian and Martin Williams, "Nonverbal Concomitants of Perceived and Intended Persuasiveness," *Journal of Personality and Social Psychology* 13 (1969), 37–58.

47. William J. Seiler, "The Conjunctive Influence of Source Credibility and the Use of Visual Materials on Communication Effectiveness," *Southern Speech Communication Journal* 37 (Winter 1971), 174–185.

48. William S. Howell and Ernest G. Bormann, *Presentational Speaking for Business and the Professions* (New York: Harper & Row, 1979), p. 30.

49. Adapted from Hamilton with Parker, *Communicating for Results*, p. 409.

50. Abraham Maslow, *Motivation and Personality* (New York: Harper & Brothers, 1954).

51. F. J. Boster and P. Mongeau, "Fear-Arousing Persuasive Messages," in R. N. Bostrom, ed., *Communication Yearbook* (Beverly Hills, CA: Sage, 1984), pp. 330–375.

52. S. R. Sutton and J. R. Eiser, "The Effect of Fear-Arousing Communications on Cigarette Smoking: An Expectancy-Value Approach," *Journal of Behavioral Medicine* 7 (1984), 13–33.

53. J. E. Maddux and R. W. Rogers, "Protection Motivation and Self-Efficacy: A Revised Theory of Fear Appeals and Attitude Change," *Journal of Experimental Social Psychology* 19 (1983), 469–479; R. W. Rogers, "A Protection Motivation Theory of Fear Appeals and Attitude Change," *Journal of Psychology* 91 (1975), 93–114.

54. Kim Witte, "Putting the Fear Back into Fear Appeals: The Extended Parallel Process Model," *Communication Monographs* 59 (December 1992), 329–349; Kim Witte, "The Role of Threat and Efficacy in AIDS Prevention," *International Quarterly of Community Health Education* 12 (1992), 225–249. For a discussion of why more research is needed to support the role of efficacy in persuasion, see Chaiken and Eagly, *Psychology of Attitudes*, pp. 440–447.

55. Herrick, *Argumentation*, p. 230.

Organizing Your Arguments So They FLOW

Step 1: FOCUS Audience Attention and Interest

Begin with an Attention-Getter

Motivate Your Audience to Listen

Establish Your Credibility

Step 2: LEAD IN to Your Topic

State Your Position—Unless the Audience Is Hostile

Preview Your Main Points

Include Background Information on the Problem (optional)

Clarify Any Unfamiliar Terms (optional)

Step 3: ORGANIZE and SUPPORT Your Main Points

Suggested Patterns of Organization

Deciding Which Pattern to Use

Quiz: Testing Your Knowledge of Persuasive Patterns

Step 4: WRAP-UP

Summarize Arguments, Position, or Recommendations

Visualize the Future

Challenge or Appeal for Action

Refocus Interest in a Memorable Way

Using the Motivated Sequence

Summary

Practice Suggestions

Notes

AS YOU KNOW FROM CHAPTER 13, although there are many similarities between informative and persuasive speeches, there are very important differences as well. The basic steps of the FLOW sequence as used in persuasive speeches are outlined in Figure 15.1. You will notice that the main differences occur in the organization and wrap-up steps. As you are already aware, the order in which you prepare the steps of the FLOW sequence is different from the order in which you actually present them in a speech—preparation normally should begin with the organization step (step 3). However, so you can see the FLOW sequence, this chapter will describe each step in the order in which you will present it in your speech.

Step 1: FOCUS Audience Attention and Interest

▼ ▼ ▼

Since the focus step in the persuasive speech is basically the same as the focus step in the informative speech, this chapter will include a brief review only. However, if you have questions, it would be a good idea to go back to Chapter 11 and reread step 1 before preparing your actual speech.

Begin with an Attention-Getter

Although getting audience interest right at the beginning of any speech is always important, it's even more important when persuasion is your intention. If audience members are not paying attention to your arguments, they certainly will not be persuaded by them. Based on your topic, specific audience interests, and your own preferences, you will want to select one of a variety of attention-getters described with examples in Chapter 11.

The type of attention-getter that will work best depends on what type of audience you have—friendly, neutral, uninterested, or hostile (see Chapter 5). Humor works especially well for the friendly audience; well-supported statistics or a detailed, factual instance are ideal for the neutral audience; a colorful, yet professional visual aid or startling facts may surprise the uninterested audience into listening; and a powerful quotation by a well-known authority or by a member of their own group will work best for the hostile audience. Novel information works with all types of audiences. Julia Hughes Jones, auditor for the state of Arkansas, used novel information in her speech "A Greater Voice in Action" to focus her audience's attention on the importance of voting:

> I am here today to help you celebrate, along with people all across the country, the anniversary of women's suffrage in the United States. . . .
>
> Many of you realize that suffrage means the right to vote, but it also implies the responsibility to vote.
>
> Why is a vote important? Many times, a single vote has changed the course of history.

FLOW Sequence for Persuasive Speeches

FOCUS audience attention and interest:
  I. Begin with attention-getter
  II. Motivate audience to listen
  III. Establish credibility

LEAD IN to topic:
  I. State position (unless audience hostile)
  II. Preview main points
  III. Include background of problem (optional)
  IV. Clarify terms (optional)

ORGANIZE AND SUPPORT main points:
  I. Use a persuasive pattern of organization
    A. Claim pattern
    B. Causal pattern
      1. Cause-effect-solution
      2. Cause-effect-action
    C. Problem-solution pattern
      1. Problem-solution-benefits
      2. Problem-solution-action
    D. Comparative advantages pattern
    E. Criteria satisfaction pattern
  II. Use a variety of verbal supporting materials
    A. Supports that prove and clarify
      1. Expert opinion
      2. Statistics
      3. Instances (detailed and brief)
      4. Literal comparisons
    B. Supports that clarify only
      1. Explanation
      2. Figurative comparisons
      3. Fables, sayings, poems, and rhymes
      4. Demonstrations
  III. Use visual supporting materials

WRAP UP:
  I. Summarize arguments, position, or recommendations
  II. Visualize future
  III. Challenge or appeal to action
  IV. Refocus interest in memorable way

Figure 15.1
The FLOW Sequence as Used with Persuasive Speeches

More than a thousand years ago in Greece, an entire meeting of the Church Synod was devoted to one question: Is a woman a human being or an animal? It was finally settled by vote, and the consensus was that we do indeed belong to the human race. It passed, however, by just one vote.

Remember:

Attention-getters may include . . .

▶ A detailed instance (factual or hypothetical).

▶ Two or more brief instances.

▶ A joke or humorous instance.

▶ A quote or paraphrase.

▶ One or more startling facts.

▶ A rhetorical or actual question.

▶ Reference to a special occasion or event.

▶ A fable, saying, poem, or rhyme.

▶ A brief demonstration.

Other situations where one vote has made a difference:

▶ In 1776, *one vote* gave America the English language instead of German.

▶ In 1845, *one vote* brought Texas and California into the Union.

▶ In 1868, *one vote* saved President Andrew Johnson from impeachment.

▶ In 1923, *one vote* determined the leader of a new political party in Munich. His name was Adolf Hitler.

▶ In 1960, *one vote* change in each precinct in Illinois would have defeated John F. Kennedy.

History has proven the enormous power of *one single vote*. Yet, many women, even today, believe their vote doesn't matter; and their voices are not heard.[1]

Motivate Your Audience to Listen

In Chapter 4 you learned that getting listener attention at the beginning of your speech isn't enough—you have to motivate audience members to want to listen throughout the entire speech. To do this, you must convince them that your speech will benefit them or people they care about in some way (see Figure 4.2 for a list of audience motivators). As you saw in Chapter 14, another word for audience motivation is audience "needs." Use Maslow's five categories of basic human needs (physiological, safety, social, esteem, and self-actualization) to determine your specific audience's needs. To be persuasive, you must show how your plan or position will help fulfill one or more of these needs.

Persuasive speakers commonly combine the attention and motivation steps as Jenny Clanton did in her award-winning speech "Plutonium 238." As you

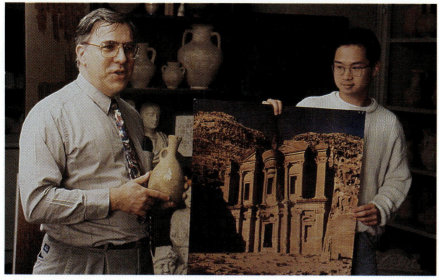

This ancient vase and picture of the ruin where it was found grabbed the attention of the audience and helped establish a common ground between the speaker and his audience of art majors.

© Michael Newman/PhotoEdit

read the following excerpt from her speech (which combines attention and motivation), think about which basic needs she is appealing to. If you had been in the audience, would you have been stimulated and motivated to listen to her speech?

> On January 28, 1986, the American Space Program suffered the worst disaster in its more than 30-year history. The entire world was shocked when the space shuttle *Challenger* exploded seconds after lift-off, claiming the lives of seven brave astronauts and crippling our entire space agenda. I suppose the oldest cliche in our culture, spoken on battlegrounds and indeed virtually anywhere Americans die, is "We must press forward, so we can say they did not die in vain." Rest assured. They didn't. The deaths of our seven astronauts probably saved the lives of untold thousands of Americans.
>
> For, you see, if the O-rings had not failed on January 28, 1986, but rather on May 20, 1987, the next scheduled shuttle launch, in the words of Dr. John Gofman, Professor Emeritus at the University of California at Berkeley, you could have "kissed Florida goodbye."
>
> Because the next shuttle, the one that was to have explored the atmosphere of Jupiter, was to carry 47 lbs. of Plutonium 238, which, is, again according to Dr. Gofman, the most toxic substance on the face of the earth. Dr. Helen Caldicott corroborates Dr. Gofman's claim in her book, *Nuclear Madness*, when she cites studies estimating one ounce of widely dispersed Plutonium 238 particles as having the toxicity to induce lung cancer in every person on earth.[2]

Establish Your Credibility

You can establish credibility by telling about your personal experience or concerns with the topic, by noting a similarity you share with your audience, by mentioning expert sources from which you obtained your materials, or by having someone known to the audience introduce you (as Lorna did in her speech on drunk driving). Jenny Clanton established her credibility by citing expert sources. She didn't have to say, "I've carefully researched this topic"; it was obvious just from the sources she cited in her introduction.

Although beginning speakers have a tendency to omit any mention of credibility in the focus section, remember that credibility is especially important in persuasive speeches. If you wait until later in your speech, some of your listeners (especially those in a hostile audience) may have already decided that you don't have enough expertise and aren't worth listening to.

To conclude our discussion of this section, let's take a closer look at the focus step Lorna McElaney used in her speech (the complete speech appears in Chapter 13).

▼ ▼ ▼ **Focus Step:** "Drinking and Driving"

Analysis

Since Lorna's speech was given early in December, her reference to the Christmas season and the celebrating that occurs during this time was a good attention-getter.

Lorna appeals to safety and social needs in her attempt to motivate her classmates. By asking them if they have ever had one or more drinks and then driven home, she hopes to get her audience personally involved. Immediately after asking the question (most of the class raised their hands), she startles them with the example of Larry Dotson to show them that her topic is relevant. Larry was out celebrating—just like them, and he killed Natalie. Now Natalie's mother grieves—just like their mothers would.

Lorna does not mention her credibility because she was introduced by a classmate. The actual introduction to Lorna's speech is included on page 331.

Speech

The Christmas season is the time for sharing and giving and sweet memories of years gone past. There is a lot of celebrating going on, not only now, but all through the year. Everyone seems to be celebrating one thing or another. How many of you when you are out there celebrating have had a drink, or maybe two or more, and then gotten in your car and driven away? Well last year in December Larry Dotson did the same thing and he hit and killed Natalie Gale, a twenty-year-old girl, and her companion. Perhaps with greater awareness and tougher laws Natalie would be here today and her mother wouldn't be suffering the pain and anguish that she is this Christmas season. Last Christmas it was Natalie Gale; this Christmas it could be one of us.

An effective speech introduction includes more than just a focus step. The lead-in step also is very important to successful persuasion.

Step 2: LEAD IN to Your Topic
▼ ▼ ▼

In a persuasive speech, the lead-in step includes four substeps: (1) state your position, (2) preview your main points, (3) include needed background on the problem, and (4) clarify any confusing terms. These substeps can be placed in any order you prefer. In most persuasive speeches, steps 1 and 2 should definitely be included but steps 3 and 4 are optional.

State Your Position—Unless the Audience Is Hostile

Normally you will want to tell your listeners exactly where you stand on the issue and then attempt to get them to agree with you. However, if your audience is hostile to your position, you may want to omit the lead-in section almost entirely. When an audience is hostile, presenting your exact position and main points in the introduction of your speech could cause members to stop listening. A better plan would be to gradually present your main points (getting audience agreement on each point as you go if possible) and conclude with your exact position and plan. Of course, even if you decide not to state your exact position up front, the audience will still need to know your general topic.

When you state your position, don't forget that persuasive language is more dynamic and powerful than informative language—start persuading your audience right from the start. Jenny Clanton made her feelings about NASA's use of Plutonium 238 completely clear and, at the same time, challenged her audience to get involved:

> Today, when you leave this room, I want you to fully understand just what impact NASA's plans could have on this planet. I want you to become cynical. I want you to be a little scared. I want you to become angry. But most of all, I want you to begin to demand some answers.[3]

Preview Your Main Points

The value of previewing your main arguments, unless the audience is hostile, is that it further clarifies your position and lets your audience know in what direction you will be going during the speech. You don't want your listeners wondering what arguments you will present; you want them listening to the arguments as you present them. Also, don't forget that repetition improves listener retention. Therefore summarizing your arguments in the lead-in step (as well as the wrap-up step) is likely to improve audience memory. **Tip:** Present your arguments on a visual aid to ensure maximum memory from your audience (see Chapters 4 and 6).

We've heard Jenny Clanton's attention-getter and her position statement. Now let's see what she used as a preview of her main points:

> To move you in this direction I would first like to explore with you just what plutonium is and what could happen if it were released in our atmosphere. Second, let's consider NASA's argument for the safety of the plutonium as used in the shuttle program. And finally, I want to convince you that NASA's conclusions are flawed.[4]

Now that we've discussed the two substeps that should normally be included in the lead-in step of all persuasive speeches, let's look at two optional steps you may want to include: (1) needed background information and (2) clarification of confusing terms.

Include Background Information on the Problem (optional)

Persuasion is dependent on the existence of problems. Before you can recommend a solution or a plan of action, there must be a reason for it—in other words, there must be a problem serious enough to warrant change. The question is, should you discuss the problem in the lead-in section or in the body of your speech. The answer is, if you are using a problem-solution pattern to organize your main arguments (discussed later in this chapter), you will discuss the problem in the body of the speech. However, when using most other organizational patterns, you will need to present the seriousness of the problem and its potential effects on your audience during the lead-in section of your speech.

If your audience is already familiar with the problem, a brief reminder is all that is needed. However, if the problem is relatively unknown or is based on listener misconceptions, a more thorough discussion will be needed. In a speech entitled "Business and School Reform" given at the Business-Education Partnership Conference, Vern Loucks, Jr., chairman and CEO of Baxter International, didn't need to spend much time explaining the problem:

> The last thing that any of us in business can afford is the existence of a permanent and largely ignored or forgotten underclass. Yet in nearly every big city of our nation, that underclass seems entrenched in our society. That is an absolute tragedy. It's also a grim and dangerous waste. All of us in this room know and understand the correlation between academic failure and crime. All of us fully understand the negative potential of a society where a very large minority does not participate in the successes of society as a whole.[5]

Clarify Any Unfamiliar Terms (optional)

The last subtopic that is normally included in the lead-in section of a persuasive speech is the clarification of any unfamiliar terms. For example, it would be a mistake to assume that everyone in your audience knows that STD stands for "sexually transmitted disease," that MBWA stands for "management by wandering around," or that plutonium "is a man-made radioactive element which is produced in large quantities in nuclear reactors from uranium."[6] In the introduction to his speech "Attitude, Not Aptitude, Determines Altitude," Richard L. Weaver II defined what he meant by "attitude":

> Motivating oneself and motivating others begins with attitude. Motivation is *not* something that occurs outside of ourselves; it is *not* something, either, that happens *to* others. Motivation of self and others begins from the same spark, the same flame, the same raging fire that creates success in school, success in relationships, or success at work. . . . That spark is, indeed, ATTITUDE. . . .[7]

To conclude our discussion of step 2, let's take a closer look at the lead-in step Lorna McElaney used in her speech on drunk drivers:

Analysis

Since Lorna is using the problem-solution-action pattern of organization, her lead-in step does not need to include background information on the problem. Also no unusual terms need defining.

Although no optional substeps are included in Lorna's lead-in, she uses persuasive language effectively in making her exact position known and smoothly previews her three main points: problem, solutions, and recommended action.

Speech

Today, I will share with you some startling facts that show how serious a problem drunk driving has become, recommend several workable solutions, and urge you to join me in writing our senators to demand tougher laws to protect ourselves and those we love.

Now that your focus and lead-in steps have successfully set the stage for your persuasive speech, you are ready to present the body of your speech—your main arguments or points.

Step 3: ORGANIZE and SUPPORT Your Main Points

▼ ▼ ▼

In preparing the body of your persuasive speech you will need to develop your main points as well as the logical, emotional, and ethical supports for those points (covered in Chapter 14). The following discussion concentrates on patterns you can use to organize your main points. As with your informative speech, the organizational pattern you select is very important to your speaking success. Therefore think about your own persuasive speech topic as you read about each pattern and see which best fits your position statement and main points.

Suggested Patterns of Organization

Basically persuasive speakers select from five main patterns when organizing their main points: (1) claim (inductive and deductive), (2) causal, (3) problem-solution (problem-solution-benefits or problem-solution-action), (4) comparative advantages, and (5) criteria satisfaction. Figure 15.2 summarizes each pattern. (The motivated sequence is also used by persuasive speakers, but since it is a method for organizing the complete speech, not just the main arguments, it will be discussed later in this chapter.) Note that these patterns are not all-inclusive, but they represent the most often used patterns in persuasive speaking.

Figure 15.2
Organizational Patterns
for Persuasive Speeches

Persuasive Patterns

I. Claim #1
II. Claim #2
III. Claim #3

▼ **Claim Pattern**

I. Any plan must meet the
   following necessary criteria:
II. Solution X does (or does
    not) meet the criteria.

▼ **Criteria Satisfaction Pattern**

I. Cause   I. Cause
II. Effect (or) II. Effect
III. Solution   III. Action

▼ **Causal Pattern**

I. Plan X is ineffective
II. Plan Y is superior
        (or)
I. Plan X is average
II. Plan Y is far better

I. Problem   I. Problem
II. Solution (or) II. Solution
III. Benefits   III. Action

▼ **Problem-Solution Pattern**

▼ **Comparative Advantages
Pattern**

Claim pattern   In the claim pattern the problem is reviewed in the lead-in section and the reasons for believing (or not believing) a particular fact, for holding (or not holding) a particular value, or for advocating (or not advocating) a particular plan are presented in the body of the speech. Although the claim pattern is similar to the topical pattern used in informative speaking, the language is definitely persuasive.

Tricia Seeley Lewis used the claim pattern to convince in her speech on "Drug Legalization":

I. Unless you listen carefully to the pro-legalization advocates, you may miss the fallacies in their reasoning. [**claim 1**]
II. If the government does accept these fallacies and legalizes drugs, they would be putting themselves in a state of hypocrisy. [**claim 2**]
III. When drugs are used, they devastate the user and the user's family. [**claim 3**]

The claim pattern often involves the use of either inductive or deductive reasoning. As discussed in Chapter 14, inductive reasoning involves presenting the specific evidence first as you build up to your general conclusion; deductive reasoning involves presenting

Drug Legalization

Fallacious reasoning •
Government hypocrisy •
Devastation •

the position or general conclusion first and then providing the supporting evidence. For example, a speech advocating prison reform before a potentially hostile audience might use the following inductive claim pattern:[8]

I. Prison spending costs society over $20 billion each year. [**claim 1**: specific evidence]
II. Much of this expense goes to provide recreational equipment and services that even many taxpayers can't afford. [**claim 2**: specific evidence]
III. In addition, civil lawsuits filed by inmates are clogging federal and state courts. [**claim 3**: specific evidence]
IV. It's time to end the resort status of American prisons. [**claim 4**: general conclusion]

Causal pattern   The causal pattern in informative speaking uses both cause-effect and effect-cause. However, the causal pattern in persuasive speaking normally uses only cause-effect and is usually followed by a solution or action step (see Figure 15.2). Since cause-effect reasoning is used to prove, it's important that the cause-effect relationship you are presenting be real and not just a chance happening. (See Chapter 14, pp. 363–364 for a list of questions to ask that will help assure that the causal link is a real one.)

If you decide to use the causal organization pattern, it may be similar to the causal pattern used by Jeff Davidson in his speech entitled "Overworked Americans or Overwhelmed Americans? You Cannot Handle Everything":[9]

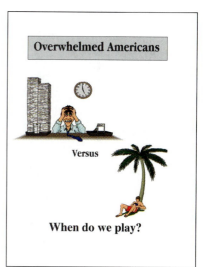

I. The overwhelmed, pressured feeling that Americans have is caused by the complexity of our society. [**cause**]
   A. Population growth
   B. Expanding volume of knowledge
   C. Mass media and electronic growth
   D. Paper trail culture
   E. Overabundance of choices
II. As complexity increases, these pressured feelings will turn into feelings of overwork and total exhaustion. [**effect**]
III. It's not too late to take control of your life. [**action**]
   A. Make choices in what to ignore.
   B. Avoid engaging in low-level decisions.
   C. Learn to enjoy yourself.

Problem-solution pattern   The problem-solution pattern can take a variety of forms. The two most popular forms are the problem-solution-benefits and the problem-solution-action patterns. Both patterns begin with a detailed discussion of the problem, its seriousness, and its effect on the audience (see Chapter 14 for suggestions on using persua-

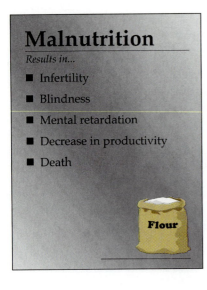

Malnutrition

Results in...

■ Infertility

■ Blindness

■ Mental retardation

■ Decrease in productivity

■ Death

Flour

Alcohol-Related Facts

■ 2 of 5 people in accident

■ 17,400 killed in U.S. last year

■ 1,800 killed in Texas last year

■ Only 20-30% conviction rate

sive appeals). Next, a solution (or solutions) is presented to solve or improve the problem. Finally, additional benefits resulting from your solution are described or a particular course of action is recommended to the audience. Nevin S. Scrimshaw used a problem-solution-benefit pattern in his speech entitled "The Consequences of Hidden Hunger":[10]

I. The magnitude and consequences of hidden hunger still devastate a large proportion of the world's population. [**problem**]

II. Hunger can be abolished as a public health problem in the world if we are willing to take the required actions. [**solution**]

III. Conquering hunger will release human potential for creating better societies. [**benefits**]

Lorna McElaney's speech on drunk drivers, located in Chapter 13, uses a problem-solution-action pattern of organization. See Figure 15.4 for a complete outline.

I. The high number of auto/alcohol-related accidents indicates a serious problem. [**problem**]
   A. Nationally, 2 of 5 involved in auto/alcohol accidents.
   B. Nationally, 17,000 killed in auto/alcohol accidents.
   C. In Texas, 1,800 killed in auto/alcohol accidents.

II. There are several workable solutions to the DWI problem. [**solutions**]
   A. Year-around sobriety checkpoints.
   B. Legal blood-alcohol level lowered from .1 to .08.
   C. Stronger penalties for drunk driving.

III. Action must be taken now. [**action**]
   A. "Lights-on-for-Life" promotion on December 16.
   B. Letter to Senator Kay Bailey Hutchison

Comparative advantages pattern   The comparative advantages pattern of organization is normally used when your audience already agrees with you on the problem but may not agree on the solution. Only a brief mention of the problem is needed during the lead-in section. The comparative advantages pattern concentrates on the advantages of one course of action over another. Usually you will want to show that your plan or course of action is superior to the current ineffective plan for a number of reasons. However, if the current plan is adequate rather than inferior, use the comparative advantages pattern to show that your plan should be adopted because of its many important advantages over the current plan. In his speech on "Aid to Russia," Lawrence M. Lesser used the comparative advantages pattern:[11]

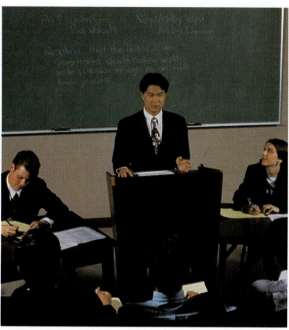

© Michelle Bridwell/PhotoEdit

Successful debaters are able to use all the persuasive patterns discussed in this chapter. This speaker is using the comparative advantages pattern to show that his plan is far superior to the one proposed by the opposing team.

I. The current method of giving aid to Russia in the form of cash grants, loans, and credit guarantees isn't working. [**current plan is ineffective**]
   A. Russia is in default on $600 million of interest payments on $4.2 billion of U.S. agricultural credit guarantees used to purchase American grain.
   B. Russia has failed to pay $200 million in debts it owes to 57 American companies.
   C. Russia has defaulted on payments on the $4.5 billion it borrowed from international lenders, forcing the U.S. to pay $180 million in loan loss claims.
II. Bartering, a concept Russia is very familiar with, is a much better way of providing aid to Russia. [**new plan is superior**]

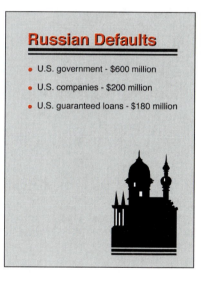

Russian Defaults

- U.S. government - $600 million
- U.S. companies - $200 million
- U.S. guaranteed loans - $180 million

Criteria satisfaction pattern   Whether you are dealing with products, services, or ideas, the criteria satisfaction pattern is a persuasive tool that works well even when audience members may oppose your position. First, you establish criteria (guidelines or rules) that should be followed when evaluating possible plans or solutions ("We all want our professors to be knowledgeable and fair"). Second, you show how your plan meets or exceeds the established criteria ("Not only is Professor X knowledgeable and fair, she is also a dynamic speaker"). Of course, it's important to carefully consider your audience's values and needs when selecting and explaining why your criteria are important. If you can get your listeners to agree with your criteria, the chances are good that they also will agree with your plan. Using the criteria satisfaction pattern, Farah M. Walters, president and CEO of University Hospitals of Cleveland and a member of President Clinton's National Health Care Reform Task Force, gave a speech called "If It's Broke, Fix It: The Significance of Health Care Reform in America":[12]

Health Care Criteria

- Security for all
- Choice of physicians
- Continuity of care
- Affordable to all
- Comprehensive coverage
- "User friendly"

I. Any health care plan should be measured against six fundamental principles: [**necessary criteria**]
  A. Provide security for all Americans.
  B. Provide choice of physician.
  C. Provide continuity of care.
  D. Be affordable to the individual, to business and to the country.
  E. Be comprehensive in terms of coverage.
  F. Be "user friendly" for consumers and providers.
II. The health care plan designed by the National Health Care Reform Task Force meets all six of these fundamental principles. [**plan meets criteria**]

Tip: Since the last criterion in your list will come right before your discussion of the "ideal" plan, it's a good idea to place your most important criterion last.

Deciding Which Pattern to Use

Which organizational pattern you choose for your persuasive speech depends on (1) whether you are giving a speech to convince or to actuate, (2) whether your position statement is written as a statement of fact, value, or policy, and (3) what your personal preferences and/or assignment requirements are.

First, the *type of speech* you plan to give (to convince or to actuate) differs in the degree of audience reaction sought. A speech to convince seeks intellectual agreement from listeners; a speech to actuate not only seeks audience agreement but also asks the audience to take a particular action. If you plan to give a speech to convince, any of the organizational patterns that do not involve action can be used successfully (the problem-solution-action and cause-result-action would not work). Basically the opposite is true for the speech to actuate—any pattern that involves action will work (the most popular pattern is the problem-solution-action pattern).

Second, your *position statement* makes a difference as to which organizational pattern you should select. For statements of fact, with which you will persuade your audience that something is or is not true, the claim and causal (cause-effect-solution) patterns are especially effective. However, for a statement of value, with which you will persuade your audience that something is or is not good, pay special attention to the claim and the criteria satisfaction patterns. Finally, for a statement of policy, with which you will persuade the audience that something should or should not be done, the problem solution or comparative advantages patterns are recommended.

The final determiner of which organizational pattern you should select for your persuasive speech is your *specific assignment and your preferences*. If the class assignment specifies which pattern to use, make sure your speech type and your position statement are compatible (see Chapter 13 for details). Your preferences also should play a role in which pattern you select.

Tip: The following pattern selection guidelines are suggested for your convenience.

For Speeches to Convince:

▶ When using a *statement of fact*, try the claim or cause-effect-solution pattern.

▶ When using a *statement of value*, try the claim or criteria satisfaction pattern.

▶ When using a *statement of policy*, try the problem-solution-benefits or comparative advantages pattern.

For Speeches to Actuate:

▶ When using a *statement of fact*, try the claim or cause-result-action pattern.

▶ When using a *statement of value*, try the claim or criteria satisfaction pattern.

▶ When using a *statement of policy*, try the problem-solution-action or comparative advantages pattern.

Quiz

Testing Your Knowledge of Persuasive Patterns

Directions: Below are six mini-outlines, each with a title and main points. Identify how the main points of each outline are organized by selecting one of the following patterns: (a) claim, (b) causal, (c) problem-solution, (d) comparative advantages, or (e) criteria satisfaction.

_____ 1. "Youth Violence"[13]

    I. The rate of youths arrested for violent crimes is up 50 percent.

    II. The rate of youths arrested for murder is up 128 percent.

(continued)

(continued)

    III. The rate of youths killed by firearms is up 59 percent.

    IV. Neighborhood prevention programs are needed to control youth violence.

_____ 2. "Senseless or Sensible Divorce?"[14]

    I. When divorce is settled in court, it's expensive and lengthy, promotes destructive competition, and clogs the court system.

    II. Divorce settled by mediation solves these problems.

    III. In addition to solving basic divorce problems, mediation has an important benefit—it allows both parties time to stabilize personally.

_____ 3. "Overweight Americans"

    I. Losing weight by dieting has very few advantages.

    II. Losing weight by lowering fat intake has several important advantages.

_____ 4. "Becoming a Blood Donor"

    I. Blood donors are crucial to alleviating America's blood shortage.

    II. Blood donors are essential if new medical treatments (such as heart and bone marrow transplants) are to continue.

    III. Blood donors are paramount in disasters like the Oklahoma bombing.

_____ 5. "Helping the Homeless"[15]

    I. Any workable solution to helping the homeless must meet the following guidelines:

        A. Respect the rights and dignity of the homeless.

        B. Require that the homeless work for shelter and food.

        C. Offer drug and alcohol abuse prevention programs.

        D. Offer hope.

    II. Our community's attempt to help the homeless by giving them money and housing violates all of the above guidelines.

_____ 6. "Good Mothers Care for Their Children at Home"

    I. Many single mothers with children must put them in day care during work hours.

    II. In several recent cases the court has taken custody from single mothers who placed their children in day care rather than caring for them at home.

    III. Such decisions are irresponsible and must be reversed.

Answers

6.   (b) cause-result-action pattern
5.   (e) criteria satisfaction pattern
4.   (a) claim pattern
3.   (d) comparative advantages pattern
2.   (c) problem-solution-benefits pattern
1.   (a) claim pattern with inductive reasoning

Now that you have made sure your main points are organized in the most persuasive pattern for your particular topic and position statement, you are ready to add a powerful conclusion.

Step 4: WRAP-UP

▼ ▼ ▼

The wrap-up step is even more important in a persuasive speech than in an informative speech because it gives you one last chance to persuade your listeners. Be sure that your language remains forceful and persuasive—now is not the time to sound uncertain. Whereas the informative wrap-up includes only two steps, the persuasive wrap-up includes four steps: (1) summarize arguments, (2) visualize the future, (3) challenge or appeal for action, and (4) refocus attention.

Summarize Arguments, Position, or Recommendations

The purpose of the summary is to remind your listeners of your general position or the specific persuasive arguments and recommendations presented in your speech. To help your audience remember specific details from your speech, use a visual aid during your summary. To conclude his speech (organized using the comparative advantages pattern), Lawrence M. Lesser summarizes why bartering is more advantageous than usual methods of giving aid to Russia:

> Grand scale barter transactions, such as a large-scale food for oil deal, and others like it, make sense for several reasons. First, the use of oil and other resources as collateral for Western loans and as payment for goods and services would enable American and other Western firms to minimize the risks of doing business today in [Russia] and protect American taxpayers against default.
>
> Second, they would advance U.S. economic and political relations with Russia. . . . And finally, agreements of this kind would further America's national security interests because they would enable us to diversify our energy resources and reduce our reliance on oil from the volatile Persian Gulf.[16]

Don't forget as you wrap up your persuasive speech to visualize the future for your audience—look them right in the eye, use forceful and dynamic delivery, and speak with emotion and sincerity.

© Mark Richards/PhotoEdit

Visualize the Future

Because your audience may not be good at doing it themselves, you need to visualize the future for them—the future without your proposal and/or the future with your proposal. This is the time to look your listeners right in the eye, to use forceful and dynamic language, and to speak with emotion and sincerity while you paint a vivid mental picture of the future. Of course, you don't want to use faulty reasoning or unethical emotional appeals (covered in Chapter 14). At the same time, you need to encourage those listeners who are almost persuaded—they just want to see how your topic relates to them one more time. Kim, another speaker on drunk driving, visualized a future with year-round sobriety checkpoints in this way:

> . . . take a moment and picture a world where we could all feel safer on our roads again. We could all go out on New Year's Eve, because, quite frankly, those of us who do drink responsibly won't go out on this night because we are afraid of the other people on the road. Families wouldn't have to be as fearful of going on a vacation over a long holiday weekend such as Memorial Day, Labor Day or the Fourth of July; they wouldn't feel as threatened by the other drivers on the road. Wouldn't this safety be worth the inconvenience of stopping at sobriety checkpoints?

Challenge or Appeal for Action

Even though you have presented your arguments and/or plan in a persuasive manner with credibility, evidence, and emotional appeal, it would be a mistake to assume that your listeners know exactly what you want them to believe or do. As stated in Chapter 13, you will be more persuasive when you specify in the wrap-up section the exact position, belief, or action you want your listeners to take.[17] You will also be more persuasive if your listeners perceive that they are capable of completing the action you are requesting of them.[18] When listeners feel that the problem you have described is a serious one ("I realize that in six months all the landfills in the state will be filled to capacity and we will have no place to put our garbage") but that they are not capable of doing anything about it ("But even if I do purchase fewer boxed and plastic wrapped items, one family isn't going to make much difference"), they will tend to reject the message and even do the opposite of what you recommend (boomerang response).[19]

Make it as easy for your listeners to comply with your request as possible. For example, if you ask them to write to their senators, have a handout with each senator's name, address, and phone number. Or, as Lorna did, have a letter already written and ask your audience to sign it. A copy of Lorna's letter (which everyone in her class signed) is shown in Figure 15.3.

Catherine B. Ahles, in a persuasive speech entitled "The Dynamics of Discovery: Creating Your Own Opportunities," issued this *challenge*:

> As you go forward to discover your world of possibilities, I challenge you to think about the seven questions I've posed tonight:
> ▸ Are you creating your own opportunities?
> ▸ Can you make more informed choices?
> ▸ How keenly are you paying attention?
> ▸ How daring are you?
> ▸ What are your convictions?
> ▸ How strong is your confidence?
> ▸ What is your personal philosophy?[20]

Joseph T. Gorman ended his presentation entitled "Facing Facts and Forging Agendas" with both a challenge and an appeal to action:

> We are in deep trouble, especially with respect to the disadvantaged—the underclass. Cleveland is but a microcosm of the entire country when it comes to education. Unless we begin right now and do everything we possibly can with a sense of urgency, we will never be in control. There is much that we can do and much that remains to be done.
>
> I have enjoyed this opportunity to talk to you about some of my favorite topics. I want to charge you up. I want you to internalize what I've said. I want you to get actively involved. I want you to go out and make a difference.[21]

Figure 15.3

Letter Lorna Asked Her
Classmates to Sign in the
Wrap-up Step of Her
Persuasive Speech

Kay Bailey Hutchison
703 Hart-Senate Office Building
Washington DC

Dear Ms. Hutchison,

As you are well aware, here in the state of Texas we have a serious problem with drinking and driving. Texas is now number one in the nation with the highest incidence of alcohol-related deaths. People who drink and drive in this state know that their chances of being pulled over for a DWI are slim. If they are stopped and arrested, their punishment is a night in jail or a fine—in other words, a slap on the hand. In order to bring senseless deaths and injury to a halt, we must change our laws. Penalties for first-time and repeat offenders must be stricter to deter people from drinking and driving.

Ohio has implemented stronger penalties for first-time and repeat offenders. For example, first-time offenders can now have their license revoked at the scene or a new license plate put on their vehicle identifying them as persons who have been pulled over for drinking and driving. Second-time offenders can have their cars impounded. Texas and all states in the nation need similar laws.

This is a very serious issue that everyone needs to be aware of—it affects us not only at holidays but all year long. We hope to see more aggressive and immediate action taken before one more death or injury occurs. We are asking you to use your influence to save lives in Texas and the nation.

Sincerely,

Refocus Interest in a Memorable Way

After the challenge or appeal to action, a final thought or attention-getter is needed to refocus audience interest and to give a feeling of closure to your speech. Any of the types of support that work well in the focus section—a detailed factual or hypothetical instance; two or more brief instances; a joke or humorous instance; a pithy quote or paraphrase; a startling fact; a rhetorical question; a fable, saying, poem, or rhyme; or a brief demonstration—can also be used effectively to end your speech.

For example, Betsy Burke concluded her speech on euthanasia in the following memorable way:

> I ask again, how long could you take walking into that hospital room and looking at your brother or father in a coma, knowing he would rather be allowed to die a natural death than to be kept alive in such a degrading manner? I've crossed that doorstep—I've gone into that hospital room, and let me tell you, it's hell. I think it's time we reconsider our laws concerning euthanasia. Don't you?[22]

If possible, relate back to your attention-getter to give the speech a nice feeling of completion. For example, if you began your speech by asking a question, either ask it again and challenge the audience to find an answer or provide the answer for the audience. If you began your speech with startling facts, end your speech with some even more startling facts. Look at the way Kim related her focus and wrap-up section in her speech on drunk driving. First, in her introduction she captured the attention of her audience with this family instance:

> On Christmas Eve six-year-old Joshua and his mother are on their way home from some last-minute shopping. Unfortunately, Santa won't be visiting Josh this year, because three blocks from home he and his mother will both be killed by a drunk driver. The driver will survive the crash, spend less than twenty-four hours in jail, plea bargain for a lesser charge, and probably never do any other jail time. Meanwhile a police officer looks for Josh's father to inform him that he no longer has a family.

Then, in her wrap-up, after summarizing, visualizing the future, and challenging her audience, Kim concluded with the following:

> And for just a moment I would like to take you back to Christmas Eve, the night that Joshua and his mother were killed by a drunk driver. The police found Josh's father; he was in the back seat of their squad car. You see he was the driver of the other vehicle, and as he had many times before, felt that he could make it home just fine. I think that a mandatory sobriety checkpoint could have possibly prevented him from killing his family.

Whatever you use to conclude your speech, remember that you want something memorable—something that will leave your listeners thinking about your speech long after it is completed, something that will make them feel glad that they came, and something that will make them feel justified in having changed their opinions.

To conclude our discussion of step 4, let's take a closer look at Lorna's wrap-up step:

Analysis

Lorna gives a summary of the three solutions she feels will reduce the accidents caused by drunk drivers. She does not summarize the action she wants from her audience since the action discussion occurred just before the wrap-up and because she had already asked her classmates to come up and sign her letter to Senator Kay Bailey Hutchison. Do you think she made the right decision?

Lorna visualizes the future as one with more senseless deaths and nothing but memories of a loved one. Also her poem is an indirect but powerful look at the future.

Lorna challenges her listeners to take action before drunks kill a loved one—a good motive appeal.

Lorna's transparency of a tombstone and concluding poem combine to create a memorable ending.

Speech

We must demand more sobriety checkpoints, a lower legal blood alcohol level, and tougher penalties for drunk driving. If we don't, we can look forward to more senseless deaths this Christmas. And next Christmas, like Natalie's mother and Officer Chick's family, it could be us with nothing but memories of someone dear. The time for action is now. [Transparency #2] Let's get these drunks off the road before they kill someone we love. I'm going to leave you with a sobering excerpt from a poem called "Prom Night" that was anonymously sent in to a local radio station.

> *I went to a party, Mom;*
> *I remembered what you said.*
> *You told me not to drink, Mom,*
> *So I drank soda instead.*
>
> *. . . . .*
>
> *This is the end, Mom.*
> *I wish I could look you in the eye*
> *To say these final words, Mom,*
> *"I love you and good-bye."*

See Figure 15.4 on pp. 408–409 for a copy of Lorna's preparation outline using the FLOW sequence.

Using the Motivated Sequence

▼ ▼ ▼

Another popular method of organizing a persuasive speech is called the "motivated sequence." Developed by communications professor Alan Monroe more than fifty years ago, it is similar to the problem-solution-action pattern and is especially effective with *speeches to actuate using a statement of policy.*[23] The motivated sequence is more than just an organizational pattern for your main points—it includes the introduction and conclusion as well. If you decide to use the motivated sequence, you will use it in place of the FLOW sequence. The motivated sequence involves five steps (attention, need, satisfaction, visualization, and action). Let's take a brief look at each step.

▶   *Attention step.* Here you grab your listeners' attention (using any of the methods described in Chapter 11) and build a desire in them to want to continue listening.

- *Need step*. Next you direct the audience's attention to a specific problem that "needs" to be solved. Describe the problem using effective credible, logical, and emotional appeals (see Chapter 14), and show how the problem relates specifically to your listeners.

- *Satisfaction step*. Next you "satisfy" the need by presenting a solution to the problem. The following basic framework is suggested: "(a) briefly state what you propose to do, (b) explain it clearly, (c) show how it remedies the problem, (d) demonstrate its workability, and (e) answer objections."[24] In demonstrating the workability and feasibility of the solution as well as answering possible audience objections, be sure to use supporting materials that will add proof to your statements (see Chapter 10).

- *Visualization step*. Next you vividly picture the future for your audience. Use either the positive, the negative, or the contrast methods. With the positive method you picture the improved future that the audience can expect when your solution is implemented. With the negative method you picture the undesirable conditions that will continue to exist or will develop if your solution is not adopted. The contrast method uses both the positive and negative methods, beginning with the negative and ending with the positive. The purpose of this step is to "intensify audience desire or willingness to act—to motivate your listeners to believe, to feel, or to act in a certain way."[25]

- *Action step*. Finally you conclude your speech by challenging your audience to take a particular action—you want a personal commitment from them. Say exactly what you want them to do and how they can do it.

Rhetoric professor Kathleen Bell describes the motivated sequence by showing how it could be used to organize a persuasive speech in favor of the "bottle bill" introduced by Senator Mark Hatfield of Oregon to Congress:

ATTENTION: Formulate a question asking what simple action could result in the benefits Senator Hatfield outlines in his bill proposal: reduce litter, create more jobs, save energy, reduce the amount of space needed for garbage disposal, and save consumers money. Then answer the questions by introducing the topic.

A nationwide bottle bill requiring a deposit of at least 5 cents on all disposable cans and throwaway bottles could make all of this possible.

NEED: Evidence can focus on problems of excess litter and garbage (remember the garbage barge no one wanted?), wasted natural resources (particularly the oil used to make disposable plastic products), and the needless cost to consumers created by the beverage companies' use of disposable cans and throwaway bottles.

SATISFACTION: Present each point of Hatfield's proposed bottle bill, explaining how each problem identified in the Need section would be improved.

VISUALIZATION: Detail the benefits of the policy by illustrating how similar bills have worked at the state level in Oregon, Vermont, Michigan, Maine, Connecticut, and Iowa.

Figure 15.4
Lorna's Persuasive
Preparation Outline

Lorna's Preparation Outline

Title: *"Drinking and Driving"* by Lorna McElaney
Position Statement: Texan citizens should demand that government representatives take stronger measures against drunk drivers.
(Speech to actuate using a statement of policy)

	Type of Source
FOCUS	
• **Attention-getter:** Christmas-celebration. *Question:* How many of you when you are out celebrating have had a drink, or maybe two or more, and gotten into your car and driven away? *Example:* Larry Dotson and Natalie Gale [Instance]	Ref. #7
• **Credibility:** [Presented in student introduction]	
• **Audience motivation:** Last Christmas it was Natalie Gale and her frined; this Christmas, it could be one of us.	
LEAD-IN	
• **Purpose/Preview:** Today I will share with you some startling facts and hopefully persuade you to join me in writing our senators to demand tougher laws to protect ourselves and those we love.	
ORGANIZED BODY with SUPPORTS	
I. **[Transparency #1] The number of auto/alcohol-related accidents indicates a serious problem. [Problem]**	
A. Nationally, 2 of 5 involved in auto/alcohol accidents. [Statistics]	Ref. #3, p. 1
B. Nationally, 17,000 killed in auto/alcohol accidents. [Statistics]	Ref. #3, p. 1
C. In Texas, 1,800 killed in auto/alcohol accidents. [Statistics]	Ref. #1, p. 11A
1. Texas #1 state in alcohol-related deaths. [Statistics]	Ref. #1, p. 11A
2. Only 20–30 percent of arrests lead to conviction. [Statistics]	
3. Example of Officer Chickl [Brief instance]	Ref. #2, p. 17A
[Transition]: What should be done? There are a lot of things that can be done.	
II. **There are several workable solution to the DWI problem. [Solution]**	
A. Year-round sobriety checkpoints. [Expert opinion]	Ref. #5, p. 7

ACTION: Outline the direct action that can be taken for national results, such as signing petitions locally and sending them to state representatives in Congress, letter-writing campaigns, and contacting state agencies for assistance.[26]

Summary
▼ ▼ ▼

Effective persuasive speeches don't happen by accident—they are carefully organized and supported. Each step of the FLOW sequence (focus, lead-in, organized body, and wrap-up) adds to the overall persuasive effect of your speech. The focus step is used basically the same as it is for informative speaking and in-

B. Legal blood-alcohol level lowered from .1 to .08. [Expert opinion and statistics]   Ref. #3, p. 5

C. Stronger penalties for drunk driving.
   1. Texas' lenient DWI laws. [Explanation]   Ref. #1, p. 11A
   2. Ohio's stricter DWI laws. [Explanation]   Ref. #4, p. 11

[Transition]: Action must be taken now. And we must all take part in that action.

III. Action must be taken now. [Action]
   A. "Lights-on-for-Life" promotion on December 16.   Ref. #6
      1. In remembrance of those killed by drunk drivers.
         [Explanation]   Personal
      2. To show government representatives we want change.
         [Explanation]
   B. Letter to Senator Kay Bailey Hutchison.

WRAP-UP
   - **Summary:** We must demand more sobriety checkpoints, a lower blood-alcohol level, and tougher penalties for drunk driving.
   - **Visualize:** If we don't—more senseless deaths. **[Transparency #2]**
   - **Challenge:** The time for action is now. Let's get these drunks off the road before they kill someone we love.
   - **Refocus:** I'm going to leave you with a sobering excerpt from a poem called "Prom Night" that was anonymously sent to a local radio station. [Poem]   Ref. #8

References:
1. Barlow, Yvonne. "Texas Alcohol Road Deaths Drop but State Has Highest Proportion of Such Fatalities, Study Shows." *The Dallas Morning News,* December 3, 1994. Sec. NEWS, p. 11A.
2. Ford, Jacquielynn. "Drunken Driver Gets Life in Death of FW Officer: Widow Gives Emotional Address." *Dallas Morning News,* Sec. NEWS, p. 17A.
3. Mothers Against Drunk Driving. *A 1994 Summary of Statistics: The Impaired Driving Problem.* Irving, Texas: MADD (Mothers Against Drunk Driving), December 1994.
4. Mothers Against Drunk Driving. *Maddvocate: A Magazine for Victims and Their Advocates,* Vol. 6, Fall 1993.
5. Mothers Against Drunk Driving. *20 X 2000: Five-Year Plan to Reduce Impaired Driving.* Dallas, Texas: MADD (Mothers Against Drunk Driving), 1994.
6. National 3D Prevention Month Coalition. *Light on for Life Handbook.* Washington, D.C.: National Highway Traffic Safety Administration, May 194.
7. North, Kim. "Sobering Message: Woman Whose Daughter Was Victim of Holiday DWI Driver Stresses Perils." *The Dallas Morning News,* December 12, 1994, Sec. NEWS, p. 17A.
8. "Prom Night." An anonymous poem read on Sunny 95 FM radio station, Dallas, Texas, October 1994.

cludes getting listener attention, motivating the audience to listen, and establishing speaker credibility. However, there are some major differences in the other three steps.

The lead-in step involves stating your position (unless the audience is hostile) and previewing main points. In addition, depending on the content and context, you might give the background of the problem and clarification of confusing terms.

The organized body step may follow any of five popular organizational patterns: claim, causal, problem-solution, comparative advantages, and criteria satisfaction. It's important to know which patterns work best for the type of speech (to convince or to actuate) and the type of position statement (fact, value, or policy) you are using. For example, speeches to convince using a statement of fact are especially effective with the claim or cause-effect-solution pattern, but the problem-solution-action pattern would be inappropriate.

As with informative speeches, the wrap-up step begins with summarizing and ends with refocusing attention in a memorable way. However, the wrap-up step also includes two special items: visualizing the future for the audience and issuing a challenge or appeal for action.

The motivated sequence is another method of organizing a persuasive speech that can be used in place of the FLOW sequence. The motivated sequence works best with speeches to actuate using a statement of policy.

Practice Suggestions
▼ ▼ ▼

1. Select a position statement of fact or value and organize your main points following the causal, comparative advantages, or criteria satisfaction pattern of organization. Compare your outline with a classmate's outline. *Or*: Select a speech to convince using a statement of fact or value and prepare a three- to four-minute mini-speech using either the causal, comparative advantages, or criteria satisfaction pattern of organization. Greatly abbreviate the focus, lead-in, and wrap-up steps so you can concentrate your efforts on the body of the speech.

2. Go back to Chapter 13 and reread Lorna's persuasive speech on drunk driving. In groups of two, write several additional persuasive transitions Lorna could have used between her problem and solution steps and between her solution and action steps. Share your transitions with another group; make revisions based on the best ideas in both groups. If possible, report the best transitions to the entire class. Discuss the importance of transitions to the persuasive process.

3. Using the persuasive preparation outline format (see Figure 13.4), make a preparation outline of Tricia Lewis's speech on drug legalization (located in Chapter 14). Compare your final outline with a classmate's outline for the same speech.

4. Read the persuasive speech by Lonnie R. Bristow entitled "Protecting Youth from the Tobacco Industry," located in Appendix C. In groups of two or three, design and produce three professional-looking transparencies (graphic and/or text visuals) that Dr. Bristow could have used in his presentation. On a day scheduled by your instructor, have all transparencies displayed and evaluated by a visiting team of three experts (made up of other instructors, and/or design professionals).

5. Using the persuasive speech evaluation form in Figure 15.5, read and evaluate one of the persuasive speeches located in Appendix C. What grade do you think the speaker deserves? Compare your evaluation with that of several other members of your class.

6. Each day that persuasive speeches are given in class, each class member should vote for the best speech of the day and the most improved speaker

Figure 15.5

Persuasive Presentation Evaluation Form

Presenter: _____ Topic: _____ Date:_____

Directions: For each step circle the number that best describes the overall performance (1 = poor; 5 = excellent).

FOCUS and LEAD-IN: 1   2   3   4   5
____ 1. Begins with good attention-getter
____ 2. Motivates audience to listen
____ 3. States qualifications
____ 4. States position and previews arguments

ORGANIZATION: 1   2   3   4   5
____ 1. Includes significant arguments
____ 2. Makes arguments clear to audience
____ 3. Uses workable pattern
____ 4. Uses smooth transitions

SUPPORTING MATERIALS: 1   2   3   4   5
____ 1. Uses interesting and convincing verbal supports
____ 2. Uses variety of verbal supports
      (check those used)
      ____ Statistics   ____ Expert opinion
      ____ Comparisons   ____ Illustrations
      ____ Examples   ____ Explanations
____ 3. Uses effective, professional visual supports

PERSUASIVENESS: 1   2   3   4   5
____ 1. Uses appropriate evidence and logic
____ 2. Appears credible
____ 3. Relates to psychological needs of listeners

WRAP-UP: 1   2   3   4   5
____ 1. Summarizes main ideas, recommendations, or position
____ 2. Visualizes future with emotion
____ 3. Asks for audience acceptance
____ 4. Refocuses interest in memorable way

DELIVERY: 1   2   3   4   5
____ 1. Has confident posture and movement
____ 2. Uses gestures effectively
____ 3. Maintains direct eye contact
____ 4. Sounds dynamic yet conversational
____ 5. Is free of distracting mannerisms
____ 6. Refers to notes only briefly
____ 7. Uses good volume
____ 8. Other:

Grade:

30
29 A
28
27
26
25 B
24
23
22
21
20 C
19
18

of the day. Give the votes to a designated person to tabulate. (Note: It's possible that the best and most improved speaker could be the same person!) At the end of each class period, the winners should be announced and their names posted in the classroom.

7. After each persuasive speech given in class, one member of the class should volunteer or be assigned by the instructor to present a one- to two-minute impromptu rebuttal or supporting speech. This is a fun way to practice your impromptu speaking.

8. Prepare a one-minute speech of introduction to give prior to a classmate's persuasive speech. Make sure each speaker in the class has someone to introduce him or her. Follow the guidelines for speeches of introduction included in Appendix A.

Notes

1. Julia Hughes Jones, "A Greater Voice in Action: Women and Equality," *Vital Speeches* 59 (1 December 1992), 109.
2. Jenny Clanton, "Plutonium 238: NASA's Fuel of Choice," *Vital Speeches* 55 (1 April 1989), 375.
3. Clanton, "Plutonium 238," 375.
4. Clanton, "Plutonium 238," 375.
5. Vern Loucks, Jr., "Business and School Reform: Accountability for Educational Change," *Vital Speeches* 59 (15 May 1993), 466.
6. Clanton, "Plutonium 238," 375.
7. Richard L. Weaver II, "Attitude, Not Aptitude, Determines Altitude: Some Assembly Required," *Vital Speeches* 59 (15 May 1993), 477.
8. Information taken from Robert James Bidinotto, "Must Our Prisons Be Resorts?" *Reader's Digest* 145 (November 1994), pp. 65–71.
9. Jeff Davidson, "Overworked Americans or Overwhelmed Americans? You Cannot Handle Everything," *Vital Speeches* 59 (15 May 1993), 470–473.
10. Nevin S. Scrimshaw, "The Consequences of Hidden Hunger: The Effect on Individuals and Societies," *Vital Speeches* 58 (15 December 1991), 138–144.
11. Lawrence M. Lesser, "Aid to Russia: Barter Transactions," *Vital Speeches* 59 (15 August 1993), 651–653.
12. Farah M. Walters, "If It's Broke, Fix It: The Significance of Health Care Reform in America," *Vital Speeches* 59 (1 September 1993), 687–691.
13. Information from Bill Moyers, "There Is So Much We Can Do," *Parade Magazine* (8 January 1995), pp. 4–6.
14. Based on information in a speech given by Carl Wayne Hensley, "Divorce—The Sensible Approach," *Vital Speeches* 60 (1 March 1994), 317–319.
15. Based on information in Randy Fitzgerald, "A Hand Up—Not A Handout," *Reader's Digest* 145 (November 1994), pp. 161–165, 168.
16. Lesser, "Aid to Russia," 653.
17. Although research in media indicates that implicit conclusions may be best when an audience is highly involved in the product (see A. G. Sawyer, "Can There Be Effective Advertising Without Explicit Conclusions? Decide for Yourself," in S. Hecker and D. W. Stewart, eds., *Nonverbal Communication in Advertising* [Lexington, MA: Heath, 1988], pp. 159–184), **most research indicates that explicit conclusions are best**. See Frank R. Kardes, "Spontaneous Inference Processing in Advertising: The Effects of Conclusion Omission and Involvement on Persuasion," *Journal of Consumer Research* 15 (September 1988), 225–233; P. C. Feingold and M. L. Knapp, "Anti-Drug Abuse Commercials," *Journal of Communication* 27 (1977), 20–28; and Steward L. Tubbs, "Explicit vs. Implicit Conclusions and Audience Commitment," *Speech Monographs* 35 (March 1968), 14–19. See Daniel J. O'Keefe, *Persuasion: Theory and Research* (Newbury, Park, CA: Sage, 1990), pp. 159–161, for a summary of related research.
18. K. H. Beck and A. L. Lund, "The Effects of Health Seriousness and Personal Efficacy upon Intentions and Behavior," *Journal of Applied Social Psychology* 11 (1981), 401–415.
19. Kim Witte, "Putting the Fear Back into Fear Appeals: The Extended Parallel Process Model," *Communication Monographs* 59 (December 1992), 329–349.

20. Catherine B. Ahles, "The Dynamics of Discovery: Creating Your Own Opportunities," *Vital Speeches* 59 (15 March 1993), 352.

21. Joseph T. Gorman, "Facing Facts and Forging Agendas," *Vital Speeches* 58 (1 December 1991), 126.

22. Student example from Rudolph F. Verderber, *Communicate!*, 8th ed. (Belmont, CA: Wadsworth, 1996), p. 436.

23. Bruce E. Gronbeck, Raymie E. McKerrow, Douglas Ehninger, and Alan H. Monroe, *Principles and Types of Speech Communication*, 12th ed. (New York: HarperCollins College, 1994), p. 196.

24. Gronbeck et al., *Principles*, p. 209.

25. Gronbeck et al., *Principles*, p. 211.

26. Kathleen Bell, *Developing Arguments: Strategies for Reaching Audiences* (Belmont, CA: Wadsworth, 1990), pp. 366–367.

16

Perfecting Language Style

Why Language Choices Are So Important

Effective Language Style

Simple Language

Specific Language

Vivid Language

Forceful Language

Stylistic Devices

Alliteration and Assonance

Antithesis

Simile and Metaphor

Onomatopoeia

Repetition and Parallelism

Hyperbole

Personification

Quiz: Testing Your Knowledge of Stylistic Devices

Language and Bias

Gender Bias

Culture Bias

Final Thought

Summary

Practice Suggestions

Notes

Read the following speaker comments and select the more persuasive one (a or b) for each set:

1. a. Although there are three arguments often presented in favor of legalizing drugs, not one of these arguments holds up under careful scrutiny. In fact, as you will see, all three arguments are based on faulty reasoning. The first fallacious argument is . . . .

    b. Let's look at three arguments in favor of drug legalization. The first argument is . . . .

2. a. When legislation on sobriety checkpoints comes up for a vote in your county, think about what I've said in making your decision.

    b. When legislation on sobriety checkpoints comes up for a vote in your county, vote "Yes." It's time we made our roads safe again.

3. a. There are three points that I'd like to cover today about the Electoral College.

    b. There are three points I'd like to cover today that will demonstrate how hopelessly out of date and ineffective the Electoral College really is.

It wasn't difficult to choose, was it? Persuasive language is generally more straightforward and forceful than informative language. Now that you have given a number of speeches and are aware of some of your delivery strengths and weaknesses (Chapter 8 covered the basics of effective verbal, visual, and vocal delivery), it is time to polish your delivery and perfect your use of language style. As a persuasive speaker your use of language can enhance the emotional impact of your message, the audience perception of you as an ethical speaker, and the clarity and impact of your arguments and evidence.

Why Language Choices Are So Important

▼ ▼ ▼

The English language certainly gives speakers plenty of choices. There are approximately 615,000 words in the *Oxford English Dictionary*,[1] and over 10,000 of these words have been added since 1961.[2] Your language choices are important for three basic reasons:

▶ *Language can add clarity to your ideas by creating mental images in the minds of your audience.* Words are powerful tools, and with words you can clarify confusing ideas by creating powerful mental images. Even though your listeners may not have experienced personally what you are talking about, they can experience it through the mental image your words create. A good mental image creates both a picture and the accompanying feelings—such as pride, frustration, sadness, or guilt.

Listeners tend to be attentive to speakers who have perfected their language style.

© *Jim Daniels/The Picture Cube*

▶ *Language can influence audience attitudes and behaviors.* Advertisers and politicians certainly know the power of language. They know that people who display bumper stickers, campaign buttons, T-shirts, or mugs with campaign or advertising logos on them are more likely to vote for the candidate or remain loyal to the product because, in using these items, they have already committed themselves.[3]

To show you how a single word can create a different emotional reaction, consider the example of the boy who called to his mother that there was a "snake." Hurrying to his aid, the boy's amused mother used a broom handle to dislodge what turned out to be a sleeping garden hose. Reread the previous sentence three times, each time inserting a different word for the word "amused": (1) frightened, (2) furious, and (3) long-suffering. Wouldn't these words have changed your overall reaction to the example? Words create emotional responses that can influence whether your listeners are impressed with your information, or persuaded to agree with your plan.

▶ *Language can add to audience interest and enjoyment.* As you know from lectures you have attended, language can be boring or it can create interest and enjoyment. You don't have to be an expert speaker to make your speeches interesting and enjoyable—just use words that are simple, specific, vivid, and forceful (as discussed in the following section).

Stop reading and take a moment to recall your previous speeches. Based on evaluation forms and audience comments, in what ways do you use language that are especially effective? What areas do you feel could use some work?

Effective Language Style

▼ ▼ ▼

S tyle basically means the way you use language to express your ideas. Although language choices must be appropriate for the situation (for example, humorous language probably wouldn't be appropriate for a funeral), generally the best language is simple, specific, vivid, and forceful.

Simple Language

The better speakers generally use simple language. Rarely are listeners impressed by speakers who use long, complicated, or technical words or who sprinkle each sentence with jargon. In other words, there is no reason to use the word "precipitation" instead of "rain" or "eschew" rather than "avoid" or "adipose" in place of "fatty" unless it's done occasionally to add humor. Have you ever heard college students complain, "Professor X is really brilliant, but he doesn't know how to talk on our level"? Maybe this sounds like a professor of yours—not much fun trying to take notes, is it? This type of language isn't used just on college campuses. For example, former President Franklin Delano Roosevelt reacted strongly to the wordiness of this government memo on wartime blackout procedures:

> Such preparations shall be made as will completely obscure all Federal buildings and non-Federal buildings occupied by the Federal Government during an air raid for any period of time from visibility by reason of internal or external illumination. Such obscuration may be obtained either by blackout construction or by termination of the illumination.[4]

Roosevelt was so offended by the poor writing that he immediately sent back this rewritten version:

> Tell them that in buildings where they have to keep the work going, to put something over the windows; and, in buildings where they can let the work stop for awhile, to turn out the lights.[5]

Using $50 words when $1 words would work just as well—or even better—is called **doublespeak.** In a speech it is even more important to avoid doublespeak and use simple, clear words because the audience can't ask for a replay.

This is in contrast to written text, which can be reread several times if necessary. The following financial item taken from the *Wall Street Journal* and reported in the *New Yorker* was discovered by Howard Kahane.[6] It's bad enough in written form; can you imagine how an audience would react to such a sentence in a speech?

> Whether increasing the after-tax return to saving in general increases saving, whether increasing the after-tax return to a particular kind of saving increases saving in total, whether increasing the after-tax return to this particular kind of saving is more effective in increasing saving than in increasing the after-tax return to other kinds of saving or to saving in total— all are unanswered questions.

Specific Language

Just because language is simple doesn't mean that it can't be highly specific. A specific word provides needed detail and clarity. Specific words are concrete rather than abstract. **Abstract words** describe intangible concepts that are generally difficult to picture (such as "devotion" or "health") while **concrete words** describe tangible things that listeners can more easily picture (such as "red apple" or "cheerful smile"). If your words are specific enough, the audience most likely will have a clear picture of your meaning. Which of the following is easier to picture?

> My dog is mischievous.

> My West Highland white terrier may look like an angel, but she has a mischievous heart. When she was a puppy, I left her alone for one hour and she peeled the wallpaper off the kitchen wall as far up as she could reach, found a loose tile on the floor and tugged it completely off the floor and then ripped it to pieces, and chewed holes in the bottom three slats of the kitchen miniblinds. One hour—one puppy! How could we name her anything else but Mischief?

Using specific language is especially important when your message is a persuasive one. Remember that the purpose of persuasion is to *influence* choices, not to *distort* or *confuse* choices. Unfortunately, instead of making sure their language is specific, some persuasive speakers consciously use ambiguous words and euphemisms as a persuasive tool to mask their exact meaning when talking to an audience who disagrees with their position.

Avoid ambiguous words   Instead of specific words, some speakers use ambiguous words. **Ambiguous** words are words with general, vague, and unclear meanings. When used accidentally (such as, "My children like our cat more than me"), they can be confusing; when used deliberately so that they will be interpreted positively by a wide range of people—even people with opposing beliefs—they are unethical.[7] For example, instead of presenting a clear stand on fiscal policy, a senator might use the ambiguous words "fiscal responsibility." Listeners who believe that the phrase means "no more deficit spending" would vote for the senator, as would listeners who believe that it means "controlling the growth of the money supply."[8] When words have unclear meanings, listeners use their own frames of reference to interpret the words. In the case of the senator, if word choices were more specific, fewer listeners would be likely to agree; therefore fewer listeners would be persuaded to vote for his or her re-election. Clearly, using ambiguous words to deceive listeners into taking an action they would not normally take is unethical.

Avoid euphemisms   **Euphemisms** are abstract words with positive overtones (connotations) substituted for specific words with negative overtones. In other words, euphemisms try to remove possible emotional overtones from words. In some cases, this might be a wise thing for a speaker to do. For example, "disabled" sounds more accepting than "handicapped," and "husky" doesn't carry the negative connotation of "fat" or "obese." Considering how emotionally charged Americans were after the space shuttle *Challenger* explosion, NASA's decision to refer to the coffins of the crew as "crew transfer containers" reflected the agency's (perhaps misguided) attempts to diminish the horror. However, when a euphemism is used to mask, mislead, or even manipulate audience response, it is unethical. For example, the phrase "ethnic cleansing" is used to describe the 1995 genocide in Bosnia.

Vivid Language

In addition to simple yet specific words, effective speakers also use vivid words. For the most impact use the active rather than the passive voice (*active*: "Jorge shoved John"; *passive*: "John was shoved by Jorge"). Vivid speakers avoid using vague references such as "It is believed," they use a variety of interesting supporting materials, and they speak directly to their listeners as though they were having a private, personal conversation with them. Vivid speakers also use words to paint a mental picture in the minds of listeners that is every bit as clear as a visual aid. In fact, vivid words are mental visual aids. Which of the following paints the clearer picture?

> A child claimed that he saw a large snake, but when his mother found it, it was only a garden hose.

> An eight-year-old boy claimed that while cleaning out his toys from under the front porch he was startled by a huge, emerald green snake lurking behind a bucket. Hurrying to his aid, the boy's amused mother used a broom handle to dislodge what turned out to be a sleeping garden hose.

Although picking an unusual word or using the stylistic devices described later in this chapter can add to the vividness of your speech, most speakers achieve vividness by choosing simple yet specific words and painting mental pictures with them. Always picture in your own mind what you are describing,

Former Texas Governor Ann Richards is known for her personable and vibrant speaking style.

© John Duricka/Wide World Photos, Inc.

and you will be surprised how easy it is to transfer this picture via vivid language to your audience.

Forceful Language

As the examples at the beginning of the chapter illustrate, the words you use in a speech can carry varying degrees of force or strength. Forceful language is especially important in persuasion—it adds to the audience's confidence in the speaker.[9]

Let's take a closer look at the third set of speaker comments from the beginning of this chapter. Statement 3a ("There are three points that I'd like to cover today about the Electoral College") not only implies (incorrectly) that this will be an informative speech but gives no indication of the speaker's position. However, statement 3b ("There are three points I'd like to cover today that will demonstrate how hopelessly out of date and ineffective the Electoral College really is") makes it clear that this will be a persuasive speech, indicates the speaker's position, and through forceful language indicates the confidence of the speaker. The persuasive process has already begun in the minds of the audience. Even in an informative speech, forceful language can give your listeners confidence in you and in your evidence.

Start by concentrating on one or two of these language characteristics. Tape-record one of your practice speech sessions and then listen and evaluate it. Add more specific and vivid words, and then record your speech again. Repeat the process until you are satisfied with your language choices.

"Let's change 'Some of us guys' to 'We the people.'"

© 1995. Reprinted courtesy of Bunny Hoest and Parade.

Stylistic Devices[10]

▼ ▼ ▼

In addition to the actual and implied meanings that words carry, words or sets of words can have a texture or "feel"—what persuasion expert Charles Larson calls the "thematic dimension" of language. This ability of words "to set a mood, develop a feeling, or generate a tone or theme [is] the most important persuasive aspect" of words.[11] If your listeners are in the correct frame of mind for a particular topic, you will have a better chance of communicating your ideas and concerns to them. Therefore using stylistic language devices to establish a mood or feeling both in the introduction and at various times during the persuasive speech is important to the success of your message.

Stylistic devices gain their entertaining and persuasive power by "departing from everyday language usage."[12] They do this in two basic ways: (1) most stylistic devices leave word meanings unchanged but rearrange sentences in unusual ways; (2) a few stylistic devices change "the main or ordinary meaning of a word" but still maintain normal sentence structure.[13] This chapter will cover several of the most popular stylistic devices: alliteration and assonance, antithesis, simile and metaphor, onomatopoeia, repetition and parallelism, hyperbole, and personification.

Alliteration and Assonance

Alliteration is the repetition of consonants (usually the first or last letter in a word), such as, "Each Wednesday, Willey washes his woolens." **Assonance** is similar except that it involves the repetition of vowel sounds, such as, "The low moans of our own soldiers. . . ."[14] Let's look at real-life examples of both alliteration and assonance. Peter G. Osgood in a speech entitled "Conveying the Environmental Message" used alliteration with the "c" sound (as well as parallelism) in this part of his wrap-up:

> It is a matter of culture and it is a matter of conversion. And finally, it is a matter of leadership, commitment and communication.[15]

In his 1961 inaugural address, former President John F. Kennedy used several stylistic devices—one of them was alliteration. How many "s" sounds do you hear in this sentence?

> So let us begin anew, remembering on both sides that civility is not a sign of weakness and sincerity is always subject to proof.[16]

In the same speech, Kennedy used assonance several times:

> . . . for only when our arms are sufficient beyond doubt . . .

> . . . instruments of peace, we renew our pledge to prevent it from becoming . . .[17]

Tip: The use of alliteration and assonance require restraint. Stylistic devices should add to, not distract from, your speech. Be especially careful with alliteration. You don't want to sound like former Vice President Spiro T. Agnew, who in a speech referred to the "nattering nabobs of negativism,"[18] or former President Warren G. Harding, who told his audience:

> Progression is not proclamation nor palaver. It is not pretense nor play on prejudice. It is not of personal pronouns, nor perennial pronouncement. It is not the perturbation of a people passion-wrought, nor a promise proposed.[19]

Antithesis

Antithesis occurs when two parallel but contrasting ideas are contained in one sentence. Effective use of antithesis brings contrasts into sharper focus for the listener,[20] which is probably why it was one of Kennedy's favorite stylistic devices. Here are three examples of antithesis from his 1961 inaugural address:

> If a free society cannot help the many who are poor, it cannot save the few who are rich.

> Let us never negotiate out of fear, but let us never fear to negotiate.

> And so, my fellow Americans, ask not what your country can do for you, ask what you can do for your country.[21]

Through metaphor and dynamic delivery, the Reverend Jesse Jackson rivets audiences.

© Ira Wyman/Sygma

Simile and Metaphor

Similes and metaphors are used to compare dissimilar items that are not of the same order or class in order to clarify one of the items. **Similes** make direct comparisons using the words *like* or *as* ("Happiness is like ice cream—both can melt away if you aren't careful"). Although **metaphors** are implied comparisons and do not use the words *like* or *as*, they speak of one item as though it were something else ("Happiness is an ice cream cone"). Just like the figurative comparisons discussed in Chapter 10, similes and metaphors create vivid images for your listeners that improve their understanding and retention of the speech. They can also be very persuasive—they can set a positive or negative tone that influences audience attitudes.

In his focus step J. Peter Grace used the following *simile* to set the tone for his speech entitled "Burning Money: The Waste of Your Tax Dollars":

> Now there's a lot of talk coming out of Washington these days about reducing the deficit and, at the same time, increasing government spending. Well, let me tell you, that's like trying to lose weight on a diet of french fries and Big Macs.[22]

Martha D. Cooper and William L. Nothstine in their book *Power Persuasion* note that metaphors "gain their power not from altering ordinary sentence structure—[as antithesis does] . . . but from altering usual meanings of words, creating new meaning."[23] In his attempt to unify the Democratic party, the Reverend Jesse Jackson uses the *metaphor* of lions and lambs in his 1988 speech to the Democratic National Convention:

> The Bible teaches that when lions and lambs lie down together none will be afraid and there will be peace in the valley. It sounds impossible. Lions

eat lambs. Lambs . . . flee from lions. Yet even lions and lambs find common ground. Why? Because neither lions nor lambs want the forest to catch on fire. Neither lions nor lambs want acid rain to fall. Neither lions nor lambs can survive a nuclear war. If lions and lambs can find common ground, surely we can as well as civilized people.[24]

John F. Kennedy's 1961 inaugural address also includes several examples of metaphor (in italic):

> . . . to assist free men and free governments in casting off the *chains of poverty* . . .

> And if a *beachhead of cooperation* may push back the *jungle of suspicion*, . . .[25]

Onomatopoeia

Although fewer speakers use onomatopoeia—"words that sound like their meanings" such as *buzz*, *boom*, *swish*, *drip*, and *ring*[26]—these words are especially good at creating a feeling or mood. Martin Luther King, Jr., used onomatopoeia many times for effect in his speeches. You are probably most familiar with his use of the word "ring" in his 1963 "I Have a Dream" speech. The way he pronounced the word "ring" in "Let freedom ring" created a powerful image of a church bell ringing. And as he repeated it over and over, the ringing seemed to get louder and more intense as he built to the memorable conclusion of his speech:

> So let freedom ring. From the prodigious hilltops of New Hampshire, let freedom ring. From the mighty mountains of New York, let freedom ring, from the heightening Alleghenies of Pennsylvania!
>   Let freedom ring from the snowcapped Rockies of Colorado!
>   Let freedom ring from the curvaceous slopes of California!
>   But not only that.
>   Let freedom ring from Stone Mountain of Georgia!
>   Let freedom ring from Lookout Mountain of Tennessee!
>   Let freedom ring from every hill and mole hill of Mississippi.
>   From every mountainside, let freedom ring, and when this happens . . . when we allow freedom to ring, when we let it ring from every village and every hamlet, from every state and every city, we will be able to speed up that day when all God's children, black men and white men, Jews and Gentiles, Protestants and Catholics, will be able to join hands and sing in the words of the old Negro spiritual, "Free at last! Free at last! Thank God Almighty, we are free at last!"[27]

Repetition and Parallelism

Did you notice as you were reading the excerpt from the famous "I Have a Dream" speech that onomatopoeia wasn't the only stylistic device that Martin Luther King, Jr., used? He used both repetition and parallelism as well. **Repetition** occurs when a word or series of words is repeated in several successive clauses or sentences (usually at the beginning of each clause or sentence). Dr.

King's repetition of "Let freedom ring" was very effective. In his "American Renewal" speech, President Bill Clinton also used repetition (as well as parallelism):

> Today we do more than celebrate America, we rededicate ourselves to the very idea of America:
>
> An idea born in revolution and renewed through two centuries of challenge;
>
> An idea tempered by the knowledge that but for fate we, the fortunate and the unfortunate, might have been each other;
>
> An idea ennobled by the faith that our nation can summon from its myriad diversity the deepest measure of unity;
>
> An idea infused with the conviction that America's long, heroic journey must go forever upward.[28]

Parallelism occurs when "groupings of similarly phrased ideas [are] presented in rapid succession."[29] As in the Martin Luther King, Jr., example, parallelism increases the pace and "therefore generates psychological momentum in listeners."[30] Franklin D. Roosevelt also was fond of using parallelism, which speech critics claim added a type of rhythm or cadence to his delivery.[31] For example, consider the following parallel sentence structure in one of his speeches:

> It cannot be a real peace if it fails to recognize brotherhood. It cannot be a lasting peace if the fruit of it is oppression. . . . It cannot be a sound peace if small nations must live in fear of powerful neighbors. It cannot be a moral peace if freedom from invasion is sold for tribute. . . . It cannot be a righteous peace if worship of God is denied.[32]

Another example of parallelism is found in the conclusion of Peter G. Osgood's speech on the environment:

> Where many see only additional problems, you need to show them opportunity; where they see unacceptable risk, you have to quantify the benefits; where they think only in terms of added cost, you have to demonstrate the potential savings.[33]

Hyperbole

A **hyperbole** is an exaggerated or distorted statement deliberately used to draw attention to a situation or problem (such as, "We either vote for this bill, or we die"). In a speech entitled "Power, Parity, Personal Responsibility, and Progress" (note the alliteration), William H. Harris used the following hyperbole and metaphor (both in italics) to impress on his audience the importance of action:

> And the answers will require creativity and discovery. I wish you Godspeed as you create and make your discoveries, but I assure you that *if you neither create nor discover in this essential arena all of us will reap a whirlwind of despair.* . . .[34]

Hyperbole also was used by Martin Luther King, Jr., in his "I've Been to the Mountain-Top" speech when he warned his audience:

R e m e m b e r :

Stylistic devices include . . .

▶ *Alliteration*—repetition of consonants (usually the first or last letter in a word).

▶ *Assonance*—repetition of vowel sounds.

▶ *Antithesis*—two parallel but contrasting ideas contained in one sentence.

▶ *Simile*—direct comparison between two items using the words *like* or *as*.

▶ *Metaphor*—implied comparison between two items without using *like* or *as*.

▶ *Onomatopoeia*—words that sound like their meaning.

▶ *Repetition*—word or series of words repeated in successive clauses or sentences.

▶ *Parallelism*—similarly phrased ideas presented in rapid succession.

▶ *Hyperbole*—statement containing deliberate exaggeration or distortion.

▶ *Personification*—human characteristics or feelings assigned to animals or things.

And in the human rights revolution, if something isn't done and done in a hurry to bring the colored peoples of the world out of their long years of poverty, their long years of hurt and neglect, the whole world is doomed.[35]

Both of these examples illustrate the ability of hyperbole to arouse emotion and stimulate thought. The danger is that listeners might not realize the exaggerated nature of this stylistic device and, instead, take it for face value; or they might view the hyperbole simply as a lie by an unethical speaker.

Personification

When an animal, object, or concept is given human characteristics or feelings (such as "Mother nature"), it is called **personification**. Used in moderation, this device is especially effective in clarifying ideas as well as arousing audience feelings. For example, to clarify the importance of keeping computers in top-notch condition, you might give the computer human characteristics, as one student did:

Your PC unit will be much more cooperative if you remember to defragment the hard drive regularly, since otherwise your computer exhausts itself rummaging through disorganized bits of files.[36]

Testing Your Knowledge
of Stylistic Devices

Directions: Below are excerpts from eight speeches. Identify what stylistic device(s) are found in each excerpt.

_____ 1. "The mother of all wars."[37] —Saddam Hussein

_____ 2. ". . . and that government of the people, by the people, and for the people, shall not perish from the earth."[38] —Abraham Lincoln

_____ 3. "America is not like a blanket—one piece of unbroken cloth, the same color, the same texture, the same size. America is more like a quilt—many patches, many pieces, many sizes, and woven and held together by a common thread."[39] —Reverend Jesse Jackson

_____ 4. ". . . attitude not aptitude determines altitude."[40] —Richard L. Weaver II

_____ 5. "Fellow citizens, we observe today not a victory of party, but a celebration of freedom. . . ."[41] —John F. Kennedy

_____ 6. "But, in a larger sense, we cannot dedicate, we cannot consecrate, we cannot hallow this ground."[42] —Abraham Lincoln

_____ 7. "Ours is a nation that has shed the blood of war and cried the tears of depression."[43] —George Bush

_____ 8. "Tax money flows into Washington, irrigating the bureaucratic gardens."[44] —James P. Pinkerton

Answers

8. Metaphor
7. Personification
6. Repetition and parallelism
5. Antithesis
4. Alliteration
3. Simile
2. Parallel repetition
1. Hyperbole

Language and Bias

▼ ▼ ▼

L anguage can indicate speaker bias as well as create listener bias. Gender and culture bias are the two most common types of bias that show up in language usage.

Gender Bias

As Chapter 8 indicated, using the pronoun "he" as a generic term to refer to both males and females should be avoided. Although you may mean both male and female when you use generic terms, "he" conjures up masculine images in the minds of many audience members.[45] A study of college students conducted in 1993 found that both male and female students tended to use masculine pronouns when referring to a person who is a judge, engineer, and lawyer, and feminine pronouns for nurses, librarians, and teachers.[46] According to Diana K. Ivy and Phil Backlund in *Exploring Gender Speak*, when speakers use generic masculine pronouns (like "he," "mankind," "sportsman," and "workmanship") or feminine terms (like "stewardess," "waitress," "actress") they are helping to maintain sex-biased perceptions.[47] Figure 8.3 lists some common masculine and feminine terms and expressions.[48] Alternative words that are not gender-based are suggested for your use. Although some of these terms may seem strange at first, they will make your communication more accurate and more effective, and you are less likely to risk offending your listeners.

Culture Bias

An important communication principle for speakers to remember is: *The only message that counts is the one that gets received.* As we discussed in Chapter 1, it doesn't matter what you meant to say or what you actually said. It is what the audience thought you said that counts. Since the meaning of words is supplied by listeners based on their own frames of reference, language must be chosen carefully. The more diverse your audience, the more likely it is that their frames of reference will be somewhat different from yours. According to the last census, 25 percent of Americans are from the Native American, African, Hispanic, or Asian cultures.[49] The most effective speakers are sensitive to the diverse backgrounds of their listeners and make their language as free of culture bias as possible.

Final Thought
▼ ▼ ▼

Now that you have learned to give several different types of speeches and know how to research, organize, develop, and deliver effective presentations, remember that "practice makes perfect." To make sure your new skills become permanent, you will want to continue speaking every chance you get. With a little bit of effort, your skills will gain polish, and you will come closer and closer to your goal of enjoying speaking. The rewards of successful public speaking are great. Good luck in your quest.

Summary
▼ ▼ ▼

Although effective organization, content, and delivery are essential for a successful speech, perfecting your language style adds the polish that makes your speech shine. The most effective language is simple, specific, vivid, and forceful. Language creates mental images in the minds of your listeners, influences audience attitudes and behaviors, and adds interest and enjoyment to your speeches. These characteristics are especially important in persuasive speaking because words can set a mood, develop a feeling, or generate a theme. If listeners are in the correct frame of mind for a particular topic, you will have a better chance of communicating your ideas and concerns to them. Of course, you must keep your speech free of gender and culture bias.

To obtain these language advantages, polished, professional speakers use a variety of stylistic devices: alliteration and assonance, antithesis, simile and metaphor, onomatopoeia, repetition and parallelism, hyperbole and personification. Begin by practicing two or three of these devices. Then, add more until you have tried them all. Select the ones that seem to be the most valuable to you and incorporate them into your own style.

Practice Suggestions
▼ ▼ ▼

1. In groups of two or three, select a well-known public figure who has a distinctive speaking style. Separate the speaker's visual and vocal techniques from his or her verbal language techniques. Try to determine what stylistic devices this person uses. Share your discoveries with another group or the entire class.

2. Retake the PRCA located in Appendix D without looking at the answers you gave at the beginning of the class. Determine your score by following the scoring instructions at the bottom of the questionnaire. Compare these scores with your previous scores. Write a brief comparison and discussion of the two scores and what these scores say about you as a speaker. Show the comparison to your instructor.

3. Read the following section from a speech on health care by James S. Todd, executive vice president, American Medical Association. How many different stylistic devices can you find? Compare answers with a classmate.

There is no quick fix. It is essential we do it right, and that will not be easy.

All any of us can do is watch—and wait—and sometimes worry.

If there is one message I have today, it is this: The physicians of America are worried.

Don't get me wrong. We're not worried that change is coming. That we welcome. What worries us is the strong possibility that real change won't occur at all.

We're worried that politics and miscalculation will conspire to keep the Administration from achieving the kind of meaningful reform the President promised during his campaign.

We're worried that the Clinton plan may be too enormous to comprehend, too complex to explain, too expensive to defend. . . .

Senator Phil Gramm says managed competition is like a five-legged animal. It might work, but we sure don't see any running around in nature. . . .

We're worried that the Administration's package of health care benefits could turn into a high-priced Christmas tree, one that's so loaded with ornaments the cost will be prohibitive.[50]

4. Select one argument that you will be using in your persuasive speech. Prepare this argument to present to your class or to a small group of students. Practice using at least two different stylistic devices in this argument.

Notes

1. Richard Lederer, *The Miracle of Language* (New York: Pocket Books, 1991), p. 24.
2. R. Gozzi, *New Words and a Changing American Culture* (Columbia: University of South Carolina Press, 1990).
3. Charles U. Larson, *Persuasion: Reception and Responsibility* (Belmont, CA: Wadsworth, 1995), p. 107.
4. John O'Hayre, *Gobbledygook Has Gotta Go*, U.S. Department of the Interior, Bureau of Land Management (Washington, DC: Government Printing Office, 1966), p. 39.
5. O'Hayre, *Gobbledygook*, p. 39.
6. Howard Kahane, *Logic and Contemporary Rhetoric*, 7th ed. (Belmont, CA: Wadsworth, 1995), p. 135.
7. Larson, *Persuasion*, p. 133.
8. Larson, *Persuasion*, p. 133–134.
9. P. Gibbons, J. Busch, and J. J. Bradac, "Powerful Versus Powerless Language: Consequences for Persuasion, Impression Formation, and Cognitive Response," *Journal of Language and Social Psychology* 10 (1991), 115–133;

J. J. Bradac and A. Mulac, "A Molecular View of Powerful and Powerless Speech Styles: Attributional Consequences of Specific Language Feature and Communication Intentions," *Communication Monographs* 51 (1984), 307–319; D. G. Linz and S. Penrod, "Increasing Attorney Persuasiveness in the Courtroom," *Law and Psychology Review* 8 (1984), 1–47.
10. This section is based on Larson, *Persuasion*, pp. 142–147.
11. Larson, *Persuasion*, p. 142.
12. Martha D. Cooper and William L. Nothstine, *Power Persuasion: Moving an Ancient Art into the Media Age* (Greenwood, IN: Educational Video Group, 1992), p. 168.
13. Cooper and Nothstine, *Power Persuasion*, p. 168.
14. Larson, *Persuasion*, p. 123.
15. Peter G. Osgood, "Conveying the Environmental Message: Getting Green is Better Than Seeing Red," *Vital Speeches* 59 (15 February 1993), 270.

16. John Fitzgerald Kennedy, "Inaugural Address: January 20, 1961," in John Graham, ed., *Great American Speeches 1898–1963: Texts and Studies* (New York: Appleton-Century-Crofts, 1970), pp. 113–116.

17. Kennedy, "Inaugural Address," pp. 113-116.

18. In Lewis D. Eigen and Jonathan P. Siegel, *The Macmillan Dictionary of Political Quotations* (New York: Macmillan, 1993), p. 70.

19. Eigen and Siegel, *Macmillan Dictionary*, p. 467.

20. Roderick P. Hart, *Modern Rhetorical Criticism* (Glenview, IL: Scott, Foresman, 1990), p. 226.

21. Kennedy, "Inaugural Address," pp. 113-116.

22. J. Peter Grace, "Burning Money: The Waste of Your Tax Dollars," *Vital Speeches* 59 (July 1, 1993), 566.

23. Cooper and Nothstine, *Power Persuasion*, p. 169.

24. Jesse L. Jackson, "The Candidate's Challenge: The Call of Conscience, The Courage of Conviction," in Cooper and Nothstine, *Power Persuasion*, p. 169.

25. Kennedy, "Inaugural Address," pp. 113-116.

26. Larson, *Persuasion*, p. 123.

27. Martin Luther King, Jr., "I Have a Dream: August 28, 1963," in Graham, *Great American Speeches*, pp. 117-121.

28. Bill Clinton, "American Renewal: We Must Care for One Another," *Vital Speeches* 59 (15 February 1993), 259.

29. Hart, *Modern Rhetorical Criticism*, pp. 226-227.

30. Hart, *Modern Rhetorical Criticism*, p. 227.

31. Harold P. Zelko, "Franklin D. Roosevelt's Rhythm in Rhetorical Style," in Graham, *Great American Speeches*, pp. 191-194.

32. Zelko, "Franklin D. Roosevelt's Rhythm," p. 194.

33. Osgood, "Conveying the Environmental Message," 270.

34. William H. Harris, "Power, Parity, Personal Responsibility, and Progress: The Agenda For African Americans in the 1990's," *Vital Speeches* 59 (15 June 1993), 536.

35. Martin Luther King, Jr., "I've Been to the Mountain-Top," in Michael C. Leff and Fred J. Kauffeld, eds., *Texts in Context: Critical Dialogues on Significant Episodes in American Political Rhetoric* (Davis, CA: Hermagoras Press, 1989), pp. 311-321.

36. Excerpted from a speech given in one of my classes.

37. The "mother of all wars" reference was used many times by Iraqi President Saddam Hussein in press releases to describe his view of the Gulf War.

38. Abraham Lincoln, "Gettysburg Address," in Philip B. Kunhardt, Jr., *A New Birth of Freedom* (Boston: Little, Brown, 1983), p. 240.

39. Jesse Jackson, "The Rainbow Coalition," in Richard L. Johannesen, R. R. Allen, and Wil A. Linkugel, *Contemporary American Speeches*, 7th ed. (Dubuque, IA: Kendall/Hunt, 1992), p. 384.

40. Richard L. Weaver II, "Attitude, Not Aptitude, Determine Altitude," *Vital Speeches* 59 (15 May 1993), 478.

41. Kennedy, "Inaugural Address," p. 318.

42. Lincoln, "Gettysburg Address," p. 240.

43. George Bush, "Transcript of President Bush's Radio Address on His Defeat at the Polls," *The New York Times* (8 November 1992), p. A26.

44. James P. Pinkerton, "The New Paradigm," in Johannesen, Allen, and Linkugel, *Contemporary American Speeches*, p. 327.

45. L. C. Hamilton, "Using Masculine Generics: Does Generic 'He' Increase Male Bias in the User's Imagery?" *Sex Roles* 19 (1988), 785-799.

46. Diana K. Ivy, L. Bullis-Moore, K. Norvell, Phil Backlund, and M. Javidi, *The Lawyer, the Babysitter, and the Student: Non-sexist Language Usage and Instruction*. Paper presented at the annual meeting of the Western States Communication Association, Albuquerque, NM, February 1993.

47. Diana K. Ivy and Phil Backlund, *Exploring Gender Speak: Personal Effectiveness in Gender Communication* (New York: McGraw-Hill, 1994), p. 75.

48. Ivy and Backlund, *Exploring Gender Speak*, pp. 78, 80, 93-94.

49. Felicity Barringer, "Census Shows Profound Change in Racial Makeup of the Nation," *New York Times* (11 March 1991), p. A1.

50. James S. Todd, "Health Care at the Brink," *Vital Speeches* 59 (15 June 1993), 523.

Special Occasion Speaking

Y OUR PUBLIC SPEAKING EXPERIENCE WILL include informative and persuasive presentations. Often, however, you will be in situations that invite a somewhat different approach to public communication. Significant events in people's lives call for public recognition. From birth announcements to eulogies, the rituals of life involve the ritual of speech making. Consider the following situations and the role a public presentation would play:

▶ You have just received an award and are asked to "say a few words."

▶ Your best friend is getting married. At the reception you are responsible for proposing a toast to the newlyweds.

▶ A local civic organization invites you to give a speech at their annual banquet.

▶ Your college roommate has just been elected class president. The campaign manager asks if you would be willing to introduce your friend, who will then make her victory speech.

▶ Your favorite uncle has just died. The family asks you to deliver a memorial speech at the funeral.

These examples represent just a few of the many special occasions where public speaking is expected.

Special Occasion Speaking: An Overview

▼ ▼ ▼

S pecial occasion speeches—or ceremonial speeches—differ from informative and persuasive speeches. Unlike informative presentations, ceremonial addresses do not offer large doses of new knowledge or present detailed instructions. Unlike persuasive presentations, special occasion speeches do not generally deal with controversial issues or attempt to change the way audiences think or act. In general, ceremonial presentations avoid controversy and reaffirm the audience's beliefs. Figure A.1 outlines the key characteristics of informative, persuasive, and special occasion speaking.

Organization of Special Occasion Speeches

Special occasion addresses, like informative and persuasive speeches, can be organized to follow the FLOW sequence. (See Chapters 11 and 15 for more detail.)

No matter whether you start your speech with a compelling story, a memorable quote, or a startling fact, you should include something in your focus step

---

Note: This appendix was written by Roy Schwartzman, Assistant Professor of Speech Communication and Director of the Basic Course, University of South Carolina, Columbia, SC.

	Informative	Persuasive	Special Occasion
Goal	Share knowledge: instruct, demonstrate	Influence belief or action: gain compliance, alter behavior	Entertain and reinforce: strengthen bonds among audience members
Sample Topic	To explain the process of public speaking	To convince listeners that they should take a course in public speaking	To congratulate students in a public speaking course after their first speech

Figure A.1
Objectives of Informative, Persuasive, and Special Occasion Speaking

that evokes the common values or feelings that have brought your audience together.[1] For example, Barbara Jordan, who delivered the keynote address at the 1976 Democratic National Convention, began her talk by pointing out how the participants were continuing a 144-year-old tradition. Also, as the first African-American woman ever to deliver the address, she acknowledged the party's role in making this part of the American Dream come true for her. After referring to the history of Democratic nominating conventions, she said, "And our meeting this week is a continuation of that tradition . . . but tonight here I am. And I feel that notwithstanding the past my presence here is one additional bit of evidence that the American Dream need not forever be deferred."[2]

Depending on your audience and the occasion, you may need to establish your credibility in the focus step as well. This is especially important if you are unknown to the audience or if your expertise on the topic is unknown.

In the second (lead-in) step of many special occasion speeches, you should clearly state the purpose of your remarks and preview your main points. However, in some speeches to commemorate, it may be more appropriate to state the purpose only. For example, in a brief toast, tribute, or eulogy, no preview is necessary.

In the third step, the organized body step, you will want to concentrate especially on making your main points clear and on supporting them with a variety of entertaining and even inspiring materials. Review Chapter 10 for a summary of the various types of supporting materials.

The wrap-up step of special occasion speeches refocuses audience interest not simply on the presentation but on who the listeners are and what they stand for. The speech gives audience members an opportunity to strengthen their sense of identity and purpose.

Since visual aids can capture audience attention rapidly and effectively, they can be especially useful in special occasion speeches. During his final State of the Union address, Ronald Reagan complained about the unnecessary complexity of congressional regulations. Instead of just talking about wasteful paperwork, Reagan placed near the podium the bound volumes of the several-thousand-page-long federal budget, which weighed in at more than twenty pounds. That gesture demonstrated more clearly than any words just how much paperwork Congress was generating.

You can use visual aids to your advantage during a special occasion speech. If you are introducing a well-known writer, you might display a stack of his books to show how productive his career has been. If you are presenting an award, you could show a chart that lists the criteria for the award and then match the recipient's accomplishments to the criteria. Keep alert to the opportunities for incorporating visual aids into special occasion speeches, especially when you want to offer audience members a concrete reminder of what they should recall from the speech.

Purposes of Special Occasion Speaking

Special occasion speaking already was well established in Greece by the fifth century B.C. In the fourth century B.C. Aristotle recognized ceremonial speeches as a class of oratory known as *epideictic* (sometimes called *epidictic*), which he defined as speeches of praise or blame.[3] These speeches would reinforce the values of the community by praising virtue and condemning vice.[4]

Today the opportunities for ceremonial speeches abound. These presentations perform an important function, because they are designed to strengthen the listeners' commitment to values they hold dear.[5] Thus, a speaker at a special occasion serves as far more than a mere ornament. Although there are many types of special occasion speeches, the following are the most common: speeches of introduction, presentations of awards, acceptance speeches, commemorative speeches (including toasts, tributes, and eulogies), and after-dinner speeches (including speeches given at graduations, conventions, meetings, and luncheons).

Speeches of Introduction
▼ ▼ ▼

The speech of introduction is one of the most common types of ceremonial oratory. The introductory speech simply prepares the audience for the featured speaker(s). Although speeches of introduction tend to be short, often five minutes or less, they must accomplish a lot. An effective speech of introduction should do the following:

▶ Tell the listeners enough about the featured speaker that they will understand why that person has been selected to speak.

▶ Encourage the audience to listen.

▶ Generate interest in the upcoming presentation.

▶ Welcome and encourage the featured speaker.[6]

Introductory speeches might seem simple: you just get up and tell the audience who will speak and what the topic will be. However, there is much more to a good speech of introduction. The introduction of a speaker prepares the audience to listen to that person. By giving listeners a basic idea of what to expect, you enable them to adapt better to the speaker and topic. An introduction also allows you to express appreciation to the speaker. If you are introducing a speaker, you might note why the topic is particularly relevant to some recent events in the community. This official recognition becomes especially important when you are representing the group that sponsored the speaker's appearance. When a speaker is being introduced, that person's reputation and credibility temporarily lie in the hands of whoever gives the introduction.[7]

To avoid the embarrassment of presenting inaccurate information, verify all facts about the speaker you will introduce. Whenever possible, get biographical information directly from the speaker.[8] This is the only way you can be certain that your information is accurate. Of course, if the person is well known, you may be able to find additional information in *Who's Who*, the *Dictionary of American Biography*, or other biographical references. You may also want to interview some of the speaker's friends or professional associates—a good source for personal anecdotes that will help reveal the speaker as an individual. Remember, however, to review your introduction with the featured speaker to ensure accuracy and reduce the risk of saying something inappropriate.[9] Imagine revealing information you thought was interesting, only to have the speaker become angry or embarrassed that you included some facts that were not supposed to be discussed publicly.

Remember that speeches of introduction are *short*. Ordinarily such a speech should last only a fraction of the time scheduled for the featured speech. Exactly how long should your introductory speech be? Rarely does an introductory speech last more than a few minutes. For example, if you are going to introduce a classmate who is delivering a seven-minute speech, your introduction should take no more than one to two minutes.

Since speeches of introduction are so common and their use is so specific, speakers can fall into the trap of using platitudes. Any speech genre that is well established invites the use of stock phrases that can instantly make a presentation seem trite. At best, such remarks will tell the audience that your presentation lacks originality. A speech of introduction filled with platitudes also sends a clear message that you did not gather specific information about the speaker. Figure A.2 lists some stock phrases to avoid when making a speech of introduction.

Also, before your speech, make absolutely sure you know how to pronounce the speaker's name. Even a slight mispronunciation can be embarrassing for you and disconcerting to the speaker. Perhaps the worst garbling of a speaker's name that I have heard happened at a banquet honoring the renowned Russian poet Yevgeny Yevtushenko. The introducer didn't make just a little slip. He mangled the Russian's name so grievously that the poet himself yelled out the correct pronunciation. The introduction ended with the unnerved introducer saying: "I present . . ." He paused, looked at his notes, gave a puzzled frown, totally mispronounced Yevtushenko's name again, and sat down. Before they applauded, most of the audience shouted in unison the correct pronunciation. The lesson is, whatever it takes, make sure you pronounce the speaker's name correctly.

Figure A.2

Stock Phrases to Avoid in Introductory Speeches[10]

1. *"Here is someone who needs no introduction . . ."* If so, then you never should have begun your speech. The audience probably will think, "Needs no introduction? Then sit down and keep quiet."
2. *"We are truly honored to have with us today . . ."* This comment is too vague to have value. You would do better to explain briefly *why* the speaker's presence is an honor.
3. *"Without further ado . . ."* You have just trivialized your own remarks, treating them as "flurry, confusion, upset, excitement, hubbub, noise, turmoil."[11] The preface "without further" labels your speech as inconsequential.
4. *"It is indeed a high privilege . . ."* This is another empty phrase that should be replaced with specifics.
5. *"On this most memorable occasion . . ."* You cannot judge now how memorable this event will be in the future. I have heard this phrase used to describe many decidedly forgettable events. I would list them, but I can't recall what they were.
6. *"We have none other than . . ."* This comment is at best redundant. It sounds as if you weren't sure whether the speaker was an impostor, and you just wanted to make sure the audience recognized him or her.

Correctness extends to the title a speaker wants you to use.[12] This point is very important because social roles and especially gender roles are changing rapidly. For example, don't assume that just because a speaker holds a Ph.D. she wants to be called "Dr." Some women prefer to be called "Ms.," others prefer their professional titles, and still others avoid all titles. Many political and religious offices carry with them titles that are part of professional etiquette. For example, judges have the title "The Honorable" before their name. Government officials have other titles appropriate to their offices (such as "Supervisor," "Congresswoman," and so on). The proper form of address is a combination of professional etiquette and the individual's preference. Instead of relying on generalizations about what "that sort" of speaker might prefer, confirm the appropriate form of address with the speaker directly.

Exactly what should your speech of introduction include? Your speech should do the following:

▶ State who you are if the audience does not know already.

▶ Highlight the speaker's name. In most cases you should mention the speaker's name early in your speech and again as the last thing you say so the audience will remember it.

▶ Recognize the reason for the occasion. Why is this speaker here now?

▶ Express appreciation to the speaker.

▶ Include only biographical information relevant to the occasion and pre-approved by the speaker.

Remember:

In speeches of introduction . . .

▶ Don't speak for too long.

▶ Don't mispronounce the featured speaker's name.

▶ Don't give inaccurate or unwanted biographical information about the featured speaker.

▶ Don't upstage the featured speaker.

▶ Don't evaluate the upcoming speech instead of letting the audience decide for itself.

▶ Whenever appropriate, add some specific, personal material that humanizes the speaker—after clearing this with him or her.

▶ Mention the topic of the speaker's talk.

A speech of introduction should focus audience attention on the featured speaker, not on you. Some speeches of introduction include so much explanation of the occasion that the audience learns little about the actual speaker. Also, be careful to avoid upstaging the speaker by making frequent references to yourself, your accomplishments, or your qualifications to give the introduction. Briefly mention who you are, then place the featured speech at the center of your presentation. Resist the temptation to evaluate the speech, because the listeners can make an informed judgment only after they have listened to the speaker. For example, don't say, "Marie's speech will be the finest presentation you'll ever hear on Haiku poetry." Specific analyses and evaluations mean little to an audience that has not yet heard what it should be appraising.

Presentations of Awards

▼ ▼ ▼

Another common ceremonial speech is the presentation of an award. This type of speech should emphasize the worthiness of the person receiving the award and explain the award's significance. An award presentation should include at least the following components:[13]

▶ The name of the award and the reason it is being given

▶ The name of the winner and his or her reason for winning

▶ The reason you are glad to present the award

The content of your presentation "should be so specific that it couldn't possibly be said about anyone else."[14] The more your remarks identify the recipient as unique, the more the audience will recognize the award as a personal distinction for the winner. Compare the impact of these fictitious presentations:

> "Now we come to the Outstanding Freshman award. And the winner is Elvira Earp. Congratulations, Elvira."

> "The award of Outstanding Freshman recognizes scholastic achievement and public service. This year's winner isn't content with a perfect 4.0 grade point average. She sets aside time from her busy schedule to work with children who have cerebral palsy. On weekends, you can find her teaching adult literacy classes at the public library. I am happy to present this award to a model for my own children: Elvira Earp."

If you had won the award, which presentation would make you feel more acknowledged?

Acceptance Speeches
▼ ▼ ▼

An acceptance speech demands more from the recipient of an award than a simple "thank you." A properly crafted acceptance concisely expresses gratitude and dignifies the occasion by recognizing the significance of the award.

Your acceptance speech should show your goodwill toward the audience, the presenter, and the sponsor of the award. The speech should do the following, although not necessarily in this order:[15]

▶ Thank the donor and presenter.

▶ Demonstrate modesty while avoiding hackneyed phrases that ring false. Don't say, "I really don't deserve this," because it insults the donors by implying that they made the wrong choice. You could, for example, show humility by pointing to how you will try to live up to the high standards of the award.

▶ Thank others who may have contributed to your success. If you have ever watched the Academy Awards on television, you'll recall that almost every acceptance speech includes a list of people the winner wishes to thank. Make sure you acknowledge those who contributed to your success, but only those who contributed directly. Giving more than a handful of thank-you's begins to sound like the recital of a grocery list—and holds about the same amount of interest for the audience.

▶ Regardless of the gift or award, express your pleasure at receiving it. I have seen some award recipients actually mock the presenter by ridiculing a gift they were given. Such behavior is rude and ungracious. Even if you think the award itself is hideous or cheap, someone has exerted effort and thought in trying to find something appropriate.

▶ Express appreciation in your conclusion. Reiterating your gratitude shows that you acknowledge the award as a favor and appreciate it.

By following these simple guidelines, you will generate an acceptance speech that is fitting and polite. Your acceptance speech also should demonstrate your understanding of the award's deeper significance. If you received the Outstanding Freshman award mentioned earlier, for example, your acceptance would call attention to its connection with the ideals of scholastic excellence and community service. Also, thinking ahead about structuring your acceptance speech in this way will help you avoid blurting out the first thought that comes to your mind in the excitement of the moment. For example, in 1984 Sally Field received the Oscar for Best Actress for her performance in *Places in the Heart.* Her acceptance speech consisted of an outburst of tears and the inane pronouncement, "You like me! You really, really like me!"

By contrast, Elie Wiesel's 1986 Nobel Peace Prize acceptance speech epitomizes an appropriate response to the situation.[16] He begins by demonstrating modesty: "It is with a profound sense of humility that I accept the honor you have chosen to bestow upon me. I know: your choice transcends me." Wiesel recognizes that the award acknowledges not simply his efforts in raising public consciousness about the Holocaust but those of others who have suffered: ". . . [T]his honor belongs .o all the survivors and their children, and through us, to the Jewish people with whose destiny I have always identified." He concludes with a brief but eloquent acknowledgment of the award and its sponsors: "Thank you, Chairman Aarvik. Thank you, members of the Nobel Committee. Thank you, people of Norway, for declaring on this singular occasion that our survival has a meaning for mankind."

Speeches to Commemorate
▼ ▼ ▼

Commemorative speeches are another type of special occasion address. These speeches formally recognize and honor a person, organization, or occasion. Commemorative speeches can occur in a variety of circumstances, from celebrating a coworker's retirement, to congratulating a friend for winning the lottery, to remembering a person who has just died. There are three basic types of commemorative speeches: tributes, eulogies, and toasts.

Tributes

An effective tribute renews the kinship between speaker and audience while recognizing the occasion. Norman Schwarzkopf's going-home speech to the troops serving in the Gulf War, included in Appendix C, provides a good example of a tribute. Schwarzkopf begins by emphasizing his closeness with the troops. Since all of them are soldiers, he praises that fact and adds "inside" references to military units in jargon that other soldiers will understand: "It's a great day to be a soldier! Big Red One, First Team, Old Ironsides, Spear Head, Hell on Wheels platoon, Jay Hawk patrol, today you're going home." His use of these terms establishes him as one of the group, in this case military personnel. Here we see one characteristic of tributes: recognizing or creating the identity of the audience.

Schwarzkopf proceeds to summarize the events that made the occasion memorable. This exemplifies a second quality of tributes—commending the audience's shared history or revered heroes: "Valiant charges by courageous men over 250 kilometers of enemy territory. Along with a force of over 1,500 tanks, almost 250 attack helicopters, over 48,500 pieces of military equipment, moving around, behind, and into the enemy and totally breaking his back and defeating him in 100 hours." Another example of evoking a revered hero occurred in Martin Luther King, Jr.'s "I Have a Dream" speech, also in Appendix C. He refers to Abraham Lincoln, the president known for his role in bringing slavery to an end, as a "great American, in whose symbolic shadow we stand today" at the Lincoln Memorial in Washington, DC.

Tributes, therefore, generally honor an individual, organization, or occasion while commending the audience's shared history or revered heroes. Some forms of tributes, however, call for special consideration.

Toasts

An abbreviated type of commemorative speech is the toast, a very brief set of remarks traditionally delivered while audience members hold aloft glasses of wine or champagne. Although toasts have evolved into symbolic gestures that might include water or no beverage at all, one element has been preserved: the speech. We hear short toasts in many contexts. The traditional Jewish toast consists of a simple "*L'chaim!*" translated, "To life!" Löwenbrau beer used to begin their commercials with the toast "Here's to good friends." When a special occasion calls for a toast, however, the remarks must be more specific.

Since toasts originated with everyone holding a glass aloft, they were brief. That custom remains unchanged—a toast rarely lasts more than a minute or two. Because of their brevity, toasts may be memorized. The speaker has very little time, and a toast is almost always on behalf of someone or something specific. As a result, the toast itself should focus on one specific quality or theme that emphasizes the reason for the occasion.

Gratuitous comments such as "Here's to the happy couple" given at a wedding fail to capitalize on the potentially dramatic effect of toasts.[17] The guests have paused to hear inspiring words, not clichés. Similarly, comments that run counter to the desired mood spell disaster. You might have heard wedding toasts in the spirit of "Here's to Bubba and Bertha. Hope this marriage turns out better than Bubba's last one. Lots of luck."

Eulogies

Another type of commemorative speech is the eulogy, which offers tribute to someone who has died (the word *eulogy* comes from the Greek for "good words"). The tradition of eulogizing probably extends to nearly the beginning of human speech. Pericles' funeral oration in 431 B.C. for those who had perished in the Peloponnesian War was the first fully recorded eulogy delivered as a public speech.[18] It exemplifies the basic format eulogies still follow. Your audience will expect a eulogy to do the following:

- Recognize the death.
- Temper the audience's grief by explaining how the deceased "lives on."
- Redefine the audience's relationship to the deceased.
- Reassure the audience that life will continue.
- Sometimes advise the audience on how the death should affect their own lives.[19]

Perhaps more than other types of ceremonial speeches, the eulogy must "reknit the community" because members have suffered a loss. In his eulogy for the astronauts who perished aboard the *Challenger* space shuttle, Ronald Reagan stressed that the tragedy had brought all Americans together in spite of their differences.[20] Speaking of his wife and himself, Reagan said, "We know we share this pain with all of the people of our country. This is truly a national loss."[21]

A brief examination of United Nations Ambassador Adlai Stevenson's 1965 eulogy for Winston Churchill shows what a eulogy can accomplish.[22]

Component of Eulogy	Fulfillment in Stevenson's Speech
Recognize the death.	Sir Winston Churchill is dead. The voice that led nations, raised armies, inspired victories and blew fresh courage into the hearts of men is silenced.
Show how the deceased lives on.	Churchill, the historian, felt the continuity of past and present, the contribution which mighty men and great events make to future experience; history's "flickering flame" lights up the past and sends its gleams into the future.
Redefine the relationship to the deceased.	One rather feels a sense of thankfulness and of encouragement that throughout so long a life, such a full measure of power, virtuosity, mastery and zest played over our human scene.
Offer reassurance.	Contemplating this completed career, we feel a sense of enlargement and exhilaration. . . . Churchill's life uplifts our hearts and fills us with fresh revelation of the scale and reach of human achievement.

Eulogies offer praise for the deceased, but the compliments must be sincere and proportionate to the actual accomplishments. Even a grief-stricken audience can recognize overly lavish praise. Claiming that the deceased was "faultless" or "perfect" rings false because everyone has shortcomings. Concentrate on the person's strengths while remaining realistic. Since a eulogist usually knows the deceased personally, some specific anecdotes that illustrate the character of the departed are especially appropriate. A poorly wrought eulogy can be interpreted as disrespectful or simply ridiculous. For example, in an episode of *Star Trek: The Next Generation*, Lieutenant Commander Data offers an overly general eulogy for a brilliant scientist who has just died: "To know him was to love him. And to love him was to know him. Those who knew him, loved him. Those who did not know him, loved him from afar." In contrast, an effective eulogy will be specific to the deceased and geared to the audience. Stevenson's moving tribute to Winston Churchill was full of quotes from Churchill and personal remembrances of the great leader's habits and mannerisms. Adapting to the dignitaries of many nations who were in attendance, Stevenson emphasized Churchill's roles in founding the United Nations and his belief that "humanity, its freedom, its survival, towered above pettier interests—national rivalries, old enmities, the bitter disputes of race and creed."[23]

After-Dinner Speeches

▼ ▼ ▼

The final type of ceremonial speech—the after-dinner speech—is far less serious than the eulogy. This type of speech gets its name from the fact that it is often delivered as the conclusion to a meeting that includes a meal. The name now signifies any speech that is light, entertaining, and often inspirational in tone.[24] Occasions for after-dinner speeches abound, and they form a part of special events such as political rallies, graduation exercises, conventions, and bar mitzvahs. It would not be exaggerating to observe, "The after-dinner speech is one of the great rituals of American public speaking and public life."[25] After-dinner speaking has become so established that it is an oratorical event at many interscholastic and intercollegiate speech contests.

Since after-dinner speeches are generally meant to be entertaining, they should avoid controversy and overly technical explanations while still reinforcing a central theme. Also, even when an after-dinner speech is humorous, there is no need to keep audience members laughing constantly. If you are asked to deliver this kind of speech, you should not feel obligated to put together a comedy monologue or an uninterrupted series of jokes. Forced humor such as this can end up detracting from your speech. Furthermore, people differ significantly in their ability to be humorous,[26] and different audiences will consider different things funny.

Be especially careful to avoid any comments that might have a chance of offending. Be aware that what you consider mild swearing could be interpreted by others as obscene, marking you as crude and inconsiderate. Ethnic, racist, sexist, and homophobic jokes are always unacceptable. The same goes for jokes that ridicule people who are mentally or physically challenged.

Ideally you should gear your choice of humor to the background and interests of your audience. This type of humor creates a sense of identification between speaker and audience. Such a feeling of collegiality helps bond the speaker and audience, letting the listeners know that the speaker is "one of us." Barbara Bush effectively established identification with her audience during her 1990 commencement address at Wellesley College. Recognizing that the graduating seniors at the women's college wanted to embark on careers traditionally closed to women, she quipped: "Who knows? Somewhere out in this audience may even be someone who will one day follow in my footsteps, and preside over the White House as the president's spouse. I wish him well!"[27] At its most powerful, humor can show that the speaker and audience share similar motivations and reactions, that the same sorts of things "make them tick."[28]

In general, the after-dinner speech will mark a specific event, so it's a good idea to reaffirm the occasion and the reason your audience has chosen to get together. You will find that vivid narratives, instances, and jokes are especially effective in bringing ideas and events to life. You can use several related items to maintain audience interest and enjoyment, or you can focus the entire speech on a single extended story or illustration. Either way, the speech should carry a lesson that applies to the specific audience.

In the following speech the speaker uses an extended illustration about messages people hear throughout life to unify a speech aimed at the life choices facing graduating seniors.

Learn to Listen with Your Heart: Farewell to Graduates

by Martha Saunders

IN THE DEPARTMENT OF Communication Arts we spend a great deal of time thinking and talking about words—the meaning of words, the persuasive value of words, the ethical implications of words and, generally, the impact of words as they are delivered in messages among people. Because of this, I was especially captured by a magazine article a few months ago which discussed how words influence people.

The article suggested that the most important messages that humans deliver to one another are usually expressed in very simple terms. I hope that doesn't

Martha Saunders, Assistant Professor of Public Relations, University of West Florida, gave this speech on October 28, 1993.

shock you now that you've spent these past few years having your minds crammed with complicated thoughts. The article went on to suggest that the *most influential messages* in our language most often come in three word phrases.

I had to agree that three-word phrases such as "I love you," or "There's no charge," or "And in conclusion" certainly were capable of prompting a strong reaction in me, and as I had hoped to impress you with profound thought today, I decided to share with you *three* three-word phrases that I have found useful as I have moved along in my life.

The first three-word phrase I've found useful in life is this: *I'll be there.* Have you ever thought about what a balm those three words can create?

I 'll be there. If you've ever had to call for a plumber over a weekend you know how really good these words can feel. Or if you've been stranded on the road with car trouble and used your last quarter to call a friend, you know how good those words can be. Think about them:

"Grandma, I'm graduating in August!" *I'll be there.*

"Roommate, I'm stuck at the office and can't get to the airport to meet my sister!" *I'll be there.*

"Mom, the baby cries all night and if I don't get some sleep I'll perish!" *I'll be there.*

Recently I was talking with a local business person who is occasionally in a position to hire UWF graduates, and she told me the single most impressive thing a job candidate can do is to demonstrate a real interest in the well-being of that business. Someone who will help further the objectives of that organization, whether or not he or she is "on the clock" is going to be a valuable person. In other words, *be somebody who will be there.*

One of my favorite stories about someone who knew how to "be there" is told of Elizabeth, the Queen Mother of England, who was asked whether the little princesses (Elizabeth and Margaret Rose) would leave England after the Blitz of 1940. The queen replied:

"The children will not leave England unless I do. I shall not leave unless their father does, and the king will not leave the country in any circumstances whatever." *I'll be there.*

The second three-word phrase I want to present to you is perhaps the hardest to learn to say—I know it was for me and sometimes still is. That is, *maybe you're right.* Think about it. If more people were to learn to say *maybe you're right* the marriage counselors would be out of business and, with a little luck, the gun shops. I know from experience it can have a disarming effect on an opponent in an argument. In fact, one of my lawyer friends uses it often in his closing remarks—and he is a *very* successful lawyer. *Maybe you're right.*

It has been my experience that when we get so hung up on getting our own way that we will not concede on *any* point, we are doing ourselves a real disservice. Make life a little easier on yourself. Remember the old saying—"There are a hundred ways to skin a cat—and every single one of them is right." *Maybe you're right.*

The third phrase I want to introduce to you I must have heard a thousand times when I was a little girl. Whenever I was faced with a hard decision I would turn to my caregiver and ask what I should do. Her response was always the same three-letter word phrase—"*Your heart knows*"—then she would go on about what she was doing.

"My heart knows?" I would think to myself. "What's that supposed to mean? I need advice here. I need for you to tell me what to do."

She would just smile and say, "*Your heart knows, honey, your heart knows.*"

But as I was an imperious child, I would throw my hand on my hip and say, "Maybe so, but my heart isn't talking!"

To this she would respond—"*Learn to listen.*"

This brings me to the point of my speech. You know, life doesn't come in the form of a degree plan. There's no Great Advisor out there who will give you a checklist and say, "Do these things and you'll earn your degree in 'life.'"

To some extent, the page is blank now. You may have a rough outline of where you're headed, but I can assure you, you won't get there without having to make some tough decisions—and decision making is never easy.

You may be able to find people to suggest what you should do, but for the most part, no one will be willing to accept the responsibility for your mistakes. You'll have to make your own choices.

My advice to you today is to *learn to listen to your heart.* The psychologists call this "turning into our subconscious." Spiritual leaders call it "turning to a higher power." Whatever you call it, there is an ability in each of you to find the right answers for your life. It's there and it's a powerful gift that all the education or degrees in the world can't acquire for you. You've had it all along—now, you're going to have to use it.

In "The Bending of the Bough," George Moore wrote: "The difficulty in life is the choice." Choose well, Graduates.

Although this commencement speech was delivered in a traditional setting with a speaker at the lectern and an attentive audience, in many cases as an after-dinner speaker you will have to compete with distractions such as courses being served, glasses being filled, plates being cleared, and servers moving around the room. Make sure you speak with sufficient volume and clear enunciation to overcome these sounds. Also remember that the attention span of your audience will be low after a heavy meal, so you should include plenty of attention-getting material throughout the speech.

Remember:

For digestible after-dinner speeches . . .

▶ Do use narratives and examples.

▶ Do use humor specific to the situation.

▶ Do keep the tone entertaining and light.

▶ Do focus your remarks on a central theme relevant to the occasion.

▶ Don't have complex or controversial content.

▶ Don't use overworked jokes, especially "A funny thing happened on the way to this speech . . ."

▶ Don't force humor; present only what you can deliver comfortably and skillfully.

▶ Don't ever use humor that can be considered racist, sexist, or otherwise offensive.

Summary
▼ ▼ ▼

Special occasion speeches reinforce the shared identity and values of an audience. Regardless of the type of special occasion speech, its objective is to strengthen the bonds that unite the listeners.

There are several types of special occasion speeches. A speech of introduction focuses attention on a subsequent speaker and prepares the audience to listen to that person. Speeches of introduction are brief and highlight the featured speaker, not the person giving the introduction.

Speeches that are presentations of awards should include not only the name of the recipient but the reason that person deserves the honor. In speeches of acceptance the recipient demonstrates humility and expresses appreciation to the sponsor of the award and to anyone who contributed to the winner's achievement.

Commemorative speeches are tributes to a person, event, or cause. Toasts are abbreviated tributes traditionally delivered at festive occasions such as weddings. Eulogies are tributes to someone who has died. When giving a eulogy, the speaker should acknowledge the death, redefine the relationship to the deceased, comfort the audience, and show what lasting contribution the deceased made.

After-dinner speeches are light, entertaining presentations that generally include humor. When using humor, tailor the humorous remarks to the audience and occasion. The more specific the jokes and anecdotes, the better the speaker and audience will identify with each other.

Notes

1. C. Perelman and L. Olbrechts-Tyteca, *The New Rhetoric: A Treatise on Argumentation*, trans. John Wilkinson and Purcell Weaver (Notre Dame: University of Notre Dame Press, 1969), p. 52.

2. Barbara Jordan, "Democratic Convention Keynote Address," in Halford Ross Ryan, ed., *Contemporary American Public Discourse*, 3rd ed. (Prospect Heights, IL: Waveland, 1992), p. 274.

3. Aristotle, *Rhetorica*, trans. W. Rhys Roberts, in W. D. Ross, ed., *The Works of Aristotle*, vol. 11 (Oxford: Clarendon, 1924), p. 1358b.

4. Aristotle, *Rhetorica*, p. 1366a.

5. Perelman and Olbrechts-Tyteca, *The New Rhetoric*, p. 50.

6. Janet Stone and Jane Bachner, *Speaking Up: A Book for Every Woman Who Wants to Speak Effectively* (New York: McGraw-Hill, 1977), pp. 141–142.

7. Karlyn Kohrs Campbell, *The Rhetorical Act*, 2nd ed. (Belmont, CA: Wadsworth, 1996), p. 126.

8. Stone and Bachner, *Speaking Up*, p. 142.

9. Campbell, *The Rhetorical Act*, p. 126.

10. List based on Joan Detz, *How to Write and Give a Speech* (New York: St. Martin's Press, 1992), p. 92.

11. *The Random House Dictionary of the English Language*, ed. Jess Stein (New York: Random House, 1983).

12. David Belson, *What to Say and How to Say It* (Secaucus, NJ: Castle, 1955), pp. 79–80.

13. Patricia Sternberg, *Speak Up! A Guide to Public Speaking* (New York: Julian Messner, 1984), pp. 134–135.

14. Detz, *How to Write*, p. 88.

15. List adapted from Richard C. Reager, Norman P. Crawford, and Edwin L. Stevens, *You Can Talk Well* (New Brunswick, NJ: Rutgers University Press, 1960), p. 155.

16. Elie Wiesel, "Acceptance of the Nobel Peace Prize," in James R. Andrews and David Zarefsky, eds., *Contemporary American Voices* (White Plains, NY: Longman, 1992), pp. 419–420.

17. An entire book has been written that covers almost every conceivable possibility for giving toasts at weddings. See Angela Lansbury, *Wedding Speeches and Toasts* (London: Ward Lock, 1994).

18. Thucydides, *History of the Peloponnesian War*, trans. Rex Warner, intro. M. I. Finley (New York: Penguin, 1972), p. 143.

19. List compiled from Kathleen Hall Jamieson and Karlyn Kohrs Campbell, "Rhetorical Hybrids: Fusions of Generic Elements," *Quarterly Journal of Speech* 68 (1982), 146-157; Karen A. Foss, "John Lennon and the Advisory Function of Eulogies," *Central States Speech Journal* 34 (1983), 187–194.

20. Reagan received high marks for his eulogy. See Steven M. Mister, "Reagan's Challenger Tribute: Combining Generic Constraints and Situational Demands," *Central States Speech Journal* 37 (1986), 158-165.

21. Ronald Reagan, Address to the Nation, 28 January 1986, *Weekly Compilation of Presidential Documents* 22.5 (3 February 1986), 104.

22. Adlai Ewing Stevenson, "Eulogy on Sir Winston Churchill," in Ryan, ed., *Contemporary American Public Discourse*, pp. 245–248.

23. Stevenson, "Eulogy," 246.

24. Reager, Crawford, and Stevens, *You Can Talk Well*, p. 149.

25. Michael Osborn and Suzanne Osborn, *Public Speaking*, 3rd ed. (Boston: Houghton Mifflin, 1994), p. 438.

26. There is some evidence that humor is related to specific personality traits and communicative abilities. See Melissa Wanzer, Melanie Booth-Butterfield, and Steven Booth-Butterfield, "The Funny People: A Source-Orientation to the Communication of Humor," *Communication Quarterly* 43 (1995), 142-154.

27. Barbara Bush, "Commencement Address at Wellesley College," in Victoria L. DeFrancisco and Marvin D. Jensen, eds., *Women's Voices in Our Time: Statements by American Leaders* (Prospect Heights, IL: Waveland, 1994), p. 92.

28. Another way of putting the matter is that the speaker and audience share the same essence or are "soul mates." For the sharing of essence as the culmination of identity, see Kenneth Burke, *A Rhetoric of Motives* (New York: Prentice-Hall, 1952), pp. 20-23.

Team Presentations

A S YOU PREPARE FOR YOUR future, have you considered the importance of teamwork? According to Robert B. Reich, author of *The Work of Nations*, in today's global market, other countries have workers willing to accept lower wages and U.S. companies are down-sizing by laying off educated professionals, middle managers, and white collar workers. As a result, the only people who are sure to have jobs are the creative problem-solvers who know how to work in teams and how to communicate concepts through oral presentations and written reports.[1] How do you feel about working in teams? When an instructor says, "Let's break into groups for the next assignment" do you view this with enthusiasm or with dread? The chances are that you have found group work to be fairly unsatisfying. But the fact is that people who can work effectively in teams are more likely to succeed in today's rapidly changing job market and to be valued by nonprofit organizations as well. Consider these examples of team presentations:

▶ You are part of a newcomer orientation team for your department or dorm. Each team member is responsible for briefing new students on a particular aspect of college life.

▶ You and three other nursing students are taking the same public speaking class. For your final class assignment, you decide to give a team presentation on AIDS. Each of you will focus on a different aspect of AIDS, and then your team will open the floor to audience questions and comments.

▶ A complex rezoning issue is up for vote in your community. To help inform the public and answer their questions, the city council has asked you and four other community members with special knowledge and differing views to present a panel discussion for broadcast on the local cable TV channel.

▶ The college administrators have announced an across-the-board budget cut for next year. A portion of the budget cut must come from student activities. The student council has appointed you and six other students to a problem-solving team. Your assignment is to decide which student activities should be cut and to present your decision to a joint meeting of administrators and student council representatives.

The above examples have probably given you a good idea of what is meant by teams and team presentations. A *team* is normally composed of three to seven members who actively work together toward a particular goal (solving a problem, gathering information, or planning an informative or persuasive presentation). A team could involve only two people, but when teams have fewer than three members, the burden of gathering sufficient information for quality decision making becomes tedious. A team of more than eight makes it difficult for all people to participate as much as they would like. Five is considered the most productive size for a team because it is large enough to supply needed information and to share the work load, yet small enough to give each member a chance for maximum participation.

Note: This appendix was written by Cheryl Hamilton with Roy Schwartzman, Assistant Professor of Speech Communication and Director of the Basic Course, University of South Carolina, Columbia, SC.

A *team presentation* involves the collaborative organization and presentation of material by team members to an audience using one of a variety of public discussion formats: forum, symposium, panel, or some combination of the three. A team presentation can be either informative or persuasive. For example, a team presentation on AIDS could be designed to present needed information to an audience or to persuade audience members that protection against AIDS is simple, effective, and affordable.

Advantages and Disadvantages of Team Presentations

▼ ▼ ▼

Understanding the positive and negative features of team presentations will enable you to maximize the benefits of teams and avoid the pitfalls. Team presentations have several advantages over individual speeches. First, teams offer the audience a broader perspective than only one person can give. A team presentation is especially good for complex or controversial topics because each member can specialize in a particular aspect of the topic. This breadth of coverage adds variety and can make the presentation more interesting for the audience.

Second, team presentations allow for shared responsibility. Research can be done more quickly and thoroughly when each member is concentrating on only one or two aspects of the topic. Also, audience questions can be directed to the team member specializing in that area. Furthermore, team members can compensate for weaknesses in one another's speaking style or general presentation skills. For some speakers this is particularly reassuring since they don't have to face the audience alone.

Third, team speaking can reinforce the idea that the topic of the presentation is particularly important. For example, when a company sends a group of people from several departments to discuss a topic, it implies widespread commitment throughout the organization. Also, strength lies in numbers. A team of authoritative speakers often can carry more weight with an audience than just one person. Remember, however, that to have the most impact, team members must establish themselves as credible speakers. (See Chapter 14 for suggestions on ways to establish credibility.)

If your past experience with group work has convinced you that "when you want it done right, you have to do it yourself," you already know that teams have some limitations. First, team presentations are far more difficult to coordinate than an individual speech. It's not easy to find free time in everyone's schedule for practice—yet practice is essential to a successful team presentation. Furthermore, each speaker's materials must fit with everyone else's. Therefore, transitions between speakers must be planned carefully, and the content of all parts of the presentation must be consistent. Obviously, the risk of inconsistency increases as the number of speakers increases. Also, all members of a team presentation must coordinate with each other to make sure their individual presentations are equally well researched and organized.

Second, team presentations have all the drawbacks of any group effort. Specifically, some members of a team might prepare poorly or become antagonistic to other team members. Squabbles and misunderstandings can ruin a team's cooperative spirit. You probably have been part of a group in which one or more members did almost nothing, so everyone else had to work that much harder to compensate. Try to prevent personal agendas and unequal participation from getting in the way of the team's objectives.

Third, team projects tend to consume more time and, if team members are salaried employees, can cost more money than individual efforts. It takes far more time to develop a team presentation than to prepare an individual speech. Practice must be more elaborate than for solo speeches, and even if one member's presentation is excellent, practice must continue until everyone's presentation is in top form. Also, when an organization sends a team to make a presentation, it means that these people are now unavailable for other tasks. In some cases it could mean that the organization must pay the travel expenses of several people instead of just one.

Now that we have defined team presentations and discussed their strengths and weaknesses, let's discuss exactly what makes a team presentation effective.

Effective Team Presentations[2]

▼ ▼ ▼

Successful team presentations have three basic characteristics: *content* is well organized, well supported, and smooth-flowing; *visual aids* are creative, professional, and effectively used; and *team performance* is smooth, polished, and dynamic. Let's look at each of these characteristics in more detail.

Content

Regardless of whether your team presentation will be informative or persuasive, each team member should prepare by following the basic steps discussed in Chapters 9 (for informative speeches) and 13 (for persuasive speeches). Each individual speech should follow the four steps of the FLOW sequence (focus, lead-in, organized body, and wrap-up). Ideas should be clearly supported with a variety of supporting materials that clarify, prove, and add interest. Detailed instances (including personal anecdotes, family stories, examples from the lives of famous people, business examples, and humorous tales) are excellent supports to capture listeners' interest and involve them in your team's content.

To make sure your team's ideas flow smoothly, each team member should prepare storyboards instead of outlines. (See Chapter 12 for more information on storyboards.) Storyboards are generally more helpful because it is easier for team members to grasp each other's ideas, visual aids, and transitions. Tape each person's storyboards to the wall or lay them out on a conference table for ease of viewing by other members. While you read them, imagine that you are an audience member. Is each presentation completely clear? Are the main points obvious? Would you have doubts about any of the main points? What additional information or visual aids would ease those doubts? Does each member's presentation flow smoothly into the next? Finding and correcting problems early in the planning process is very important. Otherwise, you may find yourselves forced to make last-minute changes requiring new visuals. Then, instead of a relaxed dry run of the entire presentation (needed before every scheduled talk), you'll have a tense, even frantic, session in which you are scrambling to pull everything together.

Visual Aids

Remember that audience members should be able to grasp visual aids within six seconds or less (as discussed in Chapter 6). All the visuals of the team should be consistent in appearance throughout the presentation—same logo (if you have one), same basic colors, and same fonts and type sizes. If one member has professional-looking transparencies and another has low-quality ones, the overall impact is diminished. Make sure your team's visuals follow the design suggestions in Chapter 7. Unless all team members are aware of and agree on what makes a quality visual aid, it's a good idea to have all the team's visuals prepared by a single team member. Prepare the visual aids early enough so that they will be available for practice and so that any needed corrections can be made. To help tie all members' presentations together and clarify the overall organization for the audience, try using a "moving agenda" transparency or chart. A moving agenda transparency lists all speakers and their topics but highlights the current speaker. This way listeners will know who's speaking (even if they were daydreaming when the speaker was introduced) and can remember names of previous speakers and keep track of the structure of the entire presentation. You can either have a separate transparency or chart for each speaker or use a single transparency with color overlays (illustrated in Figure 7.2 in Chapter 7).

Team members should practice using their visual aids in front of at least one other team member, who can offer suggestions as needed. Awkward handling of visuals can ruin the effect of a well-organized presentation. (Chapter 8 gives suggestions for effectively handling a variety of visual aids.)

You can estimate the length of the team presentation by the number of visuals you plan to use. Most speakers spend at least one minute on each visual. Therefore, twenty visual aids at one minute per visual would make for at least a twenty-minute presentation. It is very important to stay within prearranged time limits.

Team Performance

A smooth, polished, and dynamic team performance requires practice, revision, and more practice. Each member should practice alone, and then the team should have one or more dry runs of the entire presentation. Videotape the practice sessions if possible. (Check Chapter 8 for verbal, visual, and vocal pointers.) Remember that even when you are not speaking, it is important to look interested in the proceedings. If you yawn or otherwise look bored during a teammate's talk the listeners certainly will notice.

One team member needs to be the coordinator—preferably a member with both past team experience or speaking experience and leadership abilities. If the team consists of more than four or five members, it's a good idea to select a coordinator who will not be one of the presenters. This person can be more objective in critiquing and directing the presenters. During the presentation the coordinator presents the introduction and conclusion, provides transitions, and directs the question-and-answer session.

Team Presentation Formats
▼ ▼ ▼

Team presentations typically include the forum, symposium, or panel as well as any combination of the three. Any of the formats can be used for information sharing, instructional purposes, problem-solving, or persuasion.

Forum

Open audience participation is referred to as a **forum.** The term is derived from ancient Rome, where a forum referred to a public square where political and legal business was conducted. The traditional New England town meeting is a modern-day forum. When a forum is used in team presentations, it normally follows a symposium or panel (discussed below). Thus, both a panel-forum and a symposium-forum are possible. A forum may involve a simple question-and-answer period coordinated by a moderator with questions answered by team members, or it could involve a general discussion by audience and team members.

The moderator is usually a team member who is not one of the presenters. Because this role can be a difficult one, the moderator should be a good speaker and a skilled communicator who is adept at the following:[3]

▶ Stimulating the group further by posing provocative questions and presenting challenging ideas.

▶ Urging speakers to keep their comments brief so as many people as possible (or practical) may talk.

▶ Recognizing the various viewpoints and trying to give an opportunity for all of them to be heard.

Of course, at the beginning of the forum, the moderator will want to summarize the procedure as well as any ground rules (such as keep comments brief, wait to be recognized before speaking, and feel free to express opposing viewpoints). If you think the audience may be hesitant to participate, plan ahead by having one or two audience members ready to ask a question or make a comment. Political speakers often use this approach of "planting" someone in the audience to ask the first question if needed. Once one or two questions are asked, audience members normally feel free to join in.

Symposium

A *symposium* involves a series of speakers who each present a formal, five- to ten-minute speech on an aspect of the topic they have researched or have special knowledge of. The purpose of a symposium is to explore a single topic from a variety of viewpoints in order to inform and instruct and sometimes to persuade. Probably the oldest recorded symposium is one described by the Greek philosopher Plato. The event took place in Athens around 415 B.C. and consisted of seven participants presenting formal speeches on their views of the nature and definition of love.[4]

If you think of the entire symposium presentation as a speech, the coordinator handles the focus, lead-in, and wrap-up stages while the individual symposium speakers make up the organized body of the speech. In other words, it is the coordinator's responsibility to gain audience attention, introduce and clarify the topic to be covered, effectively introduce the members of the team, provide smooth transitions between speeches, and conclude the team presentation in a memorable manner.

When all speeches are finished, several procedures can be followed. For example, the symposium speakers may choose to discuss (agree or disagree with) the formal ideas presented by each speaker or to continue the discussion using the basic problem-solving process (making it a symposium-panel discussion). If the symposium was intended to educate or stimulate the audience, the moderator may invite everyone to enter the discussion after the team members have completed their panel discussion (a symposium-panel-forum) or begin the forum immediately after the symposium speakers have concluded (a symposium-forum). If a forum or panel discussion is added at the end of the symposium, the coordinator serves as moderator for these as well.

In a symposium presentation the lectern and the screen for transparencies are usually placed in the center of the front of the room, with speakers seated at tables on each side of the lectern. Or the lectern and screen can be placed to one side of the room, with the speakers seated at an angle to the audience and opposite the lectern.

Panel

In a *panel discussion* team members informally discuss a problem or topic of interest in front of an audience. No formal speeches are presented, and all panel members contribute freely and equally. A coordinator or moderator usually guides them through an organizational procedure (often the basic problem-solving procedure discussed later in this chapter). It is not unusual to find panelists disagreeing with, correcting, or interrupting each other. However, a panel discussion should have a purpose that all members agree upon, and all participants should be fully prepared for the discussion. Audience members are not involved in the discussion unless a forum is added at the completion of the panel discussion.

For effective discussion and exchange of ideas, panelists must be able to see each other as well as the audience. Two tables placed in a wide V-shape with team members seated behind the tables but facing the audience works well. Name cards (large enough for the audience to read) should be placed on the table in front of each member. A flip chart or chalkboard can be placed behind the panelists yet facing the audience.

The role of the moderator in a panel discussion is similar to that in a symposium. The coordinator should focus audience attention, introduce and clarify the topic to be covered, effectively introduce the members of the team, guide members around any procedural or personal problems, summarize the team's final results, and conclude in a memorable manner.

For panel discussions to be successful, members must (1) have good communication skills and (2) be familiar with the basic problem-solving procedure described below.

Communication Skills for Panel Members

For successful panel discussions to occur, group members must be both active listeners and open-minded participants. An episode of Geraldo Rivera's television talk show provides perhaps the most well-known example of the effect of the lack of these skills on a panel discussion. Two panels shared the stage: skinheads who were avowed racists and African-American civil rights activists. After a heated verbal exchange in which the participants neither listened actively nor displayed open-mindedness, the discussion degenerated into physical violence. Panelists threw chairs and punches, and Rivera got caught in the scuffle. He hosted the rest of the show while wearing a bandage across the bridge of his broken nose.

Active listening requires us to attend to the other team members' viewpoints. However, many times when we are discussing a problem with others, we listen selfishly. In other words, we listen to gather ammunition for our rebuttals and to determine when we can insert our viewpoints into the conversation. Specifically, the active listener does the following:

1. Listens for the other team member's complete verbal, visual, and vocal message.

2. Interprets the team member's meaning respectfully and carefully.

3. Checks the interpreted meaning for accuracy by rephrasing it for the team member.

4. Repeats steps 1–3 until the team member is satisfied with the interpretation.

After you are sure that you understand the person's argument, you may agree or disagree and present your views. This type of active listening is necessary for effective group participation.

Open-minded team members attempt to reach a decision that benefits the group or company as a whole. They work together as a team, not as unyielding individuals. However, while preparing for a panel discussion, team members sometimes become convinced that a certain solution is best. They come to the discussion prepared to convince the other team members to agree with their choice. If all participants were equally closed-minded, the discussion would degenerate into a debate. Feelings would be hurt, productivity would decrease, and the meeting would drag on without resolution.

Productive panel discussions require that members listen with an open mind to all views and try to respect those views. But open-mindedness does not mean that there can be no disagreement. Conflict over opinions can stimulate the team's thinking. If no one disagreed, the discussion might be dull and the team would likely arrive at a risky or unsuccessful decision.

The Basic Problem-Solving Procedure for Team Presentations

Many panel discussions involve problem solving and, as such, follow the basic problem-solving procedure based on John Dewey's reflective thinking process.[5] Even though the team coordinator will likely guide the team through the steps of the problem-solving process, successful team members need to be familiar with this procedure. Successful team members use the basic problem-solving procedure as a general tool to help them make decisions—whether in a private planning session or in a panel discussion in front of an audience.

Step 1. Identify the problem First, the team must agree that a problem exists and define the nature of that problem. The definition of the problem must be specific, factual, and descriptive. If you don't understand it, it's doubtful that your audience will. In defining the problem, ask the following questions:

▶ When did the problem first arise? Under what circumstances did it emerge?

▶ What is the history of the problem's development? When does it intensify or become less severe?

▶ Who is affected by this problem? How much are they affected?

▶ What are the implications of this problem? Exactly what are its financial, ethical, or health effects?

▶ When must the problem be solved? (*Note:* Just establish the time frame. Solutions will be discussed later.)

When the problem finally seems clear to everyone, test that understanding by writing down the problem *in question form.* Discuss the written question until all team members are satisfied with the wording. Then write the question on the board so the audience can see it.

You might find step 1 to be slow and painstaking. Effort at this stage, however, pays off. Without a clearly specified problem, no proposed solution can be entirely effective. Because step 1 is so time-consuming, team members often choose to complete this step ahead of the public discussion. Then, the coordinator briefly summarizes the previous discussion and reads the team's exact definition of the problem to the audience and the team begins their discussion with step 2.

Step 2. Analyze the problem   Groups that omit step 2 usually select unsound solutions because they do not know enough about the situation to make a sound decision. If you are not aware of the qualities needed in a good teacher, how can you select the best candidate from a list of applicants? Begin analyzing the problem by listing the topics and information that the team needs to discuss. Next, narrow down the list to a manageable length and discuss what is known about each item (here members share their research and personal knowledge with the team). Be sure to look at all sides of the problem and include in the discussion any opinions and objections your audience is likely to have. Informative panels use the analysis step to educate audience members; persuasive panels use the analysis step to investigate fallacious reasoning and introduce persuasive evidence.

Step 3. Establish criteria   *Criteria* are guidelines, boundaries, standards, or rules that a team agrees to follow in reaching a solution to their problem. For example, your group might agree that any solution selected should:

▶ Receive unanimous agreement by all group members.

▶ Fall within current state and national laws.

▶ Treat all persons equally.

▶ Not result in any negative consequences (such as higher costs).

You can also view the team's agreed-upon criteria as a checklist of items that any solution must meet in order to be selected. For example, a checklist of criteria for deciding which student activities to cut from the college budget might read as follows:

Any decision we reach about student activities must:

▶ Be agreeable to a majority of team members.

▶ Inconvenience the smallest number of students.

▶ Give preference to low-budget yet high-learning items.

▶ Be decided within two weeks.

Begin by making a list of all possible criteria. Then evaluate each criterion to determine its importance so the team can reduce the list of criteria to approximately three to five items. Next, divide remaining criteria into "musts" (required items) and "wants" (desired items). If an alternative fails to meet even one of the "must" criteria, it would be rejected by the team. Once the criteria have been divided into "musts" and "wants," the team should rank the "want" criteria from most to least important. There is no need to rank "must" criteria because they are all essential. "Want" criteria, however, must be ranked to be effective. For example, imagine that by using your "must" criteria you limit the possible computers to buy to two. In other words, there are two computers (solutions) that meet all of your team's "must" criteria. Suppose further that each computer meets three of your four "want" criteria. How will you decide which computer is best? You won't unless you have rank-ordered the "want" criteria. For example, if solution A meets criteria 2, 3, and 4, but solution B meets criteria 1, 2, and 3, solution B would be the best solution because it meets more of the most important "want" criteria.

Establishing criteria is a *key step* in the basic problem-solving procedure—it speeds up team decisions and improves the quality of those decisions. In fact, once the team agrees on the criteria to be used in evaluating the solutions, the most difficult part of the problem-solving process is over.

Step 4. List possible solutions   List as many solutions as are feasible within your group's time and budget limitations. Most teams have trouble listing possible solutions without evaluating them at the same time. However, all evaluations should be postponed until step 5. Don't worry about the quality of your solutions now—quantity, not quality, should be the goal in this step. Evaluating alternatives as soon as they are mentioned tends to hamper creative thinking.

One way to obtain creative, detailed lists of solutions is by *brainstorming*—the spontaneous contribution of ideas by all members of the team. Here are some suggestions for effective brainstorming:

▶ Have the team leader solicit input from each team member. Ideally, everyone should offer at least one idea at some point in the session. However, team members should feel invited, not coerced, to suggest ideas.[6]

▶ Designate one person to record *all* the ideas, no matter how far-fetched. The ideas should be listed where all team members can see them, such as on a flip chart or chalkboard. When the suggestions are listed, connections between them may begin to emerge and generate new ideas.

▶ Accept ideas as they are. Brainstorming does *not* involve editing, criticizing, or analyzing ideas. The sole purpose of brainstorming is to produce suggestions. There will be plenty of time after brainstorming for debating the merits of the proposed solutions.

▶ Give everyone equal opportunity to participate. Sometimes the leader might have to prevent someone from monopolizing the discussion. The brainstorming session should not end until everyone has made some contribution or has explicitly declined to offer input.

▶ When no more ideas are forthcoming, review the list of ideas to make sure that no important solutions were omitted.

As your team assembles its list of possible solutions, remember to include the option of "doing nothing," even if only by default. That possibility might prove unattractive, but it should be included at least as a basis for comparison to proposed alternatives.

Step 5. Evaluate solutions If the team has done a good job of establishing the criteria for evaluating solutions, the actual evaluation becomes amazingly simple. The following guidelines will enable your group to evaluate the possible options:

▶ Read through the list of solutions, eliminating those that the group feels do not meet the "must" criteria agreed to in step 3.

▶ Further reduce the list to a workable number by combining any similar alternatives.

▶ Reduce the list yet again by discussing each remaining alternative's strengths and weaknesses (referring back to relevant research presented in step 2 as needed). On the chalkboard or flip chart, make three columns. Label the left column "Proposed Solutions," the middle column "Advantages," and the right column "Disadvantages." Have one team member (or the moderator) fill in the columns as the team discusses.

▶ Take your narrowed list and determine how well each alternative meets the "want" criteria—consider the number of criteria met and the importance of criteria met. For example, on the chalkboard make a vertical list of the criteria (placing the most important criterion first) and a horizontal list of the solutions. Discuss each solution and insert a plus or minus sign to indicate how well each solution meets each criterion.

▶ Determine which alternative has the most plus marks in the most important criteria. The answer will probably be obvious. If it's not, a consensus decision (where members agree to accept a particular solution even though it may not be their first choice) is the best. If a consensus cannot be reached, the next best decision is a compromise. Voting should be used only as a last resort because it often causes resentment and unhappiness by creating winners and losers. Most group members would rather agree to a compromise than find that their preferred solution had been voted down.

When discussing each solution's merits, depersonalize the discussion by separating the person from the proposal.[7] In other words, don't mention who thought of a particular idea. Comments should focus on the merits and drawbacks of the idea, not on the personality of the member who offered the proposal.

Step 6. Discuss how to implement the solution(s) The final stage is to decide how the agreed-upon solution(s) should be put into practice. In deciding how to implement what the team has endorsed, consider these issues:

▶ Who will be responsible for overseeing implementation?

▶ When will implementation begin?

Remember:

The basic problem-solving procedure includes . . .

Step 1. Identify the problem.

Step 2. Analyze the problem.

Step 3. Establish criteria.

Step 4. List possible solutions.

Step 5. Evaluate solutions.

Step 6. Discuss how to implement solution(s).

▶ How long will implementation take? Should the solution be adopted all at once, or should it be phased in gradually?

▶ What resources (financial, personnel, time, space) are needed for the solution to take effect?

Sometimes, in discussing implementation, a team will find that a solution that seemed excellent is in fact not feasible. For example, if a school board decided to implement uniforms to solve theft of clothing at the local high school, the solution would fail if parents and students refused to comply. In cases where it is determined that the desired option will not work, the team must return to step 5 and select another possible solution.

Evaluation of Team Presentations
▼ ▼ ▼

Every team presentation should be followed by an evaluation of the presentation's strengths and weaknesses. If you are able to videotape the presentation, evaluation will be much easier. The best way for the coordinator and team presenters to determine the quality of their verbal, visual, and vocal communication is to watch a videotape of the presentation. It's also important for team members to be completely honest in evaluating each other and the team as a whole even though some members may be tempted to soft-pedal criticisms. To critique each other, your team may wish to use an evaluation form similar to the one on page 294 or page 411. When possible, it's a good idea to ask three or four audience members to fill out the form as well. Remember that evaluation is a positive tool. The more you learn about successful team presentations, the more prepared you will be for the team experiences you are likely to encounter in your future.

Summary
▼ ▼ ▼

In a team presentation three to seven people jointly present material to an audience. Team presentations can be informative or persuasive and are used in a variety of organizational and business settings. Advantages of team presentations include (1) a wide range of expertise on a single issue, (2) shared responsibility, and (3) reinforcement of a sense of importance to the topic. Disadvantages of team presentations include (1) difficulties in coordination, (2) interpersonal antagonisms, and (3) potentially high costs.

Effective team presentations include content that is well organized, well supported, and smooth-flowing; visual aids that are creative, professional, and effectively used; and a team performance that is smooth, polished, and dynamic.

Three common formats for team presentations are the forum, the symposium, and the panel discussion. A forum includes open audience participation. In a symposium several speakers give a series of formal individual presentations on a topic. A panel discussion is more informal and resembles a conversation in front of an audience.

Many panel discussions use the basic problem-solving procedure developed by Dewey, which includes these steps: (1) identify the problem, (2) analyze the problem, (3) establish criteria, (4) list possible solutions, (5) evaluate solutions, and (6) discuss how to implement the solution(s). Regardless of the type of format they plan to use in front of an audience, teams can benefit by using the problem-solving procedure in planning their presentation. The forum, symposium, and panel discussions all require thorough preparation and practice, members who are open-minded and skilled in active listening, and a coordinator who is adept in basic organizational procedure and communication.

After each team presentation, team members should evaluate each other and the presentation as a whole to determine strengths and weaknesses. If at all possible, videotape your team presentations to more clearly assess the team's verbal, visual, and vocal communication.

Notes

1. Robert B. Reich, *The Work of Nations* (New York: Vintage Books, 1992), Chapters 17 and 18.

2. Adapted from Thomas Leech, *How to Prepare, Stage, and Deliver Winning Presentations* (New York: AMACOM, 1982), pp. 333–347.

3. Gerald L. Wilson and Michael S. Hanna, *Groups in Context: Leadership and Participation in Small Groups*, 3rd ed. (New York: McGraw-Hill, 1993), p. 315.

4. W. T. Jones, *The Classical Mind: A History of Western Philosophy*, 2nd ed. (New York: Harcourt Brace Jovanovich, 1970), p. 110n.

5. John Dewey, *How We Think* (1910; Buffalo: Prometheus, 1991), pp. 72–78.

6. See Sonja K. Foss and Cindy L. Griffin, "Beyond Persuasion: A Proposal for an Invitational Rhetoric," *Communication Monographs* 62 (1995), 2–18.

7. A similar suggestion applies to classroom settings. See Roy Schwartzman, "The Winning Student: Dividends from Gaming," *Communication and Theater Association of Minnesota Journal* 21 (1994), 107–112.

Sample Speeches to Critique

Informative Speeches

"The Ishii Stick" by Eddie Osburn, student

"Canine Heartworm Disease" and preparation outline
by Karen Gemmer, student

"Plutonium 238: NASA's Fuel of Choice" by Jenny Clanton, student

Persuasive Speeches

"The Death Penalty" by Wimberly Waldroup, student

"Protecting Youth from the Tobacco Industry"
by Lonnie R. Bristow, M.D., Chair, Board of Trustees,
American Medical Association

"Successful Strategies for Achieving Your Career Goals"
by Virgis Colbert, Vice President, Plant Operations,
Miller Brewing Company

Special Occasion Speeches

"Address to Departing Troops at Dhahran"
by General H. Norman Schwarzkopf

"I Have a Dream" by Martin Luther King, Jr.

"Inaugural Address" by John F. Kennedy

Informative Speeches

▼ ▼ ▼

The Ishii Stick

by Eddie Osburn, student

In this artifact speech given the first week of class, Eddie introduces himself
by sharing something an archaeologist might uncover in his room years
in the future.

1   Hi. This is my artifact—it is an Ishii stick. It consists of a small copper rod inserted into a wooden dowel held securely by two set screws. It is used for making flint arrowheads, a process called knapping. The art of flint knapping was lost for many years. We tried to make them; we sweat and toiled and cursed and hammered away at the flint. But none of our efforts came out anything resembling that of the early Native Americans.

2   Then in the early part of this century, an Indian was found wandering in the mountains of California. This Indian had never been exposed to a white man or learned any of the white man's ways. He'd lived completely off the land and he did things in the manner that his people had always done them. His name was Ishii. That's spelled Ishii. A movie was recently made of his life called "The Last of His Tribe." Some of you may have seen it.

3   Ishii was taken to a museum in California to be studied and observed. While there, one night in an alley that was fenced off that he was allowed to exercise in, he found a broken Coke bottle. The next morning when his keepers came to his room, they found a perfect arrowhead made from this piece of glass. In wonderment they asked him how he had done it. He picked up an old nail that he had also found in this alley, and showed them a process that is known as pressure flaking. He asked for some tools to be brought to him and some flint. With these tools he fashioned a stick much like this one, and with it he made one arrowhead after another, all in near perfect condition.

4   Today there are flint knappers throughout America who are making quality arrowheads using the technique that Ishii taught us when he made this stick, appropriately called the Ishii stick. Even I have recently taken up this practice and have brought you some of my early efforts to show you—which are right here. And I do wonder if two thousand years from now when the archaeologists find my workshop and find these artifacts, if they will recognize them for what they are—only an amateur's imitations and not the authentic thing.

This speech is published by permission of Eddie Osburn.

Canine Heartworm Disease

by Karen Gemmer, student and veterinarian's technician

Over half of the students in Karen's public speaking class had one or more
dogs as pets so her topic was a good choice. Karen's preparation
outline is also included.

1   What I am holding in my hand—in this jar—is a dog's heart. And this
heart is completely infested with worms. This dog died from a very
debilitating and deadly disease called Canine Heartworm Disease.
At one time, when I thought I was going to be a veterinarian, I worked as a technician for a veterinarian. According to the journals I've read and the doctors
I've talked to, approximately fifty percent or one out of every two dogs in our
state that is unprotected against this disease will develop it. Now, that's the bad
news. The good news is—for you dog owners and future dog owners—that this
disease is entirely preventable.

2   There are three main points that I'd like to cover today about heartworm
disease [Transparency # 1] and they are: (1) What exactly is this disease? (2)
How is it spread? and (3) How can it be prevented?

3   Canine heartworm disease is exactly as its name implies—it is a disease of
the dog's heart in which worms or parasites actually live in the heart and the ad-
jacent blood vessels. Now, I'm going to bring this around so you can actually
see these worms a little more closely. These are adult heartworms. They are
about 14 inches in length and they can live at least seven years in the dog's heart.
In cases of severe infestation, there may be up to 250 worms in a heart at one
time. Now, all this time these worms are continually producing offspring called
microfilaria. The offspring are microscopic. After about six months they will
travel to the heart where they will become 14 inches long and they will block
the heart. Heartworms not only damage the heart and the arteries but, because
the rest of the body's organs are not getting as much blood as they normally
would, these other organs start to malfunction. This disease, if not prevented,
leads to congestive heart failure and death.

4   So now that we know what this disease is, how is this disease spread? It is
spread dog-to-dog by means of the mosquito. [Transparency #2] Now, let me
show you exactly how this works. Let's say the top dog there, that German shepherd, is infested with heartworm disease. That means that he does have the
adult worms living in his chest, in his heart, and he does have the microscopic
microfilaria traveling throughout his blood stream. A mosquito that comes
along and bites that German shepherd, looking for a meal, will ingest some of
that infected blood. Then when that mosquito goes along to another yard, or to
another neighborhood, or even a couple of miles away, when that mosquito
bites another dog, let's say that Dalmatian, that mosquito will inject that dog
with the infected microfilaria. That Dalmatian is now infected with this disease,
and in about six months he'll have the adult-size heartworms living in his heart.

This speech is published by permission of Karen Gemmer.

Karen's Preparation Outline

Title: "Canine Heartworm Disease" by Karen Gemmer
Exact Purpose: After listening to my speech, the audience will be aware of the existence of heartworm disease and know how to prevent it.

	Type of Source
FOCUS:	
• **Attention-getter:** What I am holding in my hand—in this jar—is a dog's heart. And this heart is completely infested with worms. This dog died from a very debilitating and deadly disease called Canine Heartworm Disease.	
• **Credibility:** At one time, when I thought I was going to be a veterinarian, I worked as a technician for a veterinarian. According to the journals I've read and the doctors I've talked to . . .	Interviews, Ref. #3
• **Audience motivation:** Approximately fifty percent or one out of every two dogs in our state that are unprotected against this disease will develop it. Now, that's the bad news. The good news is—for you dog owners and future dog owners— that this disease is entirely preventable.	

LEAD-IN
• **Purpose:** There are three main points that I'd like to cover today about heartworm disease and they are:
• **Preview:** 1) What exactly is this disease? **[Transparency #1]**
       2) How is it spread?
       3) How can it be prevented?

ORGANIZED BODY with SUPPORTS   Ref. #4
  I. **What is heartworm disease?**
    A. A parasite in the heart and adjacent blood vessels
      [Infected dog heart]
    B. Facts about adult heartworms [Explanation]
      1. 14 inches long
      2. Seven-year life span
      3. Up to 250 in heart at one time
      4. Microscopic offspring called microfilaria
    C. Damage to heart, arteries, and other organs
    D. Results: congestive heart failure and death

  [Transition:] So now that you know what this disease is, how is this disease spread?

(continued)

This disease is rapidly spreading throughout the United States. The area of the most heavy infestation is still the eastern states, as well as the southern states, and that definitely includes us. It has spread to all fifty states now, and it has even been documented in Canada.

5   Now that you realize how easily heartworm disease is spread, exactly how can we prevent this disease? There is a very easy way to do this and that's by means of a monthly medication. It's called heartworm preventative. What this medication does is actually kill, not the adult heartworms, but the microfilaria in the dog. What that means is, you can't stop the mosquitos from biting your

Karen's Preparation Outline
(continued)

II. **How is heartworm disease spread?**
   A. Spread from dog to dog by mosquito [Explanation and
      hypothetical instance]
   B. After bite, six months from microfilaria to adult worms
      [Transparency #2] [Explanation of disease cycle]
   C. Speading rapidly
      1. Disease found in all 50 states and Canada
      2. Heavy infestation in eastern and southern states

   [Transition:] Now that you know how easily heartworm disease
   is spread, exactly how can we prevent it?

III. **How is heartworm disease prevented?**
   A. Monthly medication [Explanation]
   B. Prescription from veterinarian

WRAP-UP
- **Summary:** Let's just review real fast what we have covered. All
  right, we know that this is a disease that affects the heart, as well
  as other body organs, and it's caused by a parasite. It is spread by
  the mosquito and it's very easily prevented by a monthly
  medication. **[Transparency #3]**
- **Refocus:** I have two dogs . . . [personal instance of healthy dogs].
  Because heartworm disease will strike one of every two dogs here
  in our state if they are unprotected, right now either Robin or
  Willie would have heartworm disease. So what I would like you to
  remember from today is that this disease is out there, and it is
  deadly. But if the medication is given conscientiously every month,
  it is entirely preventable.

Ref. #2

Ref. #1, pp. 1–4

Personal
observation

References: [APA editorial style]
1. American Heartworm Society. (1993). *American heartworm society recommended procedures for the diagnosis and management of heartworm infection.* Batavia, IL: American Heartworm Society.
2. Knight, D. H. (1987). Heartworm infection. In R. B. Grieve (ed.), *The veterinary clinics of North America: Vol. 17. Small animal practice* (pp. 1463–1518). New York: W. B. Sanders.
3. Personal interviews with Roger Kendrick, DVM, Eastern Hills Pet Hospital, and Gary Thayer, DVM, MS, Animal Internal Medicine Clinic.
4. Rawlings, C. A., and Calvert, C. A. (1995). Heartworm disease. In S. J. Ettinger and E. C. Feldman (eds.), *Textbook of veterinary internal medicine: Vol. I. Diseases of the dog and cat* (pp. 1046–1068). New York: W. B. Sanders.

dog, it's just going to happen. And you can't stop the mosquitos that are carrying the microfilaria from injecting it into your dog. But what you can do is kill the microfilaria, and that's what the preventative does. It stops the microfilaria from developing into the adult-size heartworms. It is a prescription medication that you do need to get from your veterinarian.

6   There is a lot more information on this disease that I wish I had the time to tell you. There's a lot of things that I think every dog lover should know about, but I do think we have covered the basics pretty well. Let's just review real fast what we have covered. All right, [Transparency #3] we know that this is a dis-

ease that affects the heart, as well as other body organs, and it's caused by a parasite. It is spread by the mosquito and it's very easily prevented by a monthly medication.

7   I have two dogs. One's a six-year-old Labrador retriever named Willie, and the other one is a German shepherd named Robin and he's thirteen years old, which in people terms means he's somewhere in his eighties. I really and truly believe that the reason he has lived so long and is doing so well is that he's had good, preventive health care all his life. Because heartworm disease will strike one out of every two dogs here in our state if they are unprotected, that means if I had not given my dogs their monthly preventative, right now either Robin or Willie would have heartworm disease. So what I would like you to remember from today is that this disease is out there, and it is deadly, but if the monthly medication is given conscientiously every month, it is entirely preventable.

8   Thank you for your attention.

Plutonium 238: NASA's Fuel of Choice

by Jenny Clanton, student and oratory winner

Jenny placed first in the Interstate Oratorical Association speech contest in
Salem, Oregon, on May 6–8, 1988.

1   On January 28, 1986, the American Space Program suffered the worst disaster in its more than 30-year history. The entire world was shocked when the space shuttle *Challenger* exploded seconds after lift-off, claiming the lives of seven brave astronauts and crippling our entire space agenda. I suppose the oldest cliché in our culture, spoken on battlegrounds and indeed virtually anywhere Americans die, is "We must press forward, so we can say they did not die in vain." Rest assured. They didn't. The deaths of our seven astronauts probably saved the lives of untold thousands of Americans.

2   For, you see, if the O-rings had not failed on January 28, 1986, but rather on May 20, 1987, the next scheduled shuttle launch, in the words of Dr. John Gofman, Professor Emeritus at the University of California at Berkeley, you could have "kissed Florida goodbye."

3   Because the next shuttle, the one that was to have explored the atmosphere of Jupiter was to carry 47 lbs. of Plutonium 238, which, is again, according to Dr. Gofman, the most toxic substance on the face of the earth. Dr. Helen Caldicott corroborates Dr. Gofman's claim in her book, *Nuclear Madness,* when she cites studies estimating one ounce of widely dispersed Plutonium 238 particles as having the toxicity to induce lung cancer in every person on earth.

4   Today, when you leave this room, I want you to fully understand just what impact NASA's plans could have on this planet. I want you to become cynical. I want you to be a little scared. I want you to become angry. But most of all, I want you to begin to demand some answers.

From *Winning Orations*, 1988, pp. 24–27. Reprinted by permission of the Interstate Oratorical Association. Reprinted from *Vital Speeches* 55 (1 April 1989), 375–376. By permission.

5   To move you in this direction I would first like to explore with you just what plutonium is and what could happen if it were released in our atmosphere. Second, let's consider NASA's argument for the safety of the plutonium as used in the shuttle program. And finally, I want to convince you that NASA's conclusions are flawed.

6   So now, let's turn our attention to the nature of plutonium. Plutonium is a man-made radioactive element which is produced in large quantities in nuclear reactors from uranium. Plutonium is a chemically reactive metal which, if exposed to air, ignites spontaneously and produces fine particles of plutonium dioxide. These particles, when dispersed by wind and inhaled by living organisms, lodge in the lungs. Lung cancer will follow—sooner or later. Once inside the human body, plutonium rests in bone tissue, causing bone cancer. Plutonium 238 is so poisonous that less than one *millionth* of a gram is a carcinogenic dose.

7   Last July, *Common Cause* magazine contacted Dr. Gofman at Berkeley and asked him to place Plutonium 238 in perspective. Before I share Dr. Gofman's assessment, please understand he's no poster-carrying "anti-nuke." Dr. Gofman was co-discoverer of Uranium 233, and he isolated the isotope first used in nuclear bombs. Dr. Gofman told Karl Grossman, author of the article "Redtape and Radio-activity" that Plutonium 238 is 300 times more radioactive than Plutonium 239, which is the isotope used in atomic bombs.

8   Dr. Richard Webb, a Nuclear Physicist and author of *The Accident Hazards of Nuclear Power Plants*, said in a similar interview that sending 46.7 lbs of Plutonium 238 into space would be the equivalent of sending five nuclear reactors up—and then hoping they wouldn't crash or explode.

9   Dr. Gofman's final assessment? It's a crazy idea, unless—unless shuttle launches are 100 percent perfect. Which is just about what NASA would have liked us to believe, and at first glance NASA's guarantees are pretty convincing.

10   NASA estimates the chance of releasing Plutonium into the environment, because of the possibility of a malfunction of the space shuttle, at .002%—that's not quite 100% perfect, but it's awfully close. NASA and the Department of Energy base their reliability figures on three factors: 1) the Titan 34D launch vehicle and its high success rate, 2) Energy Department officials in the March 10th *Aviation Week and Space Technology* magazine explain that the Plutonium would be safely contained in an unbreakable, quarter-inch thick iridium canister which would withstand pressures of over 2,000 pounds per square inch, and 3) in that same article, NASA explains there is "little public danger" because the Plutonium on board would be in the form of oxide pellets, each one-inch in diameter. If you'll remember, the danger of Plutonium is in fine particles.

11   Now, let's take a second glance. One month later, the April 28th issue of *Aviation Week and Space Technology* reported that two of the last nine Titans launched have blown-up. Two failures in nine trips is great in baseball, but not when we're dealing with nuclear payloads. That same article estimates loss of orbiter and crew, not at .002% but at 1 in 25.

12   With odds on the launch vehicle reduced to 1 in 25, the dual questions arise: just how breach-proof is that canister and, in a worst case scenario, what

could happen if the pellets of 238 were released? For the answers to those questions we go to Dr. Gary Bennett, former Director of Safety and Nuclear Operations, who not only answers those questions, but also explains why NASA is so insistent on using Plutonium.

13   Last July, Dr. Bennett told *Common Cause* that there is concern within NASA and the Department of Energy that an explosion aboard the *Galileo* spacecraft, a *Titan* or other rocket, would, in turn, set off an explosion of the booster rockets. Bennett admitted that government tests in 1984 and 1985 determined that if the shuttle exploded, and then the booster rockets exploded, there would be a likelihood of breaching the iridum canister. The Plutonium would then be vaporized and released into the environment; and there goes Florida.

14   But why would NASA take such a risk? It's really quite simple. On the one hand, Plutonium 238 is the one fuel that would enable space exploration beyond the limit of Mars. Without it, distant space exploration must wait for research to develop an equally effective, safe fuel. On the other hand, a worst case scenario would create the worst nuclear accident in history. In short, NASA weighed exploration now against the chances for disaster and opted to take the risk. The only problem is, I really don't like the idea of someone risking my life without consulting me—and I hope you don't either. By the way, there is evidence that NASA and the Department of Energy have projected some pretty horrible figures. Under the Freedom of Information Act rules, Karl Grossman was able to obtain agencies' estimates for the number of lives lost in a major accident. The only problem there is, every reference to the number of people affected is blanketed out with liquid paper and the term Exempt #1 is written over the deletion. James Lombardo of the Energy Department explains the white-outs were necessary for—you've got it—national security reasons. I would contend the national security would be threatened by mass anger over the callousness of the Energy Department, and justifiably so. Representative Edward Markey agrees, and when he was head of the House sub-committee on Energy, Conservation and Power, he uncovered most of the information I share with you today.

15   In a telephone interview last August, I asked Congressman Markey three questions: Why hasn't Congress done anything? What should be done? What can we do to help?

16   His answer to the first question was quite interesting. You may remember that shortly after the shuttle exploded and just when Congress was showing some interest in a thorough investigation of the space program, another larger, even more dramatic accident occurred—Chernobyl. The attention to Chernobyl as it related to our own power industry captured not only the attention of most Americans, but of Congress as well. Consequently, most of our nuclear experts are involved in working with Congress and the nuclear power industry.

17   And while Congress is focusing on one facet of the nuclear question, NASA and the Department of Energy are receiving much less attention. Which is why Congressman Markey helped found Space Watch.

18   Representative Markey is of the opinion that hysteria accomplishes nothing, but that all space [exploration] should be halted [until] either Plutonium

238 can be made safe, which is highly unlikely, or until an alternative fuel can be found. The burden of proof should be on NASA to prove a fuel safe, and not on the public to prove it dangerous.

19   This is where you and I come in. First, if by now you are sufficiently scared or angry, contact Space Watch through Representative Markey's office. Then, keep abreast of developments and exert pressure through your elected officials if Congress does nothing to interfere with NASA's plans. Send your objections not only to your own legislators, but to Representative Markey as well. Allow him to walk into the House with mailbag after mailbag of letters in opposition to NASA's unbridled desire to go to Jupiter. We have a friend in Congress who solicits help. The least we can do is give it to him.

20   One last thought: as of November, Plutonium 238 is *still* NASA's and the Department of Energy's fuel of choice. Dr. Bennett's last words in that July interview were, "I think you should understand there's a degree of risk with any kind of launch vehicle." But isn't that the point?

Persuasive Speeches

▼ ▼ ▼

The Death Penalty

by Wimberly Waldroup, student

Through logical reasoning, emotional appeal, and a look at arguments on both sides of the issue, Wimberly attempts to persuade her classroom audience.

1   Let the punishment fit the crime. Let the punishment fit the crime! That's what we Americans in today's society say. But what is the proper punishment for a certain crime? Is it written somewhere in some sacred book? I'm sorry to say that it is not. Capital punishment has become a subject of increasing debate through the years because of this reason. The research I've done on the death penalty for this and other classes has convinced me that it plays an important role in society.

2   I believe that the death penalty is a civilized and moral form of punishment and that it also possesses deterrent effects that protect our society. [Transparency #1]

3   To begin with, the death penalty is civilized. Murderers with a long string of heinous crimes deserve to be executed, because execution comprises the only suitable and civilized form of punishment. Professor Ernest Van den Haag in his book, *Punishing Criminals, Concerning a Very Old and Painful Question*, states, and I quote, "In capital crimes the law may inflict, as punishment on the criminal, the same physical act that constituted his crime." And that is true. If life is composed of the ultimate of goods, then death must be the greatest of punishments, and therefore appropriate in the taking of life. They balance each other

This speech is published by permission of Wimberly Waldroup.

out. What one person does to another person—what one person strips from another person, that too should be taken from him.

4   Capital punishment is a moral punishment in that it serves the function of retribution in our society. Society does not want criminals to get away with what they do. They do not want savage acts to be performed, and they express this through retribution for these acts. The retribution function of capital punishment was discussed by Lord Justice Denning before the British Royal Commission on capital punishment, and he stated, and I quote, "The punishment inflicted for grave crimes should adequately reflect the revulsion felt by the great majority of citizens for them. The ultimate justification of any punishment is that it is the emphatic denunciation by the community of a crime. And there are some murders that demand the most emphatic denunciation of all; namely, the death penalty."

5   Not only is the death penalty civilized and moral, but it also possesses deterrent effects which protect our society. In an article in the *Lincoln Review* summer 1986 edition, entitled "Capital Punishment, An Idea Whose Time Has Come Again," Professor Isaac Ehrlich argues, "There can be little doubt about the ability of the death penalty to deter. Each additional execution prevents about seven or eight people from committing murder." Why is this the case? This is the case because it instills inside criminals the mental resistance against such crimes. People will think twice about committing the act of murder if they believe that the form of punishment they are going to receive is the taking of their own life.

6   With regard to statistical evidence on the deterrence and the threat of capital punishment, there is no such data. You cannot determine the number of people who have been deterred by the threat of capital punishment. And because of this we must place great weight on the objective opinion of law enforcement officials who deal directly with these murders and potential murders every day within our system. And the vast majority of these people have said that the threat of the death penalty does deter these criminals from committing acts of murder. Sheriff Peter Pitchess of L.A. County testified before the California City Committee on the judiciary, and I quote, "I can tell you that the overwhelming majority of people in law enforcement, the ones who are seeing them not as statistics but as real live human beings, are overwhelmingly convinced that capital punishment is a deterrent."

7   Now, there are some arguments against the death penalty. And one such argument involves the deterrence of it. [Transparency #2] Supporters against the death penalty say that most acts of murder are done in the act of passion and that no kind of penalty can deter these acts. But although this is true that some homicides are committed in the act of passion, there are many, many that are premeditated, thought-out and planned. And these people know what they are doing when they do it. Moreover it is logical to think that even in the act of passion these people know in the back of their heads somewhere that they are going to get in trouble for what they are doing.

8   Now we have seen that capital punishment is a moral and civilized form of punishment, and that it does possess deterrent effects. Victims of violent crimes

and the families of these victims need justice from our court system and not lenient treatment shown to these criminals.

9   Thank you.

Protecting Youth from the Tobacco Industry
2,000 Year-Old Lessons for the Year 2000

by Lonnie R. Bristow, M.D., Chair, Board of Trustees, American Medical Association

Delivered at Indiana University, Bloomington, Indiana, January 25, 1994.

1   Good evening. I'm honored to be part of this commemoration, a celebration, if you will, of the first Surgeon General's Report on Smoking and Health exactly 30 years ago.

Joycelyn Elders, I'm sure, told you that a new report will be out next month. And a few days before that, the Journal of the American Medical Association will publish a special edition devoted entirely to smoking.

So your timing is perfect. You're just "ahead of the wave," and I can't tell you how proud I am to join forces with an audience whose efforts are crucial to the ongoing battle.

This university has long been on the front lines in the war against tobacco. I was pleased to hear you've become the first campus in the Big 10 to go virtually smoke-free.

5   But you know, when most people around the country think of Indiana University, they have an image of big time basketball and a certain big time basketball coach; perhaps eccentric, definitely with his own ways, but obviously one of the great basketball coaches in history.

This we know about him for certain: Bob Knight knows how to win.

His genius is the ability to instill his winning attitude in his teams. And then to let them ride that attitude to victory.

This doesn't happen by accident, and tonight I'm going to let you in one of Coach Knight's secrets.

He uses a book. It's not a coach's book. It's not a play book. It's a book about war, and it's 2,000 years old. It's called *The Art of War*, and it was written by Sun Tzu.

10   And if you'll indulge me, I'm going to steal a page from Coach Knight's secret little book and apply some of Sun Tzu's 2,000-year-old lessons to the Year 2000, because I believe that taking on the tobacco industry means nothing less than war.

So what does Sun Tzu say that can help us today? Let me tell you, because there is much that we can learn, and use.

First, Sun Tzu writes that you must assess the nature of any battle you plan to be part of. So listen to what we're up against.

I ask you to check your watches. Because in this hour, by the time I'm done speaking, 50 Americans will die from smoke-related diseases. By the time you

Reprinted from *Vital Speeches* 60 (15 March 1994), 333–336. By permission.

Note: Only every fifth paragraph of this speech is numbered.

sit down to breakfast in the morning, 600 more will have joined them; 8,400 by the end of the week—every week, every month, every year—until it kills nearly half-a-million Americans, year in, year out.

That's more than all the other preventable causes of death combined. Alcohol, illegal drugs, AIDS, suicide, car accidents, fires, guns—all are killers. But tobacco kills more than all of them put together.

15 These are hard, cold realities, defined by hard, cold statistics. But I'd ask you to remember this most important fact:

Every statistic is an encoded memorial to what was once a living, breathing—loving and loved—mother, father, sister, brother. Not numbers, real people, and the toll is as terrible as the most horrific war.

And don't for a minute think that the tobacco industry doesn't take these deaths seriously. They have to, because hundreds of customers are dying every day. And just like in war, they need fresh bodies to replace the old ones.

So the industry is waging an all-out war of their own for new recruits. And they will spend four billion dollars this year to promote their products.

A big chunk of that money is aimed at the hearts and minds of our kids. And they're hitting their target—some 3,000 kids start smoking every day. The average age is 12-and-a-half years.

20 If we don't get our message to them by the sixth grade—it's too late.

This, then, is the terrain of our battlefield. The landscape is littered with bodies wracked with pain, productive years cut short, friends and relatives buried before their time.

So let's go back to Sun Tzu, who tells us also that to succeed in battle, we must know the enemy.

He writes: "It is said that if you know the enemy and know yourself, you will not be imperiled in a hundred battles."

Make no mistake—our enemy is powerful. When it comes to pushing their products on our kids, the tobacco industry is creative, clever, cunning and constant.

25 Let me paint you a picture. A group of tobacco industry and advertising executives are sitting around a polished board room table. It's their "war room."

They're excited about the results of their latest ad campaign—it's been a tremendous success, one of the greatest before and after stories in tobacco history.

Before the ads, they were reaching less than one-half of one percent of their target market. But after the ads, that number skyrocketed to 33 percent.

Profits skyrocketed, too. Before the ads, sales of their product were about $6 million. After, sales approached $500 million. From six million to 500 million.

Sounds like one of the most brilliant ad campaigns in history, doesn't it? You're right. It is.

30 It's the Joe Camel Campaign, produced in the war room of RJR Nabisco. And the market they've targeted is children, kids under 18.

The sales they're pitching are illegal, and it ought to be illegal for them to even make the pitch.

But while Joe Camel is just the most obvious of tobacco's ploys, it's only one of many.

In 1981, the Federal Trade Commission forced cigarette manufacturers to reveal how they target kids. Their strategy was predictably cynical: Put a happy face on a killer. Link tobacco use to good times, good looks, popularity, independence and adventure.

You don't have to be a psychiatrist, or run an ad agency, to know that these are characteristics that most seductively appeal to kids and adolescents.

35   And to make sure they really hook them, the industry's bought its way into the world of sports. It's a rare race, game or tournament that isn't plastered with promotions, posters and ads.

Let me tell you a story about how far-reaching their power is.

Greg Louganis is perhaps the greatest diver in history. He's also a former smoker, and he tells how he began training for the 1988 Olympics, after already having won gold medals in '84.

He sought out the finest diving center in the country. While he was training, he was asked to chair the Great American Smokeout Campaign. You know, where they ask everyone to stop smoking for one day.

Louganis took the job. But there was one big problem. His training center was owned by Philip Morris. And in the time it takes to light up, his coach was on him in a flash: Drop the campaign, or drop out of training.

40   Louganis says he was young, he wanted to win—so he stayed with the Philip Morris center and left the Smokeout Campaign behind.

Greg's experience shows how insidious the tobacco industry can be. You can almost begin believing that they're everywhere, and you just might be right!

Now you know the enemy.

They've got deep pockets, long tentacles and an iron grip.

In the face of such an enemy, what can we do? How can we fight? How can we win?

45   Once again, let's turn back to Coach Knight's book of warfare. Sun Tzu says: "The rule of military operations is not to count on opponents not coming—but to rely on having ways of dealing with them" to secure victory through a variety of strategies.

So let me suggest five strategies for the American public that will take the war to the tobacco industry.

One: Attack all forms of tobacco advertising and promotion. Pack the camel off to the desert. Put the lie to their big lie.

Last year the AMA ran a contest for kids called "Just Say No to Old Joe." We wanted to get teachers and kids and classrooms involved. We had no idea what the response would be—until we received more than 175,000 posters, poems and essays from kids in every corner of the country who wanted to fight back against Joe Camel.

That tells me that there's a tremendous energy against tobacco out there, and it's just waiting to be tapped.

50   Banning ads from TV and radio back in the 60s was a start, but here we are, a generation later, and, still, we need to do more, like restrict tobacco to

tombstone ads—that would be appropriate, wouldn't it?—no models, no water-falls, no slogans, no color.

Ban billboards and other forms of ads from the arenas, the stadiums, the ballparks frequented by our kids. Persuade the government to sponsor counter ads. Keep up the drumbeat of danger to our kids. Convince them that there is no cachet to tobacco addiction.

Strategy Number Two: Get tough on access and availability.

Kids today can get tobacco products anywhere, anytime. Supermarkets, convenience stores, gas stations, vending machines—and no one pays attention to the laws that are supposed to prevent kids from buying them.

In tests around the country, minors prove they can get away with buying cigarettes three-quarters of the time. In Massachusetts, 11-year-olds were able to buy cigarettes three-quarters of the time.

55 And the industry that proclaims they don't want minors to smoke fights tooth and nail against laws that would restrict access in any way.

What can we do? For openers, take a look at tiny Woodridge, Illinois, in the western suburbs of Chicago.

In 1989, police and city officials in Woodridge drafted a law to control ciga-rettes—just like liquor. The law had provisions for licensing and enforcement. Vendors paid $50 for a license. The police set up stings to check for compliance.

If a store was caught selling to minors, they could have their license sus-pended and be fined up to $500—and that's for a first offense. Penalties in-creased after that. And kids caught with cigarettes also got a $25 ticket.

The law had a tremendous impact. Because penalties were tough, mer-chants complied. And just a year after the law went into effect, the number of kids who said they'd tried smoking was cut in half. The number who said they were regular smokers was cut by two-thirds.

60 So, here's a proven tactic in the fight against tobacco. Slap merchants on the wrist, and nothing will change. But hit them in their pocketbooks, and watch how fast they stop selling to kids. And put real teeth in the law, and you'll cut access and smoking.

Strategy Number Three: Raise taxes.

This one is simple. Kids have less money than adults. Raise the price high enough, and fewer kids will buy cigarettes.

That's exactly what happened in Canada. Between 1984 and 1991, cigarette taxes quadrupled, and teen smoking was cut in half.

Today, the United States is 19th among developed countries in taxing ciga-rettes. We can do better.

65 The AMA has called for a federal tax of $2 on every pack of cigarettes. Our main argument: Two bucks a pack will save thousands of lives.

But there's another nice advantage: we'll raise a lot of money—money the AMA would like to see used to help pay for health care for those who can't af-ford it on their own.

Here's Strategy Number Four: Improve health education in schools.

Anti-tobacco education should be systematic, age-specific and constant. Some schools don't undertake any health or drug education. And many that do, piggy-back tobacco onto their drug programs and don't emphasize it.

We want smoking and health to be an integral part of the curriculum—starting in kindergarten—so we can get to them before Joe Camel does.

70   Finally, Strategy Number Five: Keep up the pressure to change social norms against smoking.

We've already come a long way. Just ask those lonely smokers huddled in the doorways of buildings that won't let them smoke inside.

Offices, theaters, college classrooms, airplanes, taxicabs: "Please, no smoking" is more and more the rule, if it isn't already the law.

We want laws that ban smoking from all buildings.

And, of course, the tobacco industry is fighting hard to slow our momentum.

75   The Environmental Protection Agency's recent listing of sidestream smoke as a Class A carcinogen has put the fear of God into them.

Last June, I testified in support of what the EPA wanted to do. I challenged any executive of the tobacco industry to walk with me through hospital cancer wards and meet the victims of their trade.

Did I get any takers? Not one. I'm still waiting for an answer.

And now OSHA—the federal occupational safety people—has a rule that says no worker should be exposed to any known carcinogen. My guess is that the first time a worker sues, that will close the door for smoking in the workplace—once, and for all.

But we can't wait to let the courts or the government define society's perception of smoking. We must let kids know now that it's not the norm.

80   Demystify tobacco; demythologize tobacco; derail tobacco. Or a whole new generation of young Americans will fall prey to the powerful persuasions of tobacco's relentless siren song.

If we can prevent them from starting in the first place, we prevent thousands of people from dying early.

Don't forget, tobacco is an equal opportunity killer. In fact, this war is especially savage in minority communities and against minority children. And it is there, more than anyplace, that we need to put our strategies to work on the streets where they'll do the most good.

One complication is that tobacco is far down the list of crisis priorities. Economic and social issues take precedence, and, perhaps, rightly so.

Nevertheless, smoking kills almost 50,000 African Americans every year. African Americans suffer a higher incidence of respiratory diseases and cancers due to smoking than whites, and we die from those diseases more often.

85   These problems are made worse because many minorities have fewer resources with which to fight the problem. Minority communities are especially vulnerable—the kinds of targets that make tobacco executives rub their hands with glee.

You're five times more likely to see billboards pushing tobacco in African American neighborhoods than in white neighborhoods; half-again as likely to see cigarette ads in African American magazines as in general market magazines; and more likely to see tobacco as the main sponsor of minority community events.

That support comes at an awful price. It strangles the debate. It's successful because many minority organizations struggle to find funding—and the tobacco industry is more than happy to fill the gap.

How, then, can we protect our minority communities?

First, we need more data. The federal government should encourage states to do what they don't do now: Collect specific data on tobacco cessation efforts in African American, Hispanic, Asian and Native-American communities.

90 Next, there must be a greater effort at education. We must develop programs and materials that:

▶ Are tailored to minority tobacco-use patterns;

▶ Are sensitive to the special obstacles facing their communities;

▶ And make people aware of the dangers of tobacco and the tobacco industry.

Then, we need leadership. Demand that our elected leaders give the issue the attention it requires. Demand that our leaders work within the community on tobacco control. We need community-based organizations to lead the charge.

Finally, put into effect the five broad strategies I talked about earlier. Cut advertising. Restrict access. Increase cigarette taxes. Make tobacco part of every curriculum.

And do our damnedest to give tobacco the image it deserves. Not fun, but risk. Not pleasure, but disease. Not adventure, but death.

The fight, by the way, is not without its successes.

95 In 1989, RJR's marketing gurus came up with Uptown, a cigarette targeted specifically at African Americans.

The campaign was undeniably exploitive, undeniably racist.

But a coalition of church leaders, community organizations and academics joined forces and forced RJR to withdraw Uptown from the market. It's a good model of how, working together, we can defeat the tobacco industry.

It won't be easy, and it won't be quick. The tobacco industry is in for the long haul. We must be, too.

The Robert Woods Johnson Foundation recently asked the AMA to administer a $10 million grant to help 18 states develop tobacco control and prevention programs. We'll roll that out this summer.

100 And the Centers for Disease Control and National Cancer Institute are working with other states to develop similar programs.

We're also supporting several anti-tobacco initiatives in Congress. One bill would ban smoking in all public places and work places. The Synar Amendment would put teeth in youth access laws. And, of course, next month's special edition of the Journal of the AMA.

But the most important foot soldiers in this war are young men and women just like the people sitting in this room tonight.

Educate your parents, your classmates, your friends. Write and call your local or state politicians and your members of Congress.

Tell them to support the $2 tax. Tell them to support restrictions of tobacco advertising. Tell them to stand up to the tobacco industry.

105 Tell them they have a responsibility, even an obligation, to the American people to stand up to the tobacco lobby. And then tell them that you're going to hold them accountable for what they do— and what they don't do!

Sun Tzu says: "When the speed of rushing water reaches the point where it can move boulders, this is the force of momentum."

The tobacco industry is a mountainous boulder that will do everything it can to resist being moved. But we're beginning to see some strains, some cracks, some fissures in the rock. Our side is gaining momentum.

Each of us in this room tonight is only a small drop of water. But if we gather together, we can become a tidal wave that can sweep away this boulder, and save the lives of our kids.

I'm reminded of some words written by Frederick Douglass—a warrior of a different sort, from a different time.

110 This is what he said more than a hundred years ago: "The iron gate of our prison stands half open . . . one gallant rush will fling it wide."

This moment in time may not come again. It is ours to seize with one gallant rush. Let us begin now.

Successful Strategies for Achieving Your Career Goals
Write Them, Review Them, Achieve Them

by Virgis Colbert, Vice President, Plant Operations, Miller Brewing Company

Delivered to the Southeastern Wisconsin Black MBA Planning Council, Milwaukee, Wisconsin, September 21, 1993.

1 Thank you for inviting me to spend some time with you this evening. As requested, I'd like to share some thoughts with you on "Successful Strategies for Achieving Your Career Goals."

2 Someone once asked *James Lofton*, wide-receiver for the Buffalo Bills, what tricks he used to achieve success. *Lofton* replied, "One trick is to work harder than the other guy. The second trick, always hustle. Third trick, study and know what you're doing. Fourth trick, always be prepared. Fifth, never give up. *Those are my tricks.*"

3 What *Lofton* was really saying is that there are no "*tricks*" for getting ahead, but there are some very basic fundamentals of hard work and planning that can give each of us a competitive edge, if we use them.

4 I believe one of the most important fundamentals is the importance of setting goals. If I had to boil my advice about goals down to one short set of *3 bullet points*, I'd say:

▶ *First*, set very *specific* goals;

▶ *Second*, *write down* those goals; and

▶ Third, *review* them and *work toward* their accomplishment on a *daily* basis.

5 Let's review those three points very quickly.

6 The first point is to *set very specific goals*. Someone once defined a goal as "a dream with a deadline."

Reprinted from *Vital Speeches* 60 (15 December 1993), 141–143.

7   Many people have high ambitions and want to achieve success, but they never get around to defining *specifically* what they want to achieve, what *specific* position they want to fill, or what *specific* expertise they want to develop that will set them apart from their competition.

8   A goal gives you something to aim for, and not even the greatest marksmen in the world can demonstrate their shooting skill . . . until they have a target.

9   A great philosopher once said that "No wind is a fair wind if you don't know the port for which you are headed." So *strategy number one is: set a specific goal;* don't be a "wandering generality." It's much more effective in life to be a "meaningful specific" than a "wandering generality."

10   The *second strategy* is to have the courage to *write down your goals.* Many people are afraid to actually write out their goals because they are afraid they will fail to reach them, and in later years someone else may see those goals and poke fun at them for having such high ambitions.

11   We should never be afraid to set high, ambitious goals.

12   As Ralph Waldo Emerson said: "What lies *behind* us, and what lies *in front* of us, pales in significance when compared to what lies *within us.*"

13   There is a powerful, somewhat mysterious force generated when you write down your goals and frequently review them. It fixes these goals in your conscious and subconscious mind in such a way that almost everything you do will tend to move you, however slightly or subtly toward the actual realization of those goals. Things will begin to fall into place and pieces of the jigsaw puzzle of life will start to fill in the gaps.

14   Let me illustrate the power of the force that can be released when you write down your goals. A study of Yale University graduates in *1953* found that *only 3 percent* of them wrote down their goals in life. This includes actually:

- ▶ Listing their objectives
- ▶ Setting a time limit for accomplishing each goal
- ▶ Listing the people or organizations who could help them achieve these goals
- ▶ Listing the obstacles that would have to be overcome
- ▶ Spelling out what they need to know in order to achieve this goal
- ▶ Developing a plan of action, and
- ▶ Spelling out why they wanted to achieve each goal.

15   The rest of the graduating students didn't bother to write down their goals.

16   *Twenty years later,* a follow-up study revealed that *the 3 percent who had written down their goals were worth more financially than all the other 97 percent combined.*

17   That clearly illustrates the power of written goals.

18   *My third strategy* is to *review and work toward those goals on a daily basis.* That enables you to see whether you are on track to achieving them or whether you need to make some adjustments.

19   It's like the navigator of a great ship setting off on an ocean voyage. The navigator will lay out the track on a large chart, showing all the points along which the ship is to travel. This track will be frequently updated by navigational fixes, showing where the ship actually is in relation to the desired track.

20   If winds and current have blown the ship off course, it is often necessary to steer 10 degrees to the right or left in order to come back on track. It's the same in life, where we have to adjust our actions in order to get back on track and realize our goals.

21   So my first advice is to *have specific goals*. Goals will add focus to your life. They will create activity and generate the kind of excitement you need to realize your full potential.

22   Goals enable you to build a solid foundation under your dreams.

23   In addition to setting goals, there are some other suggestions I have that should apply regardless of whether you are in the corporate, government or academic environment.

24   Regardless of your profession or field of interest, *demonstrate your interest in your job* by knowing as much as you can about the organization you work for. As I said earlier, develop a clear set of personal objectives for your career, but stay flexible so that you can adapt yourself—and your objectives—to organizational changes.

25   *Present yourself well*. Dress appropriately and be cognizant of verbal and non-verbal mannerisms. Learn both the written and unwritten rules of the work place. Learn how decisions for advancement are really made, and make the adjustments.

26   Bear in mind that it's important, although sometimes difficult, for minorities and females to distinguish between racial or gender slights and general work place practices. You can handle these situations without giving up your dignity or your principles.

27   In other words, *develop an understanding of the "work place game."* The business world and many areas of the public sector play hardball. This is not a kid's game!

28   Next, *don't be ruled by your emotions*. There is a perception among some people that minorities and women will operate from an emotional basis—that they wear their feelings on their sleeves. Disprove that stereotyped notion by using logical and analytical thinking to solve problems or work place slights. Maintain a positive attitude even when it's not easy to do so.

29   *Always think positively about yourself and your ability*. If you don't, no one else will. Even more importantly, if you do, you will find that in most cases people will take you as you see yourself. If you see yourself as confident and competent, then that's the way most people are going to treat you.

30   *Be disciplined;* always *strive for excellence* without excuse. Set high goals for yourself, and conform to work place rules and expectations, because it all starts with you.

31   *Become a full member of the organization*. Be aware of how others perceive you in a social and professional sense. This doesn't mean that you have to brown

nose, but you must make certain that you are meaningfully involved in your area of the organization.

32   I have already said a great deal about the importance of goals. Let me add this: *set goals for yourself that are higher than those goals your employer has set for you.* You'll never regret it.

33   You must *function both as individuals and as members of a team* in order to be successful in the work place. Dr. Martin Luther King Jr. recognized the value of teamwork. When accepting the Nobel Peace Prize in 1964, he said: "Every time I take a flight, I am always mindful of the many people who make a successful journey possible—the known pilots and unknown ground crew."

34   The Nobel Prize, he said, was being given to one of the pilots, but he was accepting it on behalf of the crew.

35   Make an early attempt to *select a mentor* to provide you guidance in your career. That person need not necessarily be within your work place. You may utilize indirect mentors by observing those individuals in your organization who are enjoying success, and you can pattern your performance after their best traits.

36   As African-Americans, I challenge you to *accept a larger share of the responsibility for your lives.* We cannot let obstacles of racism and oppression slow us down. We must overcome racism and not give in to it.

37   And finally, I ask each of you to accept as a personal responsibility that you should *give something back to your community* by contributing money or time to positive community initiatives. This enables you to help others as you have been helped.

38   There is no royal road to learning, and there is no easy path to success, but I believe that if you practice some of these strategies and techniques, you will find that they will never let you down.

39   I would conclude with some words from the President of the Metropolitan Milwaukee YMCA:

> "Watch you thoughts; they become words.
> Watch you words; they become actions.
> Watch your actions; they become habits.
> Watch your habits; they become character.
> Watch your character; it becomes your destiny."

Special Occasion Speeches

▼ ▼ ▼

Address to Departing Troops at Dhahran

by General H. Norman Schwarzkopf

Delivered March 18, 1991, to U.S. troops as they were departing for home.

1   It's a great day to be a soldier! Big Red One, First Team, Old Ironsides, Spear Head, Hell on Wheels platoon, Jay Hawk patrol, today you're going home. You're going home to Fort Riley, Kansas, you're going home to Fort Hood, Texas, you're going home to locations all over Germany. Your country, your countrymen, your wives, your children, and your loved ones are all there waiting for you.

2   You're all going home as part of the symbolic force of all the soldiers, of all sailors, of all the airmen, all the Marines, all the Coast Guard, all the National Guard, all the Reserves, all who took part in Operation Desert Shield and Desert Storm. And your comrades in arms will be following you.

3   Hopefully in the weeks to come or the months to come, the last remaining GIs will be returning themselves and all remaining equipment and supplies to the home station. But today you're going home.

4   I can hear the war stories now. Over Lone Star beer, over Colorado Kool-aid, over some great German beer, a fire water or two and what you drink the most, that Diet Pepsi and Coca Cola. I know what glorious war stories they are going to be.

5   Valiant charges by courageous men over 250 kilometers of enemy territory. Along with a force of over 1,500 tanks, almost 250 attack helicopters, over 48,500 pieces of military equipment, moving around, behind, and into the enemy and totally breaking his back and defeating him in 100 hours. It's a war story worth telling, and every one of you deserve to tell it.

6   I ask all of you when you tell that story, don't forget to tell the whole story. Don't forget to mention the great Air Force that prepared the way for you and was overhead the entire time you fought. Don't forget the great Navy pilots that were there and the great ships that were at sea that embargoed and kept the ammunition out of the hands of the enemy. And don't ever forget to say that the 1st Tank Division of the United Kingdom was protecting your right flank. And don't ever forget to say there was an Egyptian corps protecting their right flank, and there was a task force of Saudi Arabians protecting their right flank. And two divisions of Marines out there making a hard push into Kuwait City with a fine Saudi Arabian force protecting their flank. And don't ever forget to say in your story, there were Kuwaitis, Omanis, French Foreign Legion involved because you were part of the great coalition determined not to let a petty dictator no matter what size his army, no matter how many tanks he had, no matter how

Reprinted from Richard Pyle, *Schwartzkopf: The Man, the Mission, the Triumph* (New York: Signet, 1991), pp. 265–267.

many men he had armed. Despite the fact you were badly outnumbered, you were determined to show a petty dictator that they just can't get away with bullying his neighbors and taking what they want because they think they are so tough.

7   I think you not only proved that to one petty dictator but to any petty dictator anywhere in the world that should choose to try to pull the same stunt either in the near or far future.

8   So hopefully you'll tell that war story with a lot of pride in yourselves, but don't forget to make sure that everyone understands we did it as part of a joint team, as part of an international team. We did it together, we all paid the price, we all shared in the victory

9   You served in a place I'm sure none of you thought you'd serve. You've been places you never heard of, places you can't even pronounce. But you also better take back with you some free lessons that your family, friends, and the world can hear. You're going to take back the fact that the word *Arab* isn't a bad word. That you do not judge all Arabs by the actions of a few. And I know here that we have a close, wonderful, warm, and thankful people for us being here and have expressed that thanks in many different ways. And you're going to take back the fact there are many soldiers in this world and you worry about them and you greatly respect them. And you are going to take back the fact that Islam is not a religion to be feared, it's a religion to be respected just as we respect all other religions; that's the American way.

10   It's hard for me to put into words how proud I am of you. How proud I have been to be the commander of this war. I'm proud of you, your countries are proud of you, and the world's proud of you.

11   God bless you, God's speed for your trip home, and God bless America.

I Have a Dream

by Martin Luther King, Jr., preacher and civil rights activist

Delivered August 28, 1963, on the steps of the Lincoln
Memorial before 200,000 nonviolent civil rights demonstrators.

1   I am happy to join with you today in what will go down in history as the greatest demonstration for freedom in this history of our nation.

2   Five score years ago, a great American, in whose symbolic shadow we stand today, signed the Emancipation Proclamation. This momentous decree came as a great beacon light of hope to millions of Negro slaves, who had been seared in the flames of withering injustice. It came as a joyous daybreak to end the long night of their captivity.

3   But one hundred years later, the Negro is still not free. One hundred years later, the life of the Negro is still sadly crippled by the manacles of segregation

Reprinted by arrangement with the Heirs of the Estate of Martin Luther King, Jr., c/o Joan Daves Agency as agent for the proprietor. Copyright 1963 by Martin Luther King, Jr.; copyright renewed 1991 by Coretta Scott King.

and the chains of discrimination. One hundred years later, the Negro lives on a lonely island of poverty in the midst of a vast ocean of material prosperity. One hundred years later, the Negro is still languished in the corners of American society and finds himself an exile in his own land. So we have come here today to dramatize a shameful condition.

4   In a sense, we've come to our nation's Capitol to cash a check. When the architects of our republic wrote the magnificent words of the Constitution and the Declaration of Independence, they were signing a promissory note to which every American was to fall heir. This note was a promise that all men—yes, black men as well as white men—would be guaranteed the unalienable rights of life, liberty, and the pursuit of happiness.

5   It is obvious today that America has defaulted on this promissory note insofar as her citizens of color are concerned. Instead of honoring this sacred obligation, America has given the Negro people a bad check; a check which has come back marked "insufficient funds." But we refuse to believe that the bank of justice is bankrupt. We refuse to believe that there are insufficient funds in the great vaults of opportunity of this nation. So we've come to cash this check— a check that will give us upon demand the riches of freedom and the security of justice. We have also come to this hallowed spot to remind America of the fierce urgency of *now*. This is no time to engage in the luxury of cooling off to take the tranquilizing drug of gradualism. *Now is the time* to make real the promises of Democracy. *Now is the time* to rise from the dark and desolate valley of segregation to the sunlight of racial justice. *Now is the time* to lift our nation from the quicksands of racial injustice to the solid rock of brotherhood. *Now is the time* to make justice a reality for all of God's children.

6   It would be fatal for the nation to overlook the urgency of the moment. This sweltering summer of the Negro's legitimate discontent will not pass until there is an invigorating autumn of freedom and equality. Nineteen sixty-three is not an end, but a beginning. Those who hope that the Negro needed to blow off steam and will now be content will have a rude awakening if the nation returns to business as usual. There will be neither rest nor tranquillity in America until the Negro is granted his citizenship rights. The whirlwinds of revolt will continue to shake the foundations of our nation until the bright day of justice emerges.

7   But there is something that I must say to my people who stand on the warm threshold which leads into the palace of justice. In the process of gaining our rightful place we must not be guilty of wrongful deeds. Let us not seek to satisfy our thirst for freedom by drinking from the cup of bitterness and hatred.

8   We must forever conduct our struggle on the high plane of dignity and discipline. We must not allow our creative protest to degenerate into physical violence. Again and again we must rise to the majestic heights of meeting physical force with soul force. The marvelous new militancy which has engulfed the Negro community must not lead us to a distrust of all white people, for many of our white brothers, as evidenced by their presence here today, have come to realize that their destiny is tied up with our destiny. And they have come to realize that their freedom is inextricably bound to our freedom. We cannot walk alone.

9   And as we walk we must make the pledge that we shall always march ahead. We cannot turn back. There are those who ask the devotees of civil rights,

"When will you be satisfied?" We can never be satisfied as long as the Negro is the victim of the unspeakable horrors of police brutality. We can never be satisfied as long as our bodies, heavy with the fatigue of travel, cannot gain lodging in the motels of the highways and the hotels of the cities. We cannot be satisfied as long as the Negro's basic mobility is from a smaller ghetto to a larger one. We can never be satisfied as long as our children are stripped of their selfhood and robbed of their dignity by signs stating "For Whites Only." We cannot be satisfied as long as a Negro in Mississippi cannot vote and a Negro in New York believes he has nothing for which to vote. No, no, we are not satisfied, and we will not be satisfied until justice rolls down like waters and righteousness like a mighty stream.

10 I am not unmindful that some of you have come here out of great trials and tribulations. Some of you have come fresh from narrow jail cells. Some of you have come from areas where your quest for freedom left you battered by the storms of persecution and staggered by the winds of police brutality. You have been the veterans of creative suffering. Continue to work with the faith that unearned suffering is redemptive.

11 Go back to Mississippi, go back to Alabama, go back to South Carolina, go back to Georgia, go back to Louisiana, go back to the slums and ghettos of our Northern cities knowing that somehow this situation can and will be changed. Let us not wallow in the valley of despair.

12 I say to you today, my friends, so even though we face the difficulties of today and tomorrow, I still have a dream. It is a dream deeply rooted in the American dream.

13 I have a dream that one day this nation will rise up and live out the true meaning of its creed: "We hold these truths to be self-evident; that all men are created equal."

14 I have a dream that one day on the red hills of Georgia the sons of former slaves and the sons of former slaveowners will be able to sit down together at the table of brotherhood; I have a dream—

15 That one day even the state of Mississippi, a state sweltering with the heat of injustice, sweltering with the heat of oppression, will be transformed into an oasis of freedom and justice; I have a dream—

16 That my four little children will one day live in a nation where they will not be judged by the color of their skin but by the content of their character; I have a dream today.

17 I have a dream that one day down in Alabama with its vicious racists, with its governor having his lips dripping with the words of interposition and nullification, one day right there in Alabama little black boys and black girls will be able to join hands with little white boys and white girls as sisters and brothers; I have a dream today.

18 I have a dream that one day every valley shall be exalted, every hill and mountain shall be made low, and rough places will be made plane and crooked places will be made straight, and the glory of the Lord shall be revealed, and all flesh shall see it together.

19 This is our hope. This is the faith that I go back to the South with. With this faith we will be able to hew out of the mountain of despair a stone of hope.

20   With this faith we will be able to transform the jangling discords of our nation into a beautiful symphony of brotherhood. With this faith we will be able to work together, to pray together, to struggle together, to go to jail together, to stand up for freedom together, knowing that we will be free one day.

20   This will be the day. . . . This will be the day when all of God's children will be able to sing with new meaning. "My country 'tis of thee, sweet land of liberty of thee I sing. Land where my fathers died, land of the pilgrims' pride, from every mountainside, let freedom ring," and if America is to be a great nation— this must become true.

21   So let freedom ring—from the prodigious hilltops of New Hampshire, let freedom ring; from the mighty mountains of New York, let freedom ring—from the heightening Alleghenies of Pennsylvania!

22   Let freedom ring from the snowcapped Rockies of Colorado!
Let freedom ring from the curvaceous slopes of California!
But not only that; let freedom ring from Stone Mountain of Georgia!
Let freedom ring from Lookout Mountain of Tennessee!
Let freedom ring from every hill and molehill of Mississippi. From every mountainside, let freedom ring, and when this happens . . .

23   When we allow freedom to ring, when we let it ring from every village and every hamlet, from every state and every city, we will be able to speed up that day when all of God's children, black men and white men, Jews and Gentiles, protestants and Catholics, will be able to join hands and sing in the words of the old Negro spiritual, "Free at last! free at last! thank God almighty, we are free at last!"

Inaugural Address

by John F. Kennedy, 35th president of the United States

Kennedy's inaugural address, delivered on January 20, 1961, is admired for its powerful style, as well as for its brevity.

1   *Vice President Johnson, Mr. Speaker, Mr. Chief Justice, President Eisenhower, Vice President Nixon, President Truman, Reverend Clergy, Fellow Citizens:* We observe today not a victory of party but a celebration of freedom— symbolizing an end as well as a beginning—signifying renewal as well as change. For I have sworn before you and Almighty God the same solemn oath our forebears prescribed nearly a century and three quarters ago.

2   The world is very different now. For man holds in his mortal hands the power to abolish all forms of human poverty and all forms of human life. And yet the same revolutionary beliefs for which our forebears fought are still at issue around the globe—the belief that the rights of man come not from the generosity of the state but from the hand of God.

3   We dare not forget today that we are the heirs of that first revolution. Let the word go forth from this time and place, to friend and foe alike, that the torch

Reprinted from *Contemporary American Speeches*, 7th ed., by Richard L. Johannesen, R. R. Allen, and Wil A. Linkugel (Dubuque, Iowa: Kendall/Hunt, 1992), pp. 347–350.

has been passed to a new generation of Americans—born in this century, tempered by war, disciplined by a hard and bitter peace, proud of our ancient heritage—and unwilling to witness or permit the slow undoing of those human rights to which this nation has always been committed, and to which we are committed today, at home and around the world.

4   Let every nation know, whether it wishes us well or ill, that we shall pay any price, bear any burden, meet any hardship, support any friend, or oppose any foe to assure the survival and the success of liberty.

5   This much we pledge—and more.

6   To those old allies whose cultural and spiritual origins we share, we pledge the loyalty of faithful friends. United, there is little we cannot do in a host of cooperative ventures. Divided, there is little we can do—for we dare not meet a powerful challenge at odds and split asunder.

7   To those new states whom we welcome to the ranks of the free, we pledge our word that one form of colonial control shall not have passed away merely to be replaced by a far more iron tyranny. We shall not always expect to find them supporting our view.

8   But we shall always hope to find them strongly supporting their own freedom—and to remember that, in the past, those who foolishly sought power by riding the back of the tiger ended up inside.

9   To those people in the huts and villages of half the globe struggling to break the bonds of mass misery, we pledge our best efforts to help them help themselves, for whatever period is required—not because the Communists may be doing it, not because we seek their votes, but because it is right. If a free society cannot help the many who are poor, it cannot save the few who are rich.

10   To our sister republics south of our border, we offer a special pledge—to convert our good words into good deeds—in a new alliance for progress—to assist free men and free governments in casting off the chains of poverty. But this peaceful revolution of hope cannot become the prey of hostile powers. Let all our neighbors know that we shall join with them to oppose aggression or subversion anywhere in the Americas. And let every other power know that this hemisphere intends to remain the master of its own house.

11   To that world assembly of sovereign states, the United Nations, our last best hope in an age where the instruments of war have far outpaced the instruments of peace, we renew our pledge of support—to prevent it from becoming merely a forum for invective—to strengthen its shield of the new and the weak—and to enlarge the area in which its writ may run.

12   Finally, to those nations who would make themselves our adversary, we offer not a pledge but a request: That both sides begin anew the quest for peace, before the dark powers of destruction unleashed by science engulf all humanity in planned or accidental self-destruction.

13   We dare not tempt them with weakness. For only when our arms are sufficient beyond doubt can we be certain beyond doubt that they will never be employed.

14   But neither can two great and powerful groups of nations take comfort from our present course—both sides overburdened by the cost of modern weapons, both rightly alarmed by the steady spread of the deadly atom, yet both racing to alter that uncertain balance of terror that stays the hand of mankind's final war.

15   So let us begin anew—remembering on both sides that civility is not a sign of weakness, and sincerity is always subject to proof. Let us never negotiate out of fear. But let us never fear to negotiate.

16   Let both sides explore what problems unite us instead of belaboring those problems which divide us.

17   Let both sides, for the first time, formulate serious and precise proposals for the inspection and control of arms—and bring the absolute power to destroy other nations under the absolute control of all nations.

18   Let both sides seek to invoke the wonders of science instead of its terrors. Together let us explore the stars, conquer the deserts, eradicate disease, tap the ocean depths, and encourage the arts and commerce.

19   Let both sides unite to heed in all corners of the earth the command of Isaiah—to "undo the heavy burdens . . . [and] let the oppressed go free."

20   And if a beachhead of cooperation may push back the jungle of suspicion, let both sides join in creating a new endeavor: not a new balance of power, but a new world of law, where the strong are just and the weak secure and the peace preserved.

21   All this will not be finished in the first one hundred days. Nor will it be finished in the first one thousand days, not in the life of this administration, nor even perhaps in our lifetime on this planet. But let us begin.

22   In your hands, my fellow citizens, more than mine, will rest the final success or failure of our course. Since this country was founded, each generation of Americans has been summoned to give testimony to its national loyalty. The graves of young Americans who answered the call to service surround the globe.

23   Now the trumpet summons us again—not as a call to bear arms, though arms we need—not as a call to battle, though embattled we are—but a call to bear the burden of a long twilight struggle, year in and year out, "rejoicing in hope, patient in tribulation"—a struggle against the common enemies of man: Tyranny, poverty, disease and war itself.

24   Can we forge against these enemies a grand and global alliance, North and South, East and West, that can assure a more fruitful life for all mankind? Will you join in that historic effort?

25   In the long history of the world, only a few generations have been granted the role of defending freedom in its hour of maximum danger.

26   I do not shrink from this responsibility—I welcome it. I do not believe that any of us would exchange places with any other people or any other generation. The energy, the faith, the devotion which we bring to this endeavor will light our country and all who serve it—and the glow from that fire can truly light the world.

27   And so, my fellow Americans: Ask not what your country can do for you— ask what you can do for your country.

28   My fellow citizens of the world: Ask not what America will do for you, but what together we can do for the freedom of man.

29   Finally, whether you are citizens of America or citizens of the world, ask of us here the same high standards of strength and sacrifice which we ask of you. With a good conscience our only sure reward, with history the final judge of our deeds, let us go forth to lead the land we love, asking His blessing and His help, but knowing that here on earth God's work must truly be our own.

Personal Report of Communication Apprehension (PRCA-24)

▼ ▼ ▼

Personal Report of Communication Apprehension (PRCA-24)

Name _____   Date _____

Directions: For the following questions, indicate the degree to which each statement applies to you by marking whether you:

(1) Strongly Agree   **(2)** Agree   **(3)** Are Undecided   **(4)** Disagree   **(5)** Strongly Disagree

There are no wrong or right answers. Many of the statements are similar to other statements. Do not be concerned about this. Work quickly and honestly. Record your impression as you see yourself at this point in your life.

_____ 1. I dislike participating in group discussions.

_____ 2. Generally, I am comfortable while participating in a group discussion.

_____ 3. I am tense and nervous while participating in group discussions.

_____ 4. I like to get involved in group discussions.

_____ 5. Engaging in a group discussion with new people makes me tense and nervous.

_____ 6. I am calm and relaxed while participating in a group discussion.

_____ 7. Generally, I am nervous when I have to participate in a meeting.

_____ 8. Usually I am calm and relaxed while participating in meetings.

_____ 9. I am very calm and relaxed when I am called upon to express an opinion at a meeting.

_____ 10. I am afraid to express myself at meetings.

_____ 11. Communicating at meetings usually makes me uncomfortable.

_____ 12. I am very relaxed when answering questions at a meeting.

_____ 13. While participating in a conversation with a new acquaintance, I feel very nervous.

_____ 14. I have no fear of speaking up in conversations.

_____ 15. Ordinarily I am very tense and nervous in conversations.

_____ 16. Ordinarily I am very calm and relaxed in conversations.

_____ 17. While conversing with a new acquaintance, I feel very nervous.

_____ 18. I'm afraid to speak up in conversations.

_____ 19. I have no fear of giving a speech.

_____ 20. Certain parts of my body feel very tense and rigid while giving a speech.

_____ 21. I feel relaxed while giving a speech.

_____ 22. My thoughts become confused and jumbled when I am giving a speech.

_____ 23. I face the prospect of giving a speech with confidence.

_____ 24. While giving a speech I get so nervous, I forget facts I really know.

Scoring: Four subscale scores and a total apprehension score are calculated as follows:

Group   = 18 – (score for #1) + (score for #2) – (score for #3) + (score for #4) – (score for #5) + (score for #6)
Meeting = 18 – (score for #7) + (score for #8) + (score for #9) – (score for #10) – (score for #11) + (score for #12)
Dyadic = 18 – (score for #13) + (score for #14) – (score for #15) + (score for #16) + (score for #17) – (score for #18)
Public   = 18 + (score for #19) – (score for #20) + (score for #21) – (score for #22) + (score for #23) – (score for #24)
Overall = Group total + Meeting total + Dyadic total + Public total. (Totals can range between 24 and 120.)

For each subscale total, your scores can range from a low of **6** to a high of **30**. Any score above 18 indicates some degree of apprehension.

Modified and reproduced from James D. McCroskey, *An Introduction to Rhetorical Communication*, 4th ed. (Englewood Cliffs, NJ: Prentice-Hall, 1982). Copyright by James D. McCroskey.

Index

A

Abstract language, 130, 419
Acceptance speeches, A8–A9
Acronyms, 30
Active listening, team skill, A25
After-dinner speeches, A12–A16
Alliteration, stylistic device, 423
Ambiguous language, 419–420
Analogical reasoning, 363–364
  figurative analogy, 363
  literal analogy, 363
Antithesis, stylistic device, 423
Appearance, 180, 182–183, 368–369
Alignment. *See* Design principles for
  visuals
Anxiety, coping with
  cognitive restructuring, 65
  concentration on meaning, 52–53
  deep breathing, 52
  positive imagery, 54–64
  preparation and practice, 51–52
  relaxing introduction, 52
  rhetoritherapy, 65–66
  systematic desensitization, 64–65
  visual aids, 53
Anxiety, types of
  situational, 48–50, 51–53
  trait, 48, 50–51, 54–66
Artifact speech, 33–34, 36, 38, 39,
  41, 42
Assonance, stylistic device, 423
Attention-getters, 232, 270–275
  brief instances, 271
  demonstration, 274–275
  detailed instances, 270–271
  fables/sayings/poems/rhymes, 274
  humor, 271–272
  question 273–274
  quotation, 272
  reference to occasion, 274
  startling fact, 272–273
Attitude, 107, 110

Attitude poll, 340–342
  format for, 341
  sample poll, 342
Audience analysis, 98–120
  after the speech, 117–118
  audience type, 112–115, 151, 386,
    391
  before the speech, 116–117
  demographic information,
    102–106
  for informative speeches, 216–218
  for persuasive speeches, 339–342
  psychological information,
    107–112
  situational information, 99–101
  for special occasion speeches, 35
Audience analysis, demographic
    characteristics
  age, 102–103
  cultural background, 103–104,
    105
  economic status, 105
  education, 105
  gender, 104
  group affiliation, 104
  marital status, 104
  occupation, 104
  religion, 104
  which to use, 106
Audience analysis, psychological
    characteristics
  attitudes, 107–108, 110
  beliefs, 108, 110
  hazards of incomplete, 111–112
  needs, 109–110
  values, 108–109, 110
Audience analysis, situational char-
    acteristics, 99–101
Audience types
  friendly, 112, 113, 115, 116, 386
  hostile, 112–113, 115, 116, 386,
    391

  neutral, 113, 114, 115, 116, 386
  uninterested, 113, 114, 115, 116,
    151, 386
Audiovisual aids, 188–190

B

Basic problem-solving procedure,
    for teams, A26–A30
  analyzing the problem, A27
  brainstorming, A28
  consensus decisions, A29
  establishing the problem,
    A27–A28
  evaluating solutions, A29
  identifying the problem, A26–A27
  implementing solutions, A29–A30
  listing possible solutions, A28
  summary chart of basic steps, A30
  voting to reach decisions, A29
Beginning speeches. *See* Preparation
  steps, beginning speech
Beliefs, in audience analysis, 108
  definition, 108
  in information
  in persuasion, 340
  use of, 110
Benefits (advantages), to persuasive
    proposal, 345, 395–397
Bibliography, 242
  note cards, 242
  source citations, 242
Body language. *See* Nonverbal com-
    munication; Visual delivery
Body of speech. *See* FLOW
    sequence, organize and support
Brain hemispheres, 113
  and faster comprehension, 152,
    167
  and visual aids, 131–133
Brainstorming. *See* Basic problem-
    solving procedure
Breathing, deep, 52

C

Causal reasoning, 363–364
Ceremonial speeches. *See* Special occasion speeches
Chalkboards, 149
 appropriate use, 151
 correct type size, 152
 disadvantages, 149
 usage tips, 187–188, 190
Charts. *See* Flip chart; Posters; Visual aids
Clothing, 182
Code, communication process, 7, 9, 12–13, 19, 23
 verbal, 12–13, 75, 80–81, 115, 126–127, 194–196
 visual, 12–13, 75, 80–81, 115, 126–127, 181–190, 196
 vocal, 12–13, 75, 80–81, 115, 126–127, 190–194, 197
Cognitive restructuring, 65
Color, visual aids, 20, 170–173
 background, 172
 complementary (opposite), 171
 and effect on listeners, 170
 harmonizing, 170
 hue, 170
 and persuasiveness, 350
 red-green color blindness, 172
 and saturation, 170
 twelve-hue color wheel, 170–172
 typeface or font, 167, 170–173
Color blindness, red-green, 172
Color wheel (twelve-hue), 170–172
Commemorative speeches, special occasion, A9–A12
 eulogies, A11–A12
 toasts, A10
 tributes, A9–A10
Common ground. *See* Similarity
Communication, defined, 9
Communication apprehension. *See* Anxiety, coping with; Speaker anxiety
Communication process, 9, 23
 code, 7, 9, 12–13, 19, 23
 decoding/encoding, 11–12, 80
 environment, 13–14
 feedback, 13–14, 76, 117–118
 frame of reference, 11–12, 23
 model, 10
 motivation, 11, 78–79
 noise, 13–14

speaker/listeners, 9–10
 stimulus, 10–11, 78
Communication skills, 28–32, A25–A26
Comparisons, as supporting material, 257–259
 figurative, 258–259
 literal, 257–258
Competency, 368–369
Complementary colors, 171
Computer research, 239
Computer visuals, 149–150
 advantages, 149–150
 appropriate use, 150–151
 and color, 150, 170–173
 correct type size, 158
 LCD projection, 149–150, 188
 usage tips, 188–190
Conclusion of speech. *See* FLOW sequence, wrap-up
Concrete language, 130, 419
Confidence, speaker, 182–183
Consensus, in team decision-making, A29
Contrast. *See* Design principles for visuals
Credibility, basic elements, 368–370
 competency, 368–369
 dynamism, 369–370
 objectivity, 370
 trustworthiness, 368
Credibility, speaker, 20, 82, 276–277, 339–342, 366–371, 389–390
 basic elements of, 368–370
 and evidence, 359, 364–371
 how to improve, 370–371
 as a persuasive tool, 367–368
 of sources, 83
 unethical use of, 371
 with visual aids, 34
Criteria, in problem-solving
 definition, A27
 must, A27–A28
 want, A27–A28
Critical thinking. *See* Basic problem-solving procedure; Fallacious reasoning
Cultural differences. *See* Cultural diversity
Cultural diversity, 11–12, 28–29, 75, 86, 103–104, 108
Culture bias, 429. *See also* Cultural diversity

D

Decoding, communication process, 11–12, 80
Deductive reasoning, 362–363
Deep breathing, 52
Delivery
 articulation, 193
 immediacy behaviors, 195–196
 for informative speaking, 328
 in low-light situations, 151
 methods of, 197–200
 natural and enthusiastic, 31
 nonfluencies, 368–369
 practice suggestions, 203–204
 pronunciation, 193–194
 rehearsal, 42, 200–202
 speaking rate, 89, 92
 verbal, 115, 194–197
 visual, 115, 190–194, 197
 vocal, 115, 190–194, 197
 vocal variety, 191–193
Delivery methods
 extemporaneous, 200, 222
 impromptu, 198–200
 manuscript, 197, 227, 229
 memory, 31, 197–198
Demographic audience analysis, 102–106, 276. *See also* Audience analysis, demographic characteristics
Demonstrations, as supporting material, 262–263, 274–275
Demonstration speech, 208–209
Design principles for visuals, 161–164
 alignment, 161–163, 174
 contrast, 161, 163, 173–174
 proximity, 161–163, 174
 repetition, 161–163, 174
Discussion formats. *See* Team presentation formats
Diversity. *See* Cultural diversity
Doublespeak, 418
Dynamism, 369–370

E

Emotional appeals, 371–376. *See also* Audience analysis, psychological characteristics
 and evidence, 372–373
 and fear appeals, 374–376
 and Maslow's hierarchy of needs, 373–374
 role of in persuasion, 371–372
 unethical use of, 376

W

Wrap-up step, informative,
    227–228, 268
  Q & A, 290–292
  refocus in memorable way,
    287–289
  student sample, 291

suggested length, 289
  summary, 287
Wrap-up step, persuasive, 348
  challenge or appeal for action,
    403–404
  refocus in memorable way,
    404–406

student sample, 406
  summary, 401
  taking a specific stand, 350–351
  visualize future, 402

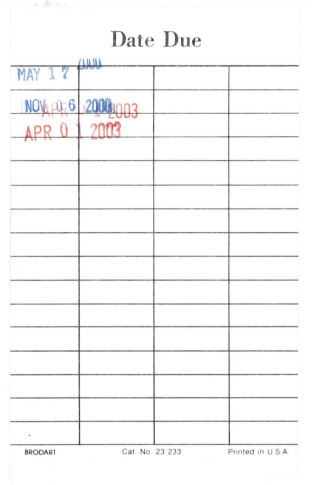

Date Due

MAY 1 7 2000

NOV 0 6 2000   APR 2 4 2003

APR 0 1 2003

BRODART   Cat. No. 23 233   Printed in U.S.A.

**OVERDUE FINES ARE
$0.25 PER DAY**

DEVRY INSTITUTE OF TECHNOLOGY
LIBRARY
MISSISSAUGA, ONTARIO

Please give us your feedback

Thank you for using *Successful Public Speaking*. I hope you have enjoyed reading it and have found it valuable in your public speaking course. In order to make the next edition even better, I'd like to know how you feel about the book. Please give me your opinions on this edition by filling out the questionnaire below. When you're done, just fold and seal the questionnaire, and drop it into the mail (postage is already paid).

Cheryl Hamilton

1. In comparison to other textbooks you have read, is *Successful Public Speaking* better, about the same, or less effective?

2. What are the three topics or parts of the book that you found most useful?

3. Which parts did you find least useful?

4. Did you find the end-of-chapter practice suggestions useful?

5. Are there any other criticisms you have of this edition?

6. How can we improve the next edition?

7. Did you use a computer in conjunction with this class? If yes, what kind and for what purpose?

May we quote your answers to all of the above questions? ___ yes ___ no

Name (optional) _____

School _____

Address _____

City/State/Zip _____

Internet address _____

Year in school and field of study _____

FOLD HERE

NO POSTAGE
NECESSARY
IF MAILED
IN THE
UNITED STATES

BUSINESS REPLY MAIL
FIRST CLASS MAIL   PERMIT NO. 34   BELMONT, CA

POSTAGE WILL BE PAID BY ADDRESSEE

Cheryl Hamilton
Wadsworth Publishing Company
An International Thompson Publishing Company
10 Davis Drive
Belmont, CA 94002-9801

FOLD HERE

DEVRY INSTITUTE OF TECHNOLOGY
LIBRARY
MISSISSAUGA, ONTARIO